OXFORD WORLD'S CLASSICS

PERCY BYSSHE SHELLEY

PERCY BYSSHE SHELLEY was born in Horsham, Sussex on 4 August 1792, the eldest child of Timothy Shelley, a landowning Whig MP and later Baronet. He was educated at Syon House Academy, Isleworth, and at 12 was sent to Eton. At 18 he went up to University College, Oxford. Five months later, together with his friend Thomas Jefferson Hogg, he was expelled from Oxford for publishing and refusing to answer questions about a pamphlet entitled *The Necessity of Atheism*. The resulting estrangement from his family was soon compounded by his elopement to Scotland in 1811 with Harriet Westbrook, daughter of the proprietor of a London coffee house. In 1814 Shelley and Harriet separated, and he eloped again, this time to the Continent, with Mary Godwin, daughter of Mary Wollstonecraft and William Godwin. Harriet committed suicide in November 1816 and Mary and Shelley married the next month. After a spell back in England they departed for Italy early in 1818, where he wrote many of his best-known works. From this self-imposed exile Shelley never returned. He drowned in the Bay of Spezia in 1822, while sailing with his friend Edward Williams, who also drowned. In the course of his brief and controversial life Shelley produced a ⸺ ⸺ ⸺ing range of poetry and prose, including numerous lyric poems, plays, longer poems, polemical pamphlets, translations, and works of criticism and political philosophy.

ZACHARY LEADER, Professor of English Literature at the University of Surrey Roehampton, has published widely on nineteenth- and twentieth-century literature. Among his books are *Revision and Romantic Authorship* (1996), *Romantic Period Writings 1798–1832: An Anthology* (co-edited with Ian Haywood) (1999) and (as editor) *The Letters of Kingsley Amis* (2000).

MICHAEL O'NEILL, Professor of English at the University of Durham, has published widely on Romantic and twentieth-century poetry. Among his books are *The Human Mind's Imaginings: Conflict and Achievement in Shelley's Poetry* (1989), *Percy Bysshe Shelley: A Literary Life* (1989), and *Romanticism and the Self-Conscious Poem* (1997).

OXFORD WORLD'S CLASSICS

Percy Bysshe Shelley
The Major Works

Edited with an Introduction and Notes by
ZACHARY LEADER *and* MICHAEL O'NEILL

OXFORD
UNIVERSITY PRESS

OXFORD
UNIVERSITY PRESS

Great Clarendon Street, Oxford OX2 6DP

Oxford University Press is a department of the University of Oxford.
It furthers the University's objective of excellence in research, scholarship,
and education by publishing worldwide in

Oxford New York

Auckland Bangkok Buenos Aires Cape Town Chennai
Dar es Salaam Delhi Hong Kong Istanbul Karachi Kolkata
Kuala Lumpur Madrid Melbourne Mexico City Mumbai Nairobi
São Paulo Shanghai Taipei Tokyo Toronto

Oxford is a registered trade mark of Oxford University Press
in the UK and in certain other countries

Published in the United States
by Oxford University Press Inc., New York

British Library Cataloguing in Publication Data

Data available

Library of Congress Cataloging in Publication Data

Data available

ISBN–13: 978–0–19–281374–9
ISBN–10: 0–19–281374–9

2

Typeset in Ehrhardt
by RefineCatch Limited, Bungay, Suffolk
Printed in Great Britain by
Clays Ltd, St Ives plc

CONTENTS

Acknowledgements   ix

Introduction   xi

Chronology   xxv

Note on the Text   xxviii

POETRY

'A Cat in distress'   1

To the Emperors of Russia and Austria Who Eyed the Battle
   of Austerlitz from the Heights whilst Buonaparte Was
   Active in the Thickest of the Fight   2

Zeinab and Kathema   3

Sonnet: On Launching Some Bottles Filled with *Knowledge*
   into the Bristol Channel   8

Sonnet: To a Balloon, Laden with *Knowledge*   9

QUEEN MAB   10

Stanzas.—April, 1814   88

'O! there are spirits of the air'   89

To Wordsworth   90

ALASTOR; OR, THE SPIRIT OF SOLITUDE   92

Mutability   112

Verses Written on Receiving a Celandine in a Letter
   from England   112

Hymn to Intellectual Beauty (versions A and B)   114/117

Mont Blanc (versions A and B)   120/124

To Constantia   128

From LAON AND CYTHNA   130

Ozymandias   198

Lines Written among the Euganean Hills   198

The Two Spirits—An Allegory   208

Stanzas Written in Dejection—December 1818, near Naples 209

Sonnet ('Lift not the painted veil') 210

JULIAN AND MADDALO 212

PROMETHEUS UNBOUND 229

THE CENCI 314

THE MASK OF ANARCHY 400

Ode to the West Wind 412

PETER BELL THE THIRD 415

Men of England: A Song 442

Lines Written during the Castlereagh Administration 443

To S. and C. 443

'What men gain fairly' 444

A New National Anthem 444

Sonnet: England in 1819 446

Love's Philosophy 446

Ode to Heaven 447

To the Lord Chancellor 448

The Sensitive Plant 450

An Exhortation 460

The Cloud 461

To a Skylark 463

Ode to Liberty 466

Sonnet ('Ye hasten to the grave!') 474

Song ('Rarely, rarely comest thou') 475

Letter to Maria Gisborne 476

To —— (Lines to a Reviewer) 484

To —— (Lines to a Critic) 485

THE WITCH OF ATLAS 486

Song of Apollo 508

Song of Pan 509

Sonnet: Political Greatness   510
The Indian Girl's Song   510
EPIPSYCHIDION   512
ADONAIS   529
To Night   546
The Aziola   547
HELLAS   548
Written on Hearing the News of the Death of Napoleon   588
'The flower that smiles today'   589
To —— ('One word is too often profaned')   590
'When the lamp is shattered'   590
To —— ('The serpent is shut out from Paradise')   591
To Jane. The Invitation   593
To Jane—The Recollection   595
The Magnetic Lady to Her Patient   597
With a Guitar. To Jane   599
To Jane ('The keen stars were twinkling')   601
Lines Written in the Bay of Lerici   602
THE TRIUMPH OF LIFE   604

PROSE

An Address to the People on the Death of the
    Princess Charlotte   623
On Love   631
On Life   633
From A Philosophical View of Reform   636
A Defence of Poetry   674

Notes   702
Further Reading   837

Ordering of Poems in Volumes Published by Shelley from
    1816 to 1822   841

Index of Titles of Poems and Prose Works   843

Index of First Lines of Poems   844

ACKNOWLEDGEMENTS

WE are grateful to various libraries and bodies for permission to quote from manuscripts in their possession. The following poems are quoted by kind permission of the Carl and Lily Pforzheimer Foundation, Inc.: 'A Cat in distress', 'To the Emperors of Russia and Austria', 'Zeinab and Kathema', 'Sonnet: On Launching Some Bottles Filled with *Knowledge* into the Bristol Channel', and 'Sonnet: To a Balloon, Laden with *Knowledge*'. The same Foundation has permitted us to use the literal transcription of *A Philosophical View of Reform* in *Shelley and His Circle*, volume vi, as copy-text for our selection from that work. We are deeply conscious of our debt to the editors of the transcription, Donald H. Reiman and Doucet Devin Fischer, and wish to thank them warmly. We, of course, take full responsibility for how we edit that transcription. We are also grateful to the Keeper of Special Collections and Western Manuscripts of the Bodleian Library, University of Oxford, for permission to quote from manuscripts in its possession (fuller details are given in our notes to each poem; relevant shelfmarks can be found under '*BSM*' in 'Abbreviations' at the head of Notes below, pp. 702–3). We are also grateful to Lord Abinger for his permission given through the Bodleian Library to use material from the Gisborne notebook (Oxford, Bodleian Library, [Abinger] Dep. d.475). For permission to publish material from the Scrope Davies Notebook, we are grateful to Barclays Bank. Other libraries and bodies which have kindly given us permission to publish texts based on manuscripts in their possession include Aberdeen University Library; the Bibliotheca Bodmeriana, Cologny-Genève; the British Library; Edinburgh University Library; Eton College Library; the Houghton Library, Harvard University; the Huntington Library, San Marino; the John Rylands University Library of Manchester; the Library of Congress; the Pierpont Morgan Library, New York; and the Syndics of Cambridge University Library.

Zachary Leader would like to thank Frank Kermode and Neil Fraistat for early advice and encouragement. Michael O'Neill would like to thank the University of Durham for research leave to work on the edition and the Arts and Humanities Research Board for an additional term of leave under its Research Leave Scheme. Both editors would like to thank Judith Luna at OUP for her patience and good sense, and Elizabeth Stratford for her meticulous copy-editing.

Many other individuals have helped us greatly. In particular we would like to thank the following for their help of various kinds: B. C. Barker-Benfield, Robert Carver, Richard Cronin, David Fuller, Basak Ertur, Doucet Devin Fischer, Gareth Reeves, Donald H. Reiman, Nicholas Roe, and Timothy Webb. Nora Crook deserves special mention for her generous readiness to discuss and expertly advise about many editorial problems. Responsibility for errors is, of course, the editors'.

The fine work of many editors of Shelley, past and present, has been of great benefit and stimulus to us. Of particular value to us among modern editions have been those of Timothy Webb for Everyman, Kelvin Everest and fellow-editors for Longman, Donald H. Reiman and Neil Fraistat for Johns Hopkins University Press, and Donald H. Reiman and Sharon B. Powers for Norton. The second edition of the Norton Shelley was published as we were going to press, but we have been able to consult it briefly. We are also indebted to the work of the editors of the *Bodleian Shelley Manuscripts* series and the relevant volumes in the *Manuscripts of the Younger Romantics* series, both under the general editorship of Donald H. Reiman.

INTRODUCTION

I

IN *A Defence of Poetry* (written in 1821) Shelley celebrates the diversity of interpretations evoked by 'high poetry' (p. 693).[1] He is certainly a poet and a man able to stimulate divided responses. The current high standing he enjoys is shown by the number of major critical studies and editions of his writing that have appeared in the last few decades.[2] Yet what held sway for many years were the correspondingly adverse judgements of T. S. Eliot, who regarded Shelley's 'ideas' as 'repellent', and F. R. Leavis, who asserted that 'feeling in Shelley's poetry is divorced from thought'.[3] Causes for divisions of opinion about Shelley are not hard to find. The incendiary violence of his political rhetoric, full of volcanic eruptions and apocalyptic conflagrations, serves non-violence. He both champions and deplores Romantic idealism, sometimes in the same poem. His language has about it a momentum that detractors find overstated and admirers applaud, as the poetry 'Sweeps through the dull dense world, compelling there | All new successions to the forms they wear' (*Adonais*, ll. 382–3).

Shelley's private life has also caused controversy. The feeling that his personal conduct proves the dangerous or liberating nature of his ideas may explain the persistence of biographical readings of his work (or refusals to read the work). To insist too literally on biographical analyses of Shelley, however, would be to ignore his own conviction that 'The poet and the man are two different natures' (*L* 2. 310).

---

[1] Dates given in this Introduction to Shelley's writings refer to the date of publication, unless, as here, stated otherwise.

[2] In *Norton*[2] the key moment for the revival of Shelley's critical fortunes is dated as circa 1960, or, more precisely, 1958–9, years that saw the publication of pioneering critical, editorial, and textual work by Harold Bloom, Lawrence John Zillman, Charles H. Taylor, Jr., and Earl R. Wasserman: see Donald H. Reiman and Neil Fraistat, 'Shelley's Reputation before 1960: A Sketch', pp. 539–49, especially pp. 547–8. (For explanation of abbreviated references, see pp. 702–3.)

[3] T. S. Eliot, *The Use of Poetry and the Use of Criticism* (London, 1933), quoted from *Selected Prose of T. S. Eliot*, ed. and intro. Frank Kermode (London, 1975), 81 (for a more respectful view of Shelley, see Eliot's comments in 'What Dante Means to Me', in *To Criticize the Critic* (London, 1965), 130–2, on *The Triumph of Life*, especially the meeting between the Poet and Rousseau, which influenced Eliot's account of the 'familiar compound ghost' in 'Little Gidding'); F. R. Leavis, 'Shelley', in *Revaluation* (1936; Harmondsworth, 1972), 208.

Arguably, this opposition simplifies; there are times when Shelley's poetry thrives on blurring the gap between 'poet' and 'man'. But even when Shelley does express private feelings, as in his responses to literary slights in poems such as 'To —— (Lines to a Critic)', he is quick to relate his feelings to an ethical issue with wider political implications (here, how best to respond to hostility). Born on 4 August 1792, a few weeks before the September Massacres in France and months before the execution of Louis XVI, Shelley spent much of his career as a poet pondering the apparent failure of the French Revolution, staging in *Prometheus Unbound* (1820) an imaginative reworking of history that results, in the literary work, in successful liberation—not only from tyranny but also from the desire for revenge. Spared the first-hand disenchantment of the previous generation of Romantic poets, Wordsworth, Coleridge, and Southey, he attacks their 'gloom' (and Byron's 'misanthropy') in the Preface to *Laon and Cythna* (1817) (p. 132). For him, all these poets served as object-lessons in how not to read history.

Personally and poetically, Shelley thrived on conflict and dissent. The 'Son of a man of fortune in Sussex', as he described his situation in a letter to Godwin (*L* 1. 227), he received the education of an aristocrat who was expected to follow his father (Sir Timothy Shelley, a landowning Whig MP) into public life. He attended Eton, where contemporaries recalled his dislike of the practice of 'fagging' (whereby younger boys acted as the servants of older boys) and the baiting to which he was subjected. He proved to be an able scholar, adept at writing Latin verse and keen on science. Yet the youthful rebel was opposed to the institutions of school, university, and church. In March 1811 he was expelled from University College, Oxford, with his friend Thomas Jefferson Hogg, after refusing to disavow authorship of a pamphlet entitled *The Necessity of Atheism* (minimally altered in a long note to *Queen Mab* (1813), included here).

Expulsion from Oxford was followed by elopement and marriage in the same year to Harriet Westbrook, daughter of John Westbrook, businessman and owner of a London coffee house. The marriage was disapproved of by Shelley's father, who effectively broke off relations with his son.[4] Harriet was Shelley's loyal companion during a period of would-be political activism, which took him to Dublin in 1812 to campaign on behalf of Catholic Emancipation and repeal of the Act of

[4] For discussion of John Westbrook and analysis of Sir Timothy Shelley's opposition to the marriage, see *SC* 2. 866–8.

Union. She is the dedicatee of *Queen Mab*, which presents the youthful poet in full revolutionary flow, attacking tyranny and religion, and rounding off his poem with fire-breathing but closely argued essays on topics such as the desirability of free love and the horrors of meat-eating. However, by 1814 the marriage was under strain, and in that year Shelley fell in love and eloped with Mary Godwin, daughter of Mary Wollstonecraft and William Godwin, the poet's intellectual mentor. In the 1790s Godwin had influenced Wordsworth and others with his dispassionate exaltation of reason in *Enquiry Concerning Political Justice* (1793). Two decades later, he had fallen so far into obscurity that the youthful Shelley was surprised to discover he was still living: 'I had enrolled your name in the list of the honorable dead', he informed a no doubt mildly startled Godwin in a letter of 3 January 1812 (*L* 1. 220). Later, Shelley outstripped Godwinian rationalism as he immersed himself in the poetry of his and previous ages, and in the writings of thinkers such as Plato. But Godwin did much to foster the poet's trust in unfettered enquiry.[5]

Shelley's refusal to abide by social convention caused great pain to himself and to others, especially the abandoned Harriet. In 1816, after a period of growing distress, she drowned herself in the Serpentine; within a month Shelley and Mary married. Yet to Virginia Woolf, at least, in a discussion of Shelley 'as son and as husband', it is apparent that 'his experiments, disastrous as they were in many ways, have helped us to greater sincerity and happiness in our own conflicts'.[6] The marriage was followed by a period of relative peace and productivity in Marlow, near Shelley's friend Thomas Love Peacock. In March 1818, though, the Shelleys set sail for Italy. This departure was prompted by several factors: the poet's financial and health problems; the wish to return Allegra, Byron's daughter by Claire Clairmont (Mary Shelley's half-sister), to her father; and Shelley's fear that his and Mary's children might be taken from them after a legal decision in March 1817 not to grant him custody of his two children by Harriet.

In Italy, Shelley and Mary experienced much suffering, at the heart of which were the deaths of their children: Clara, a year old, died in 1818 and 3-year-old William in 1819, resulting in subsequent emotional difficulties in the marriage. Shelley's work was badly received, largely on account of his heterodox views, though a number of

---

[5] See Pamela Clemit, 'Shelley's Godwin, 1812–1817', *Durham University Journal*, NS 54 (1993), 189–201.

[6] 'Not One of Us', in *The Essays of Virginia Woolf*, vol. 4: *1925–1928*, ed. Andrew McNeillie (London, 1994), 470.

reviewers recognized his poetic gifts. But his ability to communicate a fluid, dynamic vision in different literary forms is abundantly evident in his writings in Italy (1818–22), where he produced some of the finest poetry of the Romantic period. These writings include *Prometheus Unbound* and *Hellas* (1822), two lyrical dramas that take Greek models as their point of departure; *The Cenci* (1819), a five-act tragedy in blank verse; *The Mask of Anarchy* (written in 1819), a blend of masque and ballad; *Peter Bell the Third* (also written in 1819), a parody or mock-epic; *Letter to Maria Gisborne* (written in 1820), an epistle in verse; *The Witch of Atlas* (also written in 1820), a comic miniature epic or epyllion written in *ottava rima*; *Epipsychidion* (1821), a rhapsodic love poem in couplets that artfully reworks Dante's *Vita Nuova*; several Odes (including 'Ode to the West Wind' and 'Ode to Liberty', both 1820); sonnets showing formal innovation (examples are 'Ye hasten to the grave!', written in 1820, and 'England in 1819', written in 1819); shorter poems in various metrical forms (notably the poems to Jane Williams, written in 1821–2); *Adonais*, a pastoral elegy in Spenserian stanzas; and *The Triumph of Life* (written in 1822), a dream-vision written in *terza rima*. Often Shelley calls to mind a literary form or work only to offer a critique of the assumptions with which it is associated. *Adonais* ends in affirmation, but the affirmation differs from that found in elegies such as Milton's *Lycidas*: in place of Milton's Christian Heaven, Shelley puts his ambivalent trust in a self-created 'abode where the Eternal are' (l. 495). Dante's *Divine Comedy* is explicitly invoked by *The Triumph of Life* (ll. 471–6), but the Romantic poet substitutes his own blend of questioning and imagining for the theological certainties that inform the Italian poet's masterpiece.

Shelley lived in an age of turbulence, complexity, and change. More and more people lived in cities, unrepresented in Parliament. The country was locked in a war with Napoleonic France that would only come to an end with the Battle of Waterloo in 1815. After that victory a period of further reaction followed at home, a time of repression sharply analysed and attacked by Shelley, most concentratedly in 'England in 1819'.

George III was mad, and the self-indulgent Prince Regent the butt of lampoons. The government under Lord Liverpool refused to grant parliamentary reform, Catholic Emancipation, or the right to protest peacefully. Abroad, the Bourbons were restored in France and Spain, and Europe was subjected to counter-revolutionary pressures orchestrated by Metternich, Chancellor of Austria. Shelley looked eagerly for signs of social change domestically and internationally, as is evident from 'Ode to Liberty', inspired by the Spanish Revolution of 1820. His political, religious, and ethical views were underpinned by a belief in justice, equality, freedom, and the desirability of reform. In the prose work, *An Address to the People on the Death of the Princess Charlotte* (written in 1817), he shows a capacity for ironic yet visionary polemic, coupling the death of Princess Charlotte (daughter of the Prince Regent) with the executions of three labourers associated with the Pentridge Rising, which Shelley, along with other liberals, believed was fomented by a government informer. At the end, the Princess for whom Shelley enjoins his readers to mourn is not Charlotte but Liberty, whose resurrection he imagines as a 'glorious Phantom' (p. 631). The use of 'Phantom', with its implication of something yet to materialize, is characteristic. Confronted by a culture in retreat from political optimism, Shelley offers in much of his writing an ardent, self-aware Utopianism.

Shelley's interest in different poetic forms is the artistic analogue of his social experimentation and of his concern with process, in consciousness, history, and the cosmos.[7] Commitment to process, the condition of becoming, shapes his poetic practice. 'Language', he writes in *Prometheus Unbound*, is 'a perpetual Orphic song, | Which rules with daedal harmony a throng | Of thoughts and forms, which else senseless and shapeless were' (4. 415–17). In Shelley, these 'forms' negotiate with the as yet unformed. His words, whether apparently simple or evidently complex, allow us to experience the emergence of new possibilities. Turneresque in their swirls of energy, their delight in vanishings and manifestations, his descriptions of nature are the correlative of his longing for change. Reflecting on his use of different forms, Shelley worried whether 'it be wise to affect variety in composi-tions, or whether the attempt to excel in many ways does not debar from excellence in one particular kind' (*L* 2. 219). Yet it is his great distinction to be at once a poet of figurative, metrical, and syntactical constructions that mirror the desire for transformation, and a poet of audacious radical critique. Such critique is most evident in *Queen Mab*, but it is re-encountered in many later and formally quite dif-ferent poems, such as those occasioned by Shelley's revulsion from and reflections on the Peterloo Massacre of 1819 (see the notes for *The Mask of Anarchy*). In this volume, we include a good number of the

[7] For a study of 'process' in Shelley, see Jerrold E. Hogle, *Shelley's Process: Radical Transference and the Development of his Major Works* (New York, 1988) .

'popular songs' which he hoped to publish after Peterloo, but which were too outspoken to find their way into print during his lifetime. They reveal a fusion of tough political thought, sharp-edged phrasing, and grim wit.

Shelley's variety is no matter of indecisiveness or personal instability.[8] His different styles and strategies often serve a common purpose, and can frequently be explained, in the first instance, by reference to his intended audiences. This awareness of audience shows in his instruction that *Queen Mab* be printed as 'A small neat Quarto, on fine paper & so as to catch the aristocrats: They will not read it, but their sons and daughters may' (*L* 1. 361). Later, *Prometheus Unbound* was addressed to 'the more select classes of poetical readers' (Preface, p. 232), while its near-contemporary, *The Cenci*, was aimed at 'the multitude' (*L* 2. 174). Ironically, his efforts to target audiences were often thwarted while other poets—pre-eminently Byron, at once friend, rival, and Jungian shadow—enjoyed far greater popularity. If Shelley's ideas outraged conservative reviewers, his style proved too searching for popular consumption. It is easier, from this distance, to hear in his work a poetic voice able to fuse affirmation and doubt, directness and complexity. *The Mask of Anarchy*, for example, excoriates with rare satiric edge the Liverpool administration. It opens with a 'ghastly masquerade' (l. 27) in which, like the political cartoonists active in the Regency, the narrator describes meeting 'Murder on the way—| He had a mask like Castlereagh' (ll. 5–6). As the poem develops, though, its ballad stanzas accommodate more than invective; they dramatize the desirability but also the difficulty of imagining a transition from anarchic misrule to freedom. The owner of the voice which addresses the reader on this subject is hard to identify; the likely candidate, the 'Earth | Which gave the sons of England birth' (ll. 139–40), is only proposed in a prolonged 'As if' clause (see ll. 139 and 146).[9] Shelley puts the problem of speaking into the foreground to

---

[8] For the construction of a 'schizoid' Shelley, see the comments of one of his major poetic heirs, W. B. Yeats, in *A Vision* (1937; London, 1981): 'Shelley out of phase writes pamphlets, and dreams of converting the world', p. 143.

[9] Stephen C. Behrendt in *Shelley and His Audiences* (Lincoln, Nebr., 1989) comments on the 'equivocation' that Shelley creates by his use of 'As if' (quoted from Michael O'Neill (ed.), *Shelley*, Longman Critical Readers (London, 1993), 134). Susan J. Wolfson, in *Formal Charges: The Shaping of Poetry in British Romanticism* (Stanford, Calif., 1997), finds that the 'syntaxes of *As if* have a reflexive effect of restraining the political agency of the oratory to a dream', p. 198. For thought-provoking questioning of Shelley's radicalism in this poem and elsewhere, see Donald H. Reiman, 'Shelley as Agrarian Reactionary', in *Norton*[2] 589–99, esp. pp. 596–7.

bring out the fact that he is cut off, by physical exile and social class, from the group to whose defence he would leap, and to assert that poetry's voice must frequently associate itself with hope and imagination.

For many readers, Shelley is a poet who is 'tameless, and swift, and proud', words he applies in 'Ode to the West Wind' (l. 56) to himself as well as to the wind, symbol of inspiration and herald of revolution. Yet J. S. Mill's assertion that 'It is only when under the overruling influence of some one state of feeling . . . that he writes as a great poet' is only partly right.[10] If there is a presiding 'state of feeling' in the 'Ode to the West Wind', it is made up of several constituents and continually redefined. In the final section, Shelley uses his modified sonnet form (four tercets with concluding couplet) to hold together various impulses. The section's opening blend of plea and imperative—'Make me thy lyre, even as the forest is' (l. 57)— announces a recovery from the mood of the previous section, in which a time of crisis is dramatized. The desire to be 'even as the forest is' implicitly recognizes, however, that the poet cannot simplify himself into a natural object like the forest. But Shelley's way of bringing out this separation is to push to the limit the possibility of identification with the natural: 'What if my leaves are falling like its own!' (l. 58) he exclaims in a line that plays one more figurative variation on the leaves that have already brought to mind 'ghosts' (l. 3), 'Pestilence-stricken multitudes' (l. 5), 'Loose clouds' (l. 16) (and, by extension, 'tangled boughs of Heaven and Ocean' (l. 17)), and 'The sapless foliage of the ocean' (l. 40). With impassioned humour in the midst of his desire for the recovery of inspiration, Shelley sees himself as a deciduous tree whose leaves are falling.

But if he hopes that the wind 'Will take from both [poet and forest] a deep, autumnal tone, | Sweet though in sadness' (ll. 60–1), he concedes in those final words that he is investing the natural scene with emotion. Thus, the subsequent plea for unity—'Be thou me, impetuous one!' (l. 62)—has built into it an awareness that the plea cannot be successful. Long before the cry 'Bethou' is mocked by Wallace Stevens in *Notes towards a Supreme Fiction* as 'A sound like any other' that 'will end' ('It Must Change', 6), Shelley has glimpsed its necessary failure. By the poem's close it is the poet who asserts his responsibility for meaning, drawing attention to 'the incantation of this verse' (l. 65), a

---

[10] J. S. Mill, 'Two Kinds of Poetry' (1833), quoted from *Shelley: Shorter Poems and Lyrics, A Casebook*, ed. Patrick Swinden (London, 1976), 58.

moment that sharpens the immediacy of the imaginative experience.[11]
This experience is also sharpened by the image of words as scattered
'Ashes and sparks' (l. 67), reminding us of poetry's indirect and
multiple ways of working on an audience. The disseminated sparks
will kindle, the poem hopes, where they fall. As at the end of 'Mont
Blanc' (written in 1816), Shelley concludes with a question (altered
from a statement in the draft). In the earlier poem, the question teased
us into recognizing the dependence of sense-making on 'the human
mind's imaginings' (l. 143). In the 'Ode', the question looks rhetorical,
demanding the answer 'yes, Spring will not be far behind', but it
shows—covertly yet honestly—how Shelley's desires are communi-
cated through potentially unstable metaphors: in political or poetic
terms, there is no guarantee that Winter will give way to Spring.[12]

And yet it is by opening his poem to the possibility of deconstruc-
tion that Shelley persuades his reader of the need to 'believe in an
optimism in which we are our own gods' (*L* 2. 125). Often he strikes
a balance between sustaining hope and conceding that hope's only
warrant may be the need to hope. In *Julian and Maddalo* (finished in
1819), he stages a debate between optimistic and pessimistic view-
points, and while the narrator Julian articulates a Shelleyan belief in
'the power of man over his own mind' (Preface, p. 212), the poem is
resistant to interpretations that take sides. Maddalo, modelled on
Byron, is also an *alter ego* of the poet himself. Julian's enthusiasm and
Maddalo's tragic cynicism are each presented as responses to being
human that have their own authenticity. At stake for Julian, before
the encounter with the Maniac, is the belief that 'it is our will | That
thus enchains us to permitted ill' (ll. 170–1). Belief in the will's power
is central to Julian's—and Shelley's—hopes of human betterment.
Shelley's hostility to Christian orthodoxy has much to do with dislike
of the acquiescence in some supposed divine will that he saw it as
encouraging; the attractiveness to him of Godwin's *Political Justice*
derives, in large part, from that work's advocacy of tireless aspiration.
With qualifications, a vision of improvement governs Shelley's sense
of history. In *A Philosophical View of Reform* (written in 1819–20),
he traces the contest between 'the spirit of truth and the spirit of
imposture' (p. 639), and asserts confidence in the victory of the

---

[11] See James Chandler in *England in 1819* (Chicago, 1998) on the 'representation of
mutual making' in these lines; quoted from *Norton²* 718.

[12] See Ronald Tetreault's account in *The Poetry of Life: Shelley and Literary Form*
(Toronto, 1987) of how at the close of the 'Ode', 'Shelley willingly surrenders his
authority as poet to the reader' (quoted from O'Neill (ed.), *Shelley*, 140) .

former. At the same time, he grapples with 'the difficult and unbending realities of actual life' (p. 664), in keeping with his self-delineation in a letter to Leigh Hunt as 'one of those whom nothing will fully satisfy, but who [is] ready to be partially satisfied by all that is practicable' (*L* 2. 153). In *Julian and Maddalo* and *The Cenci*, the 'difficult and unbending realities of actual life' make themselves felt in the clash between theory and experience. After Julian and Maddalo have over-heard the Maniac's soliloquy, their 'argument was quite forgot' (l. 520): Maddalo modulates from his earlier despair at the human condition into a more sympathetic awareness that creativity and pain may be complementary (ll. 544–6); Julian wishes, ineffectually yet with authentic concern, that he might act as psychotherapist to the Maniac and 'find | An entrance to the caverns of his mind' (ll. 572–3) in order to 'reclaim him from his dark estate' (l. 574).

   In *The Cenci*, Shelley depicts the 'dark estate' of the human con-dition by attending to the 'caverns of the mind', or, as he calls it in the Preface to the play, 'the human heart' (p. 316). While still a teenager, Shelley had published two Gothic novels, *Zastrozzi* and *St. Irvyne* (both 1810), novels that show a relish for sensationalist plots involving vengeance, hatred, and passionate feeling. In his finest works, this strain of Gothicism transmutes, as it does in the portrait of Beatrice Cenci's father, the sadistic Count, into an altogether more harrowing awareness of the potential for evil in human beings. The play constructs traps even while voicing a desire for freedom. Beatrice, incestuously raped by her father, responds to her violation by con-triving his death. The consequence is a Romantic revenge tragedy that dramatizes with great skill knotty moral dilemmas and induces in the audience a 'restless and anatomizing casuistry' (Preface, p. 317): we want to excuse Beatrice's involvement in her father's assassination yet we 'feel', as Shelley has it, 'that she has done what needs justification'.

2

Controversy about Shelley's worth has always centred on the poet's style, described with malign brilliance by William Hazlitt as 'a passionate dream, a straining after impossibilities, a record of fond conjectures, a confused embodying of vague abstractions'.[13] This style is controversial because the demands it places on the reader are

[13] From Hazlitt's unsigned review of *PP*, in the *Edinburgh Review*, July 1824; quoted from Theodore Redpath, *The Young Romantics and Critical Opinion 1807–1824* (London, 1973), 388.

inseparable from the challenges to received ideas posed by its contents. Among these challenges is Shelley's atheism, itself by no means an uncomplicated stance in the poetry and prose.[14] Even in the hostile attack on the Christian God in *Queen Mab*, in the Note appended to the words 'There is No God!' one comes across the following: 'This negation must be understood solely to affect a creative Deity. The hypothesis of a pervading Spirit coeternal with the universe, remains unshaken' (p. 79). There is what can look like a God-shaped hole in Shelley's work, variously filled by terms such as 'Necessity', 'Power', the 'One', and 'the unknown God', terms that hover between the status of imaginative fictions and sceptical but insistent hypotheses.[15] Shelley wishes to nullify the authority of a Jehovah-like deity conceived in the image and likeness of a tyrannical earthly ruler, but he is conscious of supra-rational intimations which seem evidence of what in *A Defence of Poetry* he calls a 'divinity in man' (p. 698). His dislike of Christianity as an institution coexists with a growing admiration for the 'sublime human character of Jesus Christ', a character 'deformed', we are told in a note to *Hellas*, 'by an imputed identification with a Demon, who tempted, betrayed, and punished the innocent beings who were called into existence by his sole will' (p. 587). The rhetoric is meant to provoke, and one can hear in it the accents of the Shelley who irritated Benjamin Robert Haydon (painter and friend of Keats) by 'saying in the most feminine and gentle voice, "As to that detestable religion, the Christian . . ."'[16] But the admiration for Jesus is heartfelt, as is a quasi-religious spirit of humanist ardour, heard in the essay 'On Christianity' (written in late 1817), where Christ's teachings are interpreted in Shelleyan terms as identifying 'God' with 'all that constitutes human perfection' (*Murray*, p. 259). What is manifest in such redefinitions is not muddle but a readiness to test and explore.

In 'Hymn to Intellectual Beauty' (written in 1816) Shelley rejects as 'Frail spells' (l. 29) attempts to conjure a 'voice from some sublimer world' (l. 25). The words 'God, and ghosts, and Heaven' (version A, l. 27) merely prove the futility of any 'endeavour' (version A, l. 28) to map an other-worldly realm. But Intellectual Beauty is endowed

---

[14] See David Fuller, 'Shelley and Jesus', *Durham University Journal*, NS 54 (1993), 211–23, Robert M. Ryan, *The Romantic Reformation: Religious Politics in English Literature, 1789–1824* (Cambridge, 1997), and Martin Priestman, *Romantic Atheism: Poetry and Freethought 1780–1830* (Cambridge, 2000).

[15] See *Queen Mab*, 6. 197; 'Mont Blanc', l. 16; *Adonais*, l. 460; and *Hellas*, l. 211.

[16] Quoted from Edmund Blunden, *Shelley: A Life Story* (1946; repr. London, 1965), 143.

with the qualities of godhead and addressed with spiritual fervour as Shelley composes his own 'Frail spells'. That it is also less an abstract idea than an eroticized anima-like figure could be seen as having personal implications. A key to Shelley's development may well have been his premature expulsion from a largely female household, the older brother of four sisters, with one of whom, Elizabeth, he wrote his first collection of poems, *Victor and Cazire* (1810). In some of his mature poetry, such as *Epipsychidion*, it is possible to regard Shelley as seeking an imaginative and emotional harmony akin to that which he experienced as a child.[17] Clearly, love and desire contribute a revolutionary if troubling power to the poetry. And yet Shelley is a figure hard simply to include in or exclude from the ranks of Romantic feminism. Against his admiration for the writings of his mother-in-law, Mary Wollstonecraft, his recognition that human liberation must involve both men and women ('Can man be free if woman be a slave?', as a line in *Laon and Cythna* (1817; Canto 2, stanza 43) has it), one might point to an anti-Wollstonecraftian drive to turn women from human beings into idealized objects.

That said, Shelley is so restless and enquiring in his investigations of idealism that he can seem his own severest critic, as is at least hinted by the debate provoked by the central figure of *Alastor* (1816). Is the Poet blamed for his 'self-centred seclusion' (p. 92)? Or is he admired for a tenacity and force of quest that inspires the poem's Narrator to praise him as a 'surpassing Spirit' (l. 714)? What fascinates is the intensity with which Shelley traces the tension between awareness of subjective desire and the longing to leave behind '*self*', that burr that will cling to one' (*L* 2. 109). In 'On Love' (written in 1818), he speaks of love as 'the bond and the sanction which connects not only man with man, but with everything which exists' (p. 632). But he also stresses the unknowableness of others and the genesis of love in an imagining of our own best selves. If Shelley's poetry is often about narcissism, about the lure of falling in love with one's own ideals, it confronts the dangers of such falling in love. The boundaries the verse wishes to break down reassert themselves to productive poetic effect; so, at the close of *Epipsychidion* the poem swings between a sense that words cannot describe the union with another rapturously yearned after in the preceding lines and the admission that such a union is impossible. In the late poems to Jane Williams, poems that occupy

---

[17] See *Sperry* for the connection between the poetry and 'the grown man who sought to recreate a lost harmony through a network of extraordinarily idealized personal relationships', p. ix.

a difficult zone between friendship and love, there is once more a longing for union. Shelley describes Jane's song as 'revealing | A tone | Of some world far from ours | Where music and moonlight and feeling | Are one' ('To Jane ('The keen stars were twinkling'), ll. 20–4). The writing is balanced between a recognition that the desired world is 'far from ours' and the assertion that Jane is, indeed, 'revealing' such a world.

The boundaries between the self and the world, or the private and the public, are fluid in Shelley's work. Though his writing bears the impress of his 'individual mind' (*Peter Bell the Third*, l. 303), he gives poetry a prominent social role, and unsettles the authority of the stable ego. In the essay 'On Life' (written in 1819), he offers a sceptical interrogation of personal identity: 'the existence of distinct individual minds similar to that which is employed in now questioning its own nature, is likewise found to be a delusion' (p. 635). It is characteristic of Shelley's rapidity of thought that the passage sees individuality as 'a delusion' but admits the need to believe in a 'distinct individual mind' capable of questioning its own nature. Shelleyan doubt is never automatic or superficial; he castigates a reductive scepticism in his attack on Enlightenment 'reasoners' in *A Defence of Poetry* (Notes, p. 834). At the same time, he never loses sight of the dangers of a fixed sense of self—whether embodied in the heroic yet hate-blinded resistance of Prometheus to Jupiter, or in the Wordsworthian 'hero' of *Peter Bell the Third*, unable to 'Fancy another situation | From which to dart his contemplation | Than that wherein he stood' (ll. 300–2).

The ability to imagine a different viewpoint is, in fact, crucial to the dialogue between author and reader which Shelley's poetry encourages. An increasingly central impulse in his writing is the wish to work on the reader's imagination, so that the reader will use that imagination to 'Fancy another situation'. As Shelley explains in the Preface to *Prometheus Unbound*, he aims to avoid 'Didactic poetry', to offer, instead, 'beautiful idealisms of moral excellence' (p. 232). If in *Queen Mab* his favoured style is assertion, a capacity for which never deserts him, he develops a capacity to subsume specific ideas within a more ambitious attempt to render the reader's mind 'the receptacle of a thousand unapprehended combinations of thought' (*A Defence of Poetry*, p. 681). In *Laon and Cythna*, narrative events—the story of the education and careers of two revolutionaries—are experienced through the filter of consciousness; much of the work's most compelling writing takes us close to dream, vision, and nightmare, and employs interlacing figurative suggestions. *Prometheus Unbound* does not shy away from abstraction: the Fury's speech to Prometheus in Act 1 asserts that 'The good want power . . . | The powerful goodness want' (1. 626–7) in an incisive analysis of political malaise. Yet, in the act of imagining a millennial universe which replaces hierarchy, power, and authority with harmony, delight in otherness, and freedom, Shelley shapes a language which is symbolic and, in some respects, untranslatable. Echoes and anticipations cluster in the spirit-voiced world of the lyrical drama, until in the final Act we inhabit a genuinely Utopian poetry. Even here, Shelley does not untether his language from reality; he is still capable of plain statement—'Familiar acts are beautiful through love' (4. 403)—and he often depicts the redeemed world of his imaginings through negative epithets that bring to mind, by contrast, things as they were (or are), as when human beings are said to be 'Equal, unclassed, tribeless and nationless' (3. 4. 195).[18] Moreover, his visions of transformation, such as Ione's and Panthea's descriptions of the moon and earth in Act 4, draw on his age's scientific knowledge, gathered into a metaphorical imagination that is also fertilized by memories of passages in Milton and Dante. The lyrical drama is sharply aware of the realities which it seeks to alter. In terms of its plot, this awareness of realities other than will and desire shows in the fact that neither Prometheus' resistance nor Asia's quest for answers and trust in love will, by themselves, bring about change. Something else is needed, a favourable concatenation of events and circumstance, embodied in the form of Demogorgon, a figure needed for the wheel of history to turn.

The aspiring upward spiral, rather than the determinist, revolving cycle, is the trajectory that Shelley would prefer history to describe. But it is part of his honesty that he is able, at the end of *Hellas*, his intervention on the side of the Greeks in their War of Independence against the Turks, to admit the tragic potential that lurks inside the messianic lyric cry, 'The world's great age begins anew' (l. 1060): 'The world is weary of the past,' he concludes, 'O might it die or rest at last!' (ll. 1100–1). 'A shadow tracks thy flight of fire' (l. 3), from 'The Two Spirits—An Allegory', is a line that one can apply to many of Shelley's later poems. In *Adonais* he is on the brink of rejecting this world in favour of 'the white radiance of Eternity' (l. 463), even though life's 'dome of many-coloured glass' (l. 462) has counterbalancing attractions. The unresting drive to explore the match or

---

[18] See Timothy Webb, 'The Unascended Heaven: Negatives in *Prometheus Unbound*', in Kelvin Everest (ed.), *Shelley Revalued: Essays from the Gregynog Conference* (Leicester, 1983).

mismatch between imaginative desire and historical event pervades
his last, unfinished poem, *The Triumph of Life*, in which Shelley con-
fronts the realities of post-Napoleonic Europe. For all its political
gloom, however, *The Triumph of Life* is no straightforward retraction
of earlier aspirations. For one thing, as always in Shelley, the stylish-
ness of the writing is an advertisement for hope; for another, the quest
to understand impels the poem beyond despair, driving the Narrator,
just before the fragment breaks off, to ask, 'what is Life?' (l. 544). It
is a question that resonates because we can hear within it, after the
narrative of Rousseau's encounter with the 'shape all light' (l. 352),
a further Shelleyan question, 'what should life be?' Had Shelley
returned alive from his last, fatal boat-trip across the Gulf of Spezia,
he would have continued to pose both questions with skill, power, and
integrity.

3

This selection, organized chronologically, includes all but one of
Shelley's longer poems, from *Queen Mab* onwards, in their entirety.
Only *Laon and Cythna* (later *The Revolt of Islam*) is excerpted, though
we have found space for almost a third of its 4,818 lines, including the
Dedication, all of Cantos 1 and 2, and substantial extracts from Cantos
6–10 and 12 (plus the poem's prose Preface). In addition to a wide
range of Shelley's shorter poems, we have included a representative
sampling of his prose: the Prefaces to the longer poems, the most
important of the lengthy Notes to *Queen Mab* (which include versions
of *The Necessity of Atheism* and 'A Vindication of Natural Diet'), *An
Address to the People on the Death of the Princess Charlotte*, *A Defence of
Poetry*, almost all of *A Philosophical View of Reform*, and the essays
'On Love' and 'On Life'. Limitations of space have prevented us from
including samples of Shelley's correspondence or any of his trans-
lations. The most important of the translations are of Plato's
Symposium, canto 28 of Dante's *Purgatorio*, *The Cyclops* by Euripides,
and the late, finely wrought Englishings of scenes from Calderón and
Goethe. Shelley's extraordinary breadth of reading—including immer-
sion in the works of many Latin and Greek authors, as well as in the
King James Bible—is everywhere apparent in his poetry; the trans-
lations underline the force of his wish to achieve in his writing that
'identification of ourselves with the beautiful which exists in thought,
action or person, not our own' (*A Defence of Poetry*, p. 682).

CHRONOLOGY

1792   Born 4 Aug. at Field Place, Horsham, Sussex, the eldest child of
            Timothy Shelley, landowner, Whig MP, later Baronet (1806).

1802–4   Educated at Syon House Academy, Isleworth, near London.

1804–10   Educated at Eton.

1810   Publishes two Gothic novels, *Zastrozzi* (spring) and *St. Irvine*
            (Dec.); *Original Poetry by Victor and Cazire* (written with his sister,
            Elizabeth, published and withdrawn, Sept.); and *Posthumous
            Fragments of Margaret Nicholson* (published Nov.). At University
            College, Oxford (from Oct.).

1811   Publishes the pamphlet *The Necessity of Atheism* (Feb., written
            with fellow undergraduate Thomas Jefferson Hogg); expelled with
            Hogg (25 Mar.) for refusing to answer questions about its publica-
            tion. Meets the 16-year-old Harriet Westbrook (Jan.), elopes with
            and marries her (in Edinburgh, 29 Aug.).

1812   Visits Dublin and publishes two pamphlets on Irish political
            reform and Catholic Emancipation, *Address to the Irish People*
            and *Proposals for an Association . . . of Philanthropists* (Feb.); prints
            Declaration of Rights (Mar.). Becomes a vegetarian (Mar.). From
            9 April lives in Wales, then Lynmouth, Devon, where he is under
            government surveillance (for radical activities); writes *Letter to
            Lord Ellenborough*; his servant is imprisoned in Aug. for distri-
            buting *Declaration of Rights* and *The Devil's Walk* (written winter
            1811–12). Continued political activity in Tremadoc, North Wales
            (from Sept.), where William Madocks is building an embankment
            and model village; writes *Queen Mab*. Meets William Godwin
            (Oct.) and Thomas Love Peacock (Nov.). Copies out poems in the
            'Esdaile Notebook' (Nov.–Dec.).

1813   Leaves Tremadoc (26 Dec.), in mysterious and threatening
            circumstances; visits Dublin and Killarney (Mar.); returns to
            London (Apr.). *A Vindication of Natural Diet* privately published
            (Apr.–May, later included as a note to *Queen Mab*). *Queen Mab*
            privately and anonymously published in May. Ianthe Shelley born
            (23 June). Moves to Bracknell, Berkshire (July), near Peacock.

1814   Privately publishes and distributes *A Refutation of Deism* (late
            1813–early 1814). After a growing estrangement with Harriet,
            he meets and elopes with Mary Godwin, daughter of William
            Godwin and Mary Wollstonecraft (27 July); tours continent with
            Mary and her half-sister Claire Clairmont (returning to England
            13 Sept.). Charles Shelley born to Harriet (30 Nov.).

1815   Mary's first child born (22. Feb.); dies two weeks later. After
        death of his grandfather (5 Jan.), financial problems are partially
        alleviated in June by a settlement agreed with his father (including
        a yearly annual allowance of £1,000). Moves to Bishopsgate,
        Windsor Park (Aug.).

1816   William Shelley born to Mary (24 Jan.). Publishes *Alastor . . .
        and Other Poems* (Feb.; *Alastor* itself written in late 1815). Tours
        Switzerland with Mary and Claire (25 May–29 Aug.); meets Byron
        at Lake Geneva, where S. writes 'Hymn to Intellectual Beauty'
        and 'Mont Blanc', and Mary begins writing *Frankenstein*. Returns
        to England 8 Sept., probably leaving the so-called 'Scrope Davies
        Notebook' with Byron (a notebook not returned to Shelley and
        only rediscovered in 1976); settles in Marlow. Suicides of Mary's
        half-sister Fanny Imlay (9 Oct.) and Harriet (9 Nov.). Leigh Hunt
        introduces S. to Keats and Horace Smith (Dec.). Marries Mary
        Godwin (30 Dec.).

1817   Publishes *A Proposal for Putting Reform to the Vote* (Mar.). The
        Lord Chancellor (Lord Eldon) denies S. custody of his two
        children by Harriet (27 Mar.). Writes *Laon and Cythna* (Apr.–
        Sept.; published Dec., then immediately suppressed by publisher).
        Clara Shelley born to Mary (2 Sept.). Works on *Rosalind and Helen*
        (Sept.). Writes *An Address to the People on the Death of the Princess
        Charlotte* (11–12 Nov., a limited number probably printed in 1817
        (none survives); published posthumously, *c*.1843). Anonymous
        publication of *History of a Six Weeks' Tour* by Mary and S. (winter),
        including 'Mont Blanc'. Writes 'Ozymandias' (Dec.; published in
        the *Examiner*, in Jan. 1818).

1818   Publishes *The Revolt of Islam* (revised version of *Laon and Cythna*)
        in Jan. Leaves for Italy (13 Mar.). Meets Maria and John Gisborne
        at Livorno (Leghorn) (May). Moves to Bagni di Lucca (11 June),
        where he finishes *Rosalind and Helen*, translates Plato's *Sym-
        posium*, writes 'On Love'. Meets Byron in Venice (Aug.). Stays
        at Este, near Venice (until 5 Nov.), where he begins work on
        Julian and Maddalo, 'Lines Written among the Euganean Hills',
        and *Prometheus Unbound*. The one-year-old Clara Shelley dies in
        Venice (24 Sept.). Visits Rome (20–7 Nov.), then Naples (11 Dec.),
        where he tours Vesuvius and the Bay of Baiae and writes 'Stanzas
        Written in Dejection . . . near Naples' (Dec.).

1819   Visits Pompeii and Paestum (24–5 Feb.), returning to Rome on
        5 March. Writes Acts 2 and 3 of *Prometheus Unbound* (Mar.–Apr.),
        finishes *Julian and Maddalo* (sent to Hunt in Aug.). Publishes
        Rosalind and Helen . . . with Other Poems (spring). William Shelley
        dies (7 June, aged three-and-a-half). Returns to Livorno (Leghorn)
        (17 June), where completes *The Cenci* (8 Aug.) and has it printed in

Italy, writes *The Mask of Anarchy* (Sept.; published posthumously, 1832). Moves to Florence (2 Oct.), where he writes 'Ode to the West Wind' (late Oct.), *Peter Bell the Third* (Oct.–Nov.), 'On Life' (Nov.–Dec.), *A Philosophical View of Reform* (begun Nov.; unfinished, published posthumously, 1920), 'England in 1819' (Dec.), and Act 4 of *Prometheus Unbound* (finished in Dec.). Percy Florence Shelley born (12 Nov.). Birth of S.'s 'Neapolitan charge', 'Elena Adelaide Shelley' (27 Dec.), registered by S. as his and Mary's child (died 9 June 1820), though it is unlikely that S., Mary, or Claire Clairmont were the child's natural parents.

1820   Moves to Pisa (late Jan.), where writes 'The Sensitive Plant' and publishes *The Cenci* in England (both in spring). Moves to Livorno (15 June–4 Aug.) and writes *Letter to Maria Gisborne*, 'To a Skylark', 'Ode to Liberty'. Moves to the Baths of San Giuliano, near Pisa (Aug.–Oct.) and writes *The Witch of Atlas*, *Swellfoot the Tyrant* (published Dec., and immediately suppressed), and 'Ode to Naples'. Publishes *Prometheus Unbound . . ., with Other Poems* (Aug.). Returns to Pisa (31 Oct.), begins friendship with Emilia Viviani (Dec.) to whom *Epipsychidion* will be addressed.

1821   Edward and Jane Williams, friends of S.'s cousin Thomas Medwin, come to live in Pisa (13 Jan.). Pirated edition of *Queen Mab* published in London by William Clark (who is subsequently imprisoned for its publication). Writes *Epipsychidion* (Jan.–Feb. (though drawing on material written before S. met Viviani); published May), *A Defence of Poetry* (Feb.–Mar.; published posthumously, 1840 [1839]), *Adonais* (Apr.–June; published July), and *Hellas* (Oct.; published 1822). Byron moves to Pisa (1 Nov.).

1822   At work on *Charles the First* (Jan.). Edward Trelawny arrives in Pisa (14 Jan.). Writes poems to Jane Williams (Jan.–July), translates scenes from Goethe and Calderón (Jan.–Feb.). *Hellas* published (Feb.). Moves with family and Edward and Jane Williams to Casa Magni at San Terenzo near Lerici (30 Apr.), where he works on *The Triumph of Life* (May–July; unfinished, posthumously published 1824). On 1 July sails on new boat, the *Don Juan*, to Livorno with Edward Williams (to meet Leigh Hunt and family); on return voyage both men drown with Charles Vivian, a deckhand (8 July). Cremated on 15 Aug. on the beach between La Spezia and Leghorn (his ashes are interred in the Protestant Cemetery in Rome, 1823).

1824   Publication of *Posthumous Poems*, edited by Mary S.; withdrawn from publication because of objections of Sir Timothy.

1839   Publication of Mary S.'s editions of Shelley's poetry (the first in four volumes, the second in one volume) and prose (though the title-page is dated 1840).

NOTE ON THE TEXT

SHELLEY's texts are notoriously difficult to edit. There are two main reasons for this: at his death, he left many poems and prose works unpublished and, indeed, on occasions, unfinished; he did not see proofs for many poems that he did publish during his lifetime. For these reasons, manuscript material is of unusual importance for editors of his work. We have drawn on this manuscript material heavily in editing our texts. Along with the volumes in the *Shelley and His Circle* series, the two series published over the last two decades by Garland, the *Bodleian Shelley Manuscripts* (*BSM*) series and the relevant volumes in the *Manuscripts of the Younger Romantics* (*MYR*) series, both under the general editorship of Donald H. Reiman, have made this manuscript material more widely available. As well as photofacsimiles of the manuscripts, they nearly always include transcriptions and a wealth of detailed commentary. Because each text by Shelley presents its own problems, we have indicated in each note to the poems and prose works our copy-text, referring the reader to relevant facsimile volumes.

Our editorial policy is one of fidelity to copy-text, while retaining the freedom to emend, where appropriate, in the light of other relevant printed or manuscript authorities and our own editorial judgement. Spellings have usually been modernized; occasionally, we have kept the original spelling when modernization would involve the sacrifice of some possibility of word-play (e.g. 'wrapt') or sound value (e.g. 'sate'). Punctuation has been modernized (usually involving the elimination or insertion of commas) when not to do so presents a serious obstacle to understanding. In matters of capitalization we have followed the practice in our copy-text and other relevant printed or manuscript authorities.

The degree sign (°) indicates a note at the end of the book.

'A Cat in distress'

1

A Cat in distress
Nothing more or less
Good folks I must faithfully tell ye,
As I am a sinner
It wants for some dinner
To stuff out its own little belly.

2

You mightn't easily guess
All the modes of distress
Which torture the tenants of earth,
And the various evils
Which like many devils
Attend the poor dogs from their birth.

3

Some a living require
And others desire
An old fellow out of the way,
And which is the best
I leave to be guessed
For I cannot pretend to say.

4

One wants society
T'other variety
Others a tranquil life,
Some want food
Others as good
Only require a wife.

5

But this poor little Cat
Only wanted a rat
To stuff out its own little maw,
And 'twere as good
Had some people such food
To make them hold their jaw.

To the Emperors of Russia and Austria Who Eyed the Battle of Austerlitz from the Heights whilst Buonaparte Was Active in the Thickest of the Fight

Coward Chiefs! who while the fight
   Rages in the plain below
Hide the shame of your affright
   On yon distant mountain's brow,
Does one human feeling creep
Through your hearts' remorseless sleep?
On that silence cold and deep
   Does one impulse flow
Such as fires the Patriot's breast,
Such as breaks the Hero's rest?   10

No, cowards! ye are calm and still.
   Keen frosts that blight the human bud
Each opening petal blight and kill
   And bathe its tenderness in blood.
Ye hear the groans of those who die,
Ye hear the whistling death-shots fly.
And when the yells of Victory
   Float o'er the murdered good,
Ye smile secure.—On yonder plain
   The game, if lost, begins again.   20

Think ye the restless fiend who haunts
   The tumult of yon gory field,
Whom neither shame nor danger daunts,
   Who dares not fear, who cannot yield,
Will not with Equalizing blow
Exalt the high, abase the low,°
And in one mighty shock o'erthrow
   The slaves that sceptres wield,
Till from the ruin of the storm
   Ariseth Freedom's awful form?   30

Hushed below the battle's jar
   Night rests silent on the Heath,
Silent save when vultures soar
   Above the wounded warrior's death.
How sleep ye now, unfeeling Kings!
   Peace seldom folds her snowy wings
On poisoned memory's conscience-stings,
   Which lurk bad hearts beneath,
Nor downy beds procure repose
Where crime and terror mingle throes.   40

Yet may your terrors rest secure.
   Thou Northern chief, why startest thou?°
Pale Austria, calm those fears. Be sure°
   The tyrant needs such slaves as you.°
Think ye the world would bear his sway
Were dastards such as you away?
No! they would pluck his plumage gay
   Torn from a nation's woe,
And lay him in the oblivious gloom
Where Freedom now prepares your tomb.   50

Zeinab and Kathema

Upon the lonely beach Kathema lay;
   Against his folded arm his heart beat fast.
Through gathering tears the Sun's departing ray
   In coldness o'er his shuddering spirit passed
And all unfelt the breeze of evening came
That fanned with quivering wing his wan cheek's feeble flame.

'Oh!' cried the mourner, 'could this widowed soul
   But fly where yonder Sun now speeds to dawn.'°
He paused—a thousand thoughts began to roll;
   Like waves they swept in restless tumult on,   10
Like those fast waves that quick-succeeding beat
Without one lasting shape the beach beneath his feet.

And now the beamless, broad and yellow sphere
    Half sinking lingered on the crimson sea.
A shape of darksome distance does appear
    Within its semicircled radiancy.
All sense was gone to his betrothed one—
His eye fell on the form that dimmed the setting sun,—

He thought on his betrothed . . . for his youth
    With her that was its charm to ripeness grew.   20
All that was dear in love, or fair in truth,
    With her was shared as childhood's moments flew,
And mingled with sweet memories of her
Was life's unveiling morn with all its bliss and care,

A wild and lovely Superstition's spell—
    Love for the friend that life and freedom gave,
Youth's growing hopes that watch themselves so well,
    Passion so prompt to blight, so strong to save,
And childhood's host of memories combine
Her life and love around his being to entwine.   30

And to their wishes with its joy-mixed pain
    Just as the veil of hope began to fall,
The Christian murderers over-ran the plain,
    Ravaging, burning and polluting all.
Zeinab was reft to grace the robber's land;
Each drop of kindred blood stained the invaders' brand.

Yes! they had come their holy book to bring
    Which God's own son's apostles had compiled,
That charity and peace and love might spring
    Within a world by God's blind ire defiled,   40
But rapine, war and treachery rushed before
Their hosts, and murder dyed Kathema's bower in gore.

Therefore his soul was widowed, and alone
    He stood in the world's wide and drear expanse.
No human ear could shudder at his groan,
    No heart could thrill with his unspeaking glance,
One only hope yet lingering dared to burn,
Urging to high emprise and deeds that danger spurn.

The glow has failed on Ocean's western line,
    Faded from every moveless cloud above.   50
The moon is up—she that was wont to shine
    And bless thy childish nights of guileless love,
Unhappy one, ere Christian rapine tore
All ties, and stained thy hopes in a dear mother's gore.

The form that in the setting Sun was seen
    Now in the moonlight slowly nears the shore,
The white sails gleaming o'er the billows green
    That sparkle into foam its prow before.
A wanderer of the deep it seems to be
On high adventures bent, and feats of chivalry.   60

Then hope and wonder filled the mourner's mind.
    He gazed till vision even began to fail,
When to the pulses of the evening wind
    A little boat approaching gave its sail,
Rode o'er the slow raised surges near the strand,
Ran up the beach and gave some stranger men to land.

'If thou wilt bear me to far England's shore
    Thine is this heap, the Christian's God.'
The chief with gloating rapture viewed the ore
    And his pleased avarice gave the willing nod.   70
They reach the ship, the freshening breezes rise
And smooth and fast they speed beneath the moonlight skies.

What heart e'er felt more ardent longings now?
    What eye than his e'er beamed with riper hope
As curbed impatience on his open brow
    There painted fancy's unsuspected scope,
As all that's fair the foreign land appeared
By ever present love, wonder and hope endeared?

Meanwhile through calm and storm, through night and day,
    Unvarying in her aim the vessel went   80
As if some inward spirit ruled her way
    And her tense sails were conscious of intent,
Till Albion's cliffs gleamed o'er her plunging bow
And Albion's river floods bright sparkled round her prow.

Then on the land in joy Kathema leaped
    And kissed the soil in which his hopes were sown;
These even now in thought his heart has reaped.
    Elate of body and soul he journeyed on
And the strange things of a strange land passed by
Like motes and shadows pressed upon his charmèd eye.°   90

Yet Albion's changeful skies and chilling wind,
    The change from Cashmire's vale might well denote.
There Heaven and Earth are ever bright and kind,
    Here blights and storms and damp forever float,
Whilst hearts are more ungenial than the zone,
Gross, spiritless, alive to no pangs but their own.

There flowers and fruits are ever fair and ripe,
    Autumn there mingles with the bloom of spring,
And forms unpinched by frost or hunger's gripe,
    A natural veil o'er natural spirits fling.   100
Here, woe on all but wealth has set its foot,
Famine, disease and crime even wealth's proud gates pollute.

Unquiet death and premature decay,
    Youth tottering on the crutches of old age,
And ere the noon of manhood's riper day
    Pangs that no art of medicine can assuage,
Madness and passion ever mingling flames,
And souls that well become such miserable frames—

These are the bribes which Art to man has given
    To yield his taintless nature to her sway.   110
So might dank night with meteors tempt fair Heaven
    To blot the sunbeam and forswear the day
Till gleams of baleful light alone might show
The pestilential mists, the darkness and the woe.

Kathema little felt the sleet and wind,
    He little heeded the wide altered scene.
The flame that lived within his eager mind
    There kindled all the thoughts that once had been.
He stood alone in England's varied woe,
Safe, mid the flood of crime that round his steps did flow.   120

It was an evening when the bitterest breath
    Of dark December swept the mists along
That the lone wanderer came to a wild heath.
    Courage and hope had stayed his nature long,
Now cold and unappeasèd hunger spent
His strength; sensation failed in total languishment.

When he awaked to life cold horror crept
    Even to his heart, for a damp deathy smell
Had slowly come around him while he slept.
    He started . . . lo! the fitful moonbeams fell   130
Upon a dead and naked female form
That from a gibbet high swung to the sullen storm.°

And wildly in the wind its dark hair swung,
    Low mingling with the clangour of the chain,
Whilst ravenous birds of prey that on it clung
    In the dull ear of night poured their sad strain,
And ghastlily her shapeless visage shone
In the unsteady light, half mouldered through the bone.

Then madness seized Kathema, and his mind
    A prophecy of horror filled. He scaled   140
The gibbet which swung slowly in the wind
    High o'er the heath.—Scarcely his strength availed
To grasp the chain, when by the moonlight's gleam
His palsied gaze was fixed on Zeinab's altered frame.

Yes! in those orbs once bright with life and love
    Now full-fed worms bask in unnatural light;
That neck on which his eyes were wont to rove
    In rapture, changed by putrefaction's blight.
Now rusts the ponderous links that creak beneath
Its weight, and turns to life the frightful sport of death.°   150

Then in the moonlight played Kathema's smile
    Calmly.—In peace his spirit seemed to be.
He paused even like a man at ease awhile,
    Then spoke—'My love! I will be like to thee,
A mouldering carcase or a spirit blest,
With thee corruption's prey, or Heavens happy guest.'

He twined the chain around his neck, then leaped
    Forward, in haste to meet the life to come.
An iron-souled son of Europe might have wept
    To witness such a noble being's doom,   160
As on the death scene Heaven indignant frowned
And Night in horror drew her veil the dead around.

For they had torn his Zeinab from her home.
    Her innocent habits were all rudely shriven —°
And dragged to live in love's untimely tomb
    To prostitution, crime and woe was driven.
The human race seemed leagued against her weal,
And indignation cased her naked heart in steel.

Therefore against them she waged ruthless war
    With their own arms of bold and bloody crime,   170
Even like a mild and sweetly-beaming star
    Whose rays were wont to grace the matin prime°
Changed to a comet horrible and bright
Which wild careers awhile then sinks in dark-red night.

Thus, like its God, unjust and pitiless,
    Crimes first are made and then avenged by man,
For where's the tender heart, whose hope can bless
    Or man's, or God's, unprofitable plan,
A universe of horror and decay,
Gibbets, disease, and wars and hearts as hard as they?   180

Sonnet

On Launching Some Bottles Filled with Knowledge into the Bristol Channel

Vessels of Heavenly medicine! may the breeze
Auspicious waft your dark green forms to shore;
Safe may ye stern the wide surrounding roar°
Of the wild whirlwinds and the raging seas:
And oh! if Liberty e'er deigned to stoop

From yonder lowly throne her crownless brow,
Sure she will breathe around your emerald group
The fairest breezes of her west that blow.°
Yes! she will waft ye to some freeborn soul
Whose eyebeam, kindling as it meets your freight,   10
Her heaven-born flame on suffering Earth will light
Until its radiance gleams from pole to pole
And tyrant-hearts with powerless envy burst
To see their night of ignorance dispersed.

Sonnet

To a Balloon, Laden with Knowledge

Bright ball of flame that through the gloom of even
Silently takest thine etherial way
And with surpassing glory dimm'st each ray
Twinkling amid the dark blue Depths of Heaven,
Unlike the Fire thou bearest, soon shalt thou
Fade like a meteor in surrounding gloom,
Whilst that, unquenchable, is doomed to glow
A watch-light by the patriot's lonely tomb,
A ray of courage to the oppressed and poor,
A spark though gleaming on the hovel's hearth   10
Which through the tyrant's gilded domes shall roar,
A beacon in the darkness of the Earth,
A Sun which o'er the renovated scene
Shall dart like Truth where Falsehood yet has been.

QUEEN MAB;

A PHILOSOPHICAL POEM

WITH NOTES

ÉCRASEZ L'INFAME!

Correspondance de Voltaire.°

Avia Pieridum peragro loca, nullius ante
Trita solo; juvat integros accedere fonteis;
Atque haurire: juvatque novos decerpere flores.

    *   *   *   *   *   *   *

Unde prius nulli velarint tempora musae.
Primum quod magnis doceo de rebus; et arctis
Religionum animos nodis exsolvere pergo.—Lucret. lib. iv°

Δος που στώ, καὶ κοσμον κινησω.—Archimedes°

To Harriet * * * * *°

Whose is the love that, gleaming through the world,
Wards off the poisonous arrow of its scorn?
   Whose is the warm and partial praise,
   Virtue's most sweet reward?

Beneath whose looks did my reviving soul
Riper in truth and virtuous daring grow?
   Whose eyes have I gazed fondly on,
   And loved mankind the more?

Harriet! on thine:—thou wert my purer mind;
Thou wert the inspiration of my song;   10
   Thine are these early wilding flowers,
   Though garlanded by me.

Then press unto thy breast this pledge of love,
And know, though time may change and years may roll,
   Each flowret gathered in my heart
   It consecrates to thine.

I

How wonderful is Death,
  Death and his brother Sleep!
One, pale as yonder waning moon
  With lips of lurid blue;
The other, rosy as the morn
  When throned on ocean's wave
  It blushes o'er the world:
Yet both so passing wonderful!

  Hath then the gloomy Power
Whose reign is in the tainted sepulchres   10
  Seized on her sinless soul?
  Must then that peerless form
Which love and admiration cannot view
Without a beating heart, those azure veins
Which steal like streams along a field of snow,
  That lovely outline, which is fair
    As breathing marble, perish?
    Must putrefaction's breath
  Leave nothing of this heavenly sight
    But loathsomeness and ruin?   20
  Spare nothing but a gloomy theme,
On which the lightest heart might moralize?
  Or is it only a sweet slumber
    Stealing o'er sensation,
  Which the breath of roseate morning
    Chaseth into darkness?
    Will Ianthe wake again,°
  And give that faithful bosom joy
  Whose sleepless spirit waits to catch
Light, life and rapture from her smile?   30

    Yes! she will wake again,
Although her glowing limbs are motionless,
    And silent those sweet lips,
    Once breathing eloquence,
  That might have soothed a tiger's rage,
Or thawed the cold heart of a conqueror.
    Her dewy eyes are closed,

And on their lids, whose texture fine
Scarce hides the dark blue orbs beneath,
   The baby Sleep is pillowèd: 40
   Her golden tresses shade
   The bosom's stainless pride,
Curling like tendrils of the parasite
   Around a marble column.

   Hark! whence that rushing sound?
   'Tis like the wondrous strain
That round a lonely ruin swells,
Which, wandering on the echoing shore,
   The enthusiast hears at evening:
'Tis softer than the west wind's sigh;   50
'Tis wilder than the unmeasured notes
Of that strange lyre whose strings°
The genii of the breezes sweep:°
   Those lines of rainbow light
Are like the moonbeams when they fall
Through some cathedral window, but the tints
   Are such as may not find
   Comparison on earth.

Behold the chariot of the Fairy Queen!
Celestial coursers paw the unyielding air;   60
Their filmy pennons at her word they furl,°
And stop obedient to the reins of light:
   These the Queen of spells drew in,
   She spread a charm around the spot,
And leaning graceful from the etherial car,
   Long did she gaze, and silently,
   Upon the slumbering maid.

Oh! not the visioned poet in his dreams,
When silvery clouds float through the wildered brain,
When every sight of lovely, wild and grand   70
   Astonishes, enraptures, elevates,
   When fancy at a glance combines
   The wondrous and the beautiful,—
So bright, so fair, so wild a shape
   Hath ever yet beheld,

As that which reined the coursers of the air,
  And poured the magic of her gaze
    Upon the maiden's sleep.

    The broad and yellow moon
    Shone dimly through her form—   80
That form of faultless symmetry;
The pearly and pellucid car
  Moved not the moonlight's line:
  'Twas not an earthly pageant:
Those who had looked upon the sight,
  Passing all human glory,
  Saw not the yellow moon,
  Saw not the mortal scene,
  Heard not the night-wind's rush,
  Heard not an earthly sound,   90
  Saw but the fairy pageant,
  Heard but the heavenly strains
  That filled the lonely dwelling.

The Fairy's frame was slight, yon fibrous cloud,°
That catches but the palest tinge of even,
And which the straining eye can hardly seize
When melting into eastern twilight's shadow,
Were scarce so thin, so slight; but the fair star
That gems the glittering coronet of morn,°
Sheds not a light so mild, so powerful,   100
As that which, bursting from the Fairy's form,
Spread a purpureal halo round the scene,°
  Yet with an undulating motion,
  Swayed to her outline gracefully.

    From her celestial car
    The Fairy Queen descended,
    And thrice she waved her wand
Circled with wreaths of amaranth:°
    Her thin and misty form
    Moved with the moving air,   110
    And the clear silver tones,
    As thus she spoke, were such
As are unheard by all but gifted ear.

Fairy

Stars! your balmiest influence shed!
Elements! your wrath suspend!
Sleep, Ocean, in the rocky bounds
  That circle thy domain!
 Let not a breath be seen to stir
 Around yon grass-grown ruin's height,
  Let even the restless gossamer   120
   Sleep on the moveless air!
   Soul of Ianthe! thou,
Judged alone worthy of the envied boon
That waits the good and the sincere; that waits
Those who have struggled, and with resolute will
Vanquished earth's pride and meanness, burst the chains,
The icy chains of custom, and have shone
The day-stars of their age;—Soul of Ianthe!
    Awake! arise!

   Sudden arose   130
   Ianthe's Soul; it stood
 All beautiful in naked purity,
  The perfect semblance of its bodily frame,
Instinct with inexpressible beauty and grace.
   Each stain of earthliness
  Had passed away, it reassumed
  Its native dignity, and stood
   Immortal amid ruin.

  Upon the couch the body lay
   Wrapt in the depth of slumber:°   140
Its features were fixèd and meaningless,
  Yet animal life was there,
 And every organ yet performed
 Its natural functions: 'twas a sight
Of wonder to behold the body and soul.
 The self-same lineaments, the same
 Marks of identity were there:
Yet, oh, how different! One aspires to Heaven,
Pants for its sempiternal heritage,°

And ever changing, ever rising still, 150
    Wantons in endless being.
The other, for a time the unwilling sport
Of circumstance and passion, struggles on;
Fleets through its sad duration rapidly;
Then like an useless and worn-out machine,
    Rots, perishes, and passes.

Fairy

    Spirit! who hast dived so deep;
    Spirit! who hast soared so high;
    Thou the fearless, thou the mild,
Accept the boon thy worth hath earned, 160
    Ascend the car with me.

Spirit

    Do I dream? is this new feeling
    But a visioned ghost of slumber?
      If indeed I am a soul,
    A free, a disembodied soul,
      Speak again to me.

Fairy

I am the Fairy MAB: to me 'tis given
The wonders of the human world to keep:
The secrets of the immeasurable past,
In the unfailing consciences of men, 170
Those stern, unflattering chroniclers, I find:
The future, from the causes which arise
In each event, I gather: not the sting
Which retributive memory implants
In the hard bosom of the selfish man;
Nor that ecstatic and exulting throb
Which virtue's votary feels when he sums up
The thoughts and actions of a well-spent day,
Are unforeseen, unregistered by me:
And it is yet permitted me, to rend 180
The veil of mortal frailty, that the spirit
Clothed in its changeless purity, may know
How soonest to accomplish the great end
For which it hath its being, and may taste

That peace, which in the end all life will share.
This is the meed of virtue; happy Soul,
Ascend the car with me!

The chains of earth's immurement
Fell from Ianthe's spirit;
They shrank and brake like bandages of straw   190
Beneath a wakened giant's strength.
She knew her glorious change,
And felt in apprehension uncontrolled
New raptures opening round:
Each day-dream of her mortal life,
Each frenzied vision of the slumbers
That closed each well-spent day,
Seemed now to meet reality.

The Fairy and the Soul proceeded;
The silver clouds disparted;   200
And as the car of magic they ascended,
Again the speechless music swelled,
Again the coursers of the air
Unfurled their azure pennons, and the Queen
Shaking the beamy reins
Bade them pursue their way.

The magic car moved on.
The night was fair, and countless stars
Studded heaven's dark blue vault,—
Just o'er the eastern wave   210
Peeped the first faint smile of morn:—
The magic car moved on—
From the celestial hoofs
The atmosphere in flaming sparkles flew,
And where the burning wheels
Eddied above the mountain's loftiest peak,
Was traced a line of lightning.
Now it flew far above a rock,
The utmost verge of earth,
The rival of the Andes, whose dark brow   220
Lowered o'er the silver sea.

Far, far below the chariot's path,
   Calm as a slumbering babe,
   Tremendous Ocean lay.
The mirror of its stillness showed
   The pale and waning stars,
   The chariot's fiery track,
   And the grey light of morn
   Tinging those fleecy clouds
   That canopied the dawn.   230
  Seemed it, that the chariot's way
Lay through the midst of an immense concave,
Radiant with million constellations, tinged
   With shades of infinite colour,
   And semicircled with a belt°
   Flashing incessant meteors.

   The magic car moved on.
   As they approached their goal
The coursers seemed to gather speed;
The sea no longer was distinguished; earth   240
  Appeared a vast and shadowy sphere;
   The sun's unclouded orb
   Rolled through the black concave;°
   Its rays of rapid light
Parted around the chariot's swifter course,
  And fell, like ocean's feathery spray
   Dashed from the boiling surge
   Before a vessel's prow.

   The magic car moved on.
   Earth's distant orb appeared   250
The smallest light that twinkles in the heaven;
   Whilst round the chariot's way
   Innumerable systems rolled,°
   And countless spheres diffused
   An ever-varying glory.
  It was a sight of wonder: some
  Were hornèd like the crescent moon;
  Some shed a mild and silver beam
  Like Hesperus o'er the western sea;°
  Some dashed athwart with trains of flame,°   260

Like worlds to death and ruin driven;
Some shone like suns, and as the chariot passed,
        Eclipsed all other light.

        Spirit of Nature! here!
    In this interminable wilderness
    Of worlds, at whose immensity
        Even soaring fancy staggers,
        Here is thy fitting temple.
        Yet not the lightest leaf
    That quivers to the passing breeze   270
        Is less instinct with thee:
        Yet not the meanest worm
    That lurks in graves and fattens on the dead
        Less shares thy eternal breath.
        Spirit of Nature! thou!
        Imperishable as this scene,
        Here is thy fitting temple.

        2

If solitude hath ever led thy steps
    To the wild ocean's echoing shore,
        And thou hast lingered there,
        Until the sun's broad orb
    Seemed resting on the burnished wave,
        Thou must have marked the lines
    Of purple gold, that motionless
        Hung o'er the sinking sphere:
    Thou must have marked the billowy clouds
    Edged with intolerable radiancy   10
        Towering like rocks of jet
        Crowned with a diamond wreath.
        And yet there is a moment,
        When the sun's highest point
    Peeps like a star o'er ocean's western edge,
    When those far clouds of feathery gold,
        Shaded with deepest purple, gleam
        Like islands on a dark blue sea;

Then has thy fancy soared above the earth,
    And furled its wearied wing   20
    Within the Fairy's fane.°

    Yet not the golden islands
    Gleaming in yon flood of light,
        Nor the feathery curtains
    Stretching o'er the sun's bright couch,
    Nor the burnished ocean waves
        Paving that gorgeous dome,
  So fair, so wonderful a sight
As Mab's etherial palace could afford.
Yet likest evening's vault, that faery Hall!   30
As Heaven, low resting on the wave, it spread
        Its floors of flashing light,
        Its vast and azure dome,
        Its fertile golden islands
        Floating on a silver sea;
Whilst suns their mingling beamings darted
Through clouds of circumambient darkness,
    And pearly battlements around
  Looked o'er the immense of Heaven.

    The magic car no longer moved.   40
      The Fairy and the Spirit
      Entered the Hall of Spells:
        Those golden clouds
    That rolled in glittering billows
    Beneath the azure canopy
With the etherial footsteps trembled not:
        The light and crimson mists,
Floating to strains of thrilling melody
    Through that unearthly dwelling,
Yielded to every movement of the will.   50
Upon their passive swell the Spirit leaned,
And, for the varied bliss that pressed around,°
    Used not the glorious privilege
    Of virtue and of wisdom.

    'Spirit!' the Fairy said,
And pointed to the gorgeous dome,

'This is a wondrous sight
And mocks all human grandeur;
But, were it virtue's only meed, to dwell°
In a celestial palace, all resigned   60
To pleasurable impulses, immured
Within the prison of itself, the will
Of changeless nature would be unfulfilled.
Learn to make others happy. Spirit, come!
This is thine high reward:—the past shall rise;
Thou shalt behold the present; I will teach
        The secrets of the future.'

        The Fairy and the Spirit
Approached the overhanging battlement.—
        Below lay stretched the universe!   70
        There, far as the remotest line
        That bounds imagination's flight,
            Countless and unending orbs
        In mazy motion intermingled,
        Yet still fulfilled immutably
            Eternal nature's law.
            Above, below, around
            The circling systems formed
        A wilderness of harmony;
        Each with undeviating aim,   80
In eloquent silence, through the depths of space
        Pursued its wondrous way.

        There was a little light
That twinkled in the misty distance:
            None but a spirit's eye
            Might ken that rolling orb;
            None but a spirit's eye,
            And in no other place
But that celestial dwelling, might behold
Each action of this earth's inhabitants.   90
            But matter, space and time
In those aerial mansions cease to act;
And all-prevailing wisdom, when it reaps
The harvest of its excellence, o'erbounds

Those obstacles, of which an earthly soul
    Fears to attempt the conquest.

    The Fairy pointed to the earth.
    The Spirit's intellectual eye
    Its kindred beings recognized.
The thronging thousands, to a passing view,   100
    Seemed like an anthill's citizens.
      How wonderful! that even
The passions, prejudices, interests,
That sway the meanest being, the weak touch
      That moves the finest nerve,
      And in one human brain
Causes the faintest thought, becomes a link
    In the great chain of nature.

    'Behold', the Fairy cried,
'Palmyra's ruined palaces!—°   110
    Behold! where grandeur frowned;
    Behold! where pleasure smiled;
What now remains?—the memory
    Of senselessness and shame—
    What is immortal there?
    Nothing—it stands to tell
    A melancholy tale, to give
    An awful warning: soon
Oblivion will steal silently
    The remnant of its fame.   120
    Monarchs and conquerors there
Proud o'er prostrate millions trod—
The earthquakes of the human race;
Like them, forgotten when the ruin
    That marks their shock is past.

    'Beside the eternal Nile,
    The Pyramids have risen.
Nile shall pursue his changeless way:
    Those pyramids shall fall;
Yea! not a stone shall stand to tell   130
    The spot whereon they stood;

Their very site shall be forgotten,
 As is their builder's name!

 'Behold yon sterile spot;
Where now the wandering Arab's tent
 Flaps in the desert-blast.
There once old Salem's haughty fane°
Reared high to heaven its thousand golden domes,
 And in the blushing face of day
  Exposed its shameful glory.   140
Oh! many a widow, many an orphan cursed
The building of that fane; and many a father,
Worn out with toil and slavery, implored
The poor man's God to sweep it from the earth,
And spare his children the detested task
Of piling stone on stone, and poisoning
  The choicest days of life,
  To soothe a dotard's vanity.°
There an inhuman and uncultured race
Howled hideous praises to their Demon-God; 150
They rushed to war, tore from the mother's womb
The unborn child,—old age and infancy
Promiscuous perished; their victorious arms°
Left not a soul to breathe. Oh! they were fiends:
But what was he who taught them that the God°
Of nature and benevolence had given
A special sanction to the trade of blood?
His name and theirs are fading, and the tales
Of this barbarian nation, which imposture
Recites till terror credits, are pursuing° 160
 Itself into forgetfulness.

 'Where Athens, Rome, and Sparta stood,
There is a moral desert now:
The mean and miserable huts,
The yet more wretched palaces,
Contrasted with those ancient fanes,
Now crumbling to oblivion;
The long and lonely colonnades,
Through which the ghost of Freedom stalks,
  Seem like a well-known tune, 170

Which in some dear scene we have loved to hear,
        Remembered now in sadness.
        But, oh! how much more changed,
        How gloomier is the contrast
        Of human nature there!
Where Socrates expired, a tyrant's slave,°
A coward and a fool, spreads death around—
        Then, shuddering, meets his own.
Where Cicero and Antoninus lived,
    A cowled and hypocritical monk   180
        Prays, curses and deceives.°

        'Spirit! ten thousand years
        Have scarcely passed away,
Since, in the waste where now the savage drinks
His enemy's blood, and aping Europe's sons,
        Wakes the unholy song of war,
        Arose a stately city,°
Metropolis of the western continent:
    There, now, the mossy column-stone,
Indented by time's unrelaxing grasp,   190
        Which once appeared to brave
        All, save its country's ruin;
        There the wide forest scene,
Rude in the uncultivated loveliness
        Of gardens long run wild,
Seems, to the unwilling sojourner, whose steps
    Chance in that desert has delayed,
Thus to have stood since earth was what it is.
    Yet once it was the busiest haunt,
Whither, as to a common centre, flocked   200
    Strangers, and ships, and merchandise:
        Once peace and freedom blessed
        The cultivated plain:
        But wealth, that curse of man,
Blighted the bud of its prosperity:
Virtue and wisdom, truth and liberty,
Fled, to return not, until man shall know
    That they alone can give the bliss
        Worthy a soul that claims
    Its kindred with eternity.   210

'There's not one atom of yon earth
    But once was living man;
Nor the minutest drop of rain,
That hangeth in its thinnest cloud,
    But flowed in human veins:
    And from the burning plains
    Where Lybian monsters yell,
    From the most gloomy glens
    Of Greenland's sunless clime,
    To where the golden fields   220
    Of fertile England spread
    Their harvest to the day,
    Thou canst not find one spot
    Whereon no city stood.

    How strange is human pride!
I tell thee that those living things,
To whom the fragile blade of grass,
    That springeth in the morn
    And perisheth ere noon,
    Is an unbounded world;   230
I tell thee that those viewless beings,
Whose mansion is the smallest particle
Of the impassive atmosphere,
    Think, feel and live like man;
That their affections and antipathies,
    Like his, produce the laws
    Ruling their moral state;
    And the minutest throb
    That through their frame diffuses
    The slightest, faintest motion,   240
    Is fixed and indispensable
    As the majestic laws
    That rule yon rolling orbs.'

    The Fairy paused. The Spirit,
In ecstacy of admiration, felt
All knowledge of the past revived; the events
    Of old and wondrous times,
Which dim tradition interruptedly
Teaches the credulous vulgar, were unfolded
    In just perspective to the view;   250

Yet dim from their infinitude.
      The Spirit seemed to stand
High on an isolated pinnacle;
The flood of ages combating below,
The depth of the unbounded universe
      Above, and all around
  Nature's unchanging harmony.

3

  'Fairy!' the Spirit said,
  And on the Queen of spells
  Fixed her etherial eyes,
  'I thank thee. Thou hast given
A boon which I will not resign, and taught
A lesson not to be unlearned. I know
The past, and thence I will essay to glean
A warning for the future, so that man
May profit by his errors, and derive
    Experience from his folly: 10
For, when the power of imparting joy
Is equal to the will, the human soul
    Requires no other heaven.'

       Mab

  Turn thee, surpassing Spirit!
  Much yet remains unscanned.
  Thou knowest how great is man,
  Thou knowest his imbecility:°
  Yet learn thou what he is;
  Yet learn the lofty destiny
  Which restless time prepares   20
  For every living soul.

Behold a gorgeous palace, that, amid
Yon populous city, rears its thousand towers
And seems itself a city. Gloomy troops
Of sentinels, in stern and silent ranks,
Encompass it around: the dweller there
Cannot be free and happy; hearest thou not
The curses of the fatherless, the groans
Of those who have no friend? He passes on:

The King, the wearer of a gilded chain   30
That binds his soul to abjectness, the fool
Whom courtiers nickname monarch, whilst a slave
Even to the basest appetites—that man
Heeds not the shriek of penury; he smiles
At the deep curses which the destitute
Mutter in secret, and a sullen joy
Pervades his bloodless heart when thousands groan
But for those morsels which his wantonness
Wastes in unjoyous revelry, to save
All that they love from famine: when he hears   40
The tale of horror, to some ready-made face
Of hypocritical assent he turns,
Smothering the glow of shame, that, spite of him,
Flushes his bloated check.
                                    Now to the meal
Of silence, grandeur, and excess, he drags
His palled unwilling appetite. If gold,°
Gleaming around, and numerous viands culled
From every clime, could force the loathing sense
To overcome satiety,—if wealth
The spring it draws from poisons not,—or vice,   50
Unfeeling, stubborn vice, converteth not
Its food to deadliest venom; then that king
Is happy; and the peasant who fulfils
His unforced task, when he returns at even,
And by the blazing faggot meets again
Her welcome for whom all his toil is sped,
Tastes not a sweeter meal.
                                    Behold him now
Stretched on the gorgeous couch; his fevered brain
Reels dizzily awhile: but ah! too soon
The slumber of intemperance subsides,   60
And conscience, that undying serpent, calls
Her venomous brood to their nocturnal task.
Listen! he speaks! oh! mark that frenzied eye—
Oh! mark that deadly visage.

King
                                    No cessation!
Oh! must this last for ever! Awful death,

I wish, yet fear to clasp thee!—Not one moment
Of dreamless sleep! O dear and blessed peace!
Why dost thou shroud thy vestal purity
In penury and dungeons? wherefore lurkest
With danger, death, and solitude; yet shun'st 70
The palace I have built thee? Sacred peace!
Oh visit me but once, but pitying shed
One drop of balm upon my withered soul.

Fairy

Vain man! that palace is the virtuous heart,
And peace defileth not her snowy robes
In such a shed as thine. Hark! yet he mutters;
His slumbers are but varied agonies,
They prey like scorpions on the springs of life.
There needeth not the hell that bigots frame
To punish those who err: earth in itself 80
Contains at once the evil and the cure;
And all-sufficing nature can chastise
Those who transgress her law—she only knows
How justly to proportion to the fault
The punishment it merits.
                                   Is it strange
That this poor wretch should pride him in his woe?
Take pleasure in his abjectness, and hug
The scorpion that consumes him? Is it strange
That, placed on a conspicuous throne of thorns,
Grasping an iron sceptre, and immured 90
Within a splendid prison, whose stern bounds
Shut him from all that's good or dear on earth,
His soul asserts not its humanity?
That man's mild nature rises not in war
Against a king's employ? No—'tis not strange.
He, like the vulgar, thinks, feels, acts and lives
Just as his father did; the unconquered powers
Of precedent and custom interpose
Between a *king* and virtue. Stranger yet,
To those who know not nature, nor deduce 100
The future from the present, it may seem,
That not one slave, who suffers from the crimes
Of this unnatural being; not one wretch,

Whose children famish, and whose nuptial bed
Is earth's unpitying bosom, rears an arm
To dash him from his throne!
                         Those gilded flies
That, basking in the sunshine of a court,
Fatten on its corruption!—what are they?
—The drones of the community; they feed
On the mechanic's labour: the starved hind°   110
For them compels the stubborn glebe to yield°
Its unshared harvests; and yon squalid form,
Leaner than fleshless misery, that wastes
A sunless life in the unwholesome mine,
Drags out in labour a protracted death,
To glut their grandeur; many faint with toil,
That few may know the cares and woe of sloth.

Whence, thinkest thou, kings and parasites arose?
Whence that unnatural line of drones, who heap
Toil and unvanquishable penury   120
On those who build their palaces, and bring
Their daily bread?—From vice, black loathsome vice;
From rapine, madness, treachery, and wrong;
From all that genders misery, and makes
Of earth this thorny wilderness; from lust,
Revenge, and murder. . . . And when reason's voice,
Loud as the voice of nature, shall have waked
The nations; and mankind perceive that vice
Is discord, war, and misery; that virtue
Is peace, and happiness and harmony;   130
When man's maturer nature shall disdain
The playthings of its childhood;—kingly glare
Will lose its power to dazzle; its authority
Will silently pass by; the gorgeous throne
Shall stand unnoticed in the regal hall,
Fast falling to decay; whilst falsehood's trade
Shall be as hateful and unprofitable
As that of truth is now.
                         Where is the fame
Which the vain-glorious mighty of the earth
Seek to eternize? Oh! the faintest sound   140
From time's light footfall, the minutest wave

That swells the flood of ages, whelms in nothing
The unsubstantial bubble. Aye! today
Stern is the tyrant's mandate, red the gaze
That flashes desolation, strong the arm
That scatters multitudes. Tomorrow comes!
That mandate is a thunder-peal that died
In ages past; that gaze, a transient flash
On which the midnight closed, and on that arm
The worm has made his meal.

                    The virtuous man,   150
Who, great in his humility, as kings
Are little in their grandeur; he who leads
Invincibly a life of resolute good,
And stands amid the silent dungeon-depths
More free and fearless than the trembling judge,
Who, clothed in venal power, vainly strove
To bind the impassive spirit;—when he falls,°
His mild eye beams benevolence no more:
Withered the hand outstretched but to relieve;
Sunk reason's simple eloquence, that rolled   160
But to appal the guilty. Yes! the grave
Hath quenched that eye, and death's relentless frost
Withered that arm: but the unfading fame
Which virtue hangs upon its votary's tomb;
The deathless memory of that man, whom kings
Call to their mind and tremble; the remembrance
With which the happy spirit contemplates
Its well-spent pilgrimage on earth,
Shall never pass away.

Nature rejects the monarch, not the man;   170
The subject, not the citizen: for kings
And subjects, mutual foes, for ever play
A losing game into each other's hands,
Whose stakes are vice and misery. The man
Of virtuous soul commands not, nor obeys.
Power, like a desolating pestilence,
Pollutes whate'er it touches; and obedience,
Bane of all genius, virtue, freedom, truth,
Makes slaves of men, and, of the human frame,
A mechanized automaton.
                When Nero,   180

High over flaming Rome, with savage joy
Lowered like a fiend, drank with enraptured ear°
The shrieks of agonizing death, beheld
The frightful desolation spread, and felt
A new created sense within his soul
Thrill to the sight, and vibrate to the sound;
Thinkest thou his grandeur had not overcome
The force of human kindness? and, when Rome,
With one stern blow, hurled not the tyrant down,
Crushed not the arm red with her dearest blood,   190
Had not submissive abjectness destroyed
Nature's suggestions?
                    Look on yonder earth:
The golden harvests spring; the unfailing sun
Sheds light and life; the fruits, the flowers, the trees,
Arise in due succession; all things speak
Peace, harmony, and love. The universe,
In nature's silent eloquence, declares
That all fulfil the works of love and joy,—
All but the outcast man. He fabricates
The sword which stabs his peace; he cherisheth   200
The snakes that gnaw his heart; he raiseth up
The tyrant, whose delight is in his woe,
Whose sport is in his agony. Yon sun,
Lights it the great alone? Yon silver beams,
Sleep they less sweetly on the cottage thatch,
Than on the dome of kings? Is mother earth
A step-dame to her numerous sons, who earn
Her unshared gifts with unremitting toil;
A mother only to those puling babes
Who, nursed in ease and luxury, make men   210
The playthings of their babyhood, and mar,
In self-important childishness, that peace
Which men alone appreciate?

        Spirit of Nature! no.
The pure diffusion of thy essence throbs
    Alike in every human heart.
        Thou, aye, erectest there°
Thy throne of power unappealable:
Thou art the judge beneath whose nod

Man's brief and frail authority   220
  Is powerless as the wind
  That passeth idly by.
 Thine the tribunal which surpasseth
  The show of human justice,
   As God surpasses man.

  Spirit of Nature! thou
Life of interminable multitudes;
 Soul of those mighty spheres
Whose changeless paths through Heaven's deep silence lie;
  Soul of that smallest being,   230
   The dwelling of whose life
  Is one faint April sungleam;—
   Man, like these passive things,
Thy will unconsciously fulfilleth:
 Like theirs, his age of endless peace,
  Which time is fast maturing,
   Will swiftly, surely come;
And the unbounded frame, which thou pervadest,
   Will be without a flaw
 Marring its perfect symmetry.   240

4

How beautiful this night! the balmiest sigh,
Which vernal zephyrs breathe in evening's ear,
Were discord to the speaking quietude
That wraps this moveless scene. Heaven's ebon vault,
Studded with stars unutterably bright,
Through which the moon's unclouded grandeur rolls,
Seems like a canopy which love had spread
To curtain her sleeping world. Yon gentle hills,
Robed in a garment of untrodden snow;
Yon darksome rocks, whence icicles depend,°   10
So stainless, that their white and glittering spires
Tinge not the moon's pure beam; yon castled steep,
Whose banner hangeth o'er the time-worn tower
So idly, that rapt fancy deemeth it
A metaphor of peace;—all form a scene

Where musing solitude might love to lift
Her soul above this sphere of earthliness;
Where silence undisturbed might watch alone,
So cold, so bright, so still.
                              The orb of day,
In southern climes, o'er ocean's waveless field   20
Sinks sweetly smiling; not the faintest breath
Steals o'er the unruffled deep; the clouds of eve
Reflect unmoved the lingering beam of day;
And vesper's image on the western main
Is beautifully still. Tomorrow comes:
Cloud upon cloud, in dark and deepening mass,
Roll o'er the blackened waters; the deep roar
Of distant thunder mutters awfully;
Tempest unfolds its pinion o'er the gloom
That shrouds the boiling surge; the pitiless fiend,   30
With all his winds and lightnings, tracks his prey;
The torn deep yawns,—the vessel finds a grave
Beneath its jagged gulf.
                              Ah! whence yon glare
That fires the arch of heaven?—that dark red smoke
Blotting the silver moon? The stars are quenched
In darkness, and the pure and spangling snow
Gleams faintly through the gloom that gathers round!
Hark to that roar, whose swift and deaf'ning peals
In countless echoes through the mountains ring,
Startling pale midnight on her starry throne!   40
Now swells the intermingling din; the jar
Frequent and frightful of the bursting bomb;
The falling beam, the shriek, the groan, the shout,
The ceaseless clangour, and the rush of men
Inebriate with rage:—loud, and more loud
The discord grows; till pale death shuts the scene,
And o'er the conqueror and the conquered draws
His cold and bloody shroud.—Of all the men
Whom day's departing beam saw blooming there,
In proud and vigorous health; of all the hearts   50
That beat with anxious life at sunset there;
How few survive, how few are beating now!
All is deep silence, like the fearful calm
That slumbers in the storm's portentous pause;

Save when the frantic wail of widowed love
Comes shuddering on the blast, or the faint moan
With which some soul bursts from the frame of clay
Wrapped round its struggling powers.

                 The grey morn
Dawns on the mournful scene; the sulphurous smoke
Before the icy wind slow rolls away,   60
And the bright beams of frosty morning dance
Along the spangling snow. There tracks of blood
Even to the forest's depth, and scattered arms,
And lifeless warriors, whose hard lineaments
Death's self could change not, mark the dreadful path
Of the outsallying victors: far behind,°
Black ashes note where their proud city stood.
Within yon forest is a gloomy glen—
Each tree which guards its darkness from the day,
Waves o'er a warrior's tomb.

                   I see thee shrink,   70
Surpassing Spirit!—wert thou human else?
I see a shade of doubt and horror fleet
Across thy stainless features: yet fear not;
This is no unconnected misery,
Nor stands uncaused, and irretrievable.
Man's evil nature, that apology
Which kings who rule, and cowards who crouch, set up
For their unnumbered crimes, sheds not the blood
Which desolates the discord-wasted land.
From kings, and priests, and statesmen, war arose,   80
Whose safety is man's deep unbettered woe,
Whose grandeur his debasement. Let the axe
Strike at the root, the poison-tree will fall;°
And where its venomed exhalations spread
Ruin, and death, and woe, where millions lay
Quenching the serpent's famine, and their bones
Bleaching unburied in the putrid blast,
A garden shall arise, in loveliness
Surpassing fabled Eden.

                Hath Nature's soul,
That formed this world so beautiful, that spread   90
Earth's lap with plenty, and life's smallest chord
Strung to unchanging unison, that gave

The happy birds their dwelling in the grove,
That yielded to the wanderers of the deep
The lovely silence of the unfathomed main,
And filled the meanest worm that crawls in dust
With spirit, thought, and love; on Man alone,
Partial in causeless malice, wantonly
Heaped ruin, vice, and slavery; his soul
Blasted with withering curses; placed afar   100
The meteor-happiness, that shuns his grasp,
But serving on the frightful gulf to glare,°
Rent wide beneath his footsteps?
                               Nature!—no!
Kings, priests, and statesmen, blast the human flower
Even in its tender bud; their influence darts
Like subtle poison through the bloodless veins
Of desolate society. The child,
Ere he can lisp his mother's sacred name,
Swells with the unnatural pride of crime, and lifts
His baby-sword even in a hero's mood.   110
This infant-arm becomes the bloodiest scourge
Of devastated earth; whilst specious names,
Learnt in soft childhood's unsuspecting hour,
Serve as the sophisms with which manhood dims
Bright reason's ray, and sanctifies the sword
Upraised to shed a brother's innocent blood.
Let priest-led slaves cease to proclaim that man
Inherits vice and misery, when force
And falsehood hang even o'er the cradled babe,
Stifling with rudest grasp all natural good.   120

Ah! to the stranger-soul, when first it peeps
From its new tenement, and looks abroad
For happiness and sympathy, how stern
And desolate a tract is this wide world!
How withered all the buds of natural good!
No shade, no shelter from the sweeping storms
Of pitiless power! On its wretched frame,
Poisoned, perchance, by the disease and woe
Heaped on the wretched parent whence it sprung
By morals, law, and custom, the pure winds   130
Of heaven, that renovate the insect tribes,

May breathe not. The untainting light of day.
May visit not its longings. It is bound
Ere it has life: yea, all the chains are forged
Long ere its being: all liberty and love
And peace is torn from its defencelessness;°
Cursed from its birth, even from its cradle doomed
To abjectness and bondage!

Throughout this varied and eternal world
Soul is the only element, the block   140
That for uncounted ages has remained.
The moveless pillar of a mountain's weight
Is active, living spirit. Every grain
Is sentient both in unity and part,
And the minutest atom comprehends
A world of loves and hatreds; these beget
Evil and good: hence truth and falsehood spring;
Hence will and thought and action, all the germs
Of pain or pleasure, sympathy or hate,
That variegate the eternal universe.   150
Soul is not more polluted than the beams
Of heaven's pure orb, ere round their rapid lines
The taint of earth-born atmospheres arise.°

Man is of soul and body, formed for deeds
Of high resolve, on fancy's boldest wing
To soar unwearied, fearlessly to turn
The keenest pangs to peacefulness, and taste
The joys which mingled sense and spirit yield.
Or he is formed for abjectness and woe,
To grovel on the dunghill of his fears,   160
To shrink at every sound, to quench the flame
Of natural love in sensualism, to know
That hour as blest when on his worthless days
The frozen hand of death shall set its seal,
Yet fear the cure, though hating the disease.
The one is man that shall hereafter be;
The other, man as vice has made him now.

War is the statesman's game, the priest's delight,
The lawyer's jest, the hired assassin's trade,

And, to those royal murderers, whose mean thrones   170
Are bought by crimes of treachery and gore,
The bread they eat, the staff on which they lean.
Guards, garbed in blood-red livery, surround
Their palaces, participate the crimes°
That force defends, and from a nation's rage
Secures the crown, which all the curses reach
That famine, frenzy, woe and penury breathe.
These are the hired bravos who defend
The tyrant's throne—the bullies of his fear:°
These are the sinks and channels of worst vice,   180
The refuse of society, the dregs
Of all that is most vile: their cold hearts blend
Deceit with sternness, ignorance with pride,
All that is mean and villainous, with rage
Which hopelessness of good, and self-contempt,
Alone might kindle; they are decked in wealth,
Honour and power, then are sent abroad
To do their work. The pestilence that stalks
In gloomy triumph through some eastern land
Is less destroying. They cajole with gold,   190
And promises of fame, the thoughtless youth
Already crushed with servitude: he knows
His wretchedness too late, and cherishes
Repentance for his ruin, when his doom
Is sealed in gold and blood!
Those too the tyrant serve, who, skilled to snare
The feet of justice in the toils of law,
Stand, ready to oppress the weaker still;
And, right or wrong, will vindicate for gold,
Sneering at public virtue, which beneath   200
Their pitiless tread lies torn and trampled, where
Honour sits smiling at the sale of truth.

Then grave and hoary-headed hypocrites,
Without a hope, a passion, or a love,
Who, through a life of luxury and lies,
Have crept by flattery to the seats of power,
Support the system whence their honours flow. . . .
They have three words:—well tyrants know their use,
Well pay them for the loan, with usury

Torn from a bleeding world!—God, Hell, and Heaven.   210
A vengeful, pitiless, and almighty fiend,
Whose mercy is a nick-name for the rage
Of tameless tigers hungering for blood.
Hell, a red gulf of everlasting fire,
Where poisonous and undying worms prolong
Eternal misery to those hapless slaves
Whose life has been a penance for its crimes.
And Heaven, a meed for those who dare belie
Their human nature, quake, believe, and cringe
Before the mockeries of earthly power.°   220

These tools the tyrant tempers to his work,
Wields in his wrath, and as he wills destroys,
Omnipotent in wickedness: the while
Youth springs, age moulders, manhood tamely does
His bidding, bribed by short-lived joys to lend
Force to the weakness of his trembling arm.

They rise, they fall; one generation comes
Yielding its harvest to destruction's scythe.
It fades, another blossoms: yet behold!
Red glows the tyrant's stamp-mark on its bloom,   230
Withering and cankering deep its passive prime.
He has invented lying words and modes,
Empty and vain as his own coreless heart;
Evasive meanings, nothings of much sound,
To lure the heedless victim to the toils
Spread round the valley of its paradise.

Look to thyself, priest, conqueror, or prince!
Whether thy trade is falsehood, and thy lusts
Deep wallow in the earnings of the poor,
With whom thy master was:—or thou delight'st°   240
In numbering o'er the myriads of thy slain,
All misery weighing nothing in the scale
Against thy short-lived fame; or thou dost load
With cowardice and crime the groaning land,
A pomp-fed king. Look to thy wretched self!
Aye, art thou not the veriest slave that e'er
Crawled on the loathing earth? Are not thy days

Days of unsatisfying listlessness?
Dost thou not cry, ere night's long rack is o'er,
'When will the morning come?' Is not thy youth   250
A vain and feverish dream of sensualism?
Thy manhood blighted with unripe disease?°
Are not thy views of unregretted death
Drear, comfortless, and horrible? Thy mind,
Is it not morbid as thy nerveless frame,
Incapable of judgement, hope, or love?
And dost thou wish the errors to survive
That bar thee from all sympathies of good,
After the miserable interest
Thou hold'st in their protraction? When the grave
Has swallowed up thy memory and thyself,
Dost thou desire the bane that poisons earth
To twine its roots around thy coffined clay,
Spring from thy bones, and blossom on thy tomb,
That of its fruit thy babes may eat and die?°

5

Thus do the generations of the earth
Go to the grave, and issue from the womb,°
Surviving still the imperishable change
That renovates the world; even as the leaves
Which the keen frost-wind of the waning year
Has scattered on the forest soil, and heaped°
For many seasons there, though long they choke,
Loading with loathsome rottenness the land,
All germs of promise. Yet when the tall trees
From which they fell, shorn of their lovely shapes,   10
Lie level with the earth to moulder there,
They fertilize the land they long deformed,
Till from the breathing lawn a forest springs
Of youth, integrity, and loveliness,
Like that which gave it life, to spring and die.
Thus suicidal selfishness, that blights
The fairest feelings of the opening heart,
Is destined to decay, whilst from the soil
Shall spring all virtue, all delight, all love,

And judgment cease to wage unnatural war   20
With passion's unsubduable array.

Twin-sister of religion, selfishness!
Rival in crime and falsehood, aping all
The wanton horrors of her bloody play;
Yet frozen, unimpassioned, spiritless,
Shunning the light, and owning not its name;
Compelled, by its deformity, to screen
With flimsy veil of justice and of right,
Its unattractive lineaments, that scare
All, save the brood of ignorance: at once   30
The cause and the effect of tyranny;
Unblushing, hardened, sensual, and vile;
Dead to all love but of its abjectness,
With heart impassive by more noble powers°
Than unshared pleasure, sordid gain, or fame;
Despising its own miserable being,
Which still it longs, yet fears to disenthrall.

Hence commerce springs, the venal interchange
Of all that human art or nature yield;
Which wealth should purchase not, but want demand,   40
And natural kindness hasten to supply
From the full fountain of its boundless love,
For ever stifled, drained, and tainted now.
Commerce! beneath whose poison-breathing shade
No solitary virtue dares to spring,
But poverty and wealth with equal hand
Scatter their withering curses, and unfold
The doors of premature and violent death,
To pining famine and full-fed disease,
To all that shares the lot of human life,   50
Which poisoned body and soul, scarce drags the chain,
That lengthens as it goes and clanks behind.

Commerce has set the mark of selfishness,
The signet of its all-enslaving power
Upon a shining ore, and called it gold:
Before whose image how the vulgar great,
The vainly rich, the miserable proud,

The mob of peasants, nobles, priests, and kings,°
And with blind feelings reverence the power
That grinds them to the dust of misery.   60
But in the temple of their hireling hearts
Gold is a living god, and rules in scorn
All earthly things but virtue.

Since tyrants, by the sale of human life,
Heap luxuries to their sensualism, and fame
To their wide-wasting and insatiate pride,
Success has sanctioned to a credulous world
The ruin, the disgrace, the woe of war.
His hosts of blind and unresisting dupes
The despot numbers; from his cabinet   70
These puppets of his schemes he moves at will,
Even as the slaves by force or famine driven,
Beneath a vulgar master, to perform
A task of cold and brutal drudgery;—
Hardened to hope, insensible to fear,
Scarce living pulleys of a dead machine.
Mere wheels of work and articles of trade,
That grace the proud and noisy pomp of wealth!

The harmony and happiness of man
Yields to the wealth of nations; that which lifts°   80
His nature to the heaven of its pride,
Is bartered for the poison of his soul;
The weight that drags to earth his towering hopes,
Blighting all prospect but of selfish gain,
Withering all passion but of slavish fear,
Extinguishing all free and generous love
Of enterprise and daring, even the pulse
That fancy kindles in the beating heart
To mingle with sensation, it destroys,—
Leaves nothing but the sordid lust of self,   90
The grovelling hope of interest and gold,
Unqualified, unmingled, unredeemed
Even by hypocrisy.
                         And statesmen boast
Of wealth! The wordy eloquence that lives°
After the ruin of their hearts, can gild

The bitter poison of a nation's woe,
Can turn the worship of the servile mob
To their corrupt and glaring idol fame,
From virtue, trampled by its iron tread,
Although its dazzling pedestal be raised   100
Amid the horrors of a limb-strewn field,
With desolated dwellings smoking round.
The man of ease, who, by his warm fire-side,
To deeds of charitable intercourse
And bare fulfilment of the common laws
Of decency and prejudice, confines
The struggling nature of his human heart,
Is duped by their cold sophistry; he sheds
A passing tear perchance upon the wreck
Of earthly peace, when near his dwelling's door   110
The frightful waves are driven,—when his son
Is murdered by the tyrant, or religion
Drives his wife raving mad. But the poor man,°
Whose life is misery, and fear, and care;
Whom the morn wakens but to fruitless toil;
Who ever hears his famished offspring's scream,
Whom their pale mother's uncomplaining gaze
For ever meets, and the proud rich man's eye
Flashing command, and the heart-breaking scene
Of thousands like himself;—he little heeds   120
The rhetoric of tyranny; his hate
Is quenchless as his wrongs; he laughs to scorn
The vain and bitter mockery of words,
Feeling the horror of the tyrant's deeds,
And unrestrained but by the arm of power,
That knows and dreads his enmity.

The iron rod of penury still compels
Her wretched slave to bow the knee to wealth,
And poison, with unprofitable toil,
A life too void of solace, to confirm   130
The very chains that bind him to his doom.
Nature, impartial in munificence,
Has gifted man with all-subduing will.
Matter, with all its transitory shapes,
Lies subjected and plastic at his feet,°

That, weak from bondage, tremble as they tread.
How many a rustic Milton has passed by,
Stifling the speechless longings of his heart,
In unremitting drudgery and care!
How many a vulgar Cato has compelled°   140
His energies, no longer tameless then,
To mould a pin, or fabricate a nail!
How many a Newton, to whose passive ken
Those mighty spheres that gem infinity
Were only specks of tinsel, fixed in heaven
To light the midnights of his native town!°

Yet every heart contains perfection's germ:
The wisest of the sages of the earth,
That ever from the stores of reason drew
Science and truth, and virtue's dreadless tone,   150
Were but a weak and inexperienced boy,
Proud, sensual, unimpassioned, unimbued
With pure desire and universal love,
Compared to that high being, of cloudless brain,
Untainted passion, elevated will,
Which death (who even would linger long in awe
Within his noble presence, and beneath
His changeless eyebeam) might alone subdue.
Him, every slave now dragging through the filth
Of some corrupted city his sad life,   160
Pining with famine, swol'n with luxury,
Blunting the keenness of his spiritual sense
With narrow schemings and unworthy cares,
Or madly rushing through all violent crime,
To move the deep stagnation of his soul,—
Might imitate and equal.
                                   But mean lust
Has bound its chains so tight around the earth,
That all within it but the virtuous man
Is venal: gold or fame will surely reach
The price prefixed by selfishness, to all   170
But him of resolute and unchanging will;
Whom, nor the plaudits of a servile crowd,
Nor the vile joys of tainting luxury,
Can bribe to yield his elevated soul

To tyranny or falsehood, though they wield
With blood-red hand the sceptre of the world.

All things are sold: the very light of heaven
Is venal; earth's unsparing gifts of love,
The smallest and most despicable things
That lurk in the abysses of the deep,   180
All objects of our life, even life itself,
And the poor pittance which the laws allow
Of liberty, the fellowship of man,
Those duties which his heart of human love
Should urge him to perform instinctively,
Are bought and sold as in a public mart
Of undisguising selfishness, that sets
On each its price, the stamp-mark of her reign.
Even love is sold; the solace of all woe°
Is turned to deadliest agony, old age   190
Shivers in selfish beauty's loathing arms,
And youth's corrupted impulses prepare
A life of horror from the blighting bane
Of commerce; whilst the pestilence that springs°
From unenjoying sensualism, has filled
All human life with hydra-headed woes.

Falsehood demands but gold to pay the pangs
Of outraged conscience; for the slavish priest
Sets no great value on his hireling faith:
A little passing pomp, some servile souls,   200
Whom cowardice itself might safely chain,
Or the spare mite of avarice could bribe
To deck the triumph of their languid zeal,
Can make him minister to tyranny.
More daring crime requires a loftier meed:
Without a shudder, the slave-soldier lends
His arm to murderous deeds, and steels his heart
When the dread eloquence of dying men,
Low mingling on the lonely field of fame,
Assails that nature, whose applause he sells   210
For the gross blessings of a patriot mob,
For the vile gratitude of heartless kings,
And for a cold world's good word,—viler still!

There is a nobler glory, which survives
Until our being fades, and, solacing
All human care, accompanies its change;
Deserts not virtue in the dungeon's gloom,
And, in the precincts of the palace, guides
Its footsteps through that labyrinth of crime;
Imbues his lineaments with dauntlessness,°   220
Even when, from power's avenging hand, he takes
Its sweetest, last and noblest title—death;
—The consciousness of good, which neither gold,
Nor sordid fame, nor hope of heavenly bliss,
Can purchase; but a life of resolute good,
Unalterable will, quenchless desire
Of universal happiness, the heart
That beats with it in unison, the brain,
Whose ever wakeful wisdom toils to change
Reason's rich stores for its eternal weal.   230

This commerce of sincerest virtue needs°
No mediative signs of selfishness,
No jealous intercourse of wretched gain,
No balancings of prudence, cold and long;
In just and equal measure all is weighed,
One scale contains the sum of human weal,
And one, the good man's heart.
                              How vainly seek
The selfish for that happiness denied
To aught but virtue! Blind and hardened, they,
Who hope for peace amid the storms of care,   240
Who covet power they know not how to use,
And sigh for pleasure they refuse to give,—
Madly they frustrate still their own designs;
And, where they hope that quiet to enjoy
Which virtue pictures, bitterness of soul,
Pining regrets, and vain repentances,
Disease, disgust, and lassitude, pervade
Their valueless and miserable lives.

But hoary-headed selfishness has felt
Its death-blow, and is tottering to the grave: 250
A brighter morn awaits the human day,

When every transfer of earth's natural gifts
Shall be a commerce of good words and works;
When poverty and wealth, the thirst of fame,
The fear of infamy, disease and woe,
War with its million horrors, and fierce hell
Shall live but in the memory of time,
Who, like a penitent libertine, shall start,
Look back, and shudder at his younger years.

6

All touch, all eye, all ear,
The Spirit felt the Fairy's burning speech.
   O'er the thin texture of its frame,
The varying periods painted changing glows,°
      As on a summer even,
When soul-enfolding music floats around,
   The stainless mirror of the lake
   Re-images the eastern gloom,
Mingling convulsively its purple hues
      With sunset's burnished gold.   10

      Then thus the Spirit spoke:
'It is a wild and miserable world!
      Thorny, and full of care,
Which every fiend can make his prey at will.
   O Fairy! in the lapse of years,
      Is there no hope in store?
      Will yon vast suns roll on
   Interminably, still illuming
   The night of so many wretched souls,
      And see no hope for them?   20
Will not the universal Spirit e'er
Revivify this withered limb of Heaven?'

      The Fairy calmly smiled
In comfort, and a kindling gleam of hope
   Suffused the Spirit's lineaments.
'Oh! rest thee tranquil; chase those fearful doubts,
Which ne'er could rack an everlasting soul,

That sees the chains which bind it to its doom.
Yes! crime and misery are in yonder earth,
     Falsehood, mistake, and lust;   30
     But the eternal world
Contains at once the evil and the cure.
Some eminent in virtue shall start up,
     Even in perversest time:
The truths of their pure lips, that never die,
Shall bind the scorpion falsehood with a wreath
     Of ever-living flame,
Until the monster sting itself to death.°

    'How sweet a scene will earth become!
Of purest spirits a pure dwelling-place,   40
Symphonious with the planetary spheres;°
When man, with changeless nature coalescing,
Will undertake regeneration's work,
When its ungenial poles no longer point
     To the red and baleful sun
     That faintly twinkles there.°

    'Spirit! on yonder earth,
  Falsehood now triumphs; deadly power
Has fixed its seal upon the lip of truth!
    Madness and misery are there!   50
The happiest is most wretched! Yet confide,
Until pure health-drops, from the cup of joy,
Fall like a dew of balm upon the world.
Now, to the scene I show, in silence turn,
And read the blood-stained charter of all woe,
Which nature soon, with recreating hand,
Will blot in mercy from the book of earth.
How bold the flight of passion's wandering wing,
How swift the step of reason's firmer tread,
How calm and sweet the victories of life,   60
How terrorless the triumph of the grave!
How powerless were the mightiest monarch's arm,
Vain his loud threat, and impotent his frown!
How ludicrous the priest's dogmatic roar!
The weight of his exterminating curse,
How light! and his affected charity,

To suit the pressure of the changing times,
What palpable deceit!—but for thy aid,
Religion! but for thee, prolific fiend,
Who peoplest earth with demons, hell with men,   70
And heaven with slaves!

'Thou taintest all thou lookest upon!—the stars,°
Which on thy cradle beamed so brightly sweet,
Were gods to the distempered playfulness
Of thy untutored infancy: the trees,
The grass, the clouds, the mountains, and the sea,
All living things that walk, swim, creep, or fly,
Were gods: the sun had homage, and the moon
Her worshipper. Then thou becamest, a boy,
More daring in thy frenzies: every shape,   80
Monstrous or vast, or beautifully wild,
Which, from sensation's relics, fancy culls;
The spirits of the air, the shuddering ghost,
The genii of the elements, the powers
That give a shape to nature's varied works,
Had life and place in the corrupt belief
Of thy blind heart: yet still thy youthful hands
Were pure of human blood. Then manhood gave
Its strength and ardour to thy frenzied brain;
Thine eager gaze scanned the stupendous scene,   90
Whose wonders mocked the knowledge of thy pride:
Their everlasting and unchanging laws
Reproached thine ignorance. Awhile thou stoodst
Baffled and gloomy; then thou didst sum up
The elements of all that thou didst know;
The changing seasons, winter's leafless reign,
The budding of the heaven-breathing trees,
The eternal orbs that beautify the night,
The sun-rise, and the setting of the moon,
Earthquakes and wars, and poisons and disease,   100
And all their causes, to an abstract point
Converging, thou didst bend, and called it GOD!
The self-sufficing, the omnipotent,
The merciful, and the avenging God!
Who, prototype of human misrule, sits
High in heaven's realm, upon a golden throne,

Even like an earthly king; and whose dread work,
Hell, gapes forever for the unhappy slaves
Of fate, whom he created in his sport,
To triumph in their torments when they fell!   110
Earth heard the name; earth trembled, as the smoke°
Of his revenge ascended up to heaven,
Blotting the constellations; and the cries
Of millions, butchered in sweet confidence
And unsuspecting peace, even when the bonds
Of safety were confirmed by wordy oaths
Sworn in his dreadful name, rung through the land;
Whilst innocent babes writhed on thy stubborn spear.
And thou didst laugh to hear the mother's shriek
Of maniac gladness, as the sacred steel   120
Felt cold in her torn entrails!

'Religion! thou wert then in manhood's prime:
But age crept on: one God would not suffice
For senile puerility; thou framedst
A tale to suit thy dotage, and to glut
Thy misery-thirsting soul, that the mad fiend
Thy wickedness had pictured, might afford
A plea for sating the unnatural thirst
For murder, rapine, violence, and crime,
That still consumed thy being, even when   130
Thou heard'st the step of fate;—that flames might light
Thy funeral scene, and the shrill horrent shrieks°
Of parents dying on the pile that burned
To light their children to thy paths, the roar
Of the encircling flames, the exulting cries
Of thine apostles, loud commingling there,
          Might sate thine hungry ear
          Even on the bed of death!

'But now contempt is mocking thy grey hairs;
Thou art descending to the darksome grave,   140
Unhonoured and unpitied, but by those
Whose pride is passing by like thine, and sheds,
Like thine, a glare that fades before the sun
Of truth, and shines but in the dreadful night
That long has lowered above the ruined world.

'Throughout these infinite orbs of mingling light,
Of which yon earth is one, is wide diffused
A spirit of activity and life,
That knows no term, cessation, or decay;
That fades not when the lamp of earthly life,   150
Extinguished in the dampness of the grave,
Awhile there slumbers, more than when the babe
In the dim newness of its being feels
The impulses of sublunary things,°
And all is wonder to unpractised sense:
But, active, steadfast, and eternal, still
Guides the fierce whirlwind, in the tempest roars,
Cheers in the day, breathes in the balmy groves,
Strengthens in health, and poisons in disease;
And in the storm of change, that ceaselessly   160
Rolls round the eternal universe, and shakes
Its undecaying battlement, presides,
Apportioning with irresistible law
The place each spring of its machine shall fill;
So that, when waves on waves tumultuous heap
Confusion to the clouds, and fiercely driven
Heaven's lightnings scorch the uprooted ocean-fords,
Whilst, to the eye of shipwrecked mariner,
Lone sitting on the bare and shuddering rock,
All seems unlinked contingency and chance: 170
No atom of this turbulence fulfils
A vague and unnecessitated task,
Or acts but as it must and ought to act.°
Even the minutest molecule of light,
That in an April sunbeam's fleeting glow
Fulfils its destined, though invisible work,
The universal Spirit guides; nor less,
When merciless ambition, or mad zeal,
Has led two hosts of dupes to battle-field,
That, blind, they there may dig each other's graves,   180
And call the sad work glory, does it rule
All passions: not a thought, a will, an act,
No working of the tyrant's moody mind,
Nor one misgiving of the slaves who boast
Their servitude, to hide the shame they feel,
Nor the events enchaining every will,

That from the depths of unrecorded time
Have drawn all-influencing virtue, pass
Unrecognized, or unforeseen by thee,
Soul of the Universe! eternal spring   190
Of life and death, of happiness and woe,
Of all that chequers the phantasmal scene
That floats before our eyes in wavering light,
Which gleams but on the darkness of our prison,
          Whose chains and massy walls
          We feel, but cannot see.°

'Spirit of Nature! all-sufficing Power,
Necessity! thou mother of the world!°
Unlike the God of human error, thou
Requirest no prayers or praises; the caprice   200
Of man's weak will belongs no more to thee
Than do the changeful passions of his breast
To thy unvarying harmony: the slave,
Whose horrible lusts spread misery o'er the world.
And the good man, who lifts, with virtuous pride,
His being, in the sight of happiness,
That springs from his own works; the poison-tree,
Beneath whose shade all life is withered up,
And the fair oak, whose leafy dome affords
A temple where the vows of happy love   210
Are registered, are equal in thy sight:
No love, no hate thou cherishest; revenge
And favouritism, and worst desire of fame
Thou knowest not: all that the wide world contains
Are but thy passive instruments, and thou
Regard'st them all with an impartial eye,
Whose joy or pain thy nature cannot feel,
     Because thou hast not human sense,
     Because thou art not human mind.

     'Yes! when the sweeping storm of time   220
Has sung its death-dirge o'er the ruined fanes
And broken altars of the almighty fiend,
Whose name usurps thy honours, and the blood
Through centuries clotted there, has floated down
The tainted flood of ages, shalt thou live

Unchangeable! A shrine is raised to thee,
   Which, nor the tempest breath of time,
   Nor the interminable flood,
   Over earth's slight pageant rolling,
     Availeth to destroy,—   230
The sensitive extension of the world,°
   That wondrous and eternal fane,
Where pain and pleasure, good and evil join,
To do the will of strong necessity,
   And life, in multitudinous shapes,
Still pressing forward where no term can be,
   Like hungry and unresting flame
Curls round the eternal columns of its strength.'°

7

Spirit

I was an infant when my mother went
To see an atheist burned. She took me there:
The dark-robed priests were met around the pile;
The multitude was gazing silently;
And as the culprit passed with dauntless mien,
Tempered disdain in his unaltering eye,
Mixed with a quiet smile, shone calmly forth:
The thirsty fire crept round his manly limbs;
His resolute eyes were scorched to blindness soon;
His death-pang rent my heart! the insensate mob   10
Uttered a cry of triumph, and I wept.
'Weep not, child!' cried my mother, 'for that man
Has said, "There is no God."'

Fairy

            There is no God!°
Nature confirms the faith his death-groan sealed:
Let heaven and earth, let man's revolving race,
His ceaseless generations tell their tale;
Let every part depending on the chain
That links it to the whole, point to the hand
That grasps its term! let every seed that falls
In silent eloquence unfold its store   20

Of argument: infinity within,
Infinity without, belie creation;
The exterminable spirit it contains
Is nature's only God; but human pride
Is skilful to invent most serious names
To hide its ignorance.
                    The name of God
Has fenced about all crime with holiness,
Himself the creature of his worshippers,
Whose names and attributes and passions change,
Seeva, Buddh, Foh, Jehovah, God, or Lord,°   30
Even with the human dupes who build his shrines,
Still serving o'er the war-polluted world
For desolation's watch-word; whether hosts
Stain his death-blushing chariot wheels, as on
Triumphantly they roll, whilst Brahmins raise
A sacred hymn to mingle with the groans;°
Or countless partners of his power divide
His tyranny to weakness; or the smoke
Of burning towns, the cries of female helplessness,
Unarmed old age, and youth, and infancy,   40
Horribly massacred, ascend to heaven
In honour of his name; or, last and worst,
Earth groans beneath religion's iron age,°
And priests dare babble of a God of peace,
Even whilst their hands are red with guiltless blood,
Murdering the while, uprooting every germ
Of truth, exterminating, spoiling all,
Making the earth a slaughter-house!

         O Spirit! through the sense
By which thy inner nature was apprised   50
   Of outward shows, vague dreams have rolled,
   And varied reminiscences have waked
         Tablets that never fade;°
   All things have been imprinted there,
   The stars, the sea, the earth, the sky,
Even the unshapeliest lineaments
      Of wild and fleeting visions
         Have left a record there
         To testify of earth.

These are my empire, for to me is given   60
The wonders of the human world to keep,
And fancy's thin creations to endow
With manner, being, and reality;
Therefore a wondrous phantom, from the dreams
Of human error's dense and purblind faith,°
I will evoke, to meet thy questioning.
      Ahasuerus, rise!°

      A strange and woe-worn wight°
   Arose beside the battlement,
      And stood unmoving there.   70
His inessential figure cast no shade
      Upon the golden floor;
His port and mien bore mark of many years,
And chronicles of untold ancientness
Were legible within his beamless eye:
   Yet his cheek bore the mark of youth;
Freshness and vigour knit his manly frame;
The wisdom of old age was mingled there
   With youth's primaeval dauntlessness;
      And inexpressible woe,   80
Chastened by fearless resignation, gave
An awful grace to his all-speaking brow.

Spirit

Is there a God?

Ahasuerus

Is there a God!—aye, an almighty God,
And vengeful as almighty! Once his voice
Was heard on earth: earth shuddered at the sound;
The fiery-visaged firmament expressed
Abhorrence, and the grave of nature yawned
To swallow all the dauntless and the good
That dared to hurl defiance at his throne,   90
Girt as it was with power. None but slaves
Survived,—cold-blooded slaves, who did the work
Of tyrannous omnipotence; whose souls
No honest indignation ever urged
To elevated daring, to one deed

Which gross and sensual self did not pollute.
These slaves built temples for the omnipotent fiend,
Gorgeous and vast: the costly altars smoked
With human blood, and hideous paeans rung
Through all the long-drawn aisles. A murderer heard°   100
His voice in Egypt, one whose gifts and arts
Had raised him to his eminence in power,
Accomplice of omnipotence in crime,
And confidant of the all-knowing one.
     These were Jehovah's words:

'From an eternity of idleness
I, God, awoke; in seven days' toil made earth
From nothing; rested, and created man:
I placed him in a paradise, and there
Planted the tree of evil, so that he   110
Might eat and perish, and my soul procure
Wherewith to sate its malice, and to turn,
Even like a heartless conqueror of the earth,
All misery to my fame. The race of men
Chosen to my honour, with impunity
May sate the lusts I planted in their heart.
Here I command thee hence to lead them on,
Until, with hardened feet, their conquering troops
Wade on the promised soil through woman's blood,
And make my name be dreaded through the land.   120
Yet ever burning flame and ceaseless woe
Shall be the doom of their eternal souls,
With every soul on this ungrateful earth,
Virtuous or vicious, weak or strong,—even all
Shall perish, to fulfil the blind revenge
(Which you, to men, call justice) of their God.'

           The murderer's brow
Quivered with horror.
            'God omnipotent,
Is there no mercy? must our punishment
Be endless? will long ages roll away,   130
And see no term? Oh! wherefore hast thou made
In mockery and wrath this evil earth?
Mercy becomes the powerful—be but just:

O God! repent and save.'
                              'One way remains:
I will beget a son, and he shall bear
The sins of all the world; he shall arise°
In an unnoticed corner of the earth,
And there shall die upon a cross, and purge
The universal crime; so that the few
On whom my grace descends, those who are marked   140
As vessels to the honour of their God,
May credit this strange sacrifice, and save
Their souls alive: millions shall live and die,
Who ne'er shall call upon their Saviour's name,
But, unredeemed, go to the gaping grave.
Thousands shall deem it an old woman's tale,
Such as the nurses frighten babes withal:
These in a gulf of anguish and of flame
Shall curse their reprobation endlessly,
Yet tenfold pangs shall force them to avow,   150
Even on their beds of torment, where they howl,
My honour, and the justice of their doom.
What then avail their virtuous deeds, their thoughts
Of purity, with radiant genius bright,
Or lit with human reason's earthly ray?
Many are called, but few will I elect.
Do thou my bidding, Moses!'
                              Even the murderer's cheek
Was blanched with horror, and his quivering lips
Scarce faintly uttered—'O almighty one,
I tremble and obey!'   160

O Spirit! centuries have set their seal
On this heart of many wounds, and loaded brain,
Since the Incarnate came: humbly he came,
Veiling his horrible Godhead in the shape
Of man, scorned by the world, his name unheard,
Save by the rabble of his native town,
Even as a parish demagogue. He led
The crowd; he taught them justice, truth, and peace,
In semblance; but he lit within their souls
The quenchless flames of zeal, and blessed the sword   170
He brought on earth to satiate with the blood

Of truth and freedom his malignant soul.
At length his mortal frame was led to death.
I stood beside him: on the torturing cross
No pain assailed his unterrestrial sense;
And yet he groaned. Indignantly I summed
The massacres and miseries which his name
Had sanctioned in my country, and I cried,
'Go! go!' in mockery.
A smile of godlike malice reillumined   180
His fading lineaments.—'I go', he cried,
'But thou shalt wander o'er the unquiet earth
Eternally.'——The dampness of the grave
Bathed my imperishable front. I fell,
And long lay tranced upon the charmèd soil.
When I awoke hell burned within my brain,
Which staggered on its seat; for all around
The mouldering relics of my kindred lay,
Even as the Almighty's ire arrested them.
And in their various attitudes of death   190
My murdered children's mute and eyeless skulls
Glared ghastily upon me.°
                                            But my soul,
From sight and sense of the polluting woe
Of tyranny, had long learned to prefer
Hell's freedom to the servitude of heaven.°
Therefore I rose, and dauntlessly began
My lonely and unending pilgrimage,
Resolved to wage unweariable war
With my almighty tyrant, and to hurl
Defiance at his impotence to harm   200
Beyond the curse I bore. The very hand
That barred my passage to the peaceful grave
Has crushed the earth to misery, and given
Its empire to the chosen of his slaves.
These have I seen, even from the earliest dawn
Of weak, unstable and precarious power,
Then preaching peace, as now they practise war;
So, when they turned but from the massacre°
Of unoffending infidels, to quench
Their thirst for ruin in the very blood   210
That flowed in their own veins, and pitiless zeal

Froze every human feeling, as the wife
Sheathed in her husband's heart the sacred steel,
Even whilst its hopes were dreaming of her love;
And friends to friends, brothers to brothers stood
Opposed in bloodiest battle-field, and war,
Scarce satiable by fate's last death-draught waged,
Drunk from the winepress of the Almighty's wrath;°
Whilst the red cross, in mockery of peace,
Pointed to victory! When the fray was done,   220
No remnant of the exterminated faith
Survived to tell its ruin, but the flesh,
With putrid smoke poisoning the atmosphere,
That rotted on the half-extinguished pile.

Yes! I have seen God's worshippers unsheathe
The sword of his revenge, when grace descended,
Confirming all unnatural impulses,
To sanctify their desolating deeds;
And frantic priests waved the ill-omened cross
O'er the unhappy earth: then shone the sun   230
On showers of gore from the upflashing steel
Of safe assassination, and all crime
Made stingless by the spirits of the Lord,
And blood-red rainbows canopied the land.

Spirit! no year of my eventful being
Has passed unstained by crime and misery,
Which flows from God's own faith. I've marked his slaves
With tongues whose lies are venomous, beguile
The insensate mob, and, whilst one hand was red
With murder, feign to stretch the other out   240
For brotherhood and peace; and that they now
Babble of love and mercy, whilst their deeds
Are marked with all the narrowness and crime
That freedom's young arm dare not yet chastise,
Reason may claim our gratitude, who now
Establishing the imperishable throne
Of truth, and stubborn virtue, maketh vain
The unprevailing malice of my foe,
Whose bootless rage heaps torments for the brave,
Adds impotent eternities to pain,   250

Whilst keenest disappointment racks his breast,
To see the smiles of peace around them play,
To frustrate or to sanctify their doom.

Thus have I stood,—through a wild waste of years
Struggling with whirlwinds of mad agony,
Yet peaceful, and serene, and self-enshrined,
Mocking my powerless tyrant's horrible curse
With stubborn and unalterable will,
Even as a giant oak, which heaven's fierce flame
Had scathèd in the wilderness, to stand   260
A monument of fadeless ruin there;
Yet peacefully and movelessly it braves
The midnight conflict of the wintry storm,
    As in the sunlight's calm it spreads
    Its worn and withered arms on high
To meet the quiet of a summer's noon.

        The Fairy waved her wand:
        Ahasuerus fled
Fast as the shapes of mingled shade and mist,
That lurk in the glens of a twilight grove,   270
        Flee from the morning beam:
    The matter of which dreams are made
    Not more endowed with actual life
    Than this phantasmal portraiture
    Of wandering human thought.

8

The present and the past thou hast beheld:
It was a desolate sight. Now, Spirit, learn
    The secrets of the future.—Time!
Unfold the brooding pinion of thy gloom,
Render thou up thy half-devoured babes,°
And from the cradles of eternity,
Where millions lie lulled to their portioned sleep
By the deep murmuring stream of passing things,
Tear thou that gloomy shroud.—Spirit, behold
        Thy glorious destiny!   10

Joy to the Spirit came.
Through the wide rent in Time's eternal veil,
Hope was seen beaming through the mists of fear:
Earth was no longer hell;
Love, freedom, health, had given
Their ripeness to the manhood of its prime,
And all its pulses beat
Symphonious to the planetary spheres:
Then dulcet music swelled
Concordant with the life-strings of the soul;   20
It throbbed in sweet and languid beatings there,
Catching new life from transitory death,—
Like the vague sighings of a wind at even,
That wakes the wavelets of the slumbering sea
And dies on the creation of its breath,
And sinks and rises, fails and swells by fits,
Was the pure stream of feeling
That sprung from these sweet notes,
And o'er the Spirit's human sympathies
With mild and gentle motion calmly flowed.   30

Joy to the Spirit came,—
Such joy as when a lover sees
The chosen of his soul in happiness,
And witnesses her peace
Whose woe to him were bitterer than death,
Sees her unfaded cheek
Glow mantling in first luxury of health,
Thrills with her lovely eyes,
Which like two stars amid the heaving main
Sparkle through liquid bliss.   40

Then in her triumph spoke the Fairy Queen:
'I will not call the ghost of ages gone
To unfold the frightful secrets of its lore;
The present now is past,
And those events that desolate the earth
Have faded from the memory of Time,
Who dares not give reality to that
Whose being I annul. To me is given
The wonders of the human world to keep,

Space, matter, time, and mind. Futurity   50
Exposes now its treasure; let the sight
Renew and strengthen all thy failing hope.
O human Spirit! spur thee to the goal
Where virtue fixes universal peace,
And midst the ebb and flow of human things,
Show somewhat stable, somewhat certain still,
A lighthouse o'er the wild of dreary waves.

'The habitable earth is full of bliss;
Those wastes of frozen billows that were hurled
By everlasting snowstorms round the poles,   60
Where matter dared not vegetate or live,
But ceaseless frost round the vast solitude
Bound its broad zone of stillness, are unloosed;
And fragrant zephyrs there from spicy isles
Ruffle the placid ocean-deep, that rolls
Its broad, bright surges to the sloping sand,
Whose roar is wakened into echoings sweet
To murmur through the heaven-breathing groves
And melodize with man's blest nature there.

'Those deserts of immeasurable sand,   70
Whose age-collected fervours scarce allowed
A bird to live, a blade of grass to spring,
Where the shrill chirp of the green lizard's love
Broke on the sultry silentness alone,
Now teem with countless rills and shady woods,
Corn-fields and pastures and white cottages;
And where the startled wilderness beheld
A savage conqueror stained in kindred blood,
A tigress sating with the flesh of lambs
The unnatural famine of her toothless cubs,   80
Whilst shouts and howlings through the desert rang,
Sloping and smooth the daisy-spangled lawn,
Offering sweet incense to the sunrise, smiles
To see a babe before his mother's door,
            Sharing his morning's meal
      With the green and golden basilisk°
            That comes to lick his feet.

'Those trackless deeps, where many a weary sail
Has seen above the illimitable plain,
Morning on night, and night on morning rise,   90
Whilst still no land to greet the wanderer spread
Its shadowy mountains on the sun-bright sea,
Where the loud roarings of the tempest-waves
So long have mingled with the gusty wind
In melancholy loneliness, and swept
The desert of those ocean solitudes,
But vocal to the seabird's harrowing shriek,°
The bellowing monster, and the rushing storm,
Now to the sweet and many mingling sounds
Of kindliest human impulses respond.   100
Those lonely realms bright garden-isles begem,
With lightsome clouds and shining seas between,
And fertile valleys, resonant with bliss,
Whilst green woods overcanopy the wave,
Which like a toil-worn labourer leaps to shore,
To meet the kisses of the flowrets there.

'All things are recreated, and the flame
Of consentaneous love inspires all life:°
The fertile bosom of the earth gives suck
To myriads, who still grow beneath her care,   110
Rewarding her with their pure perfectness:
The balmy breathings of the wind inhale
Her virtues, and diffuse them all abroad:
Health floats amid the gentle atmosphere,
Glows in the fruits, and mantles on the stream:
No storms deform the beaming brow of heaven,
Nor scatter in the freshness of its pride
The foliage of the ever verdant trees;
But fruits are ever ripe, flowers ever fair,
And autumn proudly bears her matron grace,   120
Kindling a flush on the fair cheek of spring,
Whose virgin bloom beneath the ruddy fruit
Reflects its tint and blushes into love.

'The lion now forgets to thirst for blood:
There might you see him sporting in the sun
Beside the dreadless kid; his claws are sheathed,°

His teeth are harmless, custom's force has made°
His nature as the nature of a lamb.
Like passion's fruit, the nightshade's tempting bane
Poisons no more the pleasure it bestows: 130
All bitterness is past; the cup of joy
Unmingled mantles to the goblet's brim,
And courts the thirsty lips it fled before.

'But chief, ambiguous man, he that can know
More misery, and dream more joy than all;
Whose keen sensations thrill within his breast
To mingle with a loftier instinct there,
Lending their power to pleasure and to pain,
Yet raising, sharpening, and refining each;
Who stands amid the ever-varying world,   140
The burden or the glory of the earth;
He chief perceives the change, his being notes
The gradual renovation, and defines
Each movement of its progress on his mind.

'Man, where the gloom of the long polar night
Lowers o'er the snow-clad rocks and frozen soil,
Where scarce the hardiest herb that braves the frost
Basks in the moonlight's ineffectual glow,
Shrank with the plants, and darkened with the night;
His chilled and narrow energies, his heart,   150
Insensible to courage, truth, or love,
His stunted stature and imbecile frame,
Marked him for some abortion of the earth,
Fit compeer of the bears that roamed around,
Whose habits and enjoyments were his own:
His life a feverish dream of stagnant woe,
Whose meagre wants, but scantily fulfilled,
Apprised him ever of the joyless length
Which his short being's wretchedness had reached;
His death a pang which famine, cold and toil   160
Long on the mind, whilst yet the vital spark
Clung to the body stubbornly, had brought:
All was inflicted here that earth's revenge
Could wreak on the infringers of her law;
One curse alone was spared—the name of God.

'Nor where the tropics bound the realms of day
With a broad belt of mingling cloud and flame,
Where blue mists through the unmoving atmosphere
Scattered the seeds of pestilence, and fed
Unnatural vegetation, where the land   170
Teemed with all earthquake, tempest and disease,
Was man a nobler being; slavery
Had crushed him to his country's bloodstained dust;
Or he was bartered for the fame of power,
Which all internal impulses destroying,
Makes human will an article of trade;
Or he was changed with Christians for their gold,
And dragged to distant isles, where to the sound
Of the flesh-mangling scourge, he does the work
Of all-polluting luxury and wealth,   180
Which doubly visits on the tyrants' heads
The long-protracted fullness of their woe;
Or he was led to legal butchery,°
To turn to worms beneath that burning sun,
Where kings first leagued against the rights of men,
And priests first traded with the name of God.°

'Even where the milder zone afforded man
A seeming shelter, yet contagion there,
Blighting his being with unnumbered ills,
Spread like a quenchless fire; nor truth till late   190
Availed to arrest its progress, or create
That peace which first in bloodless victory waved
Her snowy standard o'er this favoured clime:
There man was long the train-bearer of slaves,
The mimic of surrounding misery,
The jackal of ambition's lion-rage,
The bloodhound of religion's hungry zeal.

'Here now the human being stands adorning
This loveliest earth with taintless body and mind;
Blessed from his birth with all bland impulses,   200
Which gently in his noble bosom wake
All kindly passions and all pure desires.
Him, still from hope to hope the bliss pursuing,
Which from the exhaustless lore of human weal

Draws on the virtuous mind, the thoughts that rise
In time-destroying infiniteness, gift
With self-enshrined eternity, that mocks°
The unprevailing hoariness of age,
And man, once fleeting o'er the transient scene
Swift as an unremembered vision, stands   210
Immortal upon earth: no longer now
He slays the lamb that looks him in the face,°
And horribly devours his mangled flesh,
Which still avenging nature's broken law,
Kindled all putrid humours in his frame,
All evil passions, and all vain belief,
Hatred, despair, and loathing in his mind,
The germs of misery, death, disease, and crime.
No longer now the wingèd habitants,
That in the woods their sweet lives sing away,   220
Flee from the form of man; but gather round,
And prune their sunny feathers on the hands°
Which little children stretch in friendly sport
Towards these dreadless partners of their play.
All things are void of terror: man has lost
His terrible prerogative, and stands
An equal amidst equals: happiness
And science dawn though late upon the earth;
Peace cheers the mind, health renovates the frame;
Disease and pleasures cease to mingle here,   230
Reason and passion cease to combat there;
Whilst each unfettered o'er the earth extend
Their all-subduing energies, and wield
The sceptre of a vast dominion there;
Whilst every shape and mode of matter lends
Its force to the omnipotence of mind,
Which from its dark mine drags the gem of truth
To decorate its paradise of peace.'

9

'O happy Earth! reality of Heaven!°
To which those restless souls that ceaselessly
Throng through the human universe, aspire;

Thou consummation of all mortal hope!
Thou glorious prize of blindly-working will!
Whose rays, diffused throughout all space and time,
Verge to one point and blend forever there:
Of purest spirits thou pure dwelling-place!
Where care and sorrow, impotence and crime,
Languor, disease, and ignorance dare not come: 10
O happy Earth, reality of Heaven!

'Genius has seen thee in her passionate dreams,
And dim forebodings of thy loveliness
Haunting the human heart, have there entwined
Those rooted hopes of some sweet place of bliss
Where friends and lovers meet to part no more.
Thou art the end of all desire and will,
The product of all action; and the souls
That by the paths of an aspiring change
Have reached thy haven of perpetual peace,   20
There rest from the eternity of toil
That framed the fabric of thy perfectness.

'Even Time, the conqueror, fled thee in his fear;
That hoary giant, who, in lonely pride,
So long had ruled the world, that nations fell
Beneath his silent footstep. Pyramids,
That for millenniums had withstood the tide
Of human things, his storm-breath drove in sand
Across that desert where their stones survived
The name of him whose pride had heaped them there.   30
Yon monarch, in his solitary pomp,
Was but the mushroom of a summer day,
That his light-wingèd footstep pressed to dust:
Time was the king of earth: all things gave way
Before him, but the fixed and virtuous will,
The sacred sympathies of soul and sense,
That mocked his fury and prepared his fall.°

'Yet slow and gradual dawned the morn of love;
Long lay the clouds of darkness o'er the scene,
Till from its native heaven they rolled away: 40
First, crime triumphant o'er all hope careered

Unblushing, undisguising, bold and strong;
Whilst falsehood, tricked in virtue's attributes,
Long sanctified all deeds of vice and woe,
Till done by her own venomous sting to death,
She left the moral world without a law,
No longer fettering passion's fearless wing,
Nor searing reason with the brand of God.°
Then steadily the happy ferment worked;
Reason was free; and wild though passion went   50
Through tangled glens and wood–embosomed meads,
Gathering a garland of the strangest flowers,
Yet like the bee returning to her queen,
She bound the sweetest on her sister's brow,
Who meek and sober kissed the sportive child,
No longer trembling at the broken rod.

'Mild was the slow necessity of death:
The tranquil Spirit failed beneath its grasp,
Without a groan, almost without a fear,
Calm as a voyager to some distant land,   60
And full of wonder, full of hope as he.
The deadly germs of languor and disease
Died in the human frame, and purity
Blest with all gifts her earthly worshippers.
How vigorous then the athletic form of age!
How clear its open and unwrinkled brow!
Where neither avarice, cunning, pride, or care,
Had stamped the seal of grey deformity
On all the mingling lineaments of time.
How lovely the intrepid front of youth!   70
Which meek–eyed courage decked with freshest grace;
Courage of soul, that dreaded not a name,
And elevated will, that journeyed on
Through life's phantasmal scene in fearlessness,
With virtue, love, and pleasure, hand in hand.

'Then, that sweet bondage which is freedom's self,°
And rivets with sensation's softest tie
The kindred sympathies of human souls,
Needed no fetters of tyrannic law:
Those delicate and timid impulses   80

In nature's primal modesty arose,
And with undoubting confidence disclosed
The growing longings of its dawning love,
Unchecked by dull and selfish chastity,
That virtue of the cheaply virtuous,
Who pride themselves in senselessness and frost.°
No longer prostitution's venomed bane
Poisoned the springs of happiness and life;
Woman and man, in confidence and love,
Equal and free and pure together trod   90
The mountain-paths of virtue, which no more
Were stained with blood from many a pilgrim's feet.

'Then, where, through distant ages, long in pride
The palace of the monarch-slave had mocked
Famine's faint groan, and penury's silent tear,
A heap of crumbling ruins stood, and threw
Year after year their stones upon the field,
Wakening a lonely echo; and the leaves
Of the old thorn, that on the topmost tower
Usurped the royal ensign's grandeur, shook   100
In the stern storm that swayed the topmost tower
And whispered strange tales in the whirlwind's ear.

'Low through the lone cathedral's roofless aisles
The melancholy winds a death-dirge sung:
It were a sight of awfulness to see
The works of faith and slavery, so vast,
So sumptuous, yet so perishing withal!
Even as the corpse that rests beneath its wall.
A thousand mourners deck the pomp of death
Today, the breathing marble glows above   110
To decorate its memory, and tongues
Are busy of its life: tomorrow, worms
In silence and in darkness seize their prey.

'Within the massy prison's mouldering courts,
Fearless and free the ruddy children played,
Weaving gay chaplets for their innocent brows
With the green ivy and the red wall-flower,
That mock the dungeon's unavailing gloom;

The ponderous chains, and gratings of strong iron,
There rusted amid heaps of broken stone   120
That mingled slowly with their native earth:
There the broad beam of day, which feebly once
Lighted the cheek of lean captivity
With a pale and sickly glare, then freely shone
On the pure smiles of infant playfulness:
No more the shuddering voice of hoarse despair
Pealed through the echoing vaults, but soothing notes
Of ivy-fingered winds and gladsome birds
And merriment were resonant around.

'These ruins soon left not a wreck behind:°   130
Their elements, wide scattered o'er the globe,
To happier shapes were moulded, and became
Ministrant to all blissful impulses:
Thus human things were perfected, and earth,
Even as a child beneath its mother's love,
Was strengthened in all excellence, and grew
Fairer and nobler with each passing year.

'Now Time his dusky pennons o'er the scene
Closes in steadfast darkness, and the past
Fades from our charmèd sight. My task is done: 140
Thy lore is learned. Earth's wonders are thine own,
With all the fear and all the hope they bring.
My spells are past: the present now recurs.
Ah me! a pathless wilderness remains
Yet unsubdued by man's reclaiming hand.

'Yet, human Spirit, bravely hold thy course,
Let virtue teach thee firmly to pursue
The gradual paths of an aspiring change:
For birth and life and death, and that strange state
Before the naked soul has found its home,   150
All tend to perfect happiness, and urge
The restless wheels of being on their way,
Whose flashing spokes, instinct with infinite life,
Bicker and burn to gain their destined goal:
For birth but wakes the spirit to the sense
Of outward shows, whose unexperienced shape

New modes of passion to its frame may lend;
Life is its state of action, and the store
Of all events is aggregated there
That variegate the eternal universe;   160
Death is a gate of dreariness and gloom,
That leads to azure isles and beaming skies
And happy regions of eternal hope.
Therefore, O Spirit! fearlessly bear on:
Though storms may break the primrose on its stalk,
Though frosts may blight the freshness of its bloom,
Yet spring's awakening breath will woo the earth,
To feed with kindliest dews its favourite flower,
That blooms in mossy banks and darksome glens,
Lighting the green wood with its sunny smile.   170

'Fear not then, Spirit, death's disrobing hand,
So welcome when the tyrant is awake,
So welcome when the bigot's hell-torch burns;
'Tis but the voyage of a darksome hour,
The transient gulf-dream of a startling sleep.
Death is no foe to virtue: earth has seen
Love's brightest roses on the scaffold bloom,
Mingling with freedom's fadeless laurels there,
And presaging the truth of visioned bliss.
Are there not hopes within thee, which this scene   180
Of linked and gradual being has confirmed?
Whose stingings bade thy heart look further still,
When to the moonlight walk by Henry led,
Sweetly and sadly thou didst talk of death?
And wilt thou rudely tear them from thy breast,
Listening supinely to a bigot's creed,
Or tamely crouching to the tyrant's rod,
Whose iron thongs are red with human gore?
Never: but bravely bearing on, thy will
Is destined an eternal war to wage   190
With tyranny and falsehood, and uproot
The germs of misery from the human heart.
Thine is the hand whose piety would soothe
The thorny pillow of unhappy crime,
Whose impotence an easy pardon gains,
Watching its wanderings as a friend's disease:

Thine is the brow whose mildness would defy
Its fiercest rage, and brave its sternest will,
When fenced by power and master of the world.
Thou art sincere and good; of resolute mind,   200
Free from heart-withering custom's cold control,
Of passion lofty, pure and unsubdued.
Earth's pride and meanness could not vanquish thee,
And therefore art thou worthy of the boon
Which thou hast now received: virtue shall keep
Thy footsteps in the path that thou hast trod,
And many days of beaming hope shall bless
Thy spotless life of sweet and sacred love.
Go, happy one, and give that bosom joy
   Whose sleepless spirit waits to catch   210
   Light, life and rapture from thy smile.'

   The fairy waves her wand of charm.
Speechless with bliss the Spirit mounts the car,
   That rolled beside the battlement,
Bending her beamy eyes in thankfulness.
   Again the enchanted steeds were yoked,
   Again the burning wheels inflame
The steep descent of heaven's untrodden way.
   Fast and far the chariot flew:
   The vast and fiery globes that rolled   220
   Around the Fairy's palace-gate
Lessened by slow degrees, and soon appeared
Such tiny twinklers as the planet orbs
That there attendant on the solar power
With borrowed light pursued their narrower way.

   Earth floated then below:
   The chariot paused a moment there;
     The Spirit then descended:
The restless coursers pawed the ungenial soil,
Snuffed the gross air, and then, their errand done,   230
Unfurled their pinions to the winds of heaven.

   The Body and the Soul united then,
A gentle start convulsed Ianthe's frame:
Her veiny eyelids quietly unclosed;

Moveless awhile the dark blue orbs remained:
She looked around in wonder and beheld
Henry, who kneeled in silence by her couch,
Watching her sleep with looks of speechless love,
    And the bright beaming stars
    That through the casement shone.   240

NOTES TO 'QUEEN MAB'°

1.242–3

The sun's unclouded orb
Rolled through the black concave.

Beyond our atmosphere the sun would appear a rayless orb of fire in the midst of a black concave. The equal diffusion of its light on earth is owing to the refraction of the rays by the atmosphere, and their reflection from other bodies. Light consists either of vibrations propagated through a subtle medium, or of numerous minute particles repelled in all directions from the luminous body. Its velocity greatly exceeds that of any substance with which we are acquainted: observations on the eclipses of Jupiter's satellites have demonstrated that light takes up no more than 8′ 7″ in passing from the sun to the earth, a distance of 95,000,000 miles.—Some idea may be gained of the immense distance of the fixed stars, when it is computed that many years would elapse before light could reach this earth from the nearest of them; yet in one year light travels 5,422,400,000,000 miles, which is a distance 5,707,600 times greater than that of the sun from the earth.°

1.252–3

Whilst round the chariot's way
Innumerable systems rolled.

The plurality of worlds,—the indefinite immensity of the universe is a most awful subject of contemplation. He who rightly feels its mystery and grandeur, is in no danger of seduction from the falsehoods of religious systems, or of deifying the principle of the universe. It is impossible to believe that the Spirit that pervades this infinite machine, begat a son upon the body of a Jewish woman; or is angered at the consequences of that necessity, which is a synonym of itself. All that miserable tale of the Devil, and Eve, and an Intercessor, with the childish mummeries of the God of the Jews, is irreconcilable with the knowledge of the stars. The works of his fingers have borne witness against him.

The nearest of the fixed stars is inconceivably distant from the earth, and they are probably proportionably distant from each other. By a calculation of the velocity of light, Syrius is supposed to be at least 54,224,000,000,000 miles from the earth.° That which appears only like a thin and silvery cloud streaking the heaven, is in effect composed of innumerable clusters of suns, each shining with its own light, and illuminating numbers of planets that revolve around them. Millions and millions of suns are ranged around us, all attended by innumerable worlds, yet calm, regular, and harmonious, all keeping the paths of immutable necessity.

4.178–9

> These are the hired bravos who defend
> The tyrant's throne.

[This Note consists of an extended quotation from the fifth essay in part 2 of Godwin's collection of essays, *The Enquirer* (1797), followed by a version of 'Falsehood and Vice: a Dialogue', 'a little poem . . . strongly expressive of my abhorrence of despotism and falsehood'. S. rescued 'Falsehood and Vice' from the 'oblivion' of the unpublished *Esdaile Notebook*, where it exists in a slightly different form. The following extract from the Note begins in the penultimate paragraph of the Godwin quotation.]

[. . .] A soldier is a man whose business it is to kill those who never offended him, and who are the innocent martyrs of other men's iniquities. Whatever may become of the abstract question of the justifiableness of war, it seems impossible that the soldier should not be a depraved and unnatural being.

To these more serious and momentous considerations it may be proper to add a recollection of the ridiculousness of the military character. Its first constituent is obedience: a soldier is, of all descriptions of men, the most completely a machine; yet his profession inevitably teaches him something of dogmatism, swaggering, and self-consequence: he is like the puppet of a showman, who, at the very time he is made to strut and swell and display the most farcical airs, we perfectly know cannot assume the most insignificant gesture, advance either to the right or the left, but as he is moved by his exhibitor.—*Godwin's Enquirer, Essay* v.

I will here subjoin a little poem,° so strongly expressive of my abhorrence of despotism and falsehood, that I fear lest it never again may be depictured so vividly. This opportunity is perhaps the only one that ever will occur of rescuing it from oblivion.

FALSEHOOD AND VICE

A DIALOGUE

> Whilst monarchs laughed upon their thrones
> To hear a famished nation's groans,
> And hugged the wealth wrung from the woe
> That makes its eyes and veins o'erflow,—
> Those thrones, high built upon the heaps

Of bones where frenzied famine sleeps,
Where slavery wields her scourge of iron,
Red with mankind's unheeded gore,
And war's mad fiends the scene environ:
Mingling with shrieks a drunken roar,   10
There Vice and Falsehood took their stand,
High raised above the unhappy land.

Falsehood

Brother! arise from the dainty fare,
Which thousands have toiled and bled to bestow;
A finer feast for thy hungry ear
Is the news that I bring of human woe.

Vice

And, secret one, what hast thou done,
To compare, in thy tumid pride, with me?
I, whose career, through the blasted year,
Has been tracked by despair and agony.   20

Falsehood

What have I done!—I have torn the robe
From baby truth's unsheltered form,
And round the desolated globe
Borne safely the bewildering charm:
My tyrant-slaves to a dungeon-floor
Have bound the fearless innocent,
And streams of fertilizing gore
Flow from her bosom's hideous rent,
Which this unfailing dagger gave. . . .
I dread that blood!—no more—this day   30
Is ours, though her eternal ray
   Must shine upon our grave.
Yet know, proud Vice, had I not given
To thee the robe I stole from heaven,
Thy shape of ugliness and fear
Had never gained admission here.

Vice

And know, that had I disdained to toil,
But sate in my loathsome cave the while,
And ne'er to these hateful sons of heaven,
GOLD, MONARCHY, and MURDER, given;   40
Hadst thou with all thine art essayed
One of thy games then to have played,

With all thine overweening boast,
Falsehood! I tell thee thou hadst lost!—
Yet wherefore this dispute?—we tend,
Fraternal, to one common end;
In this cold grave beneath my feet
Will our hopes, our fears, and our labours meet.

Falsehood

I brought my daughter, RELIGION, on earth:
She smothered Reason's babes in their birth;   50
But dreaded their mother's eye severe,—
So the crocodile slunk off slily in fear,
And loosed her bloodhounds from the den. . . .
They started from dreams of slaughtered men,
And, by the light of her poison eye,
Did her work o'er the wide earth frightfully:
The dreadful stench of her torches' flare,
Fed with human fat, polluted the air:
The curses, the shrieks, the ceaseless cries
Of the many-mingling miseries,   60
As on she trod, ascended high
And trumpeted my victory!—
Brother, tell what thou hast done.

Vice

I have extinguished the noon-day sun,
In the carnage-smoke of battles won:
Famine, murder, hell and power
Were glutted in that glorious hour
Which searchless fate had stamped for me
With the seal of her security. . . .
For the bloated wretch on yonder throne   70
Commanded the bloody fray to rise.
Like me he joyed at the stifled moan
Wrung from a nation's miseries;
While the snakes, whose slime even him *defiled*,
In ecstacies of malice smiled:
They thought 'twas theirs,—but mine the deed!
Theirs is the toil, but mine the meed—
Ten thousand victims madly bleed.
They dream that tyrants goad them there
With poisonous war to taint the air: 80
These tyrants, on their beds of thorn,
Swell with the thoughts of murderous fame,
And with their gains to lift my name.

Restless they plan from night to morn:
I—I do all; without my aid
Thy daughter, that relentless maid,
Could never o'er a death-bed urge
The fury of her venomed scourge.

Falsehood

Brother, well:—the world is ours;
And whether thou or I have won,   90
The pestilence expectant lowers
On all beneath yon blasted sun.
Our joys, our toils, our honours meet
In the milk-white and wormy winding-sheet:
A short-lived hope, unceasing care,
Some heartless scraps of godly prayer,
A moody curse, and a frenzied sleep
Ere gapes the grave's unclosing deep,
A tyrant's dream, a coward's start,
The ice that clings to a priestly heart,   100
A judge's frown, a courtier's smile,
Make the great whole for which we toil;
And, brother, whether thou or I
Have done the work of misery,
It little boots: thy toil and pain,
Without my aid, were more than vain;
And but for thee I ne'er had sate
The guardian of heaven's palace gate.

5.1–2

Thus do the generations of the earth
Go to the grave and issue from the womb.

[S.'s Note quotes Ecclesiastes 1: 4–7.]

5.4–6

Even as the leaves
Which the keen frost-wind of the waning year
Has scattered on the forest soil.

[S.'s Note quotes *Iliad* 6. 146–9.]

5.58

The mob of peasants, nobles, priests, and kings.

[S.'s Note quotes Lucretius, *De Rerum Natura* 2. 1–14.]

5.93-4

And statesmen boast
Of wealth!

[S.'s Note deplores the unequal distribution of wealth and the role of labour in society.]

5.112-13

or religion
Drives his wife raving mad.

I am acquainted with a lady of considerable accomplishments, and the mother of a numerous family, whom the Christian religion has goaded to incurable insanity. A parallel case is, I believe, within the experience of every physician.

> Nam jam saepe homines patriam, carosque parentes
> Prodiderunt, vitare Acherusia templa petentes.
> *Lucretius.*°

5.189

Even love is sold.

Not even the intercourse of the sexes is exempt from the despotism of positive institution. Law pretends even to govern the indisciplinable wanderings of passion, to put fetters on the clearest deductions of reason, and, by appeals to the will, to subdue the involuntary affections of our nature. Love is inevitably consequent upon the perception of loveliness. Love withers under constraint: its very essence is liberty: it is compatible neither with obedience, jealousy, nor fear: it is there most pure, perfect, and unlimited, where its votaries live in confidence, equality, and unreserve.

How long then ought the sexual connection to last? what law ought to specify the extent of the grievances which should limit its duration? A husband and wife ought to continue so long united as they love each other: any law which should bind them to cohabitation for one moment after the decay of their affection, would be a most intolerable tyranny, and the most unworthy of toleration. How odious an usurpation of the right of private judgment should that law be considered, which should make the ties of friendship indissoluble, in spite of the caprices, the inconstancy, the fallibility, and capacity for improvement of the human mind. And by so much would the fetters of love be heavier and more unendurable than those of friendship, as love is more vehement and capricious, more dependent on those delicate peculiarities of imagination, and less capable of reduction to the ostensible merits of the object.

The state of society in which we exist is a mixture of feudal savageness and imperfect civilization. The narrow and unenlightened morality of the

Christian religion is an aggravation of these evils. It is not even until lately that mankind have admitted that happiness is the sole end of the science of ethics, as of all other sciences; and that the fanatical idea of mortifying the flesh for the love of God has been discarded. I have heard, indeed, an ignorant collegian adduce, in favour of Christianity, its hostility to every worldly feeling!°

But if happiness be the object of morality, of all human unions and dis-unions; if the worthiness of every action is to be estimated by the quantity of pleasurable sensation it is calculated to produce, then the connection of the sexes is so long sacred as it contributes to the comfort of the parties, and is naturally dissolved when its evils are greater than its benefits. There is nothing immoral in this separation. Constancy has nothing virtuous in itself, independently of the pleasure it confers, and partakes of the temporizing spirit of vice in proportion as it endures tamely moral defects of magnitude in the object of its indiscreet choice. Love is free: to promise for ever to love the same woman, is not less absurd than to promise to believe the same creed: such a vow, in both cases, excludes us from all enquiry. The language of the votarist is this: The woman I now love may be infinitely inferior to many others; the creed I now profess may be a mass of errors and absurdities; but I exclude myself from all future information as to the amiability of the one and the truth of the other, resolving blindly, and in spite of conviction, to adhere to them. Is this the language of delicacy and reason? Is the love of such a frigid heart of more worth than its belief?

The present system of constraint does no more, in the majority of instances, than make hypocrites or open enemies. Persons of delicacy and virtue, un-happily united to one whom they find it impossible to love, spend the loveliest season of their life in unproductive efforts to appear otherwise than they are, for the sake of the feelings of their partner or the welfare of their mutual offspring: those of less generosity and refinement openly avow their dis-appointment, and linger out the remnant of that union, which only death can dissolve, in a state of incurable bickering and hostility. The early education of their children takes its colour from the squabbles of the parents; they are nursed in a systematic school of ill humour, violence, and falsehood. Had they been suffered to part at the moment when indifference rendered their union irksome, they would have been spared many years of misery: they would have connected themselves more suitably, and would have found that happiness in the society of more congenial partners which is for ever denied them by the despotism of marriage. They would have been separately useful and happy members of society, who, whilst united, were miserable, and rendered misan-thropical by misery. The conviction that wedlock is indissoluble holds out the strongest of all temptations to the perverse: they indulge without restraint in acrimony, and all the little tyrannies of domestic life, when they know that their victim is without appeal. If this connection were put on a rational basis, each would be assured that habitual ill temper would terminate in separation, and would check this vicious and dangerous propensity.

Prostitution is the legitimate offspring of marriage and its accompanying errors. Women, for no other crime than having followed the dictates of a natural appetite, are driven with fury from the comforts and sympathies of society. It is less venial than murder; and the punishment which is inflicted on her who destroys her child to escape reproach, is lighter than the life of agony and disease to which the prostitute is irrecoverably doomed. Has a woman obeyed the impulse of unerring nature;—society declares war against her, pitiless and eternal war: she must be the tame slave, she must make no reprisals; theirs is the right of persecution, hers the duty of endurance. She lives a life of infamy: the loud and bitter laugh of scorn scares her from all return. She dies of long and lingering disease: yet *she* is in fault, *she* is the criminal, *she* the forward and untameable child,—and society, forsooth, the pure and virtuous matron, who casts her as an abortion from her undefiled bosom! Society avenges herself on the criminals of her own creation; she is employed in anathematizing the vice today, which yesterday she was the most zealous to teach. Thus is formed one tenth of the population of London: meanwhile the evil is twofold. Young men, excluded by the fanatical idea of chastity from the society of modest and accomplished women, associate with these vicious and miserable beings, destroying thereby all those exquisite and delicate sensibilities whose existence cold-hearted worldlings have denied; annihilating all genuine passion, and debasing that to a selfish feeling which is the excess of generosity and devotedness. Their body and mind alike crumble into a hideous wreck of humanity; idiocy and disease become perpetuated in their miserable offspring, and distant generations suffer for the bigoted morality of their forefathers. Chastity is a monkish and evangelical superstition, a greater foe to natural temperance even than unintellectual sensuality; it strikes at the root of all domestic happiness, and consigns more than half of the human race to misery, that some few may monopolize according to law. A system could not well have been devised more studiously hostile to human happiness than marriage.

I conceive that, from the abolition of marriage, the fit and natural arrangement of sexual connection would result. I by no means assert that the intercourse would be promiscuous: on the contrary; it appears, from the relation of parent to child, that this union is generally of long duration, and marked above all others with generosity and self-devotion. But this is a subject which it is perhaps premature to discuss. That which will result from the abolition of marriage, will be natural and right, because choice and change will be exempted from restraint.

In fact, religion and morality, as they now stand, compose a practical code of misery and servitude: the genius of human happiness must tear every leaf from the accursed book of God, ere man can read the inscription on his heart. How would morality, dressed up in stiff stays and finery, start from her own disgusting image, should she look in the mirror of nature!

6.45–6

To the red and baleful sun
That faintly twinkles there.

[S's Note discusses the precession of the equinox and the possibility of there one day being 'a perfect identity between the moral and physical improvement of the human species'.]

6.171–3

No atom of this turbulence fulfils
A vague and unnecessitated task,
Or acts but as it must and ought to act.

[S's Note quotes Holbach's *Système de la Nature* (1774 edn.), 1.56.]

6.198°

Necessity, thou mother of the world!

[S.'s lengthy Note discusses the relation of necessity to liberty, morality, and divinity, drawing on the writings of Hume, Holbach, and Godwin.]

7.13

There is no God!

This negation must be understood solely to affect a creative Deity. The hypothesis of a pervading Spirit coeternal with the universe, remains unshaken.

A close examination° of the validity of the proofs adduced to support any proposition, is the only secure way of attaining truth, on the advantages of which it is unnecessary to descant: our knowledge of the existence of a Deity is a subject of such importance, that it cannot be too minutely investigated; in consequence of this conviction we proceed briefly and impartially to examine the proofs which have been adduced. It is necessary first to consider the nature of belief.

When a proposition is offered to the mind, it perceives the agreement or disagreement of the ideas of which it is composed. A perception of their agreement is termed *belief.* Many obstacles frequently prevent this perception from being immediate; these the mind attempts to remove, in order that the perception may be distinct. The mind is active in the investigation, in order to perfect the state of perception [of the relation which the component ideas of the proposition bear to each], which is passive: the investigation being confused with the perception, has induced many falsely to imagine that the mind is active in belief,—that belief is an act of volition,—in consequence of which it may be regulated by the mind. Pursuing, continuing this mistake, they have attached a degree of criminality to disbelief; of which, in its nature, it is incapable: it is equally incapable of merit.

Belief, then, is a passion, the strength of which, like every other passion, is in precise proportion to the degrees of excitement.

The degrees of excitement are three.

The senses are the sources of all knowledge to the mind; consequently their evidence claims the strongest assent.

The decision of the mind, founded upon our own experience, derived from these sources, claims the next degree.

The experience of others, which addresses itself to the former one, occupies the lowest degree.

[(A graduated scale, on which should be marked the capabilities of propositions to approach to the test of the senses, would be a just barometer of the belief which ought to be attached to them.)]

Consequently no testimony can be admitted which is contrary to reason; reason is founded on the evidence of our senses.

Every proof may be referred to one of these three divisions: it is to be considered what arguments we receive from each of them, which should convince us of the existence of a Deity.

1st. The evidence of the senses. If the Deity should appear to us, if he should convince our senses of his existence, this revolution would necessarily command belief. Those to whom the Deity has thus appeared have the strongest possible conviction of his existence. [But the God of Theologians is incapable of local visibility.]

2d. Reason. It is urged that man knows that whatever is, must either have had a beginning, or have existed from all eternity: he also knows, that whatever is not eternal must have had a cause. When this reasoning is applied to the universe, it is necessary to prove that it was created: until that is clearly demonstrated, we may reasonably suppose that it has endured from all eternity. [We must prove design before we can infer a designer. The only idea which we can form of causation is derivable from the constant conjunction of objects, and the consequent inference of one from the other.] In a case where two propositions are diametrically opposite, the mind believes that which is least° incomprehensible;—it is easier to suppose that the universe has existed from all eternity, than to conceive a being [beyond its limits] capable of creating it: if the mind sinks beneath the weight of one, is it an alleviation to increase the intolerability of the burden?

The other argument, which is founded on a man's knowledge of his own existence, stands thus. A man knows not only that he now is, but that once he was not; consequently there must have been a cause. [But our idea of causation is alone derivable from the constant conjunction of objects and the consequent inference of one from the other; and, reasoning experimentally,°] we can only infer from effects, causes exactly adequate to those effects. But there certainly is a generative power which is effected by certain instruments: we cannot prove that it is inherent in these instruments; nor is the contrary hypothesis capable of demonstration: we admit that the generative power is incomprehensible; but to suppose that the same effect is produced by an eternal, omniscient, omnipotent being,° leaves the cause in the same obscurity, but renders it more incomprehensible.

3d. Testimony. It is required that testimony should not be contrary to reason. The testimony that the Deity convinces the senses of men of his existence can only be admitted by us, if our mind considers it less probable that these men should have been deceived, than that the Deity should have appeared to them. Our reason can never admit the testimony of men, who not only declare that they were eye-witnesses of miracles, but that the Deity was irrational; for he commanded that he should be believed, he proposed the highest rewards for faith, eternal punishments for disbelief. We can only command voluntary actions; belief is not an act of volition; the mind is even passive, or involuntarily active: from this it is evident that we have no sufficient testimony, or rather that testimony is insufficient to prove the being of a God. It has been before shown that it cannot be deduced from reason. They alone, then, who have been convinced by the evidence of the senses, can believe it.

Hence it is evident that, having no proofs from either of the three sources of conviction, the mind *cannot* believe the existence of a [creative] God: it is also evident, that, as belief is a passion of the mind, no degree of criminality is attachable to disbelief; and that they only are reprehensible who neglect to remove the false medium through which their mind views any subject of discussion. Every reflecting mind must acknowledge that there is no proof of the existence of a Deity.

God is an hypothesis, and, as such, stands in need of proof: the *onus probandi* rests on the theist. Sir Isaac Newton says: *Hypotheses non fingo, quicquid enim ex phaenomenis non deducitur, hypothesis vocanda est, et hypothesis vel metaphysica, vel physicae, vel qualitatum occultarum, seu mechanicae, in philosophiâ locum non habent.*° To all proofs of the existence of a creative God apply this valuable rule. We see a variety of bodies possessing a variety of powers: we merely know their effects; we are in a state of ignorance with respect to their essences and causes. These Newton calls the phenomena of things; but the pride of philosophy is unwilling to admit its ignorance of their causes. From the phenomena, which are the objects of our senses, we attempt to infer a cause, which we call God, and gratuitously endow it with all negative and contradictory qualities. From this hypothesis we invent this general name, to conceal our ignorance of causes and essences. The being called God by no means answers with the conditions prescribed by Newton; it bears every mark of a veil woven by philosophical conceit, to hide the ignorance of philosophers even from themselves. They borrow the threads of its texture from the anthropomorphism of the vulgar. Words have been used by sophists for the same purposes, from the occult qualities of the peripatetics to the *effluvium* of Boyle and the *crinities* or *nebulae* of Herschel.° God is represented as infinite, eternal, incomprehensible; he is contained under every praedicate in non° that the logic of ignorance could fabricate. Even his worshippers allow that it is impossible to form any idea of him: they exclaim with the French poet,

Pour dire ce qu'il est, il faut être lui-même.°

Lord Bacon says, that 'atheism leaves to man reason, philosophy, natural piety, laws, reputation, and every thing that can serve to conduct him to virtue; but superstition destroys all these, and erects itself into a tyranny over the understandings of men: hence atheism never disturbs the government, but renders man more clear-sighted, since he sees nothing beyond the boundaries of the present life.'
[. . .]

7.67

Ahasuerus, rise!

[S.'s Note is a loose prose transcription of a translation of C. F. D. Schubart's poem 'Der ewige Jude. Eine lyrische Rhapsodie' (1783), about the Wandering Jew, Ahasuerus.]

7.135–6

I will beget a Son, and he shall bear
The sins of all the world.

[S.'s lengthy Note discusses the defects, illogicalities and tyrannies of the Christian religion.]

8.203–7

Him, (still from hope to hope the bliss pursuing,
Which, from the exhaustless lore of human weal
Draws on the virtuous mind,) the thoughts that rise
In time-destroying infiniteness, gift
With self-enshrined eternity, &c.°

Time is our consciousness of the succession of ideas in our mind. Vivid sensation, of either pain or pleasure, makes the time seem long, as the common phrase is, because it renders us more acutely conscious of our ideas. If a mind be conscious of an hundred ideas during one minute, by the clock, and of two hundred during another, the latter of these spaces would actually occupy so much greater extent in the mind as two exceed one in quantity. If, therefore, the human mind, by any future improvement of its sensibility, should become conscious of an infinite number of ideas in a minute, that minute would be eternity. I do not hence infer that the actual space between the birth and death of a man will ever be prolonged; but that his sensibility is perfectible, and that the number of ideas which his mind is capable of receiving is indefinite. One man is stretched on the rack during twelve hours; another sleeps soundly in his bed: the difference of time perceived by these two persons is immense; one hardly will believe that half an hour has elapsed, the other could credit that centuries had flown during his agony. Thus, the life of a man of virtue and talent, who should die in his thirtieth year, is, with regard to his own feelings, longer than that of a miserable priest-ridden slave, who dreams out a century of dullness. The one has perpetually cultivated his mental faculties, has rendered himself master of his thoughts, can abstract and generalize amid the lethargy of everyday business;—the other can slumber over the brightest moments of his being, and is unable to remember the happiest hour of his life. Perhaps the perishing ephemeron enjoys a longer life than the tortoise.

> Dark flood of time!
> Roll as it listeth thee—I measure not
> By months or moments thy ambiguous course.
> Another may stand by me on the brink
> And watch the bubble whirled beyond his ken
> That pauses at my feet. The sense of love,
> The thirst for action, and the impassioned thought
> Prolong my being: if I wake no more,
> My life more actual living will contain
> Than some grey veteran's of the world's cold school,
> Whose listless hours unprofitably roll,
> By one enthusiast feeling unredeemed.°

8.211–12°

> No longer now
> He slays the lamb that looks him in the face.

I hold that the depravity of the physical and moral nature of man originated in his unnatural habits of life. The origin of man, like that of the universe of which he is a part, is enveloped in impenetrable mystery. His generations either had a beginning, or they had not. The weight of evidence in favour of each of these suppositions seems tolerably equal; and it is perfectly unimportant to the present argument which is assumed. The language spoken however by the mythology of nearly all religions seems to prove, that at some distant period man forsook the path of nature, and sacrificed the purity and happiness of his being to unnatural appetites. The date of this event seems to have also been that of some great change in the climates of the earth, with which it has an obvious correspondence. The allegory of Adam and Eve eating of the tree of evil, and entailing upon their posterity the wrath of God, and the loss of everlasting life, admits of no other explanation than the disease and crime that have flowed from unnatural diet. Milton° was so well aware of this, that he makes Raphael thus exhibit to Adam the consequence of his disobedience.

> Immediately a place
> Before his eyes appeared: sad, noisome, dark:
> A lazar-house it seem'd; wherein were laid
> Numbers of all diseased: all maladies

Of ghastly spasm, or racking torture, qualms
Of heart-sick agony, all feverous kinds,
Convulsions, epilepsies, fierce catarrhs,
Intestine stone and ulcer, cholic pangs,
Daemoniac frenzy, moping melancholy,
And moon-struck madness, pining atrophy,
Marasmus, and wide-wasting pestilence,
Dropsies, and asthma, and joint-racking rheums.

And how many thousands more might not be added to this frightful catalogue!

The story of Prometheus is one likewise which, although universally admitted to be allegorical, has never been satisfactorily explained. Prometheus stole fire from heaven, and was chained for this crime to mount Caucasus, where a vulture continually devoured his liver, that grew to meet its hunger. Hesiod says, that, before the time of Prometheus, mankind were exempt from suffering; that they enjoyed a vigorous youth, and that death, when at length it came, approached like sleep, and gently closed their eyes. Again, so general was this opinion, that Horace,° a poet of the Augustan age, writes—

Audax omnia perpeti,
Gens humana ruit per vetitum nefas;
Audax Iapeti genus
Ignem fraude mala gentibus intulit:
Post ignem aetheriâ domo
Subductum, macies et nova febrium
Terris incubuit cohors,
Semotique prius tarda necessitas
Lethi corripuit gradum.

How plain a language is spoken by all this. Prometheus (who represents the human race) effected some great change in the condition of his nature, and applied fire to culinary purposes; thus inventing an expedient for screening from his disgust the horrors of the shambles. From this moment his vitals were devoured by the vulture of disease. It consumed his being in every shape of its loathsome and infinite variety, inducing the soul-quelling sinkings of premature and violent death. All vice arose from the ruin of healthful innocence. Tyranny, superstition, commerce, and inequality, were then first known, when reason vainly attempted to guide the wanderings of exacerbated passion. [. . .]

Man, and the animals whom he has infected with his society, or depraved by his dominion, are alone diseased. The wild hog, the mouflon,° the bison, and the wolf, are perfectly exempt from malady, and invariably die either from external violence, or natural old age. But the domestic hog, the sheep, the cow, and the dog, are subject to an incredible variety of distempers; and, like the corrupters of their nature, have physicians who thrive upon their miseries.

The supereminence of man is like Satan's, a supereminence of pain; and the majority of his species, doomed to penury, disease and crime, have reason to curse the untoward event, that by enabling him to communicate his sensations, raised him above the level of his fellow animals. But the steps that have been taken are irrevocable. The whole of human science is comprised in one question:—How can the advantages of intellect and civilization be reconciled with the liberty and pure pleasures of natural life? How can we take the benefits, and reject the evils of the system, which is now interwoven with all the fibres of our being?—I believe that abstinence from animal food and spirituous liquors would in a great measure capacitate us for the solution of this important question.

It is true, that mental and bodily derangement is attributable in part to other deviations from rectitude and nature than those which concern diet. The mistakes cherished by society respecting the connection of the sexes, whence the misery and diseases of unsatisfied celibacy, unenjoying prostitution, and the premature arrival of puberty necessarily spring; the putrid atmosphere of crowded cities; the exhalations of chemical processes; the muffling of our bodies in superfluous apparel; the absurd treatment of infants:—all these, and innumerable other causes, contribute their mite to the mass of human evil.°

Comparative anatomy teaches us that man resembles frugivorous animals in everything, and carnivorous in nothing; he has neither claws wherewith to seize his prey, nor distinct and pointed teeth to tear the living fibre. A Mandarin of the first class, with nails two inches long, would probably find them alone inefficient to hold even a hare. After every subterfuge of gluttony, the bull must be degraded into the ox, and the ram into the wether, by an unnatural and inhuman operation, that the flaccid fibre may offer a fainter resistance to rebellious nature. It is only by softening and disguising dead flesh by culinary preparation, that it is rendered susceptible of mastication or digestion; and that the sight of its bloody juices and raw horror does not excite intolerable loathing and disgust. Let the advocate of animal food force himself to a decisive experiment on its fitness, and, as Plutarch recommends, tear a living lamb with his teeth, and plunging his head into its vitals, slake his thirst with the steaming blood; when fresh from the deed of horror, let him revert to the irresistible instincts of nature that would rise in judgment against it, and say, Nature formed me for such work as this. Then, and then only, would he be consistent. [. . .]

What is the cause of morbid action in the animal system? Not the air we breathe, for our fellow denizens of nature breathe the same uninjured; not the water we drink (if remote from the pollutions of man and his inventions°), for the animals drink it too; not the earth we tread upon; not the unobscured sight of glorious nature, in the wood, the field, or the expanse of sky and ocean; nothing that we are or do in common with the undiseased inhabitants of the forest. Something then wherein we differ from them: our habit of altering our food by fire, so that our appetite is no longer a just criterion for the fitness of its gratification. Except in children, there remain no traces of that instinct which determines, in all other animals, what aliment is natural or otherwise; and so perfectly obliterated are they in the reasoning adults of our species, that it has become necessary to urge considerations drawn from comparative anatomy to prove that we are naturally frugivorous.

Crime is madness. Madness is disease. Whenever the cause of disease shall be discovered, the root, from which all vice and misery have so long over-shadowed the globe, will lie bare to the axe. All the exertions of man, from that moment, may be considered as tending to the clear profit of his species. No sane mind in a sane body resolves upon a real crime. It is a man of violent passions, blood-shot eyes, and swollen veins, that alone can grasp the knife of murder. The system of a simple diet promises no Utopian advantages. It is no mere reform of legislation, whilst the furious passions and evil propensities of the human heart, in which it had its origin, are still unassuaged. It strikes at the root of all evil, and is an experiment which may be tried with success, not alone by nations, but by small societies, families, and even individuals. In no cases has a return to vegetable diet produced the slightest injury; in most it has been attended with changes undeniably beneficial. Should ever a physician be born with the genius of Locke, I am persuaded that he might trace all bodily and mental derangements to our unnatural habits, as clearly as that philoso-pher has traced all knowledge to sensation. What prolific sources of disease are not those mineral and vegetable poisons that have been introduced for its extirpation! How many thousands have become murderers and robbers, bigots and domestic tyrants, dissolute and abandoned adventurers, from the use of fermented liquors; who, had they slaked their thirst only with pure water, would have lived but to diffuse the happiness of their own unperverted feel-ings. How many groundless opinions and absurd institutions have not received a general sanction from the sottishness and intemperance of individuals! Who will assert that, had the populace of Paris satisfied their hunger at the ever-furnished table of vegetable nature, they would have lent their brutal suffrage to the proscription-list of Robespierre? Could a set of men, whose passions were not perverted by unnatural stimuli, look with coolness on an auto da fè? Is it to be believed that a being of gentle feelings, rising from his meal of roots, would take delight in sports of blood? Was Nero a man of temperate life? could you read calm health in his cheek, flushed with ungovernable propensities of hatred for the human race? Did Muley Ismael's° pulse beat evenly, was his skin transparent, did his eyes beam with healthful-ness, and its invariable concomitants, cheerfulness and benignity? Though history has decided none of these questions, a child could not hesitate to answer in the negative. Surely the bile-suffused cheek of Buonaparte, his wrinkled brow, and yellow eye, the ceaseless inquietude of his nervous system, speak no less plainly the character of his unresting ambition than his murders and his victories. It is impossible, had Buonaparte descended from a race of vegetable feeders, that he could have had either the inclination or the power to ascend the throne of the Bourbons. The desire of tyranny could scarcely be excited in the individual, the power to tyrannize would certainly not be delegated by a society neither frenzied by inebriation nor rendered impotent and irrational by disease. [. . .]

[. . .] The change which would be produced by simpler habits [of diet] on political economy is sufficiently remarkable. The monopolizing eater of animal flesh would no longer destroy his constitution by devouring an acre at a meal, and many loaves of bread would cease to contribute to gout, madness and apoplexy, in the shape of a pint of porter, or a dram of gin, when appeasing the long-protracted famine of the hard-working peasant's hungry babies. The quantity of nutritious vegetable matter, consumed in fattening the carcase of an ox, would afford ten times the sustenance, undepraving indeed, and incapable of generating disease, if gathered immediately from the bosom of the earth. The most fertile districts of the habitable globe are now actually cultivated by men for animals, at a delay and waste of aliment absolutely incapable of calculation. It is only the wealthy that can, to any great degree, even now, indulge the unnatural craving for dead flesh, and they pay for the greater licence of the privilege by subjection to supernumerary diseases. Again, the spirit of the nation that should take the lead in this great reform, would insensibly become agricultural; commerce, with all its vice, selfishness and corruption, would gradually decline; more natural habits would produce gentler manners, and the excessive complication of political relations would be so far simplified, that every individual might feel and understand why he loved his country, and took a personal interest in its welfare. How would England, for example, depend on the caprices of foreign rulers, if she contained within herself all the necessaries, and despised whatever they possessed of the luxuries of life? How could they starve her into compliance with their views? Of what consequence would it be that they refused to take her woollen manufactures, when large and fertile tracts of the island ceased to be allotted to the waste of pasturage? On a natural system of diet, we should require no spices from India; no wines from Portugal, Spain, France, or Madeira; none of those multitudinous articles of luxury, for which every corner of the globe is rifled, and which are the causes of so much individual rivalship, such calamitous and sanguinary national disputes. In the history of modern times, the avarice of commercial monopoly, no less than the ambition of weak and wicked chiefs, seems to have fomented the universal discord, to have added stubbornness to the mistakes of cabinets, and indocility to the infatuation of the people. Let it ever be remembered, that it is the direct influence of commerce to make the interval between the richest and the poorest man wider and more unconquerable. Let it be remembered, that it is a foe to every thing of real worth and excellence in the human character. The odious and disgusting aristocracy of wealth is built upon the ruins of all that is good in chivalry or republicanism; and luxury is the forerunner of a barbarism scarce capable of cure. Is it impossible to realize a state of society, where all the energies of man shall be directed to the production of his solid happiness? Certainly, if this advantage (the object of all political speculation) be in any degree attainable, it is attainable only by a community which holds out no factitious incentives to the avarice and ambition of the few, and which is internally organized for the liberty, security and comfort of the many. None must be entrusted with power (and money is the completest species of power) who do not stand pledged to use it exclusively for the general benefit. But the use of animal flesh and fermented liquors, directly militates with this equality of the rights of man. The peasant cannot gratify these fashionable cravings without leaving his family to starve. Without disease and war, those sweeping curtailers of population, pasturage would include a waste too great to be afforded. The labour requisite to support a family is far lighter° than is usually supposed. The peasantry work, not only for themselves, but for the aristocracy, the army, and the manufacturers. [. . .]

I address myself not only to the young enthusiast, the ardent devotee of truth and virtue, the pure and passionate moralist, yet unvitiated by the contagion of the world. He will embrace a pure system, from its abstract truth, its beauty, its simplicity, and its promise of wide-extended benefit; unless custom has turned poison into food, he will hate the brutal pleasures of the chase by instinct; it will be a contemplation full of horror and disappointment to his mind, that beings capable of the gentlest and most admirable sympathies, should take delight in the death-pangs and last convulsions of dying animals. The elderly man, whose youth has been poisoned by intemperance, or who has lived with apparent moderation, and is afflicted with a variety of painful maladies, would find his account in a beneficial change produced without the risk of poisonous medicines. The mother, to whom the perpetual restlessness of disease, and unaccountable deaths incident to her children, are the causes of incurable unhappiness, would on this diet experience the satisfaction of beholding their perpetual healths and natural playfulness.° The most valuable lives are daily destroyed by diseases, that it is dangerous to palliate and impossible to cure by medicine. How much longer will man continue to pimp for the gluttony of death, his most insidious, implacable, and eternal foe?

Stanzas. — April, 1814

Away! the moor is dark beneath the moon,
    Rapid clouds have drank the last pale beam of even:
Away! the gathering winds will call the darkness soon,
    And profoundest midnight shroud the serene lights of heaven.

Pause not! The time is past! Every voice cries, Away!
    Tempt not with one last tear thy friend's ungentle mood:
Thy lover's eye, so glazed and cold, dares not entreat thy stay:
    Duty and dereliction guide thee back to solitude.°

Away, away! to thy sad and silent home;
    Pour bitter tears on its desolated hearth;   10
Watch the dim shades as like ghosts they go and come,
    And complicate strange webs of melancholy mirth.

The leaves of wasted autumn woods shall float around thine head:
    The blooms of dewy spring shall gleam beneath thy feet:
But thy soul or this world must fade in the frost that binds the dead,
    Ere midnight's frown and morning's smile, ere thou and
      peace may meet.

The cloud shadows of midnight possess their own repose,
    For the weary winds are silent, or the moon is in the deep:
Some respite to its turbulence unresting ocean knows;
    Whatever moves, or toils, or grieves, hath its appointed sleep.   20

Thou in the grave shalt rest—yet till the phantoms flee
    Which that house and heath and garden made dear to
      thee erewhile,
Thy remembrance, and repentance, and deep musings are not free
    From the music of two voices and the light of one sweet smile.

'O! there are spirits of the air'

Δάκρυσι διοίδω πότμον ἄποτμον°

O! there are spirits of the air,
    And genii of the evening breeze,
And gentle ghosts, with eyes as fair
    As star-beams among twilight trees:—
Such lovely ministers to meet
Oft hast thou turned from men thy lonely feet.

With mountain winds, and babbling springs,
    And moonlight seas, that are the voice
Of these inexplicable things
    Thou didst hold commune, and rejoice   10
When they did answer thee; but they
Cast, like a worthless boon, thy love away.

And thou hast sought in starry eyes
    Beams that were never meant for thine,
Another's wealth:—tame sacrifice
    To a fond faith! still dost thou pine?
Still dost thou hope that greeting hands,
Voice, looks, or lips, may answer thy demands?

Ah! wherefore didst thou build thine hope
    On the false earth's inconstancy?   20
Did thine own mind afford no scope
    Of love, or moving thoughts to thee?
That natural scenes or human smiles
Could steal the power to wind thee in their wiles?

Yes, all the faithless smiles are fled
    Whose falsehood left thee broken-hearted;
The glory of the moon is dead;
    Night's ghosts and dreams have now departed;
Thine own soul still is true to thee,
But changed to a foul fiend through misery.   30

This fiend, whose ghastly presence ever
    Beside thee like thy shadow hangs,
Dream not to chase;—the mad endeavour
    Would scourge thee to severer pangs.
Be as thou art. Thy settled fate,
Dark as it is, all change would aggravate.

To Wordsworth

Poet of Nature, thou hast wept to know
That things depart which never may return:
Childhood and youth, friendship and love's first glow,
Have fled like sweet dreams, leaving thee to mourn.
These common woes I feel. One loss is mine
Which thou too feel'st, yet I alone deplore.
Thou wert as a lone star, whose light did shine
On some frail bark in winter's midnight roar:
Thou hast like to a rock-built refuge stood

Above the blind and battling multitude: 10
In honoured poverty thy voice did weave
Songs consecrate to truth and liberty,—
Deserting these, thou leavest me to grieve,
Thus having been, that thou shouldst cease to be.

ALASTOR;

OR,

THE SPIRIT OF SOLITUDE

PREFACE

The poem entitled 'ALASTOR,' may be considered as allegorical of one of the most interesting situations of the human mind. It represents a youth of uncorrupted feelings and adventurous genius led forth by an imagination inflamed and purified through familiarity with all that is excellent and majestic, to the contemplation of the universe. He drinks deep of the fountains of knowledge, and is still insatiate. The magnificence and beauty of the external world sinks profoundly into the frame of his conceptions, and affords to their modifications a variety not to be exhausted. So long as it is possible for his desires to point towards objects thus infinite and unmeasured, he is joyous, and tranquil, and self-possessed. But the period arrives when these objects cease to suffice. His mind is at length suddenly awakened and thirsts for intercourse with an intelligence similar to itself. He images to himself the Being whom he loves. Conversant with speculations of the sublimest and most perfect natures, the vision in which he embodies his own imaginations unites all of wonderful, or wise, or beautiful, which the poet, the philosopher, or the lover could depicture. The intellectual faculties, the imagination, the functions of sense, have their respective requisitions on the sympathy of corresponding powers in other human beings. The Poet is represented as uniting these requisitions, and attaching them to a single image. He seeks in vain for a prototype of his conception. Blasted by his disappointment, he descends to an untimely grave.

The picture is not barren of instruction to actual men. The Poet's self-centred seclusion was avenged by the furies of an irresistible passion pursuing him to speedy ruin. But that Power which strikes the luminaries of the world with sudden darkness and extinction, by awakening them to too exquisite a perception of its influences, dooms to a slow and poisonous decay those meaner spirits that dare to abjure its dominion. Their destiny is more abject and inglorious as their delinquency is more contemptible and pernicious. They who, deluded by no generous error, instigated by no sacred thirst of doubtful knowledge, duped by no illustrious superstition, loving nothing on this earth, and cherishing no hopes beyond, yet keep aloof from sympathies with their kind, rejoicing neither in human joy nor mourning with human grief; these, and such as they, have their apportioned curse. They languish, because none feel with them their common nature. They are morally dead. They are neither friends, nor lovers, nor fathers, nor citizens of the world, nor benefactors of their country. Among those who attempt to exist without human sympathy, the pure and tender-hearted perish through the intensity and passion of their search after its communities, when the vacancy of their spirit suddenly makes itself felt. All else,° selfish, blind, and torpid, are those unforeseeing multitudes who constitute, together with their own, the lasting misery and loneliness of the world. Those who love not their fellow-beings, live unfruitful lives, and prepare for their old age a miserable grave.

> 'The good die first,
> And those whose hearts are dry as summer dust,
> Burn to the socket!'°

Nondum amabam, et amare amabam, quaerebam quid amarem, amans amare!

Confess. St. August.

Earth, ocean, air, beloved brotherhood!
If our great Mother has imbued my soul
With aught of natural piety to feel°
Your love, and recompense the boon with mine;
If dewy morn, and odorous noon, and even,
With sunset and its gorgeous ministers,
And solemn midnight's tingling silentness;
If autumn's hollow sighs in the sere wood,
And winter robing with pure snow and crowns
Of starry ice the grey grass and bare boughs;   10
If spring's voluptuous pantings when she breathes
Her first sweet kisses, have been dear to me;
If no bright bird, insect, or gentle beast
I consciously have injured, but still loved
And cherished these my kindred; then forgive
This boast, beloved brethren, and withdraw

No portion of your wonted favour now!
   Mother of this unfathomable world!
Favour my solemn song, for I have loved
Thee ever, and thee only; I have watched   20
Thy shadow, and the darkness of thy steps,
And my heart ever gazes on the depth
Of thy deep mysteries. I have made my bed
In charnels and on coffins, where black death
Keeps record of the trophies won from thee,
Hoping to still these obstinate questionings°
Of thee and thine, by forcing some lone ghost
Thy messenger, to render up the tale
Of what we are. In lone and silent hours,
When night makes a weird sound of its own stillness,   30
Like an inspired and desperate alchemist
Staking his very life on some dark hope,
Have I mixed awful talk and asking looks
With my most innocent love, until strange tears
Uniting with those breathless kisses, made
Such magic as compels the charmèd night
To render up thy charge: . . . and, though ne'er yet
Thou hast unveiled thy inmost sanctuary,
Enough from incommunicable dream,
And twilight phantasms, and deep noonday thought,   40
Has shone within me, that serenely now
And moveless, as a long-forgotten lyre
Suspended in the solitary dome
Of some mysterious and deserted fane,
I wait thy breath, Great Parent, that my strain
May modulate with murmurs of the air,
And motions of the forests and the sea,
And voice of living beings, and woven hymns
Of night and day, and the deep heart of man.°

   There was a Poet whose untimely tomb   50
No human hands with pious reverence reared,
But the charmed eddies of autumnal winds
Built o'er his mouldering bones a pyramid
Of mouldering leaves in the waste wilderness:—
A lovely youth,—no mourning maiden decked
With weeping flowers, or votive cypress wreath,°
The lone couch of his everlasting sleep:—

Gentle, and brave, and generous,—no lorn bard
Breathed o'er his dark fate one melodious sigh:
He lived, he died, he sung, in solitude.   60
Strangers have wept to hear his passionate notes,
And virgins, as unknown he passed, have pined
And wasted for fond love of his wild eyes.
The fire of those soft orbs has ceased to burn,
And Silence, too enamoured of that voice,
Locks its mute music in her rugged cell.
  By solemn vision, and bright silver dream,
His infancy was nurtured. Every sight
And sound from the vast earth and ambient air,
Sent to his heart its choicest impulses.   70
The fountains of divine philosophy
Fled not his thirsting lips, and all of great,
Or good, or lovely, which the sacred past
In truth or fable consecrates, he felt
And knew. When early youth had passed, he left
His cold fireside and alienated home
To seek strange truths in undiscovered lands.
Many a wide waste and tangled wilderness
Has lured his fearless steps; and he has bought
With his sweet voice and eyes, from savage men,   80
His rest and food. Nature's most secret steps
He like her shadow has pursued, where'er
The red volcano overcanopies
Its fields of snow and pinnacles of ice
With burning smoke, or where bitumen lakes°
On black bare pointed islets ever beat
With sluggish surge, or where the secret caves
Rugged and dark, winding among the springs
Of fire and poison, inaccessible
To avarice or pride, their starry domes   90
Of diamond and of gold expand above
Numberless and immeasurable halls,
Frequent with crystal column, and clear shrines
Of pearl, and thrones radiant with chrysolite.°
Nor had that scene of ampler majesty
Than gems or gold, the varying roof of heaven
And the green earth lost in his heart its claims
To love and wonder; he would linger long

In lonesome vales, making the wild his home,
Until the doves and squirrels would partake   100
From his innocuous hand his bloodless food,
Lured by the gentle meaning of his looks,
And the wild antelope, that starts whene'er
The dry leaf rustles in the brake, suspend
Her timid steps to gaze upon a form
More graceful than her own.
                              His wandering step
Obedient to high thoughts, has visited
The awful ruins of the days of old:
Athens, and Tyre, and Balbec, and the waste
Where stood Jerusalem, the fallen towers   110
Of Babylon, the eternal pyramids,
Memphis and Thebes, and whatsoe'er of strange
Sculptured on alabaster obelisk,
Or jasper tomb, or mutilated sphynx,
Dark Ethiopia in her desert hills
Conceals. Among the ruined temples there,
Stupendous columns, and wild images
Of more than man, where marble daemons watch°
The Zodiac's brazen mystery, and dead men
Hang their mute thoughts on the mute walls around,°   120
He lingered, poring on memorials
Of the world's youth, through the long burning day
Gazed on those speechless shapes, nor, when the moon
Filled the mysterious halls with floating shades
Suspended he that task, but ever gazed
And gazed, till meaning on his vacant mind
Flashed like strong inspiration, and he saw
The thrilling secrets of the birth of time.°
    Meanwhile an Arab maiden brought his food,
Her daily portion, from her father's tent,   130
And spread her matting for his couch, and stole
From duties and repose to tend his steps:—
Enamoured, yet not daring for deep awe
To speak her love:—and watched his nightly sleep,
Sleepless herself, to gaze upon his lips
Parted in slumber, whence the regular breath
Of innocent dreams arose: then, when red morn
Made paler the pale moon, to her cold home

Wildered, and wan, and panting, she returned.°
   The Poet wandering on, through Arabie   140
And Persia, and the wild Carmanian waste,
And o'er the aerial mountains which pour down
Indus and Oxus from their icy caves,
In joy and exultation held his way;
Till in the vale of Cashmire, far within°
Its loneliest dell, where odorous plants entwine
Beneath the hollow rocks a natural bower,
Beside a sparkling rivulet he stretched
His languid limbs. A vision on his sleep
There came, a dream of hopes that never yet   150
Had flushed his cheek. He dreamed a veilèd maid
Sate near him, talking in low solemn tones.
Her voice was like the voice of his own soul
Heard in the calm of thought; its music long,
Like woven sounds of streams and breezes, held
His inmost sense suspended in its web
Of many-coloured woof and shifting hues.
Knowledge and truth and virtue were her theme,
And lofty hopes of divine liberty,
Thoughts the most dear to him, and poesy,   160
Herself a poet. Soon the solemn mood
Of her pure mind kindled through all her frame
A permeating fire: wild numbers then°
She raised, with voice stifled in tremulous sobs
Subdued by its own pathos: her fair hands
Were bare alone, sweeping from some strange harp
Strange symphony, and in their branching veins
The eloquent blood told an ineffable tale.
The beating of her heart was heard to fill
The pauses of her music, and her breath   170
Tumultuously accorded with those fits
Of intermitted song. Sudden she rose,
As if her heart impatiently endured
Its bursting burden: at the sound he turned,
And saw by the warm light of their own life
Her glowing limbs beneath the sinuous veil
Of woven wind, her outspread arms now bare,
Her dark locks floating in the breath of night,
Her beamy bending eyes, her parted lips

Outstretched, and pale, and quivering eagerly.   180
His strong heart sunk and sickened with excess
Of love. He reared his shuddering limbs and quelled
His gasping breath, and spread his arms to meet
Her panting bosom: . . . she drew back a while,
Then, yielding to the irresistible joy,
With frantic gesture and short breathless cry
Folded his frame in her dissolving arms.
Now blackness veiled his dizzy eyes, and night
Involved and swallowed up the vision; sleep,
Like a dark flood suspended in its course,   190
Rolled back its impulse on his vacant brain.

   Roused by the shock he started from his trance—
The cold white light of morning, the blue moon
Low in the west, the clear and garish hills,
The distinct valley and the vacant woods,
Spread round him where he stood. Whither have fled
The hues of heaven that canopied his bower
Of yesternight? The sounds that soothed his sleep,
The mystery and the majesty of Earth,
The joy, the exultation? His wan eyes   200
Gaze on the empty scene as vacantly
As ocean's moon looks on the moon in heaven.
The spirit of sweet human love has sent
A vision to the sleep of him who spurned
Her choicest gifts. He eagerly pursues
Beyond the realms of dream that fleeting shade;
He overleaps the bounds. Alas! alas!
Were limbs, and breath, and being intertwined
Thus treacherously? Lost, lost, forever lost,
In the wide pathless desert of dim sleep,   210
That beautiful shape! Does the dark gate of death
Conduct to thy mysterious paradise,
O Sleep? Does the bright arch of rainbow clouds,
And pendent mountains seen in the calm lake,
Lead only to a black and watery depth,
While death's blue vault, with loathliest vapours hung,
Where every shade which the foul grave exhales
Hides its dead eye from the detested day,
Conduct, O Sleep, to thy delightful realms?
This doubt with sudden tide flowed on his heart,   220

The insatiate hope which it awakened, stung
His brain even like despair.
                While daylight held
The sky, the Poet kept mute conference
With his still soul. At night the passion came,
Like the fierce fiend of a distempered dream,
And shook him from his rest, and led him forth
Into the darkness.—As an eagle grasped
In folds of the green serpent, feels her breast
Burn with the poison, and precipitates°
Through night and day, tempest, and calm, and cloud,   230
Frantic with dizzying anguish, her blind flight
O'er the wide aery wilderness: thus driven°
By the bright shadow of that lovely dream,°
Beneath the cold glare of the desolate night,
Through tangled swamps and deep precipitous dells,
Startling with careless step the moon-light snake,
He fled. Red morning dawned upon his flight,
Shedding the mockery of its vital hues
Upon his cheek of death. He wandered on
Till vast Aornos seen from Petra's steep°   240
Hung o'er the low horizon like a cloud;
Through Balk, and where the desolated tombs°
Of Parthian kings scatter to every wind
Their wasting dust, wildly he wandered on,
Day after day, a weary waste of hours,
Bearing within his life the brooding care
That ever fed on its decaying flame.
And now his limbs were lean; his scattered hair
Sered by the autumn of strange suffering
Sung dirges in the wind; his listless hand   250
Hung like dead bone within its withered skin;
Life, and the lustre that consumed it, shone
As in a furnace burning secretly
From his dark eyes alone. The cottagers,
Who ministered with human charity
His human wants, beheld with wondering awe
Their fleeting visitant. The mountaineer,
Encountering on some dizzy precipice
That spectral form, deemed that the Spirit of wind
With lightning eyes, and eager breath, and feet   260

Disturbing not the drifted snow, had paused
In its career: the infant would conceal
His troubled visage in his mother's robe
In terror at the glare of those wild eyes,
To remember their strange light in many a dream
Of after-times; but youthful maidens, taught
By nature, would interpret half the woe
That wasted him, would call him with false names
Brother, and friend, would press his pallid hand
At parting, and watch, dim through tears, the path   270
Of his departure from their father's door.
   At length upon the lone Chorasmian shore°
He paused, a wide and melancholy waste
Of putrid marshes. A strong impulse urged
His steps to the seashore. A swan was there,
Beside a sluggish stream among the reeds.
It rose as he approached, and with strong wings
Scaling the upward sky, bent its bright course
High over the immeasurable main.
His eyes pursued its flight.—'Thou hast a home,   280
Beautiful bird; thou voyagest to thine home,
Where thy sweet mate will twine her downy neck
With thine, and welcome thy return with eyes
Bright in the lustre of their own fond joy.
And what am I that I should linger here,
With voice far sweeter than thy dying notes,
Spirit more vast than thine, frame more attuned
To beauty, wasting these surpassing powers
In the deaf air, to the blind earth, and heaven
That echoes not my thoughts?' A gloomy smile   290
Of desperate hope wrinkled his quivering lips.
For sleep, he knew, kept most relentlessly
Its precious charge, and silent death exposed,
Faithless perhaps as sleep, a shadowy lure,
With doubtful smile mocking its own strange charms.
   Startled by his own thoughts he looked around.
There was no fair fiend near him, not a sight
Or sound of awe but in his own deep mind.
A little shallop floating near the shore°
Caught the impatient wandering of his gaze.   300
It had been long abandoned, for its sides

Gaped wide with many a rift, and its frail joints
Swayed with the undulations of the tide.
A restless impulse urged him to embark
And meet lone Death on the drear ocean's waste;
For well he knew that mighty Shadow loves
The slimy caverns of the populous deep.
    The day was fair and sunny, sea and sky
Drank its inspiring radiance, and the wind
Swept strongly from the shore, blackening the waves.   310
Following his eager soul, the wanderer
Leaped in the boat, he spread his cloak aloft
On the bare mast, and took his lonely seat,
And felt the boat speed o'er the tranquil sea
Like a torn cloud before the hurricane.
    As one that in a silver vision floats
Obedient to the sweep of odorous winds
Upon resplendent clouds, so rapidly
Along the dark and ruffled waters fled
The straining boat.—A whirlwind swept it on,   320
With fierce gusts and precipitating force,
Through the white ridges of the chafèd sea.
The waves arose. Higher and higher still
Their fierce necks writhed beneath the tempest's scourge
Like serpents struggling in a vulture's grasp.
Calm and rejoicing in the fearful war
Of wave ruining on wave, and blast on blast°
Descending, and black flood on whirlpool driven
With dark obliterating course, he sate:
As if their genii were the ministers   330
Appointed to conduct him to the light
Of those beloved eyes, the Poet sate
Holding the steady helm. Evening came on,
The beams of sunset hung their rainbow hues
High mid the shifting domes of sheeted spray
That canopied his path o'er the waste deep;
Twilight, ascending slowly from the east,
Entwined in duskier wreaths her braided locks
O'er the fair front and radiant eyes of day;
Night followed, clad with stars. On every side   340
More horribly the multitudinous streams
Of ocean's mountainous waste to mutual war

Rushed in dark tumult thundering, as to mock
The calm and spangled sky. The little boat
Still fled before the storm; still fled, like foam
Down the steep cataract of a wintry river;
Now pausing on the edge of the riven wave;
Now leaving far behind the bursting mass
That fell, convulsing ocean. Safely fled—
As if that frail and wasted human form   350
Had been an elemental god.
                              At midnight
The moon arose: and lo! the etherial cliffs°
Of Caucasus, whose icy summits shone
Among the stars like sunlight, and around
Whose caverned base the whirlpools and the waves
Bursting and eddying irresistibly
Rage and resound for ever.—Who shall save?—
The boat fled on,—the boiling torrent drove,—
The crags closed round with black and jagged arms,
The shattered mountain overhung the sea,   360
And faster still, beyond all human speed,
Suspended on the sweep of the smooth wave,
The little boat was driven. A cavern there
Yawned, and amid its slant and winding depths
Engulfed the rushing sea. The boat fled on
With unrelaxing speed.—'Vision and Love!'
The Poet cried aloud, 'I have beheld
The path of thy departure. Sleep and death
Shall not divide us long!'
                              The boat pursued
The windings of the cavern. Daylight shone   370
At length upon that gloomy river's flow;
Now, where the fiercest war among the waves
Is calm, on the unfathomable stream
The boat moved slowly. Where the mountain, riven,
Exposed those black depths to the azure sky,
Ere yet the flood's enormous volume fell
Even to the base of Caucasus, with sound
That shook the everlasting rocks, the mass
Filled with one whirlpool all that ample chasm;
Stair above stair the eddying waters rose,   380
Circling immeasurably fast, and laved

With alternating dash the gnarlèd roots
Of mighty trees, that stretched their giant arms
In darkness over it. I' the midst was left,
Reflecting, yet distorting every cloud,
A pool of treacherous and tremendous calm.
Seized by the sway of the ascending stream,
With dizzy swiftness, round, and round, and round,
Ridge after ridge the straining boat arose,
Till on the verge of the extremest curve,   390
Where, through an opening of the rocky bank,
The waters overflow, and a smooth spot
Of glassy quiet mid those battling tides
Is left, the boat paused shuddering.—Shall it sink
Down the abyss? Shall the reverting stress
Of that resistless gulf embosom it?
Now shall it fall?—A wandering stream of wind,
Breathed from the west, has caught the expanded sail,
And, lo! with gentle motion, between banks
Of mossy slope, and on a placid stream,   400
Beneath a woven grove it sails, and, hark!
The ghastly torrent mingles its far roar
With the breeze murmuring in the musical woods.
Where the embowering trees recede, and leave
A little space of green expanse, the cove
Is closed by meeting banks, whose yellow flowers°
Forever gaze on their own drooping eyes,
Reflected in the crystal calm. The wave
Of the boat's motion marred their pensive task,
Which nought but vagrant bird, or wanton wind,   410
Or falling spear-grass, or their own decay
Had e'er disturbed before. The Poet longed
To deck with their bright hues his withered hair,
But on his heart its solitude returned,
And he forbore. Not the strong impulse hid
In those flushed cheeks, bent eyes, and shadowy frame,
Had yet performed its ministry: it hung
Upon his life, as lightning in a cloud
Gleams, hovering ere it vanish, ere the floods
Of night close over it.
                              The noonday sun   420
Now shone upon the forest, one vast mass

Of mingling shade, whose brown magnificence
A narrow vale embosoms. There, huge caves,
Scooped in the dark base of their aery rocks
Mocking its moans, respond and roar forever.°
The meeting boughs and implicated leaves°
Wove twilight o'er the Poet's path, as led
By love, or dream, or god, or mightier Death,
He sought in Nature's dearest haunt, some bank,
Her cradle, and his sepulchre. More dark   430
And dark the shades accumulate. The oak,
Expanding its immense and knotty arms,
Embraces the light beech. The pyramids
Of the tall cedar overarching, frame
Most solemn domes within, and far below,
Like clouds suspended in an emerald sky,
The ash and the acacia floating hang
Tremulous and pale. Like restless serpents, clothed
In rainbow and in fire, the parasites,
Starred with ten thousand blossoms, flow around   440
The grey trunks, and, as gamesome infants' eyes,
With gentle meanings, and most innocent wiles,
Fold their beams round the hearts of those that love,
These twine their tendrils with the wedded boughs
Uniting their close union; the woven leaves
Make net-work of the dark blue light of day,
And the night's noontide clearness, mutable
As shapes in the weird clouds. Soft mossy lawns
Beneath these canopies extend their swells,
Fragrant with perfumed herbs, and eyed with blooms   450
Minute yet beautiful. One darkest glen
Sends from its woods of musk-rose, twined with jasmine,
A soul-dissolving odour, to invite
To some more lovely mystery. Through the dell,
Silence and Twilight here, twin-sisters, keep
Their noonday watch, and sail among the shades,
Like vaporous shapes half seen; beyond, a well,
Dark, gleaming, and of most translucent wave,
Images all the woven boughs above,
And each depending leaf, and every speck   460
Of azure sky, darting between their chasms;
Nor aught else in the liquid mirror laves

Its portraiture, but some inconstant star
Between one foliaged lattice twinkling fair,
Or painted bird, sleeping beneath the moon,
Or gorgeous insect floating motionless,
Unconscious of the day, ere yet his wings
Have spread their glories to the gaze of noon.
　　Hither the Poet came. His eyes beheld
Their own wan light through the reflected lines   470
Of his thin hair, distinct in the dark depth
Of that still fountain; as the human heart,
Gazing in dreams over the gloomy grave,
Sees its own treacherous likeness there. He heard
The motion of the leaves, the grass that sprung
Startled and glanced and trembled even to feel
An unaccustomed presence, and the sound
Of the sweet brook that from the secret springs
Of that dark fountain rose. A Spirit seemed
To stand beside him—clothed in no bright robes   480
Of shadowy silver or enshrining light,
Borrowed from aught the visible world affords
Of grace, or majesty, or mystery;—
But, undulating woods, and silent well,
And leaping rivulet, and evening gloom
Now deepening the dark shades, for speech assuming
Held commune with him, as if he and it
Were all that was,—only . . . when his regard
Was raised by intense pensiveness, . . . two eyes,
Two starry eyes, hung in the gloom of thought,°   490
And seemed with their serene and azure smiles
To beckon him.
　　　　　　　Obedient to the light
That shone within his soul, he went, pursuing
The windings of the dell.—The rivulet
Wanton and wild, through many a green ravine
Beneath the forest flowed. Sometimes it fell
Among the moss with hollow harmony
Dark and profound. Now on the polished stones
It danced; like childhood laughing as it went:
Then, through the plain in tranquil wanderings crept,   500
Reflecting every herb and drooping bud
That overhung its quietness.—'O stream!

Whose source is inaccessibly profound,
Whither do thy mysterious waters tend?
Thou imagest my life. Thy darksome stillness,
Thy dazzling waves, thy loud and hollow gulfs,
Thy searchless fountain, and invisible course
Have each their type in me: and the wide sky,
And measureless ocean may declare as soon
What oozy cavern or what wandering cloud   510
Contains thy waters, as the universe
Tell where these living thoughts reside, when stretched
Upon thy flowers my bloodless limbs shall waste
I' the passing wind!'
                        Beside the grassy shore
Of the small stream he went; he did impress
On the green moss his tremulous step, that caught
Strong shuddering from his burning limbs. As one
Roused by some joyous madness from the couch
Of fever, he did move; yet, not like him,
Forgetful of the grave, where, when the flame   520
Of his frail exultation shall be spent,
He must descend. With rapid steps he went
Beneath the shade of trees, beside the flow
Of the wild babbling rivulet, and now
The forest's solemn canopies were changed
For the uniform and lightsome evening sky.°
Grey rocks did peep from the spare moss, and stemmed
The struggling brook: tall spires of windlestrae°
Threw their thin shadows down the rugged slope,
And nought but gnarlèd roots of ancient pines   530
Branchless and blasted, clenched with grasping roots
The unwilling soil. A gradual change was here,
Yet ghastly. For, as fast years flow away,
The smooth brow gathers, and the hair grows thin
And white, and where irradiate dewy eyes
Had shone, gleam stony orbs:—so from his steps
Bright flowers departed, and the beautiful shade
Of the green groves, with all their odorous winds
And musical motions. Calm, he still pursued
The stream, that with a larger volume now   540
Rolled through the labyrinthine dell; and there
Fretted a path through its descending curves

With its wintry speed. On every side now rose
Rocks, which, in unimaginable forms,
Lifted their black and barren pinnacles
In the light of evening, and its precipice°
Obscuring the ravine, disclosed above,
Mid toppling stones, black gulfs and yawning caves,
Whose windings gave ten thousand various tongues
To the loud stream. Lo! where the pass expands   550
Its stony jaws, the abrupt mountain breaks,
And seems, with its accumulated crags,
To overhang the world: for wide expand
Beneath the wan stars and descending moon
Islanded seas, blue mountains, mighty streams,
Dim tracts and vast, robed in the lustrous gloom
Of leaden-coloured even, and fiery hills
Mingling their flames with twilight, on the verge
Of the remote horizon. The near scene,
In naked and severe simplicity,   560
Made contrast with the universe. A pine,
Rock-rooted, stretched athwart the vacancy
Its swinging boughs, to each inconstant blast
Yielding one only response, at each pause
In most familiar cadence, with the howl
The thunder and the hiss of homeless streams
Mingling its solemn song, whilst the broad river,
Foaming and hurrying o'er its rugged path,
Fell into that immeasurable void
Scattering its waters to the passing winds.   570
    Yet the grey precipice and solemn pine
And torrent, were not all;—one silent nook
Was there. Even on the edge of that vast mountain,
Upheld by knotty roots and fallen rocks,
It overlooked in its serenity
The dark earth, and the bending vault of stars.
It was a tranquil spot, that seemed to smile
Even in the lap of horror. Ivy clasped
The fissured stones with its entwining arms,
And did embower with leaves forever green,   580
And berries dark, the smooth and even space
Of its inviolated floor, and here
The children of the autumnal whirlwind bore,

In wanton sport, those bright leaves, whose decay,
Red, yellow, or etherially pale,°
Rivals the pride of summer. 'Tis the haunt
Of every gentle wind, whose breath can teach
The wilds to love tranquillity. One step,
One human step alone, has ever broken
The stillness of its solitude:—one voice   590
Alone inspired its echoes,—even that voice
Which hither came, floating among the winds,
And led the loveliest among human forms
To make their wild haunts the depository
Of all the grace and beauty that endued
Its motions, render up its majesty,
Scatter its music on the unfeeling storm,
And to the damp leaves and blue cavern mould,
Nurses of rainbow flowers and branching moss,
Commit the colours of that varying cheek,   600
That snowy breast, those dark and drooping eyes.

    The dim and hornèd moon hung low, and poured
A sea of lustre on the horizon's verge
That overflowed its mountains. Yellow mist
Filled the unbounded atmosphere, and drank
Wan moonlight even to fullness: not a star
Shone, not a sound was heard; the very winds,
Danger's grim playmates, on that precipice
Slept, clasped in his embrace.—O, storm of death!
Whose sightless speed divides this sullen night: 610
And thou, colossal Skeleton, that, still
Guiding its irresistible career
In thy devastating omnipotence,
Art king of this frail world, from the red field
Of slaughter, from the reeking hospital,
The patriot's sacred couch, the snowy bed
Of innocence, the scaffold and the throne,
A mighty voice invokes thee. Ruin calls
His brother Death. A rare and regal prey
He hath prepared, prowling around the world;   620
Glutted with which thou mayst repose, and men
Go to their graves like flowers or creeping worms,
Nor ever more offer at thy dark shrine
The unheeded tribute of a broken heart.

When on the threshold of the green recess
The wanderer's footsteps fell, he knew that death
Was on him. Yet a little, ere it fled,
Did he resign his high and holy soul
To images of the majestic past,
That paused within his passive being now,   630
Like winds that bear sweet music, when they breathe
Through some dim latticed chamber. He did place
His pale lean hand upon the rugged trunk
Of the old pine. Upon an ivied stone
Reclined his languid head, his limbs did rest,
Diffused and motionless, on the smooth brink
Of that obscurest chasm;—and thus he lay,
Surrendering to their final impulses
The hovering powers of life. Hope and despair,
The torturers, slept; no mortal pain or fear   640
Marred his repose, the influxes of sense,
And his own being unalloyed by pain,
Yet feebler and more feeble, calmly fed
The stream of thought, till he lay breathing there
At peace, and faintly smiling:—his last sight
Was the great moon, which o'er the western line
Of the wide world her mighty horn suspended,
With whose dun beams inwoven darkness seemed
To mingle. Now upon the jagged hills
It rests, and still as the divided frame   650
Of the vast meteor sunk, the Poet's blood,°
That ever beat in mystic sympathy
With nature's ebb and flow, grew feebler still:
And when two lessening points of light alone°
Gleamed through the darkness, the alternate gasp
Of his faint respiration scarce did stir
The stagnate night:—till the minutest ray
Was quenched, the pulse yet lingered in his heart.
It paused—it fluttered. But when heaven remained
Utterly black, the murky shades involved   660
An image, silent, cold, and motionless,
As their own voiceless earth and vacant air.
Even as a vapour fed with golden beams
That ministered on sunlight, ere the west
Eclipses it, was now that wondrous frame—

No sense, no motion, no divinity—
A fragile lute, on whose harmonious strings
The breath of heaven did wander—a bright stream
Once fed with many-voicèd waves—a dream
Of youth, which night and time have quenched forever,   670
Still, dark, and dry, and unremembered now.
    O, for Medea's wondrous alchemy,°
Which wheresoe'er it fell made the earth gleam
With bright flowers, and the wintry boughs exhale
From vernal blooms fresh fragrance! O, that God,
Profuse of poisons, would concede the chalice
Which but one living man has drained, who now,°
Vessel of deathless wrath, a slave that feels
No proud exemption in the blighting curse
He bears, over the world wanders forever,   680
Lone as incarnate death! O, that the dream
Of dark magician in his visioned cave,
Raking the cinders of a crucible
For life and power, even when his feeble hand
Shakes in its last decay, were the true law
Of this so lovely world! But thou art fled
Like some frail exhalation; which the dawn
Robes in its golden beams,—ah! thou hast fled!
The brave, the gentle, and the beautiful,
The child of grace and genius. Heartless things   690
Are done and said i' the world, and many worms
And beasts and men live on, and mighty Earth
From sea and mountain, city and wilderness,
In vesper low or joyous orison,
Lifts still its solemn voice:—but thou art fled—
Thou canst no longer know or love the shapes
Of this phantasmal scene, who have to thee
Been purest ministers, who are, alas!
Now thou art not. Upon those pallid lips
So sweet even in their silence, on those eyes   700
That image sleep in death, upon that form
Yet safe from the worm's outrage, let no tear
Be shed—not even in thought. Nor, when those hues
Are gone, and those divinest lineaments,
Worn by the senseless wind, shall live alone°
In the frail pauses of this simple strain,

Let not high verse, mourning the memory
Of that which is no more, or painting's woe
Or sculpture, speak in feeble imagery
Their own cold powers. Art and eloquence,   710
And all the shows o' the world are frail and vain
To weep a loss that turns their lights to shade.
It is a woe too 'deep for tears,' when all°
Is reft at once, when some surpassing Spirit,
Whose light adorned the world around it, leaves
Those who remain behind, not sobs or groans,
The passionate tumult of a clinging hope;
But pale despair and cold tranquillity,
Nature's vast frame, the web of human things,
Birth and the grave, that are not as they were.   720

Mutability

We are as clouds that veil the midnight moon;
   How restlessly they speed, and gleam, and quiver,
Streaking the darkness radiantly!—yet soon
   Night closes round, and they are lost for ever:

Or like forgotten lyres, whose dissonant strings°
   Give various response to each varying blast,
To whose frail frame no second motion brings
   One mood or modulation like the last.

We rest.—A dream has power to poison sleep;
   We rise.—One wandering thought pollutes the day;   10
We feel, conceive or reason, laugh or weep;
   Embrace fond woe, or cast our cares away:

It is the same!—For, be it joy or sorrow,
   The path of its departure still is free:
Man's yesterday may ne'er be like his morrow;
   Nought may endure but Mutability.

Verses Written on Receiving a Celandine in a Letter from England

    I thought of thee, fair Celandine,
      As of a flower aery blue°
    Yet small—thy leaves methought were wet
      With the light of morning dew.
    In the same glen thy star did shine
    As the primrose and the violet,
    And the wild briar bent over thee
    And the woodland brook danced under thee.

    Lovely thou wert in thine own glen
      Ere thou didst dwell in song or story,   10
    Ere the moonlight of a Poet's mind

Had arrayed thee with the glory
Whose fountains are the hearts of men—
Many a thing of vital kind
Had fed and sheltered under thee,
Had nourished their thoughts near to thee.

Yes, gentle flower, in thy recess
    None might a sweeter aspect wear;
Thy young bud drooped so gracefully,
    Thou wert so very fair—   20
Among the fairest, ere the stress
Of exile, death and injury
Thus withering and deforming thee
Had made a mournful type of thee—

A type of that whence I and thou
    Are thus familar, Celandine—
A deathless Poet whose young prime
    Was as serene as thine;
But he is changed and withered now,°
Fallen on a cold and evil time;°   30
His heart is gone—his flame is dim,
And Infamy sits mocking him.

Celandine! Thou art pale and dead,
    Changed from thy fresh and woodland state.
Oh! that thy bard were cold, but he
    Has lived too long and late.
Would he were in an honoured grave;
But that, men say, now must not be
Since he for impious gold could sell
The love of those who loved him well.   40

That he, with all hope else of good
    Should be thus transitory
I marvel not—but that his lays
    Have spared not their own glory,
That blood, even the foul god of blood
With most inexpiable praise,
Freedom and truth left desolate,
He has been brought to celebrate!°

They were his hopes which he doth scorn;
   They were his foes the fight that won;   50
That sanction and that condemnation
   Are now forever gone.
They need them not! Truth may not mourn
That with a liar's inspiration
Her majesty he did disown
Ere he could overlive his own.

They need them not, for Liberty,
   Justice and philosophic truth
From this divine and simple song°
   Shall draw immortal youth,   60
When he and thou shalt cease to be
Or be some other thing, so long
As men may breathe or flowers may blossom
O'er the wide Earth's maternal bosom.

The stem whence thou wert disunited
   Since thy poor self was banished hither,
Now by that priest of Nature's care
   Who sent thee forth to wither
His window with its blooms has lighted,
And I shall see thy brethren there,   70
And each, like thee, will aye betoken
Love sold, hope dead, and honour broken.

Hymn to Intellectual Beauty

(VERSION A)

I

The awful shadow of some unseen Power°
   Floats though unseen amongst us,—visiting
   This various world with as inconstant wing
As summer winds that creep from flower to flower.—
Like moonbeams that behind some piny mountain shower,°
   It visits with inconstant glance

Each human heart and countenance;
Like hues and harmonies of evening,—
      Like clouds in starlight widely spread,—
      Like memory of music fled,—   10
      Like aught that for its grace may be
Dear, and yet dearer for its mystery.

                              2

Spirit of BEAUTY, that doth consecrate
    With thine own hues all thou dost shine upon
    Of human thought or form,—where art thou gone?
Why dost thou pass away and leave our state,
This dim vast vale of tears, vacant and desolate?°
      Ask why the sunlight not forever
      Weaves rainbows o'er yon mountain river,
Why aught should fail and fade that once is shown,   20
      Why fear and dream and death and birth
      Cast on the daylight of this earth
      Such gloom,—why man has such a scope
For love and hate, despondency and hope?

                              3

No voice from some sublimer world hath ever
    To sage or poet these responses given—
    Therefore the name of God, and ghosts, and Heaven,
Remain the records of their vain endeavour,
Frail spells—whose uttered charm might not avail to sever,
      From all we hear and all we see   30
      Doubt, chance, and mutability.
Thy light alone—like mist o'er mountains driven,
      Or music by the night wind sent
      Through strings of some still instrument,
      Or moonlight on a midnight stream,
Gives grace and truth to life's unquiet dream.

                              4

Love, Hope, and Self-esteem, like clouds depart°
    And come, for some uncertain moments lent.
    Man were immortal, and omnipotent,
Didst thou, unknown and awful as thou art,   40

Keep with thy glorious train firm state within his heart.
       Thou messenger of sympathies,
       That wax and wane in lovers' eyes—
Thou—that to human thought art nourishment,
       Like darkness to a dying flame!°
       Depart not as thy shadow came,
       Depart not—lest the grave should be,
Like life and fear, a dark reality.

5

While yet a boy I sought for ghosts, and sped
    Through many a listening chamber, cave and ruin,   50
    And starlight wood, with fearful steps pursuing
Hopes of high talk with the departed dead.°
I called on poisonous names with which our youth is fed,
       I was not heard—I saw them not—°
       When musing deeply on the lot
Of life, at that sweet time when winds are wooing
       All vital things that wake to bring
       News of buds and blossoming,—
       Sudden, thy shadow fell on me;
I shrieked, and clasped my hands in ecstasy!   60

6

I vowed that I would dedicate my powers
    To thee and thine—have I not kept the vow?
    With beating heart and streaming eyes, even now
I call the phantoms of a thousand hours
Each from his voiceless grave: they have in visioned bowers
       Of studious zeal or love's delight
       Outwatched with me the envious night—
They know that never joy illumed my brow
       Unlinked with hope that thou wouldst free
       This world from its dark slavery,   70
       That thou—O awful LOVELINESS,
Wouldst give whate'er these words cannot express.

7

The day becomes more solemn and serene
    When noon is past—there is a harmony

In autumn, and a lustre in its sky,
   Which through the summer is not heard or seen,
   As if it could not be, as if it had not been!
      Thus let thy power, which like the truth
      Of nature on my passive youth
Descended, to my onward life supply   80
      Its calm—to one who worships thee,
      And every form containing thee,
      Whom, SPIRIT fair, thy spells did bind
To fear himself, and love all human kind.°

Hymn to Intellectual Beauty

(VERSION B)

1

The lovely shadow of some awful Power
   Walks though unseen amongst us, visiting
   This peopled world with as inconstant wing
As summer winds that creep from flower to flower,
Like moonbeams that behind some piny mountain shower
   It visits with a wavering glance
   Each human heart and countenance;—
Like hues and harmonies of evening—
   Like clouds in starlight widely spread,
   Like memory of music fled   10
   Like aught that for its grace might be
Dear, and yet dearer for its mystery.

2

Shadow of Beauty!—that doth consecrate
   With thine own hues all thou dost fall upon
   Of human thought or form, where art thou gone?
Why dost thou pass away and leave our state
A dark deep vale of tears, vacant and desolate?
   Ask why the sunlight not forever
   Weaves rainbows o'er yon mountain river,

Ask why aught fades away that once is shown,   20
   Ask wherefore dream and death and birth
   Cast on the daylight of this earth
Such gloom,—why man has such a scope
For love and joy, despondency and hope.

3

No voice from some sublimer world hath ever
   To wisest poets these responses given,
   Therefore the name of God and Ghosts and Heaven
Remain yet records of their vain Endeavour—
Frail spells, whose uttered charm might not avail to sever
   From what we feel and what we see   30
   Doubt, Chance and mutability.
Thy shade alone like mists o'er mountains driven
   Or music by the night-wind sent
   Through strings of some mute instrument
Or moonlight on a forest stream
Gives truth and grace to life's tumultuous dream.

4

Love, hope and self-esteem like clouds depart—
   And come, for some uncertain moments lent.—
   Man were immortal and omnipotent
Didst thou, unknown and awful as thou art   40
Keep with this glorious train firm state within his heart.
   Thou messenger of sympathies
   That wax and wane in lovers' eyes,
Thou that to the poet's thought art nourishment
   As darkness to a dying flame,
   Depart not as thy shadow came!
Depart not!—lest the grave should be
Like life and fear a dark reality.

5

While yet a boy I sought for ghosts, and sped
   Through many a lonely chamber, vault and ruin   50
   And starlight wood, with fearful step pursuing

Hopes of strange converse with the storied dead.
I called on that false name with which our youth is fed:
   He heard me not—I saw them not—
   When musing deeply on the lot
Of Life, at that sweet time when winds are wooing
   All vocal things that live to bring
   News of buds and blossoming—
   Sudden thy shadow fell on me,
I shrieked and clasped my hands in ecstasy.   60

6

I vowed that I would dedicate my powers
   To thee and thine—have I not kept the vow?
   With streaming eyes and panting heart even now
I call the spectres of a thousand hours
Each from his voiceless grave, who have in visioned bowers
   Of studious zeal or love's delight
   Outwatched with me the waning night
To tell that never joy illumed my brow
   Unlinked with hope that thou wouldst free
   This world from its dark slavery,   70
   That thou, O, awful Loveliness!
Would give whate'er these words cannot express.

7

The day becomes more solemn and serene
   When noon is past—there is a harmony
   In Autumn and a lustre in the sky
Which through the summer is not heard or seen
As if it could not be—as if it had not been—
   Thus let thy shade—which like the truth
   Of Nature on my passive youth
Descended, to my onward life supply   80
   Its hues, to one that worships thee
   And every form containing thee
Whom, fleeting power! thy spells did bind
To fear himself and love all human Kind.

Mont Blanc
Lines Written in the Vale of Chamouni
(VERSION A)

I

The everlasting universe of things
Flows through the mind, and rolls its rapid waves,°
Now dark—now glittering—now reflecting gloom—
Now lending splendour, where from secret springs
The source of human thought its tribute brings
Of waters,—with a sound but half its own,°
Such as a feeble brook will oft assume
In the wild woods, among the mountains lone,
Where waterfalls around it leap for ever,
Where woods and winds contend, and a vast river   10
Over its rocks ceaselessly bursts and raves.°

2

Thus thou, Ravine of Arve—dark, deep Ravine—°
Thou many-coloured, many-voicèd vale,
Over whose pines, and crags, and caverns sail
Fast cloud shadows and sunbeams: awful scene,
Where Power in likeness of the Arve comes down
From the ice gulfs that gird his secret throne,
Bursting through these dark mountains like the flame
Of lightning through the tempest;—thou dost lie,
Thy giant brood of pines around thee clinging,   20
Children of elder time, in whose devotion
The chainless winds still come and ever came
To drink their odours, and their mighty swinging
To hear—an old and solemn harmony;
Thine earthly rainbows stretched across the sweep
Of the ethereal waterfall, whose veil
Robes some unsculptured image; the strange sleep°
Which when the voices of the desert fail
Wraps all in its own deep eternity;—
Thy caverns echoing to the Arve's commotion,   30

A loud, lone sound no other sound can tame;
Thou art pervaded with that ceaseless motion,
Thou art the path of that unresting sound—
Dizzy Ravine! and when I gaze on thee
I seem as in a trance sublime and strange
To muse on my own separate fantasy,
My own, my human mind, which passively
Now renders and receives fast influencings,
Holding an unremitting interchange
With the clear universe of things around;   40
One legion of wild thoughts, whose wandering wings
Now float above thy darkness, and now rest
Where that or thou art no unbidden guest,°
In the still cave of the witch Poesy,
Seeking among the shadows that pass by,°
Ghosts of all things that are, some shade of thee,
Some phantom, some faint image; till the breast°
From which they fled recalls them, thou art there!

3

Some say that gleams of a remoter world
Visit the soul in sleep,—that death is slumber,   50
And that its shapes the busy thoughts outnumber
Of those who wake and live.—I look on high;
Has some unknown omnipotence unfurled°
The veil of life and death? or do I lie
In dream, and does the mightier world of sleep
Spread far around and inaccessibly
Its circles? For the very spirit fails,
Driven like a homeless cloud from steep to steep
That vanishes among the viewless gales!
Far, far above, piercing the infinite sky,   60
Mont Blanc appears,—still, snowy, and serene—
Its subject mountains their unearthly forms
Pile around it, ice and rock; broad vales between
Of frozen floods, unfathomable deeps,
Blue as the overhanging heaven, that spread
And wind among the accumulated steeps;
A desert peopled by the storms alone,

Save when the eagle brings some hunter's bone,
And the wolf tracks her there—how hideously°
Its shapes are heaped around! rude, bare, and high,   70
Ghastly, and scarred, and riven.—Is this the scene
Where the old Earthquake-daemon taught her young
Ruin? Were these their toys? or did a sea
Of fire envelop once this silent snow?°
None can reply—all seems eternal now.
The wilderness has a mysterious tongue
Which teaches awful doubt, or faith so mild,°
So solemn, so serene, that man may be
But for such faith with nature reconciled;°
Thou hast a voice, great Mountain, to repeal   80
Large codes of fraud and woe; not understood
By all, but which the wise, and great, and good
Interpret, or make felt, or deeply feel.

4

The fields, the lakes, the forests, and the streams,
Ocean, and all the living things that dwell
Within the daedal earth; lightning, and rain,°
Earthquake, and fiery flood, and hurricane,
The torpor of the year when feeble dreams
Visit the hidden buds, or dreamless sleep
Holds every future leaf and flower;—the bound   90
With which from that detested trance they leap;
The works and ways of man, their death and birth,
And that of him and all that his may be;
All things that move and breathe with toil and sound
Are born and die; revolve, subside and swell.
Power dwells apart in its tranquillity
Remote, serene, and inaccessible:°
And *this*, the naked countenance of earth,
On which I gaze, even these primeval mountains
Teach the adverting mind. The glaciers creep°   100
Like snakes that watch their prey, from their far fountains,
Slow rolling on; there, many a precipice,
Frost and the Sun in scorn of mortal power
Have piled: dome, pyramid, and pinnacle,

A city of death, distinct with many a tower°
And wall impregnable of beaming ice.
Yet not a city, but a flood of ruin
Is there, that from the boundaries of the sky
Rolls its perpetual stream; vast pines are strewing
Its destined path, or in the mangled soil   110
Branchless and shattered stand; the rocks, drawn down
From yon remotest waste, have overthrown
The limits of the dead and living world,
Never to be reclaimed. The dwelling-place
Of insects, beasts, and birds, becomes its spoil;
Their food and their retreat for ever gone,
So much of life and joy is lost. The race
Of man flies far in dread; his work and dwelling
Vanish, like smoke before the tempest's stream,
And their place is not known. Below, vast caves°   120
Shine in the rushing torrents' restless gleam,
Which from those secret chasms in tumult welling°
Meet in the vale, and one majestic River,°
The breath and blood of distant lands, for ever
Rolls its loud waters to the ocean waves,
Breathes its swift vapours to the circling air.

5

Mont Blanc yet gleams on high:—the power is there,
The still and solemn power of many sights,
And many sounds, and much of life and death.
In the calm darkness of the moonless nights,   130
In the lone glare of day, the snows descend
Upon that Mountain; none beholds them there,
Nor when the flakes burn in the sinking sun,
Or the star-beams dart through them:—Winds contend
Silently there, and heap the snow with breath°
Rapid and strong, but silently! Its home
The voiceless lightning in these solitudes
Keeps innocently, and like vapour broods
Over the snow. The secret strength of things
Which governs thought, and to the infinite dome   140
Of heaven is as a law, inhabits thee!

And what were thou, and earth, and stars, and sea,
If to the human mind's imaginings
Silence and solitude were vacancy?°

Mont Blanc

(VERSION B)

Scene—Pont Pellisier in the Vale of Servox

In day the eternal universe of things
Flows through the mind, and rolls its rapid waves
Now dark, now glittering; now reflecting gloom,
Now lending splendour, where, from secret caves
The source of human thought its tribute brings
Of waters, with a sound not all its own:
Such as a feeble brook will oft assume
In the wild woods among the mountains lone
Where waterfalls around it leap forever
Where winds and woods contend, and a vast river   10
Over its rocks ceaselessly bursts and raves.

Thus thou Ravine of Arve, dark deep ravine,
Thou many coloured, many voicèd vale!
Over whose rocks and pines and caverns sail
Fast cloud shadows and sunbeams—awful scene,
Where Power in likeness of the Arve comes down
From the ice gulfs that gird his secret throne
Bursting through these dark mountains like the flame
Of lightning through the tempest—thou dost lie
Thy giant brood of pines around thee clinging   20
Children of elder time, in whose devotion
The charmèd winds still come, and ever came
To drink their odours, and their mighty swinging
To hear, an old and solemn harmony;
Thine earthly rainbows stretched across the sweep
Of the aerial waterfall, whose veil
Robes some unsculptured image; even the sleep
The sudden pause that does inhabit thee
Which when the voices of the desert fail

And its hues wane, doth blend them all and steep   30
Their periods in its own eternity;
Thy caverns echoing to the Arve's commotion
A loud lone sound no other sound can tame:
Thou art pervaded with such ceaseless motion
Thou art the path of that unresting sound:
Ravine of Arve! and when I gaze on thee
I seem as in a vision deep and strange
To muse on my own various fantasy,
My own, my human mind . . . which passively
Now renders and receives fast influencings   40
Holding an unforeseeing interchange
With the clear universe of things around:
A legion of swift thoughts, whose wandering wings
Now float above thy darkness, and now rest
Near the still cave of the witch Poesy
Seeking among the shadows that pass by,
Ghosts of the things that are, some form like thee,
Some spectre, some faint image; till the breast
From which they fled recalls them—thou art there.

Some say that gleams of a remoter world   50
Visit the soul in sleep—that death is slumber
And that its shapes the busy thoughts outnumber
Of those who wake and live. I look on high—
Has some unknown omnipotence unfurled
The veil of life and death? or do I lie
In dream, and does the mightier world of sleep
Spread far around, and inaccessibly
Its circles?—for the very spirit fails
Driven like a homeless cloud from steep to steep
That vanishes among the viewless gales.—   60
Far, far above, piercing the infinite sky
Mont Blanc appears, still, snowy and serene,
Its subject mountains their unearthly forms
Pile round it—ice and rock—broad chasms between
Of frozen waves, unfathomable deeps
Blue as the overhanging Heaven, that spread
And wind among the accumulated steeps,
Vast deserts, peopled by the storms alone
Save when the eagle brings some hunter's bone

And the wolf watches her—how hideously   70
Its rocks are heaped around, rude, bare and high,
Ghastly and scarred and riven!—is this the scene
Where the old Earthquake demon taught her young
Ruin? were these their toys? or did a sea
Of fire envelop once this silent snow?
None can reply—all seems eternal now.
This wilderness has a mysterious tongue
Which teaches awful doubt, or faith so mild
So simple, so serene that man may be
In such a faith with Nature reconciled.   80
Ye have a doctrine, Mountains, to repeal
Large codes of fraud and woe—not understood
By all, but which the wise and great and good
Interpret, or make felt, or deeply feel.

The fields, the lakes, the forests and the streams,
Ocean, and all the living things that dwell
Within the daedal Earth, lightning and rain,
Earthquake, and lava flood, and hurricane—
The torpor of the year, when feeble dreams
Visit the hidden buds, or dreamless sleep   90
Holds every future leaf and flower—the bound
With which from that detested trance they leap;
The works and ways of man, their death and birth
And that of him, and all that his may be,
All things that move and breathe with toil and sound
Are born and die, revolve, subside and swell—
Power dwells apart in deep tranquillity,
Remote, sublime, and inaccessible,
And this, the naked countenance of Earth
On which I gaze—even these primeval mountains   100
Teach the adverting mind.—the Glaciers creep
Like snakes that watch their prey, from their far fountains
Slow rolling on:—there, many a precipice
Frost and the Sun in scorn of human power
Have piled—dome, pyramid and pinnacle
A city of death, distinct with many a tower
And wall impregnable of shining ice . . .
A city's phantom . . . but a flood of ruin
Is there, that from the boundaries of the sky

Rolls its eternal stream . . . vast pines are strewing   110
Its destined path, or in the mangled soil
Branchless and shattered stand—the rocks drawn down
From yon remotest waste have overthrown
The limits of the dead and living world
Never to be reclaimed—the dwelling place
Of insects, beasts and birds becomes its spoil,
Their food and their retreat forever gone
So much of life and joy is lost—the race
Of man flies far in dread. His work and dwelling
Vanish like smoke before the tempest's stream   120
And their place is not known—below, vast caves
Shine in the gushing torrents' restless gleam
Which from those secret chasms in tumult welling
Meet in the vale—and one majestic river
The breath and blood of distant lands, forever
Rolls its loud waters to the Ocean waves,
Breathes its swift vapours to the circling air.

Mont Blanc yet gleams on high—the Power is there,
The still and solemn Power of many sights
And many sounds, and much of life and death.   130
In the calm darkness of the moonless nights
Or the lone light of day the snows descend
Upon that mountain—none beholds them there—
Nor when the sunset wraps their flakes in fire
Or the starbeams dart through them—winds contend
Silently there, and heap the snows, with breath
Blasting and swift—but silently—its home
The voiceless lightning in these solitudes
Keeps innocently, and like vapour broods
Over the snow. The secret strength of things   140
Which governs thought, and to the infinite dome
Of Heaven is as a column, rests on thee,
And what were thou and Earth and Stars and Sea
If to the human mind's imaginings
Silence and solitude were Vacancy?

To Constantia

Thy voice, slow rising like a Spirit, lingers
O'ershadowing me with soft and lulling wings;
The blood and life within thy snowy fingers
Teach witchcraft to the instrumental strings.
     My brain is wild, my breath comes quick,
     The blood is listening in my frame,
     And thronging shadows fast and thick
     Fall on my overflowing eyes,
     My heart is quivering like a flame;
As morning dew, that in the sunbeam dies,   10
I am dissolved in these consuming ecstasies.

I have no life, Constantia, but in thee;
Whilst, like the world-surrounding air, thy song
Flows on, and fills all things with melody:
Now is thy voice a tempest, swift and strong,
     On which, as one in trance, upborne
     Secure o'er woods and waves I sweep
     Rejoicing, like a cloud of morn:
     Now 'tis the breath of summer's night
     Which, where the starry waters sleep   20
Round western isles with incense-blossoms bright,
Lingering, suspends my soul in its voluptuous flight.

A deep and breathless awe, like the swift change
Of dreams unseen, but felt in youthful slumbers,
Wild, sweet, yet incommunicably strange,
Thou breathest now, in fast ascending numbers:
     The cope of Heaven seems rent and cloven°
     By the enchantment of thy strain,
     And o'er my shoulders wings are woven
     To follow its sublime career,   30
     Beyond the mighty moons that wane
Upon the verge of Nature's utmost sphere,°
Till the world's shadowy walls are past, and disappear.

Cease, cease—for such wild lessons madmen learn:
Long thus to sink,—thus to be lost and die
Perhaps is death indeed—Constantia turn!

Yes! in thine eyes a power like light doth lie,
   Even though the sounds, its voice that were,°
   Between thy lips are laid to sleep—
   Within thy breath and on thy hair   40
   Like odour it is lingering yet—
   And from thy touch like fire doth leap:
Even while I write my burning cheeks are wet—
Such things the heart can feel and learn, but not forget!

LAON AND CYTHNA;

OR,

THE REVOLUTION

OF

THE GOLDEN CITY

A Vision of the Nineteenth Century

IN THE STANZA OF SPENSER

Δοζ που στω, καὶ κοσμον κινησω.—Archimedes°

PREFACE

The Poem which I now present to the world, is an attempt from which I scarcely dare to expect success, and in which a writer of established fame might fail without disgrace. It is an experiment° on the temper of the public mind, as to how far a thirst for a happier condition of moral and political society survives, among the enlightened and refined,° the tempests which have shaken the age in which we live. I have sought to enlist the harmony of metrical language, the etherial combinations of the fancy, the rapid and subtle transitions of human passion, all those elements which essentially compose a Poem, in the cause of a liberal and comprehensive morality, and in the view of kindling within the bosoms of my readers, a virtuous enthusiasm for those doctrines of liberty and justice, that faith and hope in something good, which neither violence, nor misrepresentation, nor prejudice, can ever totally extinguish among mankind.

For this purpose I have chosen a story of human passion in its most universal character, diversified with moving and romantic adventures, and appealing, in contempt of all artificial opinions or institutions, to the common sympathies of every human breast. I have made no attempt to recommend the motives which I would substitute for those at present governing mankind by methodical and systematic argument.° I would only awaken the feelings, so that the reader should see the beauty of true virtue, and be incited to those enquiries which have led to my moral and political creed, and that of some of the sublimest intellects in the world. The Poem, therefore (with the exception of the first Canto, which is purely introductory), is narrative, not didactic. It is a succession of pictures illustrating the growth and progress of individual mind aspiring after excellence, and devoted to the love of mankind; its influence in refining and making pure the most daring and uncommon impulses of the imagination, the understanding, and the senses; its impatience at 'all the oppressions which are done under the sun';° its tendency to awaken public hope and to enlighten and improve mankind; the rapid effects of the application of that tendency; the awakening of an immense nation from their slavery and degradation to a true sense of moral dignity and freedom; the blood-less dethronement of their oppressors, and the unveiling of the religious frauds by which they had been deluded into submission; the tranquillity of successful patriotism, and the universal toleration and benevolence of true philanthropy; the treachery and barbarity of hired soldiers; vice not the object of punishment and hatred, but kindness and pity; the faithlessness of tyrants; the confederacy of the Rulers of the World, and the restoration of the expelled Dynasty by foreign arms;° the massacre and extermination of the Patriots, and the victory of established power; the consequences of legitimate despotism, civil war, famine, plague, superstition, and an utter extinction of the domestic affections; the judicial murder of the advocates of Liberty; the temporary triumph of oppression, that secure earnest of its final and inevitable fall; the transient nature of ignorance and error, and the eternity of genius and virtue. Such is the series of delineations of which the Poem consists. And if the lofty passions with which it has been my scope° to distinguish this story shall not excite in the reader a generous impulse, an ardent thirst for excellence, an interest profound and strong, such as belongs to no meaner desires—let not the failure be imputed to a natural unfitness for human sympathy in these sub-lime and animating themes. It is the business of the Poet to com-municate to others the pleasure and the enthusiasm arising out of those images and feelings, in the vivid presence of which, within his own mind, consists at once his inspiration and his reward.

The panic which, like an epidemic transport, seized upon all classes of men during the excesses consequent upon the French Revolution, is gradually giving place to sanity. It has ceased to be believed, that whole generations of mankind ought to consign themselves to a hopeless inheritance of ignorance and misery, because a nation of men who had been dupes and slaves for centuries, were incapable of conducting themselves with the wisdom and tranquillity of freemen so soon as some of their fetters were partially loosened. That their conduct could not have been marked by any other characters than ferocity and thoughtlessness, is the historical fact from which liberty derives all its recommendations, and falsehood the worst features of its deformity. There is a reflux in the tide of human things which bears the shipwrecked hopes of men into a secure haven, after the storms are past. Methinks, those who now live have survived an age of despair.

The French Revolution may be considered as one of those manifestations of a general state of feeling among civilized mankind, produced by a defect of correspondence between the knowledge existing in society and the improvement, or gradual abolition, of political institutions. The year 1788 may be assumed as the epoch of one of the most important crises produced by this feeling. The sympathies connected with that event extended to every bosom. The most generous and amiable natures were those which participated the most extensively in these sympathies. But such a degree of unmingled good was expected, as it was impossible to realize. If the Revolution had been in every respect prosperous, then misrule and superstition would lose half their claims to our abhorrence, as fetters which the captive can unlock with the slightest motion of his fingers, and which do not eat with poisonous rust into the soul. The revulsion occasioned by the atrocities° of the demagogues and the re-establishment of successive tyrannies in France was terrible, and felt in the remotest corner of the civilized world. Could they listen to the plea of reason who had groaned under the calamities of a social state, according to the provisions of which, one man riots in luxury whilst another famishes for want of bread? Can he who the day before was a trampled slave, suddenly become liberal-minded, forbearing, and independent? This is the consequence of the habits of a state of society to be produced by resolute perseverance and indefatigable hope, and long-suffering and long-believing courage, and the systematic efforts of generations of men of intellect and virtue. Such is the lesson which experience teaches now. But on the first reverses of hope in the progress of French liberty, the sanguine eagerness for good overleapt the solution of these questions, and for a time extinguished itself in the unexpectedness of their result. Thus many of the most ardent and tender-hearted of the worshippers of public good, have been morally ruined by what a partial glimpse of the events they deplored appeared to show as the melancholy desolation of all their cherished hopes. Hence gloom and misanthropy have become the characteristics of the age in which we live, the solace of a disappointment that unconsciously finds relief only in the wilful exaggeration of its own despair. This influence has tainted the literature of the age with the hopelessness of the minds from which it flows. Metaphysics,° and enquiries into moral and political science, have become little else than vain attempts to revive exploded superstitions, or sophisms like those° of Mr Malthus, calculated to lull the oppressors of mankind into a security of everlasting triumph. Our works of fiction and poetry have been overshadowed by the same infectious gloom.° But mankind appear to me to be emerging from their trance. I am aware, methinks, of a slow, gradual, silent change. In that belief I have composed the following Poem.

I do not presume to enter into competition with our greatest contemporary Poets. Yet I am unwilling to tread in the footsteps of any who have preceded me. I have sought to avoid the imitation of any style of language or versification peculiar to the original minds of which it is the character, designing that even if what I have produced be worthless, it should still be properly my own. Nor have I permitted any system relating to mere words, to divert the attention of the reader from whatever interest I may have succeeded in creating, to my own ingenuity in contriving to disgust him according to the rules of criticism. I have simply clothed my thoughts in what appeared to me the most obvious and appropriate language. A person familiar with nature, and with the most celebrated productions of the human mind, can scarcely err in following the instinct, with respect to selection of language, produced by that familiarity.

There is an education peculiarly fitted for a Poet, without which, genius and sensibility can hardly fill the circle of their capacities. No education indeed can entitle to this appellation a dull and unobservant mind, or one, though neither dull nor unobservant, in which the channels of communication between thought and expression have been obstructed or closed. How far it is my fortune to belong to either of the latter classes, I cannot know. I aspire to be something better. The circumstances of my accidental education° have been favourable to this ambition. I have been familiar from boyhood with mountains and lakes, and the sea, and the solitude of forests: Danger which sports upon the brink of precipices, has been my playmate. I have trodden the glaciers of the Alps, and lived under the eye of Mont Blanc. I have been a wanderer among distant fields. I have sailed down mighty rivers, and seen the sun rise and set, and the stars come forth, whilst I have sailed night and day down a rapid stream among mountains. I have seen populous cities, and have watched the passions which rise and spread, and sink and change amongst assembled multitudes of men. I have seen the theatre of the more visible ravages of tyranny and war, cities and villages reduced to scattered groups of black and roof-less houses, and the naked inhabitants sitting famished upon their deso-lated thresholds. I have conversed with living men of genius. The poetry of ancient Greece and Rome, and modern Italy, and our own country, has been to me like external nature, a passion and an enjoy-ment. Such are the sources from which the materials for the imagery of my Poem have been drawn. I have considered Poetry in its most comprehensive sense, and have read the Poets and the Historians and the Metaphysicians° whose writings have been accessible to me, and have looked upon the beautiful and majestic scenery of the earth as common sources of those elements which it is the province of the Poet to embody and combine. Yet the experience and the feelings to which I refer, do not in themselves constitute men Poets, but only prepares them to be the auditors of those who are. How far I shall be found to possess that more essential attribute of Poetry, the power of awakening in others sensations like those which animate my own bosom, is that which, to speak sincerely, I know not; and which with an acquiescent and contented spirit, I expect to be taught by the effect which I shall produce upon those whom I now address.

I have avoided, as I have said before, the imitation of any con-temporary style. But there must be a resemblance which does not depend upon their own will, between all the writers of any particular age. They cannot escape from subjection to a common influence which arises out of an infinite combination of circumstances belonging to the times in which they live, though each is in a degree the author of the very influence by which his being is thus pervaded. Thus, the tragic Poets of the age of Pericles;° the Italian revivers of ancient learning; those mighty intellects of our own country that succeeded the Reformation, the translators of the Bible, Shakespeare, Spenser, the Dramatists of the reign of Elizabeth, and Lord Bacon;° the colder spirits of the interval that succeeded—all resemble each other and differ from every other in their several classes. In this view of things, Ford° can no more be called the imitator of Shakespeare, than Shakespeare the imitator of Ford. There were perhaps few other points of resemblance between these two men than that which the universal and inevitable influence of their age produced. And this is an influence which neither the meanest scribbler, nor the sublimest genius of any era can escape; and which I have not attempted to escape.

I have adopted the stanza of Spenser (a measure inexpressibly beautiful) not because I consider it a finer model of poetical harmony than the blank verse of Shakespeare and Milton, but because in the latter there is no shelter for mediocrity: you must either succeed or fail. This perhaps an aspiring spirit should desire. But I was enticed also, by the brilliancy and magnificence of sound which a mind that has been nourished upon musical thoughts can produce by a just and harmonious arrangement of the pauses of this measure. Yet there will be found some instances where I have completely failed in this attempt, and one, which I here request the reader to consider as an erratum, where there is left most inadvertently an alexandrine in the middle of a stanza.°

But in this, as in every other respect, I have written fearlessly. It is the misfortune of this age, that its Writers, too thoughtless of immortality, are exquisitely sensible to temporary praise or blame. They write with the fear of Reviews before their eyes. This system of criticism° sprang up in that torpid interval when Poetry was not. Poetry, and the art which professes to regulate and limit its powers, cannot subsist together. Longinus° could not have been the contemporary of Homer, nor Boileau of Horace. Yet this species of criticism never presumed to assert an understanding of its own: it has always, unlike true science, followed, not preceded the opinion of mankind, and would even now bribe with worthless adulation some of our greatest Poets to impose gratuitous fetters on their own imaginations, and become unconscious accomplices in the daily murder of all genius either not so aspiring or not so fortunate as their own. I have sought therefore to write, as I believe that Homer, Shakespeare, and Milton wrote, with an utter disregard of anonymous censure.° I am certain that calumny and misrepresentation, though it may move me to compassion, cannot disturb my peace. I shall understand the expressive silence of those sagacious enemies who dare not trust themselves to speak. I shall endeavour to extract from the midst of insult, and contempt, and maledictions, those admonitions which may tend to correct whatever imperfections such censurers may discover in this my first serious appeal to the Public.° If certain Critics were as clear-sighted as they are malignant, how great would be the benefit to be derived from their virulent writings! As it is, I fear I shall be malicious enough to be amused with their paltry tricks and lame invectives. Should the Public judge that my composition is worthless, I shall indeed bow before the tribunal from which Milton received his crown of immortality, and shall seek to gather, if I live, strength from that defeat, which may nerve me to some new enterprise of thought which may *not* be worthless. I cannot conceive that Lucretius,° when he meditated that poem whose doctrines are yet the basis of our metaphysical knowledge, and whose eloquence has been the wonder of mankind, wrote in awe of such censure as the hired sophists of the impure and superstitious noblemen of Rome might affix to what he should produce. It was at the period when Greece was led captive, and Asia made tributary to the Republic, fast verging itself to slavery and ruin, that a multitude of Syrian captives, bigoted to the worship of their obscene Ashtaroth,° and the unworthy successors of Socrates and Zeno,° found there a precarious subsistence by administering, under the name of freedmen, to the vices and vanities of the great. These wretched men were skilled to plead, with a superficial but plausible set of sophisms, in favour of that contempt for virtue which is the portion of slaves, and that faith in portents, the most fatal substitute for benevolence in the imaginations of men, which arising from the enslaved communities of the East, then first began to overwhelm the western nations in its stream. Were these the kind of men whose disapprobation the wise and lofty-minded Lucretius should have regarded with a salutary awe? The latest and perhaps the meanest of those who follow in his footsteps,° would disdain to hold life on such conditions.

The Poem now presented to the Public occupied little more than six months in the composition. That period has been devoted to the task with unremitting ardour and enthusiasm. I have exercised a watchful and earnest criticism on my work as it grew under my hands. I would willingly have sent it forth to the world with that perfection which long labour and revision is said to bestow. But I found that if I should gain something in exactness by this method, I might lose much of the newness and energy of imagery and language as it flowed fresh from my mind. And although the mere composition occupied no more than six months, the thoughts thus arranged were slowly gathered in as many years.°

I trust that the reader will carefully distinguish between those opinions which have a dramatic propriety in reference to the characters which they are designed to elucidate, and such as are properly my own. The erroneous and degrading idea which men have conceived of a Supreme Being, for instance, is spoken against, but not the Supreme Being itself. The belief which some superstitious persons whom I have brought upon the stage, express in the cruelty and malevolence of God,° is widely different from my own. In recommending also a great

and important change in the spirit which animates the social institu-
tions of mankind, I have avoided all flattery to those violent and malig-
nant passions of our nature, which are ever on the watch to mingle
with and to alloy the most beneficial innovations. There is no quarter
given to Revenge, or Envy, or Prejudice. Love is celebrated everywhere
as the sole law which should govern the moral world,

In the personal conduct of my Hero and Heroine, there is one
circumstance which was intended to startle the reader from the trance
of ordinary life. It was my object to break through the crust of those
outworn opinions on which established institutions depend. I have
appealed therefore to the most universal of all feelings, and have
endeavoured to strengthen the moral sense, by forbidding it to waste
its energies in seeking to avoid actions which are only crimes of
convention. It is because there is so great a multitude of artificial
vices, that there are so few real virtues. Those feelings alone which are
benevolent or malevolent, are essentially good or bad. The circum-
stance of which I speak, was introduced, however, merely to accustom
men to that charity and toleration which the exhibition of a practice
widely differing from their own, has a tendency to promote.° Nothing
indeed can be more mischievous, than many actions innocent in
themselves, which might bring down upon individuals the bigoted
contempt and rage of the multitude.°

DEDICATION

There is no danger to a man, that knows
What life and death is: there's not any law
Exceeds his knowledge: neither is it lawful
That he should stoop to any other law.

Chapman°

TO

MARY — —°

I

So now my summer-task is ended, Mary,
And I return to thee, mine own heart's home;
As to his Queen some victor Knight of Faery,°
Earning bright spoils for her enchanted dome;
Nor thou disdain, that ere my fame become
A star among the stars of mortal night,

If it indeed may cleave its natal gloom,
Its doubtful promise thus I would unite
With thy beloved name, thou Child of love and light.°

2

The toil which stole from thee so many an hour,   10
Is ended,—and the fruit is at thy feet!
No longer where the woods to frame a bower
With interlacèd branches mix and meet,
Or where with sound like many voices sweet,
Water-falls leap among wild islands green,
Which framed for my lone boat a lone retreat°
Of moss-grown trees and weeds, shall I be seen:
But beside thee, where still my heart has ever been.

3

Thoughts of great deeds were mine, dear Friend, when first
The clouds which wrap this world from youth did pass.   20
I do remember well the hour which burst
My spirit's sleep: a fresh May-dawn it was,
When I walked forth upon the glittering grass,
And wept, I knew not why; until there rose
From the near school-room, voices, that, alas!
Were but one echo from a world of woes—
The harsh and grating strife of tyrants and of foes.°

4

And then I clasped my hands and looked around—
—But none was near to mock my streaming eyes,
Which poured their warm drops on the sunny ground—   30
So without shame, I spake:—'I will be wise,
And just, and free, and mild, if in me lies
Such power, for I grow weary to behold
The selfish and the strong still tyrannize
Without reproach or check.' I then controlled
My tears, my heart grew calm, and I was meek and bold.

5

And from that hour did I with earnest thought
Heap knowledge from forbidden mines of lore,°

Yet nothing that my tyrants knew or taught
I cared to learn, but from that secret store   40
Wrought linkèd armour for my soul, before
It might walk forth to war among mankind;
Thus power and hope were strengthened more and more
Within me, till there came upon my mind
A sense of loneliness, a thirst with which I pined.

6

Alas, that love should be a blight and snare
To those who seek all sympathies in one!—°
Such once I sought in vain; then black despair,
The shadow of a starless night, was thrown
Over the world in which I moved alone:—   50
Yet never found I one not false to me,
Hard hearts, and cold, like weights of icy stone
Which crushed and withered mine, that could not be
Aught but a lifeless clog, until revived by thee.°

7

Thou Friend, whose presence on my wintry heart
Fell, like bright Spring upon some herbless plain;
How beautiful and calm and free thou wert
In thy young wisdom, when the mortal chain
Of Custom thou didst burst and rend in twain,°
And walked as free as light the clouds among,   60
Which many an envious slave then breathed in vain°
From his dim dungeon, and my spirit sprung
To meet thee from the woes which had begirt it long.

8

No more alone through the world's wilderness,
Although I trod the paths of high intent,
I journeyed now: no more companionless,
Where solitude is like despair, I went.—
There is the wisdom of a stern content
When Poverty can blight the just and good,°
When Infamy dares mock the innocent,°   70
And cherished friends turn with the multitude
To trample: this was ours, and we unshaken stood!

9

Now has descended a serener hour,
And with inconstant fortune, friends return;
Though suffering leaves the knowledge and the power
Which says:—Let scorn be not repaid with scorn.
And from thy side two gentle babes are born°
To fill our home with smiles, and thus are we
Most fortunate beneath life's beaming morn;
And these delights, and thou, have been to me   80
The parents of the Song I consecrate to thee.

10

Is it, that now my inexperienced fingers
But strike the prelude of a loftier strain?
Or, must the lyre on which my spirit lingers
Soon pause in silence, ne'er to sound again,
Though it might shake the Anarch Custom's reign,°
And charm the minds of men to Truth's own sway
Holier than was Amphion's? I would fain°
Reply in hope—but I am worn away,
And Death and Love are yet contending for their prey.°   90

11

And what art thou? I know, but dare not speak:
Time may interpret to his silent years.
Yet in the paleness of thy thoughtful cheek,
And in the light thine ample forehead wears,
And in thy sweetest smiles, and in thy tears,
And in thy gentle speech, a prophecy
Is whispered, to subdue my fondest fears:
And through thine eyes, even in thy soul I see
A lamp of vestal fire burning internally.°

12

They say that thou wert lovely from thy birth,   100
Of glorious parents, thou aspiring Child.
I wonder not—for One then left this earth°
Whose life was like a setting planet mild,
Which clothed thee in the radiance undefiled

Of its departing glory; still her fame
Shines on thee, through the tempests dark and wild
Which shake these latter days; and thou canst claim
The shelter, from thy Sire, of an immortal name.°

13

One voice came forth from many a mighty spirit,
Which was the echo of three thousand years;   110
And the tumultuous world stood mute to hear it,
As some lone man who in a desert hears
The music of his home:—unwonted fears
Fell on the pale oppressors of our race,
And Faith, and Custom, and low-thoughted cares,
Like thunder-stricken dragons, for a space
Left the torn human heart, their food and dwelling-place.

14

Truth's deathless voice pauses among mankind!
If there must be no response to my cry—
If men must rise and stamp with fury blind   120
On his pure name who loves them,—thou and I,
Sweet Friend! can look from our tranquillity
Like lamps into the world's tempestuous night,—
Two tranquil stars, while clouds are passing by
Which wrap them from the foundering seaman's sight,
That burn from year to year with unextinguished light.

ὅσαις δὲ βροτὸν ἔθνος ἀγλαΐαις ἁπτόμεσθα,
    περαίνει πρὸς ἔσχατον
πλόον· ναυσὶ δ᾽ οὔτε πεζὸς ἰὼν ἂν εὕροις
ἐς Ὑπερβορέων ἀγῶνα θαυματὰν ὁδόν.

Pind. *Pyth X*°

Canto First

1

When the last hope of trampled France had failed°
Like a brief dream of unremaining glory,
From visions of despair I rose, and scaled

The peak of an aerial promontory,   130
Whose caverned base with the vexed surge was hoary;
And saw the golden dawn break forth, and waken
Each cloud, and every wave:—but transitory
The calm: for sudden, the firm earth was shaken,
As if by the last wreck its frame were overtaken.°

2

So as I stood, one blast of muttering thunder
Burst in far peals along the waveless deep,
When, gathering fast, around, above and under,
Long trains of tremulous mist began to creep,
Until their complicating lines did steep°   140
The orient sun in shadow:—not a sound
Was heard; one horrible repose did keep°
The forests and the floods, and all around
Darkness more dread than night was poured upon the ground.

3

Hark! 'tis the rushing of a wind that sweeps
Earth and the ocean. See! the lightnings yawn°
Deluging Heaven with fire, and the lashed deeps
Glitter and boil beneath: it rages on,
One mighty stream, whirlwind and waves upthrown,
Lightning, and hail, and darkness eddying by.   150
There is a pause—the sea-birds, that were gone
Into their caves to shriek, come forth, to spy
What calm has fall'n on earth, what light is in the sky.

4

For, where the irresistible storm had cloven
That fearful darkness, the blue sky was seen
Fretted with many a fair cloud interwoven°
Most delicately, and the ocean green,
Beneath that opening spot of blue serene,
Quivered like burning emerald: calm was spread
On all below; but far on high, between   160
Earth and the upper air, the vast clouds fled,
Countless and swift as leaves on autumn's tempest shed.

5

For ever, as the war became more fierce
Between the whirlwinds and the rack on high,°
That spot grew more serene; blue light did pierce
The woof of those white clouds, which seemed to lie
Far, deep, and motionless; while through the sky
The pallid semicircle of the moon
Passed on, in slow and moving majesty;
Its upper horn arrayed in mists, which soon   170
But slowly fled, like dew beneath the beams of noon.

6

I could not choose but gaze; a fascination°
Dwelt in that moon, and sky, and clouds, which drew
My fancy thither, and in expectation
Of what I knew not, I remained:—the hue
Of the white moon, amid that heaven so blue,
Suddenly stained with shadow did appear;
A speck, a cloud, a shape, approaching grew,
Like a great ship in the sun's sinking sphere
Beheld afar at sea, and swift it came anear.   180

7

Even like a bark, which from a chasm of mountains,
Dark, vast, and overhanging, on a river
Which there collects the strength of all its fountains,
Comes forth, whilst with the speed its frame doth quiver,
Sails, oars, and stream, tending to one endeavour;
So, from that chasm of light a wingèd Form
On all the winds of heaven approaching ever
Floated, dilating as it came: the storm
Pursued it with fierce blasts, and lightnings swift and warm.

8

A course precipitous, of dizzy speed,   190
Suspending thought and breath; a monstrous sight!
For in the air do I behold indeed
An Eagle and a Serpent wreathed in fight:—°
And now relaxing its impetuous flight,
Before the aerial rock on which I stood,

The Eagle, hovering, wheeled to left and right,
And hung with lingering wings over the flood,
And startled with its yells the wide air's solitude.

9

A shaft of light upon its wings descended,
And every golden feather gleamed therein—   200
Feather and scale inextricably blended.
The Serpent's mailed and many-coloured skin
Shone through the plumes its coils were twined within
By many a swollen and knotted fold, and high
And far, the neck receding lithe and thin,
Sustained a crested head, which warily
Shifted and glanced before the Eagle's steadfast eye.°

10

Around, around, in ceaseless circles wheeling
With clang of wings and scream, the Eagle sailed°
Incessantly—sometimes on high concealing   210
Its lessening orbs, sometimes as if it failed,
Drooped through the air; and still it shrieked and wailed,
And casting back its eager head, with beak°
And talon unremittingly assailed
The wreathèd Serpent, who did ever seek
Upon his enemy's heart a mortal wound to wreak.

11

What life, what power, was kindled and arose
Within the sphere of that appalling fray!
For, from the encounter of those wondrous foes,
A vapour like the sea's suspended spray   220
Hung gathered: in the void air, far away,
Floated the shattered plumes; bright scales did leap,
Where'er the Eagle's talons made their way,
Like sparks into the darkness;—as they sweep,°
Blood stains the snowy foam of the tumultuous deep.

12

Swift chances in that combat—many a check,
And many a change, a dark and wild turmoil;

Sometimes the Snake around his enemy's neck
Locked in stiff rings his adamantine coil,
Until the Eagle, faint with pain and toil,   230
Remitted his strong flight, and near the sea
Languidly fluttered, hopeless so to foil
His adversary, who then reared on high
His red and burning crest, radiant with victory.

13

Then on the white edge of the bursting surge,
Where they had sunk together, would the Snake
Relax his suffocating grasp, and scourge
The wind with his wild writhings; for to break
That chain of torment, the vast bird would shake
The strength of his unconquerable wings   240
As in despair, and with his sinewy neck,
Dissolve in sudden shock those linkèd rings,
Then soar—as swift as smoke from a volcano springs.

14

Wile baffled wile, and strength encountered strength,
Thus long, but unprevailing:—the event°
Of that portentous fight appeared at length:°
Until the lamp of day was almost spent
It had endured, when lifeless, stark, and rent,°
Hung high that mighty Serpent, and at last
Fell to the sea, while o'er the continent,   250
With clang of wings and scream the Eagle passed,
Heavily borne away on the exhausted blast.

15

And with it fled the tempest, so that ocean
And earth and sky shone through the atmosphere—
Only, 'twas strange to see the red commotion
Of waves like mountains o'er the sinking sphere
Of sunset sweep, and their fierce roar to hear
Amid the calm: down the steep path I wound
To the seashore—the evening was most clear
And beautiful, and there the sea I found   260
Calm as a cradled child in dreamless slumber bound.

16

There was a Woman, beautiful as morning,
Sitting beneath the rocks, upon the sand
Of the waste sea—fair as one flower adorning
An icy wilderness—each delicate hand
Lay crossed upon her bosom, and the band
Of her dark hair had fall'n, and so she sate
Looking upon the waves; on the bare strand
Upon the sea-mark a small boat did wait,°
Fair as herself, like Love by Hope left desolate.   270

17

It seemed that this fair Shape had looked upon
That unimaginable fight, and now
That her sweet eyes were weary of the sun,
As brightly it illustrated her woe;
For in the tears which silently to flow
Paused not, its lustre hung: she watching aye
The foam-wreathes which the faint tide wove below
Upon the spangled sands, groaned heavily,
And after every groan looked up over the sea.

18

And when she saw the wounded Serpent make   280
His path between the waves, her lips grew pale,
Parted, and quivered; the tears ceased to break
From her immovable eyes; no voice of wail°
Escaped her; but she rose, and on the gale
Loosening her star-bright robe and shadowy hair
Poured forth her voice; the caverns of the vale
That opened to the ocean, caught it there,
And filled with silver sounds the overflowing air.

19

She spake in language whose strange melody
Might not belong to earth. I heard, alone,°   290
What made its music more melodious be,
The pity and the love of every tone;
But to the Snake those accents sweet were known
His native tongue and hers; nor did he beat

The hoar spray idly then, but winding on
Through the green shadows of the waves that meet
Near to the shore, did pause beside her snowy feet.

20

Then on the sands the Woman sate again,
And wept and clasped her hands, and all between,
Renewed the unintelligible strain   300
Of her melodious voice and eloquent mien;
And she unveiled her bosom, and the green
And glancing shadows of the sea did play
O'er its marmoreal depth:—one moment seen,°
For ere the next, the Serpent did obey
Her voice, and, coiled in rest in her embrace it lay.

21

Then she arose, and smiled on me with eyes
Serene yet sorrowing, like that planet fair,
While yet the day-light lingereth in the skies
Which cleaves with arrowy beams the dark-red air,   310
And said: 'To grieve is wise, but the despair
Was weak and vain which led thee here from sleep:
This shalt thou know, and more, if thou dost dare
With me and with this Serpent, o'er the deep,
A voyage divine and strange, companionship to keep.'

22

Her voice was like the wildest, saddest tone,
Yet sweet, of some loved voice heard long ago.
I wept. Shall this fair woman all alone,
Over the sea with that fierce Serpent go?
His head is on her heart, and who can know   320
How soon he may devour his feeble prey?—
Such were my thoughts, when the tide 'gan to flow;
And that strange boat, like the moon's shade, did sway
Amid reflected stars that in the waters lay.

23

A boat of rare device, which had no sail°
But its own curvèd prow of thin moonstone,

Wrought like a web of texture fine and frail,
To catch those gentlest winds which are not known
To breathe, but by the steady speed alone
With which it cleaves the sparkling sea; and now   330
We are embarked, the mountains hang and frown
Over the starry deep that gleams below,
A vast and dim expanse, as o'er the waves we go.°

24

And as we sailed, a strange and awful tale
That Woman told, like such mysterious dream
As makes the slumberer's cheek with wonder pale!
'Twas midnight, and around, a shoreless stream,
Wide ocean rolled, when that majestic theme
Shrined in her heart found utterance, and she bent
Her looks on mine; those eyes a kindling beam   340
Of love divine into my spirit sent,
And ere her lips could move, made the air eloquent.

25

'Speak not to me, but hear! much shalt thou learn,
Much must remain unthought, and more untold,
In the dark Future's ever-flowing urn:°
Know then, that from the depth of ages old,
Two Powers o'er mortal things dominion hold,
Ruling the world with a divided lot,
Immortal, all pervading, manifold,
Twin Genii, equal Gods—when life and thought°   350
Sprang forth, they burst the womb of inessential Nought.°

26

'The earliest dweller of the world alone,
Stood on the verge of chaos: Lo! afar
O'er the wide wild abyss two meteors shone,
Sprung from the depth of its tempestuous jar:°
A blood-red Comet and the Morning Star°
Mingling their beams in combat—as he stood,
All thoughts within his mind waged mutual war,
In dreadful sympathy—when to the flood°
That fair Star fell, he turned and shed his brother's blood.   360

27

'Thus evil triumphed, and the Spirit of evil,
One Power of many shapes which none may know,°
One Shape of many names; the Fiend did revel
In victory, reigning o'er a world of woe,
For the new race of man went to and fro,
Famished and homeless, loathed and loathing, wild,
And hating good—for his immortal foe,
He changed from starry shape, beauteous and mild,°
To a dire Snake, with man and beast unreconciled.

28

'The darkness lingering o'er the dawn of things,   370
Was Evil's breath and life: this made him strong
To soar aloft with overshadowing wings;
And the great Spirit of Good did creep among
The nations of mankind, and every tongue
Cursed, and blasphemed him as he passed; for none
Knew good from evil, though their names were hung
In mockery o'er the fane where many a groan,°
As King, and Lord, and God, the conquering Fiend did own.°

29

'The fiend, whose name was Legion; Death, Decay,
Earthquake and Blight, and Want, and Madness pale,   380
Wingèd and wan diseases, an array
Numerous as leaves that strew the autumnal gale;
Poison, a snake in flowers, beneath the veil
Of food and mirth, hiding his mortal head;
And, without whom all these might nought avail,
Fear, Hatred, Faith, and Tyranny, who spread
Those subtle nets which snare the living and the dead.

30

'His spirit is their power, and they his slaves
In air, and light, and thought, and language dwell;
And keep their state from palaces to graves,   390
In all resorts of men—invisible,
But when, in ebon mirror, Nightmare fell
To tyrant or impostor bids them rise,

Black-wingèd demon forms—whom, from the hell,
His reign and dwelling beneath nether skies,°
He loosens to their dark and blasting ministries.°

31

'In the world's youth his empire was as firm
As its foundations—soon the Spirit of Good,
Though in the likeness of a loathsome worm,
Sprang from the billows of the formless flood,   400
Which shrank and fled; and with that fiend of blood
Renewed the doubtful war—thrones then first shook,
And earth's immense and trampled multitude,
In hope on their own powers began to look,
And Fear, the demon pale, his sanguine shrine forsook.°

32

'Then Greece arose, and to its bards and sages,
In dream, the golden-pinioned Genii came,
Even where they slept amid the night of ages,
Steeping their hearts in the divinest flame,
Which thy breath kindled, Power of holiest name!   410
And oft in cycles since, when darkness gave
New weapons to thy foe, their sunlike fame
Upon the combat shone—a light to save,°
Like Paradise spread forth beyond the shadowy grave.

33

'Such is this conflict—when mankind doth strive
With its oppressors in a strife of blood,
Or when free thoughts, like lightnings are alive;
And in each bosom of the multitude
Justice and truth, with custom's hydra brood,°
Wage silent war;—when priests and kings dissemble   420
In smiles or frowns their fierce disquietude,
When round pure hearts, a host of hopes assemble,
The Snake and Eagle meet—the world's foundations tremble!

34

'Thou hast beheld that fight—when to thy home
Thou dost return, steep not its hearth in tears;

Though thou may'st hear that earth is now become
The tyrant's garbage, which to his compeers,°
The vile reward of their dishonoured years,
He will dividing give.—The victor Fiend
Omnipotent of yore, now quails, and fears   430
His triumph dearly won, which soon will lend
An impulse swift and sure to his approaching end.

35

'List, stranger list, mine is an human form,
Like that thou wearest—touch me—shrink not now!
My hand thou feel'st is not a ghost's, but warm
With human blood.—'Twas many years ago,
Since first my thirsting soul aspired to know
The secrets of this wondrous world, when deep
My heart was pierced with sympathy, for woe
Which could not be mine own—and thought did keep   440
In dream, unnatural watch beside an infant's sleep.°

36

'Woe could not be mine own, since far from men
I dwelt, a free and happy orphan child,
By the seashore, in a deep mountain glen;
And near the waves, and through the forests wild,
I roamed, to storm and darkness reconciled:
For I was calm while tempest shook the sky:
But when the breathless heavens in beauty smiled,
I wept, sweet tears, yet too tumultuously
For peace, and clasped my hands aloft in ecstacy.   450

37

'These were forebodings of my fate—before
A woman's heart beat in my virgin breast,
It had been nurtured in divinest lore:
A dying poet gave me books, and blest°
With wild but holy talk the sweet unrest
In which I watched him as he died away—
A youth with hoary hair—a fleeting guest
Of our lone mountains—and this lore did sway
My spirit like a storm, contending there alway.

38

'Thus the dark tale which history doth unfold,   460
I knew, but not, methinks, as others know,
For they weep not; and Wisdom had unrolled
The clouds which hide the gulf of mortal woe:
To few can she that warning vision show,
For I loved all things with intense devotion;
So that when Hope's deep source in fullest flow,°
Like earthquake did uplift the stagnant ocean
Of human thoughts—mine shook beneath the wide emotion.

39

'When first the living blood through all these veins
Kindled a thought in sense, great France sprang forth,   470
And seized, as if to break, the ponderous chains
Which bind in woe the nations of the earth.
I saw, and started from my cottage hearth;
And to the clouds and waves in tameless gladness,
Shrieked, till they caught immeasurable mirth—
And laughed in light and music: soon, sweet madness
Was poured upon my heart, a soft and thrilling sadness.

40

'Deep slumber fell on me:—my dreams were fire,
Soft and delightful thoughts did rest and hover
Like shadows o'er my brain; and strange desire,   480
The tempest of a passion, raging over
My tranquil soul, its depths with light did cover,
Which passed; and calm, and darkness, sweeter far
Came—then I loved; but not a human lover!
For when I rose from sleep, the Morning Star°
Shone through the woodbine wreaths which round my
          casement were.

41

''Twas like an eye which seemed to smile on me.
I watched, till by the sun made pale, it sank
Under the billows of the heaving sea;
But from its beams deep love my spirit drank,   490

And to my brain the boundless world now shrank
Into one thought—one image—yes, for ever!
Even like the dayspring, poured on vapours dank,
The beams of that one Star did shoot and quiver
Through my benighted mind—and were extinguished never.

42

'The day passed thus: at night, methought in dream
A shape of speechless beauty did appear:°
It stood like light on a careering stream
Of golden clouds which shook the atmosphere;
A wingèd youth, his radiant brow did wear   500
The Morning Star: a wild dissolving bliss
Over my frame he breathed, approaching near,
And bent his eyes of kindling tenderness
Near mine, and on my lips impressed a lingering kiss,

43

'And said: "a Spirit loves thee, mortal maiden,
How wilt thou prove thy worth?" Then joy and sleep
Together fled, my soul was deeply laden,
And to the shore I went to muse and weep;
But as I moved, over my heart did creep
A joy less soft, but more profound and strong   510
Than my sweet dream; and it forbade to keep
The path of the seashore: that Spirit's tongue
Seemed whispering in my heart, and bore my steps along.

44

'How, to that vast and peopled city led,°
Which was a field of holy warfare then,
I walked among the dying and the dead,
And shared in fearless deeds with evil men,
Calm as an angel in the dragon's den—
How I braved death for liberty and truth,
And spurned at peace, and power, and fame; and when   520
Those hopes had lost the glory of their youth,
How sadly I returned—might move the hearer's ruth:°

45

'Warm tears throng fast! the tale may not be said—
Know then, that when this grief had been subdued,
I was not left, like others, cold and dead;°
The Spirit whom I loved, in solitude
Sustained his child: the tempest-shaken wood,
The waves, the fountains, and the hush of night—
These were his voice, and well I understood
His smile divine, when the calm sea was bright   530
With silent stars, and Heaven was breathless with delight.

46

'In lonely glens, amid the roar of rivers,
When the dim nights were moonless, have I known
Joys which no tongue can tell; my pale lip quivers
When thought revisits them:—know thou alone,
That after many wondrous years were flown,
I was awakened by a shriek of woe;
And over me a mystic robe was thrown,
By viewless hands, and a bright Star did glow
Before my steps—the Snake then met his mortal foe.'   540

47

'Thou fearest not then the Serpent on thy heart?'
'Fear it!' she said, with brief and passionate cry,
And spake no more: that silence made me start—
I looked, and we were sailing pleasantly,
Swift as a cloud between the sea and sky;
Beneath the rising moon seen far away,
Mountains of ice, like sapphire, piled on high
Hemming the horizon round, in silence lay
On the still waters—these we did approach alway.

48

And swift and swifter grew the vessel's motion,   550
So that a dizzy trance fell on my brain—
Wild music woke me: we had passed the ocean
Which girds the pole, Nature's remotest reign—
And we glode fast o'er a pellucid plain
Of waters, azure with the noontide day.

Etherial mountains shone around—a Fane
Stood in the midst, girt by green isles which lay
On the blue sunny deep, resplendent far away.°

49

It was a Temple, such as mortal hand
Has never built, nor ecstasy, nor dream,   560
Reared in the cities of enchanted land:
'Twas likest Heaven, ere yet day's purple stream
Ebbs o'er the western forest, while the gleam
Of the unrisen moon among the clouds
Is gathering—when with many a golden beam
The thronging constellations rush in crowds,
Paving with fire the sky and the marmoreal floods;

50

Like what may be conceived of this vast dome,°
When from the depths which thought can seldom pierce
Genius beholds it rise, his native home,   570
Girt by the deserts of the Universe.
Yet, nor in painting's light, or mightier verse,
Or sculpture's marble language can invest
That shape to mortal sense—such glooms immerse
That incommunicable sight, and rest
Upon the labouring brain and overburdened breast.

51

Winding among the lawny islands fair,
Whose blosmy forests starred the shadowy deep,°
The wingless boat paused where an ivory stair
Its fretwork in the crystal sea did steep,   580
Encircling that vast Fane's aerial heap:°
We disembarked, and through a portal wide
We passed—whose roof of moonstone carved, did keep
A glimmering o'er the forms on every side,
Sculptures like life and thought; immovable, deep-eyed.

52

We came to a vast hall, whose glorious roof
Was diamond, which had drunk the lightning's sheen

In darkness, and now poured it through the woof
Of spell-inwoven clouds hung there to screen
Its blinding splendour—through such veil was seen   590
That work of subtlest power, divine and rare;
Orb above orb, with starry shapes between,
And hornèd moons, and meteors strange and fair,
On night-black columns poised—one hollow hemisphere!

53

Ten thousand columns in that quivering light
Distinct—between whose shafts wound far away
The long and labyrinthine aisles—more bright
With their own radiance than the Heaven of Day;
And on the jasper walls around, there lay
Paintings, the poesy of mightiest thought,   600
Which did the Spirit's history display;
A tale of passionate change, divinely taught,
Which, in their wingèd dance, unconscious Genii wrought.

54

Beneath, there sate on many a sapphire throne,
The Great, who had departed from mankind,
A mighty Senate;—some whose white hair shone
Like mountain snow, mild, beautiful, and blind;°
Some, female forms, whose gestures beamed with mind;
And ardent youths, and children bright and fair;
And some had lyres whose strings were intertwined   610
With pale and clinging flames, which ever there
Waked faint yet thrilling sounds that pierced the crystal air.

55

One seat was vacant in the midst, a throne,
Reared on a pyramid like sculptured flame,
Distinct with circling steps which rested on
Their own deep fire—soon as the Woman came
Into that hall, she shrieked the Spirit's name
And fell; and vanished slowly from the sight.
Darkness arose from her dissolving frame,
Which gathering, filled that dome of woven light,   620
Blotting its spherèd stars with supernatural night.°

56

Then first, two glittering lights were seen to glide
In circles on the amethystine floor,
Small serpent eyes trailing from side to side,
Like meteors on a river's grassy shore,°
They round each other rolled, dilating more
And more—then rose, commingling into one,
One clear and mighty planet hanging o'er
A cloud of deepest shadow, which was thrown
Athwart the glowing steps and the crystalline throne.   630

57

The cloud which rested on that cone of flame
Was cloven; beneath the planet sate a Form,°
Fairer than tongue can speak or thought may frame,
The radiance of whose limbs rose-like and warm
Flowed forth, and did with softest light inform°
The shadowy dome, the sculptures, and the state
Of those assembled shapes—with clinging charm
Sinking upon their hearts and mine—He sate
Majestic, yet most mild—calm, yet compassionate.

58

Wonder and joy a passing faintness threw   640
Over my brow—a hand supported me,
Whose touch was magic strength: an eye of blue
Looked into mine, like moonlight, soothingly;
And a voice said—'Thou must a listener be
This day—two mighty Spirits now return,
Like birds of calm, from the world's raging sea,
They pour fresh light from Hope's immortal urn;
A tale of human power—despair not—list and learn!'

59

I looked, and lo! one stood forth eloquently,°
His eyes were dark and deep, and the clear brow   650
Which shadowed them was like the morning sky,
The cloudless Heaven of Spring, when in their flow
Through the bright air, the soft winds as they blow
Wake the green world—his gestures did obey

The oracular mind that made his features glow,
And where his curvèd lips half open lay,
Passion's divinest stream had made impetuous way.

60

Beneath the darkness of his outspread hair
He stood thus beautiful: but there was One°
Who sate beside him like his shadow there,   660
And held his hand—far lovelier—she was known
To be thus fair, by the few lines alone°
Which through her floating locks and gathered cloak
Glances of soul-dissolving glory, shone:—
None else beheld her eyes—in him they woke
Memories which found a tongue, as thus he silence broke.

Canto Second

1

The starlight smile of children, the sweet looks
Of women, the fair breast from which I fed,
The murmur of the unreposing brooks,
And the green light which, shifting overhead,   670
Some tangled bower of vines around me shed,
The shells on the sea-sand, and the wild flowers,
The lamp-light through the rafters cheerly spread,
And on the twining flax—in life's young hours
These sights and sounds did nurse my spirit's folded powers.

2

In Argolis, beside the echoing sea,°
Such impulses within my mortal frame
Arose, and they were dear to memory,
Like tokens of the dead:—but others came
Soon, in another shape: the wondrous fame   680
Of the past world, the vital words and deeds
Of minds whom neither time nor change can tame,
Traditions dark and old, whence evil creeds
Start forth, and whose dim shade a stream of poison feeds.

3

I heard, as all have heard, the various story
Of human life, and wept unwilling tears.
Feeble historians of its shame and glory,
False disputants on all its hopes and fears,
Victims who worshipped ruin,—chroniclers
Of daily scorn, and slaves who loathed their state   690
Yet flattering power had given its ministers
A throne of judgement in the grave:—'twas fate,°
That among such as these my youth should seek its mate.

4

The land in which I lived, by a fell bane°
Was withered up. Tyrants dwelt side by side,
And stabled in our homes,—until the chain
Stifled the captive's cry, and to abide
That blasting curse men had no shame—all vied
In evil, slave and despot; fear with lust,
Strange fellowship through mutual hate had tied,   700
Like two dark serpents tangled in the dust,
Which on the paths of men their mingling poison thrust.

5

Earth, our bright home, its mountains and its waters,
And the etherial shapes which are suspended
Over its green expanse, and those fair daughters,
The clouds, of Sun and Ocean, who have blended
The colours of the air since first extended
It cradled the young world, none wandered forth
To see or feel: a darkness had descended
On every heart: the light which shows its worth,°
Must among gentle thoughts and fearless take its birth.

6

This vital world, this home of happy spirits,
Was as a dungeon to my blasted kind,
All that despair from murdered hope inherits
They sought, and in their helpless misery blind,
A deeper prison and heavier chains did find,°
And stronger tyrants:—a dark gulf before,

The realm of a stern Ruler, yawned; behind,°
Terror and Time conflicting drove, and bore°
On their tempestuous flood the shrieking wretch from shore.   720

7

Out of that Ocean's wrecks had Guilt and Woe
Framed a dark dwelling for their homeless thought,°
And, starting at the ghosts which to and fro
Glide o'er its dim and gloomy strand, had brought
The worship thence which they each other taught.
Well might men loathe their life, well might they turn
Even to the ills again from which they sought
Such refuge after death!—well might they learn
To gaze on this fair world with hopeless unconcern!

8

For they all pined in bondage: body and soul,   730
Tyrant and slave, victim and torturer, bent
Before one Power, to which supreme control
Over their will by their own weakness lent,
Made all its many names omnipotent;
All symbols of things evil, all divine;
And hymns of blood or mockery, which rent
The air from all its fanes, did intertwine°
Imposture's impious toils round each discordant shrine.

9

I heard as all have heard, life's various story,
And in no careless heart transcribed the tale;   740
But, from the sneers of men who had grown hoary
In shame and scorn, from groans of crowds made pale
By famine, from a mother's desolate wail
O'er her polluted child, from innocent blood°
Poured on the earth, and brows anxious and pale
With the heart's warfare; did I gather food
To feed my many thoughts: a tameless multitude!

10

I wandered through the wrecks of days departed
Far by the desolated shore, when even°

O'er the still sea and jagged islets darted 750
The light of moonrise; in the northern Heaven,
Among the clouds near the horizon driven,
The mountains lay beneath one planet pale;
Around me, broken tombs and columns riven
Looked vast in twilight, and the sorrowing gale
Waked in those ruins grey its everlasting wail!

11

I knew not who had framed these wonders then,
Nor had I heard the story of their deeds;
But dwellings of a race of mightier men,
And monuments of less ungentle creeds 760
Tell their own tale to him who wisely heeds
The language which they speak; and now, to me
The moonlight making pale the blooming weeds,
The bright stars shining in the breathless sea,
Interpreted those scrolls of mortal mystery.

12

Such man has been, and such may yet become!
Aye, wiser, greater, gentler, even than they
Who on the fragments of yon shattered dome
Have stamped the sign of power—I felt the sway
Of the vast stream of ages bear away 770
My floating thoughts—my heart beat loud and fast—
Even as a storm let loose beneath the ray
Of the still moon, my spirit onward passed
Beneath truth's steady beams upon its tumult cast.

13

It shall be thus no more! too long, too long,
Sons of the glorious dead, have ye lain bound°
In darkness and in ruin.—Hope is strong,
Justice and Truth their wingèd child have found—°
Awake! arise! until the mighty sound
Of your career shall scatter in its gust 780
The thrones of the oppressor, and the ground
Hide the last altar's unregarded dust,
Whose Idol has so long betrayed your impious trust.°

14

It must be so—I will arise and waken
The multitude, and like a sulphurous hill,
Which on a sudden from its snows has shaken
The swoon of ages, it shall burst and fill
The world with cleansing fire: it must, it will—
It may not be restrained!—and who shall stand
Amid the rocking earthquake steadfast still,   790
But Laon? on high Freedom's desert land
A tower whose marble walls the leaguèd storms withstand!

15

One summer night, in commune with the hope
Thus deeply fed, amid those ruins grey
I watched, beneath the dark sky's starry cope;
And ever from that hour upon me lay
The burden of this hope, and night or day,
In vision or in dream, clove to my breast:
Among mankind, or when gone far away
To the lone shores and mountains, 'twas a guest   800
Which followed where I fled, and watched when I did rest.

16

These hopes found words through which my spirit sought
To weave a bondage of such sympathy,
As might create some response to the thought
Which ruled me now—and as the vapours lie
Bright in the outspread morning's radiancy,
So were these thoughts invested with the light
Of language: and all bosoms made reply
On which its lustre streamed, whene'er it might
Through darkness wide and deep those trancèd spirits smite.   810

17

Yes, many an eye with dizzy tears was dim,
And oft I thought to clasp my own heart's brother,
When I could feel the listener's senses swim,
And hear his breath its own swift gaspings smother
Even as my words evoked them—and another,
And yet another, I did fondly deem,

Felt that we all were sons of one great mother;
And the cold truth such sad reverse did seem,
As to awake in grief from some delightful dream.

18

Yes, oft beside the ruined labyrinth   820
Which skirts the hoary caves of the green deep,
Did Laon and his friend on one grey plinth,°
Round whose worn base the wild waves hiss and leap,
Resting at eve, a lofty converse keep:
And that this friend was false, may now be said
Calmly—that he like other men could weep
Tears which are lies, and could betray and spread
Snares for that guileless heart which for his own had bled.°

19

Then, had no great aim recompensed my sorrow,
I must have sought dark respite from its stress   830
In dreamless rest, in sleep that sees no morrow—
For to tread life's dismaying wilderness
Without one smile to cheer, one voice to bless,
Amid the snares and scoffs of humankind,
Is hard—but I betrayed it not, nor less
With love that scorned return, sought to unbind
The interwoven clouds which make its wisdom blind.°

20

With deathless minds which leave where they have passed
A path of light, my soul communion knew;
Till from that glorious intercourse, at last,   840
As from a mine of magic store, I drew
Words which were weapons;—round my heart there grew
The adamantine armour of their power,
And from my fancy wings of golden hue
Sprang forth—yet not alone from wisdom's tower,
A minister of truth, these plumes young Laon bore.

21

I had a little sister, whose fair eyes°
Were lodestars of delight, which drew me home°

When I might wander forth; nor did I prize
Aught human thing beneath Heaven's mighty dome   850
Beyond this child: so when sad hours were come,
And baffled hope like ice still clung to me,
Since kin were cold, and friends had now become
Heartless and false, I turned from all, to be,
Cythna, the only source of tears and smiles to thee.

22

What wert thou then? A child most infantine,
Yet wandering far beyond that innocent age
In all but its sweet looks and mien divine;
Even then, methought, with the world's tyrant rage
A patient warfare thy young heart did wage,   860
When those soft eyes of scarcely conscious thought,
Some tale, or thine own fancies would engage
To overflow with tears, or converse fraught
With passion, o'er their depths its fleeting light had wrought.

23

She moved upon this earth a shape of brightness,
A power, that from its objects scarcely drew
One impulse of her being—in her lightness
Most like some radiant cloud of morning dew,
Which wanders through the waste air's pathless blue,
To nourish some far desert: she did seem   870
Beside me, gathering beauty as she grew,
Like the bright shade of some immortal dream
Which walks, when tempest sleeps, the wave of life's dark stream.

24

As mine own shadow was this child to me,
A second self, far dearer and more fair;
Which clothed in undissolving radiancy,
All those steep paths which languor and despair
Of human things, had made so dark and bare,
But which I trod alone—nor, till bereft
Of friends, and overcome by lonely care,   880
Knew I what solace for that loss was left,
Though by a bitter wound my trusting heart was cleft.

25

Once she was dear, now she was all I had
To love in human life—this sister sweet,°
This child of twelve years old—so she was made°
My sole associate, and her willing feet
Wandered with mine where earth and ocean meet,
Beyond the aerial mountains whose vast cells°
The unreposing billows ever beat,
Through forests wide and old, and lawny dells,   890
Where boughs of incense droop over the emerald wells.

26

And warm and light I felt her clasping hand
When twined in mine: she followed where I went,
Through the lone paths of our immortal land.
It had no waste, but some memorial lent
Which strung me to my toil—some monument°
Vital with mind: then, Cythna by my side,
Until the bright and beaming day were spent,
Would rest, with looks entreating to abide,
Too earnest and too sweet ever to be denied.   900

27

And soon I could not have refused her—thus
Forever, day and night, we two were ne'er
Parted, but when brief sleep divided us:
And when the pauses of the lulling air°
Of noon beside the sea, had made a lair
For her soothed senses, in my arms she slept,
And I kept watch over her slumbers there,
While, as the shifting visions o'er her swept,
Amid her innocent rest by turns she smiled and wept.

28

And, in the murmur of her dreams was heard   910
Sometimes the name of Laon: suddenly
She would arise, and like the secret bird°
Whom sunset wakens, fill the shore and sky
With her sweet accents—a wild melody!
Hymns which my soul had woven to Freedom, strong

The source of passion whence they rose, to be;°
Triumphant strains, which, like a spirit's tongue,
To the enchanted waves that child of glory sung,

29

Her white arms lifted through the shadowy stream
Of her loose hair—oh, excellently great   920
Seemed to me then my purpose, the vast theme
Of those impassioned songs, when Cythna sate
Amid the calm which rapture doth create
After its tumult, her heart vibrating,
Her spirit o'er the ocean's floating state
From her deep eyes far wandering, on the wing
Of visions that were mine, beyond its utmost spring.

30

For, before Cythna loved it, had my song
Peopled with thoughts the boundless universe,
A mighty congregation, which were strong   930
Where'er they trod the darkness to disperse
The cloud of that unutterable curse
Which clings upon mankind:—all things became
Slaves to my holy and heroic verse,
Earth, sea and sky, the planets, life and fame
And fate, or whate'er else binds the world's wondrous frame.

31

And this beloved child thus felt the sway
Of my conceptions, gathering like a cloud
The very wind on which it rolls away:
Hers too were all my thoughts, ere yet endowed   940
With music and with light, their fountains flowed
In poesy; and her still and earnest face,
Pallid with feelings which intensely glowed
Within, was turned on mine with speechless grace,
Watching the hopes which there her heart had learned to trace.°

32

In me, communion with this purest being
Kindled intenser zeal, and made me wise

In knowledge, which in hers mine own mind seeing,
Left in the human world few mysteries:
How without fear of evil or disguise   950
Was Cythna!—what a spirit strong and mild,
Which death, or pain or peril could despise,
Yet melt in tenderness! what genius wild
Yet mighty, was enclosed within one simple child!

33

New lore was this—old age with its grey hair,
And wrinkled legends of unworthy things,
And icy sneers, is nought: it cannot dare
To burst the chains which life for ever flings
On the entangled soul's aspiring wings,
So is it cold and cruel, and is made   960
The careless slave of that dark power which brings
Evil, like blight on man, who still betrayed,
Laughs o'er the grave in which his living hopes are laid.

34

Nor are the strong and the severe to keep
The empire of the world: thus Cythna taught
Even in the visions of her eloquent sleep,
Unconscious of the power through which she wrought
The woof of such intelligible thought,
As from the tranquil strength which cradled lay
In her smile-peopled rest, my spirit sought   970
Why the deceiver and the slave has sway
O'er heralds so divine of truth's arising day.

35

Within that fairest form, the female mind
Untainted by the poison clouds which rest
On the dark world, a sacred home did find:
But else, from the wide earth's maternal breast,
Victorious Evil, which had dispossessed
All native power, had those fair children torn,
And made them slaves to soothe his vile unrest,
And minister to lust its joys forlorn,   980
Till they had learned to breathe the atmosphere of scorn.

36

This misery was but coldly felt, till she°
Became my only friend, who had indued
My purpose with a wider sympathy;
Thus, Cythna mourned with me the servitude
In which the half of humankind were mewed,°
Victims of lust and hate, the slaves of slaves;
She mourned that grace and power were thrown as food
To the hyena lust, who, among graves,
Over his loathed meal, laughing in agony, raves.   990

37

And I, still gazing on that glorious child,
Even as these thoughts flushed o'er her.—'Cythna sweet,°
Well with the world art thou unreconciled;
Never will peace and human nature meet
Till free and equal man and woman greet
Domestic peace; and ere this power can make
In human hearts its calm and holy seat,
This slavery must be broken'—as I spake,
From Cythna's eyes a light of exultation brake.

38

She replied earnestly:—'It shall be mine,   1000
This task, mine, Laon!—thou hast much to gain;
Nor wilt thou at poor Cythna's pride repine,
If she should lead a happy female train
To meet thee over the rejoicing plain,
When myriads at thy call shall throng around
The Golden City'—Then the child did strain°
My arm upon her tremulous heart, and wound
Her own about my neck, till some reply she found.

39

I smiled, and spake not—'wherefore dost thou smile
At what I say? Laon, I am not weak,   1010
And though my cheek might become pale the while,
With thee, if thou desirest, will I seek
Through their array of banded slaves to wreak
Ruin upon the tyrants. I had thought

It was more hard to turn my unpractised cheek
To scorn and shame, and this beloved spot
And thee, O dearest friend, to leave and murmur not.

40

'Whence came I what I am? thou, Laon, knowest
How a young child should thus undaunted be;
Methinks, it is a power which thou bestowest,   1020
Through which I seek, by most resembling thee,
So to become most good, and great and free,
Yet far beyond this Ocean's utmost roar
In towers and huts are many like to me,
Who, could they see thine eyes, or feel such lore
As I have learnt from them, like me would fear no more.

41

'Think'st thou that I shall speak unskilfully,
And none will heed me? I remember now,
How once, a slave in tortures doomed to die,
Was saved, because in accents sweet and low   1030
He sung a song his Judge loved long ago,
As he was led to death.—All shall relent
Who hear me—tears as mine have flowed, shall flow,
Hearts beat as mine now beats, with such intent
As renovates the world; a will omnipotent!

42

'Yes, I will tread Pride's golden palaces,
Through Penury's roofless huts and squalid cells
Will I descend, where'er in abjectness
Woman with some vile slave her tyrant dwells,
There with the music of thine own sweet spells   1040
Will disenchant the captives, and will pour
For the despairing, from the crystal wells
Of thy deep spirit, reason's mighty lore,
And power shall then abound, and hope arise once more.

43

'Can man be free if woman be a slave?
Chain one who lives, and breathes this boundless air

To the corruption of a closèd grave!
Can they whose mates are beasts, condemned to bear
Scorn, heavier far than toil or anguish, dare
To trample their oppressors? in their home   1050
Among their babes, thou knowest a curse would wear
The shape of woman—hoary crime would come°
Behind, and fraud rebuild religion's tottering dome.

44

'I am a child:—I would not yet depart.
When I go forth alone, bearing the lamp
Aloft which thou hast kindled in my heart,
Millions of slaves from many a dungeon damp
Shall leap in joy, as the benumbing cramp
Of ages leaves their limbs—no ill may harm
Thy Cythna ever—truth her radiant stamp   1060
Has fixed, as an invulnerable charm
Upon her children's brow, dark falsehood to disarm.

45

'Wait yet awhile for the appointed day—
Thou wilt depart, and I with tears shall stand
Watching thy dim sail skirt the ocean grey;
Amid the dwellers of this lonely land
I shall remain alone—and thy command
Shall then dissolve the world's unquiet trance,
And, multitudinous as the desert sand
Borne on the storm, its millions shall advance,   1070
Thronging round thee, the light of their deliverance.

46

'Then, like the forests of some pathless mountain,
Which from remotest glens two warring winds
Involve in fire, which not the loosened fountain
Of broadest floods might quench, shall all the kinds
Of evil, catch from our uniting minds
The spark which must consume them;—Cythna then
Will have cast off the impotence that binds
Her childhood now, and through the paths of men
Will pass, as the charmèd bird that haunts the serpent's den. 1080

47

'We part!—O Laon, I must dare nor tremble°
To meet those looks no more!—Oh, heavy stroke,
Sweet brother of my soul! can I dissemble
The agony of this thought?'—As thus she spoke
The gathered sobs her quivering accents broke,
And in my arms she hid her beating breast.
I remained still for tears—sudden she woke
As one awakes from sleep, and wildly pressed
My bosom, her whole frame impetuously possessed.

48

'We part to meet again—but yon blue waste,   1090
Yon desert wide and deep holds no recess,
Within whose happy silence, thus embraced
We might survive all ills in one caress:
Nor doth the grave—I fear 'tis passionless—
Nor yon cold vacant Heaven:—we meet again
Within the minds of men, whose lips shall bless
Our memory, and whose hopes its light retain
When these dissevered bones are trodden in the plain.'

49

I could not speak, though she had ceased, for now
The fountains of her feeling, swift and deep,   1100
Seemed to suspend the tumult of their flow;
So we arose, and by the starlight steep
Went homeward—neither did we speak nor weep,
But pale, were calm with passion—thus subdued
Like evening shades that o'er the mountains creep,
We moved towards our home; where, in this mood,
Each from the other sought refuge in solitude.

From *Canto Sixth*

28

The autumnal winds, as if spellbound, had made
A natural couch of leaves in that recess°
Which seasons none disturbed, but in the shade   2580

Of flowering parasites, did spring love to dress°
With their sweet blooms the wintry loneliness
Of those dead leaves, shedding their stars, whene'er
The wandering wind her nurslings might caress;
Whose intertwining fingers ever there,°
Made music wild and soft that filled the listening air.

29

We know not where we go, or what sweet dream
May pilot us through caverns strange and fair
Of far and pathless passion, while the stream
Of life, our bark doth on its whirlpools bear,   2590
Spreading swift wings as sails to the dim air;
Nor should we seek to know, so the devotion
Of love and gentle thoughts be heard still there
Louder and louder from the utmost Ocean
Of universal life, attuning its commotion.

30

To the pure all things are pure! Oblivion wrapped°
Our spirits, and the fearful overthrow
Of public hope was from our being snapped,
Though linkèd years had bound it there; for now
A power, a thirst, a knowledge, which below   2600
All thoughts, like light beyond the atmosphere,
Clothing its clouds with grace, doth ever flow,
Came on us, as we sate in silence there,
Beneath the golden stars of the clear azure air.

31

In silence which doth follow talk that causes
The baffled heart to speak with sighs and tears,
When wildering passion swalloweth up the pauses
Of inexpressive speech:—the youthful years
Which we together passed, their hopes and fears,
The common blood which ran within our frames,°   2610
That likeness of the features which endears
The thoughts expressed by them, our very names,°
And all the wingèd hours which speechless memory claims,

32

Had found a voice:—and ere that voice did pass,
The night grew damp and dim, and through a rent
Of the ruin where we sate, from the morass,
A wandering Meteor by some wild wind sent,°
Hung high in the green dome, to which it lent
A faint and pallid lustre; while the song
Of blasts, in which its blue hair quivering bent,°   2620
Strewed strangest sounds the moving leaves among;
A wondrous light, the sound as of a spirit's tongue.

33

The Meteor showed the leaves on which we sate,
And Cythna's glowing arms, and the thick ties°
Of her soft hair which bent with gathered weight
My neck near hers, her dark and deepening eyes,
Which, as twin phantoms of one star that lies
O'er a dim well, move, though the star reposes,
Swam in our mute and liquid ecstacies,
Her marble brow, and eager lips, like roses,   2630
With their own fragrance pale, which spring but half uncloses.

34

The Meteor to its far morass returned:
The beating of our veins one interval
Made still; and then I felt the blood that burned°
Within her frame, mingle with mine, and fall
Around my heart like fire; and over all
A mist was spread, the sickness of a deep
And speechless swoon of joy, as might befall
Two disunited spirits when they leap
In union from this earth's obscure and fading sleep.   2640

35

Was it one moment that confounded thus
All thought, all sense, all feeling, into one
Unutterable power, which shielded us
Even from our own cold looks, when we had gone
Into a wide and wild oblivion

Of tumult and of tenderness? or now
Had ages, such as make the moon and sun,
The seasons, and mankind their changes know,
Left fear and time unfelt by us alone below?°

36

I know not. What are kisses whose fire clasps   2650
The failing heart in languishment, or limb
Twined within limb? or the quick dying gasps
Of the life meeting, when the faint eyes swim
Through tears of a wide mist boundless and dim,
In one caress? What is the strong control
Which leads the heart that dizzy steep to climb,
Where far over the world those vapours roll,
Which blend two restless frames in one reposing soul?

37

It is the shadow which doth float unseen,°
But not unfelt, o'er blind mortality,   2660
Whose divine darkness fled not from that green
And lone recess, where lapped in peace did lie
Our linkèd frames; till, from the changing sky,
That night and still another day had fled;
And then I saw and felt. The moon was high,
And clouds, as of a coming storm, were spread
Under its orb,—loud winds were gathering overhead.

From *Canto Seventh*

30

'We live in our own world, and mine was made°
From glorious fantasies of hope departed:
Aye we are darkened with their floating shade,°
Or cast a lustre on them—time imparted
Such power to me, I became fearless-hearted,°
My eye and voice grew firm, calm was my mind,
And piercing, like the morn, now it has darted
Its lustre on all hidden things, behind
Yon dim and fading clouds which load the weary wind.

31

'My mind became the book through which I grew   3100
Wise in all human wisdom, and its cave,
Which like a mine I rifled through and through,
To me the keeping of its secrets gave—
One mind, the type of all, the moveless wave°
Whose calm reflects all moving things that are,
Necessity, and love, and life, the grave,
And sympathy, fountains of hope and fear;
Justice, and truth, and time, and the world's natural sphere.

32

'And on the sand would I make signs to range
These woofs, as they were woven, of my thought;   3110
Clear, elemental shapes, whose smallest change
A subtler language within language wrought:
The key of truths which once were dimly taught
In old Crotona;—and sweet melodies°
Of love, in that lorn solitude I caught
From mine own voice in dream, when thy dear eyes
Shone through my sleep, and did that utterance harmonize.

33

'Thy songs were winds whereon I fled at will,
As in a wingèd chariot, o'er the plain
Of crystal youth; and thou wert there to fill   3120
My heart with joy, and there we sate again
On the grey margin of the glimmering main,
Happy as then but wiser far, for we
Smiled on the flowery grave in which were lain
Fear, Faith, and Slavery; and mankind was free,
Equal, and pure and wise, in wisdom's prophecy.

34

'For to my will my fancies were as slaves
To do their sweet and subtle ministries;
And oft from that bright fountain's shadowy waves
They would make human throngs gather and rise   3130
To combat with my overflowing eyes,
And voice made deep with passion—thus I grew

Familiar with the shock and the surprise
And war of earthly minds, from which I drew
The power which has been mine to frame their thoughts anew.

35

'And thus my prison was the populous earth—
Where I saw—even as misery dreams of morn
Before the east has given its glory birth—
Religion's pomp made desolate by the scorn
Of Wisdom's faintest smile, and thrones uptorn,   3140
And dwellings of mild people interspersed
With undivided fields of ripening corn,
And love made free,—a hope which we have nursed
Even with our blood and tears,—until its glory burst.

36

'All is not lost! there is some recompense
For hope whose fountain can be thus profound,
Even throned Evil's splendid impotence,°
Girt by its hell of power, the secret sound
Of hymns to truth and freedom—the dread bound
Of life and death passed fearlessly and well,   3150
Dungeons wherein the high resolve is found,
Racks which degraded woman's greatness tell,
And what may else be good and irresistible.

37

'Such are the thoughts which, like the fires that flare
In storm-encompassed isles, we cherish yet
In this dark ruin—such were mine even there;°
As in its sleep some odorous violet,
While yet its leaves with nightly dews are wet,
Breathes in prophetic dreams of day's uprise,
Or, as ere Scythian frost in fear has met°   3160
Spring's messengers descending from the skies,
The buds foreknow their life—this hope must ever rise.

38

'So years had passed, when sudden earthquake rent
The depth of ocean, and the cavern cracked

With sound, as if the world's wide continent
Had fallen in universal ruin wracked;
And through the cleft streamed in one cataract
The stifling waters:—when I woke, the flood
Whose banded waves that crystal cave had sacked
Was ebbing round me, and my bright abode   3170
Before me yawned—a chasm desert, and bare, and broad.

39

'Above me was the sky, beneath the sea:
I stood upon a point of shattered stone,
And heard loose rocks rushing tumultuously
With splash and shock into the deep—anon
All ceased, and there was silence wide and lone.
I felt that I was free! the Ocean-spray
Quivered beneath my feet, the broad Heaven shone
Around, and in my hair the winds did play
Lingering as they pursued their unimpeded way.'   3180

From *Canto Eighth*

4

' "What dream ye? Your own hands have built a home,°
Even for yourselves on a beloved shore:
For some, fond eyes are pining till they come,
How they will greet him when his toils are o'er,
And laughing babes rush from the well-known door!   3230
Is this your care? ye toil for your own good—
Ye feel and think—has some immortal power
Such purposes? or in a human mood,
Dream ye that God thus builds for man in solitude?°

5

' "What then is God? ye mock yourselves, and give
A human heart to what ye cannot know:
As if the cause of life could think and live!
'Twere as if man's own works should feel, and show
The hopes, and fears, and thoughts from which they flow,
And he be like to them. Lo! Plague is free   3240

To waste, Blight, Poison, Earthquake, Hail, and Snow,
Disease, and Want, and worse Necessity
Of hate and ill, and Pride, and Fear, and Tyranny.

6

'"What then is God? Some moon-struck sophist stood
Watching the shade from his own soul upthrown
Fill Heaven and darken Earth, and in such mood
The Form he saw and worshipped was his own,
His likeness in the world's vast mirror shown;
And 'twere an innocent dream, but that a faith
Nursed by fear's dew of poison, grows thereon,   3250
And that men say, God has appointed Death°
On all who scorn his will, to wreak immortal wrath.

7

'"Men say they have seen God, and heard from God,
Or known from others who have known such things,
And that his will is all our law, a rod°
To scourge us into slaves—that Priests and Kings,
Custom, domestic sway, aye, all that brings
Man's freeborn soul beneath the oppressor's heel,
Are his strong ministers, and that the stings
Of death will make the wise his vengeance feel,   3260
Though truth and virtue arm their hearts with tenfold steel.

8

'"And it is said, that God will punish wrong;°
Yes, add despair to crime, and pain to pain!
And his red hell's undying snakes among,°
Will bind the wretch on whom he fixed a stain,
Which, like a plague, a burden, and a bane,
Clung to him while he lived;—for, love and hate,
Virtue and vice, they say, are difference vain—
The will of strength is right—this human state
Tyrants, that they may rule, with lies thus desolate.   3270

9

'"Alas, what strength? opinion is more frail
Than yon dim cloud now fading on the moon

Even while we gaze, though it awhile avail
To hide the orb of truth—and every throne
Of Earth or Heaven, though shadow, rests thereon,°
One shape of many names:—for this ye plough
The barren waves of ocean, hence each one
Is slave or tyrant; all betray and bow,
Command, or kill, or fear, or wreak, or suffer woe.

10

' "Its names are each a sign which maketh holy   3280
All power—aye, the ghost, the dream, the shade
Of power,—lust, falsehood, hate, and pride, and folly;
The pattern whence all fraud and wrong is made,
A law to which mankind has been betrayed;
And human love is as the name well known
Of a dear mother, whom the murderer laid
In bloody grave, and into darkness thrown,
Gathered her wildered babes around him as his own.

11

' "O love! who to the hearts of wandering men
Art as the calm to Ocean's weary waves!   3290
Justice, or truth, or joy! those only can
From slavery and religion's labyrinth caves
Guide us, as one clear star the seaman saves,—
To give to all an equal share of good,
To track the steps of freedom though through graves
She pass, to suffer all in patient mood,
To weep for crime, though stained with thy friend's dearest blood°

12

' "To feel the peace of self-contentment's lot,
To own all sympathies, and outrage none,
And in the inmost bowers of sense and thought,   3300
Until life's sunny day is quite gone down,
To sit and smile with Joy, or, not alone,
To kiss salt tears from the worn cheek of Woe;
To live, as if to love and live were one,—
This is not faith or law, nor those who bow
To thrones on Heaven or Earth, such destiny may know.

13

'"But children near their parents tremble now,
Because they must obey—one rules another,
For it is said God rules both high and low,
And man is made the captive of his brother,°   3310
And Hate is throned on high with Fear her mother,
Above the Highest—and those fountain-cells,
Whence love yet flowed when faith had choked all other,
Are darkened—Woman, as the bond-slave, dwells
Of man, a slave; and life is poisoned in its wells.

14

'"Man seeks for gold in mines, that he may weave
A lasting chain for his own slavery;—
In fear and restless care that he may live
He toils for others, who must ever be
The joyless thralls of like captivity;   3320
He murders, for his chiefs delight in ruin;
He builds the altar, that its idol's fee
May be his very blood; he is pursuing
O, blind and willing wretch! his own obscure undoing.

15

'"Woman!—she is his slave, she has become
A thing I weep to speak—the child of scorn,
The outcast of a desolated home.
Falsehood, and fear, and toil, like waves have worn
Channels upon her cheek, which smiles adorn,
As calm decks the false Ocean:—well ye know   3330
What Woman is, for none of Woman born,
Can choose but drain the bitter dregs of woe,
Which ever from the oppressed to the oppressors flow.°

16

'"This need not be; ye might arise, and will
That gold should lose its power, and thrones their glory;
That love, which none may bind, be free to fill
The world, like light; and evil faith, grown hoary
With crime, be quenched and die.—Yon promontory
Even now eclipses the descending moon!—

Dungeons and palaces are transitory—   3340
High temples fade like vapour—Man alone
Remains, whose will has power when all beside is gone.

17

' "Let all be free and equal!—from your hearts
I feel an echo; through my inmost frame
Like sweetest sound, seeking its mate, it darts—
Whence come ye, friends? alas, I cannot name
All that I read of sorrow, toil, and shame,
On your worn faces; as in legends old
Which make immortal the disastrous fame
Of conquerors and impostors false and bold,   3350
The discord of your hearts, I in your looks behold.

18

' "Whence come ye, friends? from pouring human blood
Forth on the earth? or bring ye steel and gold,
That Kings may dupe and slay the multitude?
Or from the famished poor, pale, weak, and cold,
Bear ye the earnings of their toil? unfold!
Speak! are your hands in slaughter's sanguine hue
Stained freshly? have your hearts in guile grown old?
Know yourselves thus! ye shall be pure as dew,
And I will be a friend and sister unto you.   3360

19

' "Disguise it not—we have one human heart—°
All mortal thoughts confess a common home:
Blush not for what may to thyself impart
Stains of inevitable crime: the doom
Is this, which has, or may, or must become
Thine, and all humankind's. Ye are the spoil
Which Time thus marks for the devouring tomb,
Thou and thy thoughts and they, and all the toil°
Wherewith ye twine the rings of life's perpetual coil.

20

' "Disguise it not—ye blush for what ye hate,   3370
And Enmity is sister unto Shame;

Look on your mind—it is the book of fate—
Ah! it is dark with many a blazoned name
Of misery—all are mirrors of the same;
But the dark fiend who with his iron pen
Dipped in scorn's fiery poison makes his fame
Enduring there, would o'er the heads of men
Pass harmless, if they scorned to make their hearts his den.

21

'"Yes, it is Hate, that shapeless fiendly thing
Of many names, all evil, some divine,   3380
Whom self-contempt arms with a mortal sting;
Which, when the heart its snaky folds entwine
Is wasted quite, and when it doth repine
To gorge such bitter prey, on all beside
It turns with ninefold rage, as with its twine
When Amphisbaena some fair bird has tied,°
Soon o'er the putrid mass he threats on every side.

22

'"Reproach not thine own soul, but know thyself,
Nor hate another's crime, nor loathe thine own.
It is the dark idolatry of self,   3390
Which, when our thoughts and actions once are gone,
Demands that man should weep, and bleed, and groan;
O vacant expiation! be at rest.—
The past is Death's, the future is thine own;
And love and joy can make the foulest breast
A paradise of flowers, where peace might build her nest."'

From *Canto Ninth*

21

'The blasts of autumn drive the wingèd seeds°
Over the earth,—next come the snows, and rain,   3650
And frosts, and storms, which dreary winter leads
Out of his Scythian cave, a savage train;
Behold! Spring sweeps over the world again,
Shedding soft dews from her etherial wings;

Flowers on the mountains, fruits over the plain,
And music on the waves and woods she flings,
And love on all that lives, and calm on lifeless things.

22

'O Spring, of hope, and love, and youth, and gladness
Wind-wingèd emblem ! brightest, best and fairest!
Whence comest thou, when, with dark winter's sadness   3660
The tears that fade in sunny smiles thou sharest?
Sister of joy, thou art the child who wearest
Thy mother's dying smile, tender and sweet;
Thy mother Autumn, for whose grave thou bearest
Fresh flowers, and beams like flowers, with gentle feet,
Disturbing not the leaves which are her winding-sheet.

23

'Virtue, and Hope, and Love, like light and Heaven,
Surround the world.—We are their chosen slaves.
Has not the whirlwind of our spirit driven
Truth's deathless germs to thought's remotest caves?°   3670
Lo, Winter comes!—the grief of many graves,
The frost of death, the tempest of the sword,
The flood of tyranny, whose sanguine waves°
Stagnate like ice at Faith, the enchanter's word,
And bind all human hearts in its repose abhorred.

24

'The seeds are sleeping in the soil: meanwhile
The tyrant peoples dungeons with his prey,
Pale victims on the guarded scaffold smile
Because they cannot speak; and, day by day,
The moon of wasting Science wanes away   3680
Among her stars, and in that darkness vast
The sons of earth to their foul idols pray,
And grey Priests triumph, and like blight or blast
A shade of selfish care o'er human looks is cast.

25

'This is the winter of the world;—and here
We die, even as the winds of Autumn fade,

Expiring in the frore and foggy air.—
Behold! Spring comes, though we must pass, who made
The promise of its birth,—even as the shade
Which from our death, as from a mountain, flings   3690
The future, a broad sunrise; thus arrayed°
As with the plumes of overshadowing wings,
From its dark gulf of chains, Earth like an eagle springs.

26

'O dearest love! we shall be dead and cold
Before this morn may on the world arise;
Wouldst thou the glory of its dawn behold?
Alas! gaze not on me, but turn thine eyes
On thine own heart—it is a paradise°
Which everlasting spring has made its own,
And while drear Winter fills the naked skies,   3700
Sweet streams of sunny thought, and flowers fresh blown,
Are there, and weave their sounds and odours into one.

27

'In their own hearts the earnest of the hope
Which made them great, the good will ever find;
And though some envious shade may interlope
Between the effect and it, One comes behind,
Who aye the future to the past will bind—
Necessity, whose sightless strength forever
Evil with evil, good with good must wind
In bands of union, which no power may sever: 3710
They must bring forth their kind, and be divided never!°

28

'The good and mighty of departed ages
Are in their graves, the innocent and free,
Heroes, and Poets, and prevailing Sages,°
Who leave the vesture of their majesty
To adorn and clothe this naked world;—and we
Are like to them—such perish, but they leave
All hope, or love, or truth, or liberty,
Whose forms their mighty spirits could conceive
To be a rule and law to ages that survive.   3720

29

'So be the turf heaped over our remains
Even in our happy youth, and that strange lot,
Whate'er it be, when in these mingling veins
The blood is still, be ours; let sense and thought
Pass from our being, or be numbered not
Among the things that are; let those who come
Behind, for whom our steadfast will has bought
A calm inheritance, a glorious doom,
Insult with careless tread our undivided tomb.

30

'Our many thoughts and deeds, our life and love,   3730
Our happiness, and all that we have been,
Immortally must live, and burn and move,
When we shall be no more;—the world has seen
A type of peace; and as some most serene
And lovely spot to a poor maniac's eye,
After long years, some sweet and moving scene
Of youthful hope returning suddenly,
Quells his long madness—thus man shall remember thee.

31

'And Calumny meanwhile shall feed on us,
As worms devour the dead, and near the throne   3740
And at the altar, most accepted thus
Shall sneers and curses be;—what we have done
None shall dare vouch, though it be truly known;
That record shall remain, when they must pass
Who built their pride on its oblivion;
And fame, in human hope which sculptured was,
Survive the perished scrolls of unenduring brass.

32

'The while we two, beloved, must depart,
And Sense and Reason, those enchanters fair,
Whose wand of power is hope, would bid the heart   3750
That gazed beyond the wormy grave despair:
These eyes, these lips, this blood, seems darkly there
To fade in hideous ruin; no calm sleep
Peopling with golden dreams the stagnant air,

Seems our obscure and rotting eyes to steep
In joy;—but senseless death—a ruin dark and deep!

33

'These are blind fancies—reason cannot know
What sense can neither feel, nor thought conceive;
There is delusion in the world—and woe,
And fear, and pain—we know not whence we live,   3760
Or why, or how, or what mute Power may give
Their being to each plant, and star, and beast,
Or even these thoughts:—Come near me! I do weave
A chain I cannot break—I am possessed
With thoughts too swift and strong for one lone human breast.

34

'Yes, yes—thy kiss is sweet, thy lips are warm—
O! willingly, beloved, would these eyes,
Might they no more drink being from thy form,
Even as to sleep whence we again arise,
Close their faint orbs in death: I fear nor prize   3770
Aught that can now betide, unshared by thee—
Yes, Love when wisdom fails makes Cythna wise:
Darkness and death, if death be true, must be
Dearer than life and hope, if unenjoyed with thee.

35

'Alas, our thoughts flow on with stream, whose waters
Return not to their fountain—Earth and Heaven,
The Ocean and the Sun, the clouds their daughters,
Winter, and Spring, and Morn, and Noon, and Even,
All that we are or know, is darkly driven
Towards one gulf—Lo! what a change is come   3780
Since I first spake—but time shall be forgiven,
Though it change all but thee!'—She ceased, night's gloom
Meanwhile had fallen on earth from the sky's sunless dome.

36

Though she had ceased, her countenance uplifted
To Heaven, still spake, with solemn glory bright;
Her dark deep eyes, her lips, whose motions gifted
The air they breathed with love, her locks undight;

'Fair star of life and love,' I cried, 'my soul's delight,
Why lookest thou on the crystalline skies?
O, that my spirit were yon Heaven of night,   3790
Which gazes on thee with its thousand eyes!'°
She turned to me and smiled—that smile was Paradise!

From *Canto Tenth*

17

Day after day, when the year wanes, the frosts°
Strip its green crown of leaves, till all is bare;
So on those strange and congregated hosts
Came Famine, a swift shadow, and the air   3940
Groaned with the burden of a new despair;
Famine, than whom Misrule no deadlier daughter
Feeds from her thousand breasts, though sleeping there
With lidless eyes, lie Faith, and Plague, and Slaughter,
A ghastly brood; conceived of Lethe's sullen water.°

18

There was no food, the corn was trampled down,
The flocks and herds had perished; on the shore
The dead and putrid fish were ever thrown;
The deeps were foodless, and the winds no more
Creaked with the weight of birds, but as before   3950
Those wingèd things sprang forth, were void of shade;
The vines and orchards, Autumn's golden store,
Were burned;—so that the meanest food was weighed
With gold, and Avarice died before the god it made.

19

There was no corn—in the wide market-place
All loathliest things, even human flesh, was sold;
They weighed it in small scales—and many a face
Was fixed in eager horror then: his gold
The miser brought; the tender maid, grown bold
Through hunger, bared her scornèd charms in vain;   3960
The mother brought her eldest born, controlled
By instinct blind as love, but turned again
And bade her infant suck, and died in silent pain.

20

Then fell blue Plague upon the race of man.°
'O, for the sheathèd steel, so late which gave
Oblivion to the dead, when the streets ran
With brothers' blood! O, that the earthquake's grave
Would gape, or Ocean lift its stifling wave!'
Vain cries—throughout the streets, thousands pursued
Each by his fiery torture howl and rave,   3970
Or sit, in frenzy's unimagined mood,
Upon fresh heaps of dead; a ghastly multitude.

21

It was not hunger now, but thirst. Each well
Was choked with rotting corpses, and became
A cauldron of green mist made visible
At sunrise. Thither still the myriads came,
Seeking to quench the agony of the flame,
Which raged like poison through their bursting veins;
Naked they were from torture, without shame,
Spotted with nameless scars and lurid blains,°   3980
Childhood, and youth, and age, writhing in savage pains.

22

It was not thirst but madness! many saw
Their own lean image everywhere, it went
A ghastlier self beside them, till the awe
Of that dread sight to self-destruction sent
Those shrieking victims; some, ere life was spent,
Sought, with a horrid sympathy, to shed
Contagion on the sound; and others rent
Their matted hair, and cried aloud, 'We tread
On fire! Almighty God his hell on earth has spread!'°   3990

23

Sometimes the living by the dead were hid.
Near the great fountain in the public square,
Where corpses made a crumbling pyramid
Under the sun, was heard one stifled prayer
For life, in the hot silence of the air;
And strange 'twas, amid that hideous heap to see

Some shrouded in their long and golden hair,
As if not dead, but slumbering quietly
Like forms which sculptors carve, then love to agony.°

24

Famine had spared the palace of the king:—   4000
He rioted in festival the while,
He and his guards and priests; but Plague did fling
One shadow upon all. Famine can smile°
On him who brings it food and pass, with guile
Of thankful falsehood, like a courtier grey,
The house-dog of the throne; but many a mile
Comes Plague, a wingèd wolf, who loathes alway
The garbage and the scum that strangers make her prey.°

25

So, near the throne, amid the gorgeous feast,
Sheathed in resplendent arms, or loosely dight°   4010
To luxury, ere the mockery yet had ceased
That lingered on his lips, the warrior's might
Was loosened, and a new and ghastlier night
In dreams of frenzy lapped his eyes; he fell
Headlong, or with stiff eyeballs sate upright
Among the guests, or raving mad, did tell
Strange truths; a dying seer of dark oppression's hell.

26

The Princes and the Priests were pale with terror;
That monstrous faith wherewith they ruled mankind,
Fell, like a shaft loosed by the bowman's error,   4020
On their own hearts: they sought and they could find
No refuge—'twas the blind who led the blind!
So, through the desolate streets to the high fane
Of their Almighty God, the armies wind°
In sad procession: each among the train
To his own Idol lifts his supplications vain.

27

'O God!' they cried, 'we know our secret pride
Has scorned thee, and thy worship, and thy name;

Secure in human power we have defied
Thy fearful might; we bend in fear and shame   4030
Before thy presence; with the dust we claim
Kindred; be merciful, O King of Heaven!
Most justly have we suffered for thy fame
Made dim, but be at length our sins forgiven,
Ere to despair and death thy worshippers be driven.

28

'O God Almighty! thou alone hast power!°
Who can resist thy will? who can restrain
Thy wrath, when on the guilty thou dost shower
The shafts of thy revenge, a blistering rain?
Greatest and best, be merciful again!   4040
Have we not stabbed thine enemies, and made
The Earth an altar, and the Heavens a fane,
Where thou wert worshipped with their blood, and laid
Those hearts in dust which would thy searchless works
        have weighed?

29

'Well didst thou loosen on this impious City
Thine angels of revenge: recall them now;
Thy worshippers, abased, here kneel for pity,
And bind their souls by an immortal vow:
We swear by thee! and to our oath do thou
Give sanction, from thine hell of fiends and flame,   4050
That we will kill with fire and torments slow,
The last of those who mocked thy holy name,
And scorned the sacred laws thy prophets did proclaim.'

30

Thus they with trembling limbs and pallid lips
Worshipped their own hearts' image, dim and vast,°
Scared by the shade wherewith they would eclipse
The light of other minds;—troubled they passed
From the great Temple;—fiercely still and fast
The arrows of the plague among them fell,
And they on one another gazed aghast,   4060
And through the hosts contention wild befell,
As each of his own God the wondrous works did tell.°

31

And Oromaze, and Christ, and Mahomet,
Moses, and Buddh, Zerdusht, and Brahm, and Foh,°
A tumult of strange names, which never met
Before, as watchwords of a single woe,
Arose; each raging votary 'gan to throw
Aloft his armèd hands, and each did howl
'Our God alone is God!' and slaughter now
Would have gone forth, when from beneath a cowl   4070
A voice came forth, which pierced like ice through every soul.

32

He was a Christian Priest from whom it came,°
A zealous man, who led the legioned west
With words which faith and pride had steeped in flame,
To quell the rebel Atheists; a dire guest
Even to his friends was he, for in his breast
Did hate and guile lie watchful, intertwined,
Twin serpents in one deep and winding nest;
He loathed all faith beside his own, and pined
To wreak his fear of God in vengeance on mankind.   4080

33

But more he loathed and hated the clear light
Of wisdom and free thought, and more did fear,
Lest, kindled once, its beams might pierce the night,
Even where his Idol stood; for, far and near
Did many a heart in Europe leap to hear
That faith and tyranny were trampled down;
Many a pale victim, doomed for truth to share
The murderer's cell, or see, with helpless groan,
The priests his children drag for slaves to serve their own.

34

He dared not kill the infidels with fire   4090
Or steel, in Europe: the slow agonies
Of legal torture mocked his keen desire:
So he made truce with those who did despise
His cradled Idol, and the sacrifice
Of God to God's own wrath,—that Islam's creed°
Might crush for him those deadlier enemies;

For fear of God did in his bosom breed
A jealous hate of man, an unreposing need.

35

'Peace! Peace!' he cried, 'when we are dead, the Day
Of Judgement comes, and all shall surely know   4100
Whose God is God, each fearfully shall pay
The errors of his faith in endless woe!
But there is sent a mortal vengeance now
On earth, because an impious race had spurned
Him whom we all adore,—a subtle foe,
By whom for ye this dread reward was earned,
And thrones, which rest on faith in God, nigh overturned.°

36

'Think ye, because ye weep, and kneel, and pray,
That God will lull the pestilence? it rose
Even from beneath his throne, where, many a day   4110
His mercy soothed it to a dark repose:
It walks upon the earth to judge his foes,
And what are thou and I, that he should deign
To curb his ghastly minister, or close
The gates of death, ere they receive the twain°
Who shook with mortal spells his undefended reign?

37

'Aye, there is famine in the gulf of hell,
Its giant worms of fire for ever yawn,—
Their lurid eyes are on us! those who fell
By the swift shafts of pestilence ere dawn,   4120
Are in their jaws! they hunger for the spawn
Of Satan, their own brethren, who were sent
To make our souls their spoil. See! See! they fawn
Like dogs, and they will sleep with luxury spent,
When those detested hearts their iron fangs have rent!

38

'Our God may then lull Pestilence to sleep:—
Pile high the pyre of expiation now!
A forest's spoil of boughs, and on the heap
Pour venomous gums, which sullenly and slow,

When touched by flame, shall burn, and melt, and flow,   4130
A stream of clinging fire,—and fix on high
A net of iron, and spread forth below
A couch of snakes, and scorpions, and the fry
Of centipedes and worms, earth's hellish progeny!

39

'Let Laon and Laone on that pyre,
Linked tight with burning brass, perish!—then pray
That, with this sacrifice, the withering ire
Of God may be appeased.' He ceased, and they°
A space stood silent, as far, far away
The echoes of his voice among them died;   4140
And he knelt down upon the dust, alway
Muttering the curses of his speechless pride,°
Whilst shame, and fear, and awe, the armies did divide.

From *Canto Twelfth*

25

'When the consuming flames had wrapped ye round,°
The hope which I had cherished went away;
I fell in agony on the senseless ground,
And hid mine eyes in dust, and far astray
My mind was gone, when bright, like dawning day,   4670
The Spectre of the Plague before me flew,
And breathed upon my lips, and seemed to say,
'They wait for thee, beloved;'—then I knew
The death-mark on my breast, and became calm anew.°

26

'It was the calm of love—for I was dying.
I saw the black and half-extinguished pyre
In its own grey and shrunken ashes lying;
The pitchy smoke of the departed fire
Still hung in many a hollow dome and spire
Above the towers like night; beneath whose shade   4680
Awed by the ending of their own desire
The armies stood; a vacancy was made
In expectation's depth, and so they stood dismayed.

27

'The frightful silence of that altered mood,
The tortures of the dying clove alone,
Till one uprose among the multitude,
And said—"The flood of time is rolling on,
We stand upon its brink, whilst *they* are gone
To glide in peace down death's mysterious stream.
Have ye done well? they moulder flesh and bone,   4690
Who might have made this life's envenomed dream
A sweeter draught than ye will ever taste, I deem.

28

'"These perish as the good and great of yore
Have perished, and their murderers will repent,
Yes, vain and barren tears shall flow before
Yon smoke has faded from the firmament
Even for this cause, that ye who must lament
The death of those that made this world so fair,
Cannot recall them now; but then is lent
To man the wisdom of a high despair,   4700
When such can die, and he live on and linger here.

29

'"Ay, ye may fear not now the Pestilence,
From fabled hell as by a charm withdrawn;
All power and faith must pass, since calmly hence
In torment and in fire have Atheists gone;°
And ye must sadly turn away, and mourn
In secret, to his home each one returning,
And to long ages shall this hour be known;
And slowly shall its memory, ever burning,
Fill this dark night of things with an eternal morning.   4710

30

'"For me the world is grown too void and cold,
Since hope pursues immortal destiny
With steps thus slow—therefore shall ye behold
How Atheists and Republicans can die—°
Tell to your children this!" then suddenly
He sheathed a dagger in his heart and fell;
My brain grew dark in death, and yet to me

There came a murmur from the crowd, to tell
Of deep and mighty change which suddenly befell.

31

'Then suddenly I stood, a wingèd Thought,   4720
Before the immortal Senate, and the seat
Of that star-shining spirit, whence is wrought
The strength of its dominion, good and great,
The better Genius of this world's estate.
His realm around one mighty Fane is spread,
Elysian islands bright and fortunate,
Calm dwellings of the free and happy dead,
Where I am sent to lead!' these wingèd words she said,

32

And with the silence of her eloquent smile,
Bade us embark in her divine canoe;   4730
Then at the helm we took our seat, the while
Above her head those plumes of dazzling hue
Into the winds' invisible stream she threw,
Sitting beside the prow: like gossamer,
On the swift breath of morn, the vessel flew
O'er the bright whirlpools of that fountain fair,
Whose shores receded fast, whilst we seemed lingering there;

33

Till down that mighty stream, dark, calm, and fleet,
Between a chasm of cedarn mountains riven,°
Chased by the thronging winds whose viewless feet,   4740
As swift as twinkling beams, had, under Heaven,
From woods and waves wild sounds and odours driven,
The boat fled visibly—three nights and days,
Borne like a cloud through morn, and noon, and even,
We sailed along the winding watery ways
Of the vast stream, a long and labyrinthine maze.

34

A scene of joy and wonder to behold
That river's shapes and shadows changing ever,
Where the broad sunrise filled with deepening gold
Its whirlpools, where all hues did spread and quiver,   4750
And where melodious falls did burst and shiver

Among rocks clad with flowers, the foam and spray
Sparkled like stars upon the sunny river,
Or when the moonlight poured a holier day,
One vast and glittering lake around green islands lay.

35

Morn, noon, and even, that boat of pearl outran
The streams which bore it, like the arrowy cloud
Of tempest, or the speedier thought of man,
Which flieth forth and cannot make abode,
Sometimes through forests, deep like night, we glode,   4760
Between the walls of mighty mountains crowned
With Cyclopean piles, whose turrets proud,°
The homes of the departed, dimly frowned
O'er the bright waves which girt their dark foundations round.

36

Sometimes between the wide and flowering meadows,
Mile after mile we sailed, and 'twas delight
To see far off the sunbeams chase the shadows
Over the grass; sometimes beneath the night
Of wide and vaulted caves, whose roofs were bright
With starry gems, we fled, whilst from their deep   4770
And dark-green chasms, shades beautiful and white,
Amid sweet sounds across our path would sweep,
Like swift and lovely dreams that walk the waves of sleep.

37

And ever as we sailed, our minds were full
Of love and wisdom, which would overflow
In converse wild, and sweet, and wonderful;
And in quick smiles whose light would come and go,
Like music o'er wide waves, and in the flow
Of sudden tears, and in the mute caress—
For a deep shade was cleft, and we did know,   4780
That virtue, though obscured on Earth, not less
Survives all mortal change in lasting loveliness.

38

Three days and nights we sailed, as thought and feeling
Number delightful hours—for through the sky°

The spherèd lamps of day and night, revealing
New changes and new glories, rolled on high,
Sun, Moon, and moonlike lamps, the progeny
Of a diviner Heaven, serene and fair:
On the fourth day, wild as a wind-wrought sea
The stream became, and fast and faster bare   4790
The spirit-wingèd boat, steadily speeding there.

39

Steady and swift, where the waves rolled like mountains
Within the vast ravine, whose rifts did pour
Tumultuous floods from their ten thousand fountains,
The thunder of whose earth-uplifting roar
Made the air sweep in whirlwinds from the shore,
Calm as a shade, the boat of that fair child
Securely fled, that rapid stress before,
Amid the topmost spray, and sunbows wild,°
Wreathed in the silver mist: in joy and pride we smiled.   4800

40

The torrent of that wide and raging river
Is passed and our aerial speed suspended.
We look behind; a golden mist did quiver
When its wild surges with the lake were blended:
Our bark hung there, as on a line suspended°
Between two heavens, that windless waveless lake;
Which four great cataracts from four vales, attended
By mists, aye feed; from rocks and clouds they break,
And of that azure sea a silent refuge make.

41

Motionless resting on the lake awhile,   4810
I saw its marge of snow-bright mountains rear
Their peaks aloft, I saw each radiant isle,
And in the midst, afar, even like a sphere°
Hung in one hollow sky, did there appear
The Temple of the Spirit; on the sound
Which issued thence, drawn nearer and more near,
Like the swift moon this glorious earth around,
The charmèd boat approached, and there its haven found.°

Ozymandias

I met a traveller from an antique land
Who said—'Two vast and trunkless legs of stone
Stand in the desert. Near them, on the sand,
Half sunk, a shattered visage lies, whose frown,
And wrinkled lip, and sneer of cold command,
Tell that its sculptor well those passions read
Which yet survive, stamped on these lifeless things,
The hand that mocked them and the heart that fed;°
And on the pedestal these words appear:
"My name is Ozymandias, King of Kings: 10
Look on my Works, ye Mighty, and despair!"
Nothing beside remains. Round the decay
Of that colossal Wreck, boundless and bare
The lone and level sands stretch far away.'

Lines Written among the Euganean Hills
October, 1818

Many a green isle needs must be
In the deep wide sea of misery,°
Or the mariner, worn and wan,
Never thus could voyage on
Day and night, and night and day,
Drifting on his dreary way,
With the solid darkness black
Closing round his vessel's track;
Whilst above the sunless sky,
Big with clouds, hangs heavily,   10
And behind the tempest fleet
Hurries on with lightning feet,
Riving sail, and cord, and plank,
Till the ship has almost drank
Death from the o'er-brimming deep;
And sinks down, down, like that sleep
When the dreamer seems to be
Weltering through eternity;

And the dim low line before
Of a dark and distant shore 20
Still recedes, as ever still
Longing with divided will,
But no power to seek or shun,
He is ever drifted on
O'er the unreposing wave
To the haven of the grave.
What, if there no friends will greet;
What, if there no heart will meet
His with love's impatient beat;
Wander wheresoe'er he may, 30
Can he dream before that day
To find refuge from distress
In friendship's smile, in love's caress?
Then 'twill wreak him little woe°
Whether such there be or no:
Senseless is the breast, and cold,
Which relenting love would fold;
Bloodless are the veins and chill
Which the pulse of pain did fill;
Every little living nerve 40
That from bitter words did swerve
Round the tortured lips and brow,
Are like sapless leaflets now
Frozen upon December's bough.
On the beach of a northern sea
Which tempests shake eternally,
As once the wretch there lay to sleep,
Lies a solitary heap,
One white skull and seven dry bones,
On the margin of the stones, 50
Where a few grey rushes stand,
Boundaries of the sea and land:
Nor is heard one voice of wail
But the sea-mews, as they sail°
O'er the billows of the gale;
Or the whirlwind up and down
Howling, like a slaughtered town,
When a king in glory rides
Through the pomp of fratricides:

Those unburied bones around   60
There is many a mournful sound;
There is no lament for him,
Like a sunless vapour dim
Who once clothed with life and thought
What now moves nor murmurs not.°

Aye, many flowering islands lie
In the waters of wide Agony:
To such a one this morn was led,
My bark by soft winds piloted:
'Mid the mountains Euganean   70
I stood listening to the paean,
With which the legioned rooks did hail
The sun's uprise majestical;
Gathering round with wings all hoar,
Through the dewy mist they soar
Like grey shades, till th' eastern heaven
Bursts, and then, as clouds of even,
Flecked with fire and azure lie
In the unfathomable sky,
So their plumes of purple grain,   80
Starred with drops of golden rain,
Gleam above the sunlight woods,
As in silent multitudes
On the morning's fitful gale
Through the broken mist they sail,
And the vapours cloven and gleaming
Follow down the dark steep streaming,
Till all is bright, and clear, and still,
Round the solitary hill.

Beneath is spread like a green sea   90
The waveless plain of Lombardy,
Bounded by the vaporous air,
Islanded by cities fair;
Underneath day's azure eyes
Ocean's nursling, Venice lies,
A peopled labyrinth of walls,
Amphitrite's destined halls,°
Which her hoary sire now paves

With his blue and beaming waves.
Lo! the sun upsprings behind,   100
Broad, red, radiant, half reclined
On the level quivering line
Of the waters crystalline;
And before that chasm of light,
As within a furnace bright,
Column, tower, and dome, and spire,
Shine like obelisks of fire,
Pointing with inconstant motion
From the altar of dark ocean
To the sapphire-tinted skies;   110
As the flames of sacrifice
From the marble shrines did rise,
As to pierce the dome of gold
Where Apollo spoke of old.°

Sun-girt City, thou hast been
Ocean's child, and then his queen;
Now is come a darker day,°
And thou soon must be his prey,
If the power that raised thee here
Hallow so thy watery bier.   120
A less drear ruin then than now,
With thy conquest-branded brow
Stooping to the slave of slaves°
From thy throne, among the waves
Wilt thou be, when the sea-mew
Flies, as once before it flew,
O'er thine isles depopulate,
And all is in its ancient state,
Save where many a palace gate
With green sea-flowers overgrown   130
Like a rock of ocean's own,
Topples o'er the abandoned sea
As the tides change sullenly.
The fisher on his watery way,
Wandering at the close of day,
Will spread his sail and seize his oar
Till he pass the gloomy shore,
Lest thy dead should, from their sleep

Bursting o'er the starlight deep,
Lead a rapid masque of death   140
O'er the waters of his path.

Those who alone thy towers behold
Quivering through aerial gold,
As I now behold them here,
Would imagine not they were
Sepulchres, where human forms,
Like pollution-nourished worms
To the corpse of greatness cling,
Murdered, and now mouldering:
But if Freedom should awake   150
In her omnipotence, and shake
From the Celtic Anarch's hold°
All the keys of dungeons cold,
Where a hundred cities lie
Chained like thee, ingloriously,
Thou and all thy sister band
Might adorn this sunny land,
Twining memories of old time
With new virtues more sublime;
If not, perish thou and they,   160
Clouds which stain truth's rising day
By her sun consumed away,
Earth can spare ye: while like flowers,
In the waste of years and hours,
From your dust new nations spring
With more kindly blossoming.

Perish—let there only be
Floating o'er thy hearthless sea,
As the garment of the sky
Clothes the world immortally,   170
One remembrance, more sublime
Than the tattered pall of time,
Which scarce hides thy visage wan;—
That a tempest-cleaving Swan°
Of the songs of Albion,
Driven from his ancestral streams
By the might of evil dreams,°

Found a nest in thee; and Ocean
Welcomed him with such emotion
That its joy grew his, and sprung   180
From his lips like music flung
O'er a mighty thunder-fit,
Chastening terror:—what though yet°
Poesy's unfailing River,
Which through Albion winds forever,
Lashing with melodious wave
Many a sacred Poet's grave,
Mourn its latest nursling fled?
What though thou with all thy dead
Scarce can for this fame repay   190
Aught thine own—oh, rather say,
Though thy sins and slaveries foul
Overcloud a sunlike soul?
As the ghost of Homer clings
Round Scamander's wasting springs;°
As divinest Shakespeare's might
Fills Avon and the world with light
Like Omniscient power, which he
Imaged 'mid mortality;
As the love from Petrarch's urn°   200
Yet amid yon hills doth burn,
A quenchless lamp by which the heart
Sees things unearthly; so thou art,
Mighty Spirit—so shall be
The City that did refuge thee.

Lo, the sun floats up the sky
Like thought-wingèd Liberty,
Till the universal light
Seems to level plain and height;
From the sea a mist has spread,   210
And the beams of morn lie dead
On the towers of Venice now,
Like its glory long ago.
By the skirts of that grey cloud
Many-domèd Padua proud
Stands, a peopled solitude,
'Mid the harvest-shining plain,

Where the peasant heaps his grain
In the garner of his foe,°
And the milk-white oxen slow   220
With the purple vintage strain,
Heaped upon the creaking wain,
That the brutal Celt may swill
Drunken sleep with savage will;
And the sickle to the sword
Lies unchanged, though many a lord,
Like a weed whose shade is poison,
Overgrows this region's foison,°
Sheaves of whom are ripe to come
To destruction's harvest home: 230
Men must reap the things they sow,
Force from force must ever flow,
Or worse; but 'tis a bitter woe
That love or reason cannot change
The despot's rage, the slave's revenge.

Padua, thou within whose walls
Those mute guests at festivals,
Son and Mother, Death and Sin,
Played at dice for Ezzelin,
Till Death cried, 'I win, I win!'   240
And Sin cursed to lose the wager,
But Death promised, to assuage her,
That he would petition for
Her to be made Vice-Emperor,
When the destined years were o'er,
Over all between the Po
And the eastern Alpine snow,
Under the mighty Austrian.°
Sin smiled so as Sin only can,
And since that time, aye, long before,   250
Both have ruled from shore to shore,
That incestuous pair, who follow
Tyrants as the sun the swallow,
As Repentance follows Crime,
And as changes follow Time.

In thine halls the lamp of learning,
Padua, now no more is burning;°

Like a meteor, whose wild way°
Is lost over the grave of day,
It gleams betrayed and to betray: 260
Once remotest nations came
To adore that sacred flame,
When it lit not many a hearth
On this cold and gloomy earth:
Now new fires from antique light
Spring beneath the wide world's might;
But their spark lies dead in thee,
Trampled out by tyranny.
As the Norway woodman quells,
In the depth of piny dells,   270
One light flame among the brakes,
While the boundless forest shakes,
And its mighty trunks are torn
By the fire thus lowly born:
The spark beneath his feet is dead,
He starts to see the flames it fed
Howling through the darkened sky
With a myriad tongues victoriously,
And sinks down in fear: so thou,°
O tyranny, beholdest now   280
Light around thee, and thou hearest
The loud flames ascend, and fearest:
Grovel on the earth: aye, hide
In the dust thy purple pride!

Noon descends around me now:
'Tis the noon of autumn's glow,
When a soft and purple mist
Like a vaporous amethyst,
Or an air-dissolvèd star
Mingling light and fragrance, far   290
From the curved horizon's bound
To the point of heaven's profound,
Fills the overflowing sky;
And the plains that silent lie
Underneath, the leaves unsodden
Where the infant frost has trodden
With his morning-wingèd feet,

Whose bright print is gleaming yet;
And the red and golden vines,
Piercing with their trellised lines   300
The rough, dark-skirted wilderness;
The dun and bladed grass no less,
Pointing from this hoary tower
In the windless air; the flower
Glimmering at my feet; the line
Of the olive-sandalled Apennine
In the south dimly islanded;
And the Alps, whose snows are spread
High between the clouds and sun;
And of living things each one;   310
And my spirit which so long
Darkened this swift stream of song,
Interpenetrated lie
By the glory of the sky:
Be it love, light, harmony,
Odour, or the soul of all
Which from heaven like dew doth fall,
Or the mind which feeds this verse
Peopling the lone universe.

Noon descends, and after noon   320
Autumn's evening meets me soon,
Leading the infantine moon,
And that one star, which to her°
Almost seems to minister
Half the crimson light she brings
From the sunset's radiant springs:
And the soft dreams of the morn
(Which like wingèd winds had borne
To that silent isle, which lies
'Mid remembered agonies,   330
The frail bark of this lone being)
Pass, to other sufferers fleeing,
And its ancient pilot, Pain,
Sits beside the helm again.

Other flowering isles must be
In the sea of life and agony:

Other spirits float and flee
O'er that gulf: even now, perhaps,
On some rock the wild wave wraps,
With folded wings they waiting sit   340
For my bark, to pilot it
To some calm and blooming cove,
Where for me, and those I love,
May a windless bower be built,
Far from passion, pain, and guilt,
In a dell 'mid lawny hills,
Which the wild sea-murmur fills,
And soft sunshine, and the sound
Of old forests echoing round,
And the light and smell divine   350
Of all flowers that breathe and shine:
We may live so happy there,
That the spirits of the air,
Envying us, may even entice
To our healing paradise
The polluting multitude;°
But their rage would be subdued
By that clime divine and calm,
And the winds whose wings rain balm
On the uplifted soul, and leaves   360
Under which the bright sea heaves;°
While each breathless interval
In their whisperings musical
The inspirèd soul supplies
With its own deep melodies,
And the love which heals all strife
Circling, like the breath of life,
All things in that sweet abode
With its own mild brotherhood:
They, not it, would change; and soon   370
Every sprite beneath the moon°
Would repent its envy vain,
And the earth grow young again.°

The Two Spirits—An Allegory

First Spirit

O Thou who plumed with strong desire°
Would float above the Earth—beware!
A shadow tracks thy flight of fire—°
      Night is coming.
Bright are the regions of the air
And when winds and beams [   ]°
It were delight to wander there—
      Night is coming!

Second Spirit

The deathless stars are bright above
If I should cross the shade of night. —°   10
Within my heart is the lamp of love
      And that is day—
And the moon will smile with gentle light
On my golden plumes where'er they move;
The meteors will linger around my flight
      And make night day.

First Spirit

But if the whirlwinds of darkness waken
Eclipse and Lightning and stormy rain—°
See, the bounds of the air are shaken,
      Night is coming.   20
And swift the clouds of the hurricane°
Yon declining sun have overtaken,
The clash of the hail sweeps o'er the plain—
      Night is coming.

Second Spirit

I see the glare and I hear the sound;
I'll sail on the flood of the tempest dark
With the calm within and light around
      Which makes night day;
And thou, when the gloom is deep and stark,
Look from thy dull earth slumberbound—   30
My moonlike flight thou then may'st mark
      On high, far away.

Some say there is a precipice
Where one vast pine hangs frozen to ruin
O'er piles of snow and chasms of ice
      Mid Alpine mountains;
And that the languid storm pursuing°
That wingèd shape forever flies
Round those hoar branches, aye renewing
      Its aery fountains.   40

Some say when the nights are dry and clear
And the death-dews sleep on the morass,
Sweet whispers are heard by the traveller
      Which make night day—
And a shape like his early love doth pass
Upborne by her wild and glittering hair,
And when he awakes on the fragrant grass
      He finds night day.

Stanzas Written in Dejection— December 1818, near Naples

The Sun is warm, the sky is clear,
The waves are dancing fast and bright,
Blue isles and snowy mountains wear
The purple noon's transparent might,
The breath of the moist earth is light
Around its unexpanded buds;
Like many a voice of one delight
The winds, the birds, the Ocean-floods;
The City's voice itself is soft, like Solitude's.

I see the Deep's untrampled floor°   10
With green and purple seaweeds strown,
I see the waves upon the shore°
Like light dissolved in star-showers, thrown;
I sit upon the sands alone;
The lightning of the noontide Ocean
Is flashing round me, and a tone

Arises from its measured motion,
How sweet! did any heart now share in my emotion.

Alas, I have nor hope nor health,
Nor peace within nor calm around,   20
Nor that content surpassing wealth
The sage in meditation found,°
And walked with inward glory crowned;
Nor fame nor power nor love nor leisure—
Others I see whom these surround,
Smiling they live and call life pleasure:
To me that cup has been dealt in another measure.°

Yet now despair itself is mild
Even as the winds and waters are;
I could lie down like a tired child   30
And weep away the life of care
Which I have borne and yet must bear,
Till Death like Sleep might steal on me,
And I might feel in the warm air
My cheek grow cold, and hear the sea
Breathe o'er my dying brain its last monotony.

Some might lament that I were cold,
As I, when this sweet day is gone,
Which my lost heart, too soon grown old,
Insults with this untimely moan—°   40
They might lament,—for I am one
Whom men love not, and yet regret;
Unlike this Day, which, when the Sun
Shall on its stainless glory set,
Will linger though enjoyed, like joy in Memory yet.

Sonnet ('*Lift not the painted veil*')

Lift not the painted veil which those who live°
Call Life; though unreal shapes be pictured there,
And it but mimic all we would believe
With colours idly spread,—behind, lurk Fear

And Hope, twin Destinies, who ever weave
Their shadows o'er the chasm, sightless and drear.°

I knew one who had lifted it . . . he sought,
For his lost heart was tender, things to love
But found them not, alas; nor was there aught
The world contains, the which he could approve.   10
Through the unheeding many he did move,
A splendour among shadows, a bright blot
Upon this gloomy world, a Spirit that strove°
For truth, and like the Preacher, found it not.°

JULIAN AND MADDALO

A CONVERSATION

The meadows with fresh streams, the bees with thyme,
The goats with the green leaves of budding spring,
Are saturated not—nor Love with tears.

Virgil's Gallus°

[PREFACE]

Count Maddalo is a Venetian nobleman of ancient family and of great
fortune, who, without mixing much in the society of his countrymen,
resides chiefly at his magnificent palace in that city. He is a person
of the most consummate genius; and capable, if he would direct his
energies to such an end, of becoming the redeemer of his degraded
country. But it is his weakness to be proud: he derives, from a com-
parison of his own extraordinary mind with the dwarfish intellects
that surround him, an intense apprehension of the nothingness of
human life. His passions and his powers are incomparably greater than
those of other men, and instead of the latter having been employed in
curbing the former, they have mutually lent each other strength. His
ambition preys upon itself, for want of objects which it can consider
worthy of exertion. I say that Maddalo is proud, because I can find no
other word to express the concentered° and impatient feelings which
consume him; but it is on his own hopes and affections only that he
seems to trample, for in social life no human being can be more gentle,
patient, and unassuming than Maddalo. He is cheerful, frank, and
witty. His more serious conversation is a sort of intoxication; men are
held by it as by a spell. He has travelled much; and there is an inexpres-
sible charm in his relation of his adventures in different countries.°

Julian is an Englishman of good family, passionately attached to
those philosophical notions which assert the power of man over his
own mind, and the immense improvements of which, by the extinc-
tion of certain moral superstitions, human society may be yet sus-
ceptible. Without concealing the evil in the world, he is for ever
speculating how good may be made superior. He is a complete infidel,
and a scoffer at all things reputed holy; and Maddalo takes a wicked
pleasure in drawing out his taunts against religion. What Maddalo
thinks on these matters is not exactly known. Julian, in spite of his

heterodox opinions, is conjectured by his friends to possess some good qualities. How far this is possible, the pious reader will determine. Julian is rather serious.°

Of the Maniac° I can give no information. He seems by his own account to have been disappointed in love. He was evidently a very cultivated and amiable person when in his right senses. His story, told at length, might be like many other stories of the same kind: the unconnected exclamations of his agony will perhaps be found a sufficient comment for the text of every heart.

I rode one evening with Count Maddalo
Upon the bank of land which breaks the flow°
Of Adria towards Venice:—a bare strand°
Of hillocks, heaped from ever-shifting sand,
Matted with thistles and amphibious weeds,
Such as from earth's embrace the salt ooze breeds,
Is this;—an uninhabitable sea-side
Which the lone fisher, when his nets are dried,
Abandons; and no other object breaks
The waste, but one dwarf tree and some few stakes   10
Broken and unrepaired, and the tide makes
A narrow space of level sand thereon,
Where 'twas our wont to ride while day went down.
This ride was my delight.—I love all waste
And solitary places; where we taste
The pleasure of believing what we see
Is boundless, as we wish our souls to be:°
And such was this wide ocean, and this shore
More barren than its billows;—and yet more
Than all, with a remembered friend I love   20
To ride as then I rode;—for the winds drove
The living spray along the sunny air
Into our faces; the blue heavens were bare,°
Stripped to their depths by the awakening North,
And from the waves, sound like delight broke forth°
Harmonizing with solitude, and sent
Into our hearts aerial merriment.
So, as we rode, we talked; and the swift thought,
Winging itself with laughter, lingered not
But flew from brain to brain,—such glee was ours—   30
Charged with light memories of remembered hours,

None slow enough for sadness; till we came
Homeward, which always makes the spirit tame.
This day had been cheerful but cold, and now
The sun was sinking, and the wind also.
Our talk grew somewhat serious, as may be
Talk interrupted with such raillery
As mocks itself, because it cannot scorn
The thoughts it would extinguish:—'twas forlorn
Yet pleasing, such as once, so poets tell,   40
The devils held within the dales of Hell
Concerning God, freewill and destiny:
Of all that earth has been or yet may be,
All that vain men imagine or believe,
Or hope can paint or suffering may achieve,°
We descanted, and I (for ever still°
Is it not wise to make the best of ill?)
Argued against despondency, but pride
Made my companion take the darker side.
The sense that he was greater than his kind   50
Had struck, methinks, his eagle spirit blind
By gazing on its own exceeding light.
—Meanwhile the sun paused ere it should alight,
Over the horizon of the mountains;—Oh,
How beautiful is sunset, when the glow
Of Heaven descends upon a land like thee,
Thou Paradise of exiles, Italy!
Thy mountains, seas and vineyards and the towers
Of cities they encircle!—it was ours
To stand on thee, beholding it; and then   60
Just where we had dismounted, the Count's men
Were waiting for us with the gondola.—
As those who pause on some delightful way
Though bent on pleasant pilgrimage, we stood°
Looking upon the evening and the flood
Which lay between the city and the shore
Paved with the image of the sky . . . the hoar°
And aery Alps towards the North appeared
Through mist, an heaven-sustaining bulwark reared
Between the East and West; and half the sky   70
Was roofed with clouds of rich emblazonry
Dark purple at the zenith, which still grew

Down the steep West into a wondrous hue
Brighter than burning gold, even to the rent
Where the swift sun yet paused in his descent
Among the many-folded hills: they were
Those famous Euganean hills, which bear
As seen from Lido through the harbour piles
The likeness of a clump of peakèd isles—
And then—as if the Earth and Sea had been   80
Dissolved into one lake of fire, were seen
Those mountains towering as from waves of flame
Around the vaporous sun, from which there came
The inmost purple spirit of light, and made
Their very peaks transparent. 'Ere it fade,'
Said my companion, 'I will show you soon
A better station'—so, o'er the lagoon
We glided, and from that funereal bark
I leaned, and saw the city, and could mark
How from their many isles in evening's gleam   90
Its temples and its palaces did seem
Like fabrics of enchantment piled to Heaven.°
I was about to speak, when—'We are even
Now at the point I meant,' said Maddalo,
And bade the gondolieri cease to row.°
'Look, Julian, on the West, and listen well
If you hear not a deep and heavy bell.'
I looked, and saw between us and the sun
A building on an island; such a one
As age to age might add, for uses vile,   100
A windowless, deformed and dreary pile,
And on the top an open tower, where hung
A bell, which in the radiance swayed and swung.
We could just hear its hoarse and iron tongue.°
The broad sun sunk behind it, and it tolled
In strong and black relief.—'What we behold
Shall be the madhouse and its belfry tower,'°
Said Maddalo, 'and ever at this hour
Those who may cross the water hear that bell
Which calls the maniacs each one from his cell   110
To vespers.'—'As much skill as need to pray
In thanks or hope for their dark lot have they
To their stern maker,' I replied. 'O ho!

You talk as in years past,' said Maddalo.
' 'Tis strange men change not. You were ever still
Among Christ's flock a perilous infidel,
A wolf for the meek lambs—if you can't swim
Beware of Providence.' I looked on him,°
But the gay smile had faded in his eye.
'And such,'—he cried, 'is our mortality   120
And this must be the emblem and the sign
Of what should be eternal and divine!—
And like that black and dreary bell, the soul,
Hung in a heaven-illumined tower, must toll
Our thoughts and our desires to meet below
Round the rent heart and pray—as madmen do
For what? they know not, till the night of death
As sunset that strange vision, severeth
Our memory from itself, and us from all
We sought and yet were baffled!' I recall   130
The sense of what he said, although I mar
The force of his expressions. The broad star
Of day meanwhile had sunk behind the hill
And the black bell became invisible
And the red tower looked grey, and all between
The churches, ships and palaces were seen
Huddled in gloom;—into the purple sea
The orange hues of heaven sunk silently.
We hardly spoke, and soon the gondola
Conveyed me to my lodgings by the way.   140

    The following morn was rainy, cold and dim.
Ere Maddalo arose, I called on him,
And whilst I waited with his child I played.°
A lovelier toy sweet Nature never made,
A serious, subtle, wild, yet gentle being,
Graceful without design and unforeseeing,
With eyes—oh speak not of her eyes!—which seem
Twin mirrors of Italian Heaven, yet gleam
With such deep meaning, as we never see
But in the human countenance: with me   150
She was a special favourite. I had nursed
Her fine and feeble limbs when she came first
To this bleak world; and she yet seemed to know

On second sight her ancient playfellow,
Less changed than she was by six months or so;
For after her first shyness was worn out
We sate there, rolling billiard balls about.
When the Count entered—salutations past—
'The words you spoke last night might well have cast
A darkness on my spirit—if man be   160
The passive thing you say, I should not see
Much harm in the religions and old saws°
(Though I may never own such leaden laws)
Which break a teachless nature to the yoke:°
Mine is another faith'—thus much I spoke,
And noting he replied not, added: 'See
This lovely child, blithe, innocent and free;
She spends a happy time with little care
While we to such sick thoughts subjected are
As came on you last night—it is our will   170
That thus enchains us to permitted ill—
We might be otherwise—we might be all
We dream of happy, high, majestical.
Where is the love, beauty and truth we seek
But in our mind? and if we were not weak
Should we be less in deed than in desire?'
'Aye, if we were not weak—and we aspire
How vainly to be strong!' said Maddalo;
'You talk Utopia.' 'It remains to know,'
I then rejoined, 'and those who try may find   180
How strong the chains are which our spirits bind—
Brittle perchance as straw . . . We are assured
Much may be conquered, much may be endured
Of what degrades and crushes us. We know
That we have power over ourselves to do
And suffer—what, we know not till we try;
But something nobler than to live and die—
So taught those kings of old philosophy
Who reigned, before Religion made men blind;°
And those who suffer with their suffering kind   190
Yet feel their faith, religion.' 'My dear friend,'°
Said Maddalo, 'my judgement will not bend
To your opinion, though I think you might
Make such a system refutation-tight

As far as words go. I knew one like you
Who to this city came some months ago
With whom I argued in this sort, and he
Is now gone mad,—and so he answered me.
Poor fellow! but if you would like to go
We'll visit him, and his wild talk will show   200
How vain are such aspiring theories.'
'I hope to prove the induction otherwise,
And that a want of that true theory, still
Which seeks a "soul of goodness" in things ill°
Or in himself or others has thus bowed
His being—there are some by nature proud,
Who patient in all else demand but this:
To love and be beloved with gentleness;
And being scorned, what wonder if they die
Some living death? this is not destiny   210
But man's own wilful ill.' As thus I spoke°
Servants announced the gondola, and we
Through the fast-falling rain and high-wrought sea
Sailed to the island where the madhouse stands.
We disembarked. The clap of tortured hands,
Fierce yells and howlings and lamentings keen,
And laughter where complaint had merrier been,
Moans, shrieks and curses and blaspheming prayers
Accosted us. We climbed the oozy stairs
Into an old courtyard. I heard on high,   220
Then, fragments of most touching melody
But looking up saw not the singer there—
Through the black bars in the tempestuous air
I saw, like weeds on a wrecked palace growing,
Long tangled locks flung wildly forth, and flowing,
Of those who on a sudden were beguiled
Into strange silence, and looked forth and smiled
Hearing sweet sounds.—Then I: 'Methinks there were
A cure of these with patience and kind care
If music can thus move . . . but what is he   230
Whom we seek here?' 'Of his sad history
I know but this,' said Maddalo: 'he came
To Venice a dejected man, and fame
Said he was wealthy, or he had been so:
Some thought the loss of fortune wrought him woe;

But he was ever talking in such sort
As you do—far more sadly—he seemed hurt,
Even as a man with his peculiar wrong,
To hear but of the oppression of the strong,
Or those absurd deceits (I think with you   240
In some respects, you know) which carry through
The excellent impostors of this earth
When they outface detection—he had worth,
Poor fellow! but a humourist in his way'—°
'Alas, what drove him mad?' 'I cannot say;
A lady came with him from France, and when
She left him and returned, he wandered then
About yon lonely isles of desert sand
Till he grew wild—he had no cash or land
Remaining,—the police had brought him here—   250
Some fancy took him and he would not bear
Removal; so I fitted up for him
Those rooms beside the sea, to please his whim
And sent him busts and books and urns for flowers
Which had adorned his life in happier hours,
And instruments of music—you may guess
A stranger could do little more or less
For one so gentle and unfortunate,
And those are his sweet strains which charm the weight
From madmen's chains, and made this Hell appear   260
A heaven of sacred silence, hushed to hear.'—
'Nay, this was kind of you—he had no claim
As the world says'—'None—but the very same
Which I on all mankind were I as he
Fallen to such deep reverse;—his melody°
Is interrupted now—we hear the din
Of madmen, shriek on shriek again begin;
Let us now visit him; after this strain
He ever communes with himself again,
And sees nor hears not any.' Having said   270
These words we called the keeper, and he led
To an apartment opening on the sea.—
There the poor wretch was sitting mournfully
Near a piano, his pale fingers twined
One with the other, and the ooze and wind
Rushed through an open casement, and did sway

His hair, and starred it with the brackish spray;
His head was leaning on a music book,
And he was muttering, and his lean limbs shook.
His lips were pressed against a folded leaf   280
In hue too beautiful for health, and grief
Smiled in their motions as they lay apart—°
As one who wrought from his own fervid heart
The eloquence of passion, soon he raised
His sad meek face and eyes lustrous and glazed
And spoke—sometimes as one who wrote and thought
His words might move some heart that heeded not
If sent to distant lands: and then as one
Reproaching deeds never to be undone
With wondering self-compassion; then his speech   290
Was lost in grief, and then his words came each
Unmodulated, cold, expressionless;
But that from one jarred accent you might guess
It was despair made them so uniform:
And all the while the loud and gusty storm
Hissed through the window, and we stood behind
Stealing his accents from the envious wind
Unseen. I yet remember what he said
Distinctly: such impression his words made.

      'Month after month,' he cried, 'to bear this load   300
And as a jade urged by the whip and goad°
To drag life on, which like a heavy chain
Lengthens behind with many a link of pain!—
And not to speak my grief—O not to dare
To give a human voice to my despair
But live and move, and wretched thing! smile on
As if I never went aside to groan
And wear this mask of falsehood even to those
Who are most dear—not for my own repose—
Alas, no scorn or pain or hate could be   310
So heavy as that falsehood is to me—
But that I cannot bear more altered faces
Than needs must be, more changed and cold embraces,
More misery, disappointment and mistrust
To own me for their father . . . Would the dust
Were covered in upon my body now!

That the life ceased to toil within my brow!
And then these thoughts would at the least be fled;
Let us not fear such pain can vex the dead.

'What Power delights to torture us? I know   320
That to myself I do not wholly owe
What now I suffer, though in part I may.
Alas, none strewed sweet flowers upon the way
Where wandering heedlessly, I met pale Pain,
My shadow, which will leave me not again—
If I have erred, there was no joy in error,
But pain and insult and unrest and terror;
I have not as some do, bought penitence
With pleasure, and a dark yet sweet offence,
For then,—if love and tenderness and truth   330
Had overlived hope's momentary youth,
My creed should have redeemed me from repenting,
But loathèd scorn and outrage unrelenting
Met love excited by far other seeming
Until the end was gained . . . as one from dreaming
Of sweetest peace, I woke, and found my state
Such as it is.—
                    'O Thou, my spirit's mate°
Who, for thou art compassionate and wise,
Wouldst pity me from thy most gentle eyes
If this sad writing thou shouldst ever see—   340
My secret groans must be unheard by thee,
Thou wouldst weep tears bitter as blood to know
Thy lost friend's incommunicable woe.

'Ye few by whom my nature has been weighed
In friendship, let me not that name degrade
By placing on your hearts the secret load
Which crushes mine to dust. There is one road
To peace and that is truth, which follow ye!
Love sometimes leads astray to misery.
Yet think not though subdued—and I may well°   350
Say that I am subdued—that the full Hell
Within me would infect the untainted breast
Of sacred nature with its own unrest;
As some perverted beings think to find

In scorn or hate a medicine for the mind
Which scorn or hate have wounded—O how vain!
The dagger heals not but may rend again . . .
Believe that I am ever still the same
In creed as in resolve, and what may tame
My heart, must leave the understanding free   360
Or all would sink in this keen agony—
Nor dream that I will join the vulgar cry,
Or with my silence sanction tyranny,
Or seek a moment's shelter from my pain
In any madness which the world calls gain,
Ambition or revenge or thoughts as stern
As those which make me what I am, or turn
To avarice or misanthropy or lust . . .
Heap on me soon, O grave, thy welcome dust!
Till then the dungeon may demand its prey,   370
And poverty and shame may meet and say—
Halting beside me on the public way—
"That love-devoted youth is ours—let's sit
Beside him—he may live some six months yet."
Or the red scaffold, as our country bends,°
May ask some willing victim, or ye friends
May fall under some sorrow which this heart
Or hand may share or vanquish or avert;
I am prepared: in truth with no proud joy
To do or suffer aught, as when a boy   380
I did devote to justice and to love
My nature, worthless now! . . .
                              'I must remove
A veil from my pent mind. 'Tis torn aside!
O, pallid as death's dedicated bride,°
Thou mockery which art sitting by my side,
Am I not wan like thee? at the grave's call
I haste, invited to thy wedding-ball
To greet the ghastly paramour, for whom
Thou hast deserted me . . . and made the tomb
Thy bridal bed . . . But I beside your feet   390
Will lie and watch ye from my winding sheet—
Thus . . . wide awake, though dead . . . yet stay, O stay!
Go not so soon—I know not what I say—
Hear but my reasons . . . I am mad, I fear,

My fancy is o'erwrought . . . thou art not here . . .
Pale art thou, 'tis most true . . . but thou art gone,
Thy work is finished . . . I am left alone!—°

    *   *   *   *   *   *   *

  'Nay, was it I who wooed thee to this breast
Which, like a serpent, thou envenomest
As in repayment of the warmth it lent?   400
Didst thou not seek me for thine own content?
Did not thy love awaken mine? I thought
That thou wert she who said, "You kiss me not
Ever, I fear you cease to love me now"—
In truth I loved even to my overthrow°
Her, who would fain forget these words: but they
Cling to her mind, and cannot pass away.

    *   *   *   *   *   *   *

  'You say that I am proud—that when I speak
My lip is tortured with the wrongs which break
The spirit it expresses . . . Never one   410
Humbled himself before, as I have done!
Even the instinctive worm on which we tread
Turns, though it wound not—then with prostrate head
Sinks in the dust and writhes like me—and dies?
No: wears a living death of agonies!
As the slow shadows of the pointed grass
Mark the eternal periods, his pangs pass
Slow, ever-moving,—making moments be°
As mine seem—each an immortality!

    *   *   *   *   *   *   *

  'That you had never seen me—never heard   420
My voice, and more than all had ne'er endured
The deep pollution of my loathed embrace—
That your eyes ne'er had lied love in my face—
That, like some maniac monk, I had torn out
The nerves of manhood by their bleeding root
With mine own quivering fingers, so that ne'er
Our hearts had for a moment mingled there
To disunite in horror—these were not
With thee, like some suppressed and hideous thought
Which flits athwart our musings, but can find   430

No rest within a pure and gentle mind . . .
Thou sealedst them with many a bare broad word
And cearedst my memory o'er them—for I heard°
And can forget not . . . they were ministered
One after one, those curses. Mix them up
Like self-destroying poisons in one cup,
And they will make one blessing which thou ne'er
Didst imprecate for, on me,—death.

     *   *   *   *   *   *

                           'It were
A cruel punishment for one most cruel,
If such can love, to make that love the fuel   440
Of the mind's hell; hate, scorn, remorse, despair:
But *me*—whose heart a stranger's tear might wear
As water-drops the sandy fountain-stone,
Who loved and pitied all things, and could moan
For woes which others hear not, and could see
The absent with the glance of fantasy,
And with the poor and trampled sit and weep,
Following the captive to his dungeon deep;
Me—who am as a nerve o'er which do creep
The else unfelt oppressions of this earth°   450
And was to thee the flame upon thy hearth
When all beside was cold—that thou on me
Shouldst rain these plagues of blistering agony—
Such curses are from lips once eloquent
With love's too partial praise—let none relent
Who intend deeds too dreadful for a name
Henceforth, if an example for the same
They seek . . . for thou on me lookedst so, and so—
And didst speak thus . . . and thus . . . I live to show
How much men bear and die not!

     *   *   *   *   *   *   *

                        'Thou wilt tell   460
With the grimace of hate how horrible
It was to meet my love when thine grew less;
Thou wilt admire how I could e'er address
Such features to love's work . . . this taunt, though true,
(For indeed nature nor in form nor hue
Bestowed on me her choicest workmanship)

Shall not be thy defence . . . for since thy lip
Met mine first, years long past, since thine eye kindled
With soft fire under mine, I have not dwindled
Nor changed in mind or body, or in aught   470
But as love changes what it loveth not
After long years and many trials.

                          'How vain
Are words! I thought never to speak again,
Not even in secret,—not to my own heart—
But from my lips the unwilling accents start
And from my pen the words flow as I write,°
Dazzling my eyes with scalding tears . . . my sight
Is dim to see that charactered in vain
On this unfeeling leaf which burns the brain
And eats into it . . . blotting all things fair   480
And wise and good which time had written there.

   'Those who inflict must suffer, for they see
The work of their own hearts and this must be
Our chastisement or recompense—O child!
I would that thine were like to be more mild
For both our wretched sakes . . . for thine the most
Who feelest already all that thou hast lost
Without the power to wish it thine again;
And as slow years pass, a funereal train
Each with the ghost of some lost hope or friend   490
Following it like its shadow, wilt thou bend
No thought on my dead memory?

      *   *   *   *   *   *
                         'Alas, love,
Fear me not . . . against thee I would not move
A finger in despite. Do I not live
That thou mayst have less bitter cause to grieve?
I give thee tears for scorn and love for hate,
And that thy lot may be less desolate
Than his on whom thou tramplest, I refrain
From that sweet sleep which medicines all pain.°
Then, when thou speakest of me, never say   500
"He could forgive not." Here I cast away

All human passions, all revenge, all pride;
I think, speak, act no ill; I do but hide
Under these words like embers, every spark
Of that which has consumed me—quick and dark
The grave is yawning . . . as its roof shall cover
My limbs with dust and worms under and over
So let Oblivion hide this grief . . . the air
Closes upon my accents, as despair
Upon my heart—let death upon despair!'   510

   He ceased, and overcome leant back awhile,
Then rising, with a melancholy smile
Went to a sofa, and lay down, and slept
A heavy sleep, and in his dreams he wept
And muttered some familiar name, and we
Wept without shame in his society.
I think I never was impressed so much;
The man who were not must have lacked a touch
Of human nature . . . then we lingered not,
Although our argument was quite forgot,   520
But calling the attendants, went to dine
At Maddalo's; yet neither cheer nor wine
Could give us spirits, for we talked of him
And nothing else, till daylight made stars dim;
And we agreed his was some dreadful ill
Wrought on him boldly, yet unspeakable,
By a dear friend; some deadly change in love
Of one vowed deeply which he dreamed not of;
For whose sake he, it seemed, had fixed a blot
Of falsehood on his mind which flourished not   530
But in the light of all-beholding truth;
And having stamped this canker on his youth
She had abandoned him . . . and how much more
Might be his woe, we guessed not—he had store
Of friends and fortune once, as we could guess
From his nice habits and his gentleness;
These were now lost . . . it were a grief indeed
If he had changed one unsustaining reed
For all that such a man might else adorn.
The colours of his mind seemed yet unworn;   540
For the wild language of his grief was high

Such as in measure were called poetry;
And I remember one remark which then
Maddalo made. He said: 'Most wretched men
Are cradled into poetry by wrong;
They learn in suffering what they teach in song.'

    If I had been an unconnected man
I, from this moment, should have formed some plan
Never to leave sweet Venice,—for to me
It was delight to ride by the lone sea; 550
And then, the town is silent—one may write
Or read in gondolas by day or night,
Having the little brazen lamp alight,
Unseen, uninterrupted; books are there,
Pictures, and casts from all those statues fair
Which were twin-born with poetry, and all
We seek in towns, with little to recall
Regrets for the green country. I might sit
In Maddalo's great palace, and his wit
And subtle talk would cheer the winter night 560
And make me know myself, and the firelight
Would flash upon our faces, till the day
Might dawn and make me wonder at my stay:
But I had friends in London too: the chief
Attraction here, was that I sought relief
From the deep tenderness that maniac wrought
Within me—'twas perhaps an idle thought,
But I imagined that if day by day
I watched him, and but seldom went away,
And studied all the beatings of his heart 570
With zeal, as men study some stubborn art
For their own good, and could by patience find
An entrance to the caverns of his mind,
I might reclaim him from his dark estate:
In friendships I had been most fortunate—
Yet never saw I one whom I would call
More willingly my friend; and this was all
Accomplished not; such dreams of baseless good
Oft come and go in crowds and solitude
And leave no trace—but what I now designed 580
Made for long years impression on my mind.

The following morning urged by my affairs
I left bright Venice.

                    After many years
And many changes I returned; the name
Of Venice, and its aspect, was the same;
But Maddalo was travelling far away
Among the mountains of Armenia.
His dog was dead. His child had now become
A woman; such as it has been my doom
To meet with few, a wonder of this earth   590
Where there is little of transcendent worth,
Like one of Shakespeare's women: kindly she
And with a manner beyond courtesy
Received her father's friend; and when I asked
Of the lorn maniac, she her memory tasked
And told as she had heard the mournful tale:
'That the poor sufferer's health began to fail°
Two years from my departure, but that then
The Lady who had left him, came again.
Her mien had been imperious, but she now   600
Looked meek—perhaps remorse had brought her low.
Her coming made him better, and they stayed
Together at my father's—for I played
As I remember with the lady's shawl—
I might be six years old—but after all
She left him' . . . 'Why, her heart must have been tough:
How did it end?' 'And was not this enough?
They met—they parted'—'Child, is there no more?'
'Something within that interval which bore
The stamp of *why* they parted, *how* they met: 610
Yet if thine aged eyes disdain to wet
Those wrinkled cheeks with youth's remembered tears,
Ask me no more, but let the silent years
Be closed and ceared over their memory°
As yon mute marble where their corpses lie.'
I urged and questioned still, she told me how
All happened—but the cold world shall not know.

PROMETHEUS UNBOUND°

A LYRICAL DRAMA°

IN FOUR ACTS

Audisne haec, Amphiarae, sub terram abdite?°

PREFACE

The Greek tragic writers, in selecting as their subject any portion of
their national history or mythology, employed in their treatment of it
a certain arbitrary discretion. They by no means conceived themselves
bound to adhere to the common interpretation or to imitate in story
as in title their rivals and predecessors. Such a system would have
amounted to a resignation of those claims to preference over their
competitors which incited the composition. The Agamemnonian story
was exhibited on the Athenian theatre with as many variations as
dramas.

I have presumed to employ a similar licence. The *Prometheus
Unbound* of Aeschylus supposed the reconciliation of Jupiter with
his victim as the price of the disclosure of the danger threatened to his
empire by the consummation of his marriage with Thetis. Thetis,
according to this view of the subject, was given in marriage to Peleus,
and Prometheus, by the permission of Jupiter, delivered from his
captivity by Hercules.° Had I framed my story on this model, I should
have done no more than have attempted to restore the lost drama of
Aeschylus; an ambition which, if my preference to this mode of treat-
ing the subject had incited me to cherish, the recollection of the high
comparison such an attempt would challenge might well abate. But, in
truth, I was averse from a catastrophe so feeble as that of reconciling
the Champion with the Oppressor of mankind. The moral interest
of the fable, which is so powerfully sustained by the sufferings and
endurance of Prometheus, would be annihilated if we could conceive
of him as unsaying his high language and quailing before his successful
and perfidious adversary. The only imaginary being resembling in any
degree Prometheus is Satan; and Prometheus is, in my judgement, a
more poetical character than Satan, because, in addition to courage,
and majesty, and firm and patient opposition to omnipotent force, he is
susceptible of being described as exempt from the taints of ambition,

envy, revenge, and a desire for personal aggrandisement, which, in the Hero of *Paradise Lost*, interfere with the interest. The character of Satan engenders in the mind a pernicious casuistry which leads us to weigh his faults with his wrongs, and to excuse the former because the latter exceed all measure. In the minds of those who consider that magnificent fiction with a religious feeling it engenders something worse. But Prometheus is, as it were, the type of the highest perfection of moral and intellectual nature, impelled by the purest and the truest motives to the best and noblest ends.

This Poem was chiefly written upon the mountainous ruins of the Baths of Caracalla, among the flowery glades, and thickets of odoriferous blossoming trees, which are extended in ever widening labyrinths upon its immense platforms and dizzy arches suspended in the air. The bright blue sky of Rome, and the effect of the vigorous awakening of spring in that divinest climate, and the new life with which it drenches the spirits even to intoxication, were the inspiration of this drama.

The imagery which I have employed will be found, in many instances, to have been drawn from the operations of the human mind, or from those external actions by which they are expressed. This is unusual in modern poetry, although Dante and Shakespeare are full of instances of the same kind: Dante indeed more than any other poet, and with greater success. But the Greek poets, as writers to whom no resource of awakening the sympathy of their contemporaries was unknown, were in the habitual use of this power; and it is the study of their works (since a higher merit would probably be denied me) to which I am willing that my readers should impute this singularity.

One word is due° in candour to the degree in which the study of contemporary writings may have tinged my composition, for such has been a topic of censure with regard to poems far more popular, and indeed more deservedly popular, than mine. It is impossible that any one who inhabits the same age with such writers as those who stand in the foremost ranks of our own, can conscientiously assure himself that his language and tone of thought may not have been modified by the study of the productions of those extraordinary intellects. It is true that, not the spirit of their genius, but the forms in which it has manifested itself, are due less to the peculiarities of their own minds than to the peculiarity of the moral and intellectual condition of the minds among which they have been produced. Thus a number of writers possess the form, whilst they want the spirit of those whom, it is alleged, they imitate; because the former is the endowment of the age in which they live, and the latter must be the uncommunicated lightning of their own mind.

The peculiar style of intense and comprehensive imagery which distinguishes the modern literature of England, has not been, as a general power, the product of the imitation of any particular writer. The mass of capabilities remains at every period materially the same; the circumstances which awaken it to action perpetually change. If England were divided into forty republics, each equal in population and extent to Athens, there is no reason to suppose but that, under institutions not more perfect than those of Athens, each would produce philosophers and poets equal to those who (if we except Shakespeare) have never been surpassed. We owe the great writers of the golden age of our literature to that fervid awakening of the public mind which shook to dust the oldest and most oppressive form of the Christian religion. We owe Milton to the progress and development of the same spirit: the sacred Milton was, let it ever be remembered, a republican, and a bold inquirer into morals and religion. The great writers of our own age are, we have reason to suppose, the companions and forerunners of some unimagined change in our social condition or the opinions which cement it. The cloud of mind is discharging its collected lightning, and the equilibrium between institutions and opinions is now restoring, or is about to be restored.

As to imitation, poetry is a mimetic art. It creates, but it creates by combination and representation. Poetical abstractions are beautiful and new, not because the portions of which they are composed had no previous existence in the mind of man or in nature, but because the whole produced by their combination has some intelligible and beautiful analogy with those sources of emotion and thought, and with the contemporary condition of them: one great poet is a masterpiece of nature which another not only ought to study but must study. He might as wisely and as easily determine that his mind should no longer be the mirror of all that is lovely in the visible universe, as exclude from his contemplation the beautiful which exists in the writings of a great contemporary. The pretence of doing it would be a presumption in any but the greatest; the effect, even in him, would be strained, unnatural, and ineffectual. A poet is the combined product of such internal powers as modify the nature of others, and of such external influences as excite and sustain these powers; he is not one, but both. Every man's mind is, in this respect, modified by all the objects of nature and art; by every word and every suggestion which he ever admitted to act upon his consciousness; it is the mirror upon which all forms are reflected, and in which they compose one form. Poets, not otherwise than philosophers, painters, sculptors and musicians, are, in one sense, the creators, and, in another, the creations, of their age. From this subjection the loftiest do not escape. There is a similarity between Homer and Hesiod, between Aeschylus and Euripides, between Virgil and Horace, between Dante and Petrarch, between Shakespeare and Fletcher, between Dryden and Pope; each has a generic resemblance under which their specific distinctions are arranged. If this similarity be the result of imitation, I am willing to confess that I have imitated.

Let this opportunity be conceded to me of acknowledging that I have what a Scotch philosopher° characteristically terms, 'a passion for reforming the world':° what passion incited him to write and publish his book, he omits to explain. For my part I had rather be damned with Plato and Lord Bacon, than go to Heaven with Paley°and Malthus.° But it is a mistake to suppose that I dedicate my poetical compositions solely to the direct enforcement of reform, or that I consider them in any degree as containing a reasoned system on the theory of human life. Didactic poetry is my abhorrence; nothing can be equally well expressed in prose that is not tedious and supererogatory in verse. My purpose has hitherto been simply to familiarize the highly refined imagination of the more select classes of poetical readers with beautiful idealisms of moral excellence; aware that until the mind can love, and admire, and trust, and hope, and endure, reasoned principles of moral conduct are seeds cast upon the highway of life, which the unconscious passenger tramples into the dust, although they would bear the harvest of his happiness. Should I live to accomplish what I purpose, that is, produce a systematical history of what appear to me to be the genuine elements of human society, let not the advocates of injustice and superstition flatter themselves that I should take Aeschylus rather than Plato as my model.

The having spoken of myself with unaffected freedom will need little apology with the candid; and let the uncandid consider that they injure me less than their own hearts and minds by misrepresentation. Whatever talents a person may possess to amuse and instruct others, be they ever so inconsiderable, he is yet bound to exert them: if his attempt be ineffectual, let the punishment of an unaccomplished purpose have been sufficient; let none trouble themselves to heap the dust of oblivion upon his efforts; the pile they raise will betray his grave which might otherwise have been unknown.

DRAMATIS PERSONAE

PROMETHEUS.   ASIA.
DEMOGORGON.   PANTHEA. } Oceanides.
JUPITER.   IONE.
The EARTH.   The PHANTASM of JUPITER.
OCEAN.   The SPIRIT of the EARTH.
APOLLO.   The SPIRIT of the MOON.
MERCURY.   SPIRITS of the HOURS.
HERCULES.   SPIRITS. ECHOES. FAUNS.
    FURIES.

Act 1°

SCENE.—*A ravine of icy rocks in the Indian Caucasus.* PROMETHEUS°
is discovered bound to the precipice. PANTHEA *and* IONE *are seated at
his feet. Time, night. During the Scene, morning slowly breaks.*

   Prometheus. Monarch of Gods and Daemons, and all Spirits°
But One, who throng those bright and rolling worlds°
Which Thou and I alone of living things
Behold with sleepless eyes, regard this Earth
Made multitudinous with thy slaves, whom thou
Requitest for knee-worship, prayer, and praise,°
And toil, and hecatombs of broken hearts,°
With fear and self-contempt and barren hope;
Whilst me, who am thy foe, eyeless in hate,°
Hast thou made reign and triumph, to thy scorn,   10
O'er mine own misery and thy vain revenge.
Three thousand years of sleep-unsheltered hours,
And moments aye divided by keen pangs
Till they seemed years, torture and solitude,
Scorn and despair,—these are mine empire:
More glorious far than that which thou surveyest
From thine unenvied throne, O Mighty God!
Almighty, had I deigned to share the shame
Of thine ill tyranny, and hung not here
Nailed to this wall of eagle-baffling mountain,°   20
Black, wintry, dead, unmeasured; without herb,

Insect, or beast, or shape or sound of life.
Ah me! alas, pain, pain ever, forever!

No change, no pause, no hope! Yet I endure.
I ask the Earth, have not the mountains felt?
I ask yon Heaven, the all-beholding Sun,
Has it not seen? The Sea, in storm or calm,
Heaven's ever-changing Shadow, spread below,
Have its deaf waves not heard my agony?
Ah me! alas, pain, pain ever, forever!   30

The crawling glaciers pierce me with the spears
Of their moon-freezing crystals; the bright chains
Eat with their burning cold into my bones.
Heaven's wingèd hound, polluting from thy lips
His beak in poison not his own, tears up
My heart; and shapeless sights come wandering by,
The ghastly people of the realm of dream,
Mocking me; and the Earthquake-fiends are charged
To wrench the rivets from my quivering wounds
When the rocks split and close again behind;   40
While from their loud abysses howling throng
The genii of the storm, urging the rage
Of whirlwind, and afflict me with keen hail.
And yet to me welcome is day and night,
Whether one breaks the hoar frost of the morn,
Or starry, dim, and slow, the other climbs
The leaden-coloured east; for then they lead°
Their wingless, crawling Hours, one among whom
—As some dark Priest hales the reluctant victim—
Shall drag thee, cruel King, to kiss the blood   50
From these pale feet, which then might trample thee
If they disdained not such a prostrate slave.
Disdain? Ah no! I pity thee. What ruin
Will hunt thee undefended through wide Heaven!
How will thy soul, cloven to its depth with terror,
Gape like a hell within! I speak in grief,
Not exultation, for I hate no more,
As then, ere misery made me wise. The curse
Once breathed on thee I would recall. Ye Mountains,°
Whose many-voicèd Echoes, through the mist   60

Of cataracts, flung the thunder of that spell!
Ye icy Springs, stagnant with wrinkling frost,
Which vibrated to hear me, and then crept
Shuddering through India! Thou serenest Air,
Through which the Sun walks burning without beams!
And ye swift Whirlwinds, who on poisèd wings
Hung mute and moveless o'er yon hushed abyss,
As thunder, louder than your own, made rock
The orbèd world—if then my words had power,   70
Though I am changed so that aught evil wish
Is dead within; although no memory be
Of what is hate—let them not lose it now!
What was that curse? for ye all heard me speak.

First Voice (*from the Mountains*)

Thrice three hundred thousand years
    O'er the Earthquake's couch we stood:
Oft, as men convulsed with fears,
    We trembled in our multitude.

Second Voice (*from the Springs*)

Thunderbolts had parched our water,
    We had been stained with bitter blood,
And had run mute, 'mid shrieks of slaughter,   80
    Through a city and a solitude.

Third Voice (*from the Air*)

I had clothed, since Earth uprose,
    Its wastes in colours not their own,°
And oft had my serene repose
    Been cloven by many a rending groan.

Fourth Voice (*from the Whirlwinds*)

We had soared beneath these mountains
    Unresting ages; nor had thunder,
Nor yon volcano's flaming fountains,
    Nor any power above or under
    Ever made us mute with wonder.   90

First Voice

But never bowed our snowy crest
As at the voice of thine unrest.

Second Voice

Never such a sound before
To the Indian waves we bore.
A pilot asleep on the howling sea
Leaped up from the deck in agony,
And heard, and cried, 'Ah, woe is me!'
And died as mad as the wild waves be.

Third Voice

By such dread words from Earth to Heaven
My still realm was never riven: 100
When its wound was closed, there stood
Darkness o'er the day like blood.°

Fourth Voice

And we shrank back: for dreams of ruin
To frozen caves our flight pursuing
Made us keep silence—thus—and thus—
Though silence is as hell to us.

The Earth. The tongueless Caverns of the craggy hills
Cried, 'Misery!' then; the hollow Heaven replied,
'Misery!' and the Ocean's purple waves,
Climbing the land, howled to the lashing winds,   110
And the pale nations heard it, 'Misery!'

Prometheus. I hear a sound of voices: not the voice
Which I gave forth. Mother, thy sons and thou
Scorn him, without whose all-enduring will
Beneath the fierce omnipotence of Jove,
Both they and thou had vanished, like thin mist
Unrolled on the morning wind. Know ye not me,
The Titan? he who made his agony
The barrier to your else all-conquering foe?
O rock-embosomed lawns and snow-fed streams,   120
Now seen athwart frore vapours, deep below,°
Through whose o'ershadowing woods I wandered once
With Asia, drinking life from her loved eyes,
Why scorns the spirit which informs ye, now
To commune with me? me alone, who checked—
As one who checks a fiend-drawn charioteer—

The falsehood and the force of him who reigns
Supreme, and with the groans of pining slaves
Fills your dim glens and liquid wildernesses?
Why answer ye not, still? Brethren!

The Earth.   They dare not.

Prometheus. Who dares? For I would hear that curse again.   130
Ha, what an awful whisper rises up!
'Tis scarce like sound: it tingles through the frame
As lightning tingles, hovering ere it strike.
Speak, Spirit! from thine inorganic voice°
I only know that thou art moving near
And love. How cursed I him?°

The Earth.   How canst thou hear
Who knowest not the language of the dead?

Prometheus. Thou art a living spirit; speak as they.

The Earth. I dare not speak like life, lest Heaven's fell King   140
Should hear, and link me to some wheel of pain°
More torturing than the one whereon I roll.
Subtle thou art and good, and though the Gods
Hear not this voice, yet thou art more than God,
Being wise and kind: earnestly hearken now.

Prometheus. Obscurely through my brain, like shadows dim,
Sweep awful thoughts, rapid and thick. I feel
Faint, like one mingled in entwining love;
Yet 'tis not pleasure.

The Earth.   No, thou canst not hear:
Thou art immortal, and this tongue is known   150
Only to those who die.

Prometheus.   And what art thou,
O melancholy Voice?

The Earth.   I am the Earth,
Thy mother; she within whose stony veins,
To the last fibre of the loftiest tree

Whose thin leaves trembled in the frozen air,
Joy ran, as blood within a living frame,
When thou didst from her bosom, like a cloud
Of glory, arise—a spirit of keen joy!
And at thy voice her pining sons uplifted
Their prostrate brows from the polluting dust,   160
And our almighty Tyrant with fierce dread
Grew pale, until his thunder chained thee here.
Then, see those million worlds which burn and roll
Around us: their inhabitants beheld
My spherèd light wane in wide Heaven; the sea
Was lifted by strange tempest, and new fire
From earthquake-rifted mountains of bright snow
Shook its portentous hair beneath Heaven's frown;
Lightning and Inundation vexed the plains;
Blue thistles bloomed in cities; foodless toads°   170
Within voluptuous chambers panting crawled;
When Plague had fallen on man and beast and worm,
And Famine; and black blight on herb and tree;
And in the corn, and vines, and meadow-grass,
Teemed ineradicable poisonous weeds
Draining their growth, for my wan breast was dry
With grief; and the thin air, my breath, was stained
With the contagion of a mother's hate°
Breathed on her child's destroyer; aye, I heard
Thy curse, the which, if thou rememberest not,   180
Yet my innumerable seas and streams,
Mountains, and caves, and winds, and yon wide air,
And the inarticulate people of the dead,
Preserve, a treasured spell. We meditate
In secret joy and hope those dreadful words
But dare not speak them.

   Prometheus.   Venerable Mother!
All else who live and suffer take from thee
Some comfort; flowers, and fruit, and happy sounds,
And love, though fleeting; these may not be mine.
But mine own words, I pray, deny me not.   190

   The Earth. They shall be told. Ere Babylon was dust,
The Magus Zoroaster, my dead child,°

Met his own image walking in the garden.
That apparition, sole of men, he saw.
For know there are two worlds of life and death:
One that which thou beholdest; but the other
Is underneath the grave, where do inhabit
The shadows of all forms that think and live
Till death unite them and they part no more;
Dreams and the light imaginings of men,   200
And all that faith creates or love desires,
Terrible, strange, sublime and beauteous shapes.°
There thou art, and dost hang, a writhing shade,
'Mid whirlwind-shaken mountains; all the Gods
Are there, and all the Powers of nameless worlds,
Vast, sceptred Phantoms; heroes, men, and beasts;
And Demogorgon, a tremendous Gloom;°
And he, the Supreme Tyrant, on his throne
Of burning gold. Son, one of these shall utter
The curse which all remember. Call at will   210
Thine own ghost, or the ghost of Jupiter,
Hades or Typhon, or what mightier Gods
From all-prolific Evil since thy ruin
Have sprung, and trampled on my prostrate sons.
Ask, and they must reply: so the revenge
Of the Supreme may sweep through vacant shades,
As rainy wind through the abandoned gate
Of a fallen palace.

    Prometheus.   Mother, let not aught
Of that which may be evil, pass again
My lips, or those of aught resembling me.   220
Phantasm of Jupiter, arise, appear!°

Ione

    My wings are folded o'er mine ears:
        My wings are crossed over mine eyes:
    Yet through their silver shade appears,
        And through their lulling plumes arise,
    A Shape, a throng of sounds:
        May it be no ill to thee
    O thou of many wounds!

Near whom, for our sweet sister's sake,
Ever thus we watch and wake.   230

Panthea°

The sound is of whirlwind underground,
    Earthquake, and fire, and mountains cloven;
The Shape is awful like the sound,
    Clothed in dark purple, star-inwoven.
A sceptre of pale gold,
    To stay steps proud, o'er the slow cloud,
His veinèd hand doth hold.
Cruel he looks, but calm and strong,
Like one who does, not suffers wrong.

Phantasm of Jupiter. Why have the secret powers of this
    strange world   240
Driven me, a frail and empty phantom, hither
On direst storms? What unaccustomed sounds
Are hovering on my lips, unlike the voice
With which our pallid race hold ghastly talk
In darkness? And, proud sufferer, who art thou?

Prometheus. Tremendous Image, as thou art must be
He whom thou shadowest forth. I am his foe,
The Titan. Speak the words which I would hear,
Although no thought inform thine empty voice.

The Earth. Listen! And though your echoes must be mute,   250
Grey mountains, and old woods, and haunted springs,
Prophetic caves, and isle-surrounded streams,
Rejoice to hear what yet ye cannot speak.

Phantasm. A spirit seizes me and speaks within:
It tears me as fire tears a thunder-cloud.

Panthea. See, how he lifts his mighty looks, the Heaven
Darkens above.

Ione.   He speaks! O shelter me!

Prometheus. I see the curse on gestures proud and cold,   260
And looks of firm defiance, and calm hate,

And such despair as mocks itself with smiles,
Written as on a scroll . . . yet speak—O speak!

Phantasm

    Fiend, I defy thee! with a calm, fixed mind,
        All that thou canst inflict I bid thee do;
    Foul Tyrant both of Gods and Humankind,
        One only being shalt thou not subdue.
Rain then thy plagues upon me here,
Ghastly disease, and frenzying fear;
And let alternate frost and fire
Eat into me, and be thine ire
Lightning, and cutting hail, and legioned forms   270
Of furies, driving by upon the wounding storms.

    Aye, do thy worst. Thou art omnipotent.
        O'er all things but thyself I gave thee power,
    And my own will. Be thy swift mischiefs sent
        To blast mankind, from yon etherial tower.
Let thy malignant spirit move
Its darkness over those I love:
On me and mine I imprecate
The utmost torture of thy hate,
And thus devote to sleepless agony   280
This undeclining head while thou must reign on high.

    But thou, who art the God and Lord: O thou
        Who fillest with thy soul this world of woe,
    To whom all things of Earth and Heaven do bow
        In fear and worship: all-prevailing foe!
I curse thee! let a sufferer's curse
Clasp thee, his torturer, like remorse,
Till thine Infinity shall be
A robe of envenomed agony;
And thine Omnipotence a crown of pain   290
To cling like burning gold round thy dissolving brain.

    Heap on thy soul, by virtue of this Curse,
        Ill deeds; then be thou damned, beholding good;°
    Both infinite as is the universe,
        And thou, and thy self-torturing solitude.

An awful image of calm power
Though now thou sittest, let the hour
Come, when thou must appear to be
That which thou art internally,
And after many a false and fruitless crime   300
Scorn track thy lagging fall through boundless space and time.

Prometheus. Were these my words, O Parent?

The Earth.   They were thine.

Prometheus. It doth repent me: words are quick and vain;
Grief for a while is blind, and so was mine.
I wish no living thing to suffer pain.

The Earth

Misery, oh misery to me,
That Jove at length should vanquish thee.
Wail, howl aloud, Land and Sea,
The Earth's rent heart shall answer ye.
Howl, Spirits of the living and the dead;   310
Your refuge, your defence lies fallen and vanquishèd.

First Echo

Lies fallen and vanquishèd?

Second Echo

Fallen and vanquishèd!

Ione

Fear not: 'tis but some passing spasm,
    The Titan is unvanquished still.
But see, where through the azure chasm
    Of yon forked and snowy hill,
Trampling the slant winds on high
    With golden-sandalled feet, that glow
Under plumes of purple dye,   320
Like rose-ensanguined ivory,
    A Shape comes now,
Stretching on high from his right hand
A serpent-cinctured wand.

Panthea. 'Tis Jove's world-wandering herald, Mercury.°

Ione

And who are those with hydra tresses
    And iron wings that climb the wind,
Whom the frowning God represses
    Like vapours steaming up behind,
Clanging loud, an endless crowd—   330

Panthea

These are Jove's tempest-walking hounds,°
    Whom he gluts with groans and blood,
When charioted on sulphurous cloud
    He bursts Heaven's bounds.

Ione

Are they now led from the thin dead,
    On new pangs to be fed?

Panthea. The Titan looks as ever, firm, not proud.

First Fury. Ha! I scent life!

Second Fury.   Let me but look into his eyes!

Third Fury. The hope of torturing him smells like a heap
Of corpses to a death-bird after battle.   340

First Fury. Darest thou delay, O Herald? take cheer, Hounds
Of Hell: what if the Son of Maia soon
Should make us food and sport? Who can please long
The Omnipotent?

Mercury.   Back to your towers of iron,
And gnash beside the streams of fire and wail°
Your foodless teeth! . . . Geryon, arise! and Gorgon,°
Chimaera, and thou Sphinx, subtlest of fiends,°
Who ministered to Thebes Heaven's poisoned wine,
Unnatural love, and more unnatural hate:°
These shall perform your task.

First Fury.   Oh, mercy! mercy!   350
We die with our desire: drive us not back!

Mercury.   Crouch then in silence.
                                        Awful Sufferer,
To thee unwilling, most unwillingly
I come, by the great Father's will driven down,
To execute a doom of new revenge.
Alas! I pity thee, and hate myself
That I can do no more—aye from thy sight
Returning, for a season, Heaven seems Hell,
So thy worn form pursues me night and day,
Smiling reproach. Wise art thou, firm and good,   360
But vainly wouldst stand forth alone in strife
Against the Omnipotent; as yon clear lamps
That measure and divide the weary years
From which there is no refuge, long have taught,
And long must teach. Even now thy Torturer arms
With the strange might of unimagined pains
The powers who scheme slow agonies in Hell,
And my commission is to lead them here,
Or what more subtle, foul or savage fiends
People the abyss, and leave them to their task.   370
Be it not so . . . there is a secret known
To thee, and to none else of living things,
Which may transfer the sceptre of wide Heaven,
The fear of which perplexes the Supreme:
Clothe it in words, and bid it clasp his throne
In intercession; bend thy soul in prayer,
And like a suppliant in some gorgeous fane,
Let the will kneel within thy haughty heart;
For benefits and meek submission tame
The fiercest and the mightiest.

Prometheus.   Evil minds   380
Change good to their own nature. I gave all
He has; and in return he chains me here
Years, ages, night and day: whether the Sun
Split my parched skin, or in the moony night
The crystal-wingèd snow cling round my hair:
Whilst my beloved race is trampled down

By his thought-executing ministers.°
Such is the tyrant's recompense—'tis just:
He who is evil can receive no good;
And for a world bestowed, or a friend lost,   390
He can feel hate, fear, shame; not gratitude:
He but requites me for his own misdeed.
Kindness to such is keen reproach, which breaks
With bitter stings the light sleep of Revenge.
Submission, thou dost know, I cannot try:
For what submission but that fatal word,
The death-seal of mankind's captivity,
Like the Sicilian's hair-suspended sword°
Which trembles o'er his crown, would he accept,
Or could I yield? Which yet I will not yield.   400
Let others flatter Crime, where it sits throned
In brief Omnipotence; secure are they:
For Justice, when triumphant, will weep down
Pity, not punishment, on her own wrongs,
Too much avenged by those who err. I wait,
Enduring thus, the retributive hour
Which since we spake is even nearer now.
But hark, the hell-hounds clamour: fear delay:
Behold! Heaven lowers under thy Father's frown.

    Mercury. Oh, that we might be spared: I to inflict,   410
And thou to suffer! Once more answer me:
Thou knowest not the period of Jove's power?

    Prometheus. I know but this, that it must come.

    Mercury.   Alas!
Thou canst not count thy years to come of pain?

    Prometheus. They last while Jove must reign; nor more, nor less
Do I desire or fear.

    Mercury.   Yet pause, and plunge
Into Eternity, where recorded time,
Even all that we imagine, age on age,
Seems but a point, and the reluctant mind
Flags wearily in its unending flight,   420

Till it sink, dizzy, blind, lost, shelterless;
Perchance it has not numbered the slow years
Which thou must spend in torture, unreprieved.

Prometheus. Perchance no thought can count them, yet they pass.

Mercury. If thou might'st dwell among the Gods the while,
Lapped in voluptuous joy?

Prometheus.   I would not quit
This bleak ravine, these unrepentant pains.

Mercury. Alas! I wonder at, yet pity thee.

Prometheus. Pity the self-despising slaves of Heaven,
Not me, within whose mind sits peace serene,   430
As light in the sun, throned: how vain is talk!
Call up the fiends.

Ione.   O sister, look! White fire
Has cloven to the roots yon huge snow-loaded cedar;
How fearfully God's thunder howls behind!

Mercury. I must obey his words and thine: alas!
Most heavily remorse hangs at my heart!

Panthea. See where the child of Heaven with wingèd feet
Runs down the slanted sunlight of the dawn.

Ione. Dear sister, close thy plumes over thine eyes
Lest thou behold and die—they come, they come   440
Blackening the birth of day with countless wings,
And hollow underneath, like death.

First Fury.   Prometheus!

Second Fury. Immortal Titan!

Third Fury.   Champion of Heaven's slaves!

Prometheus. He whom some dreadful voice invokes is here,

Prometheus, the chained Titan. Horrible forms,
What and who are ye? Never yet there came
Phantasms so foul through monster-teeming Hell
From the all-miscreative brain of Jove;
Whilst I behold such execrable shapes,
Methinks I grow like what I contemplate,   450
And laugh and stare in loathsome sympathy.

    First Fury. We are the ministers of pain, and fear,
And disappointment, and mistrust, and hate,
And clinging crime; and as lean dogs pursue
Through wood and lake some struck and sobbing fawn,
We track all things that weep, and bleed, and live,
When the great King betrays them to our will.

    Prometheus. O many fearful natures in one name,
I know ye; and these lakes and echoes know
The darkness and the clangour of your wings.   460
But why more hideous than your loathèd selves
Gather ye up in legions from the deep?

    Second Fury. We knew not that: Sisters, rejoice, rejoice!

    Prometheus. Can aught exult in its deformity?

    Second Fury. The beauty of delight makes lovers glad,
Gazing on one another: so are we.
As from the rose which the pale priestess kneels
To gather for her festal crown of flowers
The aerial crimson falls, flushing her cheek,
So from our victim's destined agony   470
The shade which is our form invests us round,
Else are we shapeless as our mother Night.

    Prometheus. I laugh your power, and his who sent you here,
To lowest scorn. Pour forth the cup of pain.

    First Fury. Thou thinkest we will rend thee bone from bone,
And nerve from nerve, working like fire within?

    Prometheus. Pain is my element, as hate is thine;
Ye rend me now: I care not.

Second Fury.   Dost imagine
We will but laugh into thy lidless eyes?

Prometheus. I weigh not what ye do, but what ye suffer,   480
Being evil. Cruel was the Power which called
You, or aught else so wretched, into light.

Third Fury. Thou think'st we will live through thee, one by one,
Like animal life, and though we can obscure not
The soul which burns within, that we will dwell
Beside it, like a vain loud multitude
Vexing the self-content of wisest men:
That we will be dread thought beneath thy brain,
And foul desire round thine astonished heart,
And blood within thy labyrinthine veins   490
Crawling like agony?

Prometheus.   Why, ye are thus now:
Yet am I king over myself, and rule
The torturing and conflicting throngs within,
As Jove rules you when Hell grows mutinous.

Chorus of Furies

From the ends of the earth, from the ends of the earth,
Where the night has its grave and the morning its birth,
          Come, come, come!
O ye who shake hills with the scream of your mirth
When cities sink howling in ruin; and ye
Who with wingless footsteps trample the sea,   500
And close upon Shipwreck and Famine's track
Sit chattering with joy on the foodless wreck;
          Come, come, come!
Leave the bed, low, cold, and red,
Strewed beneath a nation dead;
Leave the hatred, as in ashes
     Fire is left for future burning:
It will burst in bloodier flashes
     When ye stir it, soon returning;
Leave the self-contempt implanted   510
In young spirits, sense-enchanted,
     Misery's yet unkindled fuel;

        Leave Hell's secrets half unchanted
          To the maniac dreamer: cruel
      More than ye can be with hate
          Is he with fear.
              Come, come, come!
    We are steaming up from Hell's wide gate,
      And we burden the blasts of the atmosphere,
      But vainly we toil till ye come here.   520

Ione. Sister, I hear the thunder of new wings.

Panthea. These solid mountains quiver with the sound
Even as the tremulous air: their shadows make
The space within my plumes more black than night.

First Fury

      Your call was as a wingèd car,
      Driven on whirlwinds fast and far;
      It rapt us from red gulfs of war.

Second Fury

      From wide cities, famine-wasted;

Third Fury

      Groans half heard, and blood untasted;

Fourth Fury

      Kingly conclaves stern and cold,°   530
      Where blood with gold is bought and sold;

Fifth Fury

      From the furnace, white and hot,
      In which—

A Fury

            Speak not—whisper not:
    I know all that ye would tell,
    But to speak might break the spell
    Which must bend the Invincible,
      The stern of thought;
    He yet defies the deepest power of Hell.

Fury

Tear the veil!

Another Fury

It is torn!

Chorus

The pale stars of the morn
Shine on a misery, dire to be borne,   540
Dost thou faint, mighty Titan? We laugh thee to scorn.
Dost thou boast the clear knowledge thou waken'dst for man?
Then was kindled within him a thirst which outran
Those perishing waters; a thirst of fierce fever,
Hope, love, doubt, desire—which consume him for ever.
    One came forth of gentle worth.°
    Smiling on the sanguine earth;
    His words outlived him, like swift poison
        Withering up truth, peace, and pity.
    Look where round the wide horizon   550
        Many a million-peopled city
    Vomits smoke in the bright air.
    Hark that outcry of despair!
    'Tis his mild and gentle ghost
        Wailing for the faith he kindled.
    Look again, the flames almost
        To a glow-worm's lamp have dwindled:
    The survivors round the embers
        Gather in dread.
          Joy, joy, joy!   560
Past ages crowd on thee, but each one remembers,
And the future is dark, and the present is spread
Like a pillow of thorns for thy slumberless head.°

Semichorus 1

    Drops of bloody agony flow
    From his white and quivering brow.
    Grant a little respite now:
    See, a disenchanted nation°
    Springs like day from desolation;
    To Truth its state is dedicate,

And Freedom leads it forth, her mate;   570
A legioned band of linkèd brothers,
Whom Love calls children—

Semichorus 2

                              'Tis another's—
        See how kindred murder kin:
        'Tis the vintage-time for death and sin:
        Blood, like new wine, bubbles within;
              Till Despair smothers
        The struggling world, which slaves and tyrants win.°
                                        [*All the* FURIES *vanish, except one.*

Ione. Hark, sister! what a low yet dreadful groan
Quite unsuppressed is tearing up the heart
Of the good Titan, as storms tear the deep,   580
And beasts hear the sea moan in inland caves.
Darest thou observe how the fiends torture him?

Panthea. Alas! I looked forth twice, but will no more.

Ione. What didst thou see?

Panthea.   A woeful sight: a youth
With patient looks nailed to a crucifix.

Ione. What next?

Panthea.   The heaven around, the earth below
Was peopled with thick shapes of human death,
All horrible, and wrought by human hands,
And some appeared the work of human hearts,
For men were slowly killed by frowns and smiles: 590
And other sights too foul to speak and live
Were wandering by. Let us not tempt worse fear
By looking forth: those groans are grief enough.

Fury. Behold, an emblem: those who do endure
Deep wrongs for man, and scorn, and chains, but heap
Thousandfold torment on themselves and him.

Prometheus. Remit the anguish of that lighted stare;
Close those wan lips; let that thorn-wounded brow
Stream not with blood; it mingles with thy tears!
Fix, fix those tortured orbs in peace and death,   600
So thy sick throes shake not that crucifix,
So those pale fingers play not with thy gore.
O horrible! Thy name I will not speak,
It hath become a curse. I see, I see
The wise, the mild, the lofty, and the just,
Whom thy slaves hate for being like to thee,
Some hunted by foul lies from their heart's home,
An early-chosen, late-lamented home,
As hooded ounces cling to the driven hind;°
Some linked to corpses in unwholesome cells;   610
Some—hear I not the multitude laugh loud?—
Impaled in lingering fire: and mighty realms
Float by my feet, like sea-uprooted isles,
Whose sons are kneaded down in common blood
By the red light of their own burning homes.

Fury. Blood thou canst see, and fire; and canst hear groans:
Worse things unheard, unseen, remain behind.

Prometheus. Worse?

Fury.   In each human heart terror survives
The ravin it has gorged: the loftiest fear
All that they would disdain to think were true: 620
Hypocrisy and custom make their minds
The fanes of many a worship, now outworn.
They dare not devise good for man's estate,
And yet they know not that they do not dare.
The good want power, but to weep barren tears.
The powerful goodness want: worse need for them.
The wise want love; and those who love want wisdom;
And all best things are thus confused to ill.
Many are strong and rich, and would be just,
But live among their suffering fellow-men   630
As if none felt: they know not what they do.°

Prometheus. Thy words are like a cloud of wingèd snakes;
And yet I pity those they torture not.

Fury. Thou pitiest them? I speak no more!   [*Vanishes*.

Prometheus.   Ah woe!
Ah woe! Alas! pain, pain ever, forever!
I close my tearless eyes, but see more clear
Thy works within my woe-illumèd mind,
Thou subtle tyrant! Peace is in the grave.
The grave hides all things beautiful and good:
I am a God and cannot find it there: 640
Nor would I seek it: for, though dread revenge,
This is defeat, fierce King, not victory!
The sights with which thou torturest gird my soul
With new endurance, till the hour arrives
When they shall be no types of things which are.

Panthea. Alas! what sawest thou more?

Prometheus.   There are two woes:
To speak and to behold; thou spare me one.
Names are there, Nature's sacred watch-words, they
Were borne aloft in bright emblazonry;
The nations thronged around, and cried aloud,   650
As with one voice, 'Truth, liberty, and love!'
Suddenly fierce confusion fell from Heaven
Among them: there was strife, deceit, and fear;
Tyrants rushed in, and did divide the spoil.
This was the shadow of the truth I saw.

The Earth. I felt thy torture, Son, with such mixed joy
As pain and virtue give. To cheer thy state,
I bid ascend those subtle and fair spirits,°
Whose homes are the dim caves of human thought,
And who inhabit, as birds wing the wind,   660
Its world-surrounding ether: they behold
Beyond that twilight realm, as in a glass,
The future: may they speak comfort to thee!

Panthea. Look, sister, where a troop of spirits gather,
Like flocks of clouds in spring's delightful weather,
Thronging in the blue air!

Ione.   And see! more come,
Like fountain-vapours when the winds are dumb,
That climb up the ravine in scattered lines.
And hark! is it the music of the pines?
Is it the lake? Is it the waterfall?   670

Panthea. 'Tis something sadder, sweeter far than all.

Chorus of Spirits

From unremembered ages we
Gentle guides and guardians be
Of Heaven-oppressed mortality;
And we breathe, and sicken not,
The atmosphere of human thought:
Be it dim, and dank, and grey,
Like a storm-extinguished day,
Travelled o'er by dying gleams;
    Be it bright as all between   680
Cloudless skies and windless streams,
    Silent, liquid, and serene;
As the birds within the wind,
    As the fish within the wave,
As the thoughts of man's own mind
    Float through all above the grave,
We make there our liquid lair,
Voyaging cloudlike and unpent
Through the boundless element:
Thence we bear the prophecy   690
Which begins and ends in thee!

Ione. More yet come, one by one: the air around them
Looks radiant as the air around a star.

First Spirit

On a battle-trumpet's blast
I fled hither, fast, fast, fast,
'Mid the darkness upward cast.
From the dust of creeds outworn,
From the tyrant's banner torn,
Gathering round me, onward borne,

There was mingled many a cry—   700
'Freedom! Hope! Death! Victory!'
Till they faded through the sky;
And one sound above, around,
One sound beneath, around, above,
Was moving; 'twas the soul of love;
'Twas the hope, the prophecy,
Which begins and ends in thee.

Second Spirit

A rainbow's arch stood on the sea
Which rocked beneath, immovably;
And the triumphant storm did flee,   710
Like a conqueror, swift and proud,
Between, with many a captive cloud,
A shapeless, dark and rapid crowd,
Each by lightning riven in half:
I heard the thunder hoarsely laugh.
Mighty fleets were strewn like chaff
And spread beneath a hell of death
O'er the white waters. I alit
On a great ship lightning-split,
And speeded hither on the sigh   720
Of one who gave an enemy
His plank, then plunged aside to die.°

Third Spirit

I sate beside a sage's bed,
And the lamp was burning red
Near the book where he had fed,
When a Dream with plumes of flame
To his pillow hovering came,
And I knew it was the same
Which had kindled long ago
Pity, eloquence, and woe;   730
And the world awhile below
Wore the shade its lustre made.
It has borne me here as fleet
As Desire's lightning feet:
I must ride it back ere morrow,
Or the sage will wake in sorrow.

Fourth Spirit

On a poet's lips I slept
Dreaming like a love-adept
In the sound his breathing kept;
Nor seeks nor finds he mortal blisses,   740
But feeds on the aerial kisses
Of shapes that haunt thought's wildernesses.
He will watch from dawn to gloom
The lake-reflected sun illume
The yellow bees i' the ivy-bloom,
Nor heed nor see what things they be;
But from these create he can
Forms more real than living man,
Nurslings of immortality!
One of these awakened me,   750
And I sped to succour thee.

Ione. Behold'st thou not two shapes from the east and west
Come, as two doves to one beloved nest,
Twin nurslings of the all-sustaining air,
On swift still wings glide down the atmosphere?
And hark! their sweet, sad voices! 'tis despair
Mingled with love and then dissolved in sound.

Panthea. Canst thou speak, sister? all my words are drowned.

Ione. Their beauty gives me voice. See how they float
On their sustaining wings of skiey grain.   760
Orange and azure deepening into gold:
Their soft smiles light the air like a star's fire.

Chorus of Spirits

Hast thou beheld the form of Love?

Fifth Spirit

                                 As over wide dominions
I sped, like some swift cloud that wings the wide air's wildernesses,
That planet-crested shape swept by on lightning-braided pinions,°
Scattering the liquid joy of life from his ambrosial tresses:
His footsteps paved the world with light; but as I passed 'twas fading,
And hollow Ruin yawned behind: great sages bound in madness,

And headless patriots, and pale youths who perished,
  unupbraiding,
Gleamed in the night I wandered o'er—till thou, O King
  of sadness,   770
Turned by thy smile the worst I saw to recollected gladness.

Sixth Spirit

Ah, sister! Desolation is a delicate thing:
It walks not on the earth, it floats not on the air,
But treads with lulling footstep, and fans with silent wing
The tender hopes which in their hearts the best and gentlest bear,
Who, soothed to false repose by the fanning plumes above
And the music-stirring motion of its soft and busy feet,
Dream visions of aerial joy, and call the monster Love,
And wake, and find the shadow Pain—as he whom now we greet.°

Chorus

Though Ruin now Love's shadow be,   780
Following him destroyingly
  On Death's white and wingèd steed,
Which the fleetest cannot flee,
  Trampling down both flower and weed,
Man and beast, and foul and fair,
Like a tempest through the air;
Thou shalt quell this horseman grim,
Woundless though in heart or limb.

Prometheus

Spirits! how know ye this shall be?

Chorus

In the atmosphere we breathe,   790
As buds grow red when snow-storms flee
  From spring gathering up beneath,
Whose mild winds shake the elder brake,
And the wandering herdsmen know
That the white-thorn soon will blow:
Wisdom, Justice, Love, and Peace,
When they struggle to increase,
  Are to us as soft winds be

To shepherd boys, the prophecy
Which begins and ends in thee.   800

Ione. Where are the Spirits fled?

Panthea.   Only a sense
Remains of them, like the omnipotence
Of music, when the inspired voice and lute
Languish, ere yet the responses are mute
Which through the deep and labyrinthine soul,
Like echoes through long caverns, wind and roll.

Prometheus. How fair these air-born shapes! and yet I feel
Most vain all hope but love; and thou art far,
Asia! who, when my being overflowed,
Wert like a golden chalice to bright wine   810
Which else had sunk into the thirsty dust.
All things are still: alas! how heavily
This quiet morning weighs upon my heart;
Though I should dream, I could even sleep with grief,
If slumber were denied not. I would fain
Be what it is my destiny to be,
The saviour and the strength of suffering man,
Or sink into the original gulf of things:
There is no agony, and no solace left;
Earth can console, Heaven can torment no more.   820

Panthea. Hast thou forgotten one who watches thee
The cold dark night, and never sleeps but when
The shadow of thy spirit falls on her?

Prometheus. I said all hope was vain but love: thou lovest.

Panthea. Deeply in truth; but the Eastern star looks white,°
And Asia waits in that far Indian vale
The scene of her sad exile; rugged once
And desolate and frozen, like this ravine;
But now invested with fair flowers and herbs,
And haunted by sweet airs and sounds, which flow   830
Among the woods and waters, from the ether
Of her transforming presence—which would fade
If it were mingled not with thine. Farewell!

Act 2

SCENE I.—*Morning. A lovely vale in the Indian Caucasus.* ASIA, *alone.*

   Asia. From all the blasts of heaven thou hast descended:
Yes, like a spirit, like a thought, which makes
Unwonted tears throng to the horny eyes,
And beatings haunt the desolated heart,
Which should have learnt repose: thou hast descended
Cradled in tempests; thou dost wake, O Spring!
O child of many winds! As suddenly
Thou comest as the memory of a dream,
Which now is sad because it hath been sweet;
Like genius, or like joy which riseth up   10
As from the earth, clothing with golden clouds
The desert of our life . . .
This is the season, this the day, the hour;
At sunrise thou shouldst come, sweet sister mine,
Too long desired, too long delaying, come!
How like death-worms the wingless moments crawl!
The point of one white star is quivering still
Deep in the orange light of widening morn
Beyond the purple mountains; through a chasm
Of wind-divided mist the darker lake   20
Reflects it; now it wanes; it gleams again
As the waves fade, and as the burning threads
Of woven cloud unravel in pale air . . .
'Tis lost! and through yon peaks of cloud-like snow
The roseate sunlight quivers: hear I not
The Aeolian music of her sea-green plumes
Winnowing the crimson dawn?

                  PANTHEA *enters.*°

                  I feel, I see
Those eyes which burn through smiles that fade in tears,
Like stars half quenched in mists of silver dew.
Beloved and most beautiful, who wearest   30
The shadow of that soul by which I live,
How late thou art! the spherèd sun had climbed
The sea, my heart was sick with hope, before
The printless air felt thy belated plumes.

Panthea. Pardon, great Sister! but my wings were faint
With the delight of a remembered dream,
As are the noon-tide plumes of summer winds
Satiate with sweet flowers. I was wont to sleep
Peacefully, and awake refreshed and calm,
Before the sacred Titan's fall, and thy   40
Unhappy love, had made, through use and pity,
Both love and woe familiar to my heart
As they had grown to thine: erewhile I slept°
Under the glaucous caverns of old Ocean°
Within dim bowers of green and purple moss,
Our young Ione's soft and milky arms
Locked then, as now, behind my dark, moist hair,
While my shut eyes and cheek were pressed within
The folded depth of her life-breathing bosom:
But not as now, since I am made the wind   50
Which fails beneath the music that I bear
Of thy most wordless converse; since dissolved
Into the sense with which love talks, my rest
Was troubled and yet sweet; my waking hours
Too full of care and pain.

    Asia.   Lift up thine eyes,
And let me read thy dream.

    Panthea.   As I have said,
With our sea-sister at his feet I slept.
The mountain mists, condensing at our voice
Under the moon, had spread their snowy flakes,
From the keen ice shielding our linkèd sleep.   60
Then two dreams came. One, I remember not.
But in the other, his pale, wound-worn limbs
Fell from Prometheus, and the azure night
Grew radiant with the glory of that form
Which lives unchanged within, and his voice fell
Like music which makes giddy the dim brain,
Faint with intoxication of keen joy:
'Sister of her whose footsteps pave the world
With loveliness—more fair than aught but her,
Whose shadow thou art—lift thine eyes on me.'   70
I lifted them: the overpowering light

Of that immortal shape was shadowed o'er
By love; which, from his soft and flowing limbs,
And passion-parted lips, and keen, faint eyes,
Steamed forth like vaporous fire; an atmosphere
Which wrapped me in its all-dissolving power,
As the warm ether of the morning sun
Wraps ere it drinks some cloud of wandering dew.
I saw not, heard not, moved not, only felt
His presence flow and mingle through my blood   80
Till it became his life, and his grew mine,
And I was thus absorbed—until it passed,
And like the vapours when the sun sinks down,
Gathering again in drops upon the pines,
And tremulous as they, in the deep night
My being was condensed; and as the rays
Of thought were slowly gathered, I could hear
His voice, whose accents lingered ere they died
Like footsteps of far melody: thy name
Among the many sounds alone I heard   90
Of what might be articulate; though still
I listened through the night when sound was none.
Ione wakened then, and said to me:
'Canst thou divine what troubles me to-night?
I always knew what I desired before,
Nor ever found delight to wish in vain.
But now I cannot tell thee what I seek;
I know not; something sweet, since it is sweet
Even to desire; it is thy sport, false sister!
Thou hast discovered some enchantment old,   100
Whose spells have stolen my spirit as I slept
And mingled it with thine;—for when just now
We kissed, I felt within thy parted lips
The sweet air that sustained me, and the warmth
Of the life-blood, for loss of which I faint,
Quivered between our intertwining arms.'
I answered not, for the Eastern star grew pale,
But fled to thee.

   Asia.   Thou speakest, but thy words
Are as the air: I feel them not . . . Oh, lift
Thine eyes that I may read his written soul!   110

Panthea. I lift them, though they droop beneath the load
Of that they would express: what canst thou see
But thine own fairest shadow imaged there?

Asia. Thine eyes are like the deep, blue, boundless heaven
Contracted to two circles underneath
Their long, fine lashes: dark, far, measureless,
Orb within orb, and line through line inwoven.

Panthea. Why lookest thou as if a spirit passed?

Asia. There is a change; beyond their inmost depth
I see a shade, a shape: 'tis He, arrayed   120
In the soft light of his own smiles, which spread
Like radiance from the cloud-surrounded moon.
Prometheus, it is thine! depart not yet!
Say not those smiles that we shall meet again
Within that bright pavilion which their beams
Shall build o'er the waste world? The dream is told.
What shape is that between us? Its rude hair°
Roughens the wind that lifts it; its regard
Is wild and quick, yet 'tis a thing of air
For through its grey robe gleams the golden dew   130
Whose stars the noon has quenched not.

                              Dream
                        Follow! Follow!

Panthea. It is mine other dream.

Asia.   It disappears.

Panthea. It passes now into my mind. Methought
As we sat here, the flower-infolding buds
Burst on yon lightning-blasted almond tree,°
When swift from the white Scythian wilderness°
A wind swept forth wrinkling the Earth with frost.
I looked, and all the blossoms were blown down;
But on each leaf was stamped, as the blue bells
Of Hyacinth tell Apollo's written grief,°   140
O, FOLLOW, FOLLOW!

Asia.   As you speak, your words
Fill, pause by pause, my own forgotten sleep
With shapes. Methought among these lawns together
We wandered, underneath the young grey dawn,
And multitudes of dense, white, fleecy clouds
Were wandering in thick flocks along the mountains,
Shepherded by the slow, unwilling wind;
And the white dew on the new-bladed grass,
Just piercing the dark earth, hung silently;
And there was more which I remember not: 150
But on the shadows of the moving clouds
Athwart the purple mountain slope, was written
FOLLOW, O, FOLLOW! as they vanished by,
And on each herb, from which Heaven's dew had fallen,
The like was stamped, as with a withering fire.
A wind arose among the pines; it shook
The clinging music from their boughs, and then
Low, sweet, faint sounds, like the farewell of ghosts,
Were heard: O, FOLLOW, FOLLOW, FOLLOW ME!
And then I said: 'Panthea, look on me'.   160
But in the depth of those beloved eyes
Still I saw, FOLLOW, FOLLOW!

Echo
Follow, follow!

Panthea. The crags, this clear spring morning, mock our voices
As they were spirit-tongued.

Asia.   It is some being
Around the crags. What fine clear sounds! O, list!

Echoes, unseen
Echoes we: listen!
We cannot stay:
As dew-stars glisten
Then fade away—
Child of Ocean!   170

Asia. Hark! Spirits speak! The liquid responses
Of their aerial tongues yet sound.

Panthea.   I hear.

Echoes

O, follow, follow,
   As our voice recedeth
Through the caverns hollow,
   Where the forest spreadeth;

(*More distant*)

O, follow, follow;
Through the caverns hollow;
As the song floats thou pursue;
Where the wild bee never flew,   180
Through the noon-tide darkness deep,
By the odour-breathing sleep
Of faint nightflowers, and the waves
At the fountain-lighted caves,
While our music, wild and sweet,
Mocks thy gently falling feet,
   Child of Ocean!

Asia. Shall we pursue the sound? It grows more faint
And distant.

Panthea.   List! the strain floats nearer now.

Echoes

In the world unknown   190
   Sleeps a voice unspoken;
By thy step alone
   Can its rest be broken;
     Child of Ocean!

Asia. How the notes sink upon the ebbing wind!

Echoes

O, follow, follow
Through the caverns hollow;
As the song floats thou pursue,
By the woodland noon-tide dew;
By the forests, lakes, and fountains,   200

Through the many-folded mountains;
To the rents, and gulfs, and chasms,
Where the Earth reposed from spasms,
On the day when He and thou
Parted, to commingle now;
        Child of Ocean!

Asia. Come, sweet Panthea, link thy hand in mine,
And follow, ere the voices fade away.

SCENE 2.—*A forest, intermingled with rocks and caverns.* ASIA *and*
PANTHEA *pass into it.* Two young FAUNS *are sitting on a rock, listening.*

Semichorus 1 of Spirits

The path through which that lovely twain
    Have passed, by cedar, pine, and yew,°
    And each dark tree that ever grew,
    Is curtained out from Heaven's wide blue;
Nor sun, nor moon, nor wind, nor rain,
        Can pierce its interwoven bowers;
    Nor aught, save where some cloud of dew,
Drifted along the earth-creeping breeze
Between the trunks of the hoar trees,
        Hangs each a pearl in the pale flowers°   10
    Of the green laurel, blown anew;
And bends, and then fades silently,
One frail and fair anemone:
Or when some star of many a one
That climbs and wanders through steep night,
Has found the cleft through which alone
Beams fall from high those depths upon,
Ere it is borne away, away,
By the swift Heavens that cannot stay,
It scatters drops of golden light,   20
Like lines of rain that ne'er unite:
And the gloom divine is all around;
And underneath is the mossy ground.

Semichorus 2

There the voluptuous nightingales
    Are awake through all the broad noonday.

When one with bliss or sadness fails,
  And through the windless ivy-boughs,
  Sick with sweet love, droops dying away
On its mate's music-panting bosom;
Another from the swinging blossom,   30
   Watching to catch the languid close
  Of the last strain, then lifts on high
  The wings of the weak melody,
Till some new stream of feeling bear
  The song, and all the woods are mute;
When there is heard through the dim air
The rush of wings, and rising there
  Like many a lake-surrounded flute,
Sounds overflow the listener's brain
So sweet, that joy is almost pain.   40

Semichorus 1

There those enchanted eddies play
  Of echoes, music-tongued, which draw,
  By Demogorgon's mighty law,
  With melting rapture, or sweet awe,
All spirits on that secret way,
  As inland boats are driven to Ocean
Down streams made strong with mountain-thaw;
   And first there comes a gentle sound
   To those in talk or slumber bound,
  And wakes the destined; soft emotion°   50
Attracts, impels them: those who saw
  Say from the breathing earth behind°
  There steams a plume-uplifting wind
Which drives them on their path, while they
  Believe their own swift wings and feet
The sweet desires within obey:
And so they float upon their way,
Until, still sweet, but loud and strong,
The storm of sound is driven along,
  Sucked up and hurrying: as they fleet   60
  Behind, its gathering billows meet
And to the fatal mountain bear
Like clouds amid the yielding air.

First Faun. Canst thou imagine where those spirits live
Which make such delicate music in the woods?
We haunt within the least frequented caves
And closest coverts, and we know these wilds,
Yet never meet them, though we hear them oft:
Where may they hide themselves?

   Second Faun.   'Tis hard to tell:
I have heard those more skilled in spirits say,   70
The bubbles, which the enchantment of the sun
Sucks from the pale faint water-flowers that pave
The oozy bottom of clear lakes and pools,
Are the pavilions where such dwell and float
Under the green and golden atmosphere
Which noontide kindles through the woven leaves;
And when these burst, and the thin fiery air,
The which they breathed within those lucent domes,
Ascends to flow like meteors through the night,
They ride on them, and rein their headlong speed,   80
And bow their burning crests, and glide in fire
Under the waters of the earth again.°

   First Faun. If such live thus, have others other lives,
Under pink blossoms or within the bells
Of meadow flowers, or folded violets deep,
Or on their dying odours, when they die,
Or in the sunlight of the spherèd dew?

   Second Faun. Aye, many more, which we may well divine.
But should we stay to speak, noontide would come,
And thwart Silenus find his goats undrawn,°   90
And grudge to sing those wise and lovely songs
Of fate, and chance, and God, and Chaos old,
And Love, and the chained Titan's woeful doom,
And how he shall be loosed, and make the earth
One brotherhood: delightful strains which cheer
Our solitary twilights, and which charm
To silence the unenvying nightingales.

SCENE 3.—*A pinnacle of rock among mountains.* ASIA *and* PANTHEA.

   Panthea. Hither the sound has borne us—to the realm
Of Demogorgon, and the mighty portal,
Like a volcano's meteor-breathing chasm,°
Whence the oracular vapour is hurled up°
Which lonely men drink wandering in their youth,
And call truth, virtue, love, genius, or joy,
That maddening wine of life, whose dregs they drain
To deep intoxication, and uplift,
Like Maenads who cry loud, Evoe! Evoe!°
The voice which is contagion to the world.°   10

   Asia. Fit throne for such a Power! Magnificent!
How glorious art thou, Earth! and if thou be
The shadow of some spirit lovelier still,
Though evil stain its work, and it should be
Like its creation, weak yet beautiful,
I could fall down and worship that and thee.
Even now my heart adoreth—Wonderful!
Look, sister, ere the vapour dim thy brain:
Beneath is a wide plain of billowy mist,
As a lake, paving in the morning sky,   20
With azure waves which burst in silver light,
Some Indian vale. Behold it, rolling on
Under the curdling winds, and islanding
The peak whereon we stand—midway, around,
Encinctured by the dark and blooming forests,
Dim twilight lawns and stream-illumèd caves,
And wind-enchanted shapes of wandering mist;
And far on high the keen sky-cleaving mountains
From icy spires of sunlike radiance fling
The dawn, as lifted Ocean's dazzling spray,   30
From some Atlantic islet scattered up,
Spangles the wind with lamp-like water-drops.
The vale is girdled with their walls, a howl
Of cataracts from their thaw-cloven ravines
Satiates the listening wind, continuous, vast,
Awful as silence. Hark! the rushing snow!
The sun-awakened avalanche! whose mass,
Thrice sifted by the storm, had gathered there

Flake after flake, in heaven-defying minds
As thought by thought is piled, till some great truth   40
Is loosened, and the nations echo round,
Shaken to their roots, as do the mountains now.°

   Panthea. Look how the gusty sea of mist is breaking
In crimson foam, even at our feet! it rises
As Ocean at the enchantment of the moon
Round foodless men wrecked on some oozy isle.

   Asia. The fragments of the cloud are scattered up;
The wind that lifts them disentwines my hair;
Its billows now sweep o'er mine eyes—my brain
Grows dizzy—seest those shapes within the mist?   50

   Panthea. A countenance with beckoning smiles—there burns
An azure fire within its golden locks!
Another and another—hark! they speak!

Song of Spirits

> To the deep, to the deep,
>   Down, down!
> Through the shade of sleep,
> Through the cloudy strife
> Of Death and of Life;
> Through the veil and the bar
> Of things which seem and are,°   60
> Even to the steps of the remotest throne,
>   Down, down!
>
> While the sound whirls around,
>   Down, down!
> As the fawn draws the hound,
> As the lightning the vapour,
> As a weak moth the taper;
> Death, despair; love, sorrow;
> Time both; today, tomorrow;
> As steel obeys the Spirit of the stone,°   70
>   Down, down!
>
> Through the grey, void abysm,
>   Down, down!

Where the air is no prism,
And the moon and stars are not,
And the cavern-crags wear not
The radiance of Heaven,
Nor the gloom to Earth given;
Where there is One pervading, One alone,
          Down, down!   80

In the depth of the deep,
          Down, down!
Like veiled lightning asleep,
Like the spark nursed in embers,
The last look Love remembers,
Like a diamond, which shines
On the dark wealth of mines,
A spell is treasured but for thee alone.
          Down, down!

We have bound thee, we guide thee   90
          Down, down!
With the bright form beside thee;
Resist not the weakness—
Such strength is in meekness
That the Eternal, the Immortal,°
Must unloose through life's portal
The snake-like Doom coiled underneath his throne°
          By that alone.

SCENE 4.—*The Cave of* DEMOGORGON. ASIA *and* PANTHEA.

Panthea. What veilèd form sits on that ebon throne?

Asia. The veil has fallen!

Panthea.   I see a mighty Darkness
Filling the seat of power; and rays of gloom
Dart round, as light from the meridian sun,
Ungazed upon and shapeless; neither limb,°
Nor form, nor outline; yet we feel it is
A living Spirit.

Demogorgon. Ask what thou wouldst know.

Asia. What canst thou tell?

Demogorgon.   All things thou dar'st demand.

Asia. Who made the living world?

Demogorgon.   God.

Asia.   Who made all
That it contains—thought, passion, reason, will,   10
Imagination?

Demogorgon. God: Almighty God.

Asia. Who made that sense which, when the winds of spring
In rarest visitation, or the voice
Of one beloved heard in youth alone,
Fills the faint eyes with falling tears which dim
The radiant looks of unbewailing flowers,
And leaves this peopled earth a solitude
When it returns no more?

Demogorgon.   Merciful God.

Asia. And who made terror, madness, crime, remorse,
Which from the links of the great chain of things   20
To every thought within the mind of man
Sway and drag heavily, and each one reels°
Under the load towards the pit of death;
Abandoned hope, and love that turns to hate;
And self-contempt, bitterer to drink than blood;
Pain, whose unheeded and familiar speech
Is howling, and keen shrieks, day after day;
And Hell, or the sharp fear of Hell?

Demogorgon.   He reigns.

Asia Utter his name: a world pining in pain
Asks but his name: curses shall drag him down.   30

Demogorgon. He reigns.

Asia.   I feel, I know it: who?

Demogorgon.   He reigns.

Asia. Who reigns? There was the Heaven and Earth at first,°
And Light and Love; then Saturn, from whose throne
Time fell, an envious shadow; such the state
Of the earth's primal spirits beneath his sway,
As the calm joy of flowers and living leaves
Before the wind or sun has withered them
And semivital worms; but he refused
The birthrights of their being, knowledge, power,
The skill which wields the elements, the thought   40
Which pierces this dim universe like light,
Self-empire, and the majesty of love;
For thirst of which they fainted. Then Prometheus
Gave wisdom, which is strength, to Jupiter,
And with this law alone, 'Let man be free,'
Clothed him with the dominion of wide Heaven.
To know nor faith, nor love, nor law; to be
Omnipotent but friendless is to reign;
And Jove now reigned; for on the race of man
First famine, and then toil, and then disease,   50
Strife, wounds, and ghastly death unseen before,
Fell; and the unseasonable seasons drove,°
With alternating shafts of frost and fire,
Their shelterless, pale tribes to mountain caves:
And in their desert hearts fierce wants he sent,
And mad disquietudes, and shadows idle
Of unreal good, which levied mutual war,
So ruining the lair wherein they raged.
Prometheus saw, and waked the legioned hopes
Which sleep within folded Elysian flowers,   60
Nepenthe, Moly, Amaranth, fadeless blooms,°
That they might hide with thin and rainbow wings
The shape of Death; and Love he sent to bind
The disunited tendrils of that vine
Which bears the wine of life, the human heart;
And he tamed fire which, like some beast of prey
Most terrible, but lovely, played beneath
The frown of man; and tortured to his will

Iron and gold, the slaves and signs of power,
And gems and poisons, and all subtlest forms   70
Hidden beneath the mountains and the waves.
He gave man speech, and speech created thought,
Which is the measure of the universe;
And Science struck the thrones of earth and heaven,
Which shook, but fell not; and the harmonious mind
Poured itself forth in all-prophetic song;
And music lifted up the listening spirit
Until it walked, exempt from mortal care,
Godlike, o'er the clear billows of sweet sound;°
And human hands first mimicked and then mocked,°   80
With moulded limbs more lovely than its own,
The human form, till marble grew divine,
And mothers, gazing, drank the love men see
Reflected in their race, behold, and perish.°
He told the hidden power of herbs and springs,
And Disease drank and slept. Death grew like sleep.
He taught the implicated orbits woven°
Of the wide-wandering stars; and how the sun°
Changes his lair, and by what secret spell°
The pale moon is transformed, when her broad eye   90
Gazes not on the interlunar sea:°
He taught to rule, as life directs the limbs,
The tempest-wingèd chariots of the Ocean,
And the Celt knew the Indian. Cities then
Were built, and through their snow-like columns flowed
The warm winds, and the azure ether shone,
And the blue sea and shadowy hills were seen.
Such, the alleviations of his state,
Prometheus gave to man, for which he hangs
Withering in destined pain: but who rains down   100
Evil, the immedicable plague, which, while°
Man looks on his creation like a God
And sees that it is glorious, drives him on,°
The wreck of his own will, the scorn of earth,
The outcast, the abandoned, the alone?
Not Jove: while yet his frown shook heaven, aye, when
His adversary from adamantine chains°
Cursed him, he trembled like a slave. Declare
Who is his master? Is he too a slave?

Demogorgon. All spirits are enslaved which serve things evil. 110
Thou knowest if Jupiter be such or no.

Asia. Whom called'st thou God?

Demogorgon.   I spoke but as ye speak,
For Jove is the supreme of living things.

Asia. Who is the master of the slave?

Demogorgon.   If the abysm
Could vomit forth its secrets:—but a voice
Is wanting, the deep truth is imageless;
For what would it avail to bid thee gaze
On the revolving world? What to bid speak
Fate, Time, Occasion, Chance and Change? To these
All things are subject but eternal Love.   120

Asia. So much I asked before, and my heart gave
The response thou hast given; and of such truths
Each to itself must be the oracle.
One more demand; and do thou answer me
As my own soul would answer, did it know
That which I ask. Prometheus shall arise
Henceforth the sun of this rejoicing world:
When shall the destined hour arrive?

Demogorgon.   Behold!

Asia. The rocks are cloven, and through the purple night
I see cars drawn by rainbow-wingèd steeds   130
Which trample the dim winds: in each there stands
A wild-eyed charioteer, urging their flight.
Some look behind, as fiends pursued them there,
And yet I see no shapes but the keen stars;
Others, with burning eyes, lean forth, and drink,
With eager lips the wind of their own speed,
As if the thing they loved fled on before,
And now, even now, they clasped it. Their bright locks
Stream like a comet's flashing hair: they all
Sweep onward.

Demogorgon.   These are the immortal Hours,   140
Of whom thou didst demand. One waits for thee.

Asia. A spirit with a dreadful countenance°
Checks its dark chariot by the craggy gulf.
Unlike thy brethren, ghastly charioteer,
What art thou? Whither wouldst thou bear me? Speak!

Spirit. I am the shadow of a destiny
More dread than is my aspect: ere yon planet
Has set, the Darkness which ascends with me
Shall wrap in lasting night Heaven's kingless throne.

Asia. What meanest thou?

Panthea.   That terrible shadow floats   150
Up from its throne, as may the lurid smoke
Of earthquake-ruined cities o'er the sea.
Lo! it ascends the car; the coursers fly
Terrified: watch its path among the stars
Blackening the night!

Asia.   Thus I am answered: strange!

Panthea. See, near the verge, another chariot stays;
An ivory shell inlaid with crimson fire,°
Which comes and goes within its sculptured rim
Of delicate strange tracery; the young spirit
That guides it has the dove-like eyes of hope;   160
How its soft smiles attract the soul! as light
Lures wingèd insects through the lampless air.

Spirit

My coursers are fed with the lightning,
    They drink of the whirlwind's stream,
And when the red morning is bright'ning
    They bathe in the fresh sunbeam;
    They have strength for their swiftness I deem:
Then ascend with me, daughter of Ocean.

I desire: and their speed makes night kindle;
    I fear: they outstrip the Typhoon;   170

> Ere the cloud piled on Atlas can dwindle
> We encircle the earth and the moon:
> We shall rest from long labours at noon:
> Then ascend with me, daughter of Ocean.

SCENE 5.—*The car pauses within a cloud on the top of a snowy mountain.*
ASIA, PANTHEA, *and the* SPIRIT OF THE HOUR.

Spirit

> On the brink of the night and the morning
>   My coursers are wont to respire;°
> But the Earth has just whispered a warning
>   That their flight must be swifter than fire:
>   They shall drink the hot speed of desire!

Asia. Thou breathest on their nostrils, but my breath
Would give them swifter speed.

Spirit.   Alas! it could not.°

Panthea. O Spirit! pause, and tell whence is the light
Which fills this cloud—the sun is yet unrisen.

Spirit. The sun will rise not until noon. Apollo   10
Is held in heaven by wonder; and the light
Which fills this vapour, as the aerial hue
Of fountain-gazing roses fills the water,
Flows from thy mighty sister.°

Panthea.   Yes, I feel—

Asia. What is it with thee, sister? Thou art pale.

Panthea. How thou art changed! I dare not look on thee;
I feel, but see thee not. I scarce endure
The radiance of thy beauty. Some good change
Is working in the elements, which suffer
Thy presence thus unveiled. The Nereids tell°   20
That on the day when the clear hyaline°
Was cloven at thine uprise, and thou didst stand
Within a veinèd shell, which floated on
Over the calm floor of the crystal sea,

Among the Aegean isles, and by the shores
Which bear thy name, love, like the atmosphere
Of the sun's fire filling the living world,
Burst from thee, and illumined earth and heaven
And the deep ocean and the sunless caves,
And all that dwells within them; till grief cast°   30
Eclipse upon the soul from which it came:
Such art thou now; nor is it I alone,
Thy sister, thy companion, thine own chosen one,
But the whole world which seeks thy sympathy.
Hearest thou not sounds i' the air which speak the love
Of all articulate beings? Feelest thou not
The inanimate winds enamoured of thee? List!   [*Music.*

   Asia. Thy words are sweeter than aught else but his
Whose echoes they are: yet all love is sweet,
Given or returned. Common as light is love,   40
And its familiar voice wearies not ever.
Like the wide heaven, the all-sustaining air,
It makes the reptile equal to the God:
They who inspire it most are fortunate,
As I am now; but those who feel it most
Are happier still, after long sufferings,
As I shall soon become.

   Panthea.   List! Spirits speak.

              Voice (in the air, singing)

   Life of Life! thy lips enkindle
     With their love the breath between them;
   And thy smiles before they dwindle   50
     Make the cold air fire; then screen them
   In those looks, where whoso gazes
   Faints, entangled in their mazes.

   Child of Light! thy limbs are burning
     Through the vest which seems to hide them,
   As the radiant lines of morning
     Through the clouds ere they divide them;
   And this atmosphere divinest
   Shrouds thee wheresoe'er thou shinest.

Fair are others; none beholds thee,
  But thy voice sounds low and tender
Like the fairest, for it folds thee
  From the sight, that liquid splendour,
And all feel, yet see thee never,
As I feel now, lost forever!

Lamp of Earth! where'er thou movest
  Its dim shapes are clad with brightness,
And the souls of whom thou lovest
  Walk upon the winds with lightness,
Till they fail, as I am failing,°   70
Dizzy, lost, yet unbewailing!

Asia

My soul is an enchanted boat,
  Which, like a sleeping swan, doth float
Upon the silver waves of thy sweet singing;
  And thine doth like an angel sit
  Beside the helm conducting it,
Whilst all the winds with melody are ringing.
  It seems to float ever, forever,
  Upon that many-winding river,
Between mountains, woods, abysses,   80
  A paradise of wildernesses!
Till, like one in slumber bound
Borne to the ocean, I float down, around,
Into a sea profound, of ever-spreading sound:

  Meanwhile thy spirit lifts its pinions
  In music's most serene dominions,
Catching the winds that fan that happy heaven;
  And we sail on, away, afar,
  Without a course, without a star,
But by the instinct of sweet music driven;   90
  Till through Elysian garden islets
  By thee, most beautiful of pilots,
  Where never mortal pinnace glided,
  The boat of my desire is guided:
Realms where the air we breathe is love,
Which in the winds and on the waves doth move,
Harmonizing this earth with what we feel above.

   We have passed Age's icy caves,
   And Manhood's dark and tossing waves,
And Youth's smooth ocean, smiling to betray: 100
   Beyond the glassy gulfs we flee
   Of shadow-peopled Infancy,
Through Death and Birth, to a diviner day;°
   A paradise of vaulted bowers
   Lit by downward-gazing flowers,
   And watery paths that wind between
   Wildernesses calm and green,
Peopled by shapes too bright to see,
And rest, having beheld; somewhat like thee;
Which walk upon the sea, and chant melodiously!°   110

Act 3

SCENE 1.—*Heaven.* JUPITER *on his throne;* THETIS *and the other Deities assembled.*

Jupiter. Ye congregated Powers of Heaven, who share
The glory and the strength of him ye serve,
Rejoice! henceforth I am omnipotent.
All else has been subdued to me; alone
The soul of man, like unextinguished fire,
Yet burns towards Heaven with fierce reproach, and doubt,
And lamentation, and reluctant prayer,
Hurling up insurrection, which might make
Our antique empire insecure, though built
On eldest faith, and Hell's coeval, fear;   10
And though my curses through the pendulous air,°
Like snow on herbless peaks, fall flake by flake,°
And cling to it; though under my wrath's night
It climb the crags of life, step after step,
Which wound it, as ice wounds unsandalled feet,
It yet remains supreme o'er misery,
Aspiring, unrepressed, yet soon to fall:
Even now have I begotten a strange wonder,
That fatal child, the terror of the earth,°
Who waits but till the destined hour arrive,   20
Bearing from Demogorgon's vacant throne
The dreadful might of ever-living limbs
Which clothed that awful spirit unbeheld,
To redescend, and trample out the spark.

Pour forth Heaven's wine, Idaean Ganymede,°
And let it fill the daedal cups like fire,
And from the flower-inwoven soil divine
Ye all-triumphant harmonies arise,
As dew from earth under the twilight stars:
Drink! be the nectar circling through your veins   30
The soul of joy, ye ever-living Gods,
Till exultation burst in one wide voice
Like music from Elysian winds.
          And thou

Ascend beside me, veilèd in the light
Of the desire which makes thee one with me,
Thetis, bright image of eternity!°
When thou didst cry, 'Insufferable might!
God! Spare me! I sustain not the quick flames,
The penetrating presence; all my being,°
Like him whom the Numidian seps did thaw   40
Into a dew with poison, is dissolved,°
Sinking through its foundations': even then
Two mighty spirits, mingling, made a third
Mightier than either, which, unbodied now,
Between us floats, felt, although unbeheld,
Waiting the incarnation, which ascends
(Hear ye the thunder of the fiery wheels
Griding the winds?) from Demogorgon's throne.°
Victory! victory! Feel'st thou not, O world,
The earthquake of his chariot thundering up   50
Olympus?

The Car of the HOUR *arrives.* DEMOGORGON *descends, and
moves towards the throne of* JUPITER.

Awful shape, what art thou? Speak!

Demogorgon. Eternity. Demand no direr name.
Descend, and follow me down the abyss.
I am thy child, as thou wert Saturn's child;
Mightier than thee: and we must dwell together
Henceforth in darkness. Lift thy lightnings not.
The tyranny of Heaven none may retain,
Or reassume, or hold, succeeding thee:
Yet if thou wilt, as 'tis the destiny
Of trodden worms to writhe till they are dead,   60
Put forth thy might.

Jupiter.   Detested prodigy!
Even thus beneath the deep Titanian prisons°
I trample thee! thou lingerest?
                                Mercy! mercy!
No pity, no release, no respite! Oh,
That thou wouldst make mine enemy my judge,

Even where he hangs, seared by my long revenge,
On Caucasus! He would not doom me thus.
Gentle, and just, and dreadless, is he not
The monarch of the world? What then art thou?
No refuge! no appeal!

                Sink with me then,   70
We two will sink on the wide waves of ruin,
Even as a vulture and a snake outspent
Drop, twisted in inextricable fight,
Into a shoreless sea. Let Hell unlock
Its mounded oceans of tempestuous fire,
And whelm on them into the bottomless void
This desolated world, and thee, and me,
The conqueror and the conquered, and the wreck
Of that for which they combated.

                    Ai! Ai!°
The elements obey me not. I sink   80
Dizzily down, ever, forever, down.
And, like a cloud, mine enemy above
Darkens my fall with victory! Ai, Ai!

SCENE 2.—*The mouth of a great river in the island Atlantis.*° OCEAN° *is discovered reclining near the shore*; APOLLO° *stands beside him.*

   Ocean. He fell, thou sayest, beneath his conqueror's frown?

   Apollo. Aye, when the strife was ended which made dim
The orb I rule, and shook the solid stars.
The terrors of his eye illumined Heaven
With sanguine light, through the thick ragged skirts
Of the victorious Darkness, as he fell:
Like the last glare of day's red agony,
Which, from a rent among the fiery clouds,
Burns far along the tempest-wrinkled deep.

   Ocean. He sunk to the abyss? To the dark void?   10

   Apollo. An eagle so caught in some bursting cloud
On Caucasus, his thunder-baffled wings
Entangled in the whirlwind, and his eyes,
Which gazed on the undazzling sun, now blinded
By the white lightning, while the ponderous hail

Beats on his struggling form, which sinks at length
Prone, and the aerial ice clings over it.

Ocean. Henceforth the fields of Heaven-reflecting sea
Which are my realm, will heave, unstained with blood,°
Beneath the uplifting winds, like plains of corn   20
Swayed by the summer air; my streams will flow
Round many-peopled continents, and round
Fortunate isles; and from their glassy thrones
Blue Proteus and his humid nymphs shall mark
The shadow of fair ships, as mortals see
The floating bark of the light-laden moon
With that white star, its sightless pilot's crest,°
Borne down the rapid sunset's ebbing sea;
Tracking their path no more by blood and groans
And desolation, and the mingled voice   30
Of slavery and command; but by the light
Of wave-reflected flowers, and floating odours,
And music soft, and mild, free, gentle voices,
That sweetest music, such as spirits love.

Apollo. And I shall gaze not on the deeds which make
My mind obscure with sorrow, as eclipse
Darkens the sphere I guide; but list, I hear
The small, clear, silver lute of the young Spirit
That sits i' the morning star.

Ocean.   Thou must away;
Thy steeds will pause at even, till when, farewell.   40
The loud deep calls me home even now to feed it
With azure calm out of the emerald urns
Which stand forever full beside my throne.
Behold the Nereids under the green sea,
Their wavering limbs borne on the wind-like streams,
Their white arms lifted o'er their streaming hair,
With garlands pied and starry sea-flower crowns,
Hastening to grace their mighty sister's joy.
                                    [*A sound of waves is heard.*
It is the unpastured sea hungering for calm.°
Peace, monster; I come now. Farewell.

Apollo.   Farewell.   50

SCENE 3.—*Caucasus*. PROMETHEUS, HERCULES, IONE, *the* EARTH, SPIRITS. ASIA, *and* PANTHEA, *borne in the Car with the* SPIRIT OF THE HOUR.

[HERCULES *unbinds* PROMETHEUS, *who descends*.

Hercules. Most glorious among spirits, thus doth strength
To wisdom, courage, and long-suffering love,
And thee, who art the form they animate,
Minister, like a slave.

Prometheus.   Thy gentle words
Are sweeter even than freedom long desired
And long delayed.
                              Asia, thou light of life,
Shadow of beauty unbeheld; and ye,
Fair sister-nymphs, who made long years of pain
Sweet to remember, through your love and care;
Henceforth we will not part. There is a Cave°   10
All overgrown with trailing odorous plants,
Which curtain out the day with leaves and flowers,
And paved with veinèd emerald, and a fountain
Leaps in the midst with an awakening sound.
From its curved roof the mountain's frozen tears,
Like snow, or silver, or long diamond spires,
Hang downward, raining forth a doubtful light;
And there is heard the ever-moving air,
Whispering without from tree to tree, and birds,
And bees; and all around are mossy seats,   20
And the rough walls are clothed with long soft grass;
A simple dwelling, which shall be our own;
Where we will sit and talk of time and change,
As the world ebbs and flows, ourselves unchanged.°
What can hide man from mutability?
And if ye sigh, then I will smile; and thou,
Ione, shall chant fragments of sea-music,
Until I weep, when ye shall smile away
The tears she brought, which yet were sweet to shed.
We will entangle buds and flowers, and beams   30
Which twinkle on the fountain's brim, and make
Strange combinations out of common things,

Like human babes in their brief innocence;
And we will search, with looks and words of love,
For hidden thoughts, each lovelier than the last,
Our unexhausted spirits; and like lutes
Touched by the skill of the enamoured wind,
Weave harmonies divine, yet ever new,
From difference sweet where discord cannot be;
And hither come, sped on the charmèd winds   40
Which meet from all the points of heaven, as bees
From every flower aerial Enna feeds°
At their known island-homes in Himera,°
The echoes of the human world, which tell
Of the low voice of love, almost unheard,
And dove-eyed pity's murmured pain, and music,
Itself the echo of the heart, and all
That tempers or improves man's life, now free;
And lovely apparitions, dim at first,
Then radiant, as the mind, arising bright   50
From the embrace of beauty, whence the forms
Of which these are the phantoms, casts on them
The gathered rays which are reality,°
Shall visit us, the progeny immortal
Of Painting, Sculpture, and rapt Poesy,
And arts, though unimagined, yet to be.
The wandering voices and the shadows these
Of all that man becomes, the mediators
Of that best worship, love, by him and us
Given and returned; swift shapes and sounds, which grow   60
More fair and soft as man grows wise and kind,
And veil by veil, evil and error fall:
Such virtue has the cave and place around.
                            [*Turning to the* SPIRIT OF THE HOUR.
For thee, fair Spirit, one toil remains. Ione,
Give her that curvèd shell, which Proteus old°
Made Asia's nuptial boon, breathing within it
A voice to be accomplished, and which thou
Didst hide in grass under the hollow rock.

    Ione. Thou most desired Hour, more loved and lovely
Than all thy sisters, this is the mystic shell;   70
See the pale azure fading into silver

Lining it with a soft yet glowing light:
Looks it not like lulled music sleeping there?

   Spirit. It seems in truth the fairest shell of Ocean:
Its sound must be at once both sweet and strange.

   Prometheus. Go, borne over the cities of mankind
On whirlwind-footed coursers: once again
Outspeed the sun around the orbèd world;
And as thy chariot cleaves the kindling air,   80
Thou breathe into the many-folded shell,
Loosening its mighty music; it shall be
As thunder mingled with clear echoes: then
Return; and thou shalt dwell beside our cave.

                                           [*Kissing the ground*.

And thou, O Mother Earth!—

   The Earth.   I hear, I feel;
Thy lips are on me, and their touch runs down
Even to the adamantine central gloom
Along these marble nerves; 'tis life, 'tis joy,
And through my withered, old, and icy frame
The warmth of an immortal youth shoots down
Circling. Henceforth the many children fair   90
Folded in my sustaining arms; all plants,
And creeping forms, and insects rainbow-winged,
And birds, and beasts, and fish, and human shapes,
Which drew disease and pain from my wan bosom,
Draining the poison of despair; shall take
And interchange sweet nutriment; to me
Shall they become like sister-antelopes
By one fair dam, snow-white and swift as wind,
Nursed among lilies near a brimming stream.
The dew-mists of my sunless sleep shall float   100
Under the stars like balm: night-folded flowers
Shall suck unwithering hues in their repose:
And men and beasts in happy dreams shall gather
Strength for the coming day and all its joy:
And death shall be the last embrace of her
Who takes the life she gave, even as a mother,
Folding her child, says, 'Leave me not again.'

Asia. O mother! wherefore speak the name of death?
Cease they to love, and move, and breathe, and speak,
Who die?

The Earth. It would avail not to reply: 110
Thou art immortal, and this tongue is known
But to the uncommunicating dead.
Death is the veil which those who live call life:
They sleep, and it is lifted: and meanwhile
In mild variety the seasons mild
With rainbow-skirted showers, and odorous winds,
And long blue meteors cleansing the dull night,
And the life-kindling shafts of the keen sun's
All-piercing bow, and the dew-mingled rain
Of the calm moonbeams, a soft influence mild,   120
Shall clothe the forests and the fields, aye, even
The crag-built deserts of the barren deep,
With ever-living leaves, and fruit, and flowers.
And Thou! There is a Cavern where my spirit°
Was panted forth in anguish whilst thy pain
Made my heart mad, and those who did inhale it
Became mad too, and built a temple there,
And spoke, and were oracular, and lured
The erring nations round to mutual war,
And faithless faith, such as Jove kept with thee;   130
Which breath now rises, as among tall weeds
A violet's exhalation, and it fills
With a serener light and crimson air
Intense, yet soft, the rocks and woods around;
It feeds the quick growth of the serpent vine,
And the dark linkèd ivy tangling wild,°
And budding, blown, or odour-faded blooms
Which star the winds with points of coloured light,
As they rain through them, and bright, golden globes
Of fruit, suspended in their own green heaven;   140
And, through their veinèd leaves and amber stems,
The flowers whose purple and translucid bowls
Stand ever mantling with aerial dew,
The drink of spirits; and it circles round,
Like the soft waving wings of noonday dreams,
Inspiring calm and happy thoughts, like mine,

Now thou art thus restored. This Cave is thine.
Arise! Appear!

                [A SPIRIT *rises in the likeness of a winged child.*
          This is my torch-bearer,
Who let his lamp out in old time with gazing
On eyes from which he kindled it anew   150
With love, which is as fire, sweet daughter mine,
For such is that within thine own. Run, wayward,
And guide this company beyond the peak
Of Bacchic Nysa, Maenad-haunted mountain,°
And beyond Indus and its tribute rivers,°
Trampling the torrent streams and glassy lakes
With feet unwet, unwearied, undelaying;
And up the green ravine, across the vale,
Beside the windless and crystalline pool,
Where ever lies, on unerasing waves,   160
The image of a temple, built above,
Distinct with column, arch, and architrave,
And palm-like capital, and over-wrought,
And populous most with living imagery,
Praxitelean shapes, whose marble smiles°
Fill the hushed air with everlasting love.
It is deserted now, but once it bore
Thy name, Prometheus; there the emulous youths
Bore to thy honour through the divine gloom
The lamp which was thine emblem; even as those°   170
Who bear the untransmitted torch of hope
Into the grave, across the night of life,
As thou hast borne it most triumphantly
To this far goal of time. Depart, farewell.
Beside that temple is the destined Cave.

SCENE 4.—*A forest. In the background a Cave.* PROMETHEUS, ASIA,
PANTHEA, IONE, *and the* SPIRIT OF THE EARTH.°

   Ione. Sister, it is not earthly: how it glides
Under the leaves! how on its head there burns
A light, like a green star, whose emerald beams°
Are twined with its fair hair! how, as it moves,
The splendour drops in flakes upon the grass!
Knowest thou it?

Panthea.   It is the delicate spirit
That guides the earth through heaven. From afar
The populous constellations call that light
The loveliest of the planets; and sometimes
It floats along the spray of the salt sea,   10
Or makes its chariot of a foggy cloud,
Or walks through fields or cities while men sleep,
Or o'er the mountain tops, or down the rivers,
Or through the green waste wilderness, as now,
Wondering at all it sees. Before Jove reigned
It loved our sister Asia, and it came
Each leisure hour to drink the liquid light
Out of her eyes, for which it said it thirsted
As one bit by a dipsas; and with her°
It made its childish confidence, and told her   20
All it had known or seen, for it saw much,
Yet idly reasoned what it saw; and called her,
For whence it sprung it knew not, nor do I,
'Mother, dear mother.'

Spirit of the Earth (*running to Asia*). Mother, dearest mother;
May I then talk with thee as I was wont?
May I then hide my eyes in thy soft arms,
After thy looks have made them tired of joy?
May I then play beside thee the long noons,
When work is none in the bright silent air?

Asia. I love thee, gentlest being, and henceforth   30
Can cherish thee unenvied: speak, I pray:
Thy simple talk once solaced, now delights.

Spirit of the Earth. Mother, I am grown wiser, though a child
Cannot be wise like thee, within this day;
And happier too; happier and wiser both.
Thou knowest that toads, and snakes, and loathly worms,
And venomous and malicious beasts, and boughs
That bore ill berries in the woods, were ever
An hindrance to my walks o'er the green world:
And that, among the haunts of humankind,   40
Hard-featured men, or with proud, angry looks,
Or cold, staid gait, or false and hollow smiles,

Or the dull sneer of self-loved ignorance,
Or other such foul masks, with which ill thoughts
Hide that fair being whom we spirits call man;
And women too, ugliest of all things evil,
(Though fair, even in a world where thou art fair,
When good and kind, free and sincere like thee),
When false or frowning made me sick at heart
To pass them, though they slept, and I unseen.   50
Well, my path lately lay through a great city;
Into the woody hills surrounding it:
A sentinel was sleeping at the gate:
When there was heard a sound, so loud, it shook
The towers amid the moonlight, yet more sweet
Than any voice but thine, sweetest of all,
A long, long sound, as it would never end;
And all the inhabitants leapt suddenly
Out of their rest, and gathered in the streets,
Looking in wonder up to Heaven, while yet   60
The music pealed along. I hid myself
Within a fountain in the public square,
Where I lay like the reflex of the moon
Seen in a wave under green leaves; and soon
Those ugly human shapes and visages
Of which I spoke as having wrought me pain,
Passed floating through the air, and fading still°
Into the winds that scattered them; and those
From whom they passed seemed mild and lovely forms
After some foul disguise had fallen, and all   70
Were somewhat changed, and after brief surprise
And greetings of delighted wonder, all
Went to their sleep again: and when the dawn
Came, wouldst thou think that toads, and snakes, and efts,
Could e'er be beautiful? yet so they were,
And that with little change of shape or hue:
All things had put their evil nature off:
I cannot tell my joy, when o'er a lake,
Upon a drooping bough with nightshade twined,
I saw two azure halcyons clinging downward°   80
And thinning one bright bunch of amber berries
With quick, long beaks, and in the deep there lay
Those lovely forms imaged as in a sky;

So with my thoughts full of these happy changes,
We meet again, the happiest change of all.

    Asia. And never will we part, till thy chaste sister
Who guides the frozen and inconstant moon
Will look on thy more warm and equal light
Till her heart thaw like flakes of April snow
And love thee.

    Spirit of the Earth. What; as Asia loves Prometheus?   90

    Asia. Peace, wanton, thou art yet not old enough.
Think ye by gazing on each other's eyes
To multiply your lovely selves, and fill
With spherèd fires the interlunar air?

    Spirit of the Earth. Nay, mother, while my sister trims her lamp
'Tis hard I should go darkling.

    Asia.   Listen! look!
                              [*The* SPIRIT OF THE HOUR *enters.*

    Prometheus. We feel what thou hast heard and seen: yet speak.

    Spirit of the Hour. Soon as the sound had ceased whose thunder
      filled
The abysses of the sky and the wide earth,
There was a change: the impalpable thin air   100
And the all-circling sunlight were transformed,
As if the sense of love, dissolved in them,
Had folded itself round the spherèd world.
My vision then grew clear, and I could see
Into the mysteries of the universe.
Dizzy as with delight I floated down,
Winnowing the lightsome air with languid plumes,
My coursers sought their birthplace in the sun,
Where they henceforth will live exempt from toil,
Pasturing flowers of vegetable fire;   110
And where my moonlike car will stand within
A temple, gazed upon by Phidian forms°
Of thee, and Asia, and the Earth, and me,

And you fair nymphs, looking the love we feel,
In memory of the tidings it has borne;
Beneath a dome fretted with graven flowers,
Poised on twelve columns of resplendent stone,
And open to the bright and liquid sky.
Yoked to it by an amphisbaenic snake°
The likeness of those wingèd steeds will mock°   120
The flight from which they find repose. Alas,°
Whither has wandered now my partial tongue
When all remains untold which ye would hear?
As I have said, I floated to the earth:
It was, as it is still, the pain of bliss
To move, to breathe, to be; I wandering went
Among the haunts and dwellings of mankind,
And first was disappointed not to see
Such mighty change as I had felt within
Expressed in outward things; but soon I looked,   130
And behold, thrones were kingless, and men walked
One with the other even as spirits do:
None fawned, none trampled; hate, disdain, or fear,
Self-love or self-contempt, on human brows
No more inscribed, as o'er the gate of hell,   135
'All hope abandon, ye who enter here';°
None frowned, none trembled, none with eager fear
Gazed on another's eye of cold command,
Until the subject of a tyrant's will
Became, worse fate, the abject of his own,   140
Which spurred him, like an outspent horse, to death.
None wrought his lips in truth-entangling lines
Which smiled the lie his tongue disdained to speak;
None, with firm sneer, trod out in his own heart
The sparks of love and hope, till there remained
Those bitter ashes, a soul self-consumed,
And the wretch crept a vampire among men,
Infecting all with his own hideous ill;
None talked that common, false, cold, hollow talk
Which makes the heart deny the *yes* it breathes,   150
Yet question that unmeant hypocrisy°
With such a self-mistrust as has no name.
And women, too, frank, beautiful, and kind
As the free heaven which rains fresh light and dew

On the wide earth, passed; gentle, radiant forms,
From custom's evil taint exempt and pure;
Speaking the wisdom once they could not think,
Looking emotions once they feared to feel,
And changed to all which once they dared not be,
Yet being now, made Earth like Heaven; nor pride,   160
Nor jealousy, nor envy, nor ill shame,
The bitterest of those drops of treasured gall,
Spoilt the sweet taste of the nepenthe, love.

Thrones, altars, judgement-seats, and prisons; wherein
And beside which, by wretched men were borne
Sceptres, tiaras, swords, and chains, and tomes
Of reasoned wrong, glozed on by ignorance,
Were like those monstrous and barbaric shapes,
The ghosts of a no more remembered fame,
Which, from their unworn obelisks, look forth   170
In triumph o'er the palaces and tombs
Of those who were their conquerors, mouldering round.
These imaged to the pride of kings and priests
A dark yet mighty faith, a power as wide
As is the world it wasted, and are now
But an astonishment; even so the tools
And emblems of its last captivity,
Amid the dwellings of the peopled earth,
Stand, not o'erthrown, but unregarded now.
And those foul shapes, abhorred by God and man,   180
Which under many a name and many a form
Strange, savage, ghastly, dark, and execrable,
Were Jupiter, the tyrant of the world;
And which the nations, panic-stricken, served
With blood, and hearts broken by long hope, and love
Dragged to his altars soiled and garlandless,
And slain amid men's unreclaiming tears,°
Flattering the thing they feared, which fear was hate,
Frown, mouldering fast, o'er their abandoned shrines:
The painted veil, by those who were, called life,   190
Which mimicked, as with colours idly spread,
All men believed and hoped, is torn aside;
The loathsome mask has fallen, the man remains
Sceptreless, free, uncircumscribed, but man:

Equal, unclassed, tribeless and nationless,
Exempt from awe, worship, degree: the king,
Over himself; just, gentle, wise: but man:
Passionless? no, yet free from guilt or pain,
Which were, for his will made or suffered them,
Nor yet exempt, though ruling them like slaves,   200
From chance, and death, and mutability,
The clogs of that which else might oversoar
The loftiest star of unascended Heaven,
Pinnacled dim in the intense inane.°

Act 4

SCENE. *A Part of the Forest near the Cave of* PROMETHEUS. PANTHEA
and IONE *are sleeping: they awaken gradually during the first Song.*

Voice of Unseen Spirits

The pale stars are gone!
For the sun, their swift shepherd,
To their folds them compelling,
In the depths of the dawn,
Hastes, in meteor-eclipsing array, and they flee
Beyond his blue dwelling
As fawns flee the leopard.
But where are ye?

*A Train of dark Forms and Shadows passes by
confusedly, singing*

Here, oh, here!
We bear the bier   10
Of the Father of many a cancelled year!
Spectres we
Of the dead Hours be,
We bear Time to his tomb in eternity.°

Strew, oh, strew
Hair, not yew!
Wet the dusty pall with tears, not dew!
Be the faded flowers
Of Death's bare bowers
Spread on the corpse of the King of Hours!   20

Haste, oh, haste!
As shades are chased,
Trembling, by day, from heaven's blue waste,
We melt away,
Like dissolving spray,
From the children of a diviner day,
With the lullaby

Of winds that die
On the bosom of their own harmony!

Ione

What dark forms were they?   30

Panthea

The past Hours weak and grey,
With the spoil which their toil
        Raked together
From the conquest but One could foil.°

Ione

Have they passed?

Panthea

            They have passed;
    They outspeeded the blast,
    While 'tis said, they are fled:

Ione

Whither, oh, whither?

Panthea

To the dark, to the past, to the dead.

Voice of Unseen Spirits

Bright clouds float in heaven,   40
Dew-stars gleam on earth,
Waves assemble on ocean,
They are gathered and driven
By the storm of delight, by the panic of glee!
They shake with emotion,
They dance in their mirth.
        But where are ye?

The pine boughs are singing
Old songs with new gladness,
The billows and fountains   50
Fresh music are flinging,

Like the notes of a spirit, from land and from sea;
    The storms mock the mountains
    With the thunder of gladness.
        But where are ye?   55

Ione. What charioteers are these?

Panthea.   Where are their chariots?

        Semichorus of Hours 1

The voice of the Spirits of Air and of Earth
Have drawn back the figured curtain of sleep°
Which covered our being and darkened our birth
    In the deep.

        A Voice
    In the deep?

        Semichorus 2
        Oh, below the deep.   60

        Semichorus 1

An hundred ages we had been kept
Cradled in visions of hate and care,
And each one who waked as his brother slept
    Found the truth—

        Semichorus 2
        Worse than his visions were!

        Semichorus 1

We have heard the lute of Hope in sleep;
We have known the voice of Love in dreams;
We have felt the wand of Power, and leap—

        Semichorus 2

As the billows leap in the morning beams.

        Chorus

Weave the dance on the floor of the breeze,
    Pierce with song heaven's silent light,   70
Enchant the day that too swiftly flees,
    To check its flight ere the cave of night.

Once the hungry Hours were hounds
Which chased the day like a bleeding deer,
And it limped and stumbled with many wounds
Through the nightly dells of the desert year.

But now, oh weave the mystic measure
Of music, and dance, and shapes of light,
Let the Hours, and the spirits of might and pleasure,
Like the clouds and sunbeams, unite.

A Voice.

Unite!   80

Panthea. See, where the Spirits of the human mind
Wrapped in sweet sounds, as in bright veils, approach.

Chorus of Spirits

We join the throng
Of the dance and the song,
By the whirlwind of gladness borne along;
As the flying-fish leap
From the Indian deep,
And mix with the sea-birds half asleep.

Chorus of Hours

Whence come ye, so wild and so fleet,
For sandals of lightning are on your feet,   90
And your wings are soft and swift as thought,
And your eyes are as love which is veilèd not?

Chorus of Spirits

We come from the mind
Of human kind,
Which was late so dusk, and obscene, and blind;
Now 'tis an ocean
Of clear emotion,
A heaven of serene and mighty motion.

From that deep abyss
Of wonder and bliss,   100

Whose caverns are crystal palaces;
    From those skiey towers
    Where Thought's crowned powers
Sit watching your dance, ye happy Hours!

    From the dim recesses
    Of woven caresses,
Where lovers catch ye by your loose tresses;
    From the azure isles,
    Where sweet Wisdom smiles,
Delaying your ships with her siren wiles.°   110

    From the temples high
    Of Man's ear and eye,
Roofed over Sculpture and Poesy;
    From the murmurings
    Of the unsealed springs
Where Science bedews his daedal wings.°

    Years after years,
    Through blood and tears,
And a thick hell of hatreds and hopes and fears,
    We waded and flew,   120
    And the islets were few
Where the bud-blighted flowers of happiness grew.

    Our feet now, every palm,
    Are sandalled with calm,
And the dew of our wings is a rain of balm;
    And, beyond our eyes,
    The human love lies
Which makes all it gazes on Paradise.

Chorus of Spirits and Hours

  Then weave the web of the mystic measure;
From the depths of the sky and the ends of the earth,   130
  Come, swift Spirits of might and of pleasure,
Fill the dance and the music of mirth,
  As the waves of a thousand streams rush by
  To an ocean of splendour and harmony!

Chorus of Spirits

Our spoil is won,
Our task is done,
We are free to dive, or soar, or run;
Beyond and around,
Or within the bound
Which clips the world with darkness round.°   140

We'll pass the eyes
Of the starry skies
Into the hoar deep to colonize:
Death, Chaos, and Night,
From the sound of our flight,
Shall flee, like mist from a tempest's might.

And Earth, Air, and Light,
And the Spirit of Might,
Which drives round the stars in their fiery flight;
And Love, Thought, and Breath,   150
The powers that quell Death,
Wherever we soar shall assemble beneath.

And our singing shall build
In the void's loose field
A world for the Spirit of Wisdom to wield;
We will take our plan
From the new world of man,
And our work shall be called the Promethean.

Chorus of Hours

Break the dance, and scatter the song;
Let some depart, and some remain.   160

Semichorus 1

We, beyond heaven, are driven along—

Semichorus 2

Us the enchantments of earth retain—

Semichorus 1

Ceaseless, and rapid, and fierce, and free,

With the Spirits which build a new earth and sea,
And a Heaven where yet Heaven could never be—

Semichorus 2

Solemn, and slow and serene, and bright
Leading the Day and outspeeding the Night,
With the powers of a world of perfect light—

Semichorus 1

We whirl, singing loud, round the gathering sphere,°
Till the trees, and the beasts, and the clouds appear   170
From its chaos made calm by love, not fear—

Semichorus 2

We encircle the oceans and mountains of earth,
And the happy forms of its death and birth
Change to the music of our sweet mirth.

Chorus of Hours and Spirits

Break the dance, and scatter the song,
    Let some depart, and some remain;
Wherever we fly we lead along
In leashes, like starbeams, soft yet strong,
    The clouds that are heavy with love's sweet rain.

Panthea. Ha! they are gone!

Ione.   Yet feel you no delight   180
From the past sweetness?

Panthea.   As the bare green hill,
When some soft cloud vanishes into rain,
Laughs with a thousand drops of sunny water
To the unpavilioned sky!

Ione.   Even whilst we speak
New notes arise. What is that awful sound?

Panthea. 'Tis the deep music of the rolling world,
Kindling within the strings of the waved air
Aeolian modulations.

Ione.   Listen too,
How every pause is filled with under-notes,
Clear, silver, icy, keen, awakening tones,   190
Which pierce the sense, and live within the soul,
As the sharp stars pierce winter's crystal air
And gaze upon themselves within the sea.

Panthea. But see where, through two openings in the forest
Which hanging branches overcanopy,
And where two runnels of a rivulet,
Between the close moss, violet-inwoven,
Have made their path of melody, like sisters
Who part with sighs that they may meet in smiles,
Turning their dear disunion to an isle   200
Of lovely grief, a wood of sweet sad thoughts;
Two visions of strange radiance float upon
The ocean-like enchantment of strong sound,
Which flows intenser, keener, deeper yet
Under the ground and through the windless air.

Ione. I see a chariot like that thinnest boat
In which the mother of the months is borne
By ebbing light into her western cave
When she upsprings from interlunar dreams,
O'er which is curved an orblike canopy   210
Of gentle darkness, and the hills and woods,
Distinctly seen through that dusk aery veil,
Regard like shapes in an enchanter's glass;°
Its wheels are solid clouds, azure and gold,
Such as the genii of the thunderstorm
Pile on the floor of the illumined sea
When the sun rushes under it; they roll
And move and grow as with an inward wind.
Within it sits a wingèd infant, white
Its countenance, like the whiteness of bright snow,   220
Its plumes are as feathers of sunny frost,
Its limbs gleam white, through the wind-flowing folds
Of its white robe, woof of ethereal pearl.
Its hair is white, the brightness of white light°
Scattered in strings; yet its two eyes are heavens
Of liquid darkness, which the Deity

Within seems pouring, as a storm is poured
From jagged clouds, out of their arrowy lashes,
Tempering the cold and radiant air around
With fire that is not brightness; in its hand°   230
It sways a quivering moonbeam, from whose point
A guiding power directs the chariot's prow
Over its wheelèd clouds, which, as they roll
Over the grass and flowers and waves, wake sounds
Sweet as a singing rain of silver dew.

   Panthea. And from the other opening in the wood
Rushes, with loud and whirlwind harmony,°
A sphere, which is as many thousand spheres,
Solid as crystal, yet through all its mass
Flow, as through empty space, music and light: 240
Ten thousand orbs involving and involved,
Purple and azure, white and green and golden,
Sphere within sphere; and every space between
Peopled with unimaginable shapes,
Such as ghosts dream dwell in the lampless deep,
Yet each inter-transpicuous; and they whirl°
Over each other with a thousand motions,
Upon a thousand sightless axles spinning,
And with the force of self-destroying swiftness,
Intensely, slowly, solemnly roll on,   250
Kindling with mingled sounds, and many tones,
Intelligible words and music wild.
With mighty whirl the multitudinous Orb
Grinds the bright brook into an azure mist
Of elemental subtlety, like light;
And the wild odour of the forest flowers,
The music of the living grass and air,
The emerald light of leaf-entangled beams,
Round its intense yet self-conflicting speed,
Seem kneaded into one aerial mass   260
Which drowns the sense. Within the Orb itself,°
Pillowed upon its alabaster arms,
Like to a child o'erwearied with sweet toil,
On its own folded wings and wavy hair,
The Spirit of the Earth is laid asleep,
And you can see its little lips are moving,

Amid the changing light of their own smiles,
Like one who talks of what he loves in dream.

    Ione. 'Tis only mocking the Orb's harmony.°

    Panthea. And from a star upon its forehead, shoot,   270
Like swords of azure fire, or golden spears
With tyrant-quelling myrtle overtwined,°
Embleming Heaven and Earth united now,
Vast beams like spokes of some invisible wheel,
Which whirl as the Orb whirls, swifter than thought,
Filling the abyss with sunlike lightenings,
And perpendicular now, and now transverse,
Pierce the dark soil, and, as they pierce and pass,
Make bare the secrets of the earth's deep heart;
Infinite mine of adamant and gold,   280
Valueless stones, and unimagined gems,°
And caverns on crystalline columns poised
With vegetable silver overspread;
Wells of unfathomed fire, and water springs
Whence the great sea, even as a child, is fed,
Whose vapours clothe earth's monarch mountain-tops
With kingly, ermine snow. The beams flash on
And make appear the melancholy ruins
Of cancelled cycles; anchors, beaks of ships,
Planks turned to marble, quivers, helms, and spears,   290
And gorgon-headed targes, and the wheels
Of scythèd chariots, and the emblazonry
Of trophies, standards, and armorial beasts,
Round which death laughed, sepulchred emblems
Of dead destruction, ruin within ruin!
The wrecks beside of many a city vast,
Whose population which the earth grew over
Was mortal, but not human; see, they lie,
Their monstrous works and uncouth skeletons,
Their statues, homes, and fanes; prodigious shapes   300
Huddled in grey annihilation, split,
Jammed in the hard, black deep; and over these
The anatomies of unknown wingèd things,
And fishes which were isles of living scale,
And serpents, bony chains, twisted around
The iron crags, or within heaps of dust

To which the tortuous strength of their last pangs
Had crushed the iron crags; and over these
The jagged alligator, and the might
Of earth-convulsing behemoth, which once   310
Were monarch beasts, and on the slimy shores
And weed-overgrown continents of earth
Increased and multiplied like summer worms
On an abandoned corpse, till the blue globe
Wrapped deluge round it like a cloak, and they
Yelled, gasped, and were abolished; or some God
Whose throne was in a comet, passed, and cried,
'Be not!' And like my words they were no more.°

The Earth

The joy, the triumph, the delight, the madness!
The boundless, overflowing, bursting gladness!   320
The vaporous exultation, not to be confined!
    Ha! ha! the animation of delight
    Which wraps me, like an atmosphere of light,
And bears me as a cloud is borne by its own wind!

The Moon

    Brother mine, calm wanderer,
    Happy globe of land and air,
Some Spirit is darted like a beam from thee,
    Which penetrates my frozen frame,
    And passes with the warmth of flame,
With love, and odour, and deep melody   330
    Through me, through me!

The Earth

Ha! ha! the caverns of my hollow mountains,
My cloven fire-crags, sound-exulting fountains,
Laugh with a vast and inextinguishable laughter.
    The oceans, and the deserts, and the abysses,
    And the deep air's unmeasured wildernesses,
Answer from all their clouds and billows, echoing after.

    They cry aloud as I do: 'Sceptred Curse,
    Who all our green and azure universe
Threatenedst to muffle round with black destruction, sending 340

A solid cloud to rain hot thunder-stones,
  And splinter and knead down my children's bones,
All I bring forth, to one void mass battering and blending;

  'Until each crag-like tower, and storied column,
  Palace, and obelisk, and temple solemn,
My imperial mountains crowned with cloud, and snow and fire;
  My sea-like forests, every blade and blossom
  Which finds a grave or cradle in my bosom,
Were stamped by thy strong hate into a lifeless mire:

  'How art thou sunk, withdrawn, covered, drunk up   350
  By thirsty nothing, as the brackish cup
Drained by a desert-troop, a little drop for all!
  And from beneath, around, within, above,
  Filling thy void annihilation, love
Bursts in like light on caves cloven by the thunder-ball.'

The Moon

  The snow upon my lifeless mountains
  Is loosened into living fountains,
My solid oceans flow, and sing, and shine:
  A spirit from my heart bursts forth,
  It clothes with unexpected birth   360
My cold bare bosom: Oh, it must be thine
      On mine, on mine!

  Gazing on thee I feel, I know
  Green stalks burst forth, and bright flowers grow,
And living shapes upon my bosom move:
  Music is in the sea and air,
  Wingèd clouds soar here and there,
Dark with the rain new buds are dreaming of:
      'Tis love, all love!

The Earth

  It interpenetrates my granite mass,   370
  Through tangled roots and trodden clay doth pass
Into the utmost leaves and delicatest flowers;
  Upon the winds, among the clouds 'tis spread;
  It wakes a life in the forgotten dead,
They breathe a spirit up from their obscurest bowers.

And like a storm, bursting its cloudy prison
　　With thunder, and with whirlwind, has arisen
Out of the lampless caves of unimagined being,
　　With earthquake shock and swiftness making shiver
Thought's stagnant chaos, unremoved for ever,   380
Till hate, and fear, and pain, light-vanquished shadows, fleeing,

　　Leave Man, who was a many-sided mirror
　　Which could distort to many a shape of error
This true fair world of things—a sea reflecting love;
　　Which over all his kind, as the sun's heaven
　　Gliding o'er ocean, smooth, serene, and even,
Darting from starry depths radiance and light, doth move.

　　Leave Man, even as a leprous child is left,
　　Who follows a sick beast to some warm cleft
Of rocks, through which the might of healing springs
　　　is poured;   390
　　Then when it wanders home with rosy smile,
　　Unconscious, and its mother fears awhile
It is a spirit—then, weeps on her child restored.°

　　Man, oh, not men! a chain of linkèd thought,
　　Of love and might to be divided not,
Compelling the elements with adamantine stress;
　　As the sun rules, even with a tyrant's gaze,
　　The unquiet republic of the maze
Of planets, struggling fierce towards heaven's free wilderness.

　　Man, one harmonious soul of many a soul,   400
　　Whose nature is its own divine control,
Where all things flow to all, as rivers to the sea;
　　Familiar acts are beautiful through love;
　　Labour, and pain, and grief, in life's green grove
Sport like tame beasts—none knew how gentle they could be!

　　His will, with all mean passions, bad delights,
　　And selfish cares, its trembling satellites,
A spirit ill to guide, but mighty to obey,
　　Is as a tempest-wingèd ship, whose helm

Love rules, through waves which dare not overwhelm,   410
Forcing life's wildest shores to own its sovereign sway.

   All things confess his strength. Through the cold mass
   Of marble and of colour his dreams pass;
Bright threads whence mothers weave the robes their children wear;
   Language is a perpetual Orphic song,°
   Which rules with daedal harmony a throng
Of thoughts and forms, which else senseless and shapeless were.

   The lightning is his slave; heaven's utmost deep
   Gives up her stars, and like a flock of sheep
They pass before his eye, are numbered, and roll on!   420
   The tempest is his steed, he strides the air;
   And the abyss shouts from her depth laid bare,
'Heaven, hast thou secrets? Man unveils me; I have none.'

The Moon

   The shadow of white death has passed
   From my path in heaven at last,
A clinging shroud of solid frost and sleep;
   And through my newly-woven bowers
   Wander happy paramours,
Less mighty, but as mild as those who keep
   Thy vales more deep.   430

The Earth

   As the dissolving warmth of dawn may fold
   A half-unfrozen dew-globe, green, and gold,
And crystalline, till it becomes a wingèd mist,
   And wanders up the vault of the blue day,
   Outlives the noon, and on the sun's last ray
Hangs o'er the sea, a fleece of fire and amethyst—

The Moon

   Thou art folded, thou art lying
   In the light which is undying
Of thine own joy, and heaven's smile divine;
   All suns and constellations shower   440
   On thee a light, a life, a power

Which doth array thy sphere; thou pourest thine
    On mine, on mine!

The Earth

I spin beneath my pyramid of night°
Which points into the heavens, dreaming delight,
Murmuring victorious joy in my enchanted sleep;
    As a youth lulled in love-dreams, faintly sighing,
    Under the shadow of his beauty lying,
Which round his rest a watch of light and warmth doth keep.

The Moon

    As in the soft and sweet eclipse   450
    When soul meets soul on lovers' lips,
High hearts are calm, and brightest eyes are dull;
    So when thy shadow falls on me,
    Then am I mute and still, by thee
Covered; of thy love, Orb most beautiful,
    Full, oh, too full!

    Thou art speeding round the sun,
    Brightest world of many a one,
    Green and azure sphere, which shinest
    With a light which is divinest   460
    Among all the lamps of Heaven
    To whom life and light is given;
    I, thy crystal paramour,
    Borne beside thee by a power
    Like the polar Paradise,
    Magnet-like, of lovers' eyes;
    I, a most enamoured maiden,
    Whose weak brain is overladen
    With the pleasure of her love,
    Maniac-like around thee move,   470
    Gazing, an insatiate bride,
    On thy form from every side,
    Like a Maenad, round the cup
    Which Agave lifted up°
    In the weird Cadmaean forest.°
    Brother, wheresoe'er thou soarest
    I must hurry, whirl and follow

Through the heavens wide and hollow,
Sheltered by the warm embrace
Of thy soul from hungry space,   480
Drinking from thy sense and sight
Beauty, majesty, and might,
As a lover or chameleon
Grows like what it looks upon,
As a violet's gentle eye
Gazes on the azure sky
Until its hue grows like what it beholds,
As a grey and watery mist
Grows like solid amethyst
Athwart the western mountain it enfolds,   490
When the sunset sleeps
Upon its snow—

The Earth

And the weak day weeps°
That it should be so.
O gentle Moon, the voice of thy delight
Falls on me like thy clear and tender light
Soothing the seaman, borne the summer night
Through isles forever calm;
O gentle Moon, thy crystal accents pierce
The caverns of my pride's deep universe,   500
Charming the tiger Joy, whose tramplings fierce
Made wounds which need thy balm.

Panthea. I rise as from a bath of sparkling water,
A bath of azure light, among dark rocks,
Out of the stream of sound.

Ione.   Ah me! sweet sister,
The stream of sound has ebbed away from us,
And you pretend to rise out of its wave,
Because your words fall like the clear soft dew
Shaken from a bathing wood-nymph's limbs and hair.

Panthea. Peace! peace! a mighty Power, which is as darkness,   510
Is rising out of Earth, and from the sky
Is showered like night, and from within the air
Bursts, like eclipse which had been gathered up

Into the pores of sunlight: the bright visions,
Wherein the singing spirits rode and shone,
Gleam like pale meteors through a watery night.

Ione. There is a sense of words upon mine ear.

Panthea. An universal sound like words. Oh, list!

Demogorgon

Thou Earth, calm empire of a happy soul,
    Sphere of divinest shapes and harmonies,   520
Beautiful orb! gathering as thou dost roll
    The love which paves thy path along the skies:°

The Earth

I hear: I am as a drop of dew that dies!

Demogorgon

Thou Moon, which gazest on the nightly Earth
    With wonder, as it gazes upon thee,
Whilst each to men, and beasts, and the swift birth
    Of birds, is beauty, love, calm, harmony:

The Moon

I hear: I am a leaf shaken by thee!

Demogorgon

Ye Kings of suns and stars, Daemons and Gods,
    Etherial Dominations, who possess   530
Elysian, windless, fortunate abodes
    Beyond Heaven's constellated wilderness:

A Voice from Above

Our great Republic hears: we are blest, and bless.

Demogorgon

Ye happy dead, whom beams of brightest verse
    Are clouds to hide, not colours to portray,
Whether your nature is that universe
    Which once ye saw and suffered—

A Voice from Beneath

                     Or as they
Whom we have left, we change and pass away.

Demogorgon

Ye elemental Genii, who have homes°
    From man's high mind even to the central stone   540
Of sullen lead; from Heaven's star-fretted domes
    To the dull weed some sea-worm battens on:

A Confused Voice

We hear: thy words waken Oblivion.

Demogorgon

Spirits, whose homes are flesh: ye beasts and birds,
    Ye worms and fish; ye living leaves and buds;
Lightning and wind; and ye untameable herds,
    Meteors and mists, which throng air's solitudes:

A Voice

Thy voice to us is wind among still woods.

Demogorgon

    Man, who wert once a despot and a slave;
       A dupe and a deceiver; a decay;   550
    A traveller from the cradle to the grave
       Through the dim night of this immortal day:

All

Speak: thy strong words may never pass away.

Demogorgon

This is the day, which down the void abysm
At the Earth-born's spell yawns for Heaven's despotism,°
    And Conquest is dragged captive through the deep;°
Love, from its awful throne of patient power
In the wise heart, from the last giddy hour
    Of dread endurance, from the slippery, steep,
And narrow verge of crag-like agony, springs   560
And folds over the world its healing wings.

Gentleness, Virtue, Wisdom, and Endurance,—
These are the seals of that most firm assurance
   Which bars the pit over Destruction's strength;
And if, with infirm hand, Eternity,
Mother of many acts and hours, should free
   The serpent that would clasp her with his length,
These are the spells by which to re-assume
An empire o'er the disentangled Doom.

To suffer woes which Hope thinks infinite;   570
To forgive wrongs darker than death or night;
   To defy Power, which seems omnipotent;
To love, and bear; to hope, till Hope creates
From its own wreck the thing it contemplates;
   Neither to change, nor falter, nor repent:°
This, like thy glory, Titan, is to be
Good, great and joyous, beautiful and free;
This is alone Life, Joy, Empire, and Victory.

THE CENCI

A TRAGEDY,
IN FIVE ACTS

DEDICATION

TO

LEIGH HUNT ESQ.

My dear friend,

I inscribe with your name, from a distant country, and after an absence whose months have seemed years, this the latest of my literary efforts.

Those writings which I have hitherto published, have been little else than visions which impersonate my own apprehensions of the beautiful and the just. I can also perceive in them the literary defects incidental to youth and impatience; they are dreams of what ought to be, or may be. The drama which I now present to you is a sad reality.° I lay aside the presumptuous attitude of an instructor, and am content to paint, with such colours as my own heart furnishes, that which has been.

Had I known a person more highly endowed than yourself with all that it becomes a man to possess, I had solicited for this work the ornament of his name. One more gentle, honourable, innocent and brave; one of more exalted toleration for all who do and think evil, and yet himself more free from evil; one who knows better how to receive, and how to confer a benefit though he must ever confer far more than he can receive; one of simpler, and, in the highest sense of the word, of purer life and manners I never knew: and I had already been fortunate in friendships when your name was added to the list.

In that patient and irreconcilable enmity with domestic and political tyranny and imposture which the tenor of your life has illustrated, and which, had I health and talents should illustrate mine, let us, comforting each other in our task, live and die.

All happiness attend you!

Your affectionate friend,

PERCY B. SHELLEY.

Rome, May 29. 1819.

PREFACE°

A manuscript was communicated to me during my travels in Italy which was copied from the archives of the Cenci Palace at Rome, and contains a detailed account of the horrors which ended in the extinction of one of the noblest and richest families of that city during the Pontificate of Clement VIII,° in the year, 1599. The story is, that an old man having spent his life in debauchery and wickedness, conceived at length an implacable hatred towards his children; which showed itself towards one daughter under the form of an incestuous passion, aggravated by every circumstance of cruelty and violence. This daughter, after long and vain attempts to escape from what she considered a perpetual contamination both of body and mind, at length plotted with her mother-in-law and brother to murder their common tyrant. The young maiden who was urged to this tremendous deed by an impulse which overpowered its horror, was evidently a most gentle and amiable being, a creature formed to adorn and be admired, and thus violently thwarted from her nature by the necessity of circumstance and opinion. The deed was quickly discovered and in spite of the most earnest prayers made to the Pope by the highest persons in Rome the criminals were put to death. The old man had during his life repeatedly bought his pardon from the Pope for capital crimes of the most enormous and unspeakable kind, at the price of a hundred thousand crowns; the death therefore of his victims can scarcely be accounted for by the love of justice. The Pope, among other motives for severity, probably felt that whoever killed the Count Cenci deprived his treasury of a certain and copious source of revenue.° Such a story, if told so as to present to the reader all the feelings of those who once acted it, their hopes and fears, their confidences and misgivings, their various interests, passions and opinions acting upon and with each other, yet all conspiring to one tremendous end, would be as a light to make apparent some of the most dark and secret caverns of the human heart.

On my arrival at Rome I found that the story of the Cenci was a subject not to be mentioned in Italian society without awakening a deep and breathless interest; and that the feelings of the company never failed to incline to a romantic pity for the wrongs, and a passionate exculpation of the horrible deed to which they urged her, who has been mingled two centuries with the common dust. All ranks of people knew the outlines of this history, and participated in the overwhelming interest which it seems to have the magic of exciting in the human heart. I had a copy of Guido's picture of Beatrice which is preserved in the Colonna Palace, and my servant instantly recognized it as the portrait of *La Cenci*.°

This national and universal interest which the story produces and has produced for two centuries and among all ranks of people in a great City, where the imagination is kept for ever active and awake, first suggested to me the conception of its fitness for a dramatic purpose. In fact it is a tragedy which has already received from its capacity of awakening and sustaining the sympathy of men, approbation and success. Nothing remained as I imagined, but to clothe it to the apprehensions of my countrymen in such language and action as would bring it home to their hearts. The deepest and the sublimest tragic compositions, *King Lear* and the two plays in which the tale of Oedipus is told, were stories which already existed in tradition, as matters of popular belief and interest, before Shakespeare and Sophocles made them familiar to the sympathy of all succeeding generations of mankind.

This story of the Cenci is indeed eminently fearful and monstrous: anything like a dry exhibition of it on the stage would be insupportable. The person who would treat such a subject must increase the ideal, and diminish the actual horror of the events, so that the pleasure which arises from the poetry which exists in these tempestuous sufferings and crimes may mitigate the pain of the contemplation of the moral deformity from which they spring. There must also be nothing attempted to make the exhibition subservient to what is vulgarly termed a moral purpose. The highest moral purpose aimed at in the highest species of the drama, is the teaching the human heart, through its sympathies and antipathies, the knowledge of itself; in proportion to the possession of which knowledge, every human being is wise, just, sincere, tolerant and kind. If dogmas can do more, it is well: but a drama is no fit place for the enforcement of them. Undoubtedly, no person can be truly dishonoured by the act of another; and the fit return to make to the most enormous injuries is kindness and forbearance, and a resolution to convert the injurer from his dark passions by peace and love. Revenge, retaliation, atonement, are pernicious mistakes. If Beatrice had thought in this manner she would have been wiser and better; but she would never have been a tragic character: the few whom such an exhibition would have interested, could never have been sufficiently interested for a dramatic purpose, from the want of finding sympathy in their interest among the mass who surround them. It is in the

restless and anatomizing casuistry° with which men seek the justifica-
tion of Beatrice, yet feel that she has done what needs justification; it
is in the superstitious horror with which they contemplate alike her
wrongs and their revenge; that the dramatic character of what she did
and suffered, consists.

I have endeavoured as nearly as possible to represent the characters
as they probably were, and have sought to avoid the error of making
them actuated by my own conceptions of right or wrong, false or true,
thus under a thin veil converting names and actions of the sixteenth
century into cold impersonations of my own mind. They are repre-
sented as Catholics, and as Catholics deeply tinged with religion. To
a Protestant apprehension there will appear something unnatural
in the earnest and perpetual sentiment of the relations between God
and man which pervade the tragedy of the Cenci. It will especially be
startled at the combination of an undoubting persuasion of the truth
of the popular religion with a cool and determined perseverance in
enormous guilt. But religion in Italy is not, as in Protestant countries,
a cloak to be worn on particular days; or a passport which those who
do not wish to be railed at carry with them to exhibit; or a gloomy
passion for penetrating the impenetrable mysteries of our being,
which terrifies its possessor at the darkness of the abyss to the brink of
which it has conducted him. Religion coexists, as it were, in the mind
of an Italian Catholic with a faith in that of which all men have the
most certain knowledge. It is interwoven with the whole fabric of
life. It is adoration, faith, submission, penitence, blind admiration; not
a rule for moral conduct. It has no necessary connection with any one
virtue. The most atrocious villain may be rigidly devout, and without
any shock to established faith, confess himself to be so. Religion
pervades intensely the whole frame of society, and is according to the
temper of the mind which it inhabits, a passion, a persuasion, an
excuse, a refuge; never a check. Cenci himself built a chapel in the
court of his Palace, and dedicated it to St Thomas the Apostle, and
established masses for the peace of his soul. Thus in the first scene of
the fourth act Lucretia's design in exposing herself to the con-
sequences of an expostulation with Cenci after having administered
the opiate, was to induce him by a feigned tale to confess himself
before death; this being esteemed by Catholics as essential to salvation;
and she only relinquishes her purpose when she perceives that her
perseverance would expose Beatrice to new outrages.

I have avoided with great care in writing this play the introduction
of what is commonly called mere poetry, and I imagine there will

scarcely be found a detached simile or a single isolated description, unless Beatrice's description of the chasm appointed for her father's murder should be judged to be of that nature.°

In a dramatic composition the imagery and the passion should interpenetrate one another, the former being reserved simply for the full development and illustration of the latter. Imagination is as the immortal God which should assume flesh for the redemption of mortal passion. It is thus that the most remote and the most familiar imagery may alike be fit for dramatic purposes when employed in the illustration of strong feeling, which raises what is low, and levels to the apprehension that which is lofty, casting over all the shadow of its own greatness. In other respects I have written more carelessly; that is without an over-fastidious and learned choice of words. In this respect I entirely agree with those modern critics° who assert that in order to move men to true sympathy we must use the familiar language of men. And that our great ancestors the ancient English poets are the writers a study of whom might incite us to do that for our own age which they have done for theirs. But it must be the real language of men° in general and not that of any particular class to whose society the writer happens to belong. So much for what I have attempted; I need not be assured that success is a very different matter; particularly for one whose attention has but newly been awakened to the study of dramatic literature.

I endeavoured whilst at Rome to observe such monuments of this story as might be accessible to a stranger. The portrait of Beatrice at the Colonna Palace is admirable as a work of art: it was taken by Guido during her confinement in prison. But it is most interesting as a just representation of one of the loveliest specimens of the workmanship of Nature. There is a fixed and pale composure upon the features: she seems sad and stricken down in spirit, yet the despair thus expressed is lightened by the patience of gentleness. Her head is bound with folds of white drapery from which the yellow strings of her golden hair escape, and fall about her neck. The moulding of her face is exquisitely delicate; the eyebrows are distinct and arched: the lips have that permanent meaning of imagination and sensibility which suffering has not repressed and which it seems as if death scarcely could extinguish. Her forehead is large and clear; her eyes which we are told were remarkable for their vivacity, are swollen with weeping and lustreless, but beautifully tender and serene. In the whole mien there is a simplicity and dignity which united with her exquisite loveliness and deep sorrow are inexpressibly pathetic. Beatrice Cenci appears to have been one of those rare persons in whom energy and gentleness dwell together without destroying one another: her nature was simple and profound. The crimes and miseries in which she was an actor and a sufferer are as the mask and the mantle in which circumstances clothed her for her impersonation on the scene of the world.

The Cenci Palace is of great extent; and though in part modernized, there yet remains a vast and gloomy pile of feudal architecture in the same state as during the dreadful scenes which are the subject of this tragedy. The Palace is situated in an obscure corner of Rome, near the quarter of the Jews, and from the upper windows you see the immense ruins of Mount Palatine half hidden under their profuse overgrowth of trees. There is a court in one part of the palace (perhaps that in which Cenci built the Chapel to St Thomas), supported by granite columns and adorned with antique friezes of fine workmanship and built up, according to the ancient Italian fashion, with balcony over balcony of open work. One of the gates of the palace formed of immense stones and leading through a passage, dark and lofty and opening into gloomy subterranean chambers, struck me particularly.

Of the Castle of Petrella, I could obtain no further information than that which is to be found in the manuscript.

DRAMATIS PERSONAE

COUNT FRANCESCO CENCI.
GIACOMO. } his sons.
BERNARDO. }
CARDINAL CAMILLO.
ORSINO, a prelate.
SAVELLA, the Pope's Legate.
OLIMPIO. } Assassins.
MARZIO. }
ANDREA, servant to Cenci.
    Nobles, Judges, Guards, Servants.

LUCRETIA. Wife of Cenci, and Step-mother of his children.
BEATRICE, his daughter.

The Scene lies principally in Rome, but changes during the fourth Act to Petrella a castle among the Apulian Apennines.

Time. During the Pontificate of Clement VIII.

Act I

SCENE I.—*An apartment in the* CENCI *Palace.*
Enter COUNT CENCI, *and* CARDINAL CAMILLO.

   Camillo. That matter of the murder is hushed up.°
If you consent to yield his Holiness
Your fief that lies beyond the Pincian gate.—°
It needed all my interest in the conclave
To bend him to this point: he said that you
Bought perilous impunity with your gold;
That crimes like yours if once or twice compounded
Enriched the Church, and respited from hell
An erring soul which might repent and live:—
But that the glory and the interest   10
Of the high throne he fills, little consist
With making it a daily mart of guilt
As manifold and hideous as the deeds
Which you scarce hide from men's revolted eyes.

   Cenci. The third of my possessions—let it go!
Aye, I once heard the nephew of the Pope°
Had sent his architect to view the ground,
Meaning to build a villa on my vines
The next time I compounded with his uncle:
I little thought he should outwit me so!   20
Henceforth no witness—not the lamp—shall see
That which the vassal threatened to divulge
Whose throat is choked with dust for his reward.
The deed he saw could not have rated higher
Than his most worthless life:—it angers me!
Respited me from Hell!—So may the Devil
Respite their souls from Heaven. No doubt Pope Clement,
And his most charitable nephews, pray
That the apostle Peter and the saints
Will grant for their sake that I long enjoy   30
Strength, wealth, and pride, and lust, and length of days
Wherein to act the deeds which are the stewards
Of their revenue.—But much yet remains
To which they show no title.

   Camillo.   Oh, Count Cenci!
So much that thou mightst honourably live
And reconcile thyself with thine own heart
And with thy God, and with the offended world.
How hideously look deeds of lust and blood
Through those snow-white and venerable hairs!—
Your children should be sitting round you now,   40
But that you fear to read upon their looks
The shame and misery you have written there.
Where is your wife? Where is your gentle daughter?
Methinks her sweet looks, which make all things else
Beauteous and glad, might kill the fiend within you.
Why is she barred from all society
But her own strange and uncomplaining wrongs?
Talk with me, Count,—you know I mean you well.
I stood beside your dark and fiery youth
Watching its bold and bad career, as men   50
Watch meteors, but it vanished not—I marked
Your desperate and remorseless manhood; now
Do I behold you in dishonoured age
Charged with a thousand unrepented crimes.
Yet I have ever hoped you would amend,
And in that hope have saved your life three times.

   Cenci. For which Aldobrandino owes you now°
My fief beyond the Pincian.—Cardinal,
One thing, I pray you, recollect henceforth,
And so we shall converse with less restraint.   60
A man you knew spoke of my wife and daughter—
He was accustomed to frequent my house;
So the next day *his* wife and daughter came
And asked if I had seen him; and I smiled:
I think they never saw him any more.

   Camillo. Thou execrable man, beware!—

   Cenci.   Of thee?
Nay this is idle:—We should know each other.
As to my character for what men call crime,
Seeing I please my senses as I list,
And vindicate that right with force or guile,   70

It is a public matter, and I care not
If I discuss it with you. I may speak
Alike to you and my own conscious heart—
For you give out that you have half reformed me,
Therefore strong vanity will keep you silent
If fear should not; both will, I do not doubt.
All men delight in sensual luxury,
All men enjoy revenge; and most exult
Over the tortures they can never feel—
Flattering their secret peace with others' pain.   80
But I delight in nothing else. I love
The sight of agony, and the sense of joy,
When this shall be another's, and that mine.
And I have no remorse and little fear,
Which are, I think, the checks of other men.
This mood has grown upon me, until now
Any design my captious fancy makes
The picture of its wish, and it forms none
But such as men like you would start to know,
Is as my natural food and rest debarred   90
Until it be accomplished.

   Camillo.   Art thou not
Most miserable?

   Cenci.   Why, miserable?—
No.—I am what your theologians call
Hardened;—which they must be in impudence,
So to revile a man's peculiar taste.
True, I was happier than I am, while yet
Manhood remained to act the thing I thought;
While lust was sweeter than revenge; and now
Invention palls:—Aye, we must all grow old—
And but that there remains a deed to act   100
Whose horror might make sharp an appetite
Duller than mine—I'd do,—I know not what.
When I was young I thought of nothing else
But pleasure; and I fed on honey sweets:
Men, by St Thomas! cannot live like bees
And I grew tired:—yet, till I killed a foe,

And heard his groans, and heard his children's groans,
Knew I not what delight was else on earth,
Which now delights me little. I the rather
Look on such pangs as terror ill conceals,   110
The dry fixed eyeball; the pale quivering lip,
Which tell me that the spirit weeps within
Tears bitterer than the bloody sweat of Christ.°
I rarely kill the body which preserves,
Like a strong prison, the soul within my power,
Wherein I feed it with the breath of fear
For hourly pain.

    Camillo.   Hell's most abandoned fiend
Did never, in the drunkenness of guilt,
Speak to his heart as now you speak to me,
I thank my God that I believe you not.   120
               Enter ANDREA.

    Andrea. My Lord, a gentleman from Salamanca
Would speak with you.

    Cenci.   Bid him attend me in
The grand saloon.

                         [*Exit* ANDREA.

    Camillo.   Farewell; and I will pray
Almighty God that thy false, impious words
Tempt not his spirit to abandon thee.

                        [*Exit* CAMILLO.

    Cenci. The third of my possessions! I must use
Close husbandry, or gold, the old man's sword,
Falls from my withered hand. But yesterday
There came an order from the Pope to make
Fourfold provision for my cursèd sons;   130
Whom I had sent from Rome to Salamanca,
Hoping some accident might cut them off;
And meaning if I could to starve them there.
I pray thee, God, send some quick death upon them!
Bernardo and my wife could not be worse
If dead and damned:—then, as to Beatrice—

                    [*looking around him suspiciously*

I think they cannot hear me at that door;
What if they should? And yet I need not speak
Though the heart triumphs with itself in words.
O, thou most silent air, that shalt not hear   140
What now I think! Thou, pavement, which I tread
Towards her chamber,—let your echoes talk
Of my imperious step scorning surprise,
But not of my intent!—Andrea!°

Enter ANDREA.

    Andrea.   My lord?

    Cenci. Bid Beatrice attend me in her chamber
This evening:—no, at midnight and alone.

[Exeunt.

SCENE 2.—*A garden of the Cenci Palace.*
    Enter BEATRICE *and* ORSINO, *as in conversation.*

    Beatrice. Pervert not truth,
Orsino. You remember where we held
That conversation;—nay, we see the spot
Even from this cypress;—two long years are past
Since, on an April midnight, underneath
The moonlight ruins of mount Palatine,
I did confess to you my secret mind.
    Orsino. You said you loved me then.

    Beatrice.   You are a Priest,
Speak to me not of love.

    Orsino.   I may obtain
The dispensation of the Pope to marry.   10
Because I am a Priest do you believe
Your image, as the hunter some struck deer,
Follows me not whether I wake or sleep?

    Beatrice. As I have said, speak to me not of love;
Had you a dispensation, I have not;
Nor will I leave this home of misery
Whilst my poor Bernard, and that gentle lady
To whom I owe life, and these virtuous thoughts,

Must suffer what I still have strength to share.
Alas, Orsino! All the love that once   20
I felt for you, is turned to bitter pain.
Ours was a youthful contract, which you first
Broke, by assuming vows no Pope will loose.
And thus I love you still, but holily,
Even as a sister or a spirit might;
And so I swear a cold fidelity.
And it is well perhaps we shall not marry.
You have a sly, equivocating vein
That suits me not.—Ah, wretched that I am!
Where shall I turn? Even now you look on me   30
As you were not my friend, and as if you
Discovered that I thought so, with false smiles
Making my true suspicion seem your wrong.
Ah! no, forgive me; sorrow makes me seem
Sterner than else my nature might have been;
I have a weight of melancholy thoughts,
And they forbode,—but what can they forbode
Worse than I now endure?

    Orsino.   All will be well.
Is the petition yet prepared? You know
My zeal for all you wish, sweet Beatrice;   40
Doubt not but I will use my utmost skill
So that the Pope attend to your complaint.

    Beatrice. Your zeal for all I wish;—Ah me, you are cold!
Your utmost skill . . . speak but one word . . . (*aside*) Alas!
Weak and deserted creature that I am,
Here I stand bickering with my only friend!

                                     [*To* ORSINO.

This night my father gives a sumptuous feast,
Orsino; he has heard some happy news
From Salamanca, from my brothers there,
And with this outward show of love he mocks   50
His inward hate. 'Tis bold hypocrisy
For he would gladlier celebrate their deaths,
Which I have heard him pray for on his knees:
Great God! that such a father should be mine!
But there is mighty preparation made,

And all our kin, the Cenci, will be there,
And all the chief nobility of Rome.
And he has bidden me and my pale Mother
Attire ourselves in festival array.
Poor lady! She expects some happy change   60
In his dark spirit from this act; I none.
At supper I will give you the petition:
Till when—farewell.

   Orsino.   Farewell.

                                      [*Exit* BEATRICE.

                  I know the Pope
Will ne'er absolve me from my priestly vow
But by absolving me from the revenue
Of many a wealthy see; and, Beatrice,
I think to win thee at an easier rate.
Nor shall he read her eloquent petition:
He might bestow her on some poor relation
Of his sixth cousin, as he did her sister,   70
And I should be debarred from all access.
Then as to what she suffers from her father,
In all this there is much exaggeration:—
Old men are testy and will have their way;
A man may stab his enemy, or his vassal,
And live a free life as to wine or women,
And with a peevish temper may return
To a dull home, and rate his wife and children;
Daughters and wives call this, foul tyranny.
I shall be well content if on my conscience   80
There rest no heavier sin than what they suffer
From the devices of my love—A net
From which she shall escape not. Yet I fear
Her subtle mind, her awe-inspiring gaze,
Whose beams anatomize me nerve by nerve°
And lay me bare, and make me blush to see
My hidden thoughts.—Ah, no! A friendless girl
Who clings to me, as to her only hope:—
I were a fool, not less than if a panther
Were panic-stricken by the Antelope's eye,   90
If she escape me.

                                        [*Exit.*

SCENE 3.—*A magnificent Hall in the Cenci Palace. A Banquet.*
Enter CENCI, LUCRETIA, BEATRICE, ORSINO, CAMILLO, NOBLES.

Cenci. Welcome, my friends and Kinsmen; welcome ye,
Princes and Cardinals, pillars of the church,
Whose presence honours our festivity.
I have too long lived like an Anchorite,°
And in my absence from your merry meetings
An evil word is gone abroad of me;
But I do hope that you, my noble friends,
When you have shared the entertainment here,
And heard the pious cause for which 'tis given,
And we have pledged a health or two together,   10
Will think me flesh and blood as well as you;
Sinful indeed, for Adam made all so,
But tender-hearted, meek and pitiful.

First Guest. In truth, my Lord, you seem too light of heart,
Too sprightly and companionable a man,
To act the deeds that rumour pins on you.

                                        [*To his companion*

I never saw such blithe and open cheer
In any eye!

Second Guest. Some most desired event,
In which we all demand a common joy,
Has brought us hither; let us hear it, Count.   20

Cenci. It is indeed a most desired event.
If when a parent from a parent's heart
Lifts from this earth to the great father of all
A prayer, both when he lays him down to sleep,
And when he rises up from dreaming it;
One supplication, one desire, one hope,
That he would grant a wish for his two sons
Even all that he demands in their regard—
And suddenly beyond his dearest hope,
It is accomplished, he should then rejoice,   30
And call his friends and kinsmen to a feast,
And task their love to grace his merriment,
Then honour me thus far—for I am he.

Beatrice (*to* LUCRETIA). Great God! How horrible! Some
    dreadful ill°
Must have befallen my brothers.

   Lucretia.   Fear not, Child,
He speaks too frankly.

   Beatrice.   Ah! My blood runs cold.
I fear that wicked laughter round his eye
Which wrinkles up the skin even to the hair.

   Cenci. Here are the letters brought from Salamanca;
Beatrice, read them to your mother. God!   40
I thank thee! In one night didst thou perform,°
By ways inscrutable, the thing I sought.
My disobedient and rebellious sons
Are dead!—Why, dead!—What means this change of cheer?
You hear me not, I tell you they are dead;
And they will need no food or raiment more:
The tapers that did light them the dark way
Are their last cost. The Pope, I think, will not
Expect I should maintain them in their coffins.
Rejoice with me—my heart is wondrous glad.   50
          [LUCRETIA *sinks, half fainting;* BEATRICE *supports her.*

   Beatrice. It is not true!—Dear lady, pray look up.
Had it been true, there is a God in Heaven,
He would not live to boast of such a boon.
Unnatural man, thou knowest that it is false.

   Cenci. Aye, as the word of God; whom here I call
To witness that I speak the sober truth;—
And whose most favouring Providence was shown
Even in the manner of their deaths. For Rocco
Was kneeling at the mass, with sixteen others,
When the Church fell and crushed him to a mummy,   60
The rest escaped unhurt. Cristofano°
Was stabbed in error by a jealous man,
Whilst she he loved was sleeping with his rival;
All in the self-same hour of the same night;
Which shows that Heaven has special care of me.

I beg those friends who love me, that they mark
The day a feast upon their calenders.
It was the twenty-seventh of December:°
Aye, read the letters if you doubt my oath.
    [*The assembly appears confused; several of the guests rise.*

First Guest. Oh, horrible! I will depart.—

Second Guest.   And I.—

Third Guest.   No, stay! 70
I do believe it is some jest; though faith!
'Tis mocking us somewhat too solemnly.
I think his son has married the Infanta,°
Or found a mine of gold in El Dorado;°
'Tis but to season some such news; stay, stay!
I see 'tis only raillery by his smile.

 Cenci (*filling a bowl of wine, and lifting it up*). Oh, thou
   bright wine whose purple splendour leaps
And bubbles gaily in this golden bowl
Under the lamplight, as my spirits do,
To hear the death of my accursèd sons!   80
Could I believe thou wert their mingled blood,
Then would I taste thee like a sacrament,°
And pledge with thee the mighty Devil in Hell,
Who, if a father's curses, as men say,
Climb with swift wings after their children's souls,
And drag them from the very throne of Heaven,
Now triumphs in my triumph!—But thou art
Superfluous; I have drunken deep of joy
And I will taste no other wine tonight.
Here, Andrea! Bear the bowl around.

 A Guest (*rising*).   Thou wretch! 90
Will none among this noble company
Check the abandoned villain?

 Camillo.   For God's sake
Let me dismiss the guests! You are insane,
Some ill will come of this.

Second Guest.   Seize, silence him!

First Guest. I will!

Third Guest.   And I!

Cenci (*addressing those who rise with a threatening gesture*). Who
    moves? Who speaks?

                                    [*Turning to the Company.*
                        'Tis nothing,
Enjoy yourselves.—Beware! For my revenge
Is as the sealed commission of a king
That kills, and none dare name the murderer.
        [*The Banquet is broken up; several of the Guests are departing.*

Beatrice. I do entreat you, go not, noble guests;
What, although tyranny and impious hate   100
Stand sheltered by a father's hoary hair?
What, if 'tis he who clothed us in these limbs
Who tortures them, and triumphs? What, if we,
The desolate and the dead, were his own flesh,
His children and his wife, whom he is bound
To love and shelter? Shall we therefore find
No refuge in this merciless wide world?
Oh, think what deep wrongs must have blotted out
First love, then reverence in a child's prone mind,°
Till it thus vanquish shame and fear! O, think°   110
I have borne much, and kissed the sacred hand
Which crushed us to the earth, and thought its stroke
Was perhaps some paternal chastisement!
Have excused much, doubted; and when no doubt
Remained, have sought by patience, love and tears
To soften him, and when this could not be
I have knelt down through the long sleepless nights
And lifted up to God, the father of all,
Passionate prayers: and when these were not heard
I have still borne,—until I meet you here,   120
Princes and kinsmen, at this hideous feast
Given at my brothers' deaths. Two yet remain,
His wife remains and I, whom if ye save not,
Ye may soon share such merriment again

As fathers make over their children's graves.
Oh! Prince Colonna, thou art our near kinsman,°
Cardinal, thou art the Pope's chamberlain,
Camillo, thou art chief justiciary,
Take us away!

Cenci. (*He has been conversing with* CAMILLO *during the first part of*
BEATRICE'*s speech; he hears the conclusion, and now advances.*) I hope
my good friends here
Will think of their own daughters—or perhaps   130
Of their own throats—before they lend an ear
To this wild girl.

Beatrice (*not noticing the words of Cenci*). Dare no one look on me?
None answer? Can one tyrant overbear
The sense of many best and wisest men?
Or is it that I sue not in some form
Of scrupulous law, that ye deny my suit?
Oh, God! That I were buried with my brothers!
And that the flowers of this departed spring
Were fading on my grave! And that my father
Were celebrating now one feast for all!   140

Camillo. A bitter wish for one so young and gentle;
Can we do nothing?—

Colonna.   Nothing that I see.
Count Cenci were a dangerous enemy:
Yet I would second any one.

A Cardinal.   And I.

Cenci. Retire to your chamber, insolent girl!

Beatrice. Retire thou, impious man! Aye, hide thyself
Where never eye can look upon thee more!
Wouldst thou have honour and obedience
Who art a torturer? Father, never dream,
Though thou mayst overbear this company,   150
But ill must come of ill.—Frown not on me!°

Haste, hide thyself, lest with avenging looks
My brothers' ghosts should hunt thee from thy seat!
Cover thy face from every living eye,
And start if thou but hear a human step:
Seek out some dark and silent corner, there,
Bow thy white head before offended God,
And we will kneel around, and fervently
Pray that he pity both ourselves and thee.

   Cenci. My friends, I do lament this insane girl   160
Has spoilt the mirth of our festivity.
Good night, farewell; I will not make you longer
Spectators of our dull domestic quarrels.
Another time.—
                       [*Exeunt all but* CENCI *and* BEATRICE.
               My brain is swimming round;
Give me a bowl of wine!
(*To* BEATRICE)   Thou painted viper!
Beast that thou art! Fair and yet terrible!
I know a charm shall make thee meek and tame,
Now get thee from my sight!
                           [*Exit* BEATRICE.
               Here, Andrea,
Fill up this goblet with Greek wine. I said
I would not drink this evening; but I must;   170
For, strange to say, I feel my spirits fail
With thinking what I have decreed to do.—
                         [*Drinking the wine.*
Be thou the resolution of quick youth
Within my veins, and manhood's purpose stern,
And age's firm, cold, subtle villainy;
As if thou wert indeed my children's blood
Which I did thirst to drink! The charm works well;
It must be done; it shall be done, I swear!°
                               [*Exit.*

END OF THE FIRST ACT.

Act 2

SCENE I.—*An apartment in the Cenci Palace.*
      Enter LUCRETIA *and* BERNARDO.

Lucretia. Weep not, my gentle boy; he struck but me
Who have borne deeper wrongs. In truth, if he
Had killed me, he had done a kinder deed.
O, God Almighty, do thou look upon us,
We have no other friend but only thee!
Yet weep not; though I love you as my own
I am not your true mother.

Bernardo.   Oh more, more,
Than ever mother was to any child,
That have you been to me! Had he not been
My father, do you think that I should weep?   10

Lucretia. Alas! Poor boy, what else couldst thou have done?
          Enter BEATRICE.

Beatrice (*in a hurried voice*). Did he pass this way? Have you seen
    him, brother?
Ah! no, that is his step upon the stairs;
'Tis nearer now; his hand is on the door;
Mother, if I to thee have ever been
A duteous child, now save me! Thou, great God,
Whose image upon earth a father is,
Dost thou indeed abandon me! He comes;
The door is opening now; I see his face;
He frowns on others, but he smiles on me,   20
Even as he did after the feast last night.
         Enter a Servant.
Almighty God, how merciful thou art!
'Tis but Orsino's servant.—Well, what news?

Servant. My master bids me say, the Holy Father
Has sent back your petition thus unopened.

                    [*Giving a paper*

And he demands at what hour 'twere secure
To visit you again?

Lucretia.   At the Ave Mary.

                                                    [*Exit Servant.*

So, daughter, our last hope has failed; Ah me!
How pale you look; you tremble, and you stand
Wrapped in some fixed and fearful meditation,   30
As if one thought were over-strong for you.
Your eyes have a chill glare; O, dearest child!
Are you gone mad? If not, pray speak to me.

Beatrice. You see I am not mad; I speak to you.

Lucretia. You talked of something that your father did
After that dreadful feast? Could it be worse
Than when he smiled, and cried, 'My sons are dead!'
And every one looked in his neighbour's face
To see if others were as white as he?
At the first word he spoke I felt the blood   40
Rush to my heart, and fell into a trance;
And when it passed I sat all weak and wild;
Whilst you alone stood up, and with strong words
Checked his unnatural pride; and I could see
The devil was rebuked that lives in him.
Until this hour thus you have ever stood
Between us and your father's moody wrath°
Like a protecting presence: your firm mind
Has been our only refuge and defence:
What can have thus subdued it? What can now   50
Have given you that cold melancholy look,
Succeeding to your unaccustomed fear?

Beatrice. What is it that you say? I was just thinking
'Twere better not to struggle any more.
Men, like my father, have been dark and bloody,
Yet never—O! Before worse comes of it
'Twere wise to die: it ends in that at last.

Lucretia. Oh, talk not so, dear child! Tell me at once
What did your father do or say to you?
He stayed not after that accursèd feast   60
One moment in your chamber.—Speak to me.

Bernardo. Oh, sister, sister, prithee, speak to us!

Beatrice (*speaking very slowly with a forced calmness*). It was one
    word, Mother, one little word;
One look, one smile. (*wildly*)
                Oh! He has trampled me
Under his feet, and made the blood stream down
My pallid cheeks. And he has given us all
Ditch water, and the fever-stricken flesh
Of buffaloes, and bade us eat or starve,
And we have eaten.—He has made me look
On my beloved Bernardo, when the rust   70
Of heavy chains has gangrened his sweet limbs,
And I have never yet despaired—but now!
What would I say? (*Recovering herself*)
                Ah! no, 'tis nothing new.
The sufferings we all share have made me wild:
He only struck and cursed me as he passed;
He said, he looked, he did,—nothing at all
Beyond his wont, yet it disordered me.
Alas! I am forgetful of my duty,
I should preserve my senses for your sake.

Lucretia. Nay, Beatrice; have courage, my sweet girl.   80
If any one despairs it should be I.
Who loved him once, and now must live with him
Till God in pity call for him or me.
For you may, like your sister, find some husband,
And smile, years hence, with children round your knees;
Whilst I, then dead, and all this hideous coil°
Shall be remembered only as a dream.

Beatrice. Talk not to me, dear lady, of a husband.
Did you not nurse me when my mother died?
Did you not shield me and that dearest boy?   90
And had we any other friend but you
In infancy, with gentle words and looks,
To win our father not to murder us?
And shall I now desert you? May the ghost
Of my dead Mother plead against my soul

If I abandon her who filled the place
She left, with more, even, than a mother's love!

Bernardo. And I am of my sister's mind. Indeed
I would not leave you in this wretchedness,
Even though the Pope should make me free to live   100
In some blithe place, like others of my age,
With sports, and delicate food, and the fresh air.
Oh, never think that I will leave you, Mother!

Lucretia. My dear, dear children!
                    Enter CENCI, *suddenly.*

Cenci.   What, Beatrice here!
Come hither! (*she shrinks back, and covers her face*)
                    Nay, hide not your face, 'tis fair;
Look up! Why, yesternight you dared to look
With disobedient insolence upon me,
Bending a stern and an inquiring brow
On what I meant; whilst I then sought to hide
That which I came to tell you—but in vain.   110

Beatrice (*wildly, staggering towards the door*). Oh, that the earth
    would gape! Hide me, oh God!°

Cenci. Then it was I whose inarticulate words
Fell from my lips, and who with tottering steps
Fled from your presence, as you now from mine.
Stay, I command you—from this day and hour
Never again, I think, with fearless eye,
And brow superior, and unaltered cheek,
And that lip made for tenderness or scorn,
Shalt thou strike dumb the meanest of mankind;
Me least of all. Now get thee to thy chamber!   120
Thou too, loathed image of thy cursèd mother,
                                        [*to* BERNARDO
Thy milky, meek face makes me sick with hate!
                            [*Exeunt* BEATRICE *and* BERNARDO.
(*Aside*) So much has passed between us as must make
Me bold, her fearful.—'Tis an awful thing

To touch such mischief as I now conceive:
So men sit shivering on the dewy bank,
And try the chill stream with their feet; once in
How the delighted spirit pants for joy!

 Lucretia (*advancing timidly towards him*). Oh, husband!
  Pray forgive poor Beatrice,
She meant not any ill.

 Cenci.   Nor you perhaps?   130
Nor that young imp, whom you have taught by rote
Parricide with his alphabet? Nor Giacomo?
Nor those two most unnatural sons, who stirred
Enmity up against me with the Pope?
Whom in one night merciful God cut off:
Innocent lambs! They thought not any ill.
You were not here conspiring? You said nothing
Of how I might be dungeoned as a madman;
Or be condemned to death for some offence,
And you would be the witnesses?—This failing,   140
How just it were to hire assassins, or
Put sudden poison in my evening drink?
Or smother me when overcome by wine?
Seeing we had no other judge but God,
And he had sentenced me, and there were none
But you to be the executioners
Of his decree enregistered in heaven?
Oh, no! You said not this?

 Lucretia.   So help me God,
I never thought the things you charge me with!

 Cenci. If you dare speak that wicked lie again
I'll kill you. What! It was not by your counsel   150
That Beatrice disturbed the feast last night?
You did not hope to stir some enemies
Against me, and escape, and laugh to scorn
What every nerve of you now trembles at?
You judged that men were bolder than they are;
Few dare to stand between their grave and me.

Lucretia. Look not so dreadfully! By my salvation
I knew not aught that Beatrice designed;
Nor do I think she designed any thing   160
Until she heard you talk of her dead brothers.

Cenci. Blaspheming liar! You are damned for this!
But I will take you where you may persuade
The stones you tread on to deliver you:
For men shall there be none but those who dare
All things—not question that which I command.
On Wednesday next I shall set out: you know
That savage rock, the Castle of Petrella,
'Tis safely walled, and moated round about:
Its dungeons underground, and its thick towers   170
Never told tales; though they have heard and seen
What might make dumb things speak.—Why do you linger?
Make speediest preparation for the journey!

                                   [*Exit* LUCRETIA.

The all-beholding sun yet shines; I hear
A busy stir of men about the streets;
I see the bright sky through the window panes;
It is a garish, broad, and peering day;°
Loud, light, suspicious, full of eyes and ears,
And every little corner, nook and hole
Is penetrated with the insolent light.   180
Come, darkness! Yet, what is the day to me?°
And wherefore should I wish for night, who do
A deed which shall confound both night and day?
'Tis she shall grope through a bewildering mist
Of horror: if there be a sun in heaven°
She shall not dare to look upon its beams;
Nor feel its warmth. Let her then wish for night;
The act I think shall soon extinguish all
For me: I bear a darker deadlier gloom
Than the earth's shade, or interlunar air,   190
Or constellations quenched in murkiest cloud,
In which I walk secure and unbeheld
Towards my purpose.—Would that it were done!

                                         [*Exit.*

SCENE 2.—*A chamber in the Vatican.*
          Enter CAMILLO *and* GIACOMO, *in conversation.*

Camillo. There is an obsolete and doubtful law
By which you might obtain a bare provision
Of food and clothing—

Giacomo.   Nothing more? Alas!
Bare must be the provision which strict law
Awards, and aged, sullen avarice pays.
Why did my father not apprentice me
To some mechanic trade? I should have then
Been trained in no highborn necessities
Which I could meet not by my daily toil.
The eldest son of a rich nobleman   10
Is heir to all his incapacities;
He has wide wants, and narrow powers. If you,
Cardinal Camillo, were reduced at once
From thrice-driven beds of down, and delicate food,°
An hundred servants, and six palaces,
To that which nature doth indeed require?—

Camillo. Nay, there is reason in your plea; 'twere hard.

Giacomo. 'Tis hard for a firm man to bear: but I
Have a dear wife, a lady of high birth,
Whose dowry in ill hour I lent my father   20
Without a bond or witness to the deed:
And children, who inherit her fine senses,
The fairest creatures in this breathing world;
And she and they reproach me not. Cardinal,
Do you not think the Pope would interpose
And stretch authority beyond the law?

Camillo. Though your peculiar case is hard, I know
The Pope will not divert the course of law.
After that impious feast the other night
I spoke with him, and urged him then to check   30
Your father's cruel hand; he frowned and said,
'Children are disobedient, and they sting
Their fathers' hearts to madness and despair,

Requiting years of care with contumely.
I pity the Count Cenci from my heart;
His outraged love perhaps awakened hate,
And thus he is exasperated to ill.
In the great war between the old and young
I, who have white hairs and a tottering body,
Will keep at least blameless neutrality.'   40
                              Enter ORSINO.
You, my good lord Orsino, heard those words.
    Orsino. What words?

    Giacomo.   Alas, repeat them not again!
There then is no redress for me, at least
None but that which I may achieve myself,
Since I am driven to the brink.—But, say,
My innocent sister and my only brother
Are dying underneath my father's eye.
The memorable torturers of this land,
Galeaz Visconti, Borgia, Ezzelin,°
Never inflicted on their meanest slave   50
What these endure; shall they have no protection?

    Camillo. Why, if they would petition to the Pope
I see not how he could refuse it—yet
He holds it of most dangerous example
In aught to weaken the paternal power,
Being, as 'twere, the shadow of his own.
I pray you now excuse me. I have business
That will not bear delay.

                              [*Exit* CAMILLO.

    Giacomo.   But you, Orsino,
Have the petition: wherefore not present it?

    Orsino. I have presented it, and backed it with   60
My earnest prayers, and urgent interest;
It was returned unanswered. I doubt not
But that the strange and execrable deeds
Alleged in it—in truth they might well baffle
Any belief—have turned the Pope's displeasure
Upon the accusers from the criminal:
So I should guess from what Camillo said.

Giacomo. My friend, that palace-walking devil Gold
Has whispered silence to his Holiness:
And we are left, as scorpions ringed with fire,
What should we do but strike ourselves to death?°   70
For he who is our murderous persecutor
Is shielded by a father's holy name,
Or I would—(*stops abruptly*)

Orsino.   What? Fear not to speak your thought.
Words are but holy as the deeds they cover:
A priest who has forsworn the God he serves;
A judge who makes Truth weep at his decree;
A friend who should weave counsel, as I now,
But as the mantle of some selfish guile;
A father who is all a tyrant seems,   80
Were the profaner for his sacred name.

Giacomo. Ask me not what I think; the unwilling brain
Feigns often what it would not; and we trust
Imagination with such fantasies
As the tongue dares not fashion into words,
Which have no words, their horror makes them dim
To the mind's eye.—My heart denies itself
To think what you demand.

Orsino.   But a friend's bosom
Is as the inmost cave of our own mind
Where we sit shut from the wide gaze of day,   90
And from the all-communicating air.
You look what I suspected—

Giacomo.   Spare me now!
I am as one lost in a midnight wood
Who dares not ask some harmless passenger
The path across the wilderness, lest he,
As my thoughts are, should be—a murderer.
I know you are my friend, and all I dare
Speak to my soul that will I trust with thee.
But now my heart is heavy and would take
Lone counsel from a night of sleepless care.   100
Pardon me, that I say farewell—farewell!

I would that to my own suspected self
I could address a word so full of peace.

   Orsino. Farewell!—Be your thoughts better or more bold.
                                  [*Exit* GIACOMO.
I had disposed the Cardinal Camillo
To feed his hope with cold encouragement:
It fortunately serves my close designs
That 'tis a trick of this same family
To analyse their own and other minds.
Such self-anatomy shall teach the will   110
Dangerous secrets: for it tempts our powers,
Knowing what must be thought, and may be done,
Into the depth of darkest purposes:
So Cenci fell into the pit; even I,
Since Beatrice unveiled me to myself,
And made me shrink from what I cannot shun,
Show a poor figure to my own esteem,
To which I grow half reconciled. I'll do
As little mischief as I can; that thought
Shall fee the accuser conscience.° (*After a pause*)
                      Now what harm   120
If Cenci should be murdered?—Yet, if murdered,
Wherefore by me? And what if I could take
The profit, yet omit the sin and peril
In such an action? Of all earthly things
I fear a man whose blows outspeed his words;
And such is Cenci: and while Cenci lives
His daughter's dowry were a secret grave
If a priest wins her.—Oh, fair Beatrice!
Would that I loved thee not, or loving thee
Could but despise danger and gold and all   130
That frowns between my wish and its effect,
Or smiles beyond it! There is no escape . . .
Her bright form kneels beside me at the altar,
And follows me to the resort of men,
And fills my slumber with tumultuous dreams,
So when I wake my blood seems liquid fire;
And if I strike my damp and dizzy head
My hot palm scorches it: her very name,
But spoken by a stranger, makes my heart

Sicken and pant; and thus unprofitably   140
I clasp the phantom of unfelt delights
Till weak imagination half possesses
The self-created shadow. Yet much longer
Will I not nurse this life of feverous hours:
From the unravelled hopes of Giacomo
I must work out my own dear purposes.
I see, as from a tower, the end of all:°
Her father dead; her brother bound to me
By a dark secret, surer than the grave;
Her mother scared and unexpostulating   150
From the dread manner of her wish achieved:
And she!—Once more take courage, my faint heart;
What dares a friendless maiden matched with thee?
I have such foresight as assures success:
Some unbeheld divinity doth ever,
When dread events are near, stir up men's minds
To black suggestions; and he prospers best,
Not who becomes the instrument of ill,
But who can flatter the dark spirit, that makes
Its empire and its prey of other hearts   160
Till it become his slave . . . as I will do.   [*Exit.*

END OF THE SECOND ACT.

Act 3

SCENE I.—*An apartment in the Cenci Palace.*
                LUCRETIA, *to her enter* BEATRICE.

Beatrice (*she enters staggering, and speaks wildly*). Reach me that
        handkerchief!—My brain is hurt;
My eyes are full of blood; just wipe them for me . . .
I see but indistinctly . . .

Lucretia.   My sweet child,
You have no wound; 'tis only a cold dew
That starts from your dear brow . . . Alas! Alas!
What has befallen?

Beatrice.   How comes this hair undone?
Its wandering strings must be what blind me so,
And yet I tied it fast.—O, horrible!
The pavement sinks under my feet! The walls
Spin round! I see a woman weeping there,   10
And standing calm and motionless, whilst I
Slide giddily as the world reels . . . My God!
The beautiful blue heaven is flecked with blood!°
The sunshine on the floor is black! The air
Is changed to vapours such as the dead breathe
In charnel pits! Pah! I am choked! There creeps
A changing, black, contaminating mist
About me . . . 'tis substantial, heavy, thick,
I cannot pluck it from me, for it glues
My fingers and my limbs to one another,   20
And eats into my sinews, and dissolves
My flesh to a pollution, poisoning
The subtle, pure, and inmost spirit of life!
My God! I never knew what the mad felt
Before; for I am mad beyond all doubt!

                                                    [*More wildly*

No, I am dead! These putrefying limbs
Shut round and sepulchre the panting soul
Which would burst forth into the wandering air!

                                                    [*A pause.*

What hideous thought was that I had even now?
'Tis gone; and yet its burden remains here   30
O'er these dull eyes . . . upon this weary heart!
O, world! O, life! O, day! O, misery!

    Lucretia. What ails thee, my poor child? She answers not;
Her spirit apprehends the sense of pain,
But not its cause; suffering has dried away
The source from which it sprung . . .

    Beatrice (*franticly*).   Like Parricide.
Misery has killed its father: yet its father°
Never like mine . . . O, God! What thing am I?

    Lucretia. My dearest child, what has your father done?

    Beatrice (*doubtfully*). Who art thou, questioner? I have
     no father.   40
                               [*Aside*
She is the madhouse nurse who tends on me;
It is a piteous office.
                      [*To* LUCRETIA, *in a slow, subdued voice*
               Do you know
I thought I was that wretched Beatrice
Men speak of, whom her father sometimes hales°
From hall to hall by the entangled hair;
At others, pens up naked in damp cells
Where scaly reptiles crawl, and starves her there,
Till she will eat strange flesh. This woeful story
So did I overact in my sick dreams,
That I imagined . . . no, it cannot be!   50
Horrible things have been in this wild world,
Prodigious mixtures, and confusions strange
Of good and ill; and worse have been conceived
Than ever there was found a heart to do.
But never fancy imaged such a deed
As . . .   [*Pauses, suddenly recollecting herself*
     Who art thou? Swear to me, ere I die
With fearful expectation, that indeed
Thou art not what thou seemest . . . Mother!

Lucretia.   Oh!
My sweet child, know you . . .

Beatrice.   Yet speak it not:
For then if this be truth, that other too   60
Must be a truth, a firm enduring truth,
Linked with each lasting circumstance of life,
Never to change, never to pass away.
Why so it is. This is the Cenci palace;
Thou art Lucretia; I am Beatrice.
I have talked some wild words, but will no more.
Mother, come near me: from this point of time,
I am . . . (*Her voice dies away faintly*)

Lucretia. Alas! What has befallen thee, child?
What has thy father done?

Beatrice.   What have I done?
Am I not innocent? Is it my crime   70
That one with white hair, and imperious brow,
Who tortured me from my forgotten years,
As parents only dare, should call himself
My father, yet should be!—Oh, what am I?
What name, what place, what memory shall be mine?
What retrospects, outliving even despair?

Lucretia. He is a violent tyrant, surely, child:
We know that death alone can make us free;
His death or ours. But what can he have done
Of deadlier outrage or worse injury?   80
Thou art unlike thyself; thine eyes shoot forth
A wandering and strange spirit. Speak to me,
Unlock those pallid hands whose fingers twine
With one another.

Beatrice.   'Tis the restless life
Tortured within them. If I try to speak
I shall go mad. Aye, something must be done;
What, yet I know not . . . something which shall make°
The thing that I have suffered but a shadow
In the dread lightning which avenges it;

Brief, rapid, irreversible, destroying   90
The consequence of what it cannot cure.
Some such thing is to be endured or done:
When I know what, I shall be still and calm,
And never any thing will move me more
But now!—O blood, which art my father's blood,
Circling through these contaminated veins,
If thou, poured forth on the polluted earth,
Could wash away the crime, and punishment
By which I suffer . . . no, that cannot be!
Many might doubt there were a God above   100
Who sees and permits evil, and so die;
That faith no agony shall obscure in me.

   Lucretia. It must indeed have been some bitter wrong;
Yet what, I dare not guess. Oh, my lost child,
Hide not in proud impenetrable grief
Thy sufferings from my fear.

   Beatrice.   I hide them not.
What are the words which you would have me speak?
I, who can feign no image in my mind
Of that which has transformed me. I, whose thought
Is like a ghost shrouded and folded up   110
In its own formless horror. Of all words,
That minister to mortal intercourse,
Which wouldst thou hear? For there is none to tell
My misery: if another ever knew
Aught like to it, she died as I will die,
And left it, as I must, without a name.
Death! Death! Our law and our religion call thee
A punishment and a reward . . . Oh, which
Have I deserved?

   Lucretia.   The peace of innocence;
Till in your season you be called to heaven.   120
Whate'er you may have suffered, you have done
No evil. Death must be the punishment
Of crime, or the reward of trampling down
The thorns which God has strewed upon the path
Which leads to immortality.

Beatrice.   Aye, death . . .
The punishment of crime. I pray thee, God,
Let me not be bewildered while I judge.
If I must live day after day, and keep
These limbs, the unworthy temple of thy spirit,
As a foul den from which what thou abhorrest   130
May mock thee, unavenged . . . it shall not be!
Self-murder . . . no, that might be no escape,
For thy decree yawns like a Hell between
Our will and it:—O! In this mortal world°
There is no vindication and no law
Which can adjudge and execute the doom
Of that through which I suffer.
                         Enter ORSINO.
(*She approaches him solemnly*)   Welcome, Friend!
I have to tell you that, since last we met,
I have endured a wrong so great and strange,
That neither life nor death can give me rest.   140
Ask me not what it is, for there are deeds
Which have no form, sufferings which have no tongue.

Orsino. And what is he who has thus injured you?

Beatrice. The man they call my father: a dread name.

Orsino. It cannot be . . .

Beatrice.   What it can be, or not,
Forbear to think. It is, and it has been;
Advise me how it shall not be again.
I thought to die; but a religious awe
Restrains me, and the dread lest death itself
Might be no refuge from the consciousness   150
Of what is yet unexpiated. Oh, speak!

Orsino. Accuse him of the deed, and let the law
Avenge thee.

Beatrice.   Oh, ice-hearted counsellor!
If I could find a word that might make known
The crime of my destroyer; and that done
My tongue should like a knife tear out the secret

Which cankers my heart's core; aye, lay all bare
So that my unpolluted fame should be
With vilest gossips a stale mouthèd story;
A mock, a bye-word, an astonishment:—   160
If this were done, which never shall be done,
Think of the offender's gold, his dreaded hate,
And the strange horror of the accuser's tale,
Baffling belief, and overpowering speech;
Scarce whispered, unimaginable, wrapped
In hideous hints . . . Oh, most assured redress!

   Orsino. You will endure it then?

   Beatrice.   Endure?—Orsino,
It seems your counsel is small profit.
                  [*Turns from him, and speaks half to herself*
                Aye,
All must be suddenly resolved and done.
What is this undistinguishable mist   170
Of thoughts, which rise, like shadow after shadow,
Darkening each other?

   Orsino.   Should the offender live?
Triumph in his misdeed? and make, by use,
His crime, whate'er it is, dreadful no doubt,
Thine element; until thou mayest become
Utterly lost; subdued even to the hue
Of that which thou permittest?

   Beatrice (*to herself*).   Mighty death!
Thou double-visaged shadow! Only judge!
Rightfullest arbiter!
                [*She retires absorbed in thought.*

   Lucretia.   If the lightning
Of God has e'er descended to avenge . . .   180

   Orsino. Blaspheme not! His high Providence commits
Its glory on this earth, and their own wrongs
Into the hands of men; if they neglect
To punish crime . . .

Lucretia.   But if one, like this wretch,
Should mock, with gold, opinion, law and power?
If there be no appeal to that which makes
The guiltiest tremble? If because our wrongs,
For that they are unnatural, strange and monstrous,
Exceed all measure of belief? Oh, God!
If, for the very reasons which should make   190
Redress most swift and sure, our injurer triumphs?
And we, the victims, bear worse punishment
Than that appointed for their torturer?

Orsino.   Think not
But that there is redress where there is wrong,
So we be bold enough to seize it.

Lucretia.   How?
If there were any way to make all sure,
I know not . . . but I think it might be good
To . . .

Orsino. Why, his late outrage to Beatrice;
For it is such, as I but faintly guess,
As makes remorse dishonour, and leaves her   200
Only one duty, how she may avenge:
You, but one refuge from ills ill endured;
Me, but one counsel . . .

Lucretia.   For we cannot hope
That aid, or retribution, or resource
Will arise thence, where every other one
Might find them with less need.

                                        [BEATRICE *advances.*

Orsino.   Then . . .

Beatrice.   Peace, Orsino!
And, honoured Lady, while I speak, I pray,
That you put off, as garments overworn,
Forbearance and respect, remorse and fear,
And all the fit restraints of daily life,   210

Which have been borne from childhood, but which
   now
Would be a mockery to my holier plea.
As I have said, I have endured a wrong,
Which, though it be expressionless, is such
As asks atonement; both for what is past;
And lest I be reserved, day after day,
To load with crimes an overburdened soul,
And be . . . what ye can dream not. I have prayed
To God, and I have talked with my own heart,
And have unravelled my entangled will,   220
And have at length determined what is right.
Art thou my friend, Orsino? False or true?
Pledge thy salvation ere I speak.

  Orsino.   I swear
To dedicate my cunning, and my strength,
My silence, and whatever else is mine,
To thy commands.

  Lucretia.   You think we should devise
His death?

  Beatrice.   And execute what is devised,
And suddenly. We must be brief and bold.

  Orsino. And yet most cautious.

  Lucretia.   For the jealous laws
Would punish us with death and infamy   230
For that which it became themselves to do.

  Beatrice. Be cautious as ye may, but prompt. Orsino
What are the means?

  Orsino.   I know two dull, fierce outlaws,
Who think man's spirit as a worm's, and they
Would trample out, for any slight caprice,
The meanest or the noblest life. This mood
Is marketable here in Rome. They sell
What we now want.

Lucretia.   Tomorrow before dawn,
Cenci will take us to that lonely rock,
Petrella, in the Apulian Apennines.   240
If he arrive there . . .

Beatrice.   He must not arrive.

Orsino. Will it be dark before you reach the tower?

Lucretia. The sun will scarce be set.

Beatrice.   But I remember.
Two miles on this side of the fort, the road
Crosses a deep ravine; 'tis rough and narrow,
And winds with short turns down the precipice;
And in its depth there is a mighty rock,
Which has, from unimaginable years,
Sustained itself with terror and with toil
Over a gulf, and with the agony   250
With which it clings seems slowly coming down;
Even as a wretched soul hour after hour,
Clings to the mass of life; yet clinging, leans;
And leaning, makes more dark the dread abyss
In which it fears to fall: beneath this crag,
Huge as despair, as if in weariness,
The melancholy mountain yawns . . . below,
You hear but see not an impetuous torrent
Raging among the caverns, and a bridge
Crosses the chasm; and high above there grow,   260
With intersecting trunks, from crag to crag,
Cedars, and yews, and pines; whose tangled hair
Is matted in one solid roof of shade
By the dark ivy's twine. At noonday here
'Tis twilight, and at sunset blackest night.°

Orsino. Before you reach that bridge make some excuse
For spurring on your mules, or loitering
Until . . .

Beatrice. What sound is that?

Lucr. Hark! No, it cannot be a servant's step;
It must be Cenci, unexpectedly   270
Returned . . . Make some excuse for being here.

Beatrice (*to* ORSINO, *as she goes out*). That step we hear approach must never pass
The bridge of which we spoke.
                              [*Exeunt* LUCRETIA *and* BEATRICE.

Orsino.   What shall I do?
Cenci must find me here, and I must bear
The imperious inquisition of his looks
As to what brought me hither: let me mask
Mine own in some inane and vacant smile.
              Enter GIACOMO, *in a hurried manner.*
How! Have you ventured hither? know you then
That Cenci is from home?

Giacomo. I sought him here;
And now must wait till he returns.

Orsino.   Great God!   280
Weigh you the danger of this rashness?

Giacomo.   Aye!
Does my destroyer know his danger? We
Are now no more, as once, parent and child,
But man to man; the oppressor to the oppressed;
The slanderer to the slandered; foe to foe:
He has cast Nature off, which was his shield,
And Nature casts him off, who is her shame;
And I spurn both. Is it a father's throat
Which I will shake, and say, I ask not gold;
I ask not happy years; nor memories   290
Of tranquil childhood; nor home-sheltered love;
Though all these hast thou torn from me, and more;
But only my fair fame; only one hoard
Of peace, which I thought hidden from thy hate,
Under the penury heaped on me by thee,
Or I will . . . God can understand and pardon,
Why should I speak with man?

Orsino.   Be calm, dear friend.

Giacomo. Well, I will calmly tell you what he did.
This old Francesco Cenci, as you know,
Borrowed the dowry of my wife from me,   300
And then denied the loan; and left me so
In poverty, the which I sought to mend
By holding a poor office in the state.
It had been promised to me, and already
I bought new clothing for my ragged babes,
And my wife smiled; and my heart knew repose;
When Cenci's intercession, as I found,
Conferred this office on a wretch, whom thus
He paid for vilest service. I returned
With this ill news, and we sate sad together   310
Solacing our despondency with tears
Of such affection and unbroken faith
As temper life's worst bitterness; when he,
As he is wont, came to upbraid and curse,
Mocking our poverty, and telling us
Such was God's scourge for disobedient sons.
And then, that I might strike him dumb with shame,
I spoke of my wife's dowry; but he coined
A brief yet specious tale, how I had wasted
The sum in secret riot; and he saw   320
My wife was touched, and he went smiling forth.
And when I knew the impression he had made,
And felt my wife insult with silent scorn
My ardent truth, and look averse and cold,
I went forth too: but soon returned again;
Yet not so soon but that my wife had taught
My children her harsh thoughts, and they all cried,
'Give us clothes, father! Give us better food!
What you in one night squander were enough
For months!' I looked, and saw that home was hell.   330
And to that hell will I return no more
Until mine enemy has rendered up
Atonement, or, as he gave life to me
I will, reversing nature's law . . .

Orsino.   Trust me,

The compensation which thou seekest here
Will be denied.

    Giacomo.   Then . . . Are you not my friend?
Did you not hint at the alternative,
Upon the brink of which you see I stand,
The other day when we conversed together?
My wrongs were then less. That word parricide,   340
Although I am resolved, haunts me like fear.

    Orsino. It must be fear itself, for the bare word
Is hollow mockery. Mark, how wisest God
Draws to one point the threads of a just doom,
So sanctifying it: what you devise
Is, as it were, accomplishèd.

    Giacomo.   Is he dead?

    Orsino. His grave is ready. Know that since we met
Cenci has done an outrage to his daughter.

    Giacomo. What outrage?

    Orsino.   That she speaks not, but you may
Conceive such half conjectures as I do,   350
From her fixed paleness, and the lofty grief
Of her stern brow bent on the idle air,
And her severe unmodulated voice,
Drowning both tenderness and dread; and last
From this; that whilst her step-mother and I,
Bewildered in our horror, talked together
With obscure hints; both self-misunderstood
And darkly guessing, stumbling, in our talk,
Over the truth, and yet to its revenge,
She interrupted us, and with a look   360
Which told before she spoke it, he must die . . .

    Giacomo. It is enough. My doubts are well appeased;
There is a higher reason for the act
Than mine; there is a holier judge than me,
A more unblamed avenger. Beatrice,

Who in the gentleness of thy sweet youth
Hast never trodden on a worm, or bruised
A living flower, but thou hast pitied it
With needless tears! Fair sister, thou in whom
Men wondered how such loveliness and wisdom   370
Did not destroy each other! Is there made
Ravage of thee? O, heart, I ask no more
Justification! Shall I wait, Orsino,
Till he return, and stab him at the door?

   Orsino. Not so; some accident might interpose
To rescue him from what is now most sure;
And you are unprovided where to fly,
How to excuse or to conceal. Nay, listen:
All is contrived; success is so assured.
That . . .

Enter BEATRICE.

   Beatrice. 'Tis my brother's voice! You know me not?   380

   Giacomo. My sister, my lost sister!

   Beatrice.   Lost indeed!
I see Orsino has talked with you, and
That you conjecture things too horrible
To speak, yet far less than the truth. Now, stay not,
He might return: yet kiss me; I shall know
That then thou hast consented to his death.
Farewell, Farewell! Let piety to God,
Brotherly love, justice and clemency,
And all things that make tender hardest hearts
Make thine hard, brother. Answer not . . . farewell.   390

[Exeunt severally.

SCENE 2.—*A mean apartment in* GIACOMO's *house*.
GIACOMO, *alone*.

   Giacomo. 'Tis midnight, and Orsino comes not yet.
[Thunder, and the sound of a storm.
What! can the everlasting elements
Feel with a worm like man? If so the shaft

Of mercy-wingèd lightning would not fall
On stones and trees. My wife and children sleep:
They are now living in unmeaning dreams:
But I must wake, still doubting if that deed
Be just which was most necessary. O,
Thou unreplenished lamp! whose narrow fire
Is shaken by the wind, and on whose edge   10
Devouring darkness hovers! Thou small flame,
Which, as a dying pulse rises and falls,
Still flickerest up and down, how very soon,
Did I not feed thee, wouldst thou fail and be
As thou hadst never been! So wastes and sinks
Even now, perhaps, the life that kindled mine:
But that no power can fill with vital oil
That broken lamp of flesh. Ha! 'tis the blood°
Which fed these veins that ebbs till all is cold:
It is the form that moulded mine, which sinks   20
Into the white and yellow spasms of death:
It is the soul by which mine was arrayed
In God's immortal likeness which now stands
Naked before Heaven's judgement seat!

                                            [*A bell strikes.*

                                    One! Two!
The hours crawl on; and when my hairs are white
My son will then perhaps be waiting thus,
Tortured between just hate and vain remorse;
Chiding the tardy messenger of news
Like those which I expect. I almost wish
He be not dead, although my wrongs are great;   30
Yet . . . 'tis Orsino's step . . .

                        Enter ORSINO.
                            Speak!

    Orsino.   I am come
To say he has escaped.

    Giacomo.   Escaped!

    Orsino.   And safe.
Within Petrella. He passed by the spot
Appointed for the deed an hour too soon.

Giacomo. Are we the fools of such contingencies?
And do we waste in blind misgivings thus
The hours when we should act? Then wind and thunder,
Which seemed to howl his knell, is the loud laughter
With which Heaven mocks our weakness! I henceforth
Will ne'er repent of aught designed or done   40
But my repentance.

   Orsino.   See, the lamp is out.

   Giacomo. If no remorse is ours when the dim air
Has drank this innocent flame, why should we quail
When Cenci's life, that light by which ill spirits
See the worst deeds they prompt, shall sink for ever?
No, I am hardened.

   Orsino.   Why, what need of this?
Who feared the pale intrusion of remorse
In a just deed? Although our first plan failed
Doubt not but he will soon be laid to rest.
But light the lamp; let us not talk i' the dark.   50

   Giacomo (*lighting the lamp*). And yet once quenched I
     cannot thus relume°
My father's life: do you not think his ghost
Might plead that argument with God?

   Orsino.   Once gone
You cannot now recall your sister's peace;
Your own extinguished years of youth and hope;
Nor your wife's bitter words; nor all the taunts
Which, from the prosperous, weak misfortune takes;
Nor your dead mother; nor . . .

   Giacomo.   O, speak no more!
I am resolved, although this very hand
Must quench the life that animated it.   60

   Orsino. There is no need of that. Listen: you know
Olimpio, the castellan of Petrella°
In old Colonna's time; him whom your father

Degraded from his post? And Marzio,
That desperate wretch, whom he deprived last year
Of a reward of blood, well earned and due?

Giacomo. I knew Olimpio; and they say he hated
Old Cenci so, that in his silent rage
His lips grew white only to see him pass.
Of Marzio I know nothing.

Orsino.   Marzio's hate   70
Matches Olimpio's. I have sent these men,
But in your name, and as at your request,
To talk with Beatrice and Lucretia.
    Giacomo. Only to talk?

Orsino.   The moments which even now
Pass onward tomorrow's midnight hour
May memorize their flight with death: ere then
They must have talked, and may perhaps have done,
And made an end . . .

Giacomo.   Listen! What sound is that?

Orsino. The housedog moans, and the beams crack: nought else.

Giacomo. It is my wife complaining in her sleep: 80
I doubt not she is saying bitter things
Of me; and all my children round her dreaming
That I deny them sustenance.

Orsino.   Whilst he
Who truly took it from them, and who fills
Their hungry rest with bitterness, now sleeps
Lapped in bad pleasures, and triumphantly
Mocks thee in visions of successful hate
Too like the truth of day.

Giacomo.   If e'er he wakes
Again, I will not trust to hireling hands . . .

Orsino. Why, that were well. I must be gone; good night!   90
When next we meet—may all be done—

   Giacomo.   And all
Forgotten—Oh, that I had never been!

                                               [Exeunt.

END OF THE THIRD ACT.

Act 4

SCENE 1.—*An apartment in the Castle of Petrella.*
Enter CENCI.

Cenci. She comes not; yet I left her even now
Vanquished and faint. She knows the penalty
Of her delay: yet what if threats are vain?
Am I now not within Petrella's moat?
Or fear I still the eyes and ears of Rome?
Might I not drag her by the golden hair?
Stamp on her? Keep her sleepless till her brain
Be overworn? Tame her with chains and famine?
Less would suffice. Yet so to leave undone
What I most seek! No, 'tis her stubborn will.°   10
Which by its own consent shall stoop as low
As that which drags it down.
     Enter LUCRETIA.
       Thou loathèd wretch!
Hide thee from my abhorrence; Fly, begone!
Yet stay! Bid Beatrice come hither.

 Lucretia.   Oh,
Husband! I pray for thine own wretched sake
Heed what thou dost. A man who walks like thee
Through crimes, and through the danger of his crimes,
Each hour may stumble o'er a sudden grave.
And thou art old; thy hairs are hoary grey;
As thou wouldst save thyself from death and hell,   20
Pity thy daughter; give her to some friend
In marriage: so that she may tempt thee not
To hatred, or worse thoughts, if worse there be.

 Cenci. What! like her sister who has found a home
To mock my hate from with prosperity?
Strange ruin shall destroy both her and thee
And all that yet remain. My death may be
Rapid, her destiny outspeeds it. Go,
Bid her come hither, and before my mood
Be changed, lest I should drag her by the hair.   30

Lucretia. She sent me to thee, husband. At thy presence
She fell, as thou dost know, into a trance;
And in that trance she heard a voice which said,
'Cenci must die! Let him confess himself!
Even now the accusing Angel waits to hear
If God, to punish his enormous crimes,
Harden his dying heart!'

Cenci.   Why—such things are . . .
No doubt divine revealings may be made.
'Tis plain I have been favoured from above,
For when I cursed my sons they died.—Aye . . . so . . .   40
As to the right or wrong, that's talk . . . repentance . . .
Repentance is an easy moment's work
And more depends on God than me. Well . . . well . . .
I must give up the greater point, which was
To poison and corrupt her soul.

                    [*A pause;* LUCRETIA *approaches anxiously, and then*
                                        shrinks back as he speaks.
                              One, two;
Aye . . . Rocco and Cristofano my curse
Strangled: and Giacomo, I think, will find
Life a worse Hell than that beyond the grave:
Beatrice shall, if there be skill in hate
Die in despair, blaspheming: to Bernardo,   50
He is so innocent, I will bequeath
The memory of these deeds, and make his youth
The sepulchre of hope, where evil thoughts
Shall grow like weeds on a neglected tomb.
When all is done, out in the wide Campagna,
I will pile up my silver and my gold;
My costly robes, paintings and tapestries;
My parchments and all records of my wealth,
And make a bonfire in my joy, and leave
Of my possessions nothing but my name;   60
Which shall be an inheritance to strip
Its wearer bare as infamy. That done,
My soul, which is a scourge, will I resign
Into the hands of him who wielded it;
Be it for its own punishment or theirs,
He will not ask it of me till the lash

Be broken in its last and deepest wound;
Until its hate be all inflicted. Yet,
Lest death outspeed my purpose, let me make
Short work and sure . . .   [*Going.*

    Lucretia (*stops him*). Oh, stay! It was a feint: 70
She had no vision, and she heard no voice.
I said it but to awe thee.

    Cenci.   That is well.
Vile palterer with the sacred truth of God,
Be thy soul choked with that blaspheming lie!
For Beatrice worse terrors are in store
To bend her to my will.

    Lucretia.   Oh! to what will?
What cruel sufferings more than she has known
Canst thou inflict?

    Cenci.   Andrea! Go call my daughter,
And if she comes not tell her that I come.
What sufferings? I will drag her, step by step,   80
Through infamies unheard of among men:
She shall stand shelterless in the broad noon
Of public scorn, for acts blazoned abroad,°
One among which shall be . . . What? Canst thou guess?
She shall become (for what she most abhors
Shall have a fascination to entrap
Her loathing will) to her own conscious self
All she appears to others; and when dead,°
As she shall die unshrived and unforgiven,
A rebel to her father and her God,   90
Her corpse shall be abandoned to the hounds;
Her name shall be the terror of the earth;
Her spirit shall approach the throne of God
Plague-spotted with my curses. I will make
Body and soul a monstrous lump of ruin.
                    Enter ANDREA.

    Andrea. The lady Beatrice . . .

Cenci.   Speak, pale slave! What
Said she?

Andrea. My Lord, 'twas what she looked; she said:
'Go tell my father that I see the gulf
Of Hell between us two, which he may pass,
I will not.'

                                        [*Exit* ANDREA.

Cenci.   Go thou quick, Lucretia,   100
Tell her to come; yet let her understand
Her coming is consent: and say, moreover,
That if she come not I will curse her.

                                        [*Exit* LUCRETIA.

                         Ha!
With what but with a father's curse doth God
Panic-strike armèd victory, and make pale
Cities in their prosperity? The world's Father
Must grant a parent's prayer against his child
Be he who asks even what men call me.
Will not the deaths of her rebellious brothers
Awe her before I speak? For I on them   110
Did imprecate quick ruin, and it came.
                    Enter LUCRETIA.
Well; what? Speak, wretch!

Lucretia.   She said, 'I cannot come;
Go tell my father that I see a torrent.
Of his own blood raging between us.'

Cenci (kneeling).   God!
Hear me! If this most specious mass of flesh,°
Which thou hast made my daughter; this my blood,
This particle of my divided being;
Or rather, this my bane and my disease,
Whose sight infects and poisons me; this devil
Which sprung from me as from a hell, was meant   120
To aught good use; if her bright loveliness
Was kindled to illumine this dark world;
If nursed by thy selectest dew of love

Such virtues blossom in her as should make
The peace of life, I pray thee for my sake,
As thou the common God and Father art
Of her, and me, and all; reverse that doom!
Earth, in the name of God, let her food be
Poison, until she be encrusted round
With leprous stains! Heaven, rain upon her head   130
The blistering drops of the Maremma's dew,°
Till she be speckled like a toad; parch up
Those love-enkindled lips, warp those fine limbs
To loathèd lameness! All-beholding sun,
Strike in thine envy those life-darting eyes
With thine own blinding beams!

   Lucretia.   Peace! Peace!
For thine own sake unsay those dreadful words.
When high God grants he punishes such prayers.

   Cenci (leaping up, and throwing his right hand towards Heaven). He
      does his will, I mine! This in addition,
That if she have a child . . .

   Lucretia.   Horrible thought!

   Cenci. That if she ever have a child; and thou,°   140
Quick Nature! I adjure thee by thy God,
That thou be fruitful in her, and increase
And multiply, fulfilling his command,
And my deep imprecation! May it be
A hideous likeness of herself, that as
From a distorting mirror, she may see
Her image mixed with what she most abhors,
Smiling upon her from her nursing breast.
And that the child may from its infancy   150
Grow, day by day, more wicked and deformed,
Turning her mother's love to misery:
And that both she and it may live until
It shall repay her care and pain with hate,
Or what may else be more unnatural,
So he may hunt her through the clamorous scoffs
Of the loud world to a dishonoured grave.

Shall I revoke this curse? Go, bid her come,
Before my words are chronicled in heaven.°

                                        [*Exit* LUCRETIA.

I do not feel as if I were a man,   160
But like a fiend appointed to chastise
The offences of some unremembered world.
My blood is running up and down my veins;
A fearful pleasure makes it prick and tingle:
I feel a giddy sickness of strange awe;
My heart is beating with an expectation
Of horrid joy.

                        Enter LUCRETIA.
                        What? Speak!

   Lucretia.   She bids thee curse;
And if thy curses, as they cannot do,
Could kill her soul . . .

   Cenci.   She would not come. 'Tis well,
I can do both: first take what I demand,   170
And then extort concession. To thy chamber!
Fly ere I spurn thee: and beware this night
That thou cross not my footsteps. It were safer
To come between the tiger and his prey.

                                        [*Exit* LUCRETIA.

It must be late; mine eyes grow weary dim
With unaccustomed heaviness of sleep.
Conscience! Oh, thou most insolent of lies!
They say that sleep, that healing dew of heaven,
Steeps not in balm the foldings of the brain
Which thinks thee an impostor. I will go   180
First to belie thee with an hour of rest,
Which will be deep and calm, I feel: and then . . .
O, multitudinous Hell, the fiends will shake
Thine arches with the laughter of their joy!
There shall be lamentation heard in Heaven
As o'er an angel fallen; and upon Earth
All good shall droop and sicken, and ill things
Shall with a spirit of unnatural life
Stir and be quickened . . . even as I am now.°

                                        [*Exit.*

SCENE 2.—*Before the Castle of Petrella.*
    Enter BEATRICE *and* LUCRETIA *above on the ramparts.*

Beatrice. They come not yet.

Lucretia.   'Tis scarce midnight.

Beatrice.   How slow
Behind the course of thought, even sick with speed.
Lags leaden-footed time!

Lucretia.   The minutes pass . . .
If he should wake before the deed is done?

Beatrice. O, Mother! He must never wake again.
What thou hast said persuades me that our act
Will but dislodge a spirit of deep hell
Out of a human form.

Lucretia.   'Tis true he spoke
Of death and judgement with strange confidence
For one so wicked; as a man believing   10
In God, yet recking not of good or ill.°
And yet to die without confession! . . .

Beatrice.   Oh!
Believe that heaven is merciful and just,
And will not add our dread necessity
To the amount of his offences.
        Enter OLIMPIO *and* MARZIO, *below.*

Lucretia.   See,
They come.

Beatrice. All mortal things must hasten thus
To their dark end. Let us go down.
        [*Exeunt* LUCRETIA *and* BEATRICE *from above.*

Olimpio. How feel you to this work?

Marzio.   As one who thinks

A thousand crowns excellent market price
For an old murderer's life. Your cheeks are pale.   20

   Olimpio. It is the white reflexion of your own,
Which you call pale.

   Marzio.   Is that their natural hue?

   Olimpio. Or 'tis my hate and the deferred desire
To wreak it, which extinguishes their blood.

   Marzio. You are inclined then to this business?

   Olimpio.   Aye.
If one should bribe me with a thousand crowns
To kill a serpent which had stung my child,
I could not be more willing.
           Enter BEATRICE *and* LUCRETIA, *below*.
           Noble ladies!

   Beatrice. Are ye resolved?

   Olimpio.   Is he asleep?

   Marzio.   Is all
Quiet?

   Lucretia. I mixed an opiate with his drink: 30
He sleeps so soundly . . .

   Beatrice.   That his death will be
But as a change of sin-chastising dreams,
A dark continuance of the Hell within him,°
Which God extinguish! But ye are resolved?
Ye know it is a high and holy deed?

   Olimpio. We are resolved.

   Marzio.   As to the how this act
Be warranted, it rests with you.

   Beatrice.   Well, follow!

Olimpio. Hush! Hark! What noise is that?

Marzio.   Ha! some one comes!

Beatrice. Ye conscience-stricken cravens, rock to rest.
Your baby hearts. It is the iron gate,   40
Which ye left open, swinging to the wind,
That enters whistling as in scorn. Come, follow!
And be your steps like mine, light, quick and bold.

                                                    [*Exeunt.*

SCENE 3.—*An apartment in the Castle.*
                    Enter BEATRICE *and* LUCRETIA.

Lucretia. They are about it now.

Beatrice.   Nay, it is done.

Lucretia. I have not heard him groan.

Beatrice.   He will not groan.

Lucretia. What sound is that?

Beatrice.   List! 'tis the tread of feet
About his bed.

Lucretia.   My God!
If he be now a cold stiff corpse . . .

Beatrice.   O, fear not
What may be done, but what is left undone:
The act seals all.
                    Enter OLIMPIO *and* MARZIO.
                    Is it accomplished?

Marzio.   What?

Olimpio. Did you not call?

Beatrice.   When?

Olimpio.   Now.°

Beatrice.   I ask if all is over?

Olimpio. We dare not kill an old and sleeping man;
His thin grey hair, his stern and reverent brow,   10
His veinèd hands crossed on his heaving breast,
And the calm innocent sleep in which he lay,
Quelled me. Indeed, indeed, I cannot do it.

Marzio. But I was bolder; for I chid Olimpio,
And bade him bear his wrongs to his own grave
And leave me the reward. And now my knife
Touched the loose wrinkled throat, when the old man
Stirred in his sleep, and said, 'God! hear, O, hear,
A father's curse! What, art thou not our father?'
And then he laughed. I knew it was the ghost   20
Of my dead father speaking through his lips,
And could not kill him.

Beatrice.   Miserable slaves!
Where, if ye dare not kill a sleeping man,
Found ye the boldness to return to me
With such a deed undone? Base palterers!
Cowards and traitors! Why, the very conscience
Which ye would sell for gold and for revenge
Is an equivocation: it sleeps over°
A thousand daily acts disgracing men;
And when a deed where mercy insults heaven . . .   30
Why do I talk?
                    [*Snatching a dagger from one of them and raising it.*
              Hadst thou a tongue to say,
'She murdered her own father,' I must do it!
But never dream ye shall outlive him long!

Olimpio. Stop, for God's sake!

Marzio.   I will go back and kill him.

Olimpio. Give me the weapon, we must do thy will.

Beatrice. Take it! Depart! Return!

> [*Exeunt* OLIMPIO *and* MARZIO.
> How pale thou art!

We do but that which 'twere a deadly crime
To leave undone.

Lucretia.   Would it were done!

Beatrice.   Even whilst
That doubt is passing through your mind, the world
Is conscious of a change. Darkness and hell   40
Have swallowed up the vapour they sent forth
To blacken the sweet light of life. My breath°
Comes, methinks, lighter and the jellied blood°
Runs freely through my veins. Hark!

> *Enter* OLIMPIO *and* MARZIO.
> He is . . .

Olimpio.   Dead!

Marzio. We strangled him that there might be no blood;
And then we threw his heavy corpse i' the garden
Under the balcony; 'twill seem it fell.

Beatrice (*giving them a bag of coin*). Here take this gold, and hasten
    to your homes.
And, Marzio, because thou wast only awed
By that which made me tremble, wear thou this!   50

> [*Clothes him in a rich mantle*

It was the mantle which my grandfather
Wore in his high prosperity, and men
Envied his state: so may they envy thine.
Thou wert a weapon in the hand of God
To a just use. Live long and thrive! And, mark,
If thou hast crimes, repent: this deed is none.

> [*A horn is sounded.*

Lucretia. Hark, 'tis the castle horn; my God! it sounds
Like the last trump.

Beatrice.   Some tedious guest is coming.

Lucretia. The drawbridge is let down; there is a tramp
Of horses in the court; fly, hide yourselves!   60
                              [*Exeunt* OLIMPIO *and* MARZIO.

Beatrice. Let us retire to counterfeit deep rest;
I scarcely need to counterfeit it now:
The spirit which doth reign within these limbs
Seems strangely undisturbed. I could even sleep
Fearless and calm: all ill is surely past.

                                                [*Exeunt.*

SCENE 4.—*Another apartment in the Castle.*
Enter on one side the Legate SAVELLA *introduced by a servant, and on the
                    other* LUCRETIA *and* BERNARDO.

Savella. Lady, my duty to his Holiness
Be my excuse that thus unseasonably
I break upon your rest. I must speak with
Count Cenci; doth he sleep?

Lucretia (*in a hurried and confused manner*). I think he sleeps;
Yet wake him not, I pray, spare me awhile,
He is a wicked and a wrathful man;
Should he be roused out of his sleep tonight,
Which is, I know, a hell of angry dreams,
It were not well; indeed it were not well.
Wait till day break. . . . (*Aside*) O, I am deadly sick!   10

Savella. I grieve thus to distress you, but the Count
Must answer charges of the gravest import,
And suddenly; such my commission is.

Lucretia (*with increased agitation*). I dare not rouse him: I know
        none who dare . . .
'Twere perilous; . . . you might as safely waken
A serpent; or a corpse in which some fiend
Were laid to sleep.

Savella.   Lady, my moments here
Are counted. I must rouse him from his sleep,
Since none else dare.

Lucretia (*aside*).   O, terror! O, despair!
(*to* BERNARDO) Bernardo, conduct you the Lord Legate to   20
Your father's chamber.

                    [*Exeunt* SAVELLA *and* BERNARDO.
                    Enter BEATRICE.

Beatrice   'Tis a messenger
Come to arrest the culprit who now stands
Before the throne of unappealable God.°
Both Earth and Heaven, consenting arbiters,
Acquit our deed.

Lucretia.   Oh, agony of fear!
Would that he yet might live! Even now I heard
The Legate's followers whisper as they passed
They had a warrant for his instant death.°
All was prepared by unforbidden means
Which we must pay so dearly, having done.   30
Even now they search the tower, and find the body;
Now they suspect the truth; now they consult
Before they come to tax us with the fact;
O, horrible, 'tis all discovered!

Beatrice.   Mother,
What is done wisely, is done well. Be bold
As thou art just. 'Tis like a truant child
To fear that others know what thou hast done,
Even from thine own strong consciousness, and thus
Write on unsteady eyes and altered cheeks
All thou wouldst hide. Be faithful to thyself,   40
And fear no other witness but thy fear.
For if, as cannot be, some circumstance
Should rise in accusation, we can blind
Suspicion with such cheap astonishment,
Or overbear it with such guiltless pride,
As murderers cannot feign. The deed is done,
And what may follow now regards not me.
I am as universal as the light;
Free as the earth-surrounding air; as firm°
As the world's centre. Consequence, to me,   50

Is as the wind which strikes the solid rock
But shakes it not.

[*A cry within and tumult.*

Voices.   Murder! Murder! Murder!
            Enter BERNARDO *and* SAVELLA.

Savella (*to his followers*). Go, search the castle round; sound the
    alarm;
Look to the gates that none escape!

Beatrice.   What now?

Bernardo. I know not what to say . . . my father's dead.

Beatrice. How; dead! he only sleeps; you mistake, brother.
His sleep is very calm, very like death;
'Tis wonderful how well a tyrant sleeps.
He is not dead?

Bernardo.   Dead; murdered.

Lucretia (*with extreme agitation*). Oh, no, no,
He is not murdered though he may be dead;   60
I have alone the keys of those apartments.

Savella. Ha! Is it so?

Beatrice.   My Lord, I pray excuse us;
We will retire; my mother is not well:
She seems quite overcome with this strange horror.
                    [*Exeunt* LUCRETIA *and* BEATRICE.

Savella. Can you suspect who may have murdered him?

Bernardo. I know not what to think.

Savella.   Can you name any
Who had an interest in his death?

Bernardo.   Alas!
I can name none who had not, and those most

Who most lament that such a deed is done;
My mother, and my sister, and myself.   70

 Savella. 'Tis strange! There were clear marks of violence.
I found the old man's body in the moonlight
Hanging beneath the window of his chamber
Among the branches of a pine: he could not
Have fallen there, for all his limbs lay heaped
And effortless; 'tis true there was no blood . . . °
Favour me, Sir; it much imports your house
That all should be made clear; to tell the ladies
That I request their presence.

              [*Exit* BERNARDO.
    Enter Guards bringing in MARZIO.

 Guard.   We have one.

 Officer. My Lord, we found this ruffian and another   80
Lurking among the rocks; there is no doubt
But that they are the murderers of Count Cenci:
Each had a bag of coin; this fellow wore
A gold-inwoven robe, which shining bright
Under the dark rocks to the glimmering moon
Betrayed them to our notice: the other fell
Desperately fighting.

 Savella.   What does he confess?

 Officer. He keeps firm silence; but these lines found on him
May speak.

 Savella. Their language is at least sincere.

                 [*Reads*.
    'TO THE LADY BEATRICE.   90
   That the atonement of what my nature
   Sickens to conjecture may soon arrive,
   I send thee, at thy brother's desire, those
   Who will speak and do more than I dare
   Write . . . Thy devoted servant,
          ORSINO.'
 Enter LUCRETIA, BEATRICE *and* BERNARDO.

Knowest thou this writing, Lady?

Beatrice.   No.

Savella.   Nor thou?

Lucretia. (*Her conduct throughout the scene is marked by extreme
agitation.*) Where was it found? What is it? It should be
Orsino's hand! It speaks of that strange horror
Which never yet found utterance, but which made
Between that hapless child and her dead father
A gulf of obscure hatred.

   Savella.   Is it so?   100
Is it true, Lady, that thy father did
Such outrages as to awaken in thee
Unfilial hate?

   Beatrice.   Not hate, 'twas more than hate:
This is most true, yet wherefore question me?

   Savella. There is a deed demanding question done;
Thou hast a secret which will answer not.

   Beatrice. What sayest? My Lord, your words are bold and rash.

   Savella. I do arrest all present in the name
Of the Pope's Holiness. You must to Rome.

   Lucretia. O, not to Rome! Indeed we are not guilty.   110

   Beatrice. Guilty! Who dares talk of guilt? My Lord,
I am more innocent of parricide
Than is a child born fatherless . . . Dear Mother,
Your gentleness and patience are no shield
For this keen-judging world, this two-edged lie,
Which seems, but is not. What! will human laws,
Rather will ye who are their ministers,
Bar all access to retribution first,

And then, when heaven doth interpose to do
What ye neglect, arming familiar things   120
To the redress of an unwonted crime,
Make ye the victims who demanded it
Culprits? 'Tis ye are culprits! That poor wretch
Who stands so pale, and trembling, and amazed,
If it be true he murdered Cenci, was
A sword in the right hand of justest God,
Wherefore should I have wielded it? Unless
The crimes which mortal tongue dare never name
God therefore scruples to avenge.

    Savella.   You own
That you desired his death?

    Beatrice.   It would have been   130
A crime no less than his, if for one moment
That fierce desire had faded in my heart.
'Tis true I did believe, and hope, and pray,
Aye, I even knew . . . for God is wise and just,
That some strange sudden death hung over him.
'Tis true that this did happen, and most true
There was no other rest for me on earth,
No other hope in Heaven . . . now what of this?

    Savella. Strange thoughts beget strange deeds; and
        here are both:
I judge thee not.

    Beatrice.   And yet, if you arrest me,   140
You are the judge and executioner
Of that which is the life of life: the breath
Of accusation kills an innocent name,
And leaves for lame acquittal the poor life
Which is a mask without it. 'Tis most false
That I am guilty of foul parricide;
Although I must rejoice, for justest cause,
That other hands have sent my father's soul
To ask the mercy he denied to me.
Now leave us free: stain not a noble house   150
With vague surmises of rejected crime;
Add to our sufferings and your own neglect

No heavier sum: let them have been enough:
Leave us the wreck we have.

   Savella.   I dare not, Lady.
I pray that you prepare yourselves for Rome:
There the Pope's further pleasure will be known.

   Lucretia. O, not to Rome! O, take us not to Rome!

   Beatrice. Why not to Rome, dear mother? There as here
Our innocence is as an armèd heel
To trample accusation. God is there   160
As here, and with his shadow ever clothes
The innocent, the injured and the weak;
And such are we. Cheer up, dear Lady, lean
On me; collect your wandering thoughts. My Lord,
As soon as you have taken some refreshment,
And had all such examinations made
Upon the spot, as may be necessary
To the full understanding of this matter,
We shall be ready. Mother; will you come?

   Lucretia. Ha! they will bind us to the rack, and wrest   170
Self-accusation from our agony!
Will Giacomo be there? Orsino? Marzio?
All present; all confronted; all demanding
Each from the other's countenance the thing
Which is in every heart! O, misery!
                                   [*She faints, and is borne out.*

   Savella. She faints: an ill appearance this.

   Beatrice.   My Lord,
She knows not yet the uses of the world.
She fears that power is as a beast which grasps
And loosens not: a snake whose look transmutes
All things to guilt which is its nutriment.   180
She cannot know how well the supine slaves
Of blind authority read the truth of things
When written on a brow of guilelessness:
She sees not yet triumphant Innocence

Stand at the judgement-seat of mortal man,
A judge and an accuser of the wrong
Which drags it there. Prepare yourself, My Lord;
Our suite will join yours in the court below.

[*Exeunt.*

END OF THE FOURTH ACT.

Act 5

SCENE 1.—*An apartment in* ORSINO's *Palace.*
Enter ORSINO *and* GIACOMO.

Giacomo. Do evil deeds thus quickly come to end?
O, that the vain remorse which must chastise
Crimes done, had but as loud a voice to warn
As its keen sting is mortal to avenge!
O, that the hour when present had cast off
The mantle of its mystery, and shown
The ghastly form with which it now returns
When its scared game is roused, cheering the hounds
Of conscience to their prey! Alas! Alas!
It was a wicked thought, a piteous deed,　　　　　　　　10
To kill an old and hoary-headed father.

Orsino. It has turned out unluckily, in truth.

Giacomo. To violate the sacred doors of sleep;
To cheat kind nature of the placid death
Which she prepares for overwearied age;
To drag from Heaven an unrepentant soul
Which might have quenched in reconciling prayers
A life of burning crimes . . .

Orsino.　　　　　　　　　You cannot say
I urged you to the deed.

Giacomo.　　　　　　O, had I never
Found in thy smooth and ready countenance　　　　　20
The mirror of my darkest thoughts; hadst thou
Never with hints and questions made me look
Upon the monster of my thought, until
It grew familiar to desire . . . °

Orsino.　　　　　　　　　'Tis thus
Men cast the blame of their unprosperous acts
Upon the abettors of their own resolve;
Or anything but their weak, guilty selves.

And yet, confess the truth, it is the peril
In which you stand that gives you this pale sickness
Of penitence; confess 'tis fear disguised   30
From its own shame that takes the mantle now
Of thin remorse. What if we yet were safe?

    Giacomo. How can that be? Already Beatrice,
Lucretia and the murderer are in prison.
I doubt not officers are, whilst we speak,
Sent to arrest us.

    Orsino.   I have all prepared
For instant flight. We can escape even now,
So we take fleet occasion by the hair.

    Giacomo. Rather expire in tortures, as I may.
What! will you cast by self-accusing flight   40
Assured conviction upon Beatrice?
She, who alone in this unnatural work,
Stands like God's angel ministered upon
By fiends; avenging such a nameless wrong
As turns black parricide to piety;
Whilst we for basest ends . . . I fear, Orsino,
While I consider all your words and looks,
Comparing them with your proposal now,
That you must be a villain. For what end
Could you engage in such a perilous crime,   50
Training me on with hints, and signs, and smiles,
Even to this gulf? Thou art no liar? No,
Thou art a lie! Traitor and murderer!
Coward and slave! But, no, defend thyself;

                                [*Drawing*.

Let the sword speak what the indignant tongue
Disdains to brand thee with.

    Orsino.   Put up your weapon.°
Is it the desperation of your fear
Makes you thus rash and sudden with a friend,
Now ruined for your sake? If honest anger
Have moved you, know, that what I just proposed   60
Was but to try you. As for me, I think,

Thankless affection led me to this point,
From which, if my firm temper could repent,
I cannot now recede. Even whilst we speak
The ministers of justice wait below:
They grant me these brief moments. Now if you
Have any word of melancholy comfort
To speak to your pale wife, 'twere best to pass
Out at the postern, and avoid them so.

   Giacomo. O, generous friend! How canst thou pardon me?   70
Would that my life could purchase thine!

   Orsino.   That wish
Now comes a day too late. Haste; fare thee well!
Hear'st thou not steps along the corridor?

                                            [*Exit* GIACOMO.

I'm sorry for it; but the guards are waiting
At his own gate, and such was my contrivance
That I might rid me both of him and them.
I thought to act a solemn comedy
Upon the painted scene of this new world,
And to attain my own peculiar ends
By some such plot of mingled good and ill   80
As others weave; but there arose a Power
Which grasped and snapped the threads of my device
And turned it to a net of ruin . . . Ha!

                                            [*A shout is heard.*

Is that my name I hear proclaimed abroad?
But I will pass, wrapped in a vile disguise;
Rags on my back, and a false innocence
Upon my face, through the misdeeming crowd°
Which judges by what seems. 'Tis easy then
For a new name and for a country new,
And a new life, fashioned on old desires,   90
To change the honours of abandoned Rome.
And these must be the masks of that within,°
Which must remain unaltered . . . Oh, I fear
That what is past will never let me rest!
Why, when none else is conscious, but myself,
Of my misdeeds, should my own heart's contempt
Trouble me? Have I not the power to fly

My own reproaches? Shall I be the slave
Of . . . what? A word? which those of this false world°
Employ against each other, not themselves;   100
As men wear daggers not for self-offence.
But if I am mistaken, where shall I
Find the disguise to hide me from myself,
As now I skulk from every other eye?

                                                          [*Exit.*

SCENE 2.—*A Hall of Justice.*
    CAMILLO, *Judges etc. are discovered seated*; MARZIO *is led in.*

  First Judge. Accused, do you persist in your denial?
I ask you, are you innocent, or guilty?
I demand who were the participators
In your offence? Speak truth and the whole truth.

  Marzio. My God! I did not kill him; I know nothing;
Olimpio sold the robe to me from which
You would infer my guilt.

  Second Judge.   Away with him!

  First Judge. Dare you, with lips yet white from the rack's kiss
Speak false? Is it so soft a questioner,
That you would bandy lover's talk with it   10
Till it wind out your life and soul? Away!

  Marzio. Spare me! O, spare! I will confess.

  First Judge.   Then speak.

  Marzio. I strangled him in his sleep.

  First Judge.   Who urged you to it?

  Marzio. His own son Giacomo, and the young prelate
Orsino sent me to Petrella; there
The ladies Beatrice and Lucretia
Tempted me with a thousand crowns, and I
And my companion forthwith murdered him.
Now let me die.

First Judge.   This sounds as bad as truth. Guards, there,
Lead forth the prisoners!

    Enter LUCRETIA, BEATRICE *and* GIACOMO, *guarded.*

           Look upon this man;   20
When did you see him last?

Beatrice.   We never saw him.

Marzio. You know me too well, Lady Beatrice.

Beatrice. I know thee! How? where? when?

Marzio.   You know 'twas I
Whom you did urge with menaces and bribes
To kill your father. When the thing was done
You clothed me in a robe of woven gold
And bade me thrive: how I have thriven, you see.
You my Lord Giacomo, Lady Lucretia,
You know that what I speak is true.

 (BEATRICE *advances towards him; he covers his face, and shrinks back.*)
           O, dart
The terrible resentment of those eyes   30
On the dead earth! Turn them away from me!
They wound: 'twas torture forced the truth. My Lords,
Having said this let me be led to death.

Beatrice. Poor wretch, I pity thee: yet stay awhile.

Camillo. Guards, lead him not away.

Beatrice.   Cardinal Camillo,
You have a good repute for gentleness
And wisdom: can it be that you sit here
To countenance a wicked farce like this?
When some obscure and trembling slave is dragged
From sufferings which might shake the sternest heart 40
And bade to answer, not as he believes,
But as those may suspect or do desire
Whose questions thence suggest their own reply:
And that in peril of such hideous torments
As merciful God spares even the damned. Speak now

The thing you surely know, which is that you,
If your fine frame were stretched upon that wheel,
And you were told: 'Confess that you did poison
Your little nephew; that fair blue-eyed child
Who was the lodestar of your life': and though   50
All see, since his most swift and piteous death,
That day and night, and heaven and earth, and time,
And all the things hoped for or done therein
Are changed to you, through your exceeding grief,°
Yet you would say, 'I confess any thing,'
And beg from your tormentors, like that slave,
The refuge of dishonourable death.
I pray thee, Cardinal, that thou assert
My innocence.

    Camillo (*much moved*). What shall we think, my lords?
Shame on these tears! I thought the heart was frozen   60
Which is their fountain. I would pledge my soul
That she is guiltless.

    Judge.   Yet she must be tortured.

    Camillo. I would as soon have tortured mine own nephew
(If he now lived he would be just her age;
His hair, too, was her colour, and his eyes
Like hers in shape, but blue and not so deep)
As that most perfect image of God's love
That ever came sorrowing upon the earth.
She is as pure as speechless infancy!

    Judge. Well, be her purity on your head, my Lord,   70
If you forbid the rack. His Holiness
Enjoined us to pursue this monstrous crime
By the severest forms of law; nay even
To stretch a point against the criminals.
The prisoners stand accused of parricide
Upon such evidence as justifies
Torture.

    Beatrice. What evidence? This man's?

    Judge.   Even so.

   Beatrice (*to* MARZIO). Come near. And who art thou thus chosen forth
Out of the multitude of living men
To kill the innocent?

   Marzio.   I am Marzio,   80
Thy father's vassal.

   Beatrice.   Fix thine eyes on mine;
Answer to what I ask.

                          [*Turning to the Judges*
                 I prithee mark
His countenance: unlike bold calumny
Which sometimes dares not speak the thing it looks,
He dares not look the thing he speaks, but bends
His gaze on the blind earth.

                             [*To* MARZIO
                What! wilt thou say
That I did murder my own father?

   Marzio.   Oh!
Spare me! My brain swims round . . . I cannot speak . . .
It was that horrid torture forced the truth.   90
Take me away! Let her not look on me!
I am a guilty, miserable wretch;
I have said all I know; now, let me die!

   Beatrice. My Lords, if by my nature I had been
So stern, as to have planned the crime alleged,
Which your suspicions dictate to this slave,
And the rack makes him utter, do you think
I should have left this two-edged instrument
Of my misdeed; this man, this bloody knife
With my own name engraven on the heft,
Lying unsheathed amid a world of foes,   100
For my own death? That with such horrible need
For deepest silence, I should have neglected
So trivial a precaution, as the making
His tomb the keeper of a secret written
On a thief's memory? What is his poor life?
What are a thousand lives? A parricide

Had trampled them like dust; and, see, he lives!

[*Turning to* MARZIO

And thou . . .

   Marzio. Oh, spare me! Speak to me no more!
That stern yet piteous look, those solemn tones,
Wound worse than torture.

[*To the Judges*

             I have told it all;   110
For pity's sake lead me away to death.

   Camillo. Guards, lead him nearer the lady Beatrice,
He shrinks from her regard like autumn's leaf
From the keen breath of the serenest north.

   Beatrice. Oh, thou who tremblest on the giddy verge
Of life and death, pause ere thou answerest me;
So mayest thou answer God with less dismay:
What evil have we done thee? I, alas!
Have lived but on this earth a few sad years
And so my lot was ordered, that a father   120
First turned the moments of awakening life
To drops, each poisoning youth's sweet hope; and then
Stabbed with one blow my everlasting soul;
And my untainted fame; and even that peace
Which sleeps within the core of the heart's heart;°
But the wound was not mortal; so my hate
Became the only worship I could lift
To our great father, who in pity and love,
Armed thee, as thou dost say, to cut him off;
And thus his wrong becomes my accusation;   130
And art thou the accuser? If thou hopest
Mercy in heaven, show justice upon earth:
Worse than a bloody hand is a hard heart.
If thou hast done murders, made thy life's path
Over the trampled laws of God and man,
Rush not before thy Judge, and say: 'My Maker,
I have done this and more; for there was one
Who was most pure and innocent on earth;
And because she endured what never any
Guilty or innocent endured before: 140

Because her wrongs could not be told, not thought;
Because thy hand at length did rescue her;
I with my words killed her and all her kin.'
Think, I adjure you, what it is to slay
The reverence living in the minds of men
Towards our ancient house, and stainless fame!
Think what it is to strangle infant pity,
Cradled in the belief of guileless looks,
Till it become a crime to suffer. Think
What 'tis to blot with infamy and blood   150
All that which shows like innocence, and is,
Hear me, great God! I swear, most innocent,
So that the world lose all discrimination
Between the sly, fierce, wild regard of guilt,
And that which now compels thee to reply
To what I ask: Am I, or am I not
A parricide?

   Marzio.   Thou art not!

   Judge.   What is this?

   Marzio. I here declare those whom I did accuse
Are innocent. 'Tis I alone am guilty.

   Judge. Drag him away to torments; let them be   160
Subtle and long drawn out, to tear the folds
Of the heart's inmost cell. Unbind him not
Till he confess.

   Marzio.   Torture me as ye will:
A keener pain has wrung a higher truth°
From my last breath. She is most innocent!
Bloodhounds, not men, glut yourselves well with me;
I will not give you that fine piece of nature
To rend and ruin.

                              [*Exit* MARZIO, *guarded.*

   Camillo.   What say ye now, my Lords?

   Judge. Let tortures strain the truth till it be white°
As snow thrice sifted by the frozen wind.   170

Camillo. Yet stained with blood.

Judge (*to* BEATRICE).   Know you this paper, Lady?

Beatrice. Entrap me not with questions. Who stands here
As my accuser? Ha! wilt thou be he,
Who art my judge? Accuser, witness, judge,
What, all in one? Here is Orsino's name;°
Where is Orsino? Let his eye meet mine.
What means this scrawl? Alas! Ye know not what,
And therefore on the chance that it may be
Some evil, will ye kill us?
                              Enter an OFFICER.

Officer.   Marzio's dead.

Judge. What did he say?

Officer.   Nothing. As soon as we   180
Had bound him on the wheel, he smiled on us,
As one who baffles a deep adversary;
And holding his breath, died.

Judge.   There remains nothing
But to apply the question to those prisoners,
Who yet remain stubborn.

Camillo.   I overrule
Further proceedings, and in the behalf
Of these most innocent and noble persons
Will use my interest with the Holy Father.

Judge. Let the Pope's pleasure then be done. Meanwhile
Conduct these culprits each to separate cells;   190
And be the engines ready: for this night
If the Pope's resolution be as grave,
Pious and just as once, I'll wring the truth
Out of those nerves and sinews, groan by groan.
                                        [*Exeunt*.

SCENE 3.—*The cell of a prison.*
         BEATRICE *is discovered asleep on a couch.*
                    Enter BERNARDO.

Bernardo. How gently slumber rests upon her face,
Like the last thoughts of some day sweetly spent
Closing in night and dreams, and so prolonged.
After such torments as she bore last night,
How light and soft her breathing comes. Ay, me!
Methinks that I shall never sleep again.
But I must shake the heavenly dew of rest
From this sweet folded flower, thus . . . wake! awake!
What, sister, canst thou sleep?

Beatrice (*awaking*).   I was just dreaming
That we were all in Paradise. Thou knowest   10
This cell seems like a kind of Paradise
After our father's presence.

Bernardo.   Dear, dear sister,
Would that thy dream were not a dream! O, God!
How shall I tell?

Beatrice.   What wouldst thou tell, sweet brother?

Bernardo. Look not so calm and happy, or even whilst
I stand considering what I have to say
My heart will break.

Beatrice.   See now, thou mak'st me weep:
How very friendless thou wouldst be, dear child,
If I were dead. Say what thou hast to say.

Bernardo. They have confessed; they could endure no more   20
The tortures . . .

Beatrice.   Ha! What was there to confess?
They must have told some weak and wicked lie
To flatter their tormentors. Have they said
That they were guilty? O, white innocence,
That thou shouldst wear the mask of guilt to hide

Thine awful and serenest countenance
From those who know thee not!

      Enter JUDGE *with* LUCRETIA *and* GIACOMO, *guarded*

                     Ignoble hearts!
For some brief spasms of pain, which are at least
As mortal as the limbs through which they pass,
Are centuries of high splendour laid in dust?   30
And that eternal honour which should live
Sunlike, above the reek of mortal fame,
Changed to a mockery and a byword? What!
Will you give up these bodies to be dragged
At horses' heels, so that our hair should sweep
The footsteps of the vain and senseless crowd,
Who, that they may make our calamity
Their worship and their spectacle, will leave
The churches and the theatres as void
As their own hearts? Shall the light multitude   40
Fling, at their choice, curses or faded pity,
Sad funeral flowers to deck a living corpse,
Upon us as we pass to pass away,
And leave . . . what memory of our having been?
Infamy, blood, terror, despair? O thou,
Who wert a mother to the parentless,
Kill not thy child! Let not her wrongs kill thee!
Brother, lie down with me upon the rack,
And let us each be silent as a corpse;
It soon will be as soft as any grave.   50
'Tis but the falsehood it can wring from fear
Makes the rack cruel.

   Giacomo.   They will tear the truth
Even from thee at last, those cruel pains:
For pity's sake say thou art guilty now.

   Lucretia. O, speak the truth! Let us all quickly die;
And after death, God is our judge, not they;
He will have mercy on us.

   Bernardo.   If indeed
It can be true, say so, dear sister mine;

And then the Pope will surely pardon you,
And all be well.

Judge.   Confess, or I will warp   60
Your limbs with such keen tortures . . .

Beatrice.   Tortures! Turn
The rack henceforth into a spinning wheel!
Torture your dog, that he may tell when last
He lapped the blood his master shed . . . not me!
My pangs are of the mind, and of the heart,
And of the soul; aye, of the inmost soul,
Which weeps within tears as of burning gall
To see, in this ill world where none are true,
My kindred false to their deserted selves.
And with considering all the wretched life   70
Which I have lived, and its now wretched end,
And the small justice shown by Heaven and Earth
To me or mine; and what a tyrant thou art,
And what slaves these; and what a world we make,
The oppressor and the oppressed . . . such pangs compel
My answer. What is it thou wouldst with me?

Judge. Art thou not guilty of thy father's death?

Beatrice. Or wilt thou rather tax high-judging God
That he permitted such an act as that
Which I have suffered, and which he beheld;   80
Made it unutterable, and took from it
All refuge, all revenge, all consequence,
But that which thou hast called my father's death?
Which is or is not what men call a crime,
Which either I have done, or have not done;
Say what ye will. I shall deny no more.
If ye desire it thus, thus let it be,
And so an end of all. Now do your will;
No other pains shall force another word.°

Judge. She is convicted, but has not confessed.   90
Be it enough. Until their final sentence
Let none have converse with them. You, young Lord,
Linger not here!

Beatrice.   O, tear him not away!

Judge.   Guards, do your duty.

Bernardo (embracing BEATRICE*).* Oh! would ye divide
Body from soul?

Officer.   That is the headsman's business.
          [*Exeunt all but* LUCRETIA, BEATRICE, *and* GIACOMO.

Giacomo. Have I confessed? Is it all over now?
No hope! No refuge! O, weak, wicked tongue
Which hast destroyed me, would that thou hadst been
Cut out and thrown to dogs first! To have killed
My father first, and then betrayed my sister;   100
Aye, thee! the one thing innocent and pure
In this black guilty world, to that which I
So well deserve! My wife! my little ones!
Destitute, helpless and I . . . Father! God!
Canst thou forgive even the unforgiving,
When their full hearts break thus, thus! . . .

                              [*Covers his face and weeps*

Lucretia.   O, my child!
To what a dreadful end are we all come!
Why did I yield? Why did I not sustain
Those torments? Oh, that I were all dissolved
Into these fast and unavailing tears,   110
Which flow and feel not!

Beatrice.   What 'twas weak to do,
'Tis weaker to lament, once being done;
Take cheer! The God who knew my wrong, and made
Our speedy act the angel of his wrath,
Seems, and but seems to have abandoned us.
Let us not think that we shall die for this.
Brother, sit near me; give me your firm hand,
You had a manly heart. Bear up! Bear up!
O, dearest Lady, put your gentle head
Upon my lap, and try to sleep awhile: 120
Your eyes look pale, hollow and overworn,

With heaviness of watching and slow grief.
Come, I will sing you some low, sleepy tune,
Not cheerful, nor yet sad; some dull old thing,
Some outworn and unused monotony,
Such as our country gossips sing and spin,
Till they almost forget they live: lie down!°
So, that will do. Have I forgot the words?
Faith! They are sadder than I thought they were.

SONG

False friend, wilt thou smile or weep   130
When my life is laid asleep?
Little cares for a smile or a tear,
The clay-cold corpse upon the bier!
    Farewell! Heigh ho!
    What is this whispers low?
There is a snake in thy smile, my dear;
And bitter poison within thy tear.

Sweet sleep, were death like to thee,
Or if thou couldst mortal be,
I would close these eyes of pain;   140
When to wake? Never again.
    O, World! Farewell!
    Listen to the passing bell!
It says, thou and I must part,
With a light and a heavy heart.

[*The scene closes.*

SCENE 4.—*A Hall of the Prison.*
Enter CAMILLO *and* BERNARDO.

Camillo. The Pope is stern; not to be moved or bent.
He looked as calm and keen as is the engine
Which tortures and which kills, exempt itself
From aught that it inflicts; a marble form,
A rite, a law, a custom: not a man.
He frowned as if to frown had been the trick
Of his machinery, on the advocates
Presenting the defences, which he tore
And threw behind, muttering with hoarse, harsh voice:
'Which among ye defended their old father   10
Killed in his sleep?' Then to another: 'Thou

Dost this in virtue of thy place; 'tis well.'
He turned to me then, looking deprecation,°
And said these three words, coldly: 'They must die.'

   Bernardo. And yet you left him not?

   Camillo.   I urged him still;
Pleading, as I could guess, the devilish wrong
Which prompted your unnatural parent's death.
And he replied. 'Paolo Santa Croce
Murdered his mother yester evening,
And he is fled. Parricide grows so rife   20
That soon, for some just cause no doubt, the young
Will strangle us all, dozing in our chairs.
Authority, and power, and hoary hair
Are grown crimes capital. You are my nephew,
You come to ask their pardon; stay a moment;
Here is their sentence; never see me more
Till, to the letter, it be all fulfilled.'

   Bernardo. O, God, not so! I did believe indeed
That all you said was but sad preparation
For happy news. O, there are words and looks   30
To bend the sternest purpose! Once I knew them,
Now I forget them at my dearest need.
What think you if I seek him out, and bathe
His feet and robe with hot and bitter tears?
Importune him with prayers, vexing his brain
With my perpetual cries, until in rage
He strike me with his pastoral cross, and trample
Upon my prostrate head, so that my blood
May stain the senseless dust on which he treads,
And remorse waken mercy? I will do it!   40
O, wait till I return!   [*Rushes out.*

   Camillo.   Alas! poor boy!
A wreck-devoted seaman thus might pray
To the deaf sea.
      Enter LUCRETIA, BEATRICE *and* GIACOMO, *guarded*.

   Beatrice.   I hardly dare to fear
That thou bring'st other news than a just pardon.

    Camillo. May God in heaven be less inexorable
To the Pope's prayers, than he has been to mine.
Here is the sentence and the warrant.

    Beatrice (*wildly*).   Oh,
My God! Can it be possible I have
To die so suddenly? So young to go°
Under the obscure, cold, rotting, wormy ground!   50
To be nailed down into a narrow place;
To see no more sweet sunshine; hear no more
Blithe voice of living thing; muse not again
Upon familiar thoughts, sad, yet thus lost—
How fearful! to be nothing! Or to be . . .
What? O, where am I? Let me not go mad!°
Sweet Heaven, forgive weak thoughts! If there should be
No God, no Heaven, no Earth in the void world;
The wide, grey, lampless, deep, unpeopled world!
If all things then should be . . . my father's spirit,   60
His eye, his voice, his touch surrounding me;
The atmosphere and breath of my dead life!
If sometimes, as a shape more like himself,
Even the form which tortured me on earth,
Masked in grey hairs and wrinkles, he should come
And wind me in his hellish arms, and fix
His eyes on mine, and drag me down, down, down!
For was he not alone omnipotent
On Earth, and ever present! Even though dead,
Does not his spirit live in all that breathe,   70
And work for me and mine still the same ruin,
Scorn, pain, despair? Who ever yet returned
To teach the laws of death's untrodden realm?°
Unjust perhaps as those which drive us now,
O, whither, whither?°

    Lucretia.   Trust in God's sweet love,
The tender promises of Christ: ere night
Think we shall be in Paradise.°

    Beatrice.   'Tis past!
Whatever comes my heart shall sink no more.
And yet, I know not why, your words strike chill:

How tedious, false and cold seem all things. I°   80
Have met with much injustice in this world;
No difference has been made by God or man,
Or any power moulding my wretched lot,
'Twixt good or evil, as regarded me.
I am cut off from the only world I know,
From light, and life, and love, in youth's sweet prime.
You do well telling me to trust in God,
I hope I do trust in him. In whom else
Can any trust? And yet my heart is cold.

    (*During the latter speeches* GIACOMO *has retired conversing with*
       CAMILLO, *who now goes out;* GIACOMO *advances.*)

Giacomo. Know you not, Mother . . . Sister, know you not?   90
Bernardo even now is gone to implore
The Pope to grant our pardon.

Lucretia.   Child, perhaps
It will be granted. We may all then live
To make these woes a tale for distant years:
O, what a thought! It gushes to my heart
Like the warm blood.

Beatrice.   Yet both will soon be cold.
O, trample out that thought! Worse than despair,
Worse than the bitterness of death, is hope:
It is the only ill which can find place
Upon the giddy, sharp and narrow hour°   100
Tottering beneath us. Plead with the swift frost
That it should spare the eldest flower of spring:
Plead with awakening Earthquake, o'er whose couch
Even now a city stands, strong, fair and free;
Now stench and blackness yawns, like death. O, plead
With famine, or wind-walking Pestilence,
Blind lightning, or the deaf sea, not with man!
Cruel, cold, formal man; righteous in words,
In deeds a Cain. No, Mother, we must die:
Since such is the reward of innocent lives;   110
Such the alleviation of worst wrongs.
And whilst our murderers live, and hard, cold men,
Smiling and slow, walk through a world of tears

To death as to life's sleep; 'twere just the grave
Were some strange joy for us. Come, obscure Death,
And wind me in thine all-embracing arms!
Like a fond mother hide me in thy bosom,
And rock me to the sleep from which none wake.
Live ye, who live, subject to one another
As we were once, who now . . .

BERNARDO rushes in.

Bernardo.   Oh, horrible!   120
That tears, that looks, that hope poured forth in prayer,
Even till the heart is vacant and despairs,
Should all be vain! The ministers of death
Are waiting round the doors. I thought I saw
Blood on the face of one . . . what if 'twere fancy?
Soon the heart's blood of all I love on earth
Will sprinkle him, and he will wipe it off
As if 'twere only rain. O, life! O, world!
Cover me! let me be no more! To see
That perfect mirror of pure innocence   130
Wherein I gazed, and grew happy and good,
Shivered to dust! To see thee, Beatrice,
Who made all lovely thou didst look upon . . .
Thee, light of life . . . dead, dark! while I say, sister,
To hear I have no sister; and thou, Mother,
Whose love was a bond to all our loves . . . °
Dead! The sweet bond broken!

Enter CAMILLO and Guards.

                                 They come! Let me
Kiss those warm lips before their crimson leaves
Are blighted . . . white . . . cold. Say farewell, before
Death chokes that gentle voice! O, let me hear   140
You speak!

Beatrice. Farewell, my tender brother. Think
Of our sad fate with gentleness, as now:
And let mild, pitying thoughts lighten for thee
Thy sorrow's load. Err not in harsh despair,
But tears and patience. One thing more, my child,
For thine own sake be constant to the love
Thou bearest us; and to the faith that I,

Though wrapped in a strange cloud of crime and shame,
Lived ever holy and unstained. And though
Ill tongues shall wound me, and our common name   150
Be as a mark stamped on thine innocent brow
For men to point at as they pass, do thou
Forbear, and never think a thought unkind
Of those, who perhaps love thee in their graves.
So mayest thou die as I do; fear and pain
Being subdued. Farewell! Farewell! Farewell!

   Bernardo. I cannot say, farewell!

   Camillo.   O, Lady Beatrice!

   Beatrice. Give yourself no unnecessary pain,
My dear Lord Cardinal. Here, Mother, tie
My girdle for me, and bind up this hair   160
In any simple knot; aye, that does well.
And yours I see is coming down. How often
Have we done this for one another; now
We shall not do it any more. My Lord,
We are quite ready. Well, 'tis very well.

THE END

THE MASK OF ANARCHY

WRITTEN ON THE OCCASION OF THE
MASSACRE AT MANCHESTER

As I lay asleep in Italy°
There came a voice from over the Sea,
And with great power it forth led me
To walk in the visions of Poesy.

I met Murder on the way—
He had a mask like Castlereagh—°
Very smooth he looked, yet grim;
Seven bloodhounds followed him:°

All were fat; and well they might
Be in admirable plight,   10
For one by one, and two by two,
He tossed them human hearts to chew
Which from his wide cloak he drew.

Next came Fraud, and he had on,
Like Eldon, an erminèd gown;°
His big tears, for he wept well,
Turned to mill-stones as they fell.

And the little children, who
Round his feet played to and fro,
Thinking every tear a gem,   20
Had their brains knocked out by them.°

Clothed with the Bible, as with light,
And the shadows of the night,
Like Sidmouth, next, Hypocrisy°
On a crocodile rode by.°

And many more Destructions played
In this ghastly masquerade,
All disguised, even to the eyes,
Like Bishops, lawyers, peers or spies.

Last came Anarchy: he rode°   30
On a white horse, splashed with blood;
He was pale even to the lips,
Like Death in the Apocalypse.

And he wore a kingly crown,
And in his grasp a sceptre shone;
On his brow this mark I saw—
'I AM GOD, AND KING, AND LAW.'

With a pace stately and fast,
Over English land he passed,
Trampling to a mire of blood   40
The adoring multitude.

And a mighty troop around,
With their trampling shook the ground,
Waving each a bloody sword,
For the service of their Lord.

And with glorious triumph they
Rode through England proud and gay,
Drunk as with intoxication
Of the wine of desolation.

O'er fields and towns, from sea to sea,   50
Passed the Pageant swift and free,
Tearing up, and trampling down,
Till they came to London town:

And each dweller, panic-stricken,
Felt his heart with terror sicken
Hearing the tempestuous cry
Of the triumph of Anarchy.

For with pomp to meet him came
Clothed in arms like blood and flame,
The hired murderers, who did sing   60
'Thou art God, and Law, and King.

'We have waited, weak and lone
For thy coming, Mighty One!

Our purses are empty, our swords are cold,
Give us glory, and blood, and gold.'

Lawyers and priests, a motley crowd,
To the earth their pale brows bowed;
Like a bad prayer not overloud,
Whispering—'Thou art Law and God.'—

Then all cried with one accord   70
'Thou art King, and God, and Lord;
Anarchy, to thee we bow,
Be thy name made holy now!'

And Anarchy, the Skeleton,
Bowed and grinned to every one,
As well as if his education
Had cost ten millions to the nation.

For he knew the Palaces
Of our Kings were rightly his;
His the sceptre, crown, and globe,°   80
And the gold-inwoven robe.

So he sent his slaves before
To seize upon the Bank and Tower,°
And was proceeding with intent
To meet his pensioned Parliament°

When one fled past, a maniac maid,
And her name was Hope, she said:
But she looked more like Despair,
And she cried out in the air:

'My father Time is weak and grey   90
With waiting for a better day;
See how idiot-like he stands,
Fumbling with his palsied hands!

'He has had child after child
And the dust of death is piled
Over every one but me—
Misery, oh, Misery!'°

Then she lay down in the street,
Right before the horses' feet,
Expecting, with a patient eye,   100
Murder, Fraud and Anarchy,

When between her and her foes
A mist, a light, an image rose,
Small at first, and weak, and frail,
Like the vapour of a vale:

Till as clouds grow on the blast,
Like tower-crowned giants striding fast,
And glare with lightnings as they fly,
And speak in thunder to the sky,

It grew—a Shape arrayed in mail°   110
Brighter than the viper's scale,
And upborne on wings whose grain
Was as the light of sunny rain.

On its helm, seen far away,
A planet, like the Morning's, lay;°
And those plumes its light rained through
Like a shower of crimson dew.

With step as soft as wind it passed
O'er the heads of men—so fast
That they knew the presence there,   120
And looked—but all was empty air.

As flowers beneath May's footstep waken,
As stars from Night's loose hair are shaken,
As waves arise when loud winds call,
Thoughts sprung where'er that step did fall.

And the prostrate multitude
Looked—and ankle-deep in blood,
Hope, that maiden most serene,
Was walking with a quiet mien:

And Anarchy, the ghastly birth,   130
Lay dead earth upon the earth—
The Horse of Death tameless as wind
Fled, and with his hoofs did grind
To dust the murderers thronged behind.

A rushing light of clouds and splendour,
A sense awakening and yet tender
Was heard and felt—and at its close
These words of joy and fear arose

As if their own indignant Earth
Which gave the sons of England birth   140
Had felt their blood upon her brow,
And shuddering with a mother's throe

Had turnèd every drop of blood
By which her face had been bedewed
To an accent unwithstood—°
As if her heart cried out aloud:

'Men of England, heirs of Glory,
Heroes of unwritten story,
Nurslings of one mighty Mother,
Hopes of her, and one another,   150

'Rise like Lions after slumber
In unvanquishable number,
Shake your chains to Earth like dew
Which in sleep had fallen on you—
Ye are many—they are few.°

'What is Freedom?—ye can tell
That which slavery is, too well—
For its very name has grown
To an echo of your own.

''Tis to work and have such pay   160
As just keeps life from day to day
In your limbs, as in a cell
For the tyrants' use to dwell,

'So that ye for them are made
Loom, and plough, and sword, and spade,
With or without your own will bent
To their defence and nourishment.

''Tis to see your children weak
With their mothers pine and peak,°
When the winter winds are bleak—   170
They are dying whilst I speak.

''Tis to hunger for such diet
As the rich man in his riot
Casts to the fat dogs that lie
Surfeiting beneath his eye;

''Tis to let the Ghost of Gold°
Take from Toil a thousandfold
More than e'er its substance could
In the tyrannies of old.

'Paper coin—that forgery   180
Of the title deeds, which ye
Hold to something of the worth
Of the inheritance of Earth.

''Tis to be a slave in soul
And to hold no strong control
Over your own wills, but be
All that others make of ye.

'And at length when ye complain
With a murmur weak and vain
'Tis to see the Tyrant's crew   190
Ride over your wives and you—
Blood is on the grass like dew.

'Then it is to feel revenge
Fiercely thirsting to exchange
Blood for blood—and wrong for wrong—
Do not thus when ye are strong.

'Birds find rest, in narrow nest
When weary of their wingèd quest;
Beasts find fare, in woody lair
When storm and snow are in the air.°   200

'Asses, swine, have litter spread
And with fitting food are fed;
All things have a home but one—
Thou, oh, Englishman, hast none!°

'This is slavery—savage men
Or wild beasts within a den
Would endure not as ye do—
But such ills they never knew.

'What art thou, Freedom? O! could slaves
Answer from their living graves   210
This demand—tyrants would flee
Like a dream's dim imagery.

'Thou art not, as imposters say,
A shadow soon to pass away,
A superstition, and a name
Echoing from the cave of Fame.°

'For the labourer thou art bread,
And a comely table spread,
From his daily labour come
To a neat and happy home.   220

'Thou art clothes, and fire, and food
For the trampled multitude—
No—in countries that are free
Such starvation cannot be
As in England now we see.

'To the rich thou art a check,
When his foot is on the neck
Of his victim, thou dost make
That he treads upon a snake.°

'Thou art Justice—ne'er for gold   230
May thy righteous laws be sold
As laws are in England—thou
Shield'st alike both high and low.

'Thou art Wisdom—Freemen never
Dream that God will damn forever
All who think those things untrue
Of which Priests make such ado.

'Thou art Peace—never by thee
Would blood and treasure wasted be
As tyrants wasted them, when all   240
Leagued to quench thy flame in Gaul.°

'What if English toil and blood
Was poured forth, even as a flood?
It availed, Oh, Liberty!
To dim, but not extinguish thee.

'Thou art Love—the rich have kissed
Thy feet, and like him following Christ
Give their substance to the free
And through the rough world follow thee°

'Or turn their wealth to arms, and make   250
War for thy beloved sake
On wealth, and war, and fraud—whence they
Drew the power which is their prey.

'Science, Poetry and Thought
Are thy lamps; they make the lot
Of the dwellers in a cot
So serene, they curse it not.°

'Spirit, Patience, Gentleness,
All that can adorn and bless
Art thou—let deeds not words express   260
Thine exceeding loveliness.

'Let a great Assembly be
Of the fearless and the free

On some spot of English ground
Where the plains stretch wide around.

'Let the blue sky overhead,
The green earth on which ye tread,
All that must eternal be
Witness the solemnity.

'From the corners uttermost   270
Of the bounds of English coast,
From every hut, village and town
Where those who live and suffer moan
For others' misery or their own,

'From the workhouse and the prison
Where pale as corpses newly risen,
Women, children, young and old
Groan for pain, and weep for cold—

'From the haunts of daily life
Where is waged the daily strife   280
With common wants and common cares
Which sows the human heart with tares—°

'Lastly from the palaces
Where the murmur of distress
Echoes, like the distant sound
Of a wind alive around

'Those prison-halls of wealth and fashion
Where some few feel such compassion
For those who groan, and toil, and wail
As must make their brethren pale—   290

'Ye who suffer woes untold,
Or to feel, or to behold
Your lost country bought and sold
With a price of blood and gold—

'Let a vast Assembly be,
And with great solemnity

Declare with measured words that ye
Are, as God has made ye, free—

'Be your strong and simple words
Keen to wound as sharpened swords,   300
And wide as targes let them be°
With their shade to cover ye.

'Let the tyrants pour around
With a quick and startling sound,
Like the loosening of a sea
Troops of armed emblazonry.

'Let the charged artillery drive
Till the dead air seems alive
With the clash of clanging wheels,
And the tramp of horses' heels.   310

'Let the fixèd bayonet
Gleam with sharp desire to wet
Its bright point in English blood,
Looking keen as one for food.

'Let the horsemen's scimitars°
Wheel and flash, like sphereless stars°
Thirsting to eclipse their burning
In a sea of death and mourning.

'Stand ye calm and resolute,
Like a forest close and mute,   320
With folded arms and looks which are
Weapons of unvanquished war,

'And let Panic, who outspeeds
The career of armèd steeds,
Pass, a disregarded shade,
Through your phalanx undismayed.

'Let the laws of your own land,
Good or ill, between ye stand

Hand to hand and foot to foot,
Arbiters of the dispute, 330

'The old laws of England—they
Whose reverend heads with age are grey,
Children of a wiser day;
And whose solemn voice must be
Thine own echo—Liberty!

'On those who first should violate
Such sacred heralds in their state
Rest the blood that must ensue,
And it will not rest on you.

'And if then the tyrants dare 340
Let them ride among you there,
Slash, and stab, and maim, and hew—
What they like, that let them do.

'With folded arms and steady eyes,
And little fear, and less surprise,
Look upon them as they slay
Till their rage has died away.°

'Then they will return with shame
To the place from which they came,
And the blood thus shed will speak
In hot blushes on their cheek. 350

'Every woman in the land
Will point at them as they stand—
They will hardly dare to greet
Their acquaintance in the street.

'And the bold, true warriors
Who have hugged Danger in wars
Will turn to those who would be free,
Ashamed of such base company.

'And that slaughter to the Nation 360
Shall steam up like inspiration,

Eloquent, oracular;
A volcano heard afar.°

'And these words shall then become
Like oppression's thundered doom
Ringing through each heart and brain,
Heard again—again—again—

' "Rise like lions after slumber
In unvanquishable number—
Shake your chains to earth like dew 370
Which in sleep had fallen on you—
Ye are many—they are few"'.

Ode to the West Wind

I

O, wild West Wind, thou breath of Autumn's being,
Thou, from whose unseen presence the leaves dead
Are driven, like ghosts from an enchanter fleeing,°

Yellow, and black, and pale, and hectic red,
Pestilence-stricken multitudes: O, thou,°
Who chariotest to their dark wintry bed

The wingèd seeds, where they lie cold and low,
Each like a corpse within its grave, until
Thine azure sister of the Spring shall blow°

Her clarion o'er the dreaming earth, and fill   10
(Driving sweet buds like flocks to feed in air)
With living hues and odours plain and hill:

Wild Spirit, which art moving everywhere;
Destroyer and Preserver; hear, O, hear!°

2

Thou on whose stream, 'mid the steep sky's commotion,
Loose clouds like earth's decaying leaves are shed,°
Shook from the tangled boughs of Heaven and Ocean,°

Angels of rain and lightning: there are spread°
On the blue surface of thine airy surge,
Like the bright hair uplifted from the head   20

Of some fierce Maenad, even from the dim verge
Of the horizon to the zenith's height,
The locks of the approaching storm. Thou dirge°

Of the dying year, to which this closing night
Will be the dome of a vast sepulchre,
Vaulted with all thy congregated might

Of vapours, from whose solid atmosphere
Black rain, and fire, and hail will burst: O, hear!

3

Thou who didst waken from his summer dreams
The blue Mediterranean, where he lay,   30
Lulled by the coil of his crystalline streams,

Beside a pumice isle in Baiae's bay,°
And saw in sleep old palaces and towers
Quivering within the wave's intenser day,°

All overgrown with azure moss and flowers
So sweet, the sense faints picturing them! Thou
For whose path the Atlantic's level powers

Cleave themselves into chasms, while far below
The sea-blooms and the oozy woods which wear
The sapless foliage of the ocean, know   40

Thy voice, and suddenly grow grey with fear,
And tremble and despoil themselves: O, hear!

4

If I were a dead leaf thou mightest bear;
If I were a swift cloud to fly with thee;
A wave to pant beneath thy power, and share

The impulse of thy strength, only less free
Than thou, O, Uncontrollable! If even
I were as in my boyhood, and could be

The comrade of thy wanderings over Heaven,
As then, when to outstrip thy skiey speed   50
Scarce seemed a vision; I would ne'er have striven

As thus with thee in prayer in my sore need.°
Oh! lift me as a wave, a leaf, a cloud!
I fall upon the thorns of life! I bleed!°

A heavy weight of hours has chained and bowed
One too like thee: tameless, and swift, and proud.

5

Make me thy lyre, even as the forest is:
What if my leaves are falling like its own!
The tumult of thy mighty harmonies

Will take from both a deep, autumnal tone,   60
Sweet though in sadness. Be thou, Spirit fierce,
My spirit! Be thou me, impetuous one!

Drive my dead thoughts over the universe
Like withered leaves to quicken a new birth!
And, by the incantation of this verse,

Scatter, as from an unextinguished hearth
Ashes and sparks, my words among mankind!
Be through my lips to unawakened earth

The trumpet of a prophecy! O, wind,
If Winter comes, can Spring be far behind?°   70

PETER BELL THE THIRD

BY MICHING MALLECHO, ESQ.°

> Is it a party in a parlour—
> Crammed just as they on earth were crammed,
> Some sipping punch—some sipping tea;
> But, as you by their faces see,
> All silent and all——damned!
>
> *Peter Bell*, by W. WORDSWORTH.°

> *Ophelia*. What means this, my lord?
> *Hamlet*. Marry, this is miching mallecho; it means mischief.
>
> SHAKESPEARE.°

DEDICATION

TO

THOMAS BROWN, ESQ., THE YOUNGER, H.F.°

Dear Tom—

Allow me to request you to introduce Mr Peter Bell to the respectable family of the Fudges; although he may fall short of those very considerable personages in the more active properties which characterize the Rat and the Apostate,° I suspect that even you their historian will be forced to confess that he surpasses them in the more peculiarly legitimate qualification of intolerable dullness.

You know Mr Examiner Hunt. That murderous and smiling villain at the mere sound of whose voice our susceptible friend the *Quarterly* fell into a paroxysm of eleutherophobia° and foamed so much acrid gall that it burned the carpet in Mr Murray's upper room,° and eating a hole in the floor fell like rain upon our poor friend's head, who was scampering from room to room like a bear with a swarm of bees on his nose:—it caused an incurable ulcer and our poor friend has worn a wig ever since. Well, this monkey° suckled with tiger's milk, this odious thief, liar, scoundrel, coxcomb and monster presented me to two of the Mr Bells.° Seeing me in his presence they of course uttered very few words and those with much caution. I scarcely need observe that they only kept company with him—at least I can certainly answer for one of them—in order to observe whether they could not borrow colours from any particulars of his private life for the denunciation they mean to make of him, as the member of an 'infamous and black conspiracy for diminishing the authority of that venerable canon, which forbids any man to mar his grandmother'; the effect of which in this on our moral and religious nation is likely to answer the purpose of the controversy. My intimacy with the younger Mr Bell naturally sprung from this introduction to his brothers. And in presenting him to you, I have the satisfaction of being able to assure you that he is considerably the dullest of the three.

There is this particular advantage in an acquaintance with any one of the Peter Bells; that if you know one Peter Bell, you know three Peter Bells; they are not one but three, not three but one. An awful mystery, after having caused torrents of blood, and having been hymned by groans enough to deafen the music of the spheres, is at length illustrated to the satisfaction of all parties in the theological world, by the nature of Mr Peter Bell.

Peter is a polyhedric Peter, or a Peter with many sides. He changes colours like a chameleon, and his coat like a snake. He is a Proteus° of a Peter. He was at first sublime, pathetic, impressive, profound; then dull; then prosy and dull; and now dull—'o so' dull! it is an ultra-legitimate° dullness.

You will perceive that it is not necessary to consider Hell and the Devil as supernatural machinery. The whole scene of my epic is in 'this world which is'—so Peter informed us before his conversion to *White Obi*°—

> the world of all of us, *and where*
> *We find our happiness, or not at all.*

Let me observe that I have spent six or seven days° in composing this sublime piece;—the orb of my moonlike genius has made the fourth part of its revolution round the dull earth which you inhabit, driving you mad whilst it has retained its calmness and its splendour, and I have been fitting this its last phase 'to occupy a permanent station in the literature of my country.'

Your works, indeed, dear Tom, sell better; but mine are far superior. The public is no judge; posterity sets all to rights.

Allow me to observe that so much has been written of Peter Bell, that the present history can be considered only, like the *Iliad*, as a continuation of that series of cyclic poems which have already been candidates for bestowing immortality upon, at the same time that they receive it from, his character and adventures. In this point of view, I have violated no rule of syntax in beginning my composition with a conjunction; the full stop which closes the poem continued by me being, like the full stops at the end of the *Iliad* and *Odyssey*, a full stop of a very qualified import.

Hoping that the immortality which you have given to the Fudges, you will receive from them; and in the firm expectation that when London shall be the habitation of bitterns,° when St Paul's and Westminster Abbey shall stand, shapeless and nameless ruins in the midst of an unpeopled marsh; when the piers of Waterloo bridge shall become the nuclei of islets of reeds and osiers and cast the jagged shadows of their broken arches on the solitary stream,—some transatlantic commentator will be weighing in the scales of some new and now unimagined system of criticism, the respective merits of the Bells and the Fudges, and of their historians,

I remain, Dear Tom,
Yours sincerely,
Miching Mallecho.

December 1, 1819.

P.S. Pray excuse the date of place;° so soon as the profits of this publication come in, I mean to hire lodgings in a more respectable street.

Prologue

Peter Bells, one, two and three,
O'er the wide world wandering be:—
First, the antenatal Peter,°
Wrapped in weeds of the same metre,
The so long predestined raiment   5
Clothed in which to walk his way meant
The second Peter, whose ambition
Is to link the proposition
As the mean of two extremes—
(This was learnt from Aldric's themes)°   10
Shielding from the guilt of schism
The orthodoxal syllogism:
The first Peter—he who was
Like the shadow in the glass   15
Of the second, yet unripe;
His substantial antitype.—°
Then came Peter Bell the Second,
Who henceforward must be reckoned

The body of a double soul—
And that portion of the whole   20
Without which the rest would seem
Ends of a disjointed dream.—
And the third is he who has
O'er the grave been forced to pass
To the other side, which is,—   25
Go and try else,—just like this.

Peter Bell the First was Peter
Smugger, milder, softer, neater,
Like the soul before it is
Born from *that* world into *this*.   30
The next Peter Bell was he
Predevote like you and me°
To good or evil as may come;
His was the severer doom.—
For he was an evil Cotter°   35
And a polygamic Potter.°
And the last is Peter Bell,
Damned since our first Parents fell,
Damned eternally to Hell—
Surely he deserves it well!   40

Part First

DEATH

And Peter Bell, when he had been
   With fresh-imported Hell-fire warmed,
Grew serious—from his dress and mien
'Twas very plainly to be seen
   Peter was quite reformed.   5

His eyes turned up, his mouth turned down;
   His accent caught a nasal twang;
He oiled his hair; there might be heard°
The grace of God in every word
   Which Peter said or sang.   10

But Peter now grew old, and had
   An ill no doctor could unravel;

His torments almost drove him mad;—
Some said it was a fever bad—
    Some swore it was the gravel.°   15

His holy friends then came about
    And with long preaching and persuasion,
Convinced the patient, that without
The smallest shadow of a doubt
    He was predestined to damnation.   20

They said—'Thy name is Peter Bell;
    Thy skin is of a brimstone hue;
Alive or dead—aye, sick or well—
The one God made to rhyme with hell;
    The other, I think, rhymes with you.'°   25

Then Peter set up such a yell!—
    The nurse, who with some water gruel
Was climbing up the stairs, as well
As her old legs could climb them—fell,
    And broke them both—the fall was cruel.   30

The Parson from the casement leapt
    Into the lake of Windermere—°
And many an eel—though no adept
In God's right reason for it—kept
    Gnawing his kidneys half a year.   35

And all the rest rushed through the door,
    And tumbled over one another,
And broke their skulls.—Upon the floor
Meanwhile sate Peter Bell, and swore,
    And cursed his father and his mother;   40

And raved of God, and sin, and death,
    Blaspheming like an infidel;
And said, that with his clenchèd teeth
He'd seize the earth from underneath,
    And drag it with him down to Hell.

As he was speaking came a spasm,
    And wrenched his gnashing teeth asunder,

Like one who sees a strange phantasm
He lay,—there was a silent chasm
   Between his upper jaw and under.   50

And yellow death lay on his face;
   And a fixed smile that was not human
Told, as I understand the case,
That he was gone to the wrong place:—
   I heard all this from the old woman.

Then there came down from Langdale Pike
   A cloud with lightning, wind and hail;
It swept over the mountains like
An Ocean,—and I heard it strike
   The woods and crags of Grasmere vale.   60

And I saw the black storm come
   Nearer, minute after minute,
Its thunder made the cataracts dumb,
With hiss, and clash, and hollow hum
   It neared as if the Devil was in it.

The Devil *was* in it:—he had bought°
   Peter for half a crown; and when
The storm which bore him vanished, nought
That in the house that storm had caught
   Was ever seen again.   70

The gaping neighbours came next day—
   They found all vanished from the shore:
The Bible, whence he used to pray,
Half scorched under a hen-coop lay;
   Smashed glass—and nothing more!

Part Second

THE DEVIL

The Devil, I safely can aver,
   Has neither hoof, nor tail, nor sting;
Nor is he, as some sages swear,

A spirit, neither here nor there,
    In nothing—yet in everything.   80

He is—what we are; for sometimes°
    The Devil is a gentleman;
At others a bard bartering rhymes
For sack; a statesman spinning crimes,°
    A swindler, living as he can;

A thief, who cometh in the night,
    With whole boots and net pantaloons,
Like some one whom it were not right
To mention;—or the luckless wight
    From whom he steals nine silver spoons.   90

But in this case he did appear
    Like a slop-merchant from Wapping°
And with smug face, and eye severe
On every side did perk and peer°
    Till he saw Peter dead or napping.

He had on an upper Benjamin°
    (For he was of the driving schism)
In the which he wrapped his skin
From the storm he travelled in,
    For fear of rheumatism.   100

He called the ghost out of the corse;—
    It was exceedingly like Peter,—
Only its voice was hollow and hoarse—
It had a queerish look of course—
    Its dress too was a little neater.

The Devil knew not his name and lot;
    Peter knew not that he was Bell:
Each had an upper stream of thought,
Which made all seem as it was not;
    Fitting itself to all things well.°   110

Peter thought he had parents dear,
    Brothers, sisters, cousins, cronies,

In the fens of Lincolnshire;
He perhaps had found them there
    Had he gone and boldly shown his

Solemn phiz in his own village;°
    Where he thought, oft when a boy
He'd clomb the orchard walls to pillage°
The produce of his neighbour's tillage,
    With marvellous pride and joy.   120

And the Devil thought he had,
    Mid the misery and confusion
Of an unjust war, just made
A fortune by the gainful trade
Of giving soldiers rations bad—
    The world is full of strange delusion.

That he had a mansion planned
    In a square like Grosvenor square,°
That he was aping fashion, and
That he now came to Westmoreland   130
    To see what was romantic there.

And all this, though quite ideal,—
    Ready at a breath to vanish,—
Was a state not more unreal
Than the peace he could not feel,
    Or the care he could not banish.

After a little conversation
    The Devil told Peter, if he chose
He'd bring him to the world of fashion
By giving him a situation   140
    In his own service—and new clothes.

And Peter bowed, quite pleased and proud,
    And after waiting some few days
For a new livery—dirty yellow
Turned up with black—the wretched fellow
    Was bowled to Hell in the Devil's chaise.

Part Third

HELL

Hell is a city much like London—
    A populous and a smoky city;
There are all sorts of people undone,
And there is little or no fun done;   150
    Small justice shown, and still less pity.

There is a Castle, and a Canning,
    A Cobbett, and a Castlereagh;°
All sorts of caitiff corpses planning
All sorts of cozening for trepanning°
    Corpses less corrupt than they.

There is a * * *, who has lost°
    His wits, or sold them, none knows which;
He walks about a double ghost,
And though as thin as Fraud almost—   160
    Ever grows more grim and rich.

There is a Chancery Court, a King,°
    A manufacturing mob; a set
Of thieves who by themselves are sent
Similar thieves to represent;
    An Army;—and a public debt.

Which last is a scheme of Paper money,°
    And means—being interpreted—
'Bees, keep your wax—give us the honey
And we will plant while skies are sunny   170
    Flowers, which in winter serve instead.'

There is a great talk of Revolution—
    And a great chance of despotism—
German soldiers—camps—confusion—°
Tumults—lotteries—rage—delusion—
    Gin—suicide and methodism;°

Taxes too, on wine and bread,
　　And meat, and beer, and tea, and cheese,
From which those patriots pure are fed
Who gorge before they reel to bed   180
　　The tenfold essence of all these.

There are mincing women, mewing
　　(Like cats, who *amant misere*)°
Of their own virtue, and pursuing
Their gentler sisters to that ruin,
　　Without which—what were chastity?°

Lawyers—judges—old hobnobbers°
　　Are there—Bailiffs—Chancellors—
Bishops—great and little robbers—
Rhymesters—pamphleteers—stock-jobbers—°   190
　　Men of glory in the wars,—

Things whose trade is, over ladies
　　To lean, and flirt, and stare, and simper,
Till all that is divine in woman
Grows cruel, courteous, smooth, inhuman,
　　Crucified 'twixt a smile and whimper.

Thrusting, toiling, wailing, moiling,°
　　Frowning, preaching—such a riot!
Each with never ceasing labour
Whilst he thinks he cheats his neighbour   200
　　Cheating his own heart of quiet.

And all these meet at levees;—°
　　Dinners convivial and political;—
Suppers of epic poets;—teas,
Where small talk dies in agonies;—
　　Breakfasts professional and critical;—

Lunches and snacks so aldermanic
　　That one would furnish forth ten dinners,
Where reigns a Cretan-tonguèd panic°
Lest news Russ, Dutch, or Alemannic°   210
　　Should make some losers, and some winners

At conversazioni—balls—°
  Conventicles and drawing-rooms—°
Courts of law—committees—calls
Of a morning—clubs—book stalls—
  Churches—masquerades and tombs.

And this is Hell—and in this smother
  All are damnable and damned;
Each one damning, damns the other;
They are damned by one another,   220
  By none other are they damned.

'Tis a lie to say, 'God damns!'°
  Where was Heaven's Attorney General
When they first gave out such flams?°
Let there be an end of shams,
  They are mines of poisonous mineral.

Statesmen damn themselves to be
  Cursed; and lawyers damn their souls
To the auction of a fee;
Churchmen damn themselves to see   230
  God's sweet love in burning coals.

The rich are damned beyond all cure
  To taunt, and starve, and trample on
The weak and wretched: and the poor
Damn their broken hearts to endure
  Stripe on stripe, with groan on groan.°

Sometimes the poor are damned indeed
  To take,—not means for being blessed,—
But Cobbett's snuff, revenge; that weed°
From which the worms that it doth feed   240
  Squeeze less than they before possessed.

And some few, like we know who,°
  Damned—but God alone knows why—
To believe their minds are given
To make this ugly Hell a Heaven;
  In which faith they live and die.

Thus, as in a Town, plague-stricken,
    Each man be he sound or no
Must indifferently sicken;
As when day begins to thicken   250
    None knows a pigeon from a crow,—

So good and bad, sane and mad,
    The oppressor and the oppressed;
Those who weep to see what others
Smile to inflict upon their brothers;
    Lovers, haters, worst and best;

All are damned—they breathe an air,
    Thick, infected, joy-dispelling:
Each pursues what seems most fair,
Mining like moles, through mind, and there   260
Scoop palace-caverns vast, where Care
    In thronèd state is ever dwelling.

Part Fourth

SIN

Lo, Peter in Hell's Grosvenor square,
    A footman in the Devil's service!
And the misjudging world would swear
That every man in service there
    To virtue would prefer vice.

But Peter, though now damned, was not
    What Peter was before damnation.
Men oftentimes prepare a lot   270
Which ere it finds them, is not what
    Suits with their genuine station.

All things that Peter saw and felt
    Had a peculiar aspect to him;
And when they came within the belt
Of his own nature, seemed to melt
    Like cloud to cloud, into him.°

And so the outward world uniting
  To that within him, he became
Considerably uninviting   280
To those, who meditation slighting,
  Were moulded in a different frame.

And he scorned them, and they scorned him;
  And he scorned all they did; and they
Did all that men of their own trim°
Are wont to do to please their whim,
  Drinking, lying, swearing, play.

Such were his fellow servants; thus
  His virtue, like our own, was built
Too much on that indignant fuss   290
Hypocrite Pride stirs up in us
  To bully out another's guilt.

He had a mind which was somehow
  At once circumference and centre
Of all he might or feel or know;
Nothing went ever out, although
  Something did ever enter.

He had as much imagination
  As a pint-pot:—he never could
Fancy another situation   300
From which to dart his contemplation,
  Than that wherein he stood.

Yet his was individual mind,
  And new created all he saw
In a new manner, and refined
Those new creations, and combined
  Them, by a master-spirit's law.

Thus—though unimaginative,
  An apprehension clear, intense,
Of his mind's work, had made alive   310
The things it wrought on; I believe
  Wakening a sort of thought in sense.

But from the first 'twas Peter's drift
    To be a kind of moral eunuch.
He touched the hem of Nature's shift,
Felt faint—and never dared uplift
    The closest, all-concealing tunic.

She laughed the while, with an arch smile,
    And kissed him with a sister's kiss,
And said—'My best Diogenes,°   320
I love you well—but, if you please,
    Tempt not again my deepest bliss.

' 'Tis you are cold—for I, not coy,
    Yield love for love, frank, warm and true;
And Burns, a Scottish Peasant boy,—
His errors prove it—knew my joy
    More, learned friend, than you.

'*Bocca baciata non perde ventura*
    Anzi rinnuova come fa la luna:—°
So thought Boccaccio, whose sweet words might cure a   330
Male prude like you from what you now endure, a
    Low-tide in soul, like a stagnant laguna.'

Then Peter rubbed his eyes severe,
    And smoothed his spacious forehead down
With his broad palm;—'twixt love and fear,
He looked, as he no doubt felt, queer,
    And in his dream sate down.

The Devil was no uncommon creature;
    A leaden-witted thief—just huddled
Out of the dross and scum of nature;   340
A toadlike lump of limb and feature,°
    With mind, and heart, and fancy muddled.

He was that heavy, dull, cold thing
    The Spirit of Evil well may be:
A drone too base to have a sting,
Who gluts, and grimes his lazy wing,
    And calls lust, luxury.

Now he was quite the kind of wight°
   Round whom collect, at a fixed era,
Venison, turtle, hock and claret,—   350
Good cheer—and those who come to share it—
   And best East Indian madeira!

It was his fancy to invite
   Men of science, wit and learning
Who came to lend each other light:—
He proudly thought that his gold's might
   Had set those spirits burning.

And men of learning, science, wit,
   Considered him as you and I
Think of some rotten tree, and sit   360
Lounging and dining under it,
   Exposed to the wide sky.

And all the while, with loose fat smile
   The willing wretch sat winking there,
Believing 'twas his power that made
That jovial scene—and that all paid
   Homage to his unnoticed chair.

Though to be sure this place was Hell;
   He was the Devil—and all they—
What though the claret circled well,   370
And wit, like ocean, rose and fell?—
   Were damned eternally.

Part Fifth

GRACE

Among the guests who often stayed
   Till the Devil's petits soupers,°
A man there came, fair as a maid,°
And Peter noted what he said,
   Standing behind his master's chair.

He was a mighty poet—and
   A subtle-souled Psychologist;

All things he seemed to understand   380
Of old or new—of sea or land—
    But his own mind—which was a mist.

This was a man who might have turned
    Hell into Heaven—and so in gladness
A Heaven unto himself have earned;
But he in shadows undiscerned
    Trusted,—and damned himself to madness.

He spoke of poetry, and how
    'Divine it was—a light—a love—
A spirit which like wind doth blow   390
As it listeth, to and fro;
    A dew rained down from God above;

'A power which comes and goes like dream,
    And which none can ever trace—
Heaven's light on Earth—Truth's brightest beam.'
And when he ceased there lay the gleam
    Of those words upon his face.

Now Peter, when he heard such talk
    Would, heedless of a broken pate
Stand like a man asleep, or baulk   400
Some wishing guest of knife or fork,
    Or drop and break his master's plate.

At night he oft would start and wake
    Like a lover, and began
In a wild measure songs to make
On moor, and glen, and rocky lake,
    And on the heart of man;°

And on the universal sky—
    And the wide earth's bosom green;—
And the sweet, strange mystery   410
Of what beyond these things may lie°
    And yet remain unseen.

For in his thought he visited
    The spots in which, ere dead and damned,

He his wayward life had led;
Yet knew not whence the thoughts were fed
   Which thus his fancy crammed.

And these obscure remembrances
   Stirred such harmony in Peter,
That, whensoever he should please,   420
He could speak of rocks and trees°
   In poetic metre.

For though it was without a sense
   Of memory, yet he remembered well
Many a ditch and quickset fence;
Of lakes he had intelligence,
   He knew something of heath and fell.

He had also dim recollections
   Of pedlars tramping on their rounds,°
Milk pans and pails, and odd collections   430
Of saws, and proverbs, and reflections
   Old parsons make in burying-grounds.

But Peter's verse was clear, and came
   Announcing from the frozen hearth
Of a cold age, that none might tame
The soul of that diviner flame
   It augured to the Earth:

Like gentle rains, on the dry plains,
   Making that green which late was grey,
Or like the sudden moon, that stains   440
Some gloomy chamber's window panes
   With a broad light like day.

For language was in Peter's hand
   Like clay while he was yet a potter;
And he made songs for all the land
Sweet both to feel and understand
   As pipkins late to mountain Cotter.°

And Mr ——, the Bookseller,
   Gave twenty pounds for some:—then scorning°

A footman's yellow coat to wear,   450
Peter, too proud of heart I fear,
    Instantly gave the Devil warning.

Whereat the Devil took offence,
    And swore in his soul a great oath then,
'That for his damned impertinence,
He'd bring him to a proper sense
    Of what was due to gentlemen!'

Part Sixth

DAMNATION

'O, that mine enemy had written
    A book!'—cried Job:—A fearful curse!°
If to the Arab, as the Briton,   460
'Twas galling to be critic-bitten:—
    The Devil to Peter wished no worse.

When Peter's next new book found vent,°
    The Devil to all the first Reviews
A copy of it slyly sent
With five-pound note as compliment,
    And this short notice—'Pray abuse.'

Then *seriatim*, month and quarter,°
    Appeared such mad tirades.—One said—
'Peter seduced Mrs Foy's daughter,°   470
Then drowned the Mother in Ullswater,
    The last thing as he went to bed.'

Another—'Let him shave his head!
    Where's Dr Willis?—Or is he joking?°
What does the rascal mean or hope,
No longer imitating Pope,
    In that barbarian Shakespeare poking?'

One more,—'Is incest not enough,
    And must there be adultery too?

Grace after meat? Miscreant and liar!   480
Thief! Blackguard! Scoundrel! Fool! Hellfire
   Is twenty times too good for you.

'By that last book of yours WE think
   You've double damned yourself to scorn:
We warned you whilst yet on the brink
You stood. From your black name will shrink
   The babe that is unborn.'

All these Reviews the Devil made
   Up in a parcel, which he had
Safely to Peter's house conveyed.   490
For carriage ten-pence Peter paid—
   United them—read them—went half mad.

'What!'—Cried he, 'this is my reward
   For nights of thought, and days of toil?
Do poets, but to be abhorred
By men of whom they never heard,
   Consume their spirits' oil?

'What have I done to them?—and who
   Is Mrs. Foy? 'Tis very cruel
To speak of me and Emma so!°   500
Adultery! God defend me! Oh!
   I've half a mind to fight a duel.

'Or,' cried he, a grave look collecting,
   'Is it my genius, like the moon,
Sets those who stand her face inspecting
(That face within their brain reflecting)
   Like a crazed bell chime, out of tune?'°

For Peter did not know the town,
   But thought, as country readers do,
For half a guinea or a crown,   510
He bought oblivion or renown
   From God's own voice in a review.°

All Peter did on this occasion
   Was, writing some sad stuff in prose.
It is a dangerous invasion
When Poets criticise: their station
   Is to delight, not pose.

The Devil then sent to Leipsic fair,
   For Born's translation of Kant's book;°
A world of words, tail foremost, where   520
Right—wrong—false—true—and foul and fair
   As in a lottery wheel are shook.

Five thousand crammed octavo pages
   Of German psychologics,—he
Who his *furor verborum* assuages°
Thereon, deserves just seven months' wages
   More than will e'er be due to me.

I looked on them nine several days,
   And then I saw that they were bad;
A friend, too, spoke in their dispraise,—   530
He never read them;—with amaze
   I found Sir William Drummond had.°

When the book came, the Devil sent
   It to P. Verbovale Esquire,°
With a brief note of compliment,
By that night's Carlisle mail. It went
   And set his soul on fire.

Fire, which *ex luce praebens fumum*,°
   Made him beyond the bottom see
Of truth's clear well—when I and you, Ma'am,   540
Go, as we shall do, *subter humum*,°
   We may know more than he.

Now Peter ran to seed in soul
   Into a walking paradox;—
For he was neither part nor whole,
Nor good, nor bad—nor knave, nor fool,
   —Among the woods and rocks

Furious he rode, where late he ran,
   Lashing and spurring his lame hobby;
Turned to a formal Puritan,   550
A solemn and unsexual man,—
   He half believed *White Obi*!

This steed in vision he would ride,
   High trotting over nine-inch bridges,
With Flibbertigibbet, imp of pride,°
Mocking and mowing by his side—
A mad-brained goblin for a guide—
   Over cornfields, gates and hedges.

After these ghastly rides, he came
   Home to his heart, and found from thence   560
Much stolen of its accustomed flame;
His thoughts grew weak, drowsy, and lame
   Of their intelligence.

To Peter's view, all seemed one hue;
   He was no Whig, he was no Tory:
No Deist and no Christian he,—°
He got so subtle, that to be
   Nothing, was all his glory.

One single point in his belief
   From his organization sprung,   570
The heart-enrooted faith, the chief
Ear in his doctrine's blighted sheaf,
   That 'happiness is wrong,'

So thought Calvin and Dominic;°
   So think their fierce successors, who
Even now would neither stint nor stick
Our flesh from off our bones to pick,
   If they might 'do their do.'

His morals thus were undermined:—
   The old Peter—the hard, old Potter—   580
Was born anew within his mind:
He grew dull, harsh, sly, unrefined,
   As when he tramped beside the Otter.°

In the death hues of agony
　　Lambently flashing from a fish,
Now Peter felt amused to see
Shades, like a rainbow's, rise and flee,
　　Mixed with a certain hungry wish.°

So in his Country's dying face
　　He looked—and, lovely as she lay,   590
Seeking in vain his last embrace,
Wailing her own abandoned case,
　　With hardened sneer he turned away:

And coolly to his own Soul said;—
　　'Do you not think that we might make
A poem on her when she's dead?—
Or, no—a thought is in my head—
　　Her shroud for a new sheet I'll take:

'My wife wants one.—Let who will bury
This mangled corpse!—And I and you,   600
My dearest Soul, will then make merry,
As the Prince Regent did with Sherry,—'°
　　'Aye—and at last desert me too.'

And so his Soul would not be gay,
　　But moaned within him; like a fawn,
Moaning within a cave, it lay
Wounded and wasting, day by day,
　　Till all its life of life was gone.

As troubled skies stain waters clear,
　　The storm in Peter's heart and mind,   610
Now made his verses dark and queer;
They were the ghosts of what they were,
　　Shaking dim grave clothes in the wind.

For he now raved enormous folly
　　Of Baptisms, Sunday-schools and Graves;
'Twould make George Colman melancholy°
To have heard him, like a male Molly,°
　　Chanting those stupid staves.

Yet the Reviews, who heaped abuse
    On Peter, while he wrote for freedom,   620
So soon as in his song they spy
The folly which soothes Tyranny,
    Praise him, for those who feed 'em.

'He was a man, too great to scan;—
    A planet lost in truth's keen rays;—
His virtue, awful and prodigious;—
He was the most sublime, religious,
    Pure-minded Poet of these days.'

As soon as he read that—cried Peter,
    'Eureka! I have found the way   630
To make a better thing of metre
Than e'er was made by living creature
    Up to this blessed day.'

Then Peter wrote odes to the Devil;—
    In one of which he meekly said:—
'May Carnage and Slaughter,
Thy niece and thy daughter,°
May Rapine and Famine,
Thy gorge ever cramming,
    Glut thee with living and dead!   640

    'May death and Damnation,
    And Consternation,
Flit up from Hell with pure intent!
    Slash them at Manchester,°
    Glasgow, Leeds and Chester;
Drench all with blood from Avon to Trent.

    'Let thy body-guard yeomen
    Hew down babes and women,
And laugh with bold triumph till Heaven be rent!
    When Moloch in Jewry°   650
    Munched children with fury
It was thou, Devil, dining with pure intent.'°

Part Seventh

DOUBLE DAMNATION

The Devil now knew his proper cue,—
  Soon as he read the ode, he drove
To his friend Lord MacMurderchouse's,°
A man of interest in both houses,
  And said:—'For money or for love

'Pray find some cure or sinecure,
  To feed from the superfluous taxes
A friend of ours—a Poet—fewer   660
Have fluttered tamer to the lure
  Than he.'—His Lordship stands and racks his

Stupid brains, while one might count
  As many beads as he had boroughs,—
At length replies;—from his mean front,
Like one who rubs out an account,
  Smoothing away the unmeaning furrows:—

'It happens fortunately, dear Sir,
  I can. I hope I need require
No pledge from you, that he will stir   670
In our affairs;—like Oliver,°
  That he'll be worthy of his hire.'

These words exchanged, the news sent off
  To Peter:—home the Devil hied;
Took to his bed; he had no cough,
No doctor,—meat and drink enough,—
  Yet that same night he died.

The Devil's corpse was leaded down.—
  His decent heirs enjoyed his pelf;°
Mourning-coaches, many a one,   680
Followed his hearse along the town:—
  Where was the Devil himself?

When Peter heard of his promotion
  His eyes grew like two stars for bliss:

There was a bow of sleek devotion
Engendering in his back; each motion
 Seemed a Lord's shoe to kiss.

He hired a house, bought plate, and made°
 A genteel drive up to his door,
With sifted gravel neatly laid,—   690
As if defying all who said
 Peter was ever poor.

But a disease soon struck into
 The very life and soul of Peter—
He walked about—slept—had the hue
Of health upon his cheeks—and few
 Dug better—none a heartier eater.

And yet, a strange and horrid curse°
 Clung upon Peter, night and day—
Month after month the thing grew worse,   700
And deadlier than in this my verse
 I can find strength to say.

Peter was dull—he was at first
 Dull—O, so dull—so very dull!
Whether he talked, wrote, or rehearsed—
Still with this dullness was he cursed—
 Dull—beyond all conception—dull.—

No one could read his books—no mortal,
 But a few natural friends, would hear him:—
The parson came not near his portal;—   710
His state was like that of the immortal
 Described by Swift—no man could bear him.°

His sister, wife, and children yawned,
 With a long, slow and drear ennui,
All human patience far beyond;
Their hopes of Heaven each would have pawned,
 Anywhere else to be.

But in his verse, and in his prose,
 The essence of his dullness was

Concentred and compressed so close,—   720
'Twould have made Guatimozin doze
   On his red gridiron of brass.°

A printer's boy, folding those pages,
   Fell slumbrously upon one side;
Like those famed seven who slept three ages.°
To wakeful frenzy's vigil rages
   As opiates were the same applied.

Even the Reviewers who were hired
   To do the work of his reviewing,
With adamantine nerves, grew tired;—   730
Gaping and torpid they retired,
   To dream of what they should be doing.

And worse and worse, the drowsy curse°
   Yawned in him—till it grew a pest—
A wide contagious atmosphere,
Creeping like cold through all things near;
   A power to infect, and to infest.

His servant maids and dogs grew dull;
   His kitten, late a sportive elf;
The woods and lakes, so beautiful,   740
Of dim stupidity were full;
   All grew dull as Peter's self.

The earth under his feet—the springs,
   Which lived within it a quick life—
The Air, the Winds of many wings—
That fan it with new murmurings—
   Were dead to their harmonious strife.

The birds and beasts within the wood,
   The insects, and each creeping thing,
Were now a silent multitude;   750
Love's work was left unwrought—no brood
   Near Peter's house took wing.

And every neighbouring Cottager
   Stupidly yawned upon the other;

No jackass brayed;—no little cur
Cocked up his ears;—no man would stir
    To save a dying mother.

Yet all from that charmed district went
    But some half idiot and half knave,
Who, rather than pay any rent,   760
Would live, with marvellous content,
    Over his father's grave.

No bailiff dared within that space,
    For fear of the dull charm, to enter:
A man would bear upon his face,
For fifteen months, in any case,
    The yawn of such a venture.

Seven miles above—below—around—
    This pest of dullness holds its sway:
A ghastly life without a sound;   770
To Peter's soul the spell is bound—
    How should it ever pass away?

Men of England: A Song

Men of England, wherefore plough
For the lords who lay ye low?
Wherefore weave with toil and care
The rich robes your tyrants wear?

Wherefore feed and clothe and save
From the cradle to the grave,
Those ungrateful drones who would
Drain your sweat—nay, drink your blood?

Wherefore, Bees of England, forge
Many a weapon, chain and scourge   10
That these stingless drones may spoil
The forced produce of your toil?

Have ye leisure, comfort, calm,
Shelter, food, love's gentle balm?
Or what is it ye buy so dear
With your pain and with your fear?

The seed ye sow, another reaps:
The wealth ye find, another keeps:
The robes ye weave, another wears:
The arms ye forge, another bears.   20

Sow seed—but let no tyrant reap:
Find wealth—let no impostor heap:
Weave robes—let not the idle wear:
Forge arms—in your defence to bear.

Shrink to your cellars, holes, and cells—
In halls ye deck, another dwells.
Why shake the chains ye wrought? Ye see
The steel ye tempered glance on ye.

With plough and spade and hoe and loom
Trace your grave and build your tomb   30
And weave your winding-sheet—till fair
England be your Sepulchre.

Lines Written during the Castlereagh Administration

Corpses are cold in the tomb—
Stones on the pavement are dumb—
Abortions are dead in the womb
And their mothers look pale, like the death-white shore
    Of Albion, free no more.

Her sons are as stones in the way—
They are masses of senseless clay—
    They are trodden and move not away—
The abortion with which she travaileth
    Is Liberty, smitten to death.   10

Then trample and dance, thou Oppressor!
For thy victim is no redressor;
Thou art sole lord and possessor
Of the corpses and clods and abortions—they pave
    Thy path to the grave.

Hearest thou the festival din
Of Death and Destruction and Sin,
And Wealth crying 'Havoc!' within?
'Tis the Bacchanal triumph which makes truth dumb,
    Thine Epithalamium—   20

Aye, marry thy ghastly wife!
Let Fear and Disquiet and Strife
Spread thy couch in the chamber of life.
Marry Ruin, thou Tyrant, and Hell be thy guide°
    To the bed of the bride.

To S. and C.°

As from their ancestral oak°
    Two empty ravens wind their clarion,°
Yell by yell, and croak for croak;

When they scent the noonday smoke
  Of fresh human carrion:—

As two gibbering night-birds flit
  From their homes of deadly yew°
Through the night to frighten it—
When the moon is in a fit,°
  And the stars are none or few:—   10

As a shark and dogfish wait
  Under an Atlantic isle
For the Negroship whose freight
Is the theme of their debate,
  Wrinkling their red gills the while:—

Are ye—two vultures sick for battle,
  Two scorpions under one wet stone,
Two bloodless wolves whose dry throats rattle,
Two crows perched on the murrained cattle,
  Two vipers tangled into one.°   20

'What men gain fairly'

What men gain fairly, that should they possess
And children may inherit idleness
From him who earns it . . . this is understood—
Private injustice may be general good.
But he who gains by base and armèd wrong
Or guilty fraud, or base compliances
With those whom force or falsehood has made strong,°
May be despoiled; even as a stolen dress
Is stripped from a convicted thief and he
Left in the nakedness of infamy.

A New National Anthem

God prosper, speed, and save,
God raise from England's grave

    Her murdered Queen!
Pave with swift victory
The steps of Liberty,
Whom Britons own to be
    Immortal Queen!

See, she comes throned on high.
On swift Eternity!
    God save the Queen!
Millions on millions wait
Firm, rapid, and elate,
On her majestic state!°
    God save the Queen!

She is thine own pure soul
Moulding the mighty whole
    God save our Queen!
She is thine own deep love
Rained down from Heaven above,
Wherever she rest or move
    God save our Queen!

'Wilder her enemies
In their own dark disguise
    God save our Queen!
All earthly things that dare
Her sacred name to wear,
Strip them, as kings are, bare
    God save our Queen!

Be her eternal throne
Built in our hearts alone,
    God save our Queen!
Let the oppressor hold
Canopied seats of gold;
She sits enthroned of old
    O'er our hearts, Queen!

Lips touched by Seraphim
Breathe out the choral hymn
    God save the Queen!

Sweet as if Angels sang,
Loud as that clarion's clang   40
Wakening the world's dead gang,
          God save the Queen!°

Sonnet: England in 1819

An old, mad, blind, despised, and dying King;°
Princes, the dregs of their dull race, who flow°
Through public scorn,—mud from a muddy spring;
Rulers who neither see nor feel nor know,
But leechlike to their fainting country cling
Till they drop, blind in blood, without a blow.
A people starved and stabbed in th'untilled field;°
An army whom liberticide and prey°
Makes as a two-edged sword to all who wield;
Golden and sanguine laws which tempt and slay;°   10
Religion Christless, Godless, a book sealed;
A senate, Time's worst statute, unrepealed—°
Are graves from which a glorious Phantom may
Burst, to illumine our tempestuous day.

Love's Philosophy

The Fountains mingle with the River
    And the Rivers with the Ocean,
The winds of Heaven mix forever
    With a sweet emotion;
Nothing in the world is single,
    All things by a law divine
In one spirit meet and mingle.°
    Why not I with thine?—

See the mountains kiss high Heaven
    And the waves clasp one another;   10
No sister-flower would be forgiven
    If it disdained its brother,

And the sunlight clasps the earth
   And the moonbeams kiss the sea;—
What is all this sweet work worth°
   If thou kiss not me?

Ode to Heaven

Chorus of Spirits
First Spirit°

Palace-roof of cloudless nights!
Paradise of golden lights!
   Deep, immeasurable, vast,
Which art now, and which wert then;
   Of the present and the past,
Of the eternal where and when,
   Presence-chamber, temple, home,
   Ever-canopying dome
   Of acts and ages yet to come!

Glorious shapes have life in thee,   10
Earth, and all earth's company;
   Living globes which ever throng
Thy deep chasms and wildernesses;
   And green worlds that glide along;
And swift stars with flashing tresses;
   And icy moons most cold and bright,
   And mighty suns beyond the night,
   Atoms of intensest light!

Even thy name is as a God,
Heaven! for thou art the abode   20
   Of that Power which is the glass
Wherein man his nature sees.
   Generations as they pass
Worship thee with bended knees.
   Their unremaining Gods and they
   Like a river roll away:
   Thou remainest such—alway!°

Second Spirit°

Thou art but the mind's first chamber,
Round which its young fancies clamber,
　　Like weak insects in a cave　　　　　　　　　　30
Lighted up by stalactites;
　　But the portal of the grave,
Where a world of new delights
　　Will make thy best glories seem
　　But a dim and noonday gleam
　　From the shadow of a dream!°

Third Spirit°

Peace! the abyss is wreathed with scorn
At your presumption, atom-born!
　　What is Heaven? and what are ye
Who its brief expanse inherit?　　　　　　　　　　40
　　What are suns and spheres which flee
With the instinct of that spirit
　　Of which ye are but a part?
　　Drops which Nature's mighty heart
　　Drives through thinnest veins. Depart!

What is Heaven? a globe of dew,
Filling in the morning new
　　Some eyed flower whose young leaves waken
On an unimagined world.
　　Constellated suns unshaken,　　　　　　　　　　50
Orbits measureless, are furled
　　In that frail and fading sphere,
　　With ten millions gathered there,°
　　To tremble, gleam, and disappear!°

To the Lord Chancellor

Thy country's curse is on thee, darkest Crest
　　Of that foul, knotted, many-headed worm
Which rends our mother's bosom!—Priestly Pest!
　　Masked Resurrection of a buried form!°

Thy country's curse is on thee—Justice sold,
  Truth trampled, Nature's landmarks overthrown,
And heaps of fraud-accumulated gold
  Plead, loud as thunder, at destruction's throne.

And whilst that sure, slow Fate which ever stands
  Watching the beck of Mutability   10
Delays to execute her high commands
  And, though a nation weeps, spares thine and thee—

O let a father's curse be on thy soul,
  And let a daughter's hope be on thy tomb;
Be both, on thy grey head, a leaden cowl
  To weigh thee down to thine approaching doom.

I curse thee! By a parent's outraged love,—
  By hopes long cherished and too lately lost,—
By gentle feelings thou couldst never prove,
  By griefs which thy stern nature never crossed;   20

By those infantine smiles of happy light,
  Which were a fire within a stranger's hearth,
Quenched even when kindled, in untimely night,
  Hiding the promise of a lovely birth—°

By those unpractised accents of young speech
  Which he who is a father thought to frame
To gentlest lore, such as the wisest teach—
  Thou strike the lyre of mind!—oh, grief and shame!

By all the happy see in children's growth,
  That undeveloped flower of budding years—   30
Sweetness and sadness interwoven both,
  Source of the sweetest hopes, the saddest fears.

By all the days under a hireling's care
  Of dull constraint and bitter heaviness—
Oh, wretched ye, if any ever were—
  Sadder than orphans—why not fatherless?°

By the false cant which on their innocent lips
  Must hang like poison on an opening bloom,

By the dark creeds which cover with eclipse
   Their pathway from the cradle to the tomb—°   40

By thy complicity with lust and hate:
   Thy thirst for tears—thy hunger after gold—
The ready frauds which ever on thee wait—
   The servile arts in which thou hast grown old.—

By thy most killing sneer, and by thy smile—
   By all the snares and nets of thy black den;
And—(for thou canst outweep the crocodile)—
   By thy false tears—those millstones braining men—°

By all the hate which checks a father's love,
   By all the scorn which kills a father's care,   50
By those most impious hands, which dared remove
   Nature's high bounds—by thee—and by despair—

Yes—the despair which bids a father groan
   And cry—'My children are no longer mine—
The blood within those veins may be mine own,
   But, Tyrant, their polluted souls are thine;—'

I curse thee, though I hate thee not.—O, slave!
   If thou couldst quench that earth-consuming Hell
Of which thou art a daemon, on thy grave
   This curse should be a blessing—Fare thee well!   60

The Sensitive Plant

Part First

A Sensitive Plant in a garden grew,
And the young winds fed it with silver dew,
And it opened its fan-like leaves to the light,
And closed them beneath the kisses of night.°

And the Spring arose on the garden fair,
Like the Spirit of Love felt everywhere;
And each flower and herb on Earth's dark breast
Rose from the dreams of its wintry rest.

But none ever trembled and panted with bliss
In the garden, the field, or the wilderness,   10
Like a doe in the noontide with love's sweet want,
As the companionless Sensitive Plant.°

The snowdrop, and then the violet,
Arose from the ground with warm rain wet,
And their breath was mixed with fresh odour, sent
From the turf, like the voice and the instrument.

Then the pied wind-flowers and the tulip tall,°
And narcissi, the fairest among them all,
Who gaze on their eyes in the stream's recess,
Till they die of their own dear loveliness;   20

And the Naiad-like lily of the vale,°
Whom youth makes so fair and passion so pale,
That the light of its tremulous bells is seen
Through their pavilions of tender green;

And the hyacinth purple, and white, and blue,
Which flung from its bells a sweet peal anew
Of music so delicate, soft, and intense,
It was felt like an odour within the sense;°

And the rose like a nymph to the bath addressed,°
Which unveiled the depth of her glowing breast,   30
Till, fold after fold, to the fainting air
The soul of her beauty and love lay bare:

And the wand-like lily, which lifted up,
As a Maenad, its moonlight-coloured cup,
Till the fiery star, which is its eye,
Gazed through clear dew on the tender sky;

And the jessamine faint, and the sweet tuberose,
The sweetest flower for scent that blows;°
And all rare blossoms from every clime
Grew in that garden in perfect prime.   40

And on the stream whose inconstant bosom
Was pranked under boughs of embowering blossom°

With golden and green light, slanting through
Their heaven of many a tangled hue,

Broad water lilies lay tremulously,
And starry river-buds glimmered by,
And around them the soft stream did glide and dance
With a motion of sweet sound and radiance.

And the sinuous paths of lawn and of moss,
Which led through the garden along and across—   50
Some open at once to the sun and the breeze,
Some lost among bowers of blossoming trees—

Were all paved with daisies and delicate bells
As fair as the fabulous asphodels,°
And flow'rets which drooping as day drooped too
Fell into pavilions, white, purple, and blue,
To roof the glow-worm from the evening dew.

And from this undefilèd Paradise°
The flowers (as an infant's awakening eyes
Smile on its mother, whose singing sweet   60
Can first lull, and at last must awaken it),

When Heaven's blithe winds had unfolded them,
As mine-lamps enkindle a hidden gem,°
Shone smiling to Heaven, and every one
Shared joy in the light of the gentle sun;

For each one was interpenetrated
With the light and the odour its neighbour shed,
Like young lovers whom youth and love make dear
Wrapped and filled by their mutual atmosphere.

But the Sensitive Plant, which could give small fruit   70
Of the love which it felt from the leaf to the root,
Received more than all, it loved more than ever,
Where none wanted but it, could belong to the giver,

For the Sensitive Plant has no bright flower;
Radiance and odour are not its dower;

It loves, even like Love, its deep heart is full,
It desires what it has not, the beautiful!°

The light winds which from unsustaining wings
Shed the music of many murmurings;
The beams which dart from many a star   80
Of the flowers whose hues they bear afar;

The plumèd insects swift and free,
Like golden boats on a sunny sea,
Laden with light and odour, which pass
Over the gleam of the living grass;

The unseen clouds of the dew, which lie
Like fire in the flowers till the sun rides high,
Then wander like spirits among the spheres,
Each cloud faint with the fragrance it bears;

The quivering vapours of dim noontide,   90
Which like a sea o'er the warm earth glide,
In which every sound, and odour, and beam,
Move, as reeds in a single stream;

Each and all like ministering angels were
For the Sensitive Plant sweet joy to bear,
Whilst the lagging hours of the day went by
Like windless clouds o'er a tender sky.

And when evening descended from Heaven above,
And the Earth was all rest, and the air was all love,
And delight, though less bright, was far more deep,   100
And the day's veil fell from the world of sleep,

And the beasts, and the birds, and the insects were drowned
In an ocean of dreams without a sound,
Whose waves never mark, though they ever impress
The light sand which paves it, consciousness;

(Only overhead the sweet nightingale
Ever sang more sweet as the day might fail,

And snatches of its Elysian chant
Were mixed with the dreams of the Sensitive Plant.)°

The Sensitive Plant was the earliest   110
Up-gathered into the bosom of rest;
A sweet child weary of its delight,
The feeblest and yet the favourite,
Cradled within the embrace of night.

Part Second

There was a Power in this sweet place,°
An Eve in this Eden; a ruling grace
Which to the flowers did they waken or dream,
Was as God is to the starry scheme.

A Lady, the wonder of her kind,
Whose form was upborne by a lovely mind
Which, dilating, had moulded her mien and motion
Like a sea-flower unfolded beneath the ocean,

Tended the garden from morn to even:
And the meteors of that sublunar Heaven,   10
Like the lamps of the air when night walks forth,
Laughed round her footsteps up from the Earth!

She had no companion of mortal race,
But her tremulous breath and her flushing face
Told, whilst the morn kissed the sleep from her eyes,
That her dreams were less slumber than Paradise:

As if some bright Spirit for her sweet sake
Had deserted heaven while the stars were awake,
As if yet around her he lingering were,
Though the veil of daylight concealed him from her.   20

Her step seemed to pity the grass it pressed;
You might hear by the heaving of her breast,
That the coming and going of the wind
Brought pleasure there and left passion behind.

And wherever her airy footstep trod,
Her trailing hair from the grassy sod
Erased its light vestige, with shadowy sweep,
Like a sunny storm o'er the dark green deep.

I doubt not the flowers of that garden sweet
Rejoiced in the sound of her gentle feet;   30
I doubt not they felt the spirit that came
From her glowing fingers through all their frame.

She sprinkled bright water from the stream
On those that were faint with the sunny beam;
And out of the cups of the heavy flowers
She emptied the rain of the thunder showers.

She lifted their heads with her tender hands,
And sustained them with rods and osier bands;°
If the flowers had been her own infants she
Could never have nursed them more tenderly.   40

And all killing insects and gnawing worms,
And things of obscene and unlovely forms,
She bore in a basket of Indian woof,°
Into the rough woods far aloof,

In a basket, of grasses and wild flowers full,
The freshest her gentle hands could pull
For the poor banished insects, whose intent,
Although they did ill, was innocent.

But the bee and the beamlike ephemeris°
Whose path is the lightning's, and soft moths that kiss   50
The sweet lips of the flowers, and harm not, did she°
Make her attendant angels be.

And many an antenatal tomb,°
Where butterflies dream of the life to come,
She left clinging round the smooth and dark
Edge of the odorous cedar bark.

This fairest creature from earliest spring
Thus moved through the garden ministering

All the sweet season of summertide,
And ere the first leaf looked brown—she died!   60

Part Third

Three days the flowers of the garden fair,
Like stars when the moon is awakened, were,
Or the waves of Baiae, ere luminous°
She floats up through the smoke of Vesuvius.°

And on the fourth, the Sensitive Plant
Felt the sound of the funeral chant,
And the steps of the bearers, heavy and slow,
And the sobs of the mourners deep and low;

The weary sound and the heavy breath,
And the silent motions of passing death,   10
And the smell, cold, oppressive, and dank,
Sent through the pores of the coffin plank;

The dark grass, and the flowers among the grass,
Were bright with tears as the crowd did pass;
From their sighs the wind caught a mournful tone,
And sate in the pines, and gave groan for groan.

The garden, once fair, became cold and foul,
Like the corpse of her who had been its soul,
Which at first was lovely as if in sleep,
Then slowly changed, till it grew a heap   20
To make men tremble who never weep.

Swift summer into the autumn flowed,
And frost in the mist of the morning rode,
Though the noonday sun looked clear and bright,
Mocking the spoil of the secret night.

The rose leaves, like flakes of crimson snow,
Paved the turf and the moss below.
The lilies were drooping, and white, and wan,
Like the head and the skin of a dying man.

And Indian plants, of scent and hue 30
The sweetest that ever were fed on dew,
Leaf by leaf, day after day,
Were massed into the common clay.

And the leaves, brown, yellow, and grey, and red,
And white with the whiteness of what is dead,
Like troops of ghosts on the dry wind passed;
Their whistling noise made the birds aghast.

And the gusty winds waked the wingèd seeds,
Out of their birthplace of ugly weeds,
Till they clung round many a sweet flower's stem, 40
Which rotted into the earth with them.

The water-blooms under the rivulet
Fell from the stalks on which they were set;
And the eddies drove them here and there,
As the winds did those of the upper air.

Then the rain came down, and the broken stalks,
Were bent and tangled across the walks;
And the leafless net-work of parasite bowers
Massed into ruin; and all sweet flowers.

Between the time of the wind and the snow, 50
All loathliest weeds began to grow,
Whose coarse leaves were splashed with many a speck,
Like the water-snake's belly and the toad's back.

And thistles, and nettles, and darnels rank,°
And the dock, and henbane; and hemlock dank°
Stretched out its long and hollow shank,°
And stifled the air, till the dead wind stank.

And plants, at whose names the verse feels loath,
Filled the place with a monstrous undergrowth,
Prickly, and pulpous, and blistering, and blue,° 60
Livid, and starred with a lurid dew.°

And agarics and fungi with mildew and mould°
Started like mists from the wet ground cold;
Pale, fleshy,—as if the decaying dead
With a spirit of growth had been animated!

Their moss rotted off them, flake by flake,
Till the thick stalk stuck like a murderer's stake,
Where rags of loose flesh yet tremble on high,
Infecting the winds that wander by.°

Spawn, weeds, and filth, a leprous scum,°   70
Made the running rivulet thick and dumb
And at its outlet flags huge as stakes°
Dammed it up with roots knotted like water-snakes.

And hour by hour, when the air was still,
The vapours arose which have strength to kill:
At morn they were seen, at noon they were felt,
At night they were darkness no star could melt.

And unctuous meteors from spray to spray°
Crept and flitted in broad noonday
Unseen; every branch on which they alit   80
By a venomous blight was burned and bit.

The Sensitive Plant like one forbid°
Wept, and the tears within each lid
Of its folded leaves which together grew
Were changed to a blight of frozen glue.

For the leaves soon fell, and the branches soon
By the heavy axe of the blast were hewn;
The sap shrank to the root through every pore
As blood to a heart that will beat no more.

For Winter came—the wind was his whip—   90
One choppy finger was on his lip:°
He had torn the cataracts from the hills
And they clanked at his girdle like manacles;

His breath was a chain which without a sound
The earth, and the air, and the water bound;

He came, fiercely driven, in his chariot-throne
By the tenfold blasts of the arctic zone.

Then the weeds which were forms of living death
Fled from the frost to the earth beneath.
Their decay and sudden flight from frost   100
Was but like the vanishing of a ghost!

And under the roots of the Sensitive Plant
The moles and the dormice died for want.°
The birds dropped stiff from the frozen air
And were caught in the branches naked and bare.

First there came down a thawing rain
And its dull drops froze on the boughs again,
Then there steamed up a freezing dew
Which to the drops of the thaw-rain grew;

And a northern whirlwind, wandering about   110
Like a wolf that had smelt a dead child out,
Shook the boughs thus laden, and heavy and stiff,
And snapped them off with his rigid griff.°

When winter had gone and spring came back
The Sensitive Plant was a leafless wreck;
But the mandrakes, and toadstools, and docks, and darnels,°
Rose like the dead from their ruined charnels.

Conclusion

Whether the Sensitive Plant, or that
Which within its boughs like a spirit sat
Ere its outward form had known decay,
Now felt this change, I cannot say.

Whether that lady's gentle mind,
No longer with the form combined
Which scattered love, as stars do light,
Found sadness, where it left delight,

I dare not guess; but in this life
Of error, ignorance, and strife,   10
Where nothing is, but all things seem,
And we the shadows of the dream,°

It is a modest creed, and yet
Pleasant if one considers it,
To own that death itself must be,°
Like all the rest, a mockery.

That garden sweet, that lady fair,
And all sweet shapes and odours there,
In truth have never passed away:
'Tis we, 'tis ours, are changed; not they.   20

For love, and beauty, and delight,
There is no death nor change: their might
Exceeds our organs, which endure
No light, being themselves obscure.°

An Exhortation

Chameleons feed on light and air:
   Poets' food is love and fame:°
If in this wide world of care
   Poets could but find the same
With as little toil as they,
   Would they ever change their hue
   As the light chameleons do,
Suiting it to every ray
Twenty times a day?

Poets are on this cold earth,   10
   As chameleons might be,
Hidden from their early birth
   In a cave beneath the sea;
Where light is, chameleons change:
   Where love is not, poets do:
   Fame is love disguised: if few

Find either, never think it strange
That poets range.

Yet dare not stain with wealth or power
   A poet's free and heavenly mind: 20
If bright chameleons should devour
   Any food but beams and wind,
They would grow as earthly soon
   As their brother lizards are.
   Children of a sunnier star,
Spirits from beyond the moon,
O, refuse the boon!°

The Cloud

I bring fresh showers for the thirsting flowers,
   From the seas and the streams;
I bear light shade for the leaves when laid
   In their noon-day dreams.
From my wings are shaken the dews that waken
   The sweet buds every one,
When rocked to rest on their mother's breast,°
   As she dances about the sun.
I wield the flail of the lashing hail,
   And whiten the green plains under,   10
And then again I dissolve it in rain,
   And laugh as I pass in thunder.

I sift the snow on the mountains below,
   And their great pines groan aghast;
And all the night 'tis my pillow white,
   While I sleep in the arms of the blast.
Sublime on the towers of my skiey bowers,
   Lightning my pilot sits,°
In a cavern under is fettered the thunder,
   It struggles and howls at fits;°   20
Over earth and ocean, with gentle motion,
   This pilot is guiding me,
Lured by the love of the genii that move°
   In the depths of the purple sea;

Over the rills, and the crags, and the hills,
        Over the lakes and the plains,
Wherever he dream, under mountain or stream,
        The Spirit he loves remains;
And I all the while bask in Heaven's blue smile,
        Whilst he is dissolving in rains.   30

The sanguine sunrise, with his meteor eyes,
        And his burning plumes outspread,
Leaps on the back of my sailing rack,°
        When the morning star shines dead;°
As on the jag of a mountain crag,
        Which an earthquake rocks and swings,
An eagle alit one moment may sit
        In the light of its golden wings;
And when sunset may breathe, from the lit sea beneath,
        Its ardours of rest and of love,   40
And the crimson pall of eve may fall
        From the depths of Heaven above,°
With wings folded I rest, on mine airy nest,°
        As still as a brooding dove.°

That orbèd maiden with white fire laden,
        Whom mortals call the moon,
Glides glimmering o'er my fleece-like floor,
        By the midnight breezes strewn;
And wherever the beat of her unseen feet,
        Which only the angels hear,   50
May have broken the woof of my tent's thin roof,
        The stars peep behind her and peer;
And I laugh to see them whirl and flee,
        Like a swarm of golden bees,
When I widen the rent in my wind-built tent,
        Till the calm rivers, lakes, and seas,
Like strips of the sky fallen through me on high,
        Are each paved with the moon and these.°

I bind the sun's throne with a burning zone,°
        And the moon's with a girdle of pearl;   60
The volcanos are dim, and the stars reel and swim,
        When the whirlwinds my banner unfurl.
From cape to cape, with a bridge-like shape,

Over a torrent sea,
Sunbeam-proof, I hang like a roof,
    The mountains its columns be.
The triumphal arch through which I march
    With hurricane, fire, and snow,
When the powers of the air are chained to my chair,
    Is the million-coloured bow;   70
The sphere-fire above its soft colours wove,°
    While the moist earth was laughing below.

I am the daughter of Earth and Water,
    And the nursling of the sky;
I pass through the pores of the oceans and shores;°
    I change, but I cannot die—
For after the rain, when with never a stain,
    The pavilion of Heaven is bare,
And the winds and sunbeams, with their convex gleams,°
    Build up the blue dome of air,   80
I silently laugh at my own cenotaph,°
    And out of the caverns of rain,
Like a child from the womb, like a ghost from the tomb,
    I arise, and unbuild it again.

To a Skylark

Hail to thee, blithe Spirit!
    Bird thou never wert,
That from Heaven, or near it,
    Pourest thy full heart
In profuse strains of unpremeditated art.

Higher still and higher
    From the earth thou springest
Like a cloud of fire;°
    The blue deep thou wingest,
And singing still dost soar, and soaring ever singest.   10

In the golden lightning
    Of the sunken sun,

O'er which clouds are bright'ning,
    Thou dost float and run;
Like an unbodied joy whose race is just begun.

    The pale purple even
        Melts around thy flight;
    Like a star of Heaven,
        In the broad daylight
Thou art unseen,—but yet I hear thy shrill delight,   20

    Keen as are the arrows
        Of that silver sphere,°
    Whose intense lamp narrows
        In the white dawn clear,
Until we hardly see—we feel that it is there.

    All the earth and air
        With thy voice is loud,
    As, when night is bare,
        From one lonely cloud
The moon rains out her beams—and Heaven is overflowed.   30

    What thou art we know not;
        What is most like thee?
    From rainbow clouds there flow not
        Drops so bright to see,
As from thy presence showers a rain of melody.

    Like a poet hidden
        In the light of thought,
    Singing hymns unbidden,
        Till the world is wrought
To sympathy with hopes and fears it heeded not: 40

    Like a high-born maiden
        In a palace tower,
    Soothing her love-laden
        Soul in secret hour
With music sweet as love, which overflows her bower:

    Like a glow-worm golden
        In a dell of dew,

Scattering unbeholden
    Its aerial hue
Among the flowers and grass, which screen it from the view: 50

Like a rose embowered
    In its own green leaves,
By warm winds deflowered,
    Till the scent it gives
Makes faint with too much sweet those heavy-wingèd thieves:

Sound of vernal showers
    On the twinkling grass,
Rain-awakened flowers,
    All that ever was
Joyous, and clear, and fresh, thy music doth surpass.   60

Teach us, Sprite or Bird,
    What sweet thoughts are thine;
I have never heard
    Praise of love or wine
That panted forth a flood of rapture so divine.

Chorus Hymenaeal,°
    Or triumphal chant,
Matched with thine would be all
    But an empty vaunt,
A thing wherein we feel there is some hidden want.   70

What objects are the fountains
    Of thy happy strain?
What fields, or waves, or mountains?
    What shapes of sky or plain?
What love of thine own kind? what ignorance of pain?

With thy clear keen joyance
    Langour cannot be:
Shadow of annoyance
    Never came near thee:
Thou lovest—but ne'er knew love's sad satiety.   80

Waking or asleep,
    Thou of death must deem

Things more true and deep
        Than we mortals dream,
Or how could thy notes flow in such a crystal stream?

We look before and after,
        And pine for what is not:°
Our sincerest laughter
        With some pain is fraught;
Our sweetest songs are those that tell of saddest thought.   90

Yet if we could scorn
        Hate, and pride, and fear;
If we were things born
        Not to shed a tear,
I know not how thy joy we ever should come near.

Better than all measures
        Of delightful sound,
Better than all treasures
        That in books are found,
Thy skill to poet were, thou scorner of the ground!   100

Teach me half the gladness
        That thy brain must know,
Such harmonious madness°
        From my lips would flow,
The world should listen then—as I am listening now.

Ode to Liberty

Yet, Freedom, yet thy banner torn but flying,
Streams like a thunder-storm against the wind.

                                        Byron°

I

A glorious people vibrated again°
        The lightning of the nations: Liberty
From heart to heart, from tower to tower, o'er Spain,
        Scattering contagious fire into the sky,

Gleamed. My soul spurned the chains of its dismay,
    And, in the rapid plumes of song,
    Clothed itself, sublime and strong;
As a young eagle soars the morning clouds among,
  Hovering in verse o'er its accustomed prey;
    Till from its station in the Heaven of fame   10
The Spirit's whirlwind rapt it, and the ray°
    Of the remotest sphere of living flame
Which paves the void was from behind it flung,
  As foam from a ship's swiftness, when there came
  A voice out of the deep: I will record the same.°

2

The Sun and the serenest Moon sprang forth:
  The burning stars of the abyss were hurled
Into the depths of Heaven. The daedal earth,°
  That island in the ocean of the world,
Hung in its cloud of all-sustaining air: 20
    But this divinest universe
    Was yet a chaos and a curse,
For thou wert not: but, power from worst producing worse,°
    The spirit of the beasts was kindled there,
    And of the birds, and of the watery forms,
  And there was war among them, and despair
    Within them, raging without truce or terms:
The bosom of their violated nurse
  Groaned, for beasts warred on beasts, and worms on worms,
  And men on men; each heart was as a hell of storms.   30

3

Man, the imperial shape, then multiplied
  His generations under the pavilion
Of the Sun's throne: palace and pyramid,
  Temple and prison, to many a swarming million,
Were as to mountain-wolves their ragged caves.
    This human living multitude
    Was savage, cunning, blind, and rude,
For thou wert not; but o'er the populous solitude,
  Like one fierce cloud over a waste of waves
    Hung tyranny; beneath, sate deified   40

The sister-pest, congregator of slaves;°
  Into the shadow of her pinions wide°
Anarchs and priests, who feed on gold and blood°
  Till with the stain their inmost souls are dyed,
  Drove the astonished herds of men from every side.

4

The nodding promontories, and blue isles,
  And cloud-like mountains, and dividuous waves°
Of Greece, basked glorious in the open smiles
  Of favouring Heaven: from their enchanted caves
Prophetic echoes flung dim melody   50
      On the unapprehensive wild.
      The vine, the corn, the olive mild,
Grew savage yet, to human use unreconciled;
  And, like unfolded flowers beneath the sea,
    Like the man's thought dark in the infant's brain,
  Like aught that is which wraps what is to be,
    Art's deathless dreams lay veiled by many a vein
Of Parian stone; and, yet a speechless child,°
  Verse murmured, and Philosophy did strain
  Her lidless eyes for thee; when o'er the Aegean main   60

5

Athens arose: a city such as vision
  Builds from the purple crags and silver towers
Of battlemented cloud, as in derision
  Of kingliest masonry: the ocean-floors
Pave it; the evening sky pavilions it;°
      Its portals are inhabited
      By thunder-zonèd winds, each head
Within its cloudy wings with sunfire garlanded—
  A divine work! Athens, diviner yet,
    Gleamed with its crest of columns, on the will   70
  Of man, as on a mount of diamond, set;
    For thou wert, and thine all-creative skill
Peopled, with forms that mock the eternal dead
  In marble immortality, that hill°
  Which was thine earliest throne and latest oracle.

6

Within the surface of Time's fleeting river
  Its wrinkled image lies, as then it lay
Immovably unquiet, and forever
  It trembles, but it cannot pass away!
The voices of its bards and sages thunder   80
          With an earth-awakening blast
          Through the caverns of the past
(Religion veils her eyes; Oppression shrinks aghast);
    A wingèd sound of joy, and love, and wonder,
        Which soars where Expectation never flew,
    Rending the veil of space and time asunder!
        One ocean feeds the clouds, and streams, and dew;
One sun illumines Heaven; one spirit vast
    With life and love makes chaos ever new,
    As Athens doth the world with thy delight renew.   90

7

Then Rome was, and from thy deep bosom fairest,
    Like a wolf-cub from a Cadmaean Maenad,°
She drew the milk of greatness, though thy dearest
    From that Elysian food was yet unweanèd;°
And many a deed of terrible uprightness
          By thy sweet love was sanctified;
          And in thy smile, and by thy side,
Saintly Camillus lived, and firm Atilius died.°
    But when tears stained thy robe of vestal whiteness,
        And gold prophaned thy Capitolian throne,°   100
    Thou didst desert, with spirit-wingèd lightness,
        The senate of the tyrants: they sunk prone,
Slaves of one tyrant: Palatinus sighed
    Faint echoes of Ionian song; that tone°
    Thou didst delay to hear, lamenting to disown.°

8

From what Hyrcanian glen or frozen hill,°
    Or piny promontory of the Arctic main,
Or utmost islet inaccessible,
    Didst thou lament the ruin of thy reign,
Teaching the woods and waves, and desert rocks,   110

And every Naiad's ice-cold urn,
　　To talk in echoes sad and stern,
Of that sublimest lore which man had dared unlearn?
　　For neither didst thou watch the wizard flocks
　　　　Of the Scald's dreams, nor haunt the Druid's sleep.°
　　What if the tears rained through thy scattered locks
　　　　Were quickly dried? for thou didst groan, not weep,
When from its sea of death, to kill and burn,
　　The Galilean serpent forth did creep,°
And made thy world an undistinguishable heap.   120

9

A thousand years the Earth cried, 'Where art thou?'
　　And then the shadow of thy coming fell
On Saxon Alfred's olive-cinctured brow:°
　　And many a warrior-peopled citadel,
Like rocks which fire lifts out of the flat deep,
　　　　Arose in sacred Italy,
　　　　Frowning o'er the tempestuous sea
Of kings, and priests, and slaves, in tower-crowned majesty;
　　That multitudinous anarchy did sweep
　　　　And burst around their walls, like idle foam,
　　Whilst from the human spirit's deepest deep
　　　　Strange melody with love and awe struck dumb
Dissonant arms; and Art, which cannot die,
　　With divine wand traced on our earthly home
　　Fit imagery to pave Heaven's everlasting dome.°

10

Thou huntress swifter than the Moon! thou terror°
　　Of the world's wolves! thou bearer of the quiver,
Whose sunlike shafts pierce tempest-wingèd Error,
　　As light may pierce the clouds when they dissever
In the calm regions of the orient day!   140
　　　　Luther caught thy wakening glance—°
　　　　Like lightning, from his leaden lance
Reflected, it dissolved the visions of the trance
　　In which, as in a tomb, the nations lay;
　　　　And England's prophets hailed thee as their queen,°
　　In songs whose music cannot pass away,
　　　　Though it must flow forever: not unseen

Before the spirit-sighted countenance
  Of Milton didst thou pass, from the sad scene°
  Beyond whose night he saw, with a dejected mien.   150

11

The eager hours and unreluctant years
  As on a dawn-illumined mountain stood,
Trampling to silence their loud hopes and fears,
  Darkening each other with their multitude,
And cried aloud, 'Liberty!' Indignation
      Answered Pity from her cave;
      Death grew pale within the grave,
And Desolation howled to the destroyer, 'Save!'°
  When, like Heaven's sun girt by the exhalation
    Of its own glorious light, thou didst arise,   160
  Chasing thy foes from nation unto nation
    Like shadows: as if day had cloven the skies
At dreaming midnight o'er the western wave,
  Men started, staggering with a glad surprise,
  Under the lightnings of thine unfamiliar eyes.°

12

Thou heaven of earth! what spells could pall thee then
  In ominous eclipse? A thousand years
Bred from the slime of deep oppression's den,
  Dyed all thy liquid light with blood and tears,
Till thy sweet stars could weep the stain away;   170
      How like Bacchanals of blood°
      Round France, the ghastly vintage, stood
Destruction's sceptred slaves, and Folly's mitred brood!°
  When one, like them, but mightier far than they,°
    The Anarch of thine own bewildered powers,
  Rose: armies mingled in obscure array,
    Like clouds with clouds, darkening the sacred bowers
Of serene Heaven. He, by the past pursued,
  Rests with those dead but unforgotten hours,
  Whose ghosts scare victor kings in their ancestral towers.

13

England yet sleeps: was she not called of old?
  Spain calls her now, as with its thrilling thunder

Vesuvius wakens Etna, and the cold°
 Snow-crags by its reply are cloven in sunder:
O'er the lit waves every Aeolian isle
  From Pithecusa to Pelorus°
  Howls, and leaps, and glares in chorus:
They cry, 'Be dim; ye lamps of heaven suspended o'er us.'
 Her chains are threads of gold,—she need but smile°
  And they dissolve; but Spain's were links of steel,   190
 Till bit to dust by virtue's keenest file.
  Twins of a single destiny! appeal
To the eternal years enthroned before us,
 In the dim West; impress, as from a seal,
 All ye have thought and done! Time cannot dare conceal.

14

Tomb of Arminius! render up thy dead,°
 Till, like a standard from a watch-tower's staff,
His soul may stream over the tyrant's head;
 Thy victory shall be his epitaph,
Wild Bacchanal of truth's mysterious wine;   200
  King-deluded Germany,
  His dead spirit lives in thee.
Why do we fear or hope? thou art already free!
 And thou, lost Paradise of this divine°
  And glorious world! thou flowery wilderness!
 Thou island of eternity! thou shrine
  Where desolation, clothed with loveliness,
Worships the thing thou wert! O Italy,
 Gather thy blood into thy heart; repress
 The beasts who make their dens thy sacred palaces.   210

15

O that the free would stamp the impious name
 Of KING into the dust! or write it there,
So that this blot upon the page of fame
 Were as a serpent's path, which the light air
Erases, and the flat sands close behind!
  Ye the oracle have heard:°
  Lift the victory-flashing sword,
And cut the snaky knots of this foul gordian word,°
 Which, weak itself as stubble, yet can bind

Into a mass, irrefragably firm,   220
   The axes and the rods which awe mankind;°
   The sound has poison in it, 'tis the sperm
Of what makes life foul, cankerous, and abhorred;
   Disdain not thou, at thine appointed term,°
   To set thine armèd heel on this reluctant worm.

16

O that the wise from their bright minds would kindle
   Such lamps within the dome of this dim world,
That the pale name of PRIEST might shrink and dwindle
   Into the hell from which it first was hurled,
A scoff of impious pride from fiends impure;   230
      Till human thoughts might kneel alone,
      Each before the judgement-throne
Of its own aweless soul, or of the Power unknown!°
   O that the words which make the thoughts obscure
      From which they spring, as clouds of glimmering dew
From a white lake blot Heaven's blue portraiture,
      Were stripped of their thin masks and various hue
And frowns and smiles and splendours not their own,
   Till in the nakedness of false and true
They stand before their Lord, each to receive its due.   240

17

He who taught man to vanquish whatsoever°
   Can be between the cradle and the grave
Crowned him the King of Life. O vain endeavour!—
   If on his own high will, a willing slave,
He has enthroned the oppression and the oppressor.
      What if earth can clothe and feed
      Amplest millions at their need,
And power in thought be as the tree within the seed?
   Or what if Art, an ardent intercessor,
      Diving on fiery wings to Nature's throne,   250
Checks the great mother stooping to caress her,
      And cries: 'Give me, thy child, dominion°
Over all height and depth'?—if Life can breed
   New wants, and wealth from those who toil and groan
Rend, of thy gifts and hers, a thousandfold for one.°

18

Come Thou, but lead out of the inmost cave
   Of man's deep spirit, as the morning-star
Beckons the Sun from the Eoan wave,°
   Wisdom. I hear the pennons of her car
Self-moving, like cloud charioted by flame;   260
       Comes she not, and come ye not,
       Rulers of eternal thought,
To judge, with solemn truth, life's ill-apportioned lot?
   Blind Love, and equal Justice, and the Fame
     Of what has been, the Hope of what will be?
   O Liberty! if such could be thy name
     Wert thou disjoined from these, or they from thee:
If thine or theirs were treasures to be bought
   By blood or tears, have not the wise and free
   Wept tears, and blood like tears?—The solemn harmony   270

19

Paused, and the Spirit of that mighty singing
   To its abyss was suddenly withdrawn;
Then, as a wild swan, when sublimely winging
   Its path athwart the thunder-smoke of dawn,
Sinks headlong through the aerial golden light
       On the heavy-sounding plain,
       When the bolt has pierced its brain;
As summer clouds dissolve, unburdened of their rain;
   As a far taper fades with fading night,
     As a brief insect dies with dying day,—   280
   My song, its pinions disarrayed of might,
     Drooped; o'er it closed the echoes far away
Of the great voice which did its flight sustain,
   As waves which lately paved his watery way
   Hiss round a drowner's head in their tempestuous play.

Sonnet ('Ye hasten to the grave!')

   Ye hasten to the grave! What seek ye there,°
   Ye restless thoughts and busy purposes

Of the idle brain, which the world's livery wear?
O thou quick Heart, which pantest to possess°
All that pale Expectation feigneth fair!°
Thou vainly curious mind which wouldest guess
Whence thou didst come and whither thou must go,
And all, that never yet was known, wouldst know,
O whither hasten ye, that thus ye press
With such swift feet life's green and pleasant path,   10
Seeking alike from happiness and woe
A refuge in the cavern of grey death?
O Heart and Mind, and Thoughts, what thing do you
Hope to inherit in the grave below?

Song ('*Rarely, rarely comest thou*')

Rarely, rarely comest thou,
   Spirit of Delight!
Wherefore hast thou left me now
   Many a day and night?
Many a weary night and day
'Tis since thou art fled away.

How shall ever one like me
   Win thee back again?
With the joyous and the free
   Thou wilt scoff at pain.   10
Spirit false! thou hast forgot
All but those who need thee not.

As a lizard with the shade
   Of a trembling leaf,
Thou with sorrow art dismayed;
   Even the sighs of grief
Reproach thee, that thou art not near
And reproach thou wilt not hear.

Let me set my mournful ditty
   To a merry measure.   20
Thou wilt never come for pity—
   Thou wilt come for pleasure.

Pity then will cut away
Those cruel wings, and thou wilt stay.—

I love all that thou lovest,
    Spirit of Delight!
The fresh Earth in new leaves dressed,
    And the starry night,
Autumn evening, and the morn
When the golden mists are born.   30

I love snow, and all the forms
    Of the radiant frost;
I love waves and winds and storms—
    Everything almost
Which is nature's and may be
Untainted by man's misery.

I love tranquil solitude,
    And such society
As is quiet, wise and good;
    Between thee and me   40
What difference? but thou dost possess
The things I seek—not love them less.

I love Love—though he has wings
    And like light can flee—
But above all things,
    Spirit, I love thee—
Thou art Love and Life! O come,
Make once more my heart thy home.

Letter to Maria Gisborne

The spider spreads her webs, whether she be°
In poet's tower, cellar, or barn, or tree;
The silkworm in the dark green mulberry leaves
His winding sheet and cradle ever weaves;
So I, a thing whom moralists call worm,°
Sit spinning still round this decaying form,
From the fine threads of verse and subtle thought—°

No net of words in garish colours wrought
To catch the idle buzzers of the day—
But a soft cell, where when that fades away,°   10
Memory may clothe in wings my living name
And feed it with the asphodels of fame,
Which in those hearts that must remember me
Grow, making love an immortality.

Whoever should behold me now, I wist,°
Would think I were a mighty mechanist,°
Bent with sublime Archimedean art°
To breathe a soul into the iron heart
Of some machine portentous, or strange gin,°
Which by the force of figured spells might win°   20
Its way over the sea, and sport therein;°
For round the walls are hung dread engines, such
As Vulcan never wrought for Jove to clutch
Ixion or the Titans:—or the quick°
Wit of that man of God, St Dominic,°
To convince Atheist, Turk, or Heretic,
Or those in philanthropic council met,°
Who thought to pay some interest for the debt
They owed to Jesus Christ for their salvation,
By giving a faint foretaste of damnation   30
To Shakespeare, Sidney, Spenser and the rest
Who made our land an island of the blest,
When lamp-like Spain, who now relumes her fire
On Freedom's hearth, grew dim with Empire—°
With thumbscrews, wheels, with tooth and spike and jag,
Which fishers found under the utmost crag
Of Cornwall and the storm-encompassed isles,°
Where to the sky the rude sea rarely smiles
Unless in treacherous wrath, as on the morn
When the exulting elements in scorn   40
Satiated with destroyed destruction, lay
Sleeping in beauty on their mangled prey,
As panthers sleep;—and other strange and dread
Magical forms the brick floor overspread——
Proteus transformed to metal did not make°
More figures, or more strange; nor did he take
Such shapes of unintelligible brass,

Or heap himself in such a horrid mass
Of tin and iron not to be understood;
And forms of unimaginable wood   50
To puzzle Tubal Cain and all his brood:°
Great screws, and cones, and wheels, and groovèd blocks,
The elements of what will stand the shocks
Of wave and wind and time.—Upon the table
More knacks and quips there be than I am able°
To catalogize in this verse of mine:—°
A pretty bowl of wood, not full of wine,
But quicksilver; that dew which the gnomes drink
When at their subterranean toil they swink,°
Pledging the daemons of the earthquake, who   60
Reply to them in lava, cry halloo!
And call out to the cities o'er their head,—
Roofs, towers and shrines, the dying and the dead,
Crash through the chinks of earth—and then all quaff
Another rouse, and hold their sides and laugh.°
This quicksilver no gnome has drunk—within
The walnut bowl it lies, veinèd and thin,
In colour like the wake of light that stains
The Tuscan deep, when from the moist moon rains
The inmost shower of its white fire—the breeze   70
Is still—blue heaven smiles over the pale seas.
And in this bowl of quicksilver—for I
Yield to the impulse of an infancy
Outlasting manhood—I have made to float
A rude idealism of a paper boat:°
A hollow screw with cogs—Henry will know
The thing I mean and laugh at me—if so
He fears not I should do more mischief—next
Lie bills and calculations much perplexed,
With steamboats, frigates and machinery quaint   80
Traced over them in blue and yellow paint.
Then comes a range of mathematical
Instruments, for plans nautical and statical;°
A heap of rosin, a queer broken glass°
With ink in it, a china cup that was
What it will never be again, I think,
A thing from which sweet lips were wont to drink
The liquor doctors rail at—and which I

Will quaff in spite of them—and when we die
We'll toss up who died first of drinking tea,   90
And cry out, 'Heads or tails?' where'er we be.
Near that a dusty paint box, some odd hooks,
A half-burnt match, an ivory block, three books
Where conic sections, spherics, logarithms,
To great Laplace, from Saunderson and Sims,°
Lie heaped in their harmonious disarray
Of figures—disentangle them who may.
Baron de Tott's Memoirs beside them lie,°
And some odd volumes of old chemistry.
Near those a most inexplicable thing,   100
With lead in the middle—I'm conjecturing
How to make Henry understand—but, no—
I'll leave, as Spenser says, with many mo,°
This secret in the pregnant womb of time,°
Too vast a matter for so weak a rhyme.

And here like some weird Archimage sit I,°
Plotting dark spells and devilish enginery,
The self-impelling steam-wheels of the mind
Which pump up oaths from clergymen, and grind
The gentle spirit of our meek reviews   110
Into a powdery foam of salt abuse,
Ruffling the dull wave of their self-content.
I sit, and smile or sigh as is my bent,
But not for them—Libeccio rushes round°
With an inconstant and an idle sound,
I heed him more than them—the thundersmoke
Is gathering on the mountains, like a cloak
Folded athwart their shoulders broad and bare;
The ripe corn under the undulating air
Undulates like an ocean—and the vines   120
Are trembling wide in all their trellised lines—
The murmur of the awakening sea doth fill
The empty pauses of the blast—the hill
Looks hoary through the white electric rain—
And from the glens beyond, in sullen strain,
The interrupted thunder howls; above
One chasm of heaven smiles, like the eye of love
On the unquiet world—while such things are,

How could one worth your friendship heed this war
Of worms? the shriek of the world's carrion jays,　　　130
Their censure, or their wonder, or their praise?

You are not here . . . the quaint witch Memory sees°
In vacant chairs your absent images,
And points where once you sat, and now should be
But are not.—I demand if ever we
Shall meet as then we met—and she replies,
Veiling in awe her second-sighted eyes;°
'I know the past alone—but summon home
My sister Hope,—she speaks of all to come.'
But I, an old diviner, who know well　　　140
Every false verse of that sweet oracle,
Turned to the sad enchantress once again,°
And sought a respite from my gentle pain
In citing every passage o'er and o'er
Of our communion—how on the seashore
We watched the ocean and the sky together
Under the roof of blue Italian weather;
How I ran home through last year's thunderstorm,
And felt the transverse lightning linger warm°
Upon my cheek—and how we often made　　　150
Feasts for each other, where good will outweighed
The frugal luxury of our country cheer,
As well it might, were it less firm and clear
Than ours must ever be;—and how we spun
A shroud of talk to hide us from the sun
Of this familiar life, which seems to be
But is not,—or is but quaint mockery
Of all we would believe; or sadly blame
The jarring and inexplicable frame
Of this wrong world; and then anatomize　　　160
The purposes and thoughts of men whose eyes
Were closed in distant years—or widely guess
The issue of the earth's great business,
When we shall be as we no longer are—
Like babbling gossips safe, who hear the war
Of winds, and sigh, but tremble not—or how
You listened to some interrupted flow
Of visionary rhyme, in joy and pain°

Struck from the inmost fountains of my brain,
With little skill perhaps—or how we sought   170
Those deepest wells of passion and of thought
Wrought by wise poets in the waste of years,
Staining their sacred waters with our tears,
Quenching a thirst ever to be renewed!
Or how I, wisest lady! then indued°
The language of a land which now is free°
And winged with thoughts of truth and majesty
Flits round the tyrant's sceptre like a cloud,
And bursts the peopled prisons, and cries aloud,
'My name is Legion!'—that majestic tongue°   180
Which Calderon over the desert flung°
Of ages and of nations; and which found
An echo in our hearts, and with the sound
Startled oblivion—thou wert then to me
As is a nurse when inarticulately°
A child would talk as its grown parents do.
If living winds the rapid clouds pursue,
If hawks chase doves through the etherial way,
Huntsmen the innocent deer, and beasts their prey,
Why should not we rouse with the spirit's blast   190
Out of the forest of the pathless past
These recollected pleasures?
                                        You are now
In London, that great sea, whose ebb and flow
At once is deaf and loud, and on the shore
Vomits its wrecks, and still howls on for more.°
Yet in its depth what treasures! You will see
That which was Godwin,—greater none than he
Though fallen—and fallen on evil times—to stand
Among the spirits of our age and land
Before the dread tribunal of *to come*
The foremost—while Rebuke cowers pale and dumb.°   200
You will see Coleridge—he who sits obscure
In the exceeding lustre, and the pure
Intense irradiation of a mind,
Which, with its own internal lightning blind,
Flags wearily through darkness and despair—
A cloud-encircled meteor of the air,
A hooded eagle among blinking owls.——

You will see Hunt, one of those happy souls
Who are the salt of the earth, and without whom°   210
This world would smell like what it is—a tomb;
Who is, what others seem; his room no doubt
Is still adorned by many a cast from Shout,°
With graceful flowers tastefully placed about,
And coronals of bay from ribbons hung,
And brighter wreaths in neat disorder flung;
The gifts of the most learn'd among some dozens
Of female friends, sisters-in-law and cousins.
And there is he with his eternal puns
Which beat the dullest brain for smiles, like duns°   220
Thundering for money at a poet's door;
Alas! it is no use to say, 'I'm poor!'
Or oft in graver mood, when he will look
Things wiser than were ever read in book,
Except in Shakespeare's wisest tenderness.—°
You will see Hogg—and I cannot express
His virtues—though I know that they are great,
Because he locks, then barricades the gate
Within which they inhabit—of his wit
And wisdom, you'll cry out when you are bit.   230
He is a pearl within an oyster shell,
One of the richest of the deep;—and there°
Is English Peacock with his mountain fair
Turned into a Flamingo, that shy bird
That gleams i' the Indian air—have you not heard
When a man marries, dies, or turns Hindoo,
His best friends hear no more of him?—but you
Will see him, and will like him too, I hope,
With the milk-white Snowdonian antelope
Matched with this camelopard—his fine wit°   240
Makes such a wound, the knife is lost in it;
A strain too learned for a shallow age,
Too wise for selfish bigots; let his page
Which charms the chosen spirits of the time,
Fold itself up for the serener clime
Of years to come, and find its recompense
In that just expectation.—Wit and sense,°
Virtue and human knowledge, all that might
Make this dull world a business of delight,

Are all combined in Horace Smith.—And these,°   250
With some exceptions which I need not tease
Your patience by descanting on, are all
You and I know in London.
                     I recall
My thoughts, and bid you look upon the night.
As water does a sponge, so the moonlight
Fills the void, hollow, universal air—
What see you?—unpavilioned heaven is fair
Whether the moon, into her chamber gone,
Leaves midnight to the golden stars, or wan
Climbs with diminished beams the azure steep;   260
Or whether clouds sail o'er the inverse deep,
Piloted by the many-wandering blast,
And the rare stars rush through them dim and fast:—
All this is beautiful in every land.—
But what see you beside?—a shabby stand
Of Hackney coaches—a brick house or wall°
Fencing some lordly court, white with the scrawl°
Of our unhappy politics, or worse—
A wretched woman reeling by, whose curse
Mixed with the watchman's, partner of her trade,   270
You must accept in place of serenade—
Or yellow-haired Pollonia murmuring°
To Henry some unutterable thing.°
I see a chaos of green leaves and fruit
Built round dark caverns, even to the root
Of the living stems that feed them—in whose bowers
There sleep in their dark dew the folded flowers;
Beyond, the surface of the unsickled corn
Trembles not in the slumbering air, and borne
In circles quaint, and ever-changing dance,   280
Like wingèd stars the fire-flies flash and glance,
Pale in the open moonshine, but each one
Under the dark trees seems a little sun,
A meteor tamed, a fixed star gone astray
From the silver regions of the milky way;—
Afar the contadino's song is heard,°
Rude, but made sweet by distance—and a bird
Which cannot be the nightingale, and yet
I know none else that sings so sweet as it

At this late hour—and then all is still——   290
Now Italy or London, which you will!

Next winter you must pass with me; I'll have
My house by that time turned into a grave
Of dead despondence and low-thoughted care,°
And all the dreams which our tormentors are;
Oh! that Hunt, Hogg, Peacock and Smith were there,
With everything belonging to them fair!
We will have books, Spanish, Italian, Greek;
And ask one week to make another week
As like his father, as I'm unlike mine,   300
Which is not his fault, as you may divine.
Though we eat little flesh and drink no wine,
Yet let's be merry: we'll have tea and toast,
Custards for supper, and an endless host
Of syllabubs and jellies and mince-pies,°
And other such lady-like luxuries—
Feasting on which we will philosophize!
And we'll have fires out of the Grand Duke's wood°
To thaw the six weeks' winter in our blood.
And then we'll talk—what shall we talk about?   310
Oh! there are themes enough for many a bout
Of thought-entangled descant;—as to nerves,
With cones and parallelograms and curves
I've sworn to strangle them if once they dare
To bother me—when you are with me there—
And they shall never more sip laudanum,°
From Helicon or Himeros;—well, come,°
And in despite of God and of the devil,
We'll make our friendly philosophic revel
Outlast the leafless time—till buds and flowers   320
Warn the obscure inevitable hours
Sweet meeting by sad parting to renew—
'Tomorrow to fresh woods and pastures new.'°

To —— (*Lines to a Reviewer*)

Alas, good friend, what profit can you see
In hating such a hateless thing as me?

There is no sport in hate when all the rage
Is on one side. In vain would you assuage
Your frowns upon an unresisting smile
In which not even contempt lurks to beguile
Your heart, by some faint sympathy of hate.
O conquer what you cannot satiate!
For to your passion I am far more coy
Than ever yet was coldest maid or boy   10
In winter noon. Of your antipathy,
If I am the Narcissus, you are free,°
To pine into a sound with hating me.

To —— (*Lines to a Critic*)

1

Honey from silkworms who can gather,
   Or silk from the yellow bee?
The grass may grow in winter weather
   As soon as hate in me.

2

Hate men who cant, and men who pray,
   And men who rail, like thee;
An equal passion to repay
   They are not coy—like me.—

3

Or seek some slave of power and gold,
   To be thy dear heart's mate—   10
Thy love will move that bigot cold
   Sooner than me, thy hate.

4

A passion like the one I prove°
   Cannot divided be—
I hate thy want of truth and love—
   How should I then hate thee?

THE WITCH OF ATLAS

To Mary

(ON HER OBJECTING TO THE FOLLOWING POEM,
UPON THE SCORE OF ITS CONTAINING
NO HUMAN INTEREST)°

1

How, my dear Mary, are you critic-bitten
   (For vipers kill, though dead) by some review,
That you condemn these verses I have written
   Because they tell no story, false or true?
What, though no mice are caught by a young kitten,
   May it not leap and play as grown cats do,
Till its claws come? Prithee, for this one time,
Content thee with a visionary rhyme.

2

What hand would crush the silken-wingèd fly,°
   The youngest of inconstant April's minions,   10
Because it cannot climb the purest sky
   Where the swan sings, amid the sun's dominions?°
Not thine. Thou knowest 'tis its doom to die
   When day shall hide within her twilight pinions
The lucent eyes, and the eternal smile,
Serene as thine, which lent it life awhile.

3

To thy fair feet a wingèd Vision came°
   Whose date should have been longer than a day,
And o'er thy head did beat its wings for fame,
   And in thy sight its fading plumes display;   20
The watery bow burned in the evening flame,
   But the shower fell, the swift Sun went his way—
And that is dead.—O, let me not believe
That anything of mine is fit to live!

4

Wordsworth informs us he was nineteen years
   Considering and retouching Peter Bell;°
Watering his laurels with the killing tears
   Of slow, dull care, so that their roots to hell
Might pierce, and their wide branches blot the spheres
   Of Heaven, with dewy leaves and flowers; this well   30
May be, for Heaven and Earth conspire to foil
The over-busy gardener's blundering toil.

5

My Witch indeed is not so sweet a creature
   As Ruth or Lucy, whom his graceful praise°
Clothes for our grandsons—but she matches Peter,
   Though he took nineteen years, and she three days
In dressing. Light the vest of flowing metre
   She wears; he, proud as dandy with his stays,
Has hung upon his wiry limbs a dress
Like King Lear's 'looped and windowed raggedness.'°   40

6

If you strip Peter, you will see a fellow,
   Scorched by Hell's hyperequatorial climate°
Into a kind of a sulphureous yellow:
   A lean mark, hardly fit to fling a rhyme at;
In shape a Scaramouch, in hue Othello.°
   If you unveil my Witch, no Priest or Primate°
Can shrive you of that sin, if sin there be°
In love, when it becomes idolatry.

1

Before those cruel Twins, whom at one birth°
   Incestuous Change bore to her father Time,   50
Error and Truth, had hunted from the earth
   All those bright natures which adorned its prime,
And left us nothing to believe in, worth
   The pains of putting into learned rhyme,
A lady-witch there lived on Atlas' mountain°
Within a cavern, by a secret fountain.°

2

Her mother was one of the Atlantides:°
    The all-beholding Sun had ne'er beholden
In his wide voyage o'er continents and seas
    So fair a creature, as she lay enfolden   60
In the warm shadow of her loveliness;—
    He kissed her with his beams, and made all golden
The chamber of grey rock in which she lay—
She, in that dream of joy, dissolved away.°

3

'Tis said, she first was changed into a vapour,
    And then into a cloud, such clouds as flit,
Like splendour-wingèd moths about a taper,
    Round the red west when the sun dies in it:
And then into a meteor, such as caper
    On hill-tops when the moon is in a fit:°   70
Then, into one of those mysterious stars
Which hide themselves between the Earth and Mars.

4

Ten times the Mother of the Months had bent°
    Her bow beside the folding-star, and bidden,°
With that bright sign the billows to indent
    The sea-deserted sand—like children chidden,
At her command they ever came and went—
    Since in that cave a dewy splendour hidden
Took shape and motion: with the living form
Of this embodied Power, the cave grew warm.   80

5

A lovely lady garmented in light
    From her own beauty—deep her eyes, as are
Two openings of unfathomable night
    Seen through a Temple's cloven roof—her hair
Dark—the dim brain whirls dizzy with delight,
    Picturing her form; her soft smiles shone afar,
And her low voice was heard like love, and drew
All living things towards this wonder new.

6

And first the spotted camelopard came,°
   And then the wise and fearless elephant;   90
Then the sly serpent, in the golden flame
   Of his own volumes intervolved;—all gaunt
And sanguine beasts her gentle looks made tame.
   They drank before her at her sacred fount;
And every beast of beating heart grew bold,
Such gentleness and power even to behold.

7

The brinded lioness led forth her young,°
   That she might teach them how they should forgo
Their inborn thirst of death; the pard unstrung°
   His sinews at her feet, and sought to know   100
With looks whose motions spoke without a tongue
   How he might be as gentle as the doe.
The magic circle of her voice and eyes
All savage natures did imparadise.

8

And old Silenus, shaking a green stick°
   Of lilies, and the wood-gods in a crew°
Came, blithe, as in the olive copses thick
   Cicadae are, drunk with the noonday dew:°
And Driope and Faunus followed quick,°
   Teasing the God to sing them something new,   110
Till in this cave they found the lady lone,
Sitting upon a seat of emerald stone.

9

And Universal Pan, 'tis said, was there,°
   And though none saw him,—through the adamant
Of the deep mountains, through the trackless air,
   And through those living spirits, like a want°
He passed out of his everlasting lair
   Where the quick heart of the great world doth pant,
And felt that wondrous lady all alone—
And she felt him upon her emerald throne.   120

10

And every nymph of stream and spreading tree,
  And every shepherdess of Ocean's flocks,
Who drives her white waves over the green sea;
  And Ocean, with the brine on his grey locks,
And quaint Priapus with his company°
  All came, much wondering how the enwombèd rocks
Could have brought forth so beautiful a birth;—
Her love subdued their wonder and their mirth.

11

The herdsmen and the mountain maidens came,
  And the rude kings of pastoral Garamant—°   130
These spirits shook within them, as a flame
  Stirred by the air under a cavern gaunt:
Pigmies, and Polyphemes, by many a name,°
  Centaurs and Satyrs, and such shapes as haunt°
Wet clefts,—and lumps neither alive nor dead,
Dog-headed, bosom-eyed and bird-footed.°

12

For she was beautiful—her beauty made
  The bright world dim, and everything beside
Seemed like the fleeting image of a shade:
  No thought of living spirit could abide,   140
Which to her looks had ever been betrayed,
  On any object in the world so wide,
On any hope within the circling skies,
But on her form, and in her inmost eyes.

13

Which when the lady knew, she took her spindle
  And twined three threads of fleecy mist, and three
Long lines of light, such as the dawn may kindle°
  The clouds and waves and mountains with, and she
As many star-beams, ere their lamps could dwindle
  In the belated moon, wound skilfully;°   150
And with these threads a subtle veil she wove—
A shadow for the splendour of her love.

14

The deep recesses of her odorous dwelling
   Were stored with magic treasures—sounds of air,
Which had the power all spirits of compelling,
   Folded in cells of crystal silence there;°
Such as we hear in youth, and think the feeling
   Will never die—yet ere we are aware,
The feeling and the sound are fled and gone,
And the regret they leave remains alone.   160

15

And there lay Visions swift, and sweet, and quaint,
   Each in its thin sheath like a chrysalis;
Some eager to burst forth, some weak and faint
   With the soft burden of intensest bliss;
It was its work to bear to many a saint
   Whose heart adores the shrine which holiest is,
Even Love's—and others white, green, grey and black,
And of all shapes—and each was at her beck.

16

And odours in a kind of aviary°
   Of ever-blooming Eden-trees she kept,   170
Clipped in a floating net, a love-sick Fairy
   Had woven from dew-beams while the moon yet slept;
As bats at the wired window of a dairy,
   They beat their vans; and each was an adept,°
When loosed and missioned, making wings of winds,
To stir sweet thoughts or sad in destined minds.

17

And liquors clear and sweet, whose healthful might
   Could medicine the sick soul to happy sleep,
And change eternal death into a night
   Of glorious dreams—or if eyes needs must weep,   180
Could make their tears all wonder and delight—
   She in her crystal vials did closely keep:
If men could drink of those clear vials, 'tis said
The living were not envied of the dead.

18

Her cave was stored with scrolls of strange device,
   The works of some Saturnian Archimage,
Which taught the expiations at whose price
   Men from the Gods might win that happy age
Too lightly lost, redeeming native vice;
   And which might quench the earth-consuming rage   190
Of gold and blood—till men should live and move
Harmonious as the sacred stars above.°

19

And how all things that seem untameable,
   Not to be checked and not to be confined,
Obey the spells of wisdom's wizard skill;°
   Time, Earth and Fire—the Ocean and the Wind,
And all their shapes—and man's imperial will;
   And other scrolls whose writings did unbind
The inmost lore of Love—let the profane
Tremble to ask what secrets they contain.

20

And wondrous works of substances unknown,
   To which the enchantment of her father's power
Had changed those ragged blocks of savage stone,
   Were heaped in the recesses of her bower;
Carved lamps and chalices, and phials which shone
   In their own golden beams—each like a flower,
Out of whose depth a fire-fly shakes his light
Under a cypress in a starless night.

21

At first she lived alone in this wild home,
   And her own thoughts were each a minister,   210
Clothing themselves or with the ocean-foam,
   Or with the wind, or with the speed of fire,
To work whatever purposes might come
   Into her mind; such power her mighty Sire
Had girt them with, whether to fly or run,
Through all the regions which he shines upon.

22

The Ocean-nymphs and Hamadryades,°
    Oreads and Naiads with long weedy locks,°
Offered to do her bidding through the seas,
    Under the earth, and in the hollow rocks,°   220
And far beneath the matted roots of trees,
    And in the gnarlèd heart of stubborn oaks,
So they might live forever in the light
Of her sweet presence—each a satellite.

23

'This may not be,' the wizard maid replied;
    'The fountains where the Naiades bedew°
Their shining hair, at length are drained and dried;
    The solid oaks forget their strength, and strew
Their latest leaf upon the mountains wide;
    The boundless ocean like a drop of dew   230
Will be consumed—the stubborn centre must
Be scattered, like a cloud of summer dust.°

24

'And ye with them will perish one by one:
    If I must sigh to think that this shall be,
If I must weep when the surviving Sun
    Shall smile on your decay—Oh, ask not me
To love you till your little race is run;
    I cannot die as ye must—over me
Your leaves shall glance—the streams in which ye dwell
Shall be my paths henceforth, and so, farewell!'   240

25

She spoke and wept: the dark and azure well
    Sparkled beneath the shower of her bright tears,
And every little circlet where they fell,
    Flung to the cavern-roof inconstant spheres
And intertangled lines of light:—a knell
    Of sobbing voices came upon her ears
From those departing Forms, o'er the serene
Of the white streams and of the forest green.

26

All day the wizard lady sat aloof,
  Spelling out scrolls of dread antiquity,   250
Under the cavern's fountain-lighted roof;
  Or broidering the pictured poesy
Of some high tale upon her growing woof,°
  Which the sweet splendour of her smiles could dye
In hues outshining heaven—and ever she
Added some grace to the wrought poesy.

27

While on her hearth lay blazing many a piece
  Of sandalwood, rare gums and cinnamon;
Men scarcely know how beautiful fire is—
  Each flame of it is as a precious stone   260
Dissolved in ever-moving light, and this
  Belongs to each and all who gaze upon.
The Witch beheld it not, for in her hand
She held a woof that dimmed the burning brand.

28

This lady never slept, but lay in trance
  All night within the fountain—as in sleep.
Its emerald crags glowed in her beauty's glance:
  Through the green splendour of the water deep
She saw the constellations reel and dance
  Like fire-flies—and withal did ever keep°   270
The tenour of her contemplations calm,°
With open eyes, closed feet and folded palm.

29

And when the whirlwinds and the clouds descended
  From the white pinnacles of that cold hill,
She passed at dewfall to a space extended,
  Where in a lawn of flowering asphodel°
Amid a wood of pines and cedars blended,
  There yawned an inextinguishable well
Of crimson fire, full even to the brim
And overflowing all the margin trim.   280

30

Within the which she lay when the fierce war
　Of wintry winds shook that innocuous liquor
In many a mimic moon and bearded star°
　O'er woods and lawns—the serpent heard it flicker
In sleep, and dreaming still, he crept afar—
　And when the windless snow descended thicker
Than autumn leaves, she watched it as it came
Melt on the surface of the level flame.

31

She had a Boat which some say Vulcan wrought°
　For Venus, as the chariot of her star;　　　　　　　　290
But it was found too feeble to be fraught
　With all the ardours in that sphere which are,°
And so she sold it, and Apollo bought,
　And gave it to this daughter: from a car
Changed to the fairest and the lightest boat
Which ever upon mortal stream did float.

32

And others say, that when but three hours old,
　The first-born Love out of his cradle leapt,
And clove dun Chaos with his wings of gold,
　And like an horticultural adept,　　　　　　　　　　300
Stole a strange seed, and wrapped it up in mould,
　And sowed it in his mother's star, and kept
Watering it all the summer with sweet dew,
And with his wings fanning it as it grew.

33

The plant grew strong and green—the snowy flower
　Fell, and the long and gourd-like fruit began
To turn the light and dew by inward power
　To its own substance; woven tracery ran
Of light firm texture, ribbed and branching, o'er
　The solid rind, like a leaf's veinèd fan,　　　　　　310
Of which Love scooped this boat, and with soft motion
Piloted it round the circumfluous ocean.°

34

This boat she moored upon her fount, and lit
   A living spirit within all its frame,
Breathing the soul of swiftness into it.
   Couched on the fountain like a panther tame,
One of the twain at Evan's feet that sit;°
   Or as on Vesta's sceptre a swift flame,°
Or on blind Homer's heart a wingèd thought—
In joyous expectation lay the boat.   320

35

Then by strange art she kneaded fire and snow
   Together, tempering the repugnant mass
With liquid love—all things together grow°
   Through which the harmony of love can pass;
And a fair Shape out of her hands did flow—
   A living Image, which did far surpass
In beauty that bright shape of vital stone
Which drew the heart out of Pygmalion.°

36

A sexless thing it was, and in its growth
   It seemed to have developed no defect   330
Of either sex, yet all the grace of both—°
   In gentleness and strength its limbs were decked;
The bosom swelled lightly with its full youth—
   The countenance was such as might select
Some artist that his skill should never die,
Imaging forth such perfect purity.

37

From its smooth shoulders hung two rapid wings,
   Fit to have borne it to the seventh sphere,°
Tipped with the speed of liquid lightnings,°
   Dyed in the ardours of the atmosphere: 340
She led her creature to the boiling springs
   Where the light boat was moored, and said—'Sit here!'
And pointed to the prow, and took her seat
Beside the rudder with opposing feet.

38

And down the streams which clove those mountains vast°
    Around their inland islets, and amid
The panther-peopled forests, whose shade cast
    Darkness and odours, and a pleasure hid
In melancholy gloom, the pinnace passed;°
    By many a star-surrounded pyramid   350
Of icy crag cleaving the purple sky,
And caverns yawning round unfathomably.

39

The silver noon into that winding dell,
    With slanted gleam athwart the forest tops,
Tempered like golden evening, feebly fell;
    A green and glowing light, like that which drops
From folded lilies in which glow-worms dwell,
    When earth over her face night's mantle wraps;
Between the severed mountains lay on high
Over the stream, a narrow rift of sky.   360

40

And ever as she went, the Image lay
    With folded wings and unawakened eyes;
And o'er its gentle countenance did play
    The busy dreams, as thick as summer flies,
Chasing the rapid smiles that would not stay,
    And drinking the warm tears, and the sweet sighs
Inhaling, which, with busy murmur vain,
They had aroused from that full heart and brain.

41

And ever down the prone vale, like a cloud°
    Upon a stream of wind, the pinnace went: 370
Now lingering on the pools, in which abode
    The calm and darkness of the deep content
In which they paused; now o'er the shallow road
    Of white and dancing waters all besprent°
With sand and polished pebbles:—mortal boat
In such a shallow rapid could not float.

42

And down the earthquaking cataracts which shiver°
   Their snow-like waters into golden air,
Or under chasms unfathomable ever
   Sepulchre them, till in their rage they tear   380
A subterranean portal for the river,
   It fled—the circling sunbows did upbear°
Its fall down the hoar precipice of spray,
Lighting it far upon its lampless way.

43

And when the wizard lady would ascend
   The labyrinths of some many-winding vale,
Which to the inmost mountain upward tend—
   She called 'Hermaphroditus!' and the pale
And heavy hue which slumber could extend
   Over its lips and eyes, as on the gale   390
A rapid shadow from a slope of grass,
Into the darkness of the stream did pass.

44

And it unfurled its heaven-coloured pinions,
   With stars of fire spotting the stream below;
And from above into the Sun's dominions
   Flinging a glory, like the golden glow
In which Spring clothes her emerald-wingèd minions,
   All interwoven with fine feathery snow
And moonlight splendour of intensest rime,°
With which frost paints the pines in winter time.   400

45

And then it winnowed the Elysian air
   Which ever hung about that lady bright,
With its ethereal vans—and speeding there,
   Like a star up the torrent of the night,
Or a swift eagle in the morning glare
   Breasting the whirlwind with impetuous flight,
The pinnace, oared by those enchanted wings,
Clove the fierce streams towards their upper springs.

46

The water flashed like sunlight by the prow
   Of a noon-wandering meteor flung to Heaven;   410
The still air seemed as if its waves did flow
   In tempest down the mountains—loosely driven
The lady's radiant hair streamed to and fro:
   Beneath, the billows having vainly striven
Indignant and impetuous, roared to feel
The swift and steady motion of the keel.

47

Or, when the weary moon was in the wane,
   Or in the noon of interlunar night,
The lady-witch in visions could not chain
   Her spirit; but sailed forth under the light   420
Of shooting stars, and bade extend amain°
   Its storm-outspeeding wings, th' Hermaphrodite;
She to the Austral waters took her way,°
Beyond the fabulous Thamondocana,°

48

Where, like a meadow which no scythe has shaven,
   Which rain could never bend, or whirl-blast shake
With the Antarctic constellations paven,
   Canopus and his crew, lay th' Austral lake—°
There she would build herself a windless haven
   Out of the clouds whose moving turrets make   430
The bastions of the storm, when through the sky
The spirits of the tempest thundered by.

49

A haven beneath whose translucent floor
   The tremulous stars sparkled unfathomably,
And around which, the solid vapours hoar,
   Based on the level waters, to the sky
Lifted their dreadful crags; and like a shore
   Of wintry mountains, inaccessibly
Hemmed in with rifts and precipices grey,
   And hanging crags, many a cove and bay.   440

50

And whilst the outer lake, beneath the lash
  Of the wind's scourge, foamed like a wounded thing,
And the incessant hail with stony clash
  Ploughed up the waters, and the flagging wing
Of the roused cormorant in the lightning flash
  Looked like the wreck of some wind-wandering
Fragment of inky thundersmoke—this haven
Was as a gem to copy Heaven engraven.

51

On which that lady played her many pranks,
  Circling the image of a shooting star,   450
Even as a tiger on Hydaspes' banks°
  Outspeeds the antelopes which speediest are,
In her light boat; and many quips and cranks°
  She played upon the water, till the car
Of the late moon, like a sick matron wan,
To journey from the misty east began.

52

And then she called out of the hollow turrets
  Of those high clouds, white, golden and vermilion,
The armies of her ministering spirits—
  In mighty legions million after million   460
They came, each troop emblazoning its merits
  On meteor flags; and many a proud pavilion°
Of the intertexture of the atmosphere
They pitched upon the plain of the calm mere.°

53

They framed the imperial tent of their great Queen
  Of woven exhalations, underlaid°
With lambent lightning-fire, as may be seen°
  A dome of thin and open ivory inlaid
With crimson silk—cressets from the serene°
  Hung there, and on the water for her tread   470
A tapestry of fleece-like mist was strewn,
Dyed in the beams of the ascending moon.

54

And on a throne o'erlaid with starlight, caught
   Upon those wandering isles of aery dew,
Which highest shoals of mountain shipwreck not,
   She sate, and heard all that had happened new
Between the earth and moon, since they had brought
   The last intelligence—and now she grew
Pale as that moon lost in the watery night—
   And now she wept, and now she laughed outright.   480

55

These were tame pleasures.—She would often climb
   The steepest ladder of the crudded rack°
Up to some beakèd cape of cloud sublime,
   And like Arion on the dolphin's back°
Ride singing through the shoreless air. Oft time
   Following the serpent lightning's winding track,
She ran upon the platforms of the wind,
And laughed to hear the fire-balls roar behind.°

56

And sometimes to those streams of upper air,
   Which whirl the earth in its diurnal round,   490
She would ascend, and win the spirits there
   To let her join their chorus. Mortals found
That on those days the sky was calm and fair,
   And mystic snatches of harmonious sound
Wandered upon the earth where'er she passed,
And happy thoughts of hope, too sweet to last.

57

But her choice sport was, in the hours of sleep,
   To glide adown old Nilus, where he threads°
Egypt and Ethiopia, from the steep
   Of utmost Axumè, until he spreads,°   500
Like a calm flock of silver-fleecèd sheep,
   His waters on the plain: and crested heads
Of cities and proud temples gleam amid
And many a vapour-belted pyramid.

58

By Moeris and the Mareotid lakes,°
   Strewn with faint blooms like bridal chamber floors,
Where naked boys bridling tame water-snakes,
   Or charioteering ghastly alligators,
Had left on the sweet waters mighty wakes
   Of those huge forms—within the brazen doors   510
Of the great Labyrinth slept both boy and beast,°
Tired with the pomp of their Osirian feast.°

59

And where within the surface of the river
   The shadows of the massy temples lie,
And never are erased—but tremble ever°
   Like things which every cloud can doom to die,
Through lotus-pav'n canals, and wheresoever
   The works of man pierced that serenest sky
With tombs, and towers, and fanes, 'twas her delight°
To wander in the shadow of the night.   520

60

With motion like the spirit of that wind
   Whose soft step deepens slumber, her light feet
Passed through the peopled haunts of human kind,
   Scattering sweet visions from her presence sweet,
Through fane and palace-court and labyrinth mined
   With many a dark and subterranean street
Under the Nile; through chambers high and deep
She passed, observing mortals in their sleep.

61

A pleasure sweet doubtless it was to see
   Mortals subdued in all the shapes of sleep.   530
Here lay two sister-twins in infancy;
   There, a lone youth who in his dreams did weep;
Within, two lovers linked innocently
   In their loose locks which over both did creep
Like ivy from one stem—and there lay calm
Old age with snow-bright hair and folded palm.

62

But other troubled forms of sleep she saw,
    Not to be mirrored in a holy song—
Distortions foul of supernatural awe,
    And pale imaginings of visioned wrong,   540
And all the code of custom's lawless law
    Written upon the brows of old and young:
    'This,' said the wizard maiden, 'is the strife
Which stirs the liquid surface of man's life.'

63

And little did the sight disturb her soul—
    We, the weak mariners of that wide lake
Where'er its shores extend or billows roll,
    Our course unpiloted and starless make
O'er its wild surface to an unknown goal—
    But she in the calm depths her way could take,   550
Where in bright bowers immortal forms abide,
Beneath the weltering of the restless tide.°

64

And she saw princes couched under the glow
    Of sunlike gems: and round each temple-court
In dormitories ranged, row after row,
    She saw the priests asleep—all of one sort,
For all were educated to be so.—
    The peasants in their huts, and in the port
The sailors she saw cradled on the waves,
And the dead lulled within their dreamless graves.   560

65

And all the forms in which those spirits lay
    Were to her sight like the diaphanous
Veils, in which those sweet ladies oft array
    Their delicate limbs, who would conceal from us
Only their scorn of all concealment: they
    Move in the light of their own beauty thus.
But these and all now lay with sleep upon them,
And little thought a Witch was looking on them.

66

She all those human figures breathing there
    Beheld as living spirits—to her eyes   570
The naked beauty of the soul lay bare,
    And often through a rude and worn disguise
She saw the inner form most bright and fair—
    And then, she had a charm of strange device,
Which murmured on mute lips with tender tone,
Could make that spirit mingle with her own.

67

Alas, Aurora! what wouldst thou have given
    For such a charm when Tithon became grey?°
Or how much, Venus, of thy silver Heaven
    Wouldst thou have yielded, ere Proserpina   580
Had half (oh! why not all?) the debt forgiven
    Which dear Adonis had been doomed to pay,°
To any witch who would have taught you it?
The Heliad doth not know its value yet.°

68

'Tis said in after times her spirit free
    Knew what love was, and felt itself alone—
But holy Dian could not chaster be
    Before she stooped to kiss Endymion,°
Than now this lady—like a sexless bee
    Tasting all blossoms, and confined to none—   590
Among those mortal forms, the wizard-maiden
Passed with an eye serene and heart unladen.

69

To those she saw most beautiful, she gave
    Strange panacea in a crystal bowl.
They drank in their deep sleep of that sweet wave,
    And lived thenceforward as if some control,
Mightier than life, were in them; and the grave
    Of such, when death oppressed the weary soul,
Was as a green and overarching bower
Lit by the gems of many a starry flower.   600

70

For on the night that they were buried, she
    Restored the embalmer's ruining, and shook
The light out of the funeral lamps, to be°
    A mimic day within that deathy nook;
And she unwound the woven imagery
    Of second childhood's swaddling bands, and took
The coffin, its last cradle, from its niche,
And threw it with contempt into a ditch.

71

And there the body lay, age after age,
    Mute, breathing, beating, warm, and undecaying   610
Like one asleep in a green hermitage,
    With gentle smiles about its eyelids playing,
And living in its dreams beyond the rage
    Of death or life; while they were still arraying
In liveries ever new the rapid, blind
And fleeting generations of mankind.

72

And she would write strange dreams upon the brain
    Of those who were less beautiful, and make
All harsh and crooked purposes more vain
    Than in the desert is the serpent's wake   620
Which the sand covers—all his evil gain
    The miser in such dreams would rise and shake
Into a beggar's lap;—the lying scribe
Would his own lies betray without a bribe.

73

The priests would write an explanation full,
    Translating hieroglyphics into Greek,°
How the god Apis really was a bull,°
    And nothing more; and bid the herald stick
The same against the temple doors, and pull
    The old cant down; they licensed all to speak   630
Whate'er they thought of hawks, and cats, and geese,°
By pastoral letters to each diocese.

74

The king would dress an ape up in his crown
   And robes, and seat him on his glorious seat,
And on the right hand of the sunlike throne
   Would place a gaudy mock-bird to repeat
The chatterings of the monkey.—Every one
   Of the prone courtiers crawled to kiss the feet
Of their great Emperor when the morning came;
And kissed—alas, how many kiss the same!°   640

75

The soldiers dreamed that they were blacksmiths, and
   Walked out of quarters in somnambulism;°
Round the red anvils you might see them stand
   Like Cyclopses in Vulcan's sooty abysm,°
Beating their swords to ploughshares—in a band°
   The jailors sent those of the liberal schism
Free through the streets of Memphis; much, I wis,°
To the annoyance of king Amasis.°

76

And timid lovers who had been so coy
   They hardly knew whether they loved or not,   650
Would rise out of their rest, and take sweet joy,
   To the fulfilment of their inmost thought;
And when next day the maiden and the boy
   Met one another, both, like sinners caught,
Blushed at the thing which each believed was done
Only in fancy—till the tenth moon shone;

77

And then the Witch would let them take no ill:
   Of many thousand schemes which lovers find
The Witch found one,—and so they took their fill
   Of happiness in marriage warm and kind.   660
Friends who by practice of some envious skill
   Were torn apart, a wide wound, mind from mind!
She did unite again with visions clear
Of deep affection and of truth sincere.

78

These were the pranks she played among the cities
   Of mortal men, and what she did to sprites
And Gods, entangling them in her sweet ditties
   To do her will, and show their subtle slights,
I will declare another time; for it is
   A tale more fit for the weird winter nights°   670
Than for these garish summer days, when we°
Scarcely believe much more than we can see.

Song of Apollo

The sleepless Hours who watch me as I lie
   Curtained with star-enwoven tapestries
From the broad moonlight of the sky,
   Fanning the busy dreams from my dim eyes,
Waken me when their mother, the grey Dawn,
Tells them that Dreams and that the moon is gone.

Then I arise; and climbing Heaven's blue dome,
   I walk over the mountains and the waves,
Leaving my robe upon the Ocean foam.
   My footsteps pave the clouds with fire; the caves   10
Are filled with my bright presence, and the air
Leaves the green earth to my embraces bare.

The sunbeams are my shafts with which I kill
   Deceit, that loves the night and fears the day.
All men who do, or even imagine ill
   Fly me; and from the glory of my ray
Good minds and open actions take new might
Until diminished by the reign of night.

I feed the clouds, the rainbows and the flowers
   With their etherial colours; the moon's globe   20
And the pure stars in their eternal bowers
   Are cinctured with my power as with a robe;°
Whatever lamps on Earth or Heaven may shine
Are portions of one spirit; which is mine.

I stand at noon upon the peak of Heaven;
   Then with unwilling steps, I wander down
Into the clouds of the Atlantic even;
   For grief that I depart they weep and frown—
What look is more delightful, than the smile
With which I soothe them from the Western isle?   30

I am the eye with which the Universe
   Beholds itself, and knows it is divine;
All harmony of instrument and verse,

All prophecy and medicine are mine;
All light of art or nature;—to my song
Victory and praise, in its own right, belong.°

Song of Pan

From the forests and highlands
  We come, we come,
From the river-girt islands
  Where loud waves were dumb
Listening my sweet pipings.
      The wind in the reeds and the rushes,
      The bees in the bells of thyme,
      The birds on the myrtle bushes,
      The cicadae above in the lime,
        And the lizards below in the grass,   10
Were silent as even old Tmolus was,°
      Listening my sweet pipings.

Liquid Peneus was flowing—°
  And all dark Tempe lay
In Pelion's shadow, outgrowing°
  The light of the dying day,
  Speeded with my sweet pipings.
      The sileni and sylvans and fauns
      And the nymphs of the woods and the waves
      To the edge of the moist river-lawns   20
      And the brink of the dewy caves,
        And all that did then attend and follow,
Were as silent for love, as you now, Apollo,
      For envy of my sweet pipings.

I sang of the dancing stars,
  I sang of the daedal Earth,
And of Heaven, and the giant wars,°
  And Love, and Death, and Birth
      And then I changed my pipings,
      Singing how down the vales of Maenalus°   30
      I pursued a maiden and clasped a reed.°

    Gods and men, we are all deluded thus!—
    It breaks on our bosom and then we bleed;
        They wept as, I think, both ye now would,°
If envy or age had not frozen your blood,
        At the sorrow of my sweet pipings.

Sonnet: Political Greatness

Nor happiness, nor majesty nor fame,°
Nor peace nor strength, nor skill in arms or arts
Shepherd those herds whom Tyranny makes tame.
Verse echoes not one beating of their hearts;
History is but the shadow of their shame;
Art veils her glass, or from the pageant starts
As to oblivion their blind millions fleet,°
Staining that Heaven with obscene imagery
Of their own likeness. What are numbers, knit
By force or custom? Man, who man would be,   10
Must rule the empire of himself; in it
Must be supreme, establishing his throne
On vanquished will; quelling the anarchy
Of hopes and fears; being himself alone.

The Indian Girl's Song

    I arise from dreams of thee
    In the first sleep of night—
    The winds are breathing low
    And the stars are burning bright.
    I arise from dreams of thee—
    And a spirit in my feet
    Has borne me—Who knows how?
    To thy chamber window, sweet!—

    The wandering airs they faint
    On the dark silent stream—   10
    The champak odours fail°

Like sweet thoughts in a dream;
The nightingale's complaint—
It dies upon her heart—
As I must die on thine
O beloved as thou art!

O lift me from the grass!
I die, I faint, I fail!
Let thy love in kisses rain
On my lips and eyelids pale.   20
My cheek is cold and white, alas!
My heart beats loud and fast.
Oh press it close to thine again
Where it will break at last.

EPIPSYCHIDION

VERSES ADDRESSED TO THE NOBLE
AND UNFORTUNATE LADY
EMILIA V——

NOW IMPRISONED IN THE CONVENT OF ——

L'anima amante si slancia fuori del creato, e si crea nel infinito un Mondo tutto per essa, diverso assai da questo oscuro e pauroso baratro.

Her own words°

ADVERTISEMENT

The Writer of the following Lines died at Florence, as he was preparing for a voyage to one of the wildest of the Sporades,° which he had bought, and where he had fitted up the ruins of an old building, and where it was his hope to have realized a scheme of life, suited perhaps to that happier and better world of which he is now an inhabitant, but hardly practicable in this. His life was singular; less on account of the romantic vicissitudes which diversified it, than the ideal tinge which it received from his own character and feelings. The present Poem, like the *Vita Nuova*° of Dante, is sufficiently intelligible to a certain class of readers without a matter-of-fact history of the circumstances to which it relates; and to a certain other class it must ever remain incomprehensible, from a defect of a common organ of perception for the ideas of which it treats. Not but that, *gran vergogna sarebbe a colui, che rimasse cosa sotto veste di figura, o di colore rettorico: e domandato non sapesse denudare le sue parole da cotal veste, in guisa che avessero verace intendimento.*°

The present poem appears to have been intended by the Writer as the dedication to some longer one. The stanza on the opposite page is almost a literal translation from Dante's famous Canzone

Voi, ch'intendendo, il terzo ciel movete, &c.°

The presumptuous application of the concluding lines to his own composition will raise a smile at the expense of my unfortunate friend: be it a smile not of contempt, but pity.

S.

My Song, I fear that thou wilt find but few
Who fitly shall conceive thy reasoning,
Of such hard matter dost thou entertain;
Whence, if by misadventure, chance should bring
Thee to base company (as chance may do)
Quite unaware of what thou dost contain,
I prithee, comfort thy sweet self again,
My last delight! tell them that they are dull,
And bid them own that thou art beautiful.°

———————

Sweet Spirit! Sister of that orphan one,°
Whose empire is the name thou weepest on,°
In my heart's temple I suspend to thee
These votive wreaths of withered memory.

  Poor captive bird! who, from thy narrow cage,
Pourest such music, that it might assuage
The rugged hearts of those who prisoned thee,
Were they not deaf to all sweet melody;
This song shall be thy rose: its petals pale
Are dead, indeed, my adored Nightingale!   10
But soft and fragrant is the faded blossom,
And it has no thorn left to wound thy bosom.

  High, spirit-wingèd Heart! who dost forever
Beat thine unfeeling bars with vain endeavour,
Till those bright plumes of thought, in which arrayed
It oversoared this low and worldly shade,
Lie shattered; and thy panting, wounded breast
Stains with dear blood its unmaternal nest!
I weep vain tears: blood would less bitter be,
Yet poured forth gladlier, could it profit thee.   20

  Seraph of Heaven! too gentle to be human,
Veiling beneath that radiant form of Woman
All that is insupportable in thee
Of light, and love, and immortality!
Sweet Benediction in the eternal Curse!
Veiled Glory of this lampless Universe!
Thou Moon beyond the clouds! Thou living Form
Among the Dead! Thou Star above the Storm!
Thou Wonder, and thou Beauty, and thou Terror!

Thou Harmony of Nature's art! Thou Mirror   30
In whom, as in the splendour of the Sun,
All shapes look glorious which thou gazest on!
Ay, even the dim words which obscure thee now
Flash, lightning-like, with unaccustomed glow;
I pray thee that thou blot from this sad song
All of its much mortality and wrong,
With those clear drops, which start like sacred dew
From the twin lights thy sweet soul darkens through,
Weeping, till sorrow becomes ecstasy:
Then smile on it, so that it may not die.   40

    I never thought before my death to see
Youth's vision thus made perfect. Emily,
I love thee; though the world by no thin name
Will hide that love from its unvalued shame.°
Would we two had been twins of the same mother!°
Or, that the name my heart lent to another
Could be a sister's bond for her and thee,
Blending two beams of one eternity!
Yet were one lawful and the other true,
These names, though dear, could paint not, as is due,   50
How beyond refuge I am thine. Ah me!
I am not thine: I am a part of *thee*.

    Sweet Lamp! my moth-like Muse has burnt its wings;
Or, like a dying swan who soars and sings,
Young Love should teach Time, in his own grey style,°
All that thou art. Art thou not void of guile,
A lovely soul formed to be blessed and bless?
A well of sealed and secret happiness,°
Whose waters like blithe light and music are,
Vanquishing dissonance and gloom? A Star°   60
Which moves not in the moving Heavens, alone?
A smile amid dark frowns? a gentle tone
Amid rude voices? a beloved light?
A Solitude, a Refuge, a Delight?
A lute, which those whom love has taught to play
Make music on, to soothe the roughest day
And lull fond grief asleep? a buried treasure?
A cradle of young thoughts of wingless pleasure?

A violet-shrouded grave of Woe?—I measure
The world of fancies, seeking one like thee,   70
And find—alas! mine own infirmity.

    She met me, Stranger, upon life's rough way,°
And lured me towards sweet Death; as Night by Day,
Winter by Spring, or Sorrow by swift Hope,
Led into light, life, peace. An antelope,
In the suspended impulse of its lightness,
Were less ethereally light: the brightness
Of her divinest presence trembles through
Her limbs, as underneath a cloud of dew
Embodied in the windless Heaven of June   80
Amid the splendour-wingèd stars, the Moon
Burns, inextinguishably beautiful:
And from her lips, as from a hyacinth full
Of honey-dew, a liquid murmur drops,
Killing the sense with passion; sweet as stops°
Of planetary music heard in trance.
In her mild lights the starry spirits dance,
The sunbeams of those wells which ever leap
Under the lightnings of the soul—too deep
For the brief fathom-line of thought or sense.   90
The glory of her being, issuing thence,
Stains the dead, blank, cold air with a warm shade
Of unentangled intermixture, made
By Love, of light and motion: one intense
Diffusion, one serene Omnipresence,
Whose flowing outlines mingle in their flowing
Around her cheeks and utmost fingers glowing
With the unintermitted blood, which there
Quivers (as in a fleece of snow-like air
The crimson pulse of living morning quiver),°   100
Continuously prolonged, and ending never,
Till they are lost, and in that Beauty furled
Which penetrates and clasps and fills the world;
Scarce visible from extreme loveliness.
Warm fragrance seems to fall from her light dress,
And her loose hair; and where some heavy tress
The air of her own speed has disentwined,
The sweetness seems to satiate the faint wind;

And in the soul a wild odour is felt,
Beyond the sense, like fiery dews that melt   110
Into the bosom of a frozen bud.—
See where she stands! a mortal shape indued
With love and life and light and deity,
And motion which may change but cannot die;
An image of some bright Eternity;
A shadow of some golden dream; a Splendour
Leaving the third sphere pilotless; a tender°
Reflection of the eternal Moon of Love
Under whose motions life's dull billows move;
A Metaphor of Spring and Youth and Morning;   120
A Vision like incarnate April, warning,
With smiles and tears, Frost the Anatomy°
Into his summer grave.

                  Ah, woe is me!
What have I dared? where am I lifted? how
Shall I descend, and perish not? I know
That Love makes all things equal: I have heard
By mine own heart this joyous truth averred:
The spirit of the worm beneath the sod,
In love and worship, blends itself with God.

    Spouse! Sister! Angel! Pilot of the Fate   130
Whose course has been so starless! O too late
Beloved! O too soon adored, by me!
For in the fields of immortality
My spirit should at first have worshipped thine,
A divine presence in a place divine;
Or should have moved beside it on this earth,
A shadow of that substance, from its birth;
But not as now:—I love thee; yes, I feel
That on the fountain of my heart a seal
Is set, to keep its waters pure and bright   140
For thee, since in those *tears* thou hast delight.
We—are we not formed, as notes of music are,
For one another, though dissimilar;
Such difference without discord, as can make
Those sweetest sounds, in which all spirits shake
As trembling leaves in a continuous air?

Thy wisdom speaks in me, and bids me dare
Beacon the rocks on which high hearts are wrecked.
I never was attached to that great sect,   150
Whose doctrine is, that each one should select
Out of the crowd a mistress or a friend,
And all the rest, though fair and wise, commend
To cold oblivion, though it is in the code
Of modern morals, and the beaten road
Which those poor slaves with weary footsteps tread,
Who travel to their home among the dead
By the broad highway of the world, and so
With one chained friend, perhaps a jealous foe,
The dreariest and the longest journey go.

True Love in this differs from gold and clay,   160
That to divide is not to take away.
Love is like understanding, that grows bright.
Gazing on many truths; 'tis like thy light.
Imagination! which from earth and sky,
And from the depths of human fantasy,
As from a thousand prisms and mirrors, fills
The Universe with glorious beams, and kills
Error, the worm, with many a sun-like arrow
Of its reverberated lightning. Narrow
The heart that loves, the brain that contemplates,   170
The life that wears, the spirit that creates
One object, and one form, and builds thereby
A sepulchre for its eternity.°

Mind from its object differs most in this:
Evil from good; misery from happiness;
The baser from the nobler; the impure
And frail, from what is clear and must endure.
If you divide suffering and dross, you may
Diminish till it is consumed away;
If you divide pleasure and love and thought,   180
Each part exceeds the whole; and we know not
How much, while any yet remains unshared,
Of pleasure may be gained, of sorrow spared:
This truth is that deep well, whence sages draw
The unenvied light of hope; the eternal law°
By which those live, to whom this world of life

Is as a garden ravaged, and whose strife
Tills for the promise of a later birth
The wilderness of this Elysian earth.

There was a Being whom my spirit oft   190
Met on its visioned wanderings, far aloft,
In the clear golden prime of my youth's dawn,
Upon the fairy isles of sunny lawn,
Amid the enchanted mountains, and the caves
Of divine sleep, and on the air-like waves
Of wonder-level dream, whose tremulous floor
Paved her light steps;—on an imagined shore.
Under the grey beak of some promontory
She met me, robed in such exceeding glory,
That I beheld her not. In solitudes   200
Her voice came to me through the whispering woods,
And from the fountains, and the odours deep
Of flowers, which, like lips murmuring in their sleep
Of the sweet kisses which had lulled them there,
Breathed but of *her* to the enamoured air;
And from the breezes whether low or loud,
And from the rain of every passing cloud,
And from the singing of the summer-birds,
And from all sounds, all silence. In the words
Of antique verse and high romance,—in form   210
Sound, colour—in whatever checks that Storm
Which with the shattered present chokes the past;
And in that best philosophy, whose taste°
Makes this cold common hell, our life, a doom
As glorious as a fiery martyrdom;
Her Spirit was the harmony of truth.—

Then, from the caverns of my dreamy youth
I sprang, as one sandalled with plumes of fire,
And towards the lodestar of my one desire,
I flitted, like a dizzy moth, whose flight   220
Is as a dead leaf's in the owlet light,
When it would seek in Hesper's setting sphere°
A radiant death, a fiery sepulchre,
As if it were a lamp of earthly flame.—
But She, whom prayers or tears then could not tame,

Passed, like a God throned on a wingèd planet,
Whose burning plumes to tenfold swiftness fan it,
Into the dreary cone of our life's shade;
And as a man with mighty loss dismayed,
I would have followed, though the grave between
Yawned like a gulf whose spectres are unseen: 230
When a voice said:—'O Thou of hearts the weakest,
The phantom is beside thee whom thou seekest.'
Then I—'Where?'—the world's echo answered 'where!'
And in that silence, and in my despair,
I questioned every tongueless wind that flew
Over my tower of mourning, if it knew
Whither 'twas fled, this soul out of my soul;
And murmured names and spells which have control
Over the sightless tyrants of our fate;
But neither prayer nor verse could dissipate   240
The night which closed on her; nor uncreate
That world within this Chaos, mine and me,
Of which she was the veiled Divinity,
The world I say of thoughts that worshipped her:
And therefore I went forth, with hope and fear
And every gentle passion sick to death,
Feeding my course with expectation's breath,
Into the wintry forest of our life;°
And struggling through its error with vain strife,   250
And stumbling in my weakness and my haste,
And half bewildered by new forms, I passed
Seeking among those untaught foresters
If I could find one form resembling hers,
In which she might have masked herself from me.
There,—One, whose voice was venomed melody
Sate by a well, under blue nightshade bowers;
The breath of her false mouth was like faint flowers,
Her touch was as electric poison,—flame
Out of her looks into my vitals came,   260
And from her living cheeks and bosom flew
A killing air, which pierced like honey-dew
Into the core of my green heart, and lay
Upon its leaves; until, as hair grown grey
O'er a young brow, they hid its unblown prime
With ruins of unseasonable time.

In many mortal forms I rashly sought
The shadow of that idol of my thought.°
And some were fair—but beauty dies away:
Others were wise—but honeyed words betray: 270
And One was true—oh! why not true to me?
Then, as a hunted deer that could not flee,
I turned upon my thoughts, and stood at bay,
Wounded and weak and panting; the cold day
Trembled, for pity of my strife and pain.
When, like a noon-day dawn, there shone again
Deliverance. One stood on my path who seemed°
As like the glorious shape which I had dreamed,
As is the Moon, whose changes ever run
Into themselves, to the eternal Sun;   280
The cold chaste Moon, the Queen of Heaven's bright isles,
Who makes all beautiful on which she smiles,
That wandering shrine of soft yet icy flame
Which ever is transformed, yet still the same,
And warms not but illumines. Young and fair
As the descended Spirit of that sphere,
She hid me, as the Moon may hide the night
From its own darkness, until all was bright
Between the Heaven and Earth of my calm mind,
And, as a cloud charioted by the wind,   290
She led me to a cave in that wild place,
And sate beside me, with her downward face
Illumining my slumbers, like the Moon
Waxing and waning o'er Endymion.
And I was laid asleep, spirit and limb,°
And all my being became bright or dim
As the Moon's image in a summer sea,
According as she smiled or frowned on me;
And there I lay, within a chaste cold bed:
Alas, I then was nor alive nor dead:—   300
For at her silver voice came Death and Life,
Unmindful each of their accustomed strife,
Masked like twin babes, a sister and a brother,
The wandering hopes of one abandoned mother,°
And through the cavern without wings they flew,
And cried 'Away, he is not of our crew.'
I wept, and though it be a dream, I weep.

What storms then shook the ocean of my sleep,
Blotting that Moon, whose pale and waning lips
Then shrank as in the sickness of eclipse;—   310
And how my soul was as a lampless sea,
And who was then its Tempest;° and when She,°
The Planet of that hour, was quenched, what frost
Crept o'er those waters, till from coast to coast
The moving billows of my being fell
Into a death of ice, immoveable;—
And then—what earthquakes made it gape and split,
The white Moon smiling all the while on it,
These words conceal:—If not, each word would be°
The key of staunchless tears. Weep not for me!   320

　　At length, into the obscure Forest came
The Vision I had sought through grief and shame.
Athwart that wintry wilderness of thorns
Flashed from her motion splendour like the Morn's,
And from her presence life was radiated
Through the grey earth and branches bare and dead;
So that her way was paved, and roofed above
With flowers as soft as thoughts of budding love;
And music from her respiration spread
Like light,—all other sounds were penetrated   330
By the small, still, sweet spirit of that sound,
So that the savage winds hung mute around;
And odours warm and fresh fell from her hair
Dissolving the dull cold in the froze air:
Soft as an Incarnation of the Sun,
When light is changed to love, this glorious One
Floated into the cavern where I lay,
And called my Spirit, and the dreaming clay
Was lifted by the thing that dreamed below
As smoke by fire, and in her beauty's glow   340
I stood, and felt the dawn of my long night
Was penetrating me with living light:
I knew it was the Vision veiled from me
So many years—that it was Emily.

　　Twin Spheres of light who rule this passive Earth,°
This world of love, this *me*; and into birth

Awaken all its fruits and flowers, and dart
Magnetic might into its central heart;
And lift its billows and its mists, and guide
By everlasting laws, each wind and tide   350
To its fit cloud, and its appointed cave;
And lull its storms, each in the craggy grave
Which was its cradle, luring to faint bowers
The armies of the rainbow-wingèd showers;
And, as those married lights, which from the towers
Of Heaven look forth and fold the wandering globe
In liquid sleep and splendour, as a robe;
And all their many-mingled influence blend,
If equal, yet unlike, to one sweet end;—
So ye, bright regents, with alternate sway   360
Govern my sphere of being, night and day!
Thou, not disdaining even a borrowed might;
Thou, not eclipsing a remoter light;
And, through the shadow of the seasons three,
From Spring to Autumn's sere maturity,
Light it into the Winter of the tomb,
Where it may ripen to a brighter bloom.
Thou too, O Comet beautiful and fierce,
Who drew the heart of this frail Universe
Towards thine own; till, wrecked in that convulsion,   370
Alternating attraction and repulsion.
Thine went astray and that was rent in twain;
Oh, float into our azure heaven again!°
Be there love's folding-star at thy return;
The living Sun will feed thee from its urn
Of golden fire; the Moon will veil her horn
In thy last smiles; adoring Even and Morn
Will worship thee with incense of calm breath
And lights and shadows; as the star of Death
And Birth is worshipped by those sisters wild   380
Called Hope and Fear—upon the heart are piled
Their offerings,—of this sacrifice divine
A World shall be the altar.

                    Lady mine,
Scorn not these flowers of thought, the fading birth
Which from its heart of hearts that plant puts forth

Whose fruit, made perfect by thy sunny eyes,
Will be as of the trees of Paradise.

    The day is come, and thou wilt fly with me.
To whatsoe'er of dull mortality
Is mine, remain a vestal sister still;   390
To the intense, the deep, the imperishable,
Not mine but me, henceforth be thou united
Even as a bride, delighting and delighted.
The hour is come:—the destined Star has risen
Which shall descend upon a vacant prison.
The walls are high, the gates are strong, thick set
The sentinels—but true love never yet
Was thus constrained: it overleaps all fence:
Like lightning, with invisible violence
Piercing its continents; like Heaven's free breath,   400
Which he who grasps can hold not; liker Death,
Who rides upon a thought, and makes his way
Through temple, tower, and palace, and the array
Of arms: more strength has Love than he or they;
For it can burst his charnel, and make free
The limbs in chains, the heart in agony,
The soul in dust and chaos.

                        Emily,
A ship is floating in the harbour now,
A wind is hovering o'er the mountain's brow;
There is a path on the sea's azure floor,   410
No keel has ever ploughed that path before;
The halcyons brood around the foamless isles;°
The treacherous Ocean has forsworn its wiles;
The merry mariners are bold and free:
Say, my heart's sister, wilt thou sail with me?
Our bark is as an albatross, whose nest
Is a far Eden of the purple East;
And we between her wings will sit, while Night
And Day, and Storm, and Calm, pursue their flight,
Our ministers, along the boundless Sea,   420
Treading each other's heels, unheededly.
It is an isle under Ionian skies,°
Beautiful as a wreck of Paradise,

And, for the harbours are not safe and good,
This land would have remained a solitude
But for some pastoral people native there,
Who from the Elysian, clear, and golden air
Draw the last spirit of the age of gold,
Simple and spirited; innocent and bold.
The blue Aegean girds this chosen home,   430
With ever-changing sound and light and foam,
Kissing the sifted sands, and caverns hoar;
And all the winds wandering along the shore
Undulate with the undulating tide:
There are thick woods where sylvan forms abide;
And many a fountain, rivulet, and pond,
As clear as elemental diamond,
Or serene morning air; and far beyond,
The mossy tracks made by the goats and deer
(Which the rough shepherd treads but once a year),   440
Pierce into glades, caverns, and bowers, and halls
Built round with ivy, which the waterfalls
Illumining, with sound that never fails
Accompany the noon-day nightingales;
And all the place is peopled with sweet airs;°
The light clear element which the isle wears
Is heavy with the scent of lemon-flowers,
Which floats like mist laden with unseen showers,
And falls upon the eyelids like faint sleep;
And from the moss violets and jonquils peep,   450
And dart their arrowy odour through the brain
Till you might faint with that delicious pain.
And every motion, odour, beam, and tone,
With that deep music is in unison:
Which is a soul within the soul—they seem
Like echoes of an antenatal dream.—
It is an isle 'twixt Heaven, Air, Earth, and Sea,
Cradled, and hung in clear tranquillity;
Bright as that wandering Eden Lucifer,°
Washed by the soft blue Oceans of young air.   460
It is a favoured place. Famine or Blight,
Pestilence, War and Earthquake, never light
Upon its mountain-peaks; blind vultures, they
Sail onward far upon their fatal way:

The wingèd storms, chanting their thunder-psalm
To other lands, leave azure chasms of calm
Over this isle, or weep themselves in dew,
From which its fields and woods ever renew
Their green and golden immortality.
And from the sea there rise, and from the sky   470
There fall, clear exhalations, soft and bright,
Veil after veil, each hiding some delight,
Which Sun or Moon or zephyr draw aside,
Till the isle's beauty, like a naked bride
Glowing at once with love and loveliness,
Blushes and trembles at its own excess:
Yet, like a buried lamp, a Soul no less
Burns in the heart of this delicious isle,
An atom of th' Eternal, whose own smile
Unfolds itself, and may be felt not seen   480
O'er the grey rocks, blue waves, and forests green,
Filling their bare and void interstices.—
But the chief marvel of the wilderness
Is a lone dwelling, built by whom or how
None of the rustic island-people know:
'Tis not a tower of strength, though with its height
It overtops the woods; but, for delight,
Some wise and tender Ocean-King, ere crime
Had been invented, in the world's young prime,
Reared it, a wonder of that simple time,   490
An envy of the isles, a pleasure-house
Made sacred to his sister and his spouse.°
It scarce seems now a wreck of human art,
But, as it were Titanic; in the heart
Of Earth having assumed its form, then grown
Out of the mountains, from the living stone,
Lifting itself in caverns light and high:
For all the antique and learned imagery
Has been erased, and in the place of it
The ivy and the wild-vine interknit   500
The volumes of their many twining stems;
Parasite flowers illume with dewy gems
The lampless halls, and when they fade, the sky
Peeps through their winter-woof of tracery
With moonlight patches, or star atoms keen,

Or fragments of the day's intense serene;—
Working mosaic on their Parian floors.°
And, day and night, aloof, from the high towers
And terraces, the Earth and Ocean seem
To sleep in one another's arms, and dream   510
Of waves, flowers, clouds, woods, rocks, and all that we
Read in their smiles, and call reality.

    This isle and house are mine, and I have vowed
Thee to be lady of the solitude.—
And I have fitted up some chambers there
Looking towards the golden Eastern air,
And level with the living winds, which flow
Like waves above the living waves below.—
I have sent books and music there, and all
Those instruments with which high spirits call   520
The future from its cradle, and the past
Out of its grave, and make the present last
In thoughts and joys which sleep, but cannot die,
Folded within their own eternity.
Our simple life wants little, and true taste
Hires not the pale drudge Luxury, to waste
The scene it would adorn, and therefore still,
Nature, with all her children, haunts the hill.
The ring–dove, in the embowering ivy, yet
Keeps up her love-lament, and the owls flit   530
Round the evening tower, and the young stars glance
Between the quick bats in their twilight dance;
The spotted deer bask in the fresh moonlight
Before our gate, and the slow, silent night
Is measured by the pants of their calm sleep.
Be this our home in life, and when years heap
Their withered hours, like leaves, on our decay,
Let us become the overhanging day,
The living soul of this Elysian isle,
Conscious, inseparable, one. Meanwhile°   540
We two will rise, and sit, and walk together,
Under the roof of blue Ionian weather,
And wander in the meadows, or ascend
The mossy mountains, where the blue heavens bend
With lightest winds, to touch their paramour;

Or linger, where the pebble-paven shore,
Under the quick, faint kisses of the sea
Trembles and sparkles as with ecstasy,—
Possessing and possessed by all that is
Within that calm circumference of bliss,   550
And by each other, till to love and live
Be one:—or, at the noontide hour, arrive
Where some old cavern hoar seems yet to keep
The moonlight of the expired night asleep,
Through which the awakened day can never peep;
A veil for our seclusion, close as Night's,
Where secure sleep may kill thine innocent lights;
Sleep, the fresh dew of languid love, the rain
Whose drops quench kisses till they burn again.
And we will talk, until thought's melody   560
Become too sweet for utterance, and it die
In words, to live again in looks, which dart
With thrilling tone into the voiceless heart,
Harmonizing silence without a sound.
Our breath shall intermix, our bosoms bound.
And our veins beat together; and our lips
With other eloquence than words, eclipse
The soul that burns between them, and the wells
Which boil under our being's inmost cells,
The fountains of our deepest life, shall be   570
Confused in passion's golden purity,
As mountain-springs under the morning Sun.
We shall become the same, we shall be one
Spirit within two frames, oh! wherefore two?
One passion in twin-hearts, which grows and grew,
Till, like two meteors of expanding flame,
Those spheres instinct with it become the same,
Touch, mingle, are transfigured; ever still
Burning, yet ever inconsumable:
In one another's substance finding food,   580
Like flames too pure and light and unimbued
To nourish their bright lives with baser prey,
Which point to Heaven and cannot pass away:
One hope within two wills, one will beneath
Two overshadowing minds, one life, one death,
One Heaven, one Hell, one immortality,

And one annihilation. Woe is me!
The wingèd words on which my soul would pierce
Into the height of love's rare Universe,
Are chains of lead around its flight of fire.— 590
I pant, I sink, I tremble, I expire!

Weak Verses, go, kneel at your Sovereign's feet,
And say:—'We are the masters of thy slave;
What wouldest thou with us and ours and thine?'
Then call your sisters from Oblivion's cave,
All singing loud: 'Love's very pain is sweet,
But its reward is in the world divine
Which, if not here, it builds beyond the grave.'
So shall ye live when I am there. Then haste
Over the hearts of men, until ye meet 600
Marina, Vanna, Primus, and the rest,°
And bid them love each other and be blessed:
And leave the troop which errs, and which reproves,
And come and be my guest,—for I am Love's.°

ADONAIS

AN ELEGY ON THE DEATH OF JOHN KEATS,
AUTHOR OF 'ENDYMION', 'HYPERION' ETC.

Ἀστὴρ πρὶν μέν ἔλαμπες ενι ζῶοισιν εῶος.
Νυν δε θανῶν, λαμπεις ἔσπερος εν φθίμενοις.

Plato°

PREFACE°

Φάρμακον ἦλθε, Βίων, ποτι σον στομα, φάρμακον ἔιδες
Πῶς τευ τοῖς χέιλεσσι ποτεδραμε, κοὐκ εγλυκανθη;
Τις δὲ Θροτος τοσσοῦτον ἀνάμερος, ἢ κερκσαι τοι,
Ἤ δοῦναι λσλέοντι το φάρμακον; ἔκφυγεν ὡδαν.

Moschus, *Epitaph. Bion.*°

It is my intention to subjoin to the London edition of this poem a criticism upon the claims of its lamented object to be classed among the writers of the highest genius who have adorned our age. My known repugnance to the narrow principles of taste on which several of his earlier compositions were modelled prove° at least that I am an impartial judge. I consider the fragment of *Hyperion*,° as second to nothing that was ever produced by a writer of the same years.

John Keats, died at Rome of a consumption, in his twenty-fourth year, on the —— of —— 1821;° and was buried in the romantic and lonely cemetery of the protestants° in that city, under the pyramid which is the tomb of Cestius, and the massy walls and towers, now mouldering and desolate, which formed the circuit of ancient Rome. The cemetery is an open space among the ruins, covered in winter with violets and daisies. It might make one in love with death,° to think that one should be buried in so sweet a place.

The genius of the lamented person to whose memory I have dedi-cated these unworthy verses, was not less delicate and fragile than it was beautiful; and where canker-worms abound, what wonder, if its young flower was blighted in the bud? The savage criticism on his *Endymion*, which appeared in the *Quarterly Review*, produced the most violent effect on his susceptible mind; the agitation thus originated ended in the rupture of a blood-vessel in the lungs; a rapid consumption ensued, and the succeeding acknowledgements from more candid critics, of the true greatness of his powers, were ineffectual to heal the wound thus wantonly inflicted.

It may be well said, that these wretched men know not what they do.° They scatter their insults and their slanders without heed as to whether the poisoned shaft lights on a heart made callous by many blows, or one like Keats's composed of more penetrable stuff.° One of their associates is, to my knowledge, a most base and unprincipled calumniator.° As to *Endymion*; was it a poem, whatever might be its defects, to be treated contemptuously by those who had celebrated with various degrees of complacency and panegyric, *Paris*, and *Woman*, and a *Syrian Tale*, and Mrs Lefanu, and Mr Barrett, and Mr Howard Payne,° and a long list of the illustrious obscure? Are these the men, who in their venal good nature, presumed to draw a parallel between the Rev. Mr Milman° and Lord Byron? What gnat did they strain at here, after having swallowed all those camels?° Against what woman taken in adultery dares the foremost of these literary prostitutes to cast his opprobrious stone?° Miserable man! you, one of the meanest, have wantonly defaced one of the noblest specimens of the workmanship of God. Nor shall it be your excuse, that, murderer as you are, you have spoken daggers, but used none.°

The circumstances of the closing scene of poor Keats's life were not made known to me until the Elegy was ready for the press.° I am given to understand that the wound which his sensitive spirit had received from the criticism of *Endymion* was exasperated by the bitter sense of unrequited benefits; the poor fellow seems to have been hooted from the stage of life, no less by those on whom he had wasted the promise of his genius, than those on whom he had lavished his fortune and his care. He was accompanied to Rome, and attended in his last illness by Mr Severn,° a young artist of the highest promise, who, I have been informed, 'almost risked his own life, and sacrificed every prospect to unwearied attendance upon his dying friend.' Had I known these circumstances before the completion of my poem, I should have been tempted to add my feeble tribute of applause to the more solid recompense which the virtuous man finds in the recollection of his own motives. Mr Severn can dispense with a reward from 'such stuff as dreams are made of.'° His conduct is a golden augury of the success of his future career—may the unextinguished Spirit of his illustrious friend animate the creations of his pencil, and plead against Oblivion for his name!

1

I weep for Adonais—he is dead!
O, weep for Adonais! though our tears°
Thaw not the frost which binds so dear a head!
And thou, sad Hour, selected from all years
To mourn our loss, rouse thy obscure compeers,°
And teach them thine own sorrow, say: with me
Died Adonais; till the Future dares
Forget the Past, his fate and fame shall be
An echo and a light unto eternity!

2

Where wert thou mighty Mother, when he lay,°   10
When thy Son lay, pierced by the shaft which flies
In darkness? where was lorn Urania°
When Adonais died? With veilèd eyes,
'Mid listening Echoes, in her Paradise
She sate, while one, with soft enamoured breath,
Rekindled all the fading melodies,
With which, like flowers that mock the corse beneath,°
He had adorned and hid the coming bulk of death.

3

O, weep for Adonais—he is dead!
Wake, melancholy Mother, wake and weep!   20
Yet wherefore? Quench within their burning bed
Thy fiery tears, and let thy loud heart keep
Like his, a mute and uncomplaining sleep;
For he is gone, where all things wise and fair
Descend;—oh, dream not that the amorous Deep°
Will yet restore him to the vital air;
Death feeds on his mute voice, and laughs at our despair.

4

Most musical of mourners, weep again!
Lament anew, Urania!—He died,
Who was the Sire of an immortal strain,   30
Blind, old, and lonely, when his country's pride
The priest, the slave, and the liberticide
Trampled and mocked with many a loathèd rite

Of lust and blood; he went, unterrified,
Into the gulf of death; but his clear Sprite
Yet reigns o'er earth; the third among the sons of light.°

                              5

Most musical of mourners, weep anew!
Not all to that bright station dared to climb;
And happier they their happiness who knew,
Whose tapers yet burn through that night of time   40
In which suns perished; others more sublime,°
Struck by the envious wrath of man or God,
Have sunk, extinct in their refulgent prime;
And some yet live, treading the thorny road,
Which leads, through toil and hate, to Fame's serene abode.

                              6

But now, thy youngest, dearest one, has perished,
The nursling of thy widowhood, who grew,
Like a pale flower by some sad maiden cherished,
And fed with true love tears, instead of dew;°
Most musical of mourners, weep anew!   50
Thy extreme hope, the loveliest and the last,°
The bloom, whose petals nipped before they blew
Died on the promise of the fruit, is waste;
The broken lily lies—the storm is overpast.

                              7

To that high Capital, where kingly Death°
Keeps his pale court in beauty and decay,
He came; and bought, with price of purest breath,
A grave among the eternal.—Come away!
Haste, while the vault of blue Italian day
Is yet his fitting charnel-roof! while still   60
He lies, as if in dewy sleep he lay;
Awake him not! surely he takes his fill
Of deep and liquid rest, forgetful of all ill.°

                              8

He will awake no more, oh, never more!—
Within the twilight chamber spreads apace

The shadow of white Death, and at the door
Invisible Corruption waits to trace
His extreme way to her dim dwelling-place;
The eternal Hunger sits, but pity and awe
Soothe her pale rage, nor dares she to deface   70
So fair a prey, till darkness, and the law
Of mortal change, shall o'er his sleep the mortal curtain draw.°

9

O, weep for Adonais!—The quick Dreams,
The passion-wingèd Ministers of thought,
Who were his flocks, whom near the living streams°
Of his young spirit he fed, and whom he taught
The love which was its music, wander not,—
Wander no more, from kindling brain to brain,
But droop there, whence they sprung; and mourn their lot
Round the cold heart, where, after their sweet pain,°   80
They ne'er will gather strength, or find a home again.

10

And one with trembling hands clasps his cold head,
And fans him with her moonlight wings, and cries;
'Our love, our hope, our sorrow, is not dead;°
See, on the silken fringe of his faint eyes,
Like dew upon a sleeping flower, there lies
A tear some Dream has loosened from his brain.'
Lost Angel of a ruined Paradise!
She knew not 'twas her own; as with no stain
She faded, like a cloud which had outwept its rain.   90

11

One from a lucid urn of starry dew
Washed his light limbs as if embalming them;
Another clipped her profuse locks, and threw
The wreath upon him, like an anadem,°
Which frozen tears instead of pearls begem;
Another in her wilful grief would break
Her bow and wingèd reeds, as if to stem
A greater loss with one which was more weak;
And dull the barbèd fire against his frozen cheek.

12

Another Splendour on his mouth alit,°   100
That mouth, whence it was wont to draw the breath
Which gave it strength to pierce the guarded wit,
And pass into the panting heart beneath
With lightning and with music: the damp death
Quenched its caress upon his icy lips;
And, as a dying meteor stains a wreath
Of moonlight vapour, which the cold night clips,°
It flushed through his pale limbs, and passed to its eclipse.

13

And others came . . . Desires and Adorations,
Wingèd Persuasions and veiled Destinies,   110
Splendours, and Glooms, and glimmering Incarnations
Of hopes and fears, and twilight Fantasies;
And Sorrow, with her family of Sighs,
And Pleasure, blind with tears, led by the gleam
Of her own dying smile instead of eyes,
Came in slow pomp;—the moving pomp might seem
Like pageantry of mist on an autumnal stream.

14

All he had loved, and moulded into thought,
From shape, and hue, and odour, and sweet sound,
Lamented Adonais. Morning sought   120
Her eastern watchtower, and her hair unbound,
Wet with the tears which should adorn the ground,
Dimmed the aerial eyes that kindle day;
Afar the melancholy thunder moaned,
Pale Ocean in unquiet slumber lay,
And the wild winds flew round, sobbing in their dismay.

15

Lost Echo sits amid the voiceless mountains,
And feeds her grief with his remembered lay,
And will no more reply to winds or fountains,
Or amorous birds perched on the young green spray,   130
Or herdsman's horn, or bell at closing day;
Since she can mimic not his lips, more dear

Than those for whose disdain she pined away
Into a shadow of all sounds:—a dear
Murmur, between their songs, is all the woodmen hear.°

16

Grief made the young Spring wild, and she threw down
Her kindling buds, as if she Autumn were,
Or they dead leaves; since her delight is flown
For whom should she have waked the sullen year?
To Phoebus was not Hyacinth so dear   140
Nor to himself Narcissus, as to both
Thou Adonais: wan they stand and sere
Amid the drooping comrades of their youth,
With dew all turned to tears; odour, to sighing ruth.

17

Thy spirit's sister, the lorn nightingale
Mourns not her mate with such melodious pain;°
Not so the eagle, who like thee could scale
Heaven, and could nourish in the sun's domain
Her mighty youth with morning, doth complain,
Soaring and screaming round her empty nest,   150
As Albion wails for thee: the curse of Cain°
Light on his head who pierced thy innocent breast,
And scared the angel soul that was its earthly guest!

18

Ah woe is me! Winter is come and gone,
But grief returns with the revolving year;
The airs and streams renew their joyous tone;
The ants, the bees, the swallows reappear;
Fresh leaves and flowers deck the dead Seasons' bier;
The amorous birds now pair in every brake,
And build their mossy homes in field and brere;°   160
And the green lizard, and the golden snake,
Like unimprisoned flames, out of their trance awake.

19

Through wood and stream and field and hill and Ocean
A quickening life from the Earth's heart has burst

As it has ever done, with change and motion,
From the great morning of the world when first
God dawned on Chaos; in its steam immersed
The lamps of Heaven flash with a softer light;
All baser things pant with life's sacred thirst;
Diffuse themselves; and spend in love's delight,   170
The beauty and the joy of their renewèd might.

20

The leprous corpse touched by this spirit tender
Exhales itself in flowers of gentle breath;
Like incarnations of the stars, when splendour
Is changed to fragrance, they illumine death
And mock the merry worm that wakes beneath;
Nought we know, dies. Shall that alone which knows°
Be as a sword consumed before the sheath
By sightless lightning?—th' intense atom glows°
A moment, then is quenched in a most cold repose.   180

21

Alas! that all we loved of him should be,
But for our grief, as if it had not been,
And grief itself be mortal! Woe is me!
Whence are we, and why are we? of what scene
The actors or spectators? Great and mean
Meet massed in death, who lends what life must borrow.
As long as skies are blue, and fields are green,
Evening must usher night, night urge the morrow,
Month follow month with woe, and year wake year to sorrow.

22

He will awake no more, oh, never more!   190
'Wake thou,' cried Misery, 'childless Mother, rise
Out of thy sleep, and slake, in thy heart's core,
A wound more fierce than his with tears and sighs.'
And all the Dreams that watched Urania's eyes,
And all the Echoes whom their sister's song°
Had held in holy silence, cried: 'Arise!'
Swift as a Thought by the snake Memory stung,
From her ambrosial rest the fading Splendour sprung.°

23

She rose like an autumnal Night, that springs
Out of the East, and follows wild and drear   200
The golden Day, which, on eternal wings,
Even as a ghost abandoning a bier,
Had left the Earth a corpse. Sorrow and fear
So struck, so roused, so rapt Urania;
So saddened round her like an atmosphere
Of stormy mist; so swept her on her way
Even to the mournful place where Adonais lay.

24

Out of her secret Paradise she sped,°
Through camps and cities rough with stone, and steel,
And human hearts, which to her aery tread   210
Yielding not, wounded the invisible
Palms of her tender feet where'er they fell:°
And barbèd tongues, and thoughts more sharp than they
Rent the soft Form they never could repel,
Whose sacred blood, like the young tears of May,
Paved with eternal flowers that undeserving way.

25

In the death chamber for a moment Death,
Shamed by the presence of that living Might,
Blushed to annihilation, and the breath
Revisited those lips, and life's pale light   220
Flashed through those limbs, so late her dear delight.
'Leave me not wild and drear and comfortless,
As silent lightning leaves the starless night!
Leave me not!' cried Urania: her distress
Roused Death: Death rose and smiled, and met her vain caress.

26

'Stay yet awhile! speak to me once again;
Kiss me, so long but as a kiss may live;°
And in my heartless breast and burning brain°
That word, that kiss shall all thoughts else survive,
With food of saddest memory kept alive,   230
Now thou art dead, as if it were a part

Of thee, my Adonais! I would give
All that I am to be as thou now art!
But I am chained to Time, and cannot thence depart!

27

'Oh gentle child, beautiful as thou wert,
Why didst thou leave the trodden paths of men
Too soon, and with weak hands though mighty heart
Dare the unpastured dragon in his den?°
Defenceless as thou wert, oh where was then
Wisdom the mirrored shield, or scorn the spear?°   240
Or hadst thou waited the full cycle, when
Thy spirit should have filled its crescent sphere,
The monsters of life's waste had fled from thee like deer.

28

'The herded wolves, bold only to pursue;
The obscene ravens, clamorous o'er the dead;
The vultures to the conqueror's banner true
Who feed where Desolation first has fed,
And whose wings rain contagion;—how they fled,
When like Apollo, from his golden bow,
The Pythian of the age one arrow sped°   250
And smiled!—The spoilers tempt no second blow,
They fawn on the proud feet that spurn them lying low.

29

'The sun comes forth, and many reptiles spawn;
He sets, and each ephemeral insect then
Is gathered into death without a dawn,
And the immortal stars awake again;
So is it in the world of living men:
A godlike mind soars forth, in its delight
Making earth bare and veiling heaven, and when
It sinks, the swarms that dimmed or shared its light   260
Leave to its kindred lamps the spirit's awful night.'°

30

Thus ceased she: and the mountain shepherds came°
Their garlands sere, their magic mantles rent;

The Pilgrim of Eternity, whose fame°
Over his living head like Heaven is bent,
An early but enduring monument,
Came, veiling all the lightnings of his song
In sorrow; from her wilds Ierne sent°
The sweetest lyrist of her saddest wrong,°
And love taught grief to fall like music from his tongue.   270

31

Midst others of less note, came one frail Form,°
A phantom among men; companionless
As the last cloud of an expiring storm
Whose thunder is its knell; he, as I guess,
Had gazed on Nature's naked loveliness,
Actaeon-like, and now he fled astray°
With feeble steps o'er the world's wilderness,
And his own thoughts, along that rugged way,
Pursued, like raging hounds, their father and their prey.

32

A pardlike Spirit beautiful and swift—°   280
A Love in desolation masked;—a Power
Girt round with weakness;—it can scarce uplift
The weight of the superincumbent hour;°
It is a dying lamp, a falling shower,
A breaking billow;—even whilst we speak
Is it not broken? On the withering flower
The killing sun smiles brightly: on a cheek
The life can burn in blood, even while the heart may break.

33

His head was bound with pansies overblown,°
And faded violets, white, and pied, and blue;   290
And a light spear topped with a cypress cone,
Round whose rude shaft dark ivy tresses grew°
Yet dripping with the forest's noonday dew,
Vibrated, as the ever-beating heart
Shook the weak hand that grasped it; of that crew
He came the last, neglected and apart;
A herd-abandoned deer struck by the hunter's dart.°

34

All stood aloof, and at his partial moan°
Smiled through their tears; well knew that gentle band
Who in another's fate now wept his own;   300
As in the accents of an unknown land,
He sung new sorrow; sad Urania scanned
The Stranger's mien, and murmured: 'who art thou?'
He answered not, but with a sudden hand
Made bare his branded and ensanguined brow,
Which was like Cain's or Christ's—Oh! that it should be so!°

35

What softer voice is hushed over the dead?
Athwart what brow is that dark mantle thrown?
What form leans sadly o'er the white death-bed,
In mockery of monumental stone,   310
The heavy heart heaving without a moan?
If it be He, who, gentlest of the wise,°
Taught, soothed, loved, honoured the departed one;
Let me not vex, with inharmonious sighs
The silence of that heart's accepted sacrifice.

36

Our Adonais has drunk poison—oh!
What deaf and viperous murderer could crown
Life's early cup with such a draught of woe?
The nameless worm would now itself disown:°
It felt, yet could escape the magic tone   320
Whose prelude held all envy, hate, and wrong,
But what was howling in one breast alone,
Silent with expectation of the song,
Whose master's hand is cold, whose silver lyre unstrung.

37

Live thou, whose infamy is not thy fame!
Live! fear no heavier chastisement from me,
Thou noteless blot on a remembered name!°
But be thyself, and know thyself to be!
And ever at thy season be thou free
To spill the venom when thy fangs o'erflow: 330

Remorse and Self-contempt shall cling to thee;
Hot Shame shall burn upon thy secret brow,
And like a beaten hound tremble thou shalt—as now.

38

Nor let us weep that our delight is fled
Far from these carrion kites that scream below;
He wakes or sleeps with the enduring dead;°
Thou canst not soar where he is sitting now.—°
Dust to the dust! but the pure spirit shall flow°
Back to the burning fountain whence it came,°
A portion of the Eternal, which must glow   340
Through time and change, unquenchably the same,
Whilst thy cold embers choke the sordid hearth of shame.

39

Peace, peace! he is not dead, he doth not sleep—
He hath awakened from the dream of life—
'Tis we, who lost in stormy visions, keep
With phantoms an unprofitable strife,
And in mad trance, strike with our spirit's knife
Invulnerable nothings.—*We* decay
Like corpses in a charnel; fear and grief
Convulse us and consume us day by day,   350
And cold hopes swarm like worms within our living clay.

40

He has outsoared the shadow of our night;
Envy and calumny and hate and pain,
And that unrest which men miscall delight,
Can touch him not and torture not again;
From the contagion of the world's slow stain
He is secure, and now can never mourn
A heart grown cold, a head grown grey in vain;
Nor, when the spirit's self has ceased to burn,
With sparkless ashes load an unlamented urn.   360

41

He lives, he wakes—'tis Death is dead, not he;
Mourn not for Adonais.—Thou young Dawn°

Turn all thy dew to splendour, for from thee
The spirit thou lamentest is not gone;
Ye caverns and ye forests, cease to moan!
Cease ye faint flowers and fountains, and thou Air
Which like a mourning veil thy scarf hadst thrown
O'er the abandoned Earth, now leave it bare
Even to the joyous stars which smile on its despair!

42

He is made one with Nature: there is heard   370
His voice in all her music, from the moan
Of thunder, to the song of night's sweet bird;°
He is a presence to be felt and known
In darkness and in light, from herb and stone,
Spreading itself where'er that Power may move
Which has withdrawn his being to its own;
Which wields the world with never wearied love,
Sustains it from beneath, and kindles it above.

43

He is a portion of the loveliness
Which once he made more lovely: he doth bear   380
His part, while the one Spirit's plastic stress°
Sweeps through the dull dense world, compelling there
All new successions to the forms they wear;°
Torturing th'unwilling dross that checks its flight
To its own likeness, as each mass may bear;
And bursting in its beauty and its might
From trees and beasts and men into the Heaven's light.

44

The splendours of the firmament of time
May be eclipsed, but are extinguished not;
Like stars to their appointed height they climb   390
And death is a low mist which cannot blot
The brightness it may veil. When lofty thought
Lifts a young heart above its mortal lair,
And love and life contend in it, for what
Shall be its earthly doom, the dead live there
And move like winds of light on dark and stormy air.

45

The inheritors of unfulfilled renown°
Rose from their thrones, built beyond mortal thought,
Far in the Unapparent. Chatterton°
Rose pale, his solemn agony had not   400
Yet faded from him; Sidney, as he fought°
And as he fell and as he lived and loved
Sublimely mild, a Spirit without spot,
Arose; and Lucan, by his death approved:°
Oblivion as they rose shrank like a thing reproved.

46

And many more, whose names on Earth are dark
But whose transmitted effluence cannot die°
So long as fire outlives the parent spark,
Rose, robed in dazzling immortality.
'Thou art become as one of us,' they cry,   410
'It was for thee yon kingless sphere has long
Swung blind in unascended majesty,
Silent alone amid an Heaven of song.°
Assume thy wingèd throne, thou Vesper of our throng!'°

47

Who mourns for Adonais? oh come forth
Fond wretch! and know thyself and him aright.
Clasp with thy panting soul the pendulous Earth;°
As from a centre, dart thy spirit's light
Beyond all worlds, until its spacious might
Satiate the void circumference: then shrink   420
Even to a point within our day and night;
And keep thy heart light lest it make thee sink
When hope has kindled hope, and lured thee to the brink.°

48

Or go to Rome, which is the sepulchre°
O, not of him, but of our joy: 'tis nought
That ages, empires, and religions there
Lie buried in the ravage they have wrought;
For such as he can lend,—they borrow not
Glory from those who made the world their prey;

And he is gathered to the kings of thought 430
Who waged contention with their time's decay,
And of the past are all that cannot pass away.

49

Go thou to Rome,—at once the Paradise,
The grave, the city, and the wilderness;
And where its wrecks like shattered mountains rise,
And flowering weeds, and fragrant copses dress
The bones of Desolation's nakedness
Pass, till the Spirit of the spot shall lead
Thy footsteps to a slope of green access°
Where, like an infant's smile, over the dead, 440
A light of laughing flowers along the grass is spread.

50

And grey walls moulder round, on which dull Time°
Feeds, like slow fire upon a hoary brand;
And one keen pyramid with wedge sublime,°
Pavilioning the dust of him who planned
This refuge for his memory, doth stand
Like flame transformed to marble; and beneath,
A field is spread, on which a newer band
Have pitched in Heaven's smile their camp of death,
Welcoming him we lose with scarce extinguished breath. 450

51

Here pause: these graves are all too young as yet
To have outgrown the sorrow which consigned
Its charge to each; and if the seal is set,
Here, on one fountain of a mourning mind,
Break it not thou! too surely shalt thou find
Thine own well full, if thou returnest home,
Of tears and gall. From the world's bitter wind
Seek shelter in the shadow of the tomb.
What Adonais is, why fear we to become?

52

The One remains, the many change and pass; 460
Heaven's light forever shines, Earth's shadows fly;

Life, like a dome of many-coloured glass,
Stains the white radiance of Eternity,°
Until Death tramples it to fragments.—Die,°
If thou wouldst be with that which thou dost seek!
Follow where all is fled!—Rome's azure sky,
Flowers, ruins, statues, music, words, are weak
The glory they transfuse with fitting truth to speak.

53

Why linger, why turn back, why shrink, my Heart?
Thy hopes are gone before: from all things here   470
They have departed; thou shouldst now depart!
A light is passed from the revolving year,
And man, and woman; and what still is dear
Attracts to crush, repels to make thee wither.
The soft sky smiles,—the low wind whispers near:
'Tis Adonais calls! oh, hasten thither,
No more let Life divide what Death can join together.°

54

That Light whose smile kindles the Universe,°
That Beauty in which all things work and move,
That Benediction which the eclipsing Curse   480
Of birth can quench not, that sustaining Love
Which through the web of being blindly wove
By man and beast and earth and air and sea,
Burns bright or dim, as each are mirrors of
The fire for which all thirst, now beams on me,
Consuming the last clouds of cold mortality.°

55

The breath whose might I have invoked in song°
Descends on me; my spirit's bark is driven
Far from the shore, far from the trembling throng
Whose sails were never to the tempest given;°   490
The massy earth and spherèd skies are riven!
I am borne darkly, fearfully, afar;
Whilst burning through the inmost veil of Heaven,
The soul of Adonais, like a star,
Beacons from the abode where the Eternal are.

To Night

Swiftly walk o'er the western wave,
    Spirit of Night!
Out of the misty eastern cave
Where, all the long and lone daylight
Thou wovest dreams of joy and fear,
Which make thee terrible and dear,—
    Swift be thy flight!

Wrap thy form in a mantle grey,
    Star-inwrought!
Blind with thine hair the eyes of day,   10
Kiss her until she be wearied out—
Then wander o'er city and sea and land,
Touching all with thine opiate wand—
    Come, long-sought!

When I arose and saw the dawn
    I sighed for thee;
When Light rode high, and the dew was gone,
And noon lay heavy on flower and tree,
And the weary day turned to his rest,
Lingering like an unloved guest,   20
    I sighed for thee.

Thy brother Death came, and cried,
    'Wouldst thou me?'
Thy sweet child Sleep, the filmy-eyed,
Murmured like a noontide bee,
'Shall I nestle near thy side?
Wouldst thou me?' and I replied,
    'No, not thee!'

Death will come when thou art dead,
    Soon, too soon—   30
Sleep will come when thou art fled;
Of neither would I ask the boon
I ask of thee, beloved Night—
Swift be thine approaching flight,
    Come soon, soon!

The Aziola

'Do you not hear the Aziola cry?
Methinks she must be nigh—'
    Said Mary as we sate
In dusk, ere stars were lit or candles brought—
    And I who thought
This Aziola was some tedious woman
Asked, 'Who is Aziola?' How elate
I felt to know that it was nothing human,
No mockery of myself to fear or hate!—
    And Mary saw my soul,   10
And laughed and said—'Disquiet yourself not,
    'Tis nothing but a little downy owl.'

Sad Aziola, many an eventide
    Thy music I had heard
By wood and stream, meadow and mountainside,
    And fields and marshes wide,
Such as nor voice, nor lute, nor wind, nor bird
    The soul ever stirred—
Unlike and far sweeter than them all.
Sad Aziola, from that moment, I   20
    Loved thee and thy sad cry.

HELLAS

A LYRICAL DRAMA

Μάντις εἰμ᾽ ἐσθλῶν ἀγώνων°
Oedip. Colon.

TO

HIS EXCELLENCY

PRINCE ALEXANDER MAVROCORDATO

LATE SECRETARY FOR FOREIGN AFFAIRS

TO THE HOSPODAR° OF WALLACHIA,

THE DRAMA OF HELLAS

IS INSCRIBED

AS AN IMPERFECT TOKEN

OF THE ADMIRATION, SYMPATHY, AND FRIENDSHIP

OF

THE AUTHOR.

PISA,
November 1st, 1821.

PREFACE

The poem of *Hellas*, written at the suggestion of the events of the moment, is a mere improvise; and derives its interest (should it be found to possess any) solely from the intense sympathy which the Author feels with the cause he would celebrate.

The subject, in its present state, is insusceptible of being treated otherwise than lyrically, and if I have called this poem a drama from the circumstance of its being composed in dialogue, the licence is not greater than that which has been assumed by other poets who have called their productions epics, only because they have been divided into twelve or twenty-four books.

The *Persae* of Aeschylus afforded me the first model of my conception, although the decision of the glorious contest now waging in Greece being yet suspended forbids a catastrophe parallel to the return of Xerxes and the desolation of the Persians. I have, therefore, contented myself with exhibiting a series of lyric pictures, and with having wrought upon the curtain of futurity, which falls upon the unfinished scene, such figures of indistinct and visionary delineation as suggest the final triumph of the Greek cause as a portion of the cause of civilization and social improvement.

The drama (if drama it must be called) is, however, so inartificial that I doubt whether, if recited on the Thespian waggon to an Athenian village at the Dionysiaca, it would have obtained the prize of the goat.° I shall bear with equanimity any punishment greater than the loss of such a reward which the Aristarchi of the hour° may think fit to inflict.

The only *goat-song* which I have yet attempted° has, I confess, in spite of the unfavourable nature of the subject, received a greater and a more valuable portion of applause than I expected or than it deserved.

Common fame is the only authority which I can allege for the details which form the basis of the poem, and I must trespass upon the forgiveness of my readers for the display of newspaper erudition° to which I have been reduced. Undoubtedly, until the conclusion of the war, it will be impossible to obtain an account of it sufficiently authentic for historical materials; but poets have their privilege, and it is unquestionable that actions of the most exalted courage have been performed by the Greeks, that they have gained more than one naval victory, and that their defeat in Wallachia° was signalized by circumstances of heroism more glorious even than victory.

The apathy of the rulers of the civilized world to the astonishing circumstance of the descendants of that nation to which they owe their civilization, rising as it were from the ashes of their ruin, is something perfectly inexplicable to a mere spectator of the shows of this mortal scene. We are all Greeks. Our laws, our literature, our religion, our arts, have their root in Greece. But for Greece, Rome, the instructor, the conqueror, or the metropolis of our ancestors, would have spread no illumination with her arms, and we might still have been savages and idolaters; or, what is worse, might have arrived at such a stagnant and miserable state of social institution as China and Japan possess.

The human form and the human mind attained to a perfection in Greece which has impressed its image on those faultless productions, whose very fragments are the despair of modern art, and has propagated impulses which cannot cease, through a thousand channels of manifest or imperceptible operation, to ennoble and delight mankind until the extinction of the race.

The modern Greek is the descendant of those glorious beings whom the imagination almost refuses to figure to itself as belonging to our kind, and he inherits much of their sensibility, their rapidity of conception, their enthusiasm, and their courage. If in many instances he is degraded, by moral and political slavery to the practice of the basest vices it engenders, and that below the level of ordinary degradation; let us reflect that the corruption of the best produces the worst, and that habits which subsist only in relation to a peculiar state of social institution may be expected to cease so soon as that relation is dissolved. In fact the Greeks, since the admirable novel of *Anastasius*° could have been a faithful picture of their manners, have undergone most important changes; the flower of their youth returning to their country from the universities of Italy, Germany, and France, have communicated to their fellow-citizens the latest results of that social perfection of which their ancestors were the original source. The university of Chios contained before the breaking out of the Revolution eight hundred students, and among them several Germans and Americans. The munificence and energy of many of the Greek princes and merchants, directed to the renovation of their country with a spirit and a wisdom which has few examples, is above all praise.

The English permit their own oppressors to act according to their natural sympathy with the Turkish tyrant, and to brand upon their name the indelible blot of an alliance with the enemies of domestic happiness, of Christianity and civilization.

Russia desires to possess, not to liberate Greece; and is contented to see the Turks, its natural enemies, and the Greeks, its intended slaves, enfeeble each other until one or both fall into its net. The wise and generous policy of England would have consisted in establishing the independence of Greece, and in maintaining it both against Russia and the Turk;—but when was the oppressor generous or just?

Should the English people ever become free they will reflect upon the part which those who presume to represent their will, have played in the great drama of the revival of liberty, with feelings which it would become them to anticipate. This is the age of the war of the oppressed against the oppressors, and every one of those ringleaders of the privileged gangs of murderers and swindlers, called Sovereigns, look to each other for aid against the common enemy and suspend their mutual jealousies in the presence of a mightier fear. Of this holy alliance all the despots of the earth are virtual members. But a new

race has arisen throughout Europe, nursed in the abhorrence of the
opinions which are its chains, and she will continue to produce fresh
generations to accomplish that destiny which tyrants foresee and
dread.°

The Spanish Peninsula is already free. France is tranquil in the
enjoyment of a partial exemption from the abuses which its unnatural
and feeble government are vainly attempting to revive. The seed of
blood and misery has been sown in Italy, and a more vigorous race
is arising to go forth to the harvest. The world waits only the news
of a revolution of Germany to see the tyrants who have pinnacled
themselves on its supineness precipitated into the ruin from which
they shall never arise. Well do these destroyers of mankind know their
enemy, when they impute the insurrection in Greece to the same spirit
before which they tremble throughout the rest of Europe, and that
enemy well knows the power and the cunning of its opponents, and
watches the moment of their approaching weakness and inevitable
division to wrest the bloody sceptres from their grasp.

DRAMATIS PERSONAE

MAHMUD.
HASSAN.
DAOOD.
AHASUERUS, *a Jew.*
Chorus of Greek Captive Women.
Messengers, Slaves and Attendants.
Phantom of Mahomet the Second.

SCENE, *Constantinople.*
TIME, *Sunset.*

SCENE.—*A Terrace on the Seraglio.*°

MAHMUD (*sleeping*), *an Indian Slave sitting beside his Couch.*

Chorus of Greek Captive Women°

We strew these opiate flowers
On thy restless pillow,—
They were stripped from Orient bowers,
By the Indian billow.
Be thy sleep
Calm and deep,
Like theirs who fell, not ours who weep!

Indian

Away, unlovely dreams!
   Away, false shapes of sleep!   10
Be his, as Heaven seems,
   Clear, and bright, and deep!
Soft as love, and calm as death,
Sweet as a summer night without a breath.

Chorus

Sleep, sleep! our song is laden
   With the soul of slumber;
It was sung by a Samian maiden,°
   Whose lover was of the number
      Who now keep
      That calm sleep
Whence none may wake, where none shall weep.   20

Indian

I touch thy temples pale!
   I breathe my soul on thee!
And could my prayers avail,
   All my joy should be
Dead, and I would live to weep,
So thou mightst win one hour of quiet sleep.

Chorus

Breathe low, low
The spell of the mighty mistress now!
When Conscience lulls her sated snake,
And Tyrants sleep, let Freedom wake.   30
Breathe low—low
The words which, like secret fire, shall flow
Through the veins of the frozen earth—low, low!

Semichorus 1

Life may change, but it may fly not;
Hope may vanish, but can die not;
Truth be veiled, but still it burneth;
Love repulsed,—but it returneth

Semichorus 2

Yet were life a charnel where
Hope lay coffined with Despair;
Yet were truth a sacred lie,   40
Love were lust—

Semichorus 1

If Liberty
Lent not life its soul of light,
Hope its iris of delight,
Truth its prophet's robe to wear,
Love its power to give and bear.

Chorus

In the great morning of the world,
The spirit of God with might unfurled
The flag of Freedom over Chaos,
    And all its banded anarchs fled
Like vultures frighted from Imaus°   50
    Before an earthquake's tread.—
So from Time's tempestuous dawn
Freedom's splendour burst and shone:—
Thermopylae and Marathon°
Caught, like mountains beacon-lighted,
    The springing Fire.—The wingèd glory
On Philippi half-alighted,°
    Like an eagle on a promontory.
Its unwearied wings could fan
The quenchless ashes of Milan.°   60
From age to age, from man to man,
    It lived; and lit from land to land,
    Florence, Albion, Switzerland.—

Then night fell; and, as from night,
Re-assuming fiery flight,
From the West swift Freedom came,
    Against the course of Heaven and doom,
A second sun arrayed in flame,
    To burn, to kindle, to illume.
From far Atlantis its young beams.°   70
Chased the shadows and the dreams.
France, with all her sanguine steams,°

Hid, but quenched it not; again
Through clouds its shafts of glory rain
From utmost Germany to Spain.—

As an eagle fed with morning
Scorns the embattled tempest's warning,
When she seeks her eyrie hanging
    In the mountain-cedar's hair,
And her brood expect the clanging   80
    Of her wings through the wild air,
Sick with famine:—Freedom, so
To what of Greece remaineth now
Returns; her hoary ruins glow
Like Orient mountains lost in day;
    Beneath the safety of her wings
Her renovated nurslings prey,
    And in the naked lightnings°
Of truth they purge their dazzled eyes.
Let Freedom leave, where'er she flies,   90
A Desert or a Paradise:
    Let the beautiful and the brave
    Share her glory, or a grave.

Semichorus 1

With the gifts of gladness
    Greece did thy cradle strew;

Semichorus 2

With the tears of sadness
Greece did thy shroud bedew!

Semichorus 1

With an orphan's affection
    She followed thy bier through Time;

Semichorus 2

And at thy resurrection   100
    Reappeareth, like thou, sublime!

Semichorus 1

If Heaven should resume thee,
    To Heaven shall her spirit ascend;

Semichorus 2

If Hell should entomb thee,
   To Hell shall her high hearts bend.

Semichorus 1

If Annihilation——

Semichorus 2

   Dust let her glories be!
And a name and a nation
   Be forgotten, Freedom, with thee!

Indian

His brow grows darker—breathe not—move not!   110
He starts—he shudders—ye that love not,
With your panting loud and fast,
Have awakened him at last.

Mahmud (starting from his sleep).
Man the Seraglio-guard! make fast the gate.
What! from a cannonade of three short hours?
'Tis false! that breach towards the Bosphorus°
Cannot be practicable yet—who stirs?
Stand to the match; that when the foe prevails
One spark may mix in reconciling ruin
The conqueror and the conquered! Heave the tower   120
Into the gap—wrench off the roof!
             (Enter HASSAN.*)*
                 Ha! what!
The truth of day lightens upon my dream
And I am Mahmud still.°

Hassan.   Your Sublime Highness
Is strangely moved.

Mahmud.   The times do cast strange shadows
On those who watch and who must rule their course,
Lest they, being first in peril as in glory,
Be whelmed in the fierce ebb:—and these are of them.
Thrice has a gloomy vision hunted me
As thus from sleep into the troubled day;

It shakes me as the tempest shakes the sea,   130
Leaving no figure upon memory's glass.
Would that—no matter. Thou didst say thou knewest
A Jew, whose spirit is a chronicle
Of strange and secret and forgotten things.
I bade thee summon him:—'tis said his tribe
Dream, and are wise interpreters of dreams.

    Hassan. The Jew of whom I spake is old,—so old
He seems to have outlived a world's decay;
The hoary mountains and the wrinkled ocean   140
Seem younger still than he;—his hair and beard
Are whiter than the tempest-sifted snow;
His cold pale limbs and pulseless arteries
Are like the fibres of a cloud instinct
With light, and to the soul that quickens them
Are as the atoms of the mountain-drift
To the winter wind:—but from his eye looks forth
A life of unconsumèd thought which pierces
The present, and the past, and the to-come.
Some say that this is he whom the great prophet
Jesus, the son of Joseph, for his mockery   150
Mocked with the curse of immortality.°
Some feign that he is Enoch: others dream°
He was pre-adamite and has survived
Cycles of generation and of ruin.
The sage, in truth, by dreadful abstinence
And conquering penance of the mutinous flesh,
Deep contemplation, and unwearied study,
In years outstretched beyond the date of man,
May have attained to sovereignty and science
Over those strong and secret things and thoughts   160
Which others fear and know not.

    Mahmud.   I would talk
With this old Jew.

    Hassan.   Thy will is even now
Made known to him, where he dwells in a sea-cavern
'Mid the Demonesi, less accessible°
Than thou or God! He who would question him

Must sail alone at sunset, where the stream
Of Ocean sleeps around those foamless isles,
When the young moon is westering as now,
And evening airs wander upon the wave;
And when the pines of that bee-pasturing isle,   170
Green Erebinthus, quench the fiery shadow
Of his gilt prow within the sapphire water,
Then must the lonely helmsman cry aloud
'Ahasuerus!' and the caverns round
Will answer 'Ahasuerus!' If his prayer
Be granted, a faint meteor will arise
Lighting him over Marmora, and a wind°
Will rush out of the sighing pine-forest,
And with the wind a storm of harmony
Unutterably sweet, and pilot him   180
Through the soft twilight to the Bosphorus:
Thence at the hour and place and circumstance
Fit for the matter of their conference
The Jew appears. Few dare, and few who dare
Win the desired communion—but that shout
Bodes——   [*A shout within*

Mahmud. Evil, doubtless; like all human sounds.
Let me converse with spirits.

Hassan.   That shout again.

Mahmud. This Jew whom thou hast summoned—

Hassan.   Will be here—

Mahmud. When the omnipotent hour to which are yoked
He, I, and all things shall compel—enough.   190
Silence those mutineers—that drunken crew,
That crowd about the pilot in the storm.
Ay! strike the foremost shorter by a head!
They weary me, and I have need of rest.
Kings are like stars—they rise and set, they have
The worship of the world, but no repose.

                                                   [*Exeunt severally*.

Chorus°

Worlds on worlds are rolling ever
    From creation to decay,
Like the bubbles on a river
    Sparkling, bursting, borne away.   200
But they are still immortal
Who, through birth's orient portal
And death's dark chasm hurrying to and fro,
    Clothe their unceasing flight
    In the brief dust and light
Gathered around their chariots as they go;
      New shapes they still may weave,
      New gods, new laws receive,
Bright or dim are they as the robes they last
      On Death's bare ribs had cast.°   210

A power from the unknown God,°
    A Promethean conqueror came;
Like a triumphal path he trod
    The thorns of death and shame.
    A mortal shape to him
    Was like the vapour dim
Which the orient planet animates with light;
      Hell, Sin and Slavery came,
      Like bloodhounds mild and tame,
Nor preyed, until their Lord had taken flight;   220
      The moon of Mahomet°
      Arose, and it shall set:
While blazoned as on Heaven's immortal noon
    The cross leads generations on.

Swift as the radiant shapes of sleep
    From one whose dreams are Paradise
Fly, when the fond wretch wakes to weep,
    And day peers forth with her blank eyes;
      So fleet, so faint, so fair,
      The Powers of earth and air   230
Fled from the folding star of Bethlehem:
      Apollo, Pan, and Love,
      And even Olympian Jove

Grew weak, for killing Truth had glared on them;
        Our hills and seas and streams
        Dispeopled of their dreams,
Their waters turned to blood, their dew to tears,
        Wailed for the golden years.°
Enter MAHMUD, HASSAN, DAOOD, *and others.*

Mahmud. More gold? our ancestors bought gold with victory,
And shall I sell it for defeat?

Daood.   The Janizars°   240
Clamour for pay.

Mahmud.   Go! bid them pay themselves
With Christian blood! Are there no Grecian virgins
Whose shrieks and spasms and tears they may enjoy?
No infidel children to impale on spears?
No hoary priests after that Patriarch°
Who bent the curse against his country's heart,°
Which clove his own at last? Go! bid them kill,
Blood is the seed of gold.

Daood.   It has been sown,
And yet the harvest to the sicklemen
Is as a grain to each.

Mahmud.   Then, take this signet,   250
Unlock the seventh chamber in which lie
The treasures of victorious Solyman.°
An empire's spoil stored for a day of ruin.
O spirit of my sires! is it not come?
The prey-birds and the wolves are gorged and sleep;
But these, who spread their feast on the red earth,
Hunger for gold, which fills not.—See them fed;
Then, lead them to the rivers of fresh death.

                                              [*Exit* DAOOD.

O! miserable dawn, after a night
More glorious than the day which it usurped!   260
O, faith in God! O, power on earth! O, word
Of the great prophet, whose o'ershadowing wings

Darkened the thrones and idols of the West,
Now bright!—For thy sake cursèd be the hour,
Even as a father by an evil child,
When the orient moon of Islam rolled in triumph
From Caucasus to White Ceraunia!°
Ruin above, and anarchy below;
Terror without, and treachery within;
The chalice of destruction full, and all   270
Thirsting to drink; and who among us dares
To dash it from his lips? and where is Hope?

   Hassan. The lamp of our dominion still rides high;
One God is God—Mahomet is his prophet.
Four hundred thousand Moslems, from the limits
Of utmost Asia, irresistibly
Throng, like full clouds at the Sirocco's cry;°
But not like them to weep their strength in tears:
They bear destroying lightning, and their step
Wakes earthquake to consume and overwhelm,   280
And reign in ruin. Phrygian Olympus,
Tmolus, and Latmos, and Mycale, roughen°
With horrent arms; and lofty ships even now,
Like vapours anchored to a mountain's edge,
Freighted with fire and whirlwind, wait at Scala°
The convoy of the ever-veering wind.
Samos is drunk with blood;—the Greek has paid.
Brief victory with swift loss and long despair.
The false Moldavian serfs fled fast and far,°
When the fierce shout of 'Allah-illa-Allah!'°   290
Rose like the war-cry of the northern wind
Which kills the sluggish clouds, and leaves a flock
Of wild swans struggling with the naked storm.
So were the lost Greeks on the Danube's day!°
If night is mute, yet the returning sun
Kindles the voices of the morning birds;
Nor at thy bidding less exultingly
Than birds rejoicing in the golden day,
The Anarchies of Africa unleash°
Their tempest-wingèd cities of the sea,   300
To speak in thunder to the rebel world.
Like sulphurous clouds, half-shattered by the storm,

They sweep the pale Aegean, while the Queen
Of Ocean, bound upon her island-throne,°
Far in the West sits mourning that her sons
Who frown on Freedom spare a smile for thee:
Russia still hovers, as an eagle might
Within a cloud, near which a kite and crane
Hang tangled in inextricable fight,
To stoop upon the victor;—for she fears   310
The name of Freedom, even as she hates thine.
But recreant Austria loves thee as the Grave°
Loves Pestilence, and her slow dogs of war,
Fleshed with the chase, come up from Italy,
And howl upon their limits; for they see
The panther, Freedom, fled to her old cover,
'Mid seas and mountains, and a mightier brood
Crouch round. What Anarch wears a crown or mitre,
Or bears the sword, or grasps the key of gold,
Whose friends are not thy friends, whose foes thy foes?   320
Our arsenals and our armories are full;
Our forts defy assault; ten thousand cannon
Lie ranged upon the beach, and hour by hour
Their earth-convulsing wheels affright the city;
The galloping of fiery steeds makes pale
The Christian merchant; and the yellow Jew
Hides his hoard deeper in the faithless earth.
Like clouds, and like the shadows of the clouds,
Over the hills of Anatolia,°
Swift in wide troops the Tartar chivalry   330
Sweep;—the far flashing of their starry lances
Reverberates the dying light of day.
We have one God, one King, one Hope, one Law;°
But many-headed Insurrection stands
Divided in itself, and soon must fall.

    Mahmud.   Proud words, when deeds come short, are seasonable:
Look, Hassan, on yon crescent moon, emblazoned
Upon that shattered flag of fiery cloud
Which leads the rear of the departing day;
Wan emblem of an empire fading now!   340
See how it trembles in the blood-red air,
And like a mighty lamp whose oil is spent

Shrinks on the horizon's edge, while, from above,
One star with insolent and victorious light
Hovers above its fall, and with keen beams,
Like arrows through a fainting antelope,
Strikes its weak form to death.

   Hassan.   Even as that moon
Renews itself——

   Mahmud.   Shall we be not renewed!
Far other bark than ours were needed now
To stem the torrent of descending time: 350
The spirit that lifts the slave before his lord
Stalks through the capitals of armèd kings,
And spreads his ensign in the wilderness:
Exults in chains; and, when the rebel falls,
Cries like the blood of Abel from the dust;
And the inheritors of the earth, like beasts
When earthquake is unleashed, with idiot fear
Cower in their kingly dens—as I do now.
What were Defeat when Victory must appal?
Or Danger, when Security looks pale?—   360
How said the messenger—who, from the fort
Islanded in the Danube, saw the battle
Of Bucharest?—that—°

   Hassan.   Ibrahim's scimitar
Drew with its gleam swift victory from heaven,
To burn before him in the night of battle—
A light and a destruction.

   Mahmud.   Ay! the day
Was ours: but how?——

   Hassan.   The light Wallachians,
The Arnaut, Servian, and Albanian allies
Fled from the glance of our artillery   370
Almost before the thunderstone alit.
One half the Grecian army made a bridge
Of safe and slow retreat, with Moslem dead;
The other—

Mahmud. Speak—tremble not.—

Hassan.   Islanded
By victor myriads, formed in hollow square
With rough and steadfast front, and thrice flung back
The deluge of our foaming cavalry;
Thrice their keen wedge of battle pierced our lines.
Our baffled army trembled like one man
Before a host, and gave them space; but soon,
From the surrounding hills, the batteries blazed,   380
Kneading them down with fire and iron rain;
Yet none approached; till, like a field of corn
Under the hook of the swart sickleman,
The band, intrenched in mounds of Turkish dead,
Grew weak and few.—Then said the Pacha, 'Slaves,°
Render yourselves—they have abandoned you—
What hope of refuge, or retreat, or aid?
We grant your lives.' 'Grant that which is thine own!'
Cried one, and fell upon his sword and died!
Another—'God, and man, and hope abandon me;   390
But I to them, and to myself, remain
Constant:'—he bowed his head, and his heart burst.
A third exclaimed, 'There is a refuge, tyrant,
Where thou darest not pursue, and canst not harm,
Shouldst thou pursue; there we shall meet again.'
Then held his breath, and, after a brief spasm,
The indignant spirit cast its mortal garment
Among the slain—dead earth upon the earth!
So these survivors, each by different ways,
Some strange, all sudden, none dishonourable,   400
Met in triumphant death; and when our army
Closed in, while yet wonder, and awe, and shame,
Held back the base hyenas of the battle
That feed upon the dead and fly the living,
One rose out of the chaos of the slain:
And if it were a corpse which some dread spirit
Of the old saviours of the land we rule
Had lifted in its anger wandering by;—
Or if there burned within the dying man
Unquenchable disdain of death, and faith   410
Creating what it feigned;—I cannot tell—

But he cried, 'Phantoms of the free, we come!
Armies of the Eternal, ye who strike
To dust the citadels of sanguine kings,
And shake the souls throned on their stony hearts,
And thaw their frostwork diadems like dew;—
O ye who float around this clime, and weave
The garment of the glory which it wears,
Whose fame, though earth betray the dust it clasped,
Lies sepulchred in monumental thought;—   420
Progenitors of all that yet is great,
Ascribe to your bright senate, O accept°
In your high ministrations, us, your sons—
Us first, and the more glorious yet to come!
And ye, weak conquerors! giants who look pale
When the crushed worm rebels beneath your tread,
The vultures and the dogs, your pensioners tame,
Are overgorged; but, like oppressors, still
They crave the relic of Destruction's feast.
The exhalations and the thirsty winds   430
Are sick with blood; the dew is foul with death;
Heaven's light is quenched in slaughter: thus, where'er
Upon your camps, cities, or towers, or fleets,
The obscene birds the reeking remnants cast
Of these dead limbs,—upon your streams and mountains,
Upon your fields, your gardens, and your housetops,
Where'er the winds shall creep, or the clouds fly,
Or the dews fall, or the angry sun look down
With poisoned light—Famine and Pestilence,
And Panic, shall wage war upon our side!   440
Nature from all her boundaries is moved
Against ye: Time has found ye light as foam.
The Earth rebels; and Good and Evil stake
Their empire o'er the unborn world of men
On this one cast;—but ere the die be thrown,
The renovated genius of our race,
Proud umpire of the impious game, descends
A seraph-wingèd Victory, bestriding
The tempest of the Omnipotence of God,
Which sweeps all things to their appointed doom,   450
And you to oblivion!'—More he would have said,
But—

Mahmud. Died—as thou shouldst ere thy lips had painted
Their ruin in the hues of our success.
A rebel's crime gilt with a rebel's tongue!
Your heart is Greek, Hassan.

Hassan.   It may be so:
A spirit not my own wrenched me within,
And I have spoken words I fear and hate;
Yet would I die for—

Mahmud.   Live! O live! outlive
Me and this sinking empire. But the fleet—

Hassan. Alas!——

Mahmud.   The fleet which, like a flock of clouds   460
Chased by the wind, flies the insurgent banner.
Our wingèd castles from their merchant ships!
Our myriads before their weak pirate bands!
Our arms before their chains! our years of empire
Before their centuries of servile fear!
Death is awake! Repulse is on the waters!
They own no more the thunder-bearing banner
Of Mahmud; but, like hounds of a base breed,
Gorge from a stranger's hand, and rend their master.

Hassan. Latmos, and Ampelos, and Phanae, saw   470
The wreck—

Mahmud.   The caves of the Icarian isles°
Told each to the other in loud mockery,
And with the tongue as of a thousand echoes,
First of the sea-convulsing fight—and, then,—
Thou darest to speak—senseless are the mountains;
Interpret thou their voice!

Hassan.   My presence bore
A part in that day's shame. The Grecian fleet
Bore down at day-break from the North, and hung
As multitudinous on the ocean line,
As cranes upon the cloudless Thracian wind.   480

Our squadron, convoying ten thousand men,
Was stretching towards Nauplia when the battle°
Was kindled.—
First through the hail of our artillery
The agile Hydriote barks with press of sail°
Dashed:—ship to ship, cannon to cannon, man
To man were grappled in the embrace of war,
Inextricable but by death or victory.
The tempest of the raging fight convulsed
To its crystalline depths that stainless sea,   490
And shook Heaven's roof of golden morning clouds,
Poised on an hundred azure mountain-isles.
In the brief trances of the artillery
One cry from the destroyed and the destroyer
Rose, and a cloud of desolation wrapped
The unforeseen event, till the north wind
Sprung from the sea, lifting the heavy veil
Of battle-smoke—then victory—victory!
For, as we thought, three frigates from Algiers
Bore down from Naxos to our aid, but soon°   500
The abhorrèd cross glimmered behind, before,
Among, around us; and that fatal sign
Dried with its beams the strength in Moslem hearts,
As the sun drinks the dew.—What more? We fled!—
Our noonday path over the sanguine foam
Was beaconed—and the glare struck the sun pale—
By our consuming transports: the fierce light
Made all the shadows of our sails blood-red,
And every countenance blank. Some ships lay feeding
The ravening fire, even to the water's level;   510
Some were blown up; some, settling heavily,
Sunk; and the shrieks of our companions died
Upon the wind, that bore us fast and far,
Even after they were dead. Nine thousand perished!
We met the vultures legioned in the air
Stemming the torrent of the tainted wind;
They, screaming from their cloudy mountain peaks,
Stooped through the sulphurous battle-smoke and perched
Each on the weltering carcase that we loved,
Like its ill angel or its damnèd soul,   520
Riding upon the bosom of the sea.

We saw the dog-fish hastening to their feast.
Joy waked the voiceless people of the sea,
And ravening Famine left his ocean cave
To dwell with war, with us, and with despair.
We met night three hours to the west of Patmos°
And with night, tempest——°

Mahmud.   Cease!
                    (*Enter a Messenger.*)

  Messenger.   Your Sublime Highness,
That Christian hound, the Muscovite Ambassador,
Has left the city.—If the rebel fleet°
Had anchored in the port, had victory   530
Crowned the Greek legions in the Hippodrome,°
Panic were tamer.—Obedience and Mutiny,
Like giants in contention planet-struck,°
Stand gazing on each other.—There is peace
In Stamboul.—

  Mahmud.   Is the grave not calmer still?
Its ruins shall be mine.

  Hassan.   Fear not the Russian:
The tiger leagues not with the stag at bay
Against the hunter.—Cunning, base, and cruel,
He crouches, watching till the spoil be won,
And must be paid for his reserve in blood.   540
After the war is fought, yield the sleek Russian
That which thou canst not keep, his deserved portion
Of blood, which shall not flow through streets and fields,
Rivers and seas, like that which we may win,
But stagnate in the veins of Christian slaves!
                    (*Enter second Messenger.*)

  Second Messenger. Nauplia, Tripolizza, Mothon, Athens,
Navarin, Artas, Monembasia,°
Corinth and Thebes are carried by assault,
And every Islamite who made his dogs
Fat with the flesh of Galilean slaves   550
Passed at the edge of the sword: the lust of blood

Which made our warriors drunk, is quenched in death;
But like a fiery plague breaks out anew
In deeds which make the Christian cause look pale
In its own light. The garrison of Patras°
Has store but for ten days, nor is there hope
But from the Briton: at once slave and tyrant
His wishes still are weaker than his fears,
Or he would sell what faith may yet remain
From the oaths broke in Genoa and in Norway;°   560
And if you buy him not, your treasury
Is empty even of promises—his own coin.
The freedman of a western poet chief°
Holds Attica with seven thousand rebels,°
And has beat back the Pacha of Negropont:°
The aged Ali sits in Yanina°
A crownless metaphor of empire:
His name, that shadow of his withered might,
Holds our besieging army like a spell
In prey to famine, pest, and mutiny;   570
He, bastioned in his citadel, looks forth
Joyless upon the sapphire lake that mirrors
The ruins of the city where he reigned
Childless and sceptreless. The Greek has reaped
The costly harvest his own blood matured,
Not the sower, Ali—who has bought a truce
From Ypsilanti with ten camel loads°
Of Indian gold.
                    (*Enter a third Messenger.*)

    Mahmud.   What more?

    Third Messenger.   The Christian tribes
Of Lebanon and the Syrian wilderness
Are in revolt;—Damascus, Hems, Aleppo   580
Tremble;—the Arab menaces Medina,
The Ethiop has intrenched himself in Sennaar,°
And keeps the Egyptian rebel well employed,
Who denies homage, claims investiture
As price of tardy aid. Persia demands
The cities on the Tigris, and the Georgians
Refuse their living tribute. Crete and Cyprus,°

Like mountain-twins that from each other's veins
Catch the volcano-fire and earthquake spasm,
Shake in the general fever. Through the city,   590
Like birds before a storm, the Santons shriek,°
And prophesyings horrible and new°
Are heard among the crowd: that sea of men
Sleeps on the wrecks it made, breathless and still.
A Dervise, learned in the Koran, preaches°
That it is written how the sins of Islam
Must raise up a destroyer even now.
The Greeks expect a Saviour from the west,
Who shall not come, men say, in clouds and glory,°
But in the omnipresence of that spirit   600
In which all live and are. Ominous signs
Are blazoned broadly on the noonday sky:
One saw a red cross stamped upon the sun;
It has rained blood; and monstrous births declare
The secret wrath of Nature and her Lord.
The army encamped upon the Cydaris,°
Was roused last night by the alarm of battle,
And saw two hosts conflicting in the air,
The shadows doubtless of the unborn time
Cast on the mirror of the night. While yet   610
The fight hung balanced, there arose a storm
Which swept the phantoms from among the stars.
At the third watch the spirit of the plague
Was heard abroad flapping among the tents;
Those who relieved watch found the sentinels dead.
The last news from the camp is that a thousand
Have sickened, and——
                    (*Enter a fourth Messenger.*)

   Mahmud.   And thou, pale ghost, dim shadow
Of some untimely rumour, speak!

   Fourth Messenger.   One comes
Fainting with toil, covered with foam and blood:
He stood, he says, on Chelonites'°   620
Promontory, which o'erlooks the isles that groan°
Under the Briton's frown, and all their waters
Then trembling in the splendour of the moon,

When as the wandering clouds unveiled or hid
Her boundless light, he saw two adverse fleets
Stalk through the night in the horizon's glimmer,
Mingling fierce thunders and sulphureous gleams,°
And smoke which strangled every infant wind
That soothed the silver clouds through the deep air.
At length the battle slept, but the Sirocco   630
Awoke, and drove his flock of thunder-clouds
Over the sea-horizon, blotting out
All objects—save that in the faint moon-glimpse
He saw, or dreamed he saw, the Turkish admiral
And two the loftiest of our ships of war,
With the bright image of that Queen of Heaven
Who hid, perhaps, her face for grief, reversed;
And the abhorrèd cross—

(Enter an Attendant.)

Attendant.   Your Sublime Highness,
The Jew, who——

Mahmud.   Could not come more seasonably:
Bid him attend. I'll hear no more! too long   640
We gaze on danger through the mist of fear,
And multiply upon our shattered hopes
The images of ruin. Come what will!
Tomorrow and tomorrow are as lamps°
Set in our path to light us to the edge
Through rough and smooth, nor can we suffer aught
Which he inflicts not in whose hand we are.

[Exeunt.

Semichorus 1

Would I were the wingèd cloud
Of a tempest swift and loud,
I would scorn   650
The smile of morn
And the wave where the moonrise is born!
I would leave
The spirits of eve
A shroud for the corpse of the day to weave
From other threads than mine!

Bask in the deep blue noon divine
Who would, not I.

Semichorus 2
Whither to fly?

Semichorus 1
Where the rocks that gird th' Aegean   660
Echo to the battle paean
Of the free—
I would flee,
A tempestuous herald of victory!
My golden rain
For the Grecian slain
Should mingle in tears with the bloody main,
And my solemn thunder-knell
Should ring to the world the passing bell   670
Of tyranny!

Semichorus 2
Ha king! wilt thou chain
The rack and the rain?
Wilt thou fetter the lightning and hurricane?
The storms are free,
But we?

Chorus
O Slavery! thou frost of the world's prime,
Killing its flowers and leaving its thorns bare!
Thy touch has stamped these limbs with crime,
These brows thy branding garland bear,
But the free heart, the impassive soul   680
Scorn thy control!

Semichorus 1
Let there be light! said Liberty,
And like sunrise from the sea,
Athens arose!—Around her born,
Shone like mountains in the morn
Glorious states;—and are they now
Ashes, wrecks, oblivion?

Semichorus 2

        Go,
Where Thermae and Asopus swallowed°
   Persia, as the sand does foam.
Deluge upon deluge followed,   690
   Discord, Macedon, and Rome:
And lastly thou!

Semichorus 1

       Temples and towers,
Citadels and marts, and they
   Who live and die there, have been ours,
And may be thine, and must decay;
   But Greece and her foundations are
   Built below the tide of war,
   Based on the crystalline sea
   Of thought and its eternity;
Her citizens, imperial spirits,   700
   Rule the present from the past,
On all this world of men inherits
   Their seal is set.

Semichorus 2

       Hear ye the blast,
Whose Orphic thunder thrilling calls
From ruin her Titanian walls?
Whose spirit shakes the sapless bones
   Of Slavery? Argos, Corinth, Crete
Hear, and from their mountain thrones
   The daemons and the nymphs repeat
The harmony.

Semichorus 1

   I hear! I hear!   710

Semichorus 2

The world's eyeless charioteer,
   Destiny, is hurrying by!
What faith is crushed, what empire bleeds
Beneath her earthquake-footed steeds?
What eagle-wingèd victory sits

At her right hand? what shadow flits
Before? what splendour rolls behind?
      Ruin and renovation cry
'Who but we?'

Semichorus 1
     I hear! I hear!
  The hiss as of a rushing wind,   720
The roar as of an ocean foaming,
The thunder as of earthquake coming.
     I hear! I hear!
The crash as of an empire falling,
The shrieks as of a people calling
'Mercy! mercy!' How they thrill!
Then a shout of 'kill! kill! kill!'
And then a small still voice, thus—

Semichorus 2
                             For°
Revenge and wrong bring forth their kind,
  The foul cubs like their parents are,
Their den is in the guilty mind,
  And Conscience feeds them with despair.

Semichorus 1
In sacred Athens, near the fane
  Of Wisdom, Pity's altar stood:
Serve not the unknown God in vain,°
But pay that broken shrine again,
  Love for hate and tears for blood.
(*Enter* MAHMUD *and* AHASUERUS.)

Mahmud. Thou art a man thou sayest even as we.

Ahasuerus. No more!

Mahmud.   But raised above thy fellow men
By thought, as I by power.

Ahasuerus.   Thou sayest so.   740

Mahmud. Thou art an adept in the difficult lore
Of Greek and Frank philosophy; thou numberest°
The flowers, and thou measurest the stars;
Thou severest element from element;
Thy spirit is present in the past, and sees
The birth of this old world through all its cycles
Of desolation and of loveliness,
And when man was not, and how man became
The monarch and the slave of this low sphere,
And all its narrow circles—it is much—   750
I honour thee, and would be what thou art
Were I not what I am; but the unborn hour,
Cradled in fear and hope, conflicting storms,
Who shall unveil? Nor thou, nor I, nor any
Mighty or wise. I apprehended not
What thou hast taught me, but I now perceive
That thou art no interpreter of dreams;
Thou dost not own that art, device, or God,
Can make the future present—let it come!
Moreover thou disdainest us and ours;   760
Thou art as God, whom thou contemplatest.

Ahasuerus. Disdain thee?—not the worm beneath thy feet!
The Fathomless has care for meaner things
Than thou canst dream, and has made pride for those
Who would be what they may not, or would seem
That which they are not. Sultan! talk no more
Of thee and me, the future and the past;
But look on that which cannot change—the One,
The unborn and the undying. Earth and ocean,
Space, and the isles of life or light that gem   770
The sapphire floods of interstellar air,
This firmament pavilioned upon chaos,
With all its cressets of immortal fire,
Whose outwall, bastioned impregnably
Against the escape of boldest thoughts, repels them
As Calpe the Atlantic clouds—this Whole°
Of suns, and worlds, and men, and beasts, and flowers,
With all the silent or tempestuous workings
By which they have been, are, or cease to be,
Is but a vision;—all that it inherits°   780

Are motes of a sick eye, bubbles and dreams;°
Thought is its cradle and its grave, nor less
The future and the past are idle shadows
Of thought's eternal flight—they have no being:
Nought is but that which feels itself to be.°

   Mahmud. What meanest thou? Thy words stream like a tempest
Of dazzling mist within my brain—they shake
The earth on which I stand, and hang like night
On Heaven above me. What can they avail?
They cast on all things surest, brightest, best,   790
Doubt, insecurity, astonishment.

   Ahasuerus. Mistake me not! All is contained in each.
Dodona's forest to an acorn's cup°
Is that which has been, or will be, to that
Which is—the absent to the present. Thought
Alone, and its quick elements, Will, Passion,
Reason, Imagination, cannot die;
They are, what that which they regard appears,
The stuff whence mutability can weave
All that it hath dominion o'er, worlds, worms,   800
Empires, and superstitions. What has thought
To do with time, or place, or circumstance?
Wouldst thou behold the future?—ask and have!
Knock and it shall be opened—look and, lo!°
The coming age is shadowed on the past
As on a glass.

   Mahmud.   Wild, wilder thoughts convulse
My spirit—Did not Mahomet the Second
Win Stamboul?°

   Ahasuerus.   Thou wouldst ask that giant spirit
The written fortunes of thy house and faith.
Thou wouldst cite one out of the grave to tell   810
How what was born in blood must die.

   Mahmud.   Thy words
Have power on me! I see——

Ahasuerus.   What hearest thou?

Mahmud. A far whisper——
Terrible silence.

Ahasuerus.   What succeeds?

Mahmud.   The sound
As of the assault of an imperial city,
The hiss of inextinguishable fire,
The roar of giant cannon; the earthquaking
Fall of vast bastions and precipitous towers,
The shock of crags shot from strange engin'ry,
The clash of wheels, and clang of armèd hoofs,   820
And crash of brazen mail as of the wreck
Of adamantine mountains—the mad blast
Of trumpets, and the neigh of raging steeds,
And shrieks of women whose thrill jars the blood,
And one sweet laugh, most horrible to hear,
As of a joyous infant waked and playing
With its dead mother's breast, and now more loud
The mingled battle-cry,—ha! hear I not
'*Εν τούτῳ νικη!*' 'Allah, Illah, Allah!'°

Ahasuerus. The sulphurous mist is raised—thou seest—

Mahmud.   A chasm, 830
As of two mountains in the wall of Stamboul;
And in that ghastly breach the Islamites,
Like giants on the ruins of a world,
Stand in the light of sunrise. In the dust
Glimmers a kingless diadem, and one
Of regal port has cast himself beneath
The stream of war. Another proudly clad
In golden arms spurs a Tartarian barb°
Into the gap, and with his iron mace
Directs the torrent of that tide of men,   840
And seems—he is—Mahomet!

Ahasuerus.   What thou seest
Is but the ghost of thy forgotten dream.

A dream itself, yet less, perhaps, than that
Thou call'st reality. Thou mayst behold
How cities, on which Empire sleeps enthroned,
Bow their towered crests to mutability.
Poised by the flood, e'en on the height thou holdest,
Thou mayst now learn how the full tide of power
Ebbs to its depths.—Inheritor of glory,
Conceived in darkness, born in blood, and nourished   850
With tears and toil, thou seest the mortal throes
Of that whose birth was but the same. The Past
Now stands before thee like an Incarnation
Of the To-come; yet wouldst thou commune with
That portion of thyself which was ere thou
Didst start for this brief race whose crown is death.
Dissolve with that strong faith and fervent passion
Which called it from the uncreated deep,
Yon cloud of war, with its tempestuous phantoms
Of raging death; and draw with mighty will   860
The imperial shade hither.

                                        [*Exit* AHASUERUS.

Mahmud.   Approach!

Phantom.   I come
Thence whither thou must go! The grave is fitter
To take the living than give up the dead;
Yet has thy faith prevailed, and I am here.
The heavy fragments of the power which fell
When I arose, like shapeless crags and clouds,
Hang round my throne on the abyss, and voices
Of strange lament soothe my supreme repose,
Wailing for glory never to return.—
  A later Empire nods in its decay: 870
The autumn of a greener faith is come,
And wolfish change, like winter, howls to strip
The foliage in which Fame, the eagle, built
Her eyrie, while Dominion whelped below.
The storm is in its branches, and the frost
Is on its leaves, and the blank deep expects
Oblivion on oblivion, spoil on spoil,
Ruin on ruin:—Thou art slow, my son;

The Anarchs of the world of darkness keep
A throne for thee, round which thine empire lies   880
Boundless and mute; and for thy subjects thou,
Like us, shalt rule the ghosts of murdered life,
The phantoms of the powers who rule thee now—
Mutinous passions, and conflicting fears,
And hopes that sate themselves on dust and die!—
Stripped of their mortal strength, as thou of thine.
Islam must fall, but we will reign together
Over its ruins in the world of death:—
And if the trunk be dry, yet shall the seed
Unfold itself even in the shape of that   890
Which gathers birth in its decay. Woe! woe!
To the weak people tangled in the grasp
Of its last spasms.

   Mahmud.   Spirit, woe to all!
Woe to the wronged and the avenger! Woe
To the destroyer, woe to the destroyed!
Woe to the dupe, and woe to the deceiver!
Woe to the oppressed, and woe to the oppressor!
Woe both to those that suffer and inflict;
Those who are born and those who die! but say,
Imperial shadow of the thing I am,   900
When, how, by whom, Destruction must accomplish
Her consummation?

   Phantom.   Ask the cold pale Hour,
Rich in reversion of impending death,°
When *he* shall fall upon whose ripe grey hairs
Sit Care, and Sorrow, and Infirmity—
The weight which Crime, whose wings are plumed with years,
Leaves in his flight from ravaged heart to heart
Over the heads of men, under which burden
They bow themselves unto the grave: fond wretch!
He leans upon his crutch, and talks of years   910
To come, and how in hours of youth renewed
He will renew lost joys, and——
                 Voice without
                   Victory! Victory!
                          [The Phantom vanishes.

Mahmud. What sound of the importunate earth has broken
My mighty trance?

Voice without
Victory! Victory!

Mahmud. Weak lightning before darkness! poor faint smile
Of dying Islam! Voice which art the response
Of hollow weakness! Do I wake and live?
Were there such things, or may the unquiet brain,
Vexed by the wise mad talk of the old Jew,
Have shaped itself these shadows of its fear?°   920
It matters not!—for nought we see or dream,
Possess, or lose, or grasp at, can be worth
More than it gives or teaches. Come what may,
The future must become the past, and I
As they were to whom once this present hour,
This gloomy crag of time to which I cling,
Seemed an Elysian isle of peace and joy
Never to be attained.—I must rebuke
This drunkenness of triumph ere it die,
And dying, bring despair. Victory! poor slaves!

[*Exit Mahmud.*

Voice without

Shout in the jubilee of death! The Greeks   931
Are as a brood of lions in the net
Round which the kingly hunters of the earth
Stand smiling. Anarchs, ye whose daily food
Are curses, groans, and gold, the fruit of death
From Thule to the girdle of the world,°
Come, feast! the board groans with the flesh of men;
The cup is foaming with a nation's blood,
Famine and Thirst await! eat, drink, and die!

Semichorus 1

Victorious Wrong, with vulture scream,   940
Salutes the risen sun, pursues the flying day!
   I saw her, ghastly as a tyrant's dream,
Perch on the trembling pyramid of night,
Beneath which earth and all her realms pavilioned lay
In visions of the dawning undelight:

Who shall impede her flight?
Who rob her of her prey?
Voice without.
Victory! Victory! Russia's famished eagles°
Dare not to prey beneath the crescent's light.
Impale the remnant of the Greeks! despoil!   950
Violate! make their flesh cheaper than dust!

Semichorus 2

Thou voice which art
The herald of the ill in splendour hid!
Thou echo of the hollow heart
Of monarchy, bear me to thine abode
When desolation flashes o'er a world destroyed:
Oh, bear me to those isles of jagged cloud
Which float like mountains on the earthquake, mid
The momentary oceans of the lightning,°
Or to some toppling promontory proud   960
Of solid tempest whose black pyramid,
Riven, overhangs the founts intensely bright'ning
Of those dawn-tinted deluges of fire
Before their waves expire,
When heaven and earth are light, and only light
In the thunder night!
Voice without
Victory! Victory! Austria, Russia, England,
And that tame serpent, that poor shadow, France,
Cry peace, and that means death when monarchs speak.
Ho, there! bring torches, sharpen those red stakes,   970
These chains are light, fitter for slaves and poisoners
Than Greeks. Kill! plunder! burn! let none remain.

Semichorus 1

Alas! for Liberty!
If numbers, wealth, or unfulfilling years,
Or fate, can quell the free!
Alas! for Virtue, when
Torments, or contumely, or the sneers.°
Of erring judging men
Can break the heart where it abides.

Alas! if Love, whose smile makes this obscure world splendid,   980
    Can change with its false times and tides,
        Like hope and terror,—
           Alas for Love!
And Truth, who wanderest lone and unbefriended,
If thou canst veil thy lie-consuming mirror
        Before the dazzled eyes of Error,
        Alas for thee! Image of the Above.°

Semichorus 2

    Repulse, with plumes from conquest torn,
Led the ten thousand from the limits of the morn
        Through many an hostile Anarchy!   990
At length they wept aloud, and cried, 'The Sea! The Sea!'°
    Through exile, persecution, and despair,
        Rome was, and young Atlantis shall become°
        The wonder, or the terror, or the tomb
Of all whose step wakes power lulled in her savage lair:
        But Greece was as a hermit-child,
        Whose fairest thoughts and limbs were built
    To woman's growth, by dreams so mild,
        She knew not pain or guilt;
And now, O Victory, blush! and Empire tremble   1000
        When ye desert the free—
        If Greece must be
A wreck, yet shall its fragments reassemble,
And build themselves again impregnably
        In a diviner clime
To Amphionic music on some Cape sublime,°
Which frowns above the idle foam of Time.

Semichorus 1

    Let the tyrants rule the desert they have made;
        Let the free possess the paradise they claim;
    Be the fortune of our fierce oppressors weighed   1010
        With our ruin, our resistance, and our name!

Semichorus 2

    Our dead shall be the seed of their decay,
        Our survivors be the shadow of their pride,
    Our adversity a dream to pass away—
        Their dishonour a remembrance to abide!

Voice without

Victory! Victory! The bought Briton sends
The keys of ocean to the Islamite.—°
Now shall the blazon of the cross be veiled,
And British skill directing Othman might,°
Thunderstrike rebel victory. O keep holy   1020
This jubilee of unrevengèd blood—
Kill! crush! despoil! Let not a Greek escape!

Semichorus 1

   Darkness has dawned in the East
      On the noon of time:
   The death-birds descend to their feast,
      From the hungry clime.
   Let Freedom and Peace flee far
      To a sunnier strand,
   And follow Love's folding star
      To the Evening land!°   1030

Semichorus 2

   The young moon has fed
     Her exhausted horn,
       With the sunset's fire:
   The weak day is dead,
     But the night is not born;
And, like loveliness panting with wild desire
   While it trembles with fear and delight,
   Hesperus flies from awakening night,
And pants in its beauty and speed with light
   Fast flashing, soft, and bright.   1040
     Thou beacon of love! thou lamp of the free!
     Guide us far, far away,
To climes where now veiled by the ardour of day
     Thou art hidden
   From waves on which weary noon,
   Faints in her summer swoon,
   Between Kingless continents sinless as Eden,
   Around mountains and islands inviolably
   Pranked on the sapphire sea.°

Semichorus 1

Through the sunset of hope,   1050
Like the shapes of a dream,
What Paradise islands of glory gleam!
   Beneath Heaven's cope,
Their shadows more clear float by—
The sound of their oceans, the light of their sky,
The music and fragrance their solitudes breathe
Burst, like morning on dream, or like Heaven on death,
   Through the walls of our prison;
And Greece, which was dead, is arisen!

Chorus°

The world's great age begins anew,   1060
   The golden years return,°
The earth doth like a snake renew
   Her winter weeds outworn:°
Heaven smiles, and faiths and empires gleam,
Like wrecks of a dissolving dream.

A brighter Hellas rears its mountains
   From waves serener far;
A new Peneus rolls his fountains°
   Against the morning-star.
Where fairer Tempes bloom, there sleep   1070
Young Cyclads on a sunnier deep.°

A loftier Argo cleaves the main,°
   Fraught with a later prize;
Another Orpheus sings again,
   And loves, and weeps, and dies.°
A new Ulysses leaves once more
Calypso for his native shore.°

O, write no more the tale of Troy,
   If earth Death's scroll must be!
Nor mix with Laian rage the joy°   1080
   Which dawns upon the free:
Although a subtler Sphinx renew°
Riddles of death Thebes never knew.

Another Athens shall arise,
   And to remoter time
Bequeath, like sunset to the skies,
   The splendour of its prime,
And leave, if nought so bright may live,
All earth can take or Heaven can give.

Saturn and Love their long repose   1090
   Shall burst, more bright and good
Than all who fell, than One who rose,°
   Than many unsubdued:
Not gold, not blood, their altar dowers°
But votive tears and symbol flowers.

O cease! must hate and death return?
   Cease! must men kill and die?
Cease! drain not to its dregs the urn
   Of bitter prophecy.
The world is weary of the past,   1100
O might it die or rest at last!

NOTES TO 'HELLAS'°

Line 60

The quenchless ashes of Milan.

Milan was the centre of the resistance of the Lombard league against the Austrian tyrant. Frederic Barbarossa burnt the city to the ground, but liberty lived in its ashes, and it rose like an exhalation from its ruin. See Sismondi's *Histoire des Républiques Italiennes*, a book which has done much towards awakening the Italians to an imitation of their great ancestors.

Line 197

The Chorus.

The popular notions of Christianity are represented in this chorus as true in their relation to the worship they superseded, and that which in all probability they will supersede, without considering their merits in a relation more universal. The first stanza contrasts the immortality of the living and thinking beings which inhabit the planets, and to use a common and inadequate phrase, *clothe themselves in matter* with the transience of the noblest manifestations of the external world.

The concluding verses indicate a progressive state of more or less exalted existence, according to the degree of perfection which every distinct intelligence may have attained. Let it not be supposed that I mean to dogmatize upon a subject, concerning which all men are equally ignorant, or that I think the Gordian knot of the origin of evil can be disentangled by that or any similar assertions. The received hypothesis of a Being resembling men in the moral attributes of his nature, having called us out of non-existence, and after inflicting on us the misery of the commission of error, should superadd that of the punishment and the privations consequent upon it, still would remain inexplicable and incredible. That there is a true solution of the riddle, and that in our present state that solution is unattainable by us, are propositions which may be regarded as equally certain: meanwhile, as it is the province of the poet to attach himself to those ideas which exalt and ennoble humanity, let him be permitted to have conjectured the condition of that futurity towards which we are all impelled by an inextinguishable thirst for immortality. Until better arguments can be produced than sophisms which disgrace the cause, this desire itself must remain the strongest and the only presumption that eternity is the inheritance of every thinking being.

Line 245

No hoary priests after that Patriarch.

The Greek Patriarch after having been compelled to fulminate an anathema against the insurgents was put to death by the Turks.

Fortunately the Greeks have been taught that they cannot buy security by degradation, and the Turks, though equally cruel, are less cunning than the smooth-faced tyrants of Europe. As to the anathema, his Holiness might as well have thrown his mitre at Mount Athos for any effect that it produced. The chiefs of the Greeks are almost all men of comprehension and enlightened views on religion and politics.

Line 563

The freedman of a western poet chief.

A Greek who had been Lord Byron's servant commands the insurgents in Attica. This Greek, Lord Byron informs me, though a poet and an enthusiastic patriot, gave him rather the idea of a timid and unenterprising person. It appears that circumstances make men what they are, and that we all contain the germ of a degree of degradation or of greatness whose connexion with our character is determined by events.

Line 598

The Greeks expect a Saviour from the west.

It is reported that this Messiah had arrived at a sea-port near Lacedaemon in an American brig. The association of names and ideas is irresistibly ludicrous,

but the prevalence of such a rumour strongly marks the state of popular
enthusiasm in Greece.

Lines 814–15

The sound
As of the assault of an imperial city.

For the vision of Mahmud of the taking of Constantinople in 1453,° see
Gibbon's *Decline and Fall of the Roman Empire*, vol. xii. p. 223.

The manner of the invocation of the spirit of Mahomet the Second will be
censured as over subtle. I could easily have made the Jew a regular conjuror,
and the Phantom° an ordinary ghost. I have preferred to represent the Jew
as disclaiming all pretension, or even belief, in supernatural agency, and as
tempting Mahmud to that state of mind in which ideas may be supposed to
assume the force of sensations through the confusion of thought with the
objects of thought, and the excess of passion animating the creations of
imagination.

It is a sort of natural magic, susceptible of being exercised in a degree by
any one who should have made himself master of° the secret associations of
another's thoughts.

Line 1060

The Chorus

The final chorus is indistinct and obscure, as the event of the living drama
whose arrival it foretells. Prophecies of wars, and rumours of wars, &c. may
safely be made by poet or prophet in any age, but to anticipate however darkly
a period of regeneration and happiness is a more hazardous exercise of the
faculty which bards possess or feign. It will remind the reader 'magno *nec
proximus intervallo*'° of Isaiah and Virgil, whose ardent spirits overleaping the
actual reign of evil which we endure and bewail, already saw the possible and
perhaps approaching state of society in which the '*lion shall lie down with the
lamb*,' and 'omnis feret omnia tellus.'° Let these great names be my authority
and my excuse.

Lines 1090–1

Saturn and Love their long repose
Shall burst.

Saturn and Love were among the deities of a real or imaginary state of inno-
cence and happiness. *All* those *who fell*, or the Gods of Greece, Asia, and
Egypt; *the One who rose*, or Jesus Christ, at whose appearance the idols of the
Pagan World were amerced° of their worship,° and *the many unsubdued*,
or the monstrous objects of the idolatry of China, India, the Antarctic
islands, and the native tribes of America, certainly have reigned over the

understandings of men in conjunction or in succession, during periods in which all we know of evil has been in a state of portentous, and, until the revival of learning and the arts, perpetually increasing activity. The Grecian gods seem indeed to have been personally more innocent, although it cannot be said that as far as temperance and chastity are concerned, they gave so edifying an example as their successor. The sublime human character of Jesus Christ was deformed by an imputed identification with a Demon,° who tempted, betrayed, and punished the innocent beings who were called into existence by his sole will; and for the period of a thousand years, the spirit of this, the most just, wise and benevolent of men, has been propitiated with myriads of hecatombs° of those who approached the nearest to his innocence and his wisdom, sacrificed under every aggravation of atrocity and variety of torture.° The horrors of the Mexican, the Peruvian, and the Indian superstitions are well known.

Written on Hearing the News of the Death of Napoleon

I

What! alive and so bold, oh Earth?
    Art thou not overbold?
    What! leapest thou forth as of old
In the light of thy morning mirth,
The last of the flock of the starry fold?
Ha! leapest thou forth as of old?
Are not the limbs still when the ghost is fled,
And canst thou move, Napoleon being dead?

2

How! is not thy quick heart cold?
    What spark is alive on thy hearth?°   10
How! is not *his* death-knell knolled?
    And livest *thou* still, Mother Earth?
Thou wert warming thy fingers old
O'er the embers covered and cold
Of that most fiery spirit, when it fled—
What, Mother, do you laugh now he is dead?

3

'Who has known me of old,' replied Earth,
    'Or who has my story told?
    It is thou who art overbold.'
And the lightning of scorn laughed forth   20
As she sung, 'To my bosom I fold
All my sons when their knell is knolled,
And so with living motion all are fed
And the quick spring like weeds out of the dead.

4

'Still alive and still bold,' shouted Earth,
    'I grow bolder and still more bold.
    The dead fill me ten thousand fold
Fuller of speed and splendour and mirth.

I was cloudy, and sullen, and cold,
Like a frozen chaos uprolled,   30
Till by the spirit of the mighty dead
My heart grew warm. I feed on whom I fed.

                    5
'Aye, alive and still bold,' muttered Earth,
    'Napoleon's fierce spirit rolled,
    In terror and blood and gold,
A torrent of ruin to death from his birth.
Leave the millions who follow to mould
The metal before it be cold,
And weave into his shame, which like the dead
Shrouds me, the hopes that from his glory fled.'   40

'The flower that smiles today'

The flower that smiles today
    Tomorrow dies;
All that we wish to stay
    Tempts and then flies;
What is this world's delight?
Lightning, that mocks the night,
    Brief even as bright.—°

Virtue, how frail it is!—
    Friendship, how rare!—
Love, how it sells poor bliss   10
    For proud despair!
But these, though soon they fall,°
Survive their joy, and all°
    Which ours we call.—

Whilst skies are blue and bright,
    Whilst flowers are gay,
Whilst eyes that change ere night
    Make glad the day;
Whilst yet the calm hours creep

Dream thou—and from thy sleep 20
  Then wake to weep.

To —— ('*One word is too often profaned*')

One word is too often profaned
  For me to profane it,
One feeling too falsely disdained
  For thee to disdain it.
One hope is too like despair
  For prudence to smother,
And Pity from thee more dear
  Than that from another.

I can give not what men call love,
  But wilt thou accept not 10
The worship the heart lifts above
  And the Heavens reject not,
The desire of the moth for the star,
  Of the night for the morrow,
The devotion to something afar
  From the sphere of our sorrow?

'*When the lamp is shattered*'

When the lamp is shattered
The light in the dust lies dead—°
  When the cloud is scattered
The rainbow's glory is shed—
  When the lute is broken
Sweet tones are remembered not—
  When the lips have spoken
Loved accents are soon forgot.

  As music and splendour
Survive not the lamp and the lute, 10
  The heart's echoes render

No song when the spirit is mute—
   No song—but sad dirges
Like the wind through a ruined cell
   Or the mournful surges
That ring the dead seaman's knell.°

   When hearts have once mingled°
Love first leaves the well-built nest—
   The weak one is singled
To endure what it once possessed.   20
   O Love! who bewailest
The frailty of all things here
   Why choose you the frailest
For your cradle, your home and your bier?

   Its passions will rock thee°
As the storms rock the ravens on high—
   Bright Reason will mock thee
Like the Sun from a wintry sky—
   From thy nest every rafter
Will rot, and thine eagle home   30
   Leave thee naked to laughter
When leaves fall and cold winds come.°

To —— ('The serpent is shut out from Paradise')

1

The serpent is shut out from Paradise—
The wounded deer must seek the herb no more
In which its heart's cure lies—
The widowed dove must cease to haunt a bower
Like that from which its mate, with feignèd sighs,
Fled in the April hour—
I, too, must seldom seek again
Near happy friends a mitigated pain.

2

Of hatred I am proud,—with scorn content;
Indifference, which once hurt me, is now grown   10

Itself indifferent.
But not to speak of love, Pity alone
Can break a spirit already more than bent.
The miserable one
Turns the mind's poison into food:
Its medicine is tears, its evil, good.°

3

Therefore, if now I see you seldomer,
Dear friends, dear *friend*, know that I only fly°
Your looks, because they stir
Griefs that should sleep, and hopes that cannot die.   20
The very comfort which they minister
I scarce can bear; yet I
(So deeply is the arrow gone)
Should quickly perish if it were withdrawn.

4

When I return to my cold home, you ask
Why I am not as I have lately been?
You spoil me for the task
Of acting a forced part in life's dull scene.°
Of wearing on my brow the idle mask
Of author, great or mean,   30
In the world's carnival. I sought
Peace thus, and but in you I found it not.

5

Full half an hour today I tried my lot
With various flowers, and every one still said,
'She loves me, loves me not.'
And if this meant a Vision long since fled—
If it meant Fortune, Fame, or Peace of thought—
If it meant—(but I dread
To speak what you may know too well)—
Still there was truth in the sad oracle.   40

6

The crane o'er seas and forests seeks her home.
No bird so wild, but has its quiet nest°

When it no more would roam.
The sleepless billows on the Ocean's breast
Break like a bursting heart, and die in foam
And thus, at length, find rest.
Doubtless there is a place of peace
Where *my* weak heart and all its throbs will cease.

                              7

I asked her yesterday if she believed
That I had resolution. One who *had*   50
Would ne'er have thus relieved
His heart with words, but what his judgement bade
Would do, and leave the scorner unrelieved.—
These verses were too sad
To send to you, but that I know,
Happy yourself, you feel another's woe.

To Jane. The Invitation

Best and brightest, come away—
Fairer far than this fair day
Which like thee to those in sorrow
Comes to bid a sweet good-morrow
To the rough year just awake
In its cradle on the brake.—°
The brightest hour of unborn spring
Through the winter wandering
Found it seems this halcyon morn
To hoar February born;   10
Bending from Heaven in azure mirth
It kissed the forehead of the earth
And smiled upon the silent sea,
And bade the frozen streams be free
And waked to music all their fountains
And breathed upon the frozen mountains
And like a prophetess of May
Strewed flowers upon the barren way,
Making the wintry world appear
Like one on whom thou smilest, dear.   20

Away, away from men and towns
To the wild wood and the downs,
To the silent wilderness
Where the soul need not repress
Its music lest it should not find
An echo in another's mind,
While the touch of Nature's art
Harmonizes heart to heart.—
'I leave this notice on my door
For each accustomed visitor—   30
I am gone into the fields
To take what this sweet hour yields—
Reflection, you may come tomorrow,
Sit by the fireside with Sorrow—
You, with the unpaid bill, Despair,
You, tiresome verse-reciter Care,
I will pay you in the grave
Death will listen to your stave—
Expectation too, be off!
Today is for itself enough—   40
Hope, in pity mock not woe
With smiles, nor follow where I go;
Long having lived on thy sweet food
At length I find one moment's good
After long pain—with all your love
This you never told me of.'

Radiant Sister of the day,
Awake, arise and come away°
To the wild woods and the plains
And the pools where winter-rains   50
Image all their roof of leaves,
Where the pine its garland weaves
Of sapless green and ivy dun
Round stems that never kiss the Sun—
Where the lawns and pastures be
And the sand hills of the sea—
Where the melting hoar-frost wets
The daisy-star that never sets,°
And wind-flowers, and violets
Which yet join not scent to hue   60

Crown the pale year weak and new
When the night is left behind
In the deep east dun and blind
And the blue noon is over us,
And the multitudinous
Billows murmur at our feet
Where the earth and ocean meet
And all things seem only one°
In the universal Sun.—

To Jane—The Recollection

Feb. 2. 1822

Now the last day of many days,
All beautiful and bright as thou,
The loveliest and the last, is dead.
Rise Memory, and write its praise!
Up to thy wonted work! come, trace
The epitaph of glory fled;°
For now the Earth has changed its face,
A frown is on the Heaven's brow.

1

We wandered to the pine forest
    That skirts the Ocean foam;   10
The lightest wind was in its nest,
    The Tempest in its home;
The whispering waves were half asleep,
    The clouds were gone to play,
And on the bosom of the deep
    The smile of Heaven lay;
It seemed as if the hour were one
    Sent from beyond the skies,
Which scattered from above the sun
    A light of Paradise.   20

2

We paused amid the pines that stood
    The giants of the waste,

Tortured by storms to shapes as rude
   As serpents interlaced,
And soothed by every azure breath
   That under Heaven is blown
To harmonies and hues beneath,
   As tender as its own;
Now all the tree-tops lay asleep
   Like green waves on the sea,   30
As still as in the silent deep
   The Ocean woods may be.

3

How calm it was! the silence there
   By such a chain was bound
That even the busy woodpecker
   Made stiller with her sound
The inviolable quietness;
   The breath of peace we drew
With its soft motion made not less
   The calm that round us grew.—   40
There seemed from the remotest seat
   Of the white mountain-waste,
To the soft flower beneath our feet
   A magic circle traced,
A spirit interfused around°
   A thrilling silent life.
To momentary peace it bound
   Our mortal nature's strife;—
And still I felt the centre of
   The magic circle there   50
Was *one* fair form that filled with love
   The lifeless atmosphere.

4

We paused beside the pools that lie
   Under the forest bough—
Each seemed as 'twere, a little sky
   Gulfed in a world below;
A firmament of purple light
   Which in the dark earth lay

More boundless than the depth of night
    And purer than the day,   60
In which the lovely forests grew
    As in the upper air
More perfect, both in shape and hue,
    Than any spreading there;
There lay the glade, the neighbouring lawn,
    And through the dark green wood
The white sun twinkling like the dawn
    Out of a speckled cloud.

5

Sweet views, which in our world above
    Can never well be seen,   70
Were imaged in the water's love
    Of that fair forest green;
And all was interfused beneath
    With an Elysian glow,
An atmosphere without a breath,
    A softer day below—
Like one beloved, the scene had lent
    To the dark water's breast
Its every leaf and lineament
    With more than truth expressed;   80
Until an envious wind crept by,
    Like an unwelcome thought
Which from the mind's too faithful eye
    Blots one dear image out.—
Though thou art ever fair and kind
    And forests ever green,
Less oft is peace in ———'s mind°
    Than calm in water seen.

The Magnetic Lady to Her Patient

    'Sleep, sleep on, forget thy pain—
        My hand is on thy brow,
        My spirit on thy brain

My pity on thy heart, poor friend;
    And from my fingers flow
The powers of life, and like a sign°
Seal thee from thine hour of woe,
And brood on thee, but may not blend
        With thine.

'Sleep, sleep, sleep on—I love thee not—   10
    Yet when I think that *he*°
    Who made and makes my lot
As full of flowers, as thine of weeds,
    Might have been lost like thee,—
And that a hand which was not mine
Might then have charmed his agony
As I another's . . . my heart bleeds
        For thine.

'Sleep, sleep, and with the slumber of
    The dead and the unborn . . .   20
    Forget thy life and love;
Forget that thou must wake;—forever
    Forget the world's dull scorn.—
Forget lost health, and the divine
Feelings which died in youth's brief morn;
And forget me, for I can never
        Be thine.—

'Like a cloud big with a May shower
    My soul weeps healing rain
    On thee, thou withered flower.—   30
It breathes mute music on thy sleep—
    Its odour calms thy brain—
Its light within thy gloomy breast
Spreads, like a second youth again—
By mine thy being is to its deep
        Possessed.

'The spell is done—how feel you now?'
    'Better, quite well' replied
    The sleeper—'What would do

You good when suffering and awake,   40
   What cure your head and side?'
'What would cure that would kill me, Jane,
And as I must on earth abide
Awhile yet, tempt me not to break
     My chain.'

With a Guitar. To Jane

Ariel to *Miranda*;—Take
This slave of music for the sake
Of him who is the slave of thee;
And teach it all the harmony,
In which thou canst, and only thou,
Make the delighted spirit glow,
Till joy denies itself again
And too intense is turned to pain;
For by permission and command
Of thine own *prince Ferdinand*   10
Poor Ariel sends this silent token
Of more than ever can be spoken;
Your guardian spirit Ariel, who
From life to life must still pursue
Your happiness, for thus alone
Can Ariel ever find his own;
From Prospero's enchanted cell,
As the mighty verses tell,°
To the throne of Naples he
Lit you o'er the trackless sea,   20
Flitting on, your prow before,
Like a living meteor.
When you die, the silent Moon
In her interlunar swoon
Is not sadder in her cell
Than deserted Ariel;
When you live again on Earth°
Like an unseen Star of birth
Ariel guides you o'er the sea
Of life from your nativity;   30

Many changes have been run
Since Ferdinand and you begun
Your course of love, and Ariel still
Has tracked your steps and served your will.
Now, in humbler, happier lot
This is all remembered not;
And now, alas! the poor sprite is
Imprisoned for some fault of his
In a body like a grave.—
From you, he only dares to crave   40
For his service and his sorrow
A smile today, a song tomorrow.

The artist who this idol wrought
To echo all harmonious thought
Felled a tree, while on the steep
The woods were in their winter sleep
Rocked in that repose divine
On the wind-swept Apennine;
And dreaming, some of autumn past
And some of spring approaching fast,   50
And some of April buds and showers
And some of songs in July bowers
And all of love,—and so this tree—
O that such our death may be—
Died in sleep and felt no pain
To live in happier form again,
From which, beneath Heaven's fairest star,
The artist wrought this loved guitar,
And taught it justly to reply
To all who question skilfully   60
In language gentle as thine own;
Whispering in enamoured tone
Sweet oracles of woods and dells
And summer winds in sylvan cells.
For it had learnt all harmonies
Of the plains and of the skies,
Of the forests and of the mountains,
And the many-voicèd fountains,
The clearest echoes of the hills,
The softest notes of falling rills,   70

The melodies of birds and bees,
The murmuring of summer seas,
And pattering rain and breathing dew
And airs of evening;—and it knew
That seldom heard mysterious sound,
Which, driven on its diurnal round
As it floats through boundless day
Our world enkindles on its way—
All this it knows, but will not tell
To those who cannot question well   80
The spirit that inhabits it:
It talks according to the wit
Of its companions, and no more
Is heard than has been felt before
By those who tempt it to betray
These secrets of an elder day.—
But, sweetly as its answers will
Flatter hands of perfect skill,
It keeps its highest holiest tone
For our beloved Jane alone.—   90

To Jane ('The keen stars were twinkling')

The keen stars were twinkling
And the fair moon was rising among them,
        Dear Jane.
    The guitar was tinkling
But the notes were not sweet 'till you sung them
        Again.—
    As the moon's soft splendour
O'er the faint cold starlight of Heaven
        Is thrown—
    So your voice most tender   10
To the strings without soul had then given
        Its own.

    The stars will awaken,
Though the moon sleep a full hour later,
        Tonight;

No leaf will be shaken
While the dews of your melody scatter
Delight.
Though the sound overpowers
Sing again, with your dear voice revealing   20
A tone
Of some world far from ours,
Where music and moonlight and feeling
Are one.°

Lines Written in the Bay of Lerici

Bright wanderer, fair coquette of Heaven,
To whom alone it has been given
To change and be adored forever. . . .
Envy not this dim world, for never
But once within its shadow grew
One fair as you, but far more true.
She left me at the silent time
When the moon had ceased to climb
The azure dome of Heaven's steep,
And like an albatross asleep,   10
Balanced on her wings of light,
Hovered in the purple night,
Ere she sought her Ocean nest,
In the chambers of the west.—°
She left me, and I stayed alone
Thinking over every tone,
Which though now silent to the ear
The enchanted heart could hear
Like notes which die when born, but still
Haunt the echoes of the hill: 20
And feeling ever—O too much—
The soft vibrations of her touch
As if her gentle hand even now
Lightly trembles on my brow;
And thus although she absent were
Memory gave me all of her
That even fancy dares to claim.—

Her presence had made weak and tame
All passions, and I lived alone
In the time which is our own;   30
The past and future were forgot
As they had been, and would be, not.—°
But soon, the guardian angel gone,
The demon reassumed his throne
In my faint heart . . . I dare not speak
My thoughts; but thus disturbed and weak
I sate and watched the vessels glide
Along the Ocean bright and wide,
Like spirit-wingèd chariots sent
O'er some serenest element   40
To ministrations strange and far;
As if to some Elysian star
They sailed for drink to medicine
Such sweet and bitter pain as mine.—
And the wind that winged their flight
From the land came fresh and light,
And the scent of sleeping flowers
And the coolness of the hours
Of dew, and the sweet warmth of day
Was scattered o'er the twinkling bay;   50
And the fisher with his lamp
And spear, about the low rocks damp
Crept, and struck the fish who came
To worship the delusive flame:
Too happy, they whose pleasure sought
Extinguishes all sense and thought
Of the regret that pleasure [   ],°
Seeking life alone, not peace.°

THE TRIUMPH OF LIFE

Swift as a spirit hastening to his task
   Of glory and of good, the Sun sprang forth
Rejoicing in his splendour, and the mask

   Of darkness fell from the awakened Earth.
The smokeless altars of the mountain snows
   Flamed above crimson clouds, and at the birth

Of light, the Ocean's orison arose°
   To which the birds tempered their matin lay.
All flowers in field or forest which unclose

   Their trembling eyelids to the kiss of day,   10
Swinging their censers in the element,
   With orient incense lit by the new ray

Burned slow and inconsumably, and sent
   Their odorous sighs up to the smiling air,
And in succession due, did Continent,

   Isle, Ocean, and all things that in them wear
The form and character of mortal mould
   Rise as the Sun their father rose, to bear

Their portion of the toil which he of old
   Took as his own and then imposed on them;
But I, whom thoughts which must remain untold

   Had kept as wakeful as the stars that gem
The cone of night, now they were laid asleep,
   Stretched my faint limbs beneath the hoary stem

Which an old chestnut flung athwart the steep
   Of a green Apennine: before me fled
The night; behind me rose the day; the Deep

   Was at my feet, and Heaven above my head°
When a strange trance over my fancy grew
   Which was not slumber, for the shade it spread   30

Was so transparent that the scene came through
   As clear as when a veil of light is drawn
O'er evening hills they glimmer; and I knew

   That I had felt the freshness of that dawn,
Bathed in the same cold dew my brow and hair
   And sate as thus upon that slope of lawn

Under the self-same bough, and heard as there
   The birds, the fountains and the Ocean hold
Sweet talk in music through the enamoured air.
   And then a Vision on my brain was rolled. . . .   40

As in that trance of wondrous thought I lay
   This was the tenour of my waking dream.
Methought I sate beside a public way

   Thick strewn with summer dust, and a great stream
Of people there was hurrying to and fro°
   Numerous as gnats upon the evening gleam,

All hastening onward, yet none seemed to know
   Whither he went, or whence he came, or why
He made one of the multitude, yet so

   Was borne amid the crowd as through the sky   50
One of the million leaves of summer's bier.—
   Old age and youth, manhood and infancy,

Mixed in one mighty torrent did appear,
   Some flying from the thing they feared and some°
Seeking the object of another's fear,

   And others as with steps towards the tomb
Pored on the trodden worms that crawled beneath,
   And others mournfully within the gloom

Of their own shadow walked, and called it death . . .
   And some fled from it as it were a ghost,   60
Half fainting in the affliction of vain breath.

But more with motions which each other crossed
Pursued or shunned the shadows the clouds threw
  Or birds within the noonday ether lost,

Upon that path where flowers never grew;
  And weary with vain toil and faint for thirst
Heard not the fountains whose melodious dew

  Out of their mossy cells forever burst,
Nor felt the breeze which from the forest told
  Of grassy paths, and wood lawns interspersed   70

With overarching elms and caverns cold,
  And violet banks where sweet dreams brood, but they
Pursued their serious folly as of old . . .

  And as I gazed methought that in the way
The throng grew wilder, as the woods of June
  When the South wind shakes the extinguished day.—

And a cold glare, intenser than the noon
  But icy cold, obscured with [   ] light°
The Sun as he the stars. Like the young moon

  When on the sunlit limits of the night   80
Her white shell trembles amid crimson air,
  And whilst the sleeping tempest gathers might

Doth, as a herald of its coming, bear
  The ghost of her dead mother, whose dim form°
Bends in dark ether from her infant's chair,

  So came a chariot on the silent storm°
Of its own rushing splendour, and a Shape
  So sate within as one whom years deform

Beneath a dusky hood and double cape
  Crouching within the shadow of a tomb,   90
And o'er what seemed the head a cloud like crape°

Was bent, a dun and faint etherial gloom
Tempering the light; upon the chariot's beam
  A Janus-visaged Shadow did assume°

The guidance of that wonder-wingèd team.
  The Shapes which drew it in thick lightnings
Were lost: I heard alone on the air's soft stream

  The music of their ever-moving wings.
All the four faces of that charioteer
  Had their eyes banded . . . little profit brings   100

Speed in the van and blindness in the rear,
  Nor then avail the beams that quench the Sun
Or that his banded eyes could pierce the sphere

  Of all that is, has been, or will be done.—
So ill was the car guided, but it passed
  With solemn speed majestically on . . .

The crowd gave way, and I arose aghast
  Or seemed to rise, so mighty was the trance,
And saw like clouds upon the thunder-blast

  The million with fierce song and maniac dance   110
Raging around; such seemed the jubilee
  As when to greet some conqueror's advance

Imperial Rome poured forth her living sea
  From senate-house and prison and theatre,
When Freedom left those who upon the free

  Had bound a yoke which soon they stooped to bear.°
Nor wanted here the true similitude
  Of a triumphal pageant, for where'er

The chariot rolled a captive multitude
  Was driven; all those who had grown old in power   120
Or misery,—all who have their age subdued

By action or by suffering, and whose hour
Was drained to its last sand in weal or woe,
 So that the trunk survived both fruit and flower;

All those whose fame or infamy must grow
 Till the great winter lay the form and name°
Of their green earth with them forever low—

 All but the sacred few who could not tame°
Their spirits to the Conqueror, but as soon
 As they had touched the world with living flame   130

Fled back like eagles to their native noon,
 Or those who put aside the diadem
Of earthly thrones or gems, till the last one

 Were there; for they of Athens and Jerusalem
Were neither mid the mighty captives seen
 Nor mid the ribald crowd that followed them

Or fled before . . . Now swift, fierce and obscene,
 The wild dance maddens in the van, and those
Who lead it, fleet as shadows on the green,

 Outspeed the chariot and without repose   140
Mix with each other in tempestuous measure
 To savage music. . . . Wilder as it grows,

They, tortured by the agonizing pleasure,
 Convulsed and on the rapid whirlwinds spun
Of that fierce spirit, whose unholy leisure

 Was soothed by mischief since the world begun,
Throw back their heads and loose their streaming hair,
 And in their dance round her who dims the Sun°

Maidens and youths fling their wild arms in air
 As their feet twinkle; they recede, and now   150
Bending within each other's atmosphere

Kindle invisibly; and as they glow
Like moths by light attracted and repelled,
  Oft to new bright destruction come and go,

Till like two clouds into one vale impelled
  That shake the mountains when their lightnings mingle
And die in rain—the fiery band which held

  Their natures, snaps . . . ere the shock cease to tingle
One falls and then another in the path
  Senseless, nor is the desolation single,   160

Yet ere I can say *where* the chariot hath
  Passed over them; nor other trace I find
But as of foam after the Ocean's wrath

  Is spent upon the desert shore.—Behind,
Old men, and women foully disarrayed
  Shake their grey hair in the insulting wind,

Limp in the dance and strain with limbs decayed
  To reach the car of light which leaves them still
Farther behind and deeper in the shade.

  But not the less with impotence of will   170
They wheel, though ghastly shadows interpose
  Round them and round each other, and fulfil

Their work and to the dust whence they arose
  Sink, and corruption veils them as they lie,
And frost in these performs what fire in those.°

  Struck to the heart by this sad pageantry,
Half to myself I said, 'And what is this?
  Whose shape is that within the car? and why'—

I would have added—'is all here amiss?'
  But a voice answered . . . 'Life' . . . I turned and knew   180
(O Heaven have mercy on such wretchedness!)

That what I thought was an old root which grew
To strange distortion out of the hillside
   Was indeed one of that deluded crew,

And that the grass which methought hung so wide
   And white, was but his thin discoloured hair,
And that the holes it vainly sought to hide

   Were or had been eyes.—'If thou canst forbear
To join the dance, which I had well forborne,'
   Said the grim Feature, of my thought aware,°   190

'I will now tell that which to this deep scorn
   Led me and my companions, and relate
The progress of the pageant since the morn.

   'If thirst of knowledge doth not thus abate,
Follow it even to the night, but I
   Am weary' . . . Then like one who with the weight

Of his own words is staggered, wearily
   He paused, and ere he could resume, I cried,
'First who art thou?' . . . 'Before thy memory

   'I feared, loved, hated, suffered, did, and died,   200
And if the spark with which Heaven lit my spirit
   Earth had with purer nutriment supplied

'Corruption would not now thus much inherit
   Of what was once Rousseau—nor this disguise
Stained that within which still disdains to wear it.—

   'If I have been extinguished, yet there rise
A thousand beacons from the spark I bore.'°
   'And who are those chained to the car?' 'The wise,

'The great, the unforgotten: they who wore
   Mitres and helms and crowns, or wreaths of light,   210
Signs of thought's empire over thought; their lore

'Taught them not this—to know themselves; their might
Could not repress the mutiny within,
    And for the morn of truth they feigned, deep night

'Caught them ere evening.' 'Who is he with chin°
    Upon his breast and hands crossed on his chain?'
'The Child of a fierce hour; he sought to win

    'The world, and lost all it did contain
Of greatness, in its hope destroyed; and more
    Of fame and peace than Virtue's self can gain   220

'Without the opportunity which bore
    Him on its eagle's pinion to the peak
From which a thousand climbers have before

    'Fall'n as Napoleon fell.'—I felt my cheek
Alter to see the great form pass away
    Whose grasp had left the giant world so weak

That every pigmy kicked it as it lay—
    And much I grieved to think how power and will
In opposition rule our mortal day—

    And why God made irreconcilable   230
Good and the means of good; and for despair
    I half disdained mine eye's desire to fill

With the spent vision of the times that were
    And scarce have ceased to be . . . 'Dost thou behold,'
Said then my guide, 'those spoilers spoiled, Voltaire,

    'Frederick and Kant, Catherine and Leopold,°
Chained hoary anarch, demagogue and sage°
    Whose name the fresh world thinks already old,

'For in the battle Life and they did wage
    She remained conqueror—I was overcome   240
By my own heart alone, which neither age

'Nor tears nor infamy nor now the tomb
Could temper to its object.' 'Let them pass',°
    I cried, '—the world and its mysterious doom

'Is not so much more glorious than it was
    That I desire to worship those who drew
New figures on its false and fragile glass

    'As the old faded.'—'Figures ever new
Rise on the bubble, paint them how you may;
    We have but thrown, as those before us threw,   250

'Our shadows on it as it passed away.
    But mark, how chained to the triumphal chair
The mighty phantoms of an elder day—

    'All that is mortal of great Plato there
Expiates the joy and woe his master knew not;°
    That star that ruled his doom was far too fair—°

'And Life, where long that flower of Heaven grew not,
    Conquered the heart by love which gold or pain
Or age or sloth or slavery could subdue not—

    'And near [   ] walk the [   ] twain,   260
The tutor and his pupil, whom Dominion°
    Followed as tame as vulture in a chain.—

'The world was darkened beneath either pinion
    Of him whom from the flock of conquerors
Fame singled as her thunder-bearing minion;

    'The other long outlived both woes and wars,
Throned in new thoughts of men, and still had kept
    The jealous keys of truth's eternal doors

'If Bacon's spirit had not leapt
    Like lightning out of darkness; he compelled   270
The Proteus shape of Nature's as it slept

'To wake and to unbar the caves that held
The treasure of the secrets of its reign.—
　　See the great bards of old who inly quelled°

'The passions which they sung, as by their strain
　　May well be known: their living melody
Tempers its own contagion to the vein

　　'Of those who are infected with it—I
Have suffered what I wrote, or viler pain!

　　'And so my words were seeds of misery—°　　　　　280
Even as the deeds of others.'—'Not as theirs,'
　　I said—he pointed to a company

In which I recognized amid the heirs
　　Of Caesar's crime from him to Constantine°
The Anarchs old whose force and murderous snares

　　Had founded many a sceptre-bearing line,
And spread the plague of blood and gold abroad,
　　And Gregory and John and men divine°

Who rose like shadows between Man and god°
　　Till that eclipse, still hanging under Heaven,　　　290
Was worshipped by the world o'er which they strode

　　For the true Sun it quenched.—'Their power was given
But to destroy,' replied the leader—'I
　　Am one of those who have created, even

'If it be but a world of agony.'—
　　'Whence camest thou and whither goest thou?
How did thy course begin,' I said, 'and why?

　　'Mine eyes are sick of this perpetual flow
Of people, and my heart of one sad thought.—
　　Speak.'—'Whence I came, partly I seem to know,　　　300

'And how and by what paths I have been brought
　　To this dread pass, methinks even thou mayst guess;
Why this should be my mind can compass not,

'Whither the conqueror hurries me still less.
But follow thou, and from spectator turn
    Actor or victim in this wretchedness,

'And what thou wouldst be taught I then may learn
    From thee.—Now listen . . . In the April prime
When all the forest tops began to burn

'With kindling green, touched by the azure clime   310
Of the young year, I found myself asleep
    Under a mountain which from unknown time

'Had yawned into a cavern high and deep,
    And from it came a gentle rivulet
Whose water like clear air in its calm sweep

'Bent the soft grass and kept forever wet
The stems of the sweet flowers, and filled the grove
    With sound which all who hear must needs forget

'All pleasure and all pain, all hate and love,
    Which they had known before that hour of rest: 320
A sleeping mother then would dream not of

'The only child who died upon her breast
At eventide, a king would mourn no more
    The crown of which his brow was dispossessed

'When the sun lingered o'er the Ocean floor
    To gild his rival's new prosperity.—
Thou wouldst forget thus vainly to deplore

'Ills, which if ills, can find no cure from thee,
The thought of which no other sleep will quell
    Nor other music blot from memory—   330

'So sweet and deep is the oblivious spell.—
    Whether my life had been before that sleep
The Heaven which I imagine, or a Hell

'Like this harsh world in which I wake to weep,
I know not. I arose and for a space
    The scene of woods and waters seemed to keep,

'Though it was now broad day, a gentle trace
    Of light diviner than the common Sun°
Sheds on the common Earth, but all the place

'Was filled with many sounds woven into one   340
Oblivious melody, confusing sense
    Amid the gliding waves and shadows dun;

'And as I looked the bright omnipresence
    Of morning through the orient cavern flowed,
And the Sun's image radiantly intense

'Burned on the waters of the well that glowed
Like gold, and threaded all the forest maze
    With winding paths of emerald fire—there stood

'Amid the Sun, as he amid the blaze
    Of his own glory, on the vibrating   350
Floor of the fountain, paving with flashing rays,

    'A shape all light, which with one hand did fling°
Dew on the earth, as if she were the Dawn
    Whose invisible rain forever seemed to sing

'A silver music on the mossy lawn,
    And still before her on the dusky grass
Iris her many-coloured scarf had drawn.—°

    'In her right hand she bore a crystal glass
Mantling with bright Nepenthe;—the fierce splendour°
    Fell from her as she moved under the mass   360

'Of the deep cavern, and with palms so tender°
    Their tread broke not the mirror of its billow,
Glided along the river, and did bend her

    'Head under the dark boughs, till like a willow
Her fair hair swept the bosom of the stream
    That whispered with delight to be their pillow.—

'As one enamoured is upborne in dream
  O'er lily-paven lakes mid silver mist
To wondrous music, so this shape might seem

  'Partly to tread the waves with feet which kissed   370
The dancing foam, partly to glide along
  The airs that roughened the moist amethyst,

'Or the slant morning beams that fell among
  The trees, or the soft shadows of the trees;
And her feet ever to the ceaseless song

  'Of leaves and winds and waves and birds and bees
And falling drops moved in a measure new
  Yet sweet, as on the summer evening breeze

'Up from the lake a shape of golden dew
  Between two rocks, athwart the rising moon,   380
Dances i' the wind where eagle never flew.—

  'And still her feet, no less than the sweet tune
To which they moved, seemed as they moved, to blot
  The thoughts of him who gazed on them, and soon

'All that was seemed as if it had been not,
  As if the gazer's mind was strewn beneath
Her feet like embers, and she, thought by thought,

  'Trampled its fires into the dust of death,
As Day upon the threshold of the east
  Treads out the lamps of night, until the breath   390

'Of darkness re-illumines even the least
  Of heaven's living eyes—like day she came,
Making the night a dream; and ere she ceased

  'To move, as one between desire and shame
Suspended, I said—"If, as it doth seem,
  Thou comest from the realm without a name

' "Into this valley of perpetual dream,
  Show whence I came, and where I am, and why—
Pass not away upon the passing stream."

'"Arise and quench thy thirst," was her reply.   400
And as a shut lily, stricken by the wand
   Of dewy morning's vital alchemy,

'I rose; and, bending at her sweet command,
   Touched with faint lips the cup she raised,
And suddenly my brain became as sand

   'Where the first wave had more than half erased
The track of deer in desert Labrador,
   Whilst the fierce wolf from which they fled amazed

'Leaves his stamp visibly upon the shore
   Until the second bursts—so on my sight   410
Burst a new Vision never seen before.—

   'And the fair shape waned in the coming light
As veil by veil the silent splendour drops
   From Lucifer, amid the chrysolite

'Of sunrise ere it strikes the mountain tops—
   And as the presence of that fairest planet,
Although unseen, is felt by one who hopes

   'That his day's path may end as he began it
In that star's smile, whose light is like the scent
   Of a jonquil when evening breezes fan it,   420

'Or the soft note in which his dear lament
   The Brescian shepherd breathes, or the caress°
That turned his weary slumber to content—

   'So knew I in that light's severe excess°
The presence of that shape which on the stream
   Moved, as I moved along the wilderness,

'More dimly than a day-appearing dream,
   The ghost of a forgotten form of sleep,
A light from Heaven whose half-extinguished beam

   'Through the sick day in which we wake to weep   430
Glimmers, forever sought, forever lost.—
   So did that shape its obscure tenour keep

'Beside my path, as silent as a ghost;
　　But the new Vision, and its cold bright car,
With savage music, stunning music, crossed

　'The forest, and as if from some dread war
Triumphantly returning, the loud million
　　Fiercely extolled the fortune of her star.—

'A moving arch of victory the vermilion
　　And green and azure plumes of Iris had   440
Built high over her wind-wingèd pavilion,

　'And underneath etherial glory clad
The wilderness, and far before her flew
　　The tempest of the splendour which forbade

'Shadow to fall from leaf or stone;—the crew
　　Seemed in that light like atomies that dance°
Within a sunbeam.—Some upon the new

　'Embroidery of flowers that did enhance
The grassy vesture of the desert, played,
　　Forgetful of the chariot's swift advance;   450

'Others stood gazing till within the shade
　　Of the great mountain its light left them dim.—
Others outspeeded it, and others made

　'Circles around it like the clouds that swim
Round the high moon in a bright sea of air,
　　And more did follow, with exulting hymn,

'The chariot and the captives fettered there,
　　But all like bubbles on an eddying flood
Fell into the same track at last and were

　'Borne onward.—I among the multitude   460
Was swept; me sweetest flowers delayed not long,
　　Me not the shadow nor the solitude,

'Me not the falling stream's Lethean song,°
   Me, not the phantom of that early form
Which moved upon its motion,—but among

   'The thickest billows of the living storm
I plunged, and bared my bosom to the clime
   Of that cold light, whose airs too soon deform.—

'Before the chariot had begun to climb
   The opposing steep of that mysterious dell,   470
Behold a wonder worthy of the rhyme°

   'Of him who from the lowest depths of Hell°
Through every Paradise and through all glory
   Love led serene, and who returned to tell

'In words of hate and awe the wondrous story
   How all things are transfigured, except Love;
For deaf as is a sea which wrath makes hoary

   'The world can hear not the sweet notes that move
The sphere whose light is melody to lovers—°
   A wonder worthy of his rhyme—the grove   480

'Grew dense with shadows to its inmost covers,
   The earth was grey with phantoms, and the air
Was peopled with dim forms, as when there hovers

   'A flock of vampire-bats before the glare
Of the tropic sun, bringing ere evening
   Strange night upon some Indian isle,—thus were

'Phantoms diffused around, and some did fling
   Shadows of shadows, yet unlike themselves,°
Behind them, some like eaglets on the wing

   'Were lost in the white blaze, others like elves   490
Danced in a thousand unimagined shapes
   Upon the sunny streams and grassy shelves;

'And others sate chattering like restless apes
   On vulgar hands and over shoulders leapt;
Some made a cradle of the ermined capes

'Of kingly mantles, some upon the tiar
Of pontiffs sate like vultures, others played
   Within the crown which girt with empire

'A baby's or an idiot's brow, and made
   Their nests in it; the old anatomies°   500
Sate hatching their bare brood under the shade

   'Of demon wings, and laughed from their dead eyes
To reassume the delegated power
   Arrayed in which these worms did monarchize

'Who make this earth their charnel.—Others more
   Humble, like falcons sate upon the fist
Of common men, and round their heads did soar

   'Or like small gnats and flies as thick as mist
On evening marshes thronged about the brow
   Of lawyer, statesman, priest and theorist,   510

'And others like discoloured flakes of snow
   On fairest bosoms and the sunniest hair
Fell, and were melted by the youthful glow

   'Which they extinguished; for like tears, they were
A veil to those from whose faint lids they rained
   In drops of sorrow.—I became aware

'Of whence those forms proceeded which thus stained
   The track in which we moved; after brief space
From every form the beauty slowly waned,

   'From every firmest limb and fairest face   520
The strength and freshness fell like dust, and left
   The action and the shape without the grace

'Of life; the marble brow of youth was cleft
   With care, and in the eyes where once hope shone
Desire like a lioness bereft

   'Of its last cub, glared ere it died; each one
Of that great crowd sent forth incessantly
   These shadows, numerous as the dead leaves blown

'In Autumn evening from a poplar tree—
  Each, like himself and like each other were,   530
At first, but soon distorted, seemed to be

'Obscure clouds moulded by the casual air;
And of this stuff the car's creative ray°
  Wrought all the busy phantoms fluttering there

'As the sun shapes the clouds—thus, on the way,
  Mask after mask fell from the countenance
And form of all, and long before the day

  'Was old, the joy which waked like Heaven's glance
The sleepers in the oblivious valley, died,
  And some grew weary of the ghastly dance   540

'And fell, as I have fallen by the wayside,
  Those soonest, from whose forms most shadows passed
And least of strength and beauty did abide.'—

  'Then, what is Life?' I said . . . the cripple cast°
His eye upon the car which now had rolled
  Onward, as if that look must be the last,

And answered . . . 'Happy those for whom the fold
  Of°

PROSE

An Address to the People on the Death of the Princess Charlotte

BY THE HERMIT OF MARLOW°

'We pity the plumage, but forget the dying bird.'°

I. The Princess Charlotte is dead. She no longer moves, nor thinks, nor feels. She is as inanimate as the clay with which she is about to mingle. It is a dreadful thing to know that she is a putrid corpse, who but a few days since was full of life and hope; a woman young, innocent, and beautiful, snatched from the bosom of domestic peace, and leaving that single vacancy which none can die and leave not.

II. Thus much the death of the Princess Charlotte has in common with the death of thousands. How many women die in childbed and leave their families of motherless children and their husbands to live on, blighted by the remembrance of that heavy loss? How many women of active and energetic virtues; mild, affectionate, and wise, whose life is as a chain of happiness and union, which once being broken, leaves those whom it bound to perish, have died, and have been deplored with bitterness, which is too deep for words?° Some have perished in penury or shame, and their orphan baby has survived, a prey to the scorn and neglect of strangers. Men have watched by the bedside of their expiring wives, and have gone mad when the hideous death-rattle was heard within the throat, regardless of the rosy child sleeping in the lap of the unobservant nurse. The countenance of the physician had been read by the stare of this distracted husband, till the legible despair sunk into his heart. All this has been and is. You walk with a merry heart through the streets of this great city, and think not that such are the scenes acting all around you. You do not number in your thought the mothers who die in childbed. It is the most horrible of ruins:—In sickness, in old age, in battle, death comes as to his own home; but in the season of joy and hope, when life should succeed to life, and the assembled family expects one more, the youngest and the best beloved, that the wife, the mother—she for whom each member of the family was so dear to one another, should die!—Yet thousands of the poorest poor, whose misery is aggravated by what cannot be spoken now, suffer this. And have they no affections?° Do not their hearts beat in their bosoms, and the tears gush from their eyes? Are they not human flesh and blood? Yet none weep for them—none mourn for them—none when their coffins are carried to the grave (if indeed the parish furnishes a coffin for all) turn aside and moralize upon the sadness they have left behind.

III. The Athenians did well to celebrate, with public mourning, the death of those who had guided the republic with their valour and their understanding, or illustrated° it with their genius. Men do well to mourn for the dead: it proves that we love something beside ourselves; and he must have a hard heart who can see his friend depart to rottenness and dust, and speed him without emotion on his voyage to 'that bourne whence no traveller returns.'° To lament for those who have benefited the state, is a habit of piety yet more favourable to the cultivation of our best affections. When Milton died it had been well that the universal English nation had been clothed in solemn black, and that the muffled bells had tolled from town to town. The French nation should have enjoined a public mourning at the deaths of Rousseau and Voltaire. We cannot truly grieve for every one who dies beyond the circle of those especially dear to us; yet in the extinction of the objects of public love and admiration, and gratitude, there is something, if we enjoy a liberal mind, which has departed from within that circle. It were well done also, that men should mourn for any public calamity which has befallen their country or the world, though it be not death. This helps to maintain that connection between one man and another, and all men considered as a whole, which is the bond of social life. There should be public mourning when those events take place which make all good men mourn in their hearts,—the rule of foreign or domestic tyrants, the abuse of public faith, the wresting of old and venerable laws to the murder of the innocent, the established insecurity of all those, the flower of the nation, who cherish an unconquerable enthusiasm for public good. Thus, if Horne Tooke and Hardy° had been convicted of high treason, it had been good that there had been not only the sorrow and the indignation which would have filled all hearts, but the external symbols of grief. When the French Republic was extinguished, the world ought to have mourned.

IV. But this appeal to the feelings of men should not be made lightly, or in any manner that tends to waste, on inadequate objects, those fertilizing streams of sympathy which a public mourning should be the occasion of pouring forth. This solemnity should be used only to express a wide and intelligible calamity, and one which is felt to be such by those who feel for their country and for mankind; its character ought to be universal, not particular.

V. The news of the death of the Princess Charlotte, and of the execution of Brandreth, Ludlam, and Turner,° arrived nearly at the same time. If beauty, youth, innocence, amiable manners, and the exercise of the domestic virtues could alone justify public sorrow when they are extinguished forever, this interesting Lady would well deserve that exhibition. She was the last and the best of her race. But there were thousands of others equally distinguished as she, for private excellencies, who have been cut off in youth and hope. The accident of her birth neither made her life more virtuous nor her death more worthy of grief. For the public she had done nothing either good or evil; her education had rendered her incapable of either in a large and comprehensive sense. She was born a Princess; and those who are destined to rule mankind are dispensed with acquiring that wisdom and that experience which is necessary even to rule themselves. She was not like Lady Jane Grey, or Queen Elizabeth, a woman of profound and various learning. She had accomplished nothing,° and aspired to nothing, and could understand nothing respecting those great political questions which involve the happiness of those over whom she was destined to rule. Yet this should not be said in blame, but in compassion: let us speak no evil of the dead. Such is the misery, such the impotence of royalty.—Princes are prevented from the cradle from becoming any thing which may deserve that greatest of all rewards next to a good conscience, public admiration and regret.

VI. The execution of Brandreth, Ludlam, and Turner, is an event of quite a different character from the death of the Princess Charlotte. These men were shut up in a horrible dungeon, for many months, with the fear of a hideous death and of everlasting hell thrust before their eyes; and at last were brought to the scaffold and hung. They too had domestic affections, and were remarkable for the exercise of private virtues. Perhaps their low station permitted the growth of those affections in a degree not consistent with a more exalted rank. They had sons, and brothers, and sisters, and fathers, who loved them, it should seem, more than the Princess Charlotte could be loved by those whom the regulations of her rank had held in perpetual estrangement from her. Her husband° was to her as father, mother, and brethren. Ludlam and Turner were men of mature years, and the affections were ripened and strengthened within them. What these sufferers felt shall not be said. But what must have been the long and various agony of their kindred may be inferred from Edward Turner, who, when he saw his brother dragged along upon the hurdle,° shrieked horribly and fell in a fit, and was carried away like a corpse by two men. How fearful must have been their agony, sitting in solitude on that day when the tempestuous voice of horror from the crowd told them that the head so dear to them was severed from the body! Yes—they listened to the maddening shriek which burst from the multitude; they heard the rush of ten thousand terror-stricken feet, the groans and the hootings which told them that the mangled and distorted head was then lifted into the air. The sufferers were dead. What is death? Who dares to say that which will come after the grave?° Brandreth was calm, and evidently believed that the consequences of our errors were limited by that tremendous barrier. Ludlam and Turner were full of fears, lest God should plunge them in everlasting fire. Mr Pickering, the clergyman, was evidently anxious that Brandreth should not by a false confidence lose the single opportunity of reconciling himself with the Ruler of the future world. None knew what death was, or could know. Yet these men were presumptuously thrust into that unfathomable gulf, by other men, who knew as little and who reckoned not the present or the future sufferings of their victims. Nothing is more horrible than that man should for any cause shed the life of man. For all other calamities there is a remedy or a consolation. When that Power through which we live ceases to maintain the life which it has conferred, then is grief and agony, and the burden which must be borne: such sorrow improves the heart. But when man sheds the blood of man, revenge, and hatred, and a long train of executions, and assassinations, and proscriptions, is perpetuated to remotest time.

VII. Such are the particular, and some of the general considerations depending on° the death of these men. But however deplorable, if it were a mere private or customary grief, the public, as the public, should not mourn. But it is more than this. The events which led to the death of those unfortunate men are a public calamity. I will not impute blame to the jury who pronounced them guilty of high treason, perhaps the law requires that such should be the denomination of their offence. Some restraint ought indeed to be imposed on those thought-less men who imagine they can find in violence a remedy for violence, even if their oppressors had tempted them to this occasion of their ruin. They are instruments of evil, not so guilty as the hands that wielded them, but fit to inspire caution. But their death, by hanging and beheading, and the circumstances° of which it is the characteristic and the consequence, constitute a calamity such as the English nation ought to mourn with an unassuageable grief.

VIII. Kings and their ministers have in every age been distinguished from other men by a thirst for expenditure and bloodshed. There existed in this country, until the American war, a check,° sufficiently feeble and pliant indeed, to this desolating propensity. Until America proclaimed itself a republic, England was perhaps the freest and most glorious nation subsisting on the surface of the earth. It was not what is to the full desirable that a nation should be, but all that it can be, when it does not govern itself. The consequences however of that fundamental defect° soon became evident. The government which the imperfect constitution of our representative assembly threw into the hands of a few aristocrats, improved the method of anticipating the taxes by loans, invented by the ministers of William III, until an enormous debt had been created. In the war against the republic of France, this policy was followed up, until now, the *mere interest* of the public debt amounts to more than twice as much as the lavish expenditure of the public treasure, for maintaining the standing army, and the royal family, and the pensioners, and the placemen. The effect of this debt is to produce such an unequal distribution of the means of living, as saps the foundation of social union and civilized life. It creates a double aristocracy, instead of one which was sufficiently burdensome before, and gives twice as many people the liberty of living in luxury and idleness, on the produce of the industrious and the poor. And it does not give them this because they are more wise and meritorious than the rest, or because their leisure is spent in schemes of public good, or in those exercises of the intellect and the imagination, whose creations ennoble or adorn a country. They are not like the old aristocracy men of pride and honour, *sans peur et sans tache*,° but petty piddling slaves who have gained a right to the title of public creditors, either by gambling in the funds,° or by subserviency to government, or some other villainous trade. They are not the 'Corinthian capital of polished society,'° but the petty and creeping weeds which deface the rich tracery of its sculpture. The effect of this system is, that the day labourer gains no more now by working sixteen hours a day than he gained before by working eight. I put the thing in its simplest and most intelligible shape. The labourer, he that tills the ground and manufactures cloth, is the man who has to provide, out of what he would bring home to his wife and children, for the luxuries and comforts of those, whose claims are represented by an annuity of forty-four millions a year levied upon the English nation. Before, he supported the army and the pensioners, and the royal family, and the landholders; and this is a hard necessity to which it was well that he should submit. Many and various are the mischiefs flowing from oppression, but this is the representative of them all; namely, that one man is forced to labour for another in a degree not only not necessary to the support of the subsisting distinctions among mankind, but so as by the excess of the injustice to endanger the very foundations of all that is valuable in social order, and to provoke that anarchy which is at once the enemy of freedom, and the child and the chastiser of misrule. The nation, tottering on the brink of two chasms,° began to be weary of a continuance of such dangers and degradations, and the miseries which are the consequence of them; the public voice loudly demanded a free representation of the people. It began to be felt that no other constituted body of men could meet the difficulties which impend. Nothing but the nation itself dares to touch the question as to whether there is any remedy or no to the annual payment of forty-four millions a year, beyond the necessary expenses of state, forever and forever. A nobler spirit also went abroad, and the love of liberty, and patriotism, and the self-respect attendant on those glorious emotions, revived in the bosoms of men. The government had a desperate game to play.

IX. In the manufacturing districts of England discontent and disaffection had prevailed for many years; this was the consequence of that system of double aristocracy produced by the causes before mentioned. The manufacturers,° the helots° of our luxury, are left by this system famished, without affections, without health, without leisure or opportunity for such instruction as might counteract those habits of turbulence and dissipation, produced by the precariousness and insecurity of poverty. Here was a ready field for any adventurer who should wish for whatever purpose to incite a few ignorant men to acts of illegal outrage. So soon as it was plainly seen that the demands of the people for a free representation must be conceded if some intimidation and prejudice were not conjured up, a conspiracy of the most horrible atrocity was laid in train. It is impossible to know how far the higher members of the government are involved in the guilt of their infernal agents. It is impossible to know how numerous or how active they have been, or by what false hopes they are yet inflaming the untutored multitude to put their necks under the axe and into the halter. But thus much is known, that so soon as the whole nation lifted up its voice for parliamentary reform, spies were sent forth.° These were selected from the most worthless and infamous of mankind, and dispersed among the multitude of famished and illiterate labourers. It was their business if they found no discontent to create it. It was their business to find victims, no matter whether right or wrong. It was their business to produce upon the public an impression, that if any attempt to attain national freedom, or to diminish the burdens of debt and taxation under which we groan, were successful, the starving multitude would rush in, and confound all orders and distinctions, and institutions and laws, in common ruin. The inference with which they were required to arm the ministers was, that despotic power ought to be eternal. To produce this salutary impression, they betrayed some innocent and unsuspecting rustics° into a crime whose penalty is a hideous death. A few hungry and ignorant manufacturers seduced by the splendid promises of these remorseless blood-conspirators, collected together in what is called rebellion against the state. All was prepared, and the eighteen dragoons assembled in readiness, no doubt, conducted their astonished victims to that dungeon which they left only to be mangled by the executioner's hand. The cruel instigators of their ruin retired to enjoy the great revenues which they had earned by a life of villainy. The public voice was overpowered by the timid and the selfish, who threw the weight of fear into the scale of public opinion, and parliament confided anew to the executive government those extraordinary powers° which may never be laid down, or which may be laid down in blood, or which the regularly constituted assembly of the nation must wrest out of their hands. Our alternatives are a despotism, a revolution, or reform.

X. On the 7th of November, Brandreth, Turner, and Ludlam ascended the scaffold. We feel for Brandreth the less, because it seems he killed a man. But recollect who instigated him to the proceedings which led to murder. On the word of a dying man, Brandreth tells us, that 'OLIVER *brought him to this*'°—that, '*but for* OLIVER, *he would not have been there.*' See, too, Ludlam and Turner, with their sons and brothers, and sisters, how they kneel together in a dreadful agony of prayer. Hell is before their eyes, and they shudder and feel sick with fear, lest some unrepented or some wilful sin should seal their doom in everlasting fire. With that dreadful penalty before their eyes—with that tremendous sanction for the truth of all he spoke, Turner exclaimed loudly and distinctly, *while the executioner was putting the rope round his neck*, 'THIS IS ALL OLIVER AND THE GOVERNMENT.' What more he might have said we know not, because the chaplain prevented° any further observations. Troops of horse, with keen and glittering swords, hemmed in the multitudes collected to witness this abominable exhibition. 'When the stroke of the axe was heard, there was a burst of horror from the crowd. The instant the head was exhibited, there was a tremendous shriek set up, and the multitude ran violently in all directions, as if under the impulse of sudden frenzy. Those who resumed their stations, groaned and hooted.' It is a national calamity, that we endure men to rule over us, who sanction for whatever ends a conspiracy which is to arrive at its purpose through such a frightful pouring forth of human blood and agony. But when that purpose is to trample upon our rights and liberties forever, to present to us the alternatives of anarchy and oppression, and triumph when the astonished nation accepts the latter at their hands, to maintain a vast standing army, and add, year by year, to a public debt, which, already, they know, cannot be discharged; and which, when the delusion that supports it fails, will produce as much misery and confusion through all classes of society as it has continued to produce of famine and degradation to the undefended poor; to imprison and calumniate those who may offend them, at will; when this, if not the purpose, is the effect of that conspiracy, how ought we not to mourn?

XI. Mourn then People of England. Clothe yourselves in solemn black. Let the bells be tolled. Think of mortality and change. Shroud yourselves in solitude and the gloom of sacred sorrow. Spare no symbol of universal grief. Weep—mourn—lament. Fill the great City—fill the boundless fields, with lamentation and the echo of groans. A beautiful Princess is dead:—she who should have been the Queen of her beloved nation, and whose posterity should have ruled it forever. She loved the domestic affections, and cherished arts which adorn, and valour which defends. She was amiable and would have become wise, but she was young, and in the flower of youth the despoiler came. LIBERTY is dead. Slave! I charge thee disturb not the depth and solemnity of our grief by any meaner sorrow. If One has died who was like her that should have ruled over this land, like Liberty, young, innocent, and lovely, know that the power through which that one perished was God, and that it was a private grief. But *man* has murdered Liberty, and whilst the life was ebbing from its wound, there descended on the heads and on the hearts of every human thing, the sympathy of an universal blast and curse. Fetters heavier than iron weigh upon us, because they bind our souls. We move about in a dungeon more pestilential than damp and narrow walls, because the earth is its floor and the heavens are its roof. Let us follow the corpse of British Liberty slowly and reverentially to its tomb: and if some glorious Phantom° should appear, and make its throne of broken swords and sceptres and royal crowns trampled in the dust, let us say that the Spirit of Liberty has arisen from its grave and left all that was gross and mortal there, and kneel down and worship it as our Queen.

On Love

What is Love? Ask him who lives what is life; ask him who adores what is God.

I know not the internal constitution of other men, or even of thine whom I now address. I see that in some external attributes they resemble me, but when misled by that appearance I have thought to appeal to something in common and unburden my inmost soul to them, I have found my language misunderstood like one in a distant and savage land. The more opportunities they have afforded me for experience, the wider has appeared the interval between us, and to a greater distance have the points of sympathy been withdrawn. With a spirit ill fitted to sustain such proof, trembling and feeble through its tenderness, I have everywhere sought,° and have found only repulse and disappointment.

Thou demandest what is Love.° It is that powerful attraction towards all that we conceive or fear or hope beyond ourselves when we find within our own thoughts the chasm of an insufficient void and seek to awaken in all things that are a community with what we experience within ourselves. If we reason, we would be understood; if we imagine, we would that the airy children of our brain° were born anew within another's; if we feel, we would that another's nerves should vibrate to our own, that the beams of their eyes should kindle at once and mix and melt into our own, that lips of motionless ice should not reply to lips quivering and burning with the heart's best blood. This is Love. This is the bond and the sanction which connects not only man with man, but with everything which exists. We are born into the world, and there is something within us which from the instant that we live and move thirsts after its likeness. It is probably in correspondence with this law that the infant drains milk from the bosom of its mother. This propensity develops itself with the development of our nature. We dimly see° within our intellectual nature a miniature as it were of our entire self, yet deprived of all that we condemn or despise, the ideal prototype° of everything excellent or lovely that we are capable of conceiving as belonging to the nature of man. Not only the portrait of our external being, but an assemblage of the minutest particles of which our nature is composed: a mirror whose surface reflects only the forms of purity and brightness: a soul within our soul° that describes a circle around its proper Paradise which pain and sorrow and evil dare not overleap. To this eagerly we refer all sensations, thirsting that they should resemble or correspond with it. The discovery of its antitype:° the meeting with an understanding capable of clearly estimating the deductions of our own, an imagination which should enter into and seize upon the subtle and delicate peculiarities which we have delighted to cherish and unfold in secret, with a frame whose nerves, like the chords of two exquisite lyres strung to the accompaniment of one delightful voice, vibrate with the vibrations of our own; and a combination of all these in such proportion as the type within demands: this is the invisible and unattainable point to which Love tends; and to attain which it urges forth the powers of man to arrest the faintest shadow of that without the possession of which there is no rest or respite to the heart over which it rules. Hence in solitude, or in that deserted state when we are surrounded by human beings and yet they sympathize not with us, we love the flowers, the grass and the waters and the sky. In the motion of the very leaves of spring, in the blue air, there is then found a secret correspondence with our heart. There is eloquence in the tongueless wind, and a melody in the flowing brooks and the rustling of the reeds beside them, which by their inconceivable relation to something within the soul awaken the spirits to a dance of breathless rapture, and bring tears of mysterious tenderness to the eyes like the enthusiasm of patriotic success or the voice of one beloved singing to you alone. Sterne says that if he were in a desert he would love some cypress° . . . So soon as this want or power is dead, man becomes a living sepulchre of himself, and what yet survives is the mere husk of what once he was.

On Life

Life, and the world, or whatever we call that which we are and feel, is an astonishing thing. The mist of familiarity obscures from us the wonder of our being. We are struck with admiration at some of its transient modifications; but it is itself the great miracle. What are changes of empire, the wreck of dynasties with the opinions which supported them; what is the birth and the extinction of religions and political systems to life? What are the revolutions of the globe which we inhabit, and the operations of which it is composed, compared with life? What is the universe of stars and suns [of]° which this inhabited earth is one and their motions and their destiny compared with life? Life, the great miracle, we admire not, because it is so miraculous. It is well that we are thus shielded by the familiarity of what is at once so certain and so unfathomable from an astonishment which would otherwise absorb and overawe the functions of that which is [its]° object.

If any artist (I do not say had executed) but had merely conceived in his mind the system of the sun and stars and planets, they not existing, and had painted to us in words or upon canvas, the spectacle now afforded by the nightly cope of Heaven and illustrated it by the wisdom of astronomy, how great would be our admiration. Or had he imagined the scenery of this earth, the mountains, the seas and the rivers, and the grass and the flowers and the variety of the forms and masses of the leaves of the woods and the colours which attend the setting and the rising sun, and the hues of the atmosphere, turbid or serene, these things not before existing, truly we should have been astonished and it would have been more than a vain boast to have said of such a man, 'Non merita nome di creatore, sennon Iddio ed il Poeta.'° But now these things are looked on with little wonder and to be conscious of them with intense delight is esteemed to be the distinguishing mark of character of a refined and extraordinary person. The multitude of those men care not for them. It is thus with Life—that which includes all.

What is life? Thoughts and feelings arise, with or without our will, and we employ words to express them. We are born, and our birth is unremembered and our infancy remembered only in fragments. We live on, and in living we lose the apprehension of life. How vain it is to think that words can penetrate the mystery of our being. Rightly used they may make evident our ignorance to ourselves, and this is much.

For what are we? Whence do we come, and whither do we go? Is birth the commencement, is death the conclusion of our being? What is birth and death?

The most refined abstractions of logic conduct to a view of life which, though startling to the apprehension, is in fact that which the habitual sense of its repeated combinations has extinguished in us. It strips, as it were, the painted curtain from this scene of things. I confess that I am one of those who am unable to refuse my assent to the conclusions of those philosophers, who assert that nothing exists but as it is perceived.°

It is a decision against which all our persuasions struggle, and we must be long convicted, before we can be convinced that the solid universe of external things is 'such stuff as dreams are made of.'°— The shocking absurdities of the popular philosophy of mind and matter, and its fatal consequences in morals, their violent dogmatism concerning the source of all things, had early conducted me to materialism. This materialism is a seducing system to young and superficial minds. It allows its disciples to talk and dispenses them from thinking. But I was discontented with such a view of things as it afforded; man is a being of high aspirations 'looking both before and after,'° with° 'thoughts that wander through eternity,'° disclaiming alliance with transience and decay, incapable of imagining to himself annihilation, existing but in the future and the past, being, not what he is, but what he has been, and shall be. Whatever may be his true and final destination, there is a spirit within him at enmity with nothingness and dissolution, change and extinction.° This is the character of all life and being.—Each is at once the centre and the circumference; the point to which all things are referred, and the line within which all things are contained.—Such contemplations as these materialism and the popular philosophy of mind and matter, alike forbid; they are consistent only with the intellectual system.

It is absurd to enter into a long recapitulation of arguments sufficiently familiar to those enquiring minds whom alone a writer on abstruse subjects can be conceived to address. Perhaps the most clear and vigorous statement of the intellectual system is to be found in Sir W. Drummond's *Academical Questions*. After such an exposition it would be idle to translate into other words what could only lose its energy and fitness by the change. Examined point by point and word by word, the most discriminating intellects have been able to discover no train of thoughts in the process of its reasoning, which does not conduct inevitably to the conclusion which has been stated.

What follows from the admission? It establishes no new truth, it gives us no additional insight into our hidden nature, neither its action, nor itself. Philosophy, impatient as it may be to build, has much work yet remaining as pioneer for the overgrowth of ages. It makes one step towards this object; it destroys error, and the roots of error. It leaves, what is too often the duty of the reformer in political and ethical questions to leave, a vacancy. It reduces the mind to that freedom in which it would have acted, but for the misuse of words and signs,° the instruments of its own creation.—By signs, I would be understood in a wide sense, including what is properly meant by that term, and what I peculiarly mean. In this latter sense almost all familiar objects are signs, standing not for themselves but for others, in their capacity of suggesting one thought, which shall lead to a train of thoughts.—Our whole life is thus an education of error.

Let us recollect our sensations as children. What a distinct and intense apprehension had we of the world and of ourselves. Many of the circumstances of social life were then important to us, which are now no longer so. But that is not the point of comparison on which I mean to insist. We less habitually distinguished all that we saw and felt from ourselves. They seemed as it were to constitute one mass. There are some persons who in this respect are always children. Those who are subject to the state called reverie feel as if their nature were dissolved into the surrounding universe, or as if the surrounding universe were absorbed into their being. They are conscious of no distinction. And these are states which precede or accompany or follow an unusually intense and vivid apprehension of life. As men grow up, this power commonly decays, and they become mechanical and habitual agents. Their feelings and their reasonings are the combined result of a multitude of entangled thoughts, of a series of what are called impressions, planted by reiteration.

The view of life presented by the most refined deductions of the intellectual philosophy, is that of unity. Nothing exists but as it is perceived. The difference is merely nominal between those two classes of thought which are vulgarly distinguished by the names of ideas and of external objects. Pursuing the same thread of reasoning, the existence of distinct individual minds similar to that which is employed in now questioning its own nature, is likewise found to be a delusion. The words, *I*, *you*, *they*, are not signs of any actual difference subsisting between the assemblage of thoughts thus indicated, but are merely marks employed to denote the different modifications of the one mind. Let it not be supposed that this doctrine conducts to the monstrous presumption, that I, the person who now write and speak, am that one mind. I am but a portion of it. The words *I*, and *you* and *they* are grammatical devices invented simply for arrangement and totally devoid of the intense and exclusive sense usually attributed to them. It is difficult to find terms adequately to express so subtle a conception as that to which the intellectual philosophy has conducted us. We are on that verge where words abandon us, and what wonder if we grow dizzy to look down the dark abyss of—how little we know.

The relations of *things* remain unchanged by whatever system. By the word *things* is to be understood any object of thought, that is, any thought upon which any other thought is employed, with an apprehension of distinction. The relations of these remain unchanged; and such is the material of our knowledge.

What is the cause of life?—that is, how was it preceded,° or what agencies distinct from life, have acted or act upon life? All recorded generations of mankind have wearily busied themselves in inventing answers to this question. And the result has been . . . Religion. Yet, that the basis° of all things cannot be, as the popular philosophy alleges, mind is sufficiently evident. Mind, as far as we have any experience of its properties, and beyond that experience how vain is argument, cannot create, it can only perceive. It is said also to be the Cause. But cause is only a word expressing a certain state of the human mind with regard to the manner in which two thoughts° are apprehended to be related to each other.—If any one desires to know how unsatisfactorily the popular philosophy employs itself upon this great question, they need only impartially reflect upon the manner in which thoughts develop themselves in their minds.—It is infinitely improbable that the cause of mind, that is, of existence, is similar to mind. It is said that mind produces motion and it might as well have been said that motion produces mind.

From *A Philosophical View of Reform*

1st. Sentiment of the Necessity of change.
2nd. Practicability and Utility of such change.
3rd. State of Parties as regards it.
4th. Probable mode—Desirable mode.°

Let us believe not only that is necessary because it is just and ought to be, but necessary because it is inevitable and must be.°

Those who imagine that their personal interest is directly or indirectly concerned in maintaining the power in which they are clothed by the existing institutions of English Government do not acknowledge the necessity of a material change in those institutions. With this exception, there is no inhabitant of the British Empire of mature age and perfect understanding not fully persuaded of the necessity of Reform.

Introduction

From the dissolution of the Roman empire, that vast and successful scheme for enslaving the most civilized portion of mankind, to the epoch of two recent wars° have succeeded a series of schemes on a smaller scale, operating to the same effect. Sacred names borrowed from the life and opinions of Jesus Christ were employed as symbols of domination and imposture; and a system of liberty and equality, for such was the system preached by that great Reformer, was perverted to support oppression—. Not his doctrines, for they are too simple and direct to be susceptible of such perversion—but the mere names. Such was the origin of the Catholic Church, which, together with the several dynasties then beginning to consolidate themselves in Europe, means, being interpreted, a plan according to which the cunning and selfish few have employed the fears and hopes of the ignorant many to the establishment of their own power and the destruction of the real interest of all.

The Republics and municipal governments of Italy° opposed for some time a systematic and effectual resistance to the all-surrounding tyranny. The Lombard League defeated the armies of the despot in open field, and until Florence was betrayed to those flattered traitors [and] polished tyrants, the Medici, Freedom had one citadel wherein it could find refuge from a world which was its enemy. Florence long balanced, divided, and weakened the strength of the Empire and the Popedom. To this cause, if to anything, was due the undisputed superiority of Italy in literature and the arts over all its contemporary nations, that union of energy and of beauty which distinguish from all other poets the writings of Dante, that restlessness of fervid power which expressed itself in painting and sculpture and in rude but daring architectural forms, and from which, conjointly from the creations of Athens, its predecessor and its image, Raphael and Michelangelo drew the inspiration which created those forms and colours of what is now the astonishment of the world. The father of our own literature, Chaucer, wrought from the simple and powerful language of a nursling of this Republic the basis of our own literature. And thus we owe, among other causes, the exact condition belonging to our own intellectual existence to the generous disdain of submission which burned in the bosoms of men who filled a distant generation and inhabited another land.

When this resistance was overpowered (as what resistance to fraud and [tyranny] has not been overpowered?) another was even then maturing. The progress of philosophy and civilization which ended in that imperfect emancipation of mankind from the yoke of priests and Kings called the Reformation had already commenced. Exasperated by their long sufferings, inflamed by the sparks of that superstition from the flames of which they were emerging, the poor rose° against their natural enemies, the rich, and repaid with bloody interest the tyranny of ages. One of the signs of the times was that the oppressed peasantry rose like the negro slaves of West Indian plantations and murdered their tyrants when they were unaware. For so dear is power that the tyrants themselves neither then nor now nor ever left or leave a path to freedom but through their own blood. The contest then waged under the names of religion, which have seldom been any more [than] only the popular and visible symbols which express the degree of power in some shape or other asserted by one party and disclaimed by the other, ended; and the result, though partial and imperfect, is perhaps the most animating that the philanthropist can contemplate in the history of man. The republic of Holland, which has been so long an armoury of the arrows of learning by which superstition has been wounded even to death,° was established by this contest. What though the name of Republic—and by whom but by conscience-stricken tyrants could it be extinguished—is no more? The Republics of Switzerland derived from this event their consolidation and their union. From England then first began to pass away the strain of conquest.° The exposition° of a certain portion of religious imposture drew with it an inquiry into political imposture, and was attended with an extraordinary exertion of the energies of intellectual power. Shakespeare and Lord Bacon and the great writers of the age of Elizabeth and James I were at once the effects of this new spirit in men's minds, and the causes of its more complete development. By rapid gradation the nation was conducted to the temporary abolition of aristocracy and episcopacy, and the mighty example which, 'in teaching nations how to live,' England afforded to the world of bringing to public justice one of those chiefs° of a conspiracy of privileged murderers and robbers whose impunity has been the consecration of crime.

After the selfish passions and compromising interests of men had enlisted themselves to produce and establish the Restoration of Charles II the unequal combat was renewed under the reign of his successor, and that compromise between the unextinguishable spirit of Liberty, and the ever-watchful spirit of fraud and tyranny, called the Revolution,° had place. On this occasion Monarchy and Aristocracy and Episcopacy were at once established and limited by law. Unfortunately they lost no more in extent of power than they gained in security of possession. Meanwhile, those by whom they were established acknowledged and declared that the will of the People was the source from which these powers, in that instance, derived the right to subsist. A man has no right to be a King or Lord or a Bishop but so long as it is for the benefit of the People and so long as the People judge that it is for their benefit, that he should impersonate that character. The solemn establishment of this maxim, as the basis of our constitutional law, more than any beneficial and energetic application of it to the circumstances of this era of its promulgation, was the fruit of that vaunted event. Correlative with this series of events in England was the commencement of a new epoch in the history of the progress of civilization and society.

That superstition which has disguised itself under the name of Jesus subsisted under all its forms, even where it had been separated from those things especially considered as abuses by the multitude, in the shape of intolerant and oppressive hierarchies. Catholics massacred Protestants and Protestants proscribed Catholics, and extermination was the sanction of each faith within the limits of the power of its professors. The New Testament is in everyone's hand, and the few who ever read it with the simple sincerity of an unbiased judgement may perceive how distinct from the opinions of any of those professing themselves established° were the doctrines and the actions of Jesus Christ. At the period of the Reformation this test was applied and this judgement formed° of the then existing hierarchy, and the same compromise was then made between the spirit of truth and the spirit of imposture after [the] struggle which ploughed up the area of the human mind as was made in the particular instance of England between the spirit of freedom and the spirit of tyranny at that event called the Revolution. In both instances the maxims so solemnly recorded remain as trophies of our difficult and incomplete victory, planted on the enemies' land. *The will of the People to change their government is an acknowledged right in the Constitution of England.* The protesting against regular and graduated systems of alternate slavery and tyranny by which all except the lowest and the largest class were to be gainers in the materials of subsistence and ostentation at the expense of that class, the means being fraud or force established in the shape of feudal monarchies upon the ruins of religious dogmas which present themselves to his mind as false is the inalienable prerogative of every human being.

This new epoch was marked by the commencement of deeper enquiries into the forms of human nature than are compatible with an unreserved belief in any of those popular mistakes upon which popular systems of faith with respect to the agencies of the universe, with all their superstructure of political and religious tyranny, are built. Lord Bacon, Spinoza, Hobbes, Bayle,° Montaigne regulated the reasoning powers, criticized the past history, exposed the errors by illustrating their causes and their connection, and anatomized the inmost nature of social man. Then with a less interval of time than of genius followed Locke° and the philosophers of his exact and intelligible but superficial school. Their illustrations of some of the minor consequences of the doctrines established by the sublime genius of their predecessors were correct, popular, simple and energetic. Above all, they indicated inferences the most incompatible with the popular religions and the established governments of Europe.° Berkeley and Hume [and] Hartley°, in a later age, following the traces of these inductions, have clearly established the certainty of our ignorance with respect to those obscure questions which under the name of religious truths have been the watchwords of con[tention] and the symbols of unjust power ever since they were distorted by the narrow passions of the immediate followers of Jesus from that meaning to which philosophers are even now restoring them.—A crowd of writers in France° seized upon the most popular topics of these doctrines, and developing those particular portions of the new philosophy which conducted to inferences at war with the dreadful oppressions under which the country groaned, made familiar to mankind the falsehood of the pretences of their religious mediators and political oppressors. Considered as philosophers their error seems to have consisted chiefly of a limitedness of view; they told the truth, but not the whole truth. This might have arisen from the terrible sufferings of their countrymen inciting them rather to apply a portion of what had already been discovered to their immediate relief, than to pursue the abstractions of thought, as the great philosophers who preceded them had done, for the sake of a future and more universal advantage. Whilst that philosophy which, burying itself in the obscure parts of our nature, regards the truth and falsehood of dogmas relating to the cause of the universe, and the nature and manner of man's relation with it, was thus stripping Power of its darkest mask, Political philosophy, or that which considers the relations of Man as a social being, was assuming a precise form. This philosophy indeed sprang from and maintained a connection with that other, as its parent. What would Swift and Bolingbroke° and Sidney and Locke and Montesquieu, or even Rousseau, not to speak of political philosophers of our own age, Godwin and Bentham, have been but for Lord Bacon, Montaigne, and Spinoza, and the other great luminaries of the preceding epoch? Something excellent and eminent, no doubt, the least of these would have been, but something different from and inferior to what they are. A series of these writers illustrated with more or less success the principles of human nature as applied to man in political society. A thirst for accommodating the existing forms according to which mankind are found divided to those rules of freedom and equality which thus have been discovered as being the elementary principles according to which the happiness resulting from the social union ought to be produced and distributed, was kindled by these inquiries. Contemporary with this condition of the intell[ect] all the powers of man seemed, though in most cases under forms highly inauspicious, to develop themselves with uncommon energy. The mechanical sciences attained to a degree of perfection which, though obscurely foreseen by Lord Bacon, it had been accounted madness to have prophesied in a preceding age. Commerce was pursued with a perpetually increasing vigour, and the same area of the Earth was perpetually compelled to furnish more and more subsistence. The means and sources of knowledge were thus increased together with knowledge itself, and the instruments of knowledge. The benefit of this increase of the powers of man became, in consequence of the inartificial forms into which society continues to be distributed, an instrument of his additional evil. The capabilities of happiness were increased and applied to the augmentation of misery. Modern European society is thus an engine assumed to be for useful purposes, whose force is by a system of subtle mechanism augmented to the highest pitch, but which, instead of grinding corn or raising water, acts against itself and is perpetually wearing away and breaking to pieces the wheels of which it is composed.

The result of the labours of the political philosophers has been the establishment of the principle of Utility° as the substance, and liberty and equality as the forms, according to which the concerns of human life ought to be administered. By this test the various institutions regulating political society have been tried and, as the undigested growth of the private passions, errors, and interests of barbarians and oppressors, have been condemned. And many new theories, more or less perfect, but all superior to the mass of evil which they would supplant, have been given to the world.

The system of Government in the United States of America was the first practical illustration of the new philosophy. Sufficiently remote, it will be confessed, from the accuracy of ideal excellence is that representative system which will soon cover the extent of that vast Continent. But it is scarcely less remote from the insolent and contaminating tyrannies under which, with some limitation of these terms as regards England, Europe groaned at the period of the successful rebellion of America. America holds forth the victorious example of an immensely populous and, as far as the external arts of life are concerned, a highly civilized community administered according to republican forms. It has no King, that is, it has no officer to whom wealth and from whom corruption flows. It has no hereditary oligarchy, that is, it acknowledges no order of men privileged to cheat and insult the rest of the members of the state, and who inherit a right of legislating and judging which the principles of human nature compel them to exercise to their own profit and to the detriment of those not included within their peculiar class. It has no established Church, that is, it has no system of opinions respecting the abstrusest questions which can be topics of human thought, founded in an age of error and fanaticism, and opposed by law to all other opinions, defended by prosecutions sanctioned by enormous bounties given to idle priests and forced through the unwilling hands of those who have an interest in the cultivation and improvement of the soil, whose consequences are captivity, confiscation, infamy and ruin. It has no false representation, but a true representation. The will of the many is represented by the few in the assemblies of legislation, and by the officers of the executive entrusted with the administration of the executive power almost as directly as the will of one person can be represented by the will of another. Lastly, it has an institution by which it is honourably distinguished from all other government which ever existed. It constitutionally acknowledges the progress of human improvement, and is framed under the limitation of the probability of more simple views of political science being rendered applicable to human life. There is a law by which the Constitution is reserved for revision every ten years. Every other set of men who have assumed the office of legislating and framing institutions for future ages, with far less right to such an assumption than the founders of the American Republic, assumed that their work was the wisest and the best that could possibly have been produced; these illustrious men° looked upon the past history of their species and saw that it was the history of his mistakes, and his sufferings arising from his mistakes; they observed the superiority of their own work to all the works which had preceded it, and they judged it probable that other political institutions would be discovered bearing the same relation to those they had established which they bear to those which have preceded them. They provided therefore for the application of these contingent discoveries to the social state without the violence and misery attendant upon such change in less modest and more imperfect governments. The United States, as would have been expected from theoretical deduction, affords an example, compared with the old governments of Europe and Asia, of a free, happy and strong people. Nor let it be said that they owe their superiority rather to the situation than to their government. Give them a King, and let that King waste in luxury, riot, and bribery the same sum which now serves for the entire expenses of their government. Give them an aristocracy, and let that aristocracy legislate for the people. Give them a priesthood, and let them bribe with a tenth of the produce of the soil a certain set of men to say a certain set of words. Pledge the larger portion of them by financial subterfuges to pay the half of their property or earnings to another portion, and let the proportion of those who enjoy the fruits of the toil of others without toiling themselves be three instead of one. Give them, as you must if you give them these things, a great standing army to cut down the people if they murmur. If any American should see these words, his blood would run cold at the imagination of such a change. He well knows that the prosperity and happiness of the United States, if subjected to such institutions, [would] be no more. Give them a Court of Chancery,° and let the property, the liberty, and the interests, in the dearest concerns of life, the exercise of the most sacred rights of a social being, depend upon the will of one of the most servile creature[s] of the kingly and oligarchical and priestly power to which every man, in proportion as he is of an inquiring and philosophical mind and of a sincere and honourable disposition, is a natural and necessary enemy.

The just and successful Revolt of America corresponded with a state of public opinion in Europe of which it was the first result. The French Revolution was the second. The oppressors of mankind had enjoyed (O that we could say suffered) a long and an undisturbed reign in France, and to the pining famine, the shelterless destitution of the inhabitants of that country, had been added, and heaped up, insult harder to endure than misery. For the feudal system (the immediate causes and conditions of its institution having become obliterated) had degenerated into an instrument not only of oppression but of contumely; and both were unsparingly inflicted. Blind in the possession of strength, drunken as with the intoxication of ancestral greatness, the rulers perceived not that increase of knowledge in their subjects which made its exercise insecure. They called soldiers to hew down the people when their power was already past. The tyrants were, as usual, the aggressors. Then the oppressed, having been rendered brutal, ignorant, servile, and bloody by long slavery, having had the intellectual thirst excited in them by the progress of civilization, satiated from fountains of literature poisoned by the spirit and the form of monarchy, arose and took a dreadful revenge on their oppressors. Their desire to wreak revenge to this extent, in itself a mistake, a crime, a calamity, arose from the same source as their other miseries and errors, and affords an additional proof of the necessity of that long-delayed change which it accompanied and disgraced. If a just and necessary revolution could have been accomplished with as little expense of happiness and order in a country governed by despotic as [in] one governed by free laws, equal liberty and justice would lose their chief recommendations, and tyranny be divested of its most revolting attributes. Tyranny entrenches itself within the existing interests of that great mass of the most refined citizens of a nation and says, 'If you dare trample upon these, be free.' Though this terrible condition shall not be evaded, the world is no longer in a temper to decline the challenge.

The French were what their literature is (excluding Montaigne and Rousseau), weak, superficial, vain, with little imagination, and with passions as well as judgements cleaving to the external form of things. Not that [they] are organically different from the inhabitants of the nations who have become [. . .]° or rather not that their organical differences, whatever they may amount to, incapacitate them from arriving at the exercise of the highest powers to be attained by man. Their institutions made them what they were. Slavery and superstition, contumely and the tame endurance of contumely, and the

habits engendered from generation to generation out of this trans-
mitted inheritance of wrong, created this thing which has extin-
guished what has been called the likeness of God in man. The
Revolution in France overthrew the hierarchy, the aristocracy, and
the monarchy, and the whole of that peculiarly insolent and oppressive
system on which they were based. But as it only partially extinguished
those passions which are the spirit of these forms a reaction took place
which has restored in a certain limited degree the old system—in a
degree, indeed, exceedingly limited, and stripped of all its ancient
terrors. The lion of the Monarchy of France, with his teeth drawn and
his claws pared, now sits maintaining the formal likeness of a most
imperfect and insecure dominion. The usurpation of Bonaparte, and
then the Restoration of the Bourbons were the shapes in which this
reaction clothed itself, and the heart of every lover of liberty was
struck as with palsy by the succession of these events. But reversing
the proverbial expression of Shakespeare, it may be the good which
the Revolutionists did lives after them, their 'ills are interred with
their bones.'° But the military project of government of the great
tyrant having failed, and there being even no attempt, and, if there
were any attempt, there being not the remotest possibility of re-
establishing the enormous system of tyranny abolished by the Revolu-
tion, France is, as it were, regenerated. Its legislative assemblies are
in a certain limited degree representations of the popular will, and the
executive power is hemmed in by jealous laws. France occupies in
this respect the same situation as was occupied by England at the
restoration of Charles II. It has undergone a revolution (unlike
in the violence and calamities which attended it, because unlike in
the abuses which it was excited to put down) which may be paralleled
with that in our own country which ended in the death of Charles I.
The Authors of both revolutions proposed a greater and more
glorious object than the degraded passions of their countrymen
permitted them to attain. But in both cases abuses were abolished
which never since have dared to show their face. There remains in the
natural order of human things that the tyranny and perfidy of
the reigns of Charles II and James II (for these were less the result of
the disposition of particular men, than the vices which would have
been engendered in any but an extraordinary man by the natural
necessities of their situation), perhaps under a milder form and within
a shorter period, should produce the institution of a government
in France which may bear the same relation to the state of political
knowledge existing at the present day, as the Revolution under

William III bore to the state of political knowledge existing at that period . . .°

Lastly, in the West Indian islands, first from the disinterested yet necessarily cautious measures of the English Nation, and then from the infection of the Spirit of Liberty in France, the deepest stain upon civilized man is fading away. Two nations° of free negroes are already established; one, in pernicious mockery of the usurpation over France, an empire, the other a republic; both animating yet terrific spectacles to those who inherit around them the degradation of slavery and the peril of dominion.

Such is a slight sketch of the general condition of the hopes and aspirations of the human race to which they have been conducted, after the obliteration of the Greek republics by the successful external tyranny of Rome—its internal liberty having been first abolished—and by those miseries and superstitions which consequent upon that event ha[ve] compelled the human race to begin anew its difficult and obscure career of producing, according to the forms of society, the greatest portion of good.

Meanwhile England, the particular object for the sake of which these general considerations have been stated on the present occasion, has arrived, like the nations which surround it, at a crisis in its destiny.

The literature of England, an energetic development of which has ever followed or preceded a great and free development of the national will, has arisen, as it were, from a new birth. In spite of that low-thoughted envy which would undervalue, through a fear of comparison with its own insignificance, the eminence of contemporary merit, ours is in intellectual achievements a memorable age, and we live among such philosophers and poets as surpass beyond comparison any who have appeared in our nation since its last struggle for liberty.° For the most unfailing herald, or companion, or follower, of an universal employment of the sentiments of a nation to the production of beneficial change is poetry, meaning by poetry an intense and impassioned power of communicating intense and impassioned impressions respecting man and nature.° The persons in whom this power takes its abode may often, as far as regards many portions of their nature, have little correspondence with the spirit of good of which it is the minister.° But although they may deny and abjure, they are yet compelled to serve, that which is seated on the throne of their own soul.° And whatever systems they may professedly support, they actually advance the interests of Liberty. It is impossible to read the productions of our most celebrated writers, whatever may be their system relating to thought or expression, without being startled by the electric life which there is in their words. They measure the circumference or sound the depths of human nature with a comprehensive and all-penetrating spirit, at which they are themselves perhaps most sincerely astonished, for it [is] less their own spirit than the spirit of their age. They are the priests of an unapprehended inspiration, the mirrors of gigantic forms which futurity casts upon the present, the words which express what they conceive not, the trumpet which sings to battle and feels not what it inspires, the influence which is moved not but moves. Poets and philosophers are the unacknowledged legislators of the world.

But, omitting these more abstracted considerations, has there not been and is there not in England a desire of change arising from the profound sentiment of the exceeding inefficiency of the existing institutions to provide for the physical and intellectual happiness of the people? It is proposed in this work (1) to state and examine the present condition of this desire, (2) to elucidate its causes and its object, (3) to the[n] show the practicability and utility, nay the necessity of change, (4) to examine the state of parties as regards it, and (5) to state the probable, the possible, and the desirable mode in which it should be accomplished.

On the Sentiment of the Necessity of Change°

Two circumstances arrest the attention of those who turn their regard to the present political condition of the English nation; first, that there is an almost universal sentiment of the approach of some change to be wrought in the institutions of the government, and secondly, the necessity and desirableness of such a change. From the first of these propositions, it being matter of fact, no person addressing the public can dissent. The latter, from a general belief in which the former flows and on which it depends, is matter of opinion, but [one] which to the mind of all excepting those interested in maintaining the contrary is a doctrine so clearly established that even they, admitting that great abuses exist, are compelled to impugn it by insisting upon the specious topic that popular violence, by which they alone could be remedied, would be more injurious than the continuance of these abuses. But as those who argue thus derive for the most part great advantage and convenience from the continuance of these abuses, their estimation of the mischiefs of temporary popular violence as compared with the mischiefs of permanent tyrannical and fraudulent forms of government is likely, from the known principles of human nature, to be exaggerated. Such an estimate comes too with a worse grace from them who, if they would in opposition to their own unjust advantage take the lead in reform, might spare the nation from the inconveniences of the temporary dominion of the poor, who by means of that very degraded condition which their insurrection would be designed to ameliorate are sufficiently incapable of discerning their own genuine and permanent advantage, though surely less incapable than those whose interests consist in proposing to themselves an object perfectly opposite [to] and wholly incompatible with that advantage. These persons (I mean the government party) propose to us the dilemma of submitting to a despotism which is notoriously gathering like an avalanche year by year; or taking the risk of something which it must be confessed bears the aspect of revolution. To this alternative we are reduced by the selfishness of those who taunt us with it. And the history of the world teaches us not to hesitate an instant in the decision, if indeed the power of decision be not already past.

The establishment of King William III on the throne of England has already been referred to as a compromise between liberty and despotism. The Parliament of which that event was the act had ceased to be, in an emphatic sense, a representation of the people.° The Long Parliament, questionless, was the organ of the will of all classes of people in England since it effected the complete revolution in a tyranny consecrated by time. But since its meeting, and since its dissolution, a great change had taken place in England. Feudal manners and institutions having become obliterated, monopolies and patents having been abolished, property and personal liberty having been rendered secure, the nation advanced rapidly towards the acquirement of the elements of national prosperity. But for want of just regulations in the distribution of these elements—which is indeed the great problem of government,—the elements of prosperity and power became, when combined, the sources of despotism and misery. Population increased, a greater number of hands were employed in the labours of agriculture and commerce, towns arose where villages had been, and the proportion borne by those whose labour produces the materials of subsistence and enjoyment to those who claim for themselves a superfluity of these materials began to increase indefinitely. A fourth class therefore appeared in the nation, the unrepresented multitude. Nor was it so much that villages which sent no members to Parliament became great cities, and that towns which had been considerable enough to send members dwindled from local circumstances into villages. This

cause no doubt contributed to the general effect of rendering the
Commons House a less complete representation of the people. Yet
had this been all, though it had ceased to be a legal and actual, it might
still have been a virtual Representation of the People. But the nation
universally became multiplied into a denomination which had no con-
stitutional presence in the state. This denomination had not existed
before, or had existed only to a degree in which its interests were
sensibly interwoven with that of those who enjoyed a constitutional
presence. Thus, the proportion borne by the Englishmen who
possessed [the] faculty of suffrage to those who were excluded from
that faculty at the several periods of 1641 and 1688 had changed by
the operation of these causes from 1 to 5 to 1 to 20. The rapid and
effectual progress by which it changed from 1 to 20 to one to many
hundreds in the interval between 1688 and 1819 is a process, to those
familiar with the history of the political economy of that period, which
is rendered by these principles sufficiently intelligible. The number
therefore of those who have influence on the government, even if
numerically the same as at the former period, was relatively different.
And a sufficiently just measure is afforded of the degree in which a
country is enslaved or free, by the consideration of the relative number
of individuals who are admitted to the exercise of political rights.
Meanwhile another cause was operating of a deeper and more exten-
sive nature. Those who compose the Lords must, by the advantage of
their situation as the great landed proprietors, possess a considerable
influence over nomination to the Commons.° This influence from an
original imperfection in the equal distribution of suffrage was always
enormous, but it is only since it has been combined with the cause
before stated that it has appeared to be fraught with consequences
incompatible with public liberty. In 1641 this influence was almost
wholly inoperative to pervert the counsels of the nation from its own
advantage. But at that epoch the enormous tyranny of the agents of
the royal power weighed equally upon all denominations of men, and
united all counsels to extinguish it; add to which, the nation was in a
very considerable degree as stated before fairly represented in Parlia-
ment. The common danger which was the bond of union between the
aristocracy and the people having been destroyed, the former system-
atized their influence through the permanence of hereditary right,
whilst the latter were losing power by the inflexibility of the institu-
tions which forbade a just accommodation to their numerical increase.
After the operations of these causes had commenced, the accession of
William III placed a seal upon forty years of Revolution.

The Government of this country at the period of 1688 was regal, tempered by aristocracy, for what conditions of democracy attach to an assembly one portion of which [was] imperfectly nominated by less than a twentieth part of the people, and another perfectly nominated by the nobles? For the nobility, having by the assistance of the people imposed close limitations upon the royal power, finding that power to be its natural ally and the people (for the people from the increase of their numbers acquired greater and more important rights whilst the organ through which those rights might be asserted grew feebler in proportion to the increase of the cause of those rights and of their importance) its natural enemy, made the Crown the mask and pretence of their own authority.

At this period began that despotism of the oligarchy of party, and under colour of administering the executive power lodged in the King, represented in truth the interests of the rich. When it is said by political reasoners, speaking of the interval between 1688 and the present time, that the royal power progressively increased, they use an expression which suggests a very imperfect and partial idea. The power which has increased is that entrusted with the administration of affairs, composed of men responsible to the aristocratical assemblies, or to the reigning party in those assemblies which represents those orders of the nation which are privileged, and will retain power as long as it pleases them and must be divested of power as soon as it ceases to please them. The power which has increased therefore is the power of the rich. The name and the office of King is merely the mask of this power and is a kind of stalking-horse used to conceal these 'catchers of men'° whilst they lay their nets.—Monarchy is only the string which ties the robber's bundle. Though less contumelious and abhorrent from the dignity of human nature than an absolute monarchy, an oligarchy of this nature exacts more of suffering from the people because it reigns both by the opinion generated by imposture and the force which that opinion places within its grasp.

At the epoch adverted to, the device of public credit° was first systematically applied as an instrument of government. It was employed at the accession of William III less as a resource for meeting the financial exigencies of the state, than as a bond to connect those in the possession of property with those who had, by taking advantage of an accident of party, acceded to power. In the interval elapsed since that period it has accurately fulfilled the intention of its establishment and has continued to add strength to the government, even until the present crisis. Now this device is one of those execrable contrivances of misrule which overbalance the material of common advantage produced by the progress of civilization and increase the number of those who are idle in proportion to those who work, whilst it increases, through the factitious wants of those indolent, privileged persons, the quantity of work to be done. The rich, no longer being able to rule by force, have invented this scheme, that they may rule by fraud. [. . .]°

The existing Government of England in substituting a currency of paper to one of Gold has had no need to depreciate the currency by alloying the coin of the country; they have merely fabricated pieces of paper on which they promise to pay a certain sum. The holders of these papers came for payment in some representation of property universally exchangeable. They then declared that the persons who held the office for that payment could not be forced by law to pay. They declared subsequently that these pieces of paper were the legal coin of the country. Of this nature are all such transactions of companies and banks as consist in the circulation of promissory notes to a greater amount than the actual property possessed by those whose names they bear. They have the effect of augmenting the prices of provision, and of benefiting at the expense of the community the speculators in this traffic.—One of the vaunted effects of this system is to increase the national industry. That is, to increase the labours of the poor and those luxuries of the rich which they supply. To make a manufacturer work sixteen hours where he only worked eight. To turn children into lifeless and bloodless machines at an age when otherwise they would be at play before the cottage doors of their parents. To augment indefinitely the proportion of those who enjoy the profit of the labour of others as compared with those who exercise this labour. [. . .]°

The consequences of this transaction have been the establishment of a new aristocracy, which has its basis in fraud as the old one has its basis in force. The hereditary land-owners in England derived their title from royal grants—they are fiefs bestowed by conquerors, or church lands, or they have been bought by bankers and merchants from those persons. [. . .]

Since usage has consecrated a distortion of the word aristocracy from its primitive meaning, let me be allowed to employ the word aristocracy in that ordinary sense which signifies that class of persons who possess a right to the produce of the labour of others, without dedicating to the common service any labour in return.—This class of persons, whose existence is a prodigious anomaly in the social system, has ever constituted an inseparable portion of it, and there has never been an approach in practice towards any plan of political society modelled on equal justice, at least in the complicated mechanism of modern life. Mankind seem to acquiesce, as in a necessary condition of the imbecility of their own will and reason, in the existence of an aristocracy. With reference to this imbecility, it has doubtless been the instrument of great social advantage, although the advantage would have been greater which might have been produced according to the forms of a just distribution of the goods and evils of life. The object therefore of all enlightened legislation, and administration, is to enclose within the narrowest practicable limits this order of drones. The effect of the financial impostures of the modern rulers of England has been to increase the number of the drones. Instead of one aristocracy the condition which, in the present state of human affairs, the friends of justice and liberty are willing to subscribe as to an inevitable evil, they have supplied us with two aristocracies: the one, consisting [of] the great land proprietors and merchants who receive and interchange the produce of this country with the produce of other countries; in this, because all other great communities have as yet acquiesced in it, we acquiesce. Connected with the members of [this aristocracy] is a certain generosity and refinement of manners and opinion which, although neither philosophy nor virtue has been that acknowledged substitute for them, at least is a religion which makes respected those venerable names. The [other] is an aristocracy of attorneys and excisemen, and directors, and government pensioners, usurers, stock jobbers, country bankers, with their dependents and descendants. These are a set of pelting wretches in whose employment there is nothing to exercise, even to their distortion, the more majestic faculties of the soul. Though at the bottom it is all trick, there is something magnificent in the chivalrous disdain of infamy connected with a gentleman. There is something to which—until you see through the base falsehood upon which all inequality is founded—it is difficult for the imagination to refuse its respect in the faithful and direct dealings of the substantial merchant.° But in the habits and lives of this new aristocracy created out of an increase [in] the public calamities, and whose existence must be determined by their termination, there is nothing to qualify our disapprobation. They eat and drink and sleep and, in the intervals of those things performed with most ridiculous ceremony and accompaniments, they cringe and lie. They poison the literature of the age in which they live, by requiring either the antitype of their own mediocrity in books, or such stupid and distorted and inharmonious idealisms as alone have the power to stir their torpid imaginations. Their hopes and fears are of the narrowest description. Their domestic affections are feeble and they have no others. They think of any commerce with their species but as a means, never as an end, and as a means to the basest forms of personal advantage.

If this aristocracy had arisen from a false and depreciated currency to the exclusion of the other, its existence would have been a moral calamity and a disgrace, but it would not have constituted an oppression. But the hereditary aristocracy who held the political administration of affairs took the measures which created this other, for purposes peculiarly its own. Those measures were so contrived as in no manner to diminish the wealth and power of the contrivers. The lord does not spare himself one luxury, but the peasant and artisan are amerced° of many needful things. To support the system of social order according to its supposed unavoidable constitution, those from whose labour all those external accommodations which distinguish a civilized being from a savage arise, worked, before the institution of this double aristocracy, eight hours. And of these only the healthy were compelled to labour, the efforts of the old, the sick and the immature being dispensed with, and they maintained by the labour of the sane, for such is the plain English of the poor-rates.° That labour procured a competent share of the decencies of life, and society seemed to extend the benefits of its institution even to its most unvalued instruments. Although deprived of those resources of sentiment and knowledge which might have been their lot could the wisdom of the institutors of social forms have established a system of strict justice, yet they earned by their labour a competency in those external materials of life which, and not the loss of moral and intellectual excellence, is supposed to be the legitimate object of the desires and murmurs of the poor. Since the institution of this double aristocracy, however, they have worked not ten but twenty hours a day. Not that all the poor have rigidly worked twenty hours, but that the worth of the labour of twenty hours now, in food and clothing, is equivalent to the worth of ten hours then. And because twenty hours' labour cannot, from the nature of the human frame, be exacted from those who before performed ten, the aged and the sickly are compelled either to work or starve. Children who were exempted from labour are put in requisition, and the vigorous promise of the coming generation blighted by premature exertion. For fourteen hours' labour which they do perform, they receive—no matter in what nominal amount—the price of seven. They eat less bread, wear worse clothes, are more ignorant, immoral, miserable and desperate. This, then, is the condition of the lowest and the largest class, from whose labour the whole materials of life are wrought, of which the others are only the receivers or the consumers. They are more superstitious, for misery on earth begets a diseased expectation and panic-stricken faith in miseries beyond the grave. 'God,' they argue, 'rules this world as well as that; and assuredly since his nature is immutable, and his powerful will unchangeable, he rules them by the same laws.' The gleams of hope which speak of Paradise seem like the flames in Milton's hell only to make darkness visible, and all things take [their] colour from what surrounds them. They become revengeful [. . .].

But the condition of all other classes of society, excepting those within the privileged pale, is singularly unprosperous, and even they experience the reaction of their own short-sighted tyranny, in all those sufferings and deprivations which are not of a distinctly physical nature, in the loss of dignity, simplicity and energy, and in the possession of all those qualities which distinguish a slave-driver from a proprietor. Right Government being an institution for the purpose of securing such a moderate degree of happiness to men as has been experimentally practicable, the sure character of misgovernment is misery, and first discontent and, if that be despised, then insurrection, as the legitimate expression of that misery. The public ought to demand happiness. By a fortunate law of nature the labouring classes, when they cannot get food for their labour, are [certain] to take it by force. Laws and assemblies and courts of justice and delegated powers placed in balance or in opposition are the means and the form, but public happiness is the substance and the end of political institution. Whenever this is attainted in a nation, not from external force, but from the internal arrangement and divisions of the common burdens of defence and maintenance, then there is oppression. And then arises an alternative between Reform and the institution of a military Despotism, or a Revolution in which various parties, one striving after ill-digested systems of democracy, and the other clinging to the outworn abuses of power, leave the few who aspire to more than the former and who would overthrow the latter at whatever expense, to wait until that modified advantage which results from [this conflict] produces a small portion of that [social improvement] which, with the temperance and the toleration which both regard as a crime, might have resulted from the occasion which they let pass in a far more signal manner.

The propositions which are the consequences or the corollaries to which the preceding reasoning seems to have conducted us are—

That the majority [of the] people of England are destitute and miserable, ill-clothed, ill-fed, ill-educated.

That they know this, and that they are impatient to procure a reform of the cause of their abject and wretched state.

That a cause of this peculiar misery is the unequal distribution which, under the form of the national debt, has been surreptitiously made of the products of their labour and the products of the labour of their ancestors; for all property is the produce of labour.

That the cause of that cause is a defect in the government.

That if they knew nothing of their condition, but believed that all they endured and all [they] were deprived of arose from the unavoidable condition of human life, this belief being an error, the endurance of [which] enforces an injustice, every enlightened and honourable person, whatever may be the imagined interests of his peculiar class, ought to excite them to the discovery of the true state of the case and to the temperate but irresistible vindication of their rights.

A Reform in England is most just and necessary. What ought to be that reform?

A writer of the present day (a priest, of course, for his doctrines are those of a eunuch and of a tyrant) has stated that the evils of the poor arise from an excess of population,° and that after they have been stripped naked by the tax gatherer and reduced to bread and tea and fourteen hours of hard labour by their masters, and after the frost has bitten their defenceless limbs, and the cramp has wrung like a disease within their bones, and hunger, and the suppressed revenge of hunger, has stamped the ferocity of want like the mark of Cain upon their countenance, that the last tie by which Nature holds them to [a] benignant earth whose plenty is garnered up in the strongholds of their tyrants, is to be divided; that the single alleviation of their sufferings and their scorns, the one thing which made it impossible to degrade them below the beasts, which amid all their crimes and miseries yet separated a cynical and unmanly contamination, an anti-social cruelty, from all the soothing, elevating and harmonious gentlenesses of the sexual intercourse, and the humanizing charities of domestic life which are its appendages,—that this is to be obliterated. They are required to abstain from marrying under penalty of starvation. And it is threatened to deprive them of that property which is as strictly their birthright as a gentleman's land is his birthright, without giving them any compensation but the insulting advice to conquer, with minds undisciplined in the habits of higher gratification, a propensity which persons of the most consummate wisdom have been unable to resist, and which it is difficult to admire a person for having resisted. The doctrine of this writer is that the principle of population, when under no dominion of moral restraint, outstripping the sustenance produced by the labour of man, and that not in proportion to the number of inhabitants, but operating equally in a thinly peopled community as in one where the population is enormous, [is] not a prevention but a check. So far a man might have been conducted by a train of reasoning which, though it may be shown to be defective, would argue in the reasoner no selfish and slavish feelings. But he has the hardened insolence to propose as a remedy that the poor should be compelled (for what except compulsion is a threat of the confiscation of those funds which by the institutions of their country had been set apart for their sustenance in sickness or destitution?) to abstain from sexual intercourse, whilst the rich are to be permitted to add as many mouths to consume the products of the labour of the poor as they please.° If any new disadvantages are found to attach to the condition of social existence, those disadvantages ought not to be borne exclusively by one class of men, nor especially by that class whose ignorance leads them to exaggerate the advantages of sensual enjoyment, whose callous habits render domestic endearments more important to dispose them to resist the suggestions to violence and cruelty by which their situation ever exposes them to be tempted, and all whose other enjoyments are limited and few, whilst their sufferings are various and many. In this sense I cannot imagine how the advocates of equality could so readily have conceded [that] the unlimited operation of the principle of population affects the truth of their theories. On the contrary, the more heavy and certain are the evils of life, the more injustice is there [in] casting the burden of them exclusively on one order in the community. They seem to have conceded it merely because their opponents have insolently assumed it. Surely it is enough that the rich should possess to the exclusion of the poor all other luxuries and comforts, and wisdom, and refinement, the least envied but the most deserving of envy among all their privileges.

What is the Reform that We Desire?

Before we aspire after theoretical perfection in the amelioration of our political state, it is necessary that we possess those advantages which we have been cheated of, and [to] which the experience of modern times has proved that nations even under the present [conditions] are susceptible: first, we would regain these; second, we would establish some form of government which might secure us against such a series of events as have conducted us to a persuasion that the forms according to which it is now administered are inadequate to that purpose.

We would abolish the national debt.

We would disband the standing army.

We would, with every possible regard to the existing interests of the holders, abolish sinecures.

We would, with every possible regard to the existing interests of the holders, abolish tithes. And make all religions, all forms of opinion respecting the origin and government of the Universe, equal in the eye of the law.

We would make justice cheap, certain and speedy, and extend the institution of juries to every possible occasion of jurisprudence.

The national debt was chiefly contracted in two liberticide wars, undertaken by the privileged classes of the country°—the first, for the ineffectual purpose of tyrannizing over one portion of their subjects; the second, in order to extinguish the resolute spirit of obtaining their rights in another.

The labour which this money represents, and that which is represented by the money wrung for purposes of the same detestable character out of the people since the commencement of the American war, would, if properly employed, have covered our land with monuments of architecture exceeding the sumptuousness and the beauty of Egypt and Athens; it might have made every peasant's cottage, surrounded with its garden, a little paradise of comfort, with every convenience desirable in civilized life; neat tables and chairs, and good beds, and a nice collection of useful books; and our ships manned by sailors well-paid and well-clothed might have kept watch round this glorious island against the less enlightened nations which assuredly would have envied, until they could have imitated, its prosperity. But the labour which is expressed by these sums has been diverted from these purposes of human happiness to the promotion of slavery, or the attempt at dominion, and a great portion of the sum in question is debt and must be paid.° Is it to remain unpaid forever, an eternal rent-charge upon the land from which the inhabitants of these islands draw their subsistence? This were to pronounce the perpetual institution of two orders of aristocracy, and men are in a temper to endure one with some reluctance. Is it to be paid now? If so what are the funds, or when and how is it to be paid? The fact is that the national debt is a debt, not contracted by the whole nation towards a portion of it, but a debt contracted by the whole mass of the privileged classes towards one particular portion of those classes. If the principal were paid, the whole property of those who possess property must be valued and the public creditor, whose property would have been included in this estimate, satisfied out of the proceeds. It has been said that all the land in the nation is mortgaged for the amount of the national debt. This is a partial statement. Not only all the land in the nation but all the property of whatever denomination, all the houses and the furniture and the goods and every article of merchandise, and the property which is represented by the very money lent by the fund-holder, who is bound to pay a certain portion as debtor, whilst he is to receive another certain portion as creditor. The property of the rich is mortgaged: to use the language of the law, let the mortgagee foreclose.

If the principal of this debt were paid, after such reductions had been made so as to make an equal value, taking corn for the standard, [. . .] it would be the rich who alone could, as justly they ought to, pay it. It would be a mere transfer among persons of property.° As it is, the interest is chiefly paid by those who had no hand in the borrowing and who are sufferers in other respects from the consequences of those transactions in which the money was spent.

The payment of the principal of what is called the National debt, which it is pretended is so difficult a problem, is only difficult to those who do not see who is the creditor and who the debtor, and who the wretched sufferers from whom they both wring the taxes which under the form of interest are given by the former° [latter] and accepted by the latter [former]. It is from the labour of those who have no property that all the persons who possess property think to extort the perpetual interest of a debt, the whole of them to the part, which the latter [former] know they could not persuade the former [latter] to pay, but by conspiring with them in an imposture which makes the third class pay what the first [second] neither received by their sanction nor spent for their benefit, and what the second [first] never lent to them. They would both shift to the labour of the present and of all succeeding generations the payment of the interest of their own debt, from themselves and their posterity, because the payment of the principal would be no more than a compromise and transfer of property between each other, by which the nation would be spared forty-four millions a year, which now is paid to maintain in luxury and indolence the public debtors and to protect them from the demand of their creditors upon them, who, being part of the same body, and owing as debtors whilst they possess a claim as creditors, agree to abstain from demanding the principal which they must all unite to pay, for the sake of receiving an enormous interest which is principally wrung out of those who had no concern whatever in the transaction. One of the first acts of a reformed government would undoubtedly be an effectual scheme for compelling these to compromise their debt between themselves.

When I speak of persons of property, I mean not every man who possesses any degree of property; I mean the rich. Every man whose scope in society has a plebeian and intelligible utility, whose personal exertions are more valuable to him than his capital; every tradesman who is not a monopolist, all surgeons and physicians, and those mechanics and editors and literary men and artists, and farmers, all those persons whose profits spring from honourably and honestly exerting their own skill and wisdom or strength in greater abundance than from the employment of money to take advantage of the necessity of the starvation of their fellow citizens for their profit, are those who pay, as well as those more obviously understood by the labouring classes, the interest of the national debt. It is the interest of all these persons as well as that of the poor to insist upon the payment of the principal.

For this purpose the form ought to be as simple and succinct as possible. The operations of deciding who was to pay, at what time, and how much, and to whom, are divested of financial chicanery, problems readily to be determined. The common tribunals may possess a legal jurisdiction to award the proportion due upon the several claims of each.

There are two descriptions of property which, without entering into the subtleties of a more refined moral theory as applicable to the existing forms of society, are entitled to two very different measures of forbearance and regard. And this forbearance and regard have by political institution usually been accorded in an inverse reason from what is just and natural. Labour, industry, economy, skill, genius, or any similar powers honourably and innocently exerted are the foundations of one description of property, and all true political institution ought to defend every man in the exercise of his discretion with respect to property so acquired. Of this kind is the principal part of the property enjoyed by those who are but one degree removed from the class which subsists by daily labour. Yet there are instances of persons in this class who have procured their property by fraudulent and violent means, as there are instances in the other of persons who have acquired their property by innocent or honorable exertion. All political science abounds with limitations and exceptions. Property thus acquired men leave to their children. The absolute right becomes weakened by descent, first because it is only to avoid the greater evil of arbitrarily interfering with the discretion [of any man] in matters of property that the great evil of acknowledging any person to have an exclusive right to property who has not created it by his skill or labour is admitted, and secondly because the mode of its having been originally acquired is forgotten, and it is confounded with the property acquired in a very different manner, and the principle upon which all property justly rests, after the great principle of the general advantage, becomes thus disregarded and misunderstood. Yet the privilege of disposing of property by will is one necessarily connected with the existing forms of domestic life, and exerted merely by those who have acquired property by industry or who have preserved it by economy, would never produce any great and invidious inequality of fortune. A thousand accidents would perpetually tend to level the accidental elevation, and the signs of property would perpetually recur to those whose deserving skill might attract, or whose labour might create it.

But there is another species of property, which has its foundation in usurpation, or imposture, or violence, without which, by the nature of things, immense aggregations of possessions of gold or land could never have been accumulated. Of this nature is the principal part of the property enjoyed by the aristocracy and by the great fund-holders, the great majority of whose ancestors never either deserved it by their skill and talents or acquired and created it by their personal labour. It could not be that they deserved it, for if the honourable exertion of the most glorious imperial faculties of our nature had been the criterion of the possession of property, the posterity of Shakespeare, of Milton, of Hampden, of Lor[d Bacon]° would be the wealthiest proprietors in England. It could not be that they acquired it by legitimate industry,— for besides that the real mode of acquisition is matter of history, no honourable profession or honest trade, nor the hereditary exercise of it, ever in such numerous instances accumulated masses of property so vast as those enjoyed by the ruling orders in England. They were either grants from the feudal sovereigns whose right to what they granted was founded upon conquest or oppression, both a denial of all right; or they were the lands of the ancient Catholic clergy which, according to the most acknowledged principles of public justice, reverted to the nation at their suppression, or they were the products of patents and monopolies, an exercise of sovereignty more pernicious than direct violence to the interests of a commercial nation; or in later times such property has been accumulated by dishonourable cunning and the taking advantage of a fictitious paper currency to obtain an unfair power over labour and the fruits of labour.

Property thus accumulated being transmitted from father to son acquires, as property of the more legitimate kind loses, force and sanction, but in a more limited manner. For not only on an examination and recurrence to first principles is it seen to have been founded on a violation of all that to which the latter owes its sacredness, but it is felt in its existence and perpetuation as a public burden, and known as a rallying point to the ministers of tyranny, having the property of a snowball, gathering as it rolls, and rolling until it bursts.

Labour and skill and the immediate wages of labour and skill is a property of the most sacred and indisputable right, and the foundation of all other property. And the right [of a man] to property in the exertion of his own bodily and mental faculties, or to the undoubted produce and free reward of that exertion is the most [inalienable of rights]. If, however, he takes by violence or appropriates to himself through fraudulent cunning, or receives from another property so acquired, his claim to that property is of a far inferior force. We may acquiesce, if we evidently perceive an overbalance of public advantage in submission, under this claim; but if any public emergency should arise, at which it might be necessary as at present to satisfy by a tax on capital the claims of a part of the nation by a contribution from such national resources as may with the least injustice be appropriated to that purpose, assuredly it would not be on labour and skill, the foundation of all property, nor on the profits and savings of labour and skill, which are property itself, but on such possessions which can only be called property in a modified sense, as have from their magnitude and their nature an evident origin in violence or imposture.

The national debt, as has been stated, is a debt contracted by the whole of a particular class in the nation towards a portion of that class. It is sufficiently clear that this debt was not contracted for the purpose of the public advantage. Besides there was no authority in the nation competent to a measure of this nature. The usual vindication of national debts is that, [since] they are contracted in an overwhelming measure for the purpose of defence against a common danger, for the vindication of the rights and liberties of posterity, it is just that posterity should bear the burden of payment. This reasoning is most fallacious. The history of nations presents us with a succession of extraordinary emergencies; their existence is perpetually threatened by new and unexpected combinations and developments of foreign or internal force. Imagine a situation of equal emergency to occur to

England as that which the ruling party assume to have occurred as their excuse for burdening the nation with the perpetual payment of £45,000,000 annually. Suppose France and Russia and Austria were to enter into a league against England, the first to revenge its injuries, the second to satisfy its ambition, the third to soothe its jealousy. Could the nation bear £90,000,000 of yearly interest, must there be twice as many luxurious and idle persons, must the labourer receive for twenty-eight hours' work what he now receives for fourteen, as he now receives for fourteen what he once received for seven? But this argument [. . .]°

What is meant by a Reform of parliament? If England were a Republic governed by one assembly; if there were no chamber of hereditary aristocracy which is at once an actual and a virtual representation of all who claim through rank or wealth superiority over their countrymen; if there were no King who is as the rallying point of those whose tendency is at once to [gather] and to confer that power which is consolidated at the expense of the nation, then [. . .]°

The advocates of universal suffrage have reasoned correctly that no individual who is governed can be denied a direct share in the government of his country without supreme injustice. If we pursue the train of reasonings which have conducted to the conclusion, we discover that systems of social order still more incompatible than universal suffrage with any reasonable hope of instant accomplishment appear to be that which should result from a just combination of the elements of social life. I do not understand why those reasoners who propose at any price an immediate appeal to universal suffrage, because it is that which it is injustice to withhold, do not insist on the same ground on the immediate abolition, for instance, of monarchy and aristocracy, and the levelling of inordinate wealth, and an agrarian distribution, including the Parks and Chases of the rich, of the uncultivated districts of the country. No doubt the institution of universal suffrage would by necessary consequence tend to the abolition of these forms; because it is impossible that the people, having attained power, should fail to see what the demagogues now conceal from them [as] the legitimate consequence of the doctrines through which they had attained it. A Republic, however just in its principle and glorious in its object, would, through [the] violence and sudden change which must attend it, incur a great risk of being as rapid in its decline as in its growth.

A civil war, which might be engendered by the passions attending on this mode of reform, would confirm in the mass of the nation those military habits which have been already introduced by our tyrants, and with which liberty is incompatible. From the moment that a man is a soldier, he becomes a slave. He is taught obedience; his will is no longer, which is the most sacred prerogative of man, guided by his own judgement. He is taught to despise human life and human suffering; this is the universal distinction of slaves. He is more degraded than a murderer; he is like the bloody knife, which has stabbed, and feels not; a murderer we may abhor and despise; a soldier is by profession beyond abhorrence and below contempt.

It is better that [the people°] should be instructed in the whole truth, that they should see the clear grounds of their rights, the objects to which they ought to tend; and be impressed with the just persuasion that patience and reason and endurance [are the means of] a calm yet irresistible progress.

Probable Means

That the House of Commons should reform itself, uninfluenced by any fear that the people would, on their refusal, assume to itself that office, seems a contradiction. What need of Reform if it expresses the will, and watches over the interests of the public? And if, as is sufficiently evident, it despises that will and neglects that interest, what motives would incite it to institute a reform which the aspect of the times renders indeed sufficiently perilous, but without which there will speedily be no longer anything in England to distinguish it from the basest and most abject community of slaves that ever existed.

The great principle of Reform consists in every individual of mature age and perfect understanding giving his consent to the institution and the continued existence of the social system, which is instituted for his advantage and for the advantage of others in his situation. As in a great nation this is practically impossible, masses of individuals consent to qualify other individuals, whom they delegate to superintend their concerns. These delegates have constitutional authority to exercise the functions of sovereignty; they unite in the highest degree the legislative and executive functions. A government that is founded on any other basis is a government of fraud or force, and ought on the first convenient occasion to be overthrown. The grand principle of political reform is the natural equality of men; not with relation to their property but to their rights. That equality in possessions which Jesus Christ° so passionately taught is a moral rather than political truth,° and is such as social institutions cannot, without mischief, inflexibly secure. Morals and politics can only be considered as portions of the same science, with relation to a system of such absolute perfection as Christ and Plato and Rousseau and other reasoners have asserted, and as Godwin has, with irresistible eloquence, systematized and developed. Equality in possessions must be the last result of the utmost refinements of civilization; it is one of the conditions of that system of society towards which, with whatever hope of ultimate success, it is our duty to tend. We may and ought to advert to it, as to the elementary principle, as to the goal, unattainable perhaps by us, but which, as it were, we revive in our posterity to pursue. We derive tranquillity and courage and grandeur of soul from contemplating an object which is, because we will it, and may be, because we hope and desire it, and must be, if succeeding generations of the enlightened sincerely and earnestly seek it. [. . .]

But our present business is with the difficult and unbending realities of actual life, and when we have drawn inspiration from the great object of our hope it becomes us with patience and resolution to apply ourselves to accommodating our theories to immediate practice.

That Representative Assembly called the House of Commons ought questionless to be *immediately* nominated by the great mass of the people. The aristocracy and those who unite in their own persons the vast privileges conferred by the possession of inordinate wealth is sufficiently represented by the House of Peers and by the King. Those theorists who admire and would put into action the mechanism of what is called the British Constitution would acquiesce in this view of the question. For if the House of Peers be a permanent representative of the privileged classes, if the regal power be no more than another form, and a form still more jealously to be regarded, of the same representation; whilst the House of Commons be not chosen by the mass of the population, what becomes of that democratic element, upon the presence of which it has been supposed that the waning superiority of England over the surrounding nations has depended?

Any sudden attempt at Universal suffrage would produce an immature attempt at a Republic; it [is better] that [an] object so inexpressibly great and sacred should never have been attempted than that it should be attempted and fail. It is no prejudice to the ultimate establishment of the boldest political innovations that we temporize so as, when they shall be accomplished, they may be rendered permanent.

Considering the population of Great Britain and Ireland as twenty millions and the representative assembly as five hundred, each member ought to be the expression of the will of 40,000 persons; of these two-thirds would be women and children and persons under age; the actual number of voters therefore for each member would be 13,300. The whole extent of the empire might be divided into five hundred electoral departments or parishes, and the inhabitants assemble on a certain day to exercise their right of suffrage.

Mr Bentham and other writers have urged the admission of females to the right of suffrage; this attempt seems somewhat immature. Should my opinion be the result of despondency, the writer of these pages would be the last to withhold his vote from any system which might tend to an equal and full development of the capacities of all living beings.

The system of voting by ballot,° which some reasoners have recommended, is attended with obvious inconveniences. It withdraws the elector from the regard of his country and his neighbours, and permits him to conceal the motives of his vote, which, if concealed, cannot but be dishonourable; when, if he had known that he had to render a public account of his conduct, he would have never permitted them° to guide him.—There is in this system of voting by ballot and of electing a member of the Representative Assembly as a church-warden is elected something too mechanical. The elector and the elected ought to meet one another face to face and interchange the meanings by actual presence and share some common impulses and, in a degree, understand each other. There ought to be the common sympathy of the excitements of a popular assembly among the electors themselves. The imagination would thus be strongly excited, and a mass of generous and enlarged and popular sentiments be awakened, which would give the vitality of [. . .]°

That republican boldness of censuring and judging one another, which [is] indeed exerted in England under the title of 'public opinion', though perverted from its true uses into an instrument of prejudice and calumny, would then be applied to its genuine purposes. Year by year the people would become more susceptible of assuming forms of government more simple and beneficial. [. . .]

If the existing government shall compel the Nation to take the task of reform into its own hands, one of the most obvious consequences of such a circumstance would be the abolition of monarchy and aristocracy. Why, it will then be argued, if the subsisting condition of social forms is to be thrown into confusion, should these things be endured? Why do we now endure them? Is it because we think that an hereditary King is cheaper and wiser than an elected President, or a

House of Lords and a Bench of Bishops are institutions modelled by the wisdom of the most refined and civilized periods, beyond which the wit of mortal man can furnish nothing more perfect? In case the subsisting Government should compel the people to revolt to establish a representative assembly in defiance of them, and to assume in the defence of that assembly an attitude of resistance and defence, this question would probably be answered in a very summary manner: no friend of mankind and of his country can desire that such a crisis should suddenly arrive; but still less, once having arrived, can he hesitate under what banner to array his person and his power. At the peace, the people would have been contented with strict economy and severe retrenchment, and some direct and intelligible plan for producing that equilibrium between the capitalists and the landholders which is delusively styled the payment of the national debt. Had this system been adopted, they probably would have refrained from exacting Parliamentary Reform, the only secure guarantee that it would have been pursued.—Two years ago it might still have been possible to have commenced a system of gradual reform. The people were then insulted, tempted and betrayed,° and the petitions of a million of men rejected with disdain. Now they are more miserable, more hopeless, more impatient of their misery. Above all, they have become more universally aware of the true sources of their misery. It is possible that the period of conciliation is past, and that after having played with the confidence and cheated the expectations of the people, their passions will be too little under discipline to allow them to wait the slow, gradual and certain operation of such a Reform as we can imagine the constituted authorities to concede.

Upon the issue of this question depends the species of reform which a philosophical mind should regard with approbation. If Reform shall be begun by the existing Government, let us be contented with a limited [beginning], with any whatsoever opening; let the rotten boroughs be disfranchised, and their rights transferred to the unrepresented cities and districts of the Nation; it is no matter how slow, gradual and cautious be the change; we shall demand more and more with firmness and moderation, never anticipating, but never deferring the moment of successful opposition, so that the people may become habituated [to] exercising the functions of sovereignty, in proportion as they acquire the possession of it.

If reform could begin from within the Houses of Parliament, as constituted at present, it appears to me that what is called moderate reform, that is a suffrage whose qualification should be the possession of a certain small property, and triennial parliaments,° would be principles—a system in which, for the sake of obtaining without bloodshed or confusion ulterior° improvements of a more important character, all reformers ought to acquiesce. Not that such are first principles, or that they would produce a system of perfect social institution or one approaching to [such a system]. But nothing is more idle than to reject a limited benefit because we cannot without great sacrifices obtain an unlimited one. We might thus reject a Representative Republic, if it were attainable, on the plea that the imagination of man can conceive of something more absolutely perfect. Towards whatsoever we regard as perfect, undoubtedly it is no less our duty than it is our nature to press forward; this is the generous enthusiasm which accomplishes not indeed the consummation after which it aspires, but one which approaches it in a degree far nearer than if the whole powers had not been developed by a delusion. It is in politics rather than in religion that faith is meritorious.

If the Houses of Parliament obstinately and perpetually refuse to concede any reform to the people, my vote is for universal suffrage and equal representation.

It is asked, how shall this be accomplished, in defiance of and in opposition to the constituted authorities of the Nation, they who possess whether with or without its consent the command of a standing army and of a legion of spies and police officers and hold all the strings of that complicated mechanism with which the hopes and fears of men are moved like puppets? They would disperse any assembly really chosen by the people; they would shoot and hew down any multitude without regard to sex or age (as the Jews did the Canaanites) which might be collected in its defence; they would calumniate, imprison, starve, ruin and expatriate every person who wrote or acted, or thought, or might be suspected to think against them; misery and extermination would fill the country from one end to another.

This question I would answer by another.

Will you endure to pay the half of your earnings to maintain in luxury and idleness the confederation of your tyrants as the reward of a successful conspiracy to defraud and oppress you? Will you make your tame cowardice and the branding record of it the everlasting inheritance of your degraded posterity? Not only this: will you render by your torpid endurance this condition of things as permanent as the system of castes in India by which the same horrible injustice is perpetrated under another form?

Assuredly no Englishmen by whom these propositions are understood will answer in the affirmative; and the opposite side of the alternative remains.

When the majority in any nation arrive at a conviction that it is their duty and their interest to divest the minority of a power employed to their disadvantage, and the minority are sufficiently mistaken as to believe that their superiority is tenable, a struggle must ensue.

If the majority are enlightened, united, impelled by a uniform enthusiasm, and animated by a distinct and powerful apprehension of their object,—and full confidence in their undoubted power—the struggle is merely nominal. The minority perceive the approaches of the development of an irresistible force, by the influence of the public opinion of their weakness on those political forms of which no government but an absolute despotism is devoid. They divest themselves of their usurped distinctions; the public tranquillity is not disturbed by the revolution.

But these conditions may only be imperfectly fulfilled by the state of a people grossly oppressed and impotent to cast off the load. Their enthusiasm may have been subdued by the killing weight of toil and suffering; they may be panic-stricken and disunited by their oppressors and the demagogues; the influence of fraud may have been sufficient to weaken the union of classes which compose them by suggesting jealousies; and the position of the conspirators, although it is to be forced by repeated assaults, may be tenable until the siege can be vigorously urged. The true patriot will endeavour to enlighten and to unite the nation and animate it with enthusiasm and confidence. For this purpose he will be indefatigable in promulgating political truth. He will endeavour to rally round one standard the divided friends of liberty, and make them forget the subordinate objects with regard to which they differ, by appealing to that respecting which they are all agreed. He will promote such open confederations among men of principle and spirit as may tend to make their intentions and their efforts converge to a common centre. He will discourage all secret associations which have a tendency, by making national will develop itself in a partial and premature manner, to cause tumult and confusion. He will urge the necessity of exciting the people frequently to exercise their right of assembling, in such limited numbers as that all present may be actual parties to the proceedings of the day. Lastly, if circumstances had collected a more considerable number as at Manchester on the memorable 16th of August,° if the tyrants command their troops to fire upon them or cut them down unless they disperse, he will exhort them peaceably to risk the danger, and to expect without resistance the onset of the cavalry, and wait with folded arms the event of the fire of the artillery and receive with unshrinking bosoms the bayonets of the charging battalions. Men are every day persuaded to incur greater perils for a less manifest advantage. And this, not because active resistance is not justifiable when all other means shall have failed, but because in this instance temperance and courage would produce greater advantages than the most decisive victory. In the first place, the soldiers are men and Englishmen, and it is not to be believed that they would massacre an unresisting multitude of their countrymen drawn up in unarmed array before them and bearing in their looks a calm and deliberate resolution to perish rather than abandon the assertion of their rights. In the confusion of flight the ideas of the soldier become confused, and he massacres those who fly from him by the instinct of his trade. In the struggle of conflict and resistance he is irritated by a sense of his own danger; he is flattered by an apprehension of his magnanimity in incurring it; he considers the blood of his countrymen at once the price of his valour, the pledge of his security. He applauds himself by reflecting that these base and dishonorable motives will gain him credit among his comrades and his officers who are animated by the same, as if they were the same. But if he should observe neither resistance nor flight he would be suddenly reduced to impotence and indecision. Thus far, his ideas were governed by the same law as those of a dog who chases a flock of sheep to the corner of a field, and keeps aloof when they make the firm parade of resistance.—But the soldier is a man and an Englishman. This unexpected reception would probably throw him back upon a recollection of the true nature of the measures of which he was made the instrument, and the enemy might be converted into the ally.

The true patriot will be foremost to publish the boldest truths in the most fearless manner, yet without the slightest tincture of personal malignity. He would encourage all others to the same efforts and assist them to the utmost of his power with the resources both of his intellect and fortune. He would call upon them to despise imprisonment and persecution and lose no opportunity of bringing the public opinions and the power of the tyrants into circumstances of perpetual contest and opposition.

All might, however, be ineffectual to produce so uniform an impulse of the national will as to preclude a further struggle. The strongest argument, perhaps, for the necessity of Reform is the inoperative and unconscious abjectness to which the purposes of a considerable mass of the people are reduced. They neither know nor care. They are sinking into a resemblance with the Hindoos and the Chinese, who were once men as they are. Unless the cause which renders them passive subjects instead of active citizens be removed, they will sink with accelerated gradations into that barbaric and unnatural civilization which destroys all the differences among men. It is in vain to exhort us to wait until all men shall desire Freedom whose real interest will consist in its establishment. It is in vain to hope to enlighten them whilst their tyrants employ the utmost artifices of all their complicated engine to perpetuate the infection of every species of fanaticism and error from generation to generation. The advocates of Reform ought indeed to leave no effort unexerted, and they ought to be indefatigable in exciting all men to examine [. . .]°

But if they wait until those neutral politicians whose opinions represent the actions of this class are persuaded that [some] effectual reform is necessary, the occasion will have passed or will never arrive, and the people will have exhausted their strength in ineffectual expectation and will have sunk into incurable supineness. It was principally [through] a similar quietism that the populous and extensive nations of Asia have fallen into their existing decrepitude; and that anarchy, insecurity, ignorance and barbarism, the symptoms of the confirmed disease of monarchy, have reduced nations of the most delicate physical and intellectual organization and under the most fortunate climates of the globe to a blank in the history of man. The manufacturers° to a man are persuaded of the necessity of reform; an immense majority of the inhabitants of London [. . .]°

The reasoners who incline to the opinion that it is not sufficient that the innovators should produce a majority in the nation, but that we ought to expect such an unanimity as would preclude anything amounting to a serious dispute, are prompted to this view of the question by the dread of anarchy and massacre. Infinite and inestimable calamities belong to oppression, but the most fatal of them all is that mine of unexploded mischief which it has practised beneath the foundation of society, and with which, 'pernicious to one touch'° it [threatens] to involve the ruin of the entire building together with its own. But delay merely renders these mischief[s] more tremendous, not the less inevitable. For the utmost may now be the crisis of the social disease [which] is rendered thus periodical, chronic and incurable.

The savage brutality of the populace is proportioned to the arbitrary character of the government, and tumults and insurrections soon, as in Constantinople, become consistent with the permanence of the causing evil, of which they might have been the critical determination.

The public opinion in England ought first to [be] excited to action, and the durability of those forms within which the oppressors intrench themselves brought perpetually to the test of its operation. No law or institution can last if this opinion be distinctly pronounced against it. For this purpose government ought to be defied, in cases of questionable result, to prosecute for political libel. All questions relating to the jurisdiction of magistrates and courts of law respecting which any doubt could be raised ought to be agitated with indefatigable pertinacity. Some two or three of the popular leaders have shown the best spirit in this regard; they only want system and co-operation. The tax-gatherer ought to be compelled in every practicable instance to distrain, whilst the right to impose taxes, as was the case in the beginning of the resistance to the tyranny of Charles I, is formally contested by an overwhelming multitude of defendants before the courts of common law. Confound the subtlety of lawyers with the subtlety of the law. All of the nation would thus be excited to develop itself, and to declare whether it acquiesced in the existing forms of government.—The manner in which all questions of this nature might be decided would develop the occasions, and afford a prognostic as to the success, of more decisive measures. Simultaneously with this active and vigilant system of opposition means ought to be taken of solemnly conveying the sense of large bodies and various denominations of the people in a manner the most explicit to the existing depositaries of power. Petitions, couched in the actual language of the petitioners, and emanating from distinct assemblies, ought to load the tables of the House of Commons. The poets, philosophers and artists ought to remonstrate, and the memorials entitled their petitions might show the diverse convictions they entertain of the inevitable connection between national prosperity and freedom, and the cultivation of the imagination and the cultivation of scientific truth, and the profound development of moral and metaphysical enquiry. Suppose these memorials to be severally written by Godwin and Hazlitt and Bentham and Hunt,° they would be worthy of the age and of the cause; radiant and irresistible like the meridian Sun [they] would strike all but the eagles who dared to gaze upon its beam, with blindness and confusion. These appeals of solemn and emphatic argument from those who have already a predestined existence among posterity, would appal the enemies of mankind by their echoes from every corner of the world in which the majestic literature of England is cultivated; it would be like a voice from beyond the dead of those who will live in the memories of men, when they must be forgotten; it would be Eternity warning Time.

Let us hope that at this stage of the progress of Reform, the oppressors would feel their impotence and reluctantly and imperfectly concede some limited portion of the Rights of the people; and disgorge some morsels of their undigested prey. In this case the people ought to be exhorted by everything ultimately dear to them to pause until by the exercise of those rights which they have regained they become fitted to demand more. It is better that we gain what we demand by a process of negotiation which would occupy twenty years, than that by communicating a sudden shock to the interests of those who are the depositaries and dependents of power we should incur the calamity which their revenge might inflict upon us by giving the signal of civil war.—If, after all, they consider the chance personal ruin and the infamy of figuring on the page of history as the promoters of civil war preferable to resigning any portion how small soever of their usurped authority, we are to recollect that we possess a right beyond remonstrance. It has been acknowledged by the most approved writers on the English constitution (which is in this instance merely declaratory of the superior decisions of eternal justice) that we possess a right of resistance. The claim of the reigning family° is founded upon a memorable exertion of this solemnly recorded right.

The last resort of resistance is undoubtedly insurrection.—The right of insurrection is derived from the employment of armed force to counteract the will of the nation. Let the government disband the standing army, and the purpose of resistance would be sufficiently fulfilled by the incessant agitation of the points of dispute before the courts of common law and by an unwarlike display of the irresistible numbers and union of the people.

Before we enter into a consideration of the measures which might terminate in civil war, let us for a moment consider the nature and the consequences of war. This is the alternative which the unprincipled cunning of the tyrants has presented to us, from which we must not sh[rink]. There is secret sympathy between Destruction and Power, between Monarchy and War; and the long experience of the history of all recorded time teaches us with what success they have played into each other's hands. War is a kind of superstition; the pageantry of arms and badges corrupts the imagination of men. How far more appropriate would be the symbols of an inconsolable grief—muffled drums, and melancholy music, and arms reversed, and the livery of sorrow rather than of blood. When men mourn at funerals, for what do they mourn in comparison with the calamities which they hasten with every circumstance of festivity to suffer and to inflict. Visit in imagination the scene of a field of battle, or a city taken by assault, collect into one group the groans and the distortions of the innumerable dying, the inconsolable grief and horror of their surviving friends, the hellish exultation, and unnatural drunkenness of destruction of the conquerors, the burning of the harvests and the obliteration of the traces of cultivation.—To this, in civil war is to be added the sudden disruption of the bonds of social life, and 'father against son.'

If there had never been war, there could never have been tyranny in the world; tyrants take advantage of the mechanical organization of armies to establish and defend their encroachments.—It is thus that the mighty advantages of the French Revolution have been almost compensated by a succession of tyrants (for demagogues, oligarchies, usurpers and legitimate Kings are merely varieties of the same class) from Robespierre to Louis XVIII. War, waged from whatever motive, extinguishes the sentiment of reason and justice in the mind. The motive is forgotten, or only adverted to in a mechanical and habitual manner. A sentiment of confidence in brute force and in a contempt of death and danger is considered as the highest virtue, when in truth, however indispensable, they are merely the means and the instruments, highly capable of being perverted to destroy the cause they were assumed to promote. It is as a foppery the most intolerable to an amiable and philosophical mind.—It is like what some reasoners have observed of religious faith; no fallacious and indirect motive to action can subsist in the mind without weakening the effect of those which are genuine and true. The person who [may] think it virtuous to believe, will think a less degree of virtue attaches to good actions than if he had considered it as indifferent. The person who has been accustomed to subdue men by force will be less inclined to the trouble of convincing or persuading them.

These brief considerations suffice to show that the true friend of mankind and of his country would hesitate before he recommended measures which tend to bring down so heavy a calamity as war.

I imagine, however, that before the English Nation shall arrive at that point of moral and political degradation now occupied by the Chinese, it will be necessary to appeal to an exertion of physical strength. If the madness of parties admits no other mode of determining the question at issue [. . .]°

When the people shall have obtained, by whatever means, the victory over their oppressors and when persons appointed by them shall have taken their seats in the Representative assembly of the nation, and assumed the control of public affairs according to constitutional rules, there will remain the great task of accommodating all that can be preserved of ancient forms with the improvements of the knowledge of a more enlightened age in legislation, jurisprudence, government, and religious and academical institution. The settlement of the national debt is, on the principles before elucidated, merely circumstance of form, and however necessary and important is an affair of mere arithmetical proportions readily determined; nor can I see how those, who being deprived of their unjust advantages will probably inwardly murmur, can oppose one word of open expostulation to a measure of such irrefragable justice.—There is one thing which certain vulgar agitators endeavour to flatter the most uneducated part of the people by assiduously proposing, which they ought not to do nor to require: and that is, Retribution. Men having been injured desire to injure in return. This is falsely called an universal law of human nature; it is a law from which many are exempt, and all in proportion to their virtue and cultivation.—The savage is more revengeful than the civilized man, the ignorant and uneducated than the person of a refined and cultivated intellect; the generous and [. . .]°

A Defence of Poetry

According to one mode of regarding those two classes of mental action which are called Reason and Imagination,° the former may be considered as mind contemplating the relations borne by one thought to another, however produced; and the latter as mind, acting upon those thoughts so as to colour them with its own light, and composing from them as from elements, other thoughts, each containing within itself the principle of its own integrity. The one is the τὸ ποιειν or the principle of synthesis; and has for its objects those forms which are common to universal nature and existence itself; the other is the τὸ λογιζειν,° or principle of analysis and its action regards the relations of things, simply as relations; considering thoughts, not in their integral unity, but as the algebraical representations which conduct to certain general results. Reason is the enumeration of quantities already known; Imagination the perception of the value of those quantities, both separately and as a whole. Reason respects the differences, and Imagination the similitudes of things. Reason is to Imagination as the instrument to the agent, as the body to the spirit, as the shadow to the substance.

Poetry, in a general sense, may be defined to be 'the expression of the Imagination':° and Poetry is connate° with the origin of man. Man is an instrument over which a series of external and internal impressions are driven, like the alternations of an ever-changing wind over an Aeolian lyre; which move it, by their motion, to ever-changing melody. But there is a principle within the human being, and perhaps within all sentient beings, which acts otherwise than in the lyre, and produces not melody alone, but harmony, by an internal adjustment of the sounds or motions thus excited to the impressions which excite them. It is as if the lyre could accommodate its chords to the motions of that which strikes them, in a determined proportion of sound; even as the musician can accommodate his voice to the sound of the lyre. A child at play by itself will express its delight by its voice and motions; and every inflexion of tone and every gesture will bear exact relation to a corresponding antitype in the pleasurable impressions which awakened it; it will be the reflected image of that impression; and as the lyre trembles and sounds after the wind has died away, so the child seeks, by prolonging in its voice and motions the duration of the effect, to prolong also a consciousness of the cause. In relation to the objects which delight a child, these expressions are, what Poetry is to higher objects. The savage (for the savage is to ages what the child is to years) expresses the emotions produced in him by surrounding objects in a similar manner; and language and gesture, together with plastic or pictorial imitation, become the image of the combined effect of those objects and of his apprehension of them. Man in society, with all his passions and his pleasures, next becomes the object of the passions and pleasures of man; an additional class of emotions produces an augmented treasure of expressions, and language, gesture and the imitative arts become at once the representation and the medium, the pencil and the picture, the chisel and the statue, the chord and the harmony. The social sympathies, or those laws from which as from its elements society results, begin to develop themselves from the moment that two human beings co-exist; the future is contained within the present as the plant within the seed; and equality, diversity, unity, contrast, mutual dependence become the principles alone capable of affording the motives according to which the will of a social being is determined to action, inasmuch as he is social; and constitute pleasure in sensation, virtue in sentiment, beauty in art, truth in reasoning, and love in the intercourse of kind. Hence men, even in the infancy of society, observe a certain order in their words and actions, distinct from that of the objects and the impressions represented by them, all expression being subject to the laws of that from which it proceeds. But let us dismiss those more general considerations which might involve an enquiry into the principles of society itself, and restrict our view to the manner in which the imagination is expressed upon its forms.

In the youth of the world, men dance and sing and imitate natural objects, observing in these actions, as in all others, a certain rhythm or order. And, although all men observe a similar, they observe not the same order in the motions of the dance, in the melody of the song, in the combinations of language, in the series of their imitations of natural objects. For there is a certain order or rhythm belonging to each of these classes of mimetic representation, from which the hearer and the spectator receive an intenser and a purer pleasure than from any other: the sense of an approximation to this order has been called taste by modern writers. Every man, in the infancy of art, observes an order which approximates more or less closely to that from which this highest delight results: but the diversity is not sufficiently marked, as that its gradations should be sensible, except in those instances where the predominance of this faculty of approximation to the beautiful (for so we may be permitted to name the relation between this highest pleasure and its cause) is very great. Those in whom it exists in excess are poets, in the most universal sense of the word; and the pleasure resulting from the manner in which they express the influence of society or nature upon their own minds, communicates itself to others, and gathers a sort of reduplication from that community. Their language is vitally metaphorical;° that is, it marks the before unapprehended relations of things, and perpetuates their apprehension, until the words which represent them become through time signs for portions and classes of thoughts, instead of pictures of integral thoughts; and then, if no new poets should arise to create afresh the associations which have been thus disorganized, language will be dead to all the nobler purposes of human intercourse. These similitudes or relations are finely said by Lord Bacon to be 'the same footsteps of nature impressed upon the various subjects of the world'°—and he considers the faculty which perceives them as the storehouse of axioms common to all knowledge. In the infancy of society every author is necessarily a poet, because language itself is poetry; and to be a poet is to apprehend the true and the beautiful, in a word the good which exists in the relation, subsisting, first between existence and perception, and secondly between perception and expression. Every original language near to its source is in itself the chaos of a cyclic poem:° the copiousness of lexicography and the distinctions of grammar are the works of a later age, and are merely the catalogue and the form of the creations of Poetry.

But Poets, or those who imagine and express this indestructible order, are not only the authors of language and of music, of the dance and architecture and statuary and painting; they are the institutors of laws and the founders of civil society and the inventors of the arts of life and the teachers, who draw into a certain propinquity with the beautiful and the true that partial apprehension of the agencies of the invisible world which is called religion. Hence all original religions are allegorical or susceptible of allegory, and like Janus have a double face of false and true. Poets, according to the circumstances of the age and nation in which they appeared, were called in the earlier epochs of the world legislators or prophets:° a poet essentially comprises and unites both these characters. For he not only beholds intensely the present as it is, and discovers those laws according to which present things ought to be ordered, but he beholds the future in the present, and his thoughts are the germs of the flower and the fruit of latest time. Not that I assert poets to be prophets in the gross sense of the word, or that they can foretell the form as surely as they foreknow the spirit of events: such is the pretence of superstition which would make poetry an attribute of prophecy, rather than prophecy an attribute of poetry. A Poet participates in the eternal, the infinite and the one; as far as relates to his conceptions, time and place and number are not. The grammatical forms which express the moods of time, and the difference of persons and the distinction of place are convertible with respect to the highest poetry without injuring it as poetry, and the choruses of Aeschylus, and the Book of Job,° and Dante's *Paradise* would afford more than any other writings examples of this fact, if the limits of this paper did not forbid citation. The creations of sculpture, painting and music are illustrations still more decisive.

Language, colour, form, and religious and civil habits of action are all the instruments and the materials of poetry; they may all be called poetry by that figure of speech which considers the effect as a synonym of the cause. But poetry in a more restricted sense expresses those arrangements of language, and especially metrical language, which are created by that imperial faculty whose throne is curtained within the invisible nature of man. And this springs from the nature itself of language, which is a more direct representation of the actions and passions of our internal being, and is susceptible of more various and delicate combinations than colour, form or motion, and is more plastic and obedient to the control of that faculty of which it is the creation. For language is arbitrarily produced by the Imagination and has relation to thoughts alone; but all other materials, instruments and conditions of art have relations among each other, which limit and interpose between conception and expression. The former is as a mirror which reflects, the latter as a cloud which enfeebles, the light of which both are mediums of communication. Hence the fame of sculptors, painters and musicians, although the intrinsic powers of the great masters of these arts may yield in no degree to that of those who have employed language as the hieroglyphic° of their thoughts, has never equalled that of poets in the restricted sense of the term; as two performers of equal skill will produce unequal effects from a guitar and a harp. The fame of legislators and founders of religions, so long as their institutions last, alone seems to exceed that of poets in the restricted sense: but it can scarcely be a question whether if we deduct the celebrity which their flattery of the gross opinions of the vulgar usually conciliates, together with that which belonged to them in their higher character of poets, any excess will remain.

We have thus circumscribed the word Poetry within the limits of that art which is the most familiar and the most perfect expression of the faculty itself. It is necessary however to make the circle still narrower, and to determine the distinction between measured and unmeasured language; for the popular division into prose and verse is inadmissible in accurate philosophy.

Sounds as well as thoughts have relation both between each other and towards that which they represent, and a perception of the order of those relations, has always been found connected with a perception of the order of the relations of thoughts. Hence the language of poets has ever affected a certain uniform and harmonious recurrence of sound, without which it were not poetry, and which is scarcely less indispensable to the communication of its influence, than the words themselves without reference to that peculiar order. Hence the vanity of translation; it were as wise to cast a violet into a crucible that you might discover the formal principle of its colour and odour, as seek to transfuse from one language into another the creations of a poet. The plant must spring again from its seed or it will bear no flower—and this is the burden of the curse of Babel.

An observation of the regular mode of the occurrence of this harmony, in the language of poetical minds, together with its relation to music, produced metre, or a certain system of traditional forms of harmony and language. Yet it is by no means essential that a poet should accommodate his language to this traditional form, so that the harmony which is its spirit be observed. The practice is indeed convenient and popular and to be preferred, especially in such composition as includes much action: but every great poet must inevitably innovate upon the example of his predecessors in the exact structure of his peculiar versification. The distinction between poets and prose-writers is a vulgar error. The distinction between philosophers and poets has been anticipated. Plato was essentially a poet°—the truth and splendour of his imagery and the melody of his language is the most intense that it is possible to conceive. He rejected the measure of the epic, dramatic and lyrical forms, because he sought to kindle a harmony in thoughts divested of shape and action, and he forebore to invent any regular plan of rhythm which would include, under determinate forms, the varied pauses of his style. Cicero° sought to imitate the cadence of his periods but with little success. Lord Bacon was a poet.°—His language has a sweet and majestic rhythm which satisfies the sense no less than the almost superhuman wisdom of his philosophy satisfies the intellect; it is a strain which distends, and then bursts the circumference of the reader's mind, and pours itself forth together with it into the universal element with which it has perpetual sympathy. All the authors of revolutions in opinion are not only necessarily poets as they are inventors, nor even as their words unveil the permanent analogy of things by images which participate in the life of truth; but as their periods are harmonious and rhythmical and contain in themselves the elements of verse; being the echo of the eternal music. Nor are those supreme poets, who have employed traditional forms of rhythm on account of the form and action of their subjects, less incapable of perceiving and teaching the truth of things, than those who have omitted that form. Shakespeare, Dante and Milton (to confine ourselves to modern writers) are philosophers of the very loftiest powers.

A poem is the very image of life expressed in its eternal truth. There is this difference between a story and a poem,° that a story is a catalogue of detached facts, which have no other bond of connection than time, place, circumstance, cause and effect; the other is the creation of actions according to the unchangeable forms of human nature, as existing in the mind of the creator, which is itself the image of all other minds. The one is partial, and applies only to a definite period of time, and a certain combination of events which can never again recur; the other is universal, and contains within itself the germ of a relation to whatever motives or actions have place in the possible varieties of human nature. Time, which destroys the beauty and the use of the story of particular facts, stripped of the poetry which should invest them, augments that of Poetry; and forever develops new and wonderful applications of the eternal truth which it contains. Hence epitomes° have been called the moths of just history;° they eat out the poetry of it. The story of particular facts is as a mirror which obscures and distorts that which should be beautiful: Poetry is a mirror which makes beautiful that which is distorted.

The parts of a composition may be poetical, without the composition as a whole being a poem. A single sentence may be considered as a whole though it may be found in the midst of a series of unassimilated portions; a single word even may be a spark of inextinguishable thought. And thus all the great historians, Herodotus,° Plutarch,° Livy,° were poets; and although the plan of these writers, especially that of Livy, restrained them from developing this faculty in its highest degree, they make copious and ample amends for their subjection, by filling all the interstices of their subject with living images.

Having determined what is poetry, and who are poets, let us proceed to estimate its effects upon society.

Poetry is ever accompanied with pleasure:° all spirits on which it falls, open themselves to receive the wisdom which is mingled with its delight. In the infancy of the world, neither poets themselves nor their auditors are fully aware of the excellence of poetry: for it acts in a divine and unapprehended manner, beyond and above consciousness: and it is reserved for future generations to contemplate and measure the mighty cause and effect in all the strength and splendour of their union. Even in modern times, no living poet ever arrived at the fullness of his fame; the jury which sits in judgement upon a poet, belonging as he does to all time, must be composed of his peers: it must be impanelled° by Time from the selectest of the wise of many generations. A Poet is a nightingale who sits in darkness, and sings to cheer its own solitude with sweet sounds; his auditors are as men entranced by the melody of an unseen musician, who feel that they are moved and softened, yet know not whence or why. The poems of Homer and his contemporaries were the delight of infant Greece; they were the elements of that social system which is the column upon which all succeeding civilization has reposed. Homer embodied the ideal perfection of his age in human character; nor can we doubt that those who read his verses were awakened to an ambition of becoming like to Achilles, Hector and Ulysses: the truth and beauty of friendship, patriotism and persevering devotion to an object, were unveiled to the depths in these immortal creations: the sentiments of the auditors must have been refined and enlarged by a sympathy with such great and lovely impersonations; until from admiring they imitated, and from imitation they identified themselves with the objects of their admiration. Nor let it be objected that these characters are remote from moral perfection, and that they can by no means be considered as edifying patterns for general imitation. Every epoch under names more or less specious has deified its peculiar errors; Revenge is the naked Idol of the worship of a semi-barbarous age; and self-deceit is the veiled Image of unknown evil before which luxury and satiety lie prostrate. But a poet considers the vices of his contemporaries as the temporary dress in which his creations must be arrayed, and which cover without concealing the eternal proportions of their beauty. An epic or dramatic personage is understood to wear them around his soul, as he may the ancient armour or the modern uniform around his body; whilst it is easy to conceive a dress more graceful than either. The beauty of the internal nature cannot be so far concealed by its accidental vesture, but that the spirit of its form shall communicate itself to the very disguise; and indicate the shape it hides from the manner in which it is worn. A majestic form and graceful motions will express themselves through the most barbarous and tasteless costume. Few poets of the highest class have chosen to exhibit the beauty of their conceptions in its naked truth and splendour; and it is doubtful whether the alloy of costume, habit &c. be not necessary to temper this planetary music° for mortal ears.

The whole objection however of the immorality of poetry° rests upon a misconception of the manner in which poetry acts to produce the moral improvement of man. Ethical science arranges the elements which poetry has created, and propounds schemes and proposes examples of civil and domestic life: nor is it for want of admirable doctrines that men hate, and despise, and censure, and deceive, and subjugate one another. But poetry acts in another and a diviner manner. It awakens and enlarges the mind itself by rendering it the receptacle of a thousand unapprehended combinations of thought. Poetry lifts the veil from the hidden beauty of the world; and makes familiar objects be as if they were not familiar; it reproduces all that it represents, and the impersonations clothed in its Elysian light stand thenceforward in the minds of those who have once contemplated them, as memorials of that gentle and exalted content which extends itself over all thoughts and actions with which it co-exists. The great secret of morals is Love; or a going out of our own nature, and an identification of ourselves with the beautiful which exists in thought, action or person, not our own. A man to be greatly good, must imagine intensely and comprehensively; he must put himself in the place of another and of many others; the pains and pleasures of his species must become his own. The great instrument of moral good is the imagination: and poetry administers to the effect by acting upon the cause. Poetry enlarges the circumference of the imagination by replenishing it with thoughts of ever new delight, which have the power of attracting and assimilating to their own nature all other thoughts, and which form new intervals and interstices whose void forever craves fresh food. Poetry strengthens the faculty which is the organ of the moral nature of man in the same manner as exercise strengthens a limb. A Poet, therefore, would do ill to embody his own conceptions of right and wrong,° which are usually those of his place and time, in his poetical creations, which participate in neither. By this assumption of the inferior office of interpreting the effect, in which perhaps after all he might acquit himself but imperfectly, he would resign a glory in a participation in the cause. There was little danger that Homer or any of the eternal poets, should have so far misunderstood themselves as to have abdicated this throne of their widest dominion. Those in whom the poetical faculty, though great, is less intense as Euripides, Lucan, Tasso, Spenser, have frequently affected a moral aim; and the effect of their poetry is diminished in exact proportion to the degree in which they compel us to advert to this purpose.

Homer and the cyclic poets were followed at a certain interval by the dramatic and lyrical Poets of Athens, who flourished contemporaneously with all that is most perfect in the kindred expressions of the poetical faculty; architecture, painting, music, the dance, sculpture, philosophy, and, we may add, the forms of civil life. For although the scheme of Athenian society was deformed by many imperfections° which the poetry existing in Chivalry and Christianity have erased from the habits and institutions of modern Europe; yet never at any other period has so much energy, beauty and virtue been developed; never was blind strength and stubborn form so disciplined and rendered subject to the will of man, or that will less repugnant to the dictates of the beautiful and the true, as during the century which preceded the death of Socrates. Of no other epoch in the history of our species have we records and fragments stamped so visibly with the image of the divinity in man. But it is Poetry alone, in form, in action or in language, which has rendered this epoch memorable above all others, and the storehouse of examples to everlasting time. For written poetry existed at that epoch simultaneously with the other arts, and it is an idle enquiry to demand which gave and which received the light, which all as from a common focus have scattered over the darkest periods of succeeding time. We know no more of cause and effect than a constant conjunction of events:° Poetry is ever found to co-exist with whatever other arts contribute to the happiness and perfection of man. I appeal to what has already been established to distinguish between the cause and the effect.

It was at the period here adverted to, that the Drama had its birth; and however a succeeding writer may have equalled or surpassed those few great specimens of the Athenian drama which have been pre-served to us, it is indisputable that the art itself never was understood or practised according to the true philosophy of it, as at Athens. For the Athenians employed language, action, music, painting, the dance, and religious institution to produce a common effect in the representa-tion of the highest idealisms° of passion and of power; each division in the art was made perfect in its kind by artists of the most consummate skill, and was disciplined into a beautiful proportion and unity one towards the other. On the modern stage a few only of the elements capable of expressing the image of the poet's conception are employed at once. We have tragedy without music and dancing; and music and dancing without the highest impersonation of which they are the fit accompaniment, and both without religion and solemnity. Religious institution has indeed been usually banished from the stage. Our system of divesting the actor's face of a mask, on which the many expressions appropriated to his dramatic character might be moulded into one permanent and unchanging expression, is favourable only to a partial and inharmonious effect; it is fit for nothing but a monologue where all the attention may be directed to some great master of ideal mimicry. The modern practice of blending comedy with tragedy, though liable to great abuse in point of practice, is undoubtedly an extension of the dramatic circle; but the comedy should be as in *King Lear*, universal, ideal° and sublime. It is perhaps the intervention of this principle which determines the balance in favour of *King Lear* against the *Oedipus Tyrannus* or the *Agamemnon*, or, if you will, the trilogies° with which they are connected; unless the intense power of the choral poetry, especially that of the latter, should be considered as restoring the equilibrium. *King Lear*, if it can sustain this comparison, may be judged to be the most perfect specimen of the dramatic art existing in the world; in spite of the narrow conditions to which the poet was subjected by the ignorance of the philosophy of the Drama which has prevailed in modern Europe. Calderon in his religious Autos° has attempted to fulfil some of the high conditions of dramatic representation neglected by Shakespeare; such as the establishing a relation between the drama and religion, and the accommodating them to music and dancing, but he omits the observation of conditions still more important, and more is lost than gained by a substitution of the rigidly defined and ever-repeated idealisms of a distorted super-stition for the living impersonations of the truth of human passion.

But we digress.—The Author of the *Four Ages of Poetry* has pru-dently omitted to dispute on the effect of the Drama upon life and manners. For, if I know the knight by the device of his shield, I have only to inscribe *Philoctetes*,° or *Agamemnon*, or *Othello* upon mine to put to flight the giant sophisms° which have enchanted him, as the mirror of intolerable light, though on the arm of one of the weakest of the Paladins,° could blind and scatter whole armies of necromancers° and pagans. The connection of scenic exhibitions with the improve-ment or corruption of the manners of men has been universally recognized: in other words, the presence or absence of poetry in its most perfect and universal form has been found to be connected with good and evil in conduct or habit. The corruption which has been imputed to the drama as an effect begins, when the poetry employed in its constitution ends: I appeal to the history of manners whether the periods of the growth of the one and the decline of the other have not corresponded with an exactness equal to any other example of moral cause and effect.

The drama at Athens, or wheresoever else it may have approached to its perfection, ever co-existed with the moral and intellectual greatness of the age. The tragedies of the Athenian poets are as mirrors in which the spectator beholds himself, under a thin disguise of circumstance, stripped of all, but that ideal perfection and energy which every one feels to be the internal type of all that he loves, admires and would become. The imagination is enlarged by a sym-pathy with pains and passions so mighty that they distend in their conception the capacity of that by which they are conceived; the good affections are strengthened by pity, indignation, terror and sorrow; and an exalted calm is prolonged from the satiety of this high exercise

of them into the tumult of familiar life; even crime is disarmed of half
its horror and all its contagion by being represented as the fatal
consequence of the unfathomable agencies of nature; error is thus
divested of its wilfulness; men can no longer cherish it as the creation
of their choice. In a drama of the highest order there is little food for
censure or hatred: it teaches rather self-knowledge and self-respect.
Neither the eye or the mind can see itself unless reflected upon that
which it resembles. The drama, so long as it continues to express
poetry, is as a prismatic and many-sided mirror,° which collects the
brightest rays of human nature and divides and reproduces them from
the simplicity of these elementary forms; and touches them with
majesty and beauty, and multiplies all that it reflects, and endows it
with the power of propagating its like wherever it may fall.

But in periods of the decay of social life, the drama sympathizes
with that decay. Tragedy becomes a cold imitation of the form of
the great masterpieces of antiquity, divested of all harmonious
accompaniment of the kindred arts; and often the very form mis-
understood: or a weak attempt to teach certain doctrines, which the
writer considers as moral truths; and which are usually no more than
specious flatteries of some gross vice or weakness with which the
author in common with his auditors are infected. Hence what has
been called the classical and the domestic drama. Addison's *Cato*°
is a specimen of the one, and would it were not superfluous to cite
examples of the other! To such purposes Poetry cannot be made sub-
servient. Poetry is a sword of lightning ever unsheathed,° which con-
sumes the scabbard that would contain it. And thus we observe that
all dramatic writings of this nature are unimaginative in a singular
degree; they affect sentiment and passion which divested of imagin-
ation are other names for caprice and appetite. The period in our
own history of the grossest degradation of the drama is the reign of
Charles II when all forms in which poetry had been accustomed to
be expressed became hymns to the triumph of kingly power over
liberty and virtue. Milton stood alone illuminating an age unworthy
of him. At such periods the calculating principle pervades all the
forms of dramatic exhibition, and poetry ceases to be expressed upon
them. Comedy loses its ideal universality: wit succeeds to humour;
we laugh from self-complacency and triumph instead of pleasure;
malignity, sarcasm and contempt succeed to sympathetic merriment;
we hardly laugh, but we smile. Obscenity, which is ever blasphemy
against the divine beauty in life, becomes, from the very veil which it
assumes, more active if less disgusting: it is a monster for which the

corruption of society forever brings forth new food, which it devours in secret.

The Drama being that form under which a greater number of modes of expression of poetry are susceptible of being combined than any other, the connection of beauty and social good is more observable in the drama than in whatever other form: and it is indisputable that the highest perfection of human society has ever corresponded with the highest dramatic excellence: and that the corruption or the extinction of the drama in a nation where it has once flourished is a mark of a corruption of manners, and an extinction of the energies which sustain the soul of social life. But, as Machiavelli° says of political institutions, that life may be preserved and renewed, if men should arise capable of bringing back the drama to its principles. And this is true with respect to poetry in its most extended sense: all language, institution and form require not only to be produced but to be sustained: the office and character of a poet participates in the divine nature as regards providence no less than as regards creation.

Civil war, the spoils of Asia, and the fatal predominance first of the Macedonian, and then of the Roman arms were so many symbols of the extinction or suspension of the creative faculty in Greece. The bucolic writers° who found patronage under the lettered tyrants of Sicily and Egypt were the latest representatives of its most glorious reign. Their poetry is intensely melodious; like the odour of the tuberose it overcomes and sickens the spirit with excess of sweetness; whilst the poetry of the preceding age was as a meadow-gale of June which mingles the fragrance of all the flowers of the field and adds a quickening and harmonizing spirit of its own which endows the sense with a power of sustaining its extreme delight. The bucolic and erotic delicacy in written poetry is correlative with that softness in statuary, music and the kindred arts, and even in manners and institutions which distinguished the epoch to which we now refer. Nor is it the poetical faculty itself, or any misapplication of it, to which this want of harmony is to be imputed. An equal sensibility to the influence of the senses and the affections is to be found in the writings of Homer and Sophocles: the former especially has clothed sensual and pathetic images with irresistible attractions. Their superiority over these succeeding writers consists in the presence of those thoughts which belong to the inner faculties of our nature, not in the absence of those which are connected with the external: their incomparable perfection consists in a harmony of the union of all. It is not what the erotic poets have, but what they have not, in which their imperfection consists. It is not inasmuch as they were Poets, but inasmuch as they were not Poets, that they can be considered with any plausibility as connected with the corruption of their age. Had that corruption availed so as to extinguish in them the sensibility to pleasure, passion and natural scenery, which is imputed to them as an imperfection, the last triumph of evil would have been achieved. For the end of social corruption is to destroy all sensibility to pleasure; and therefore it is corruption. It begins at the imagination and the intellect as at the core, and distributes itself thence as a paralysing venom, through the affections into the very appetites, until all become a torpid° mass in which sense hardly survives. At the approach of such a period, Poetry ever addresses itself to those faculties which are the last to be destroyed, and its voice is heard, like the footsteps of Astraea,° departing from the world. Poetry ever communicates all the pleasure which men are capable of receiving: it is ever still the light of life; the source of whatever beautiful, or generous, or true can have place in an evil time. It will readily be confessed that those among the luxurious° citizens of Syracuse and Alexandria who were delighted with the poems of Theocritus were less cold, cruel and sensual than the remnant of their tribe. But corruption must utterly have destroyed the fabric of human society before Poetry can ever cease. The sacred links of that chain have never been entirely disjoined, which descending through the minds of many men is attached to those great minds whence as from a magnet the invisible effluence is sent forth which at once connects, animates and sustains the life of all.° It is the faculty which contains within itself the seeds at once of its own and of social renovation. And let us not circumscribe the effects of the bucolic and erotic poetry within the limits of the sensibility of those to whom it was addressed. They may have perceived the beauty of these immortal compositions, simply as fragments and isolated portions: those who are more finely organized, or born in a happier age may recognize them as episodes of that great poem, which all poets like the co-operating thoughts of one great mind have built up since the beginning of the world.

The same revolutions within a narrower sphere had place in ancient Rome: but the actions and forms of its social life never seem to have been perfectly saturated with the poetical element. The Romans appear to have considered the Greeks as the selectest treasuries of the selectest forms of manners and of nature and to have abstained from creating in measured language, sculpture, music or architecture anything which might bear a particular relation to their own condition whilst it should bear a general one to the universal constitution of the world. But we judge from partial evidence, and we judge perhaps partially. Ennius,° Varro,° Pacuvius° and Accius,° all great poets, have been lost. Lucretius is in the highest, and Virgil in a very high sense, a creator. The chosen delicacy of the expressions of the latter are as a mist of light which conceal from us the intense and exceeding truth of his conceptions of nature. Livy is instinct with poetry. Yet Horace, Catullus, Ovid, and generally the other great writers of the Virgilian age, saw man and nature in the mirror of Greece. The institutions also and the religion of Rome were less poetical than those of Greece, as the shadow is less vivid than the substance. Hence Poetry in Rome seemed to follow rather than accompany the perfection of political and domestic society. The true Poetry of Rome lived in its institutions; for whatever of beautiful, true and majestic they contained could have sprung only from the faculty which creates the order in which they consist. The life of Camillus;° the death of Regulus;° the expectation of the senators in their godlike state of the victorious Gauls;° the refusal of the republic to make peace with Hannibal after the battle of Cannae,° were not the consequences of a refined calculation of the probable personal advantage to result from such a rhythm and order in the shows of life, to those who were at once the poets and the actors of these immortal dramas. The imagination beholding the beauty of this order, created it out of itself according to its own idea: the consequence was empire, and the reward everliving fame. These things are not the less poetry *quia carent vate sacro*.° They are the episodes of that cyclic poem written by Time upon the memories of men. The Past, like an inspired rhapsodist,° fills the theatre of everlasting generations with their harmony.

At length the ancient system of religion and manners had fulfilled the circle of its revolutions. And the world would have fallen into utter anarchy and darkness, but that there were found poets among the authors of the Christian and Chivalric systems of manners and religion, who created forms of opinion and action never before conceived; which, copied into the imaginations of men, became as generals to the bewildered armies of their thoughts. It is foreign to the present purpose to touch upon the evil produced by these systems: except that we protest, on the ground of the principles already established, that no portion of it can be attributed to the poetry they contain.

It is probable that the poetry of Moses, Job, David, Solomon and Isaiah° had produced a great effect upon the mind of Jesus and his disciples. The scattered fragments preserved to us by the biographers

of this extraordinary person are all instinct with the most vivid poetry.
But his doctrines seem to have been quickly distorted. At a certain
period after the prevalence of a system of opinions founded upon
those promulgated by him, the three forms into which Plato had dis-
tributed the faculties of mind° underwent a sort of apotheosis, and
became the object of the worship of the civilized world. Here it is to be
confessed that 'Light seems to thicken', and

> the crow makes wing to the rooky wood,
> Good things of day begin to droop and drowze
> And night's black agents to their preys do rouse.°

But mark how beautiful an order has sprung from the dust and blood
of this fierce chaos! how the World, as from a resurrection, balancing
itself on the golden wings of knowledge and of hope, has reassumed its
yet unwearied flight into the Heaven of time! Listen to the music,
unheard by outward ears, which is as a ceaseless and invisible wind
nourishing its everlasting course with strength and swiftness.

The poetry in the doctrines of Jesus Christ, and the mythology and
institutions of the Celtic conquerors° of the Roman Empire, outlived
the darkness and the convulsions connected with their growth and
victory, and blended themselves into a new fabric of manners and
opinion. It is an error to impute the ignorance of the dark ages to the
Christian doctrines or to the predominance of the Celtic nations.
Whatever of evil their agencies may have contained sprung from the
extinction of the poetical principle, connected with the progress
of despotism and superstition. Men, from causes too intricate to be
here discussed, had become insensible and selfish: their own will had
become feeble, and yet they were its slaves, and thence the slaves of the
will of others: lust, fear, avarice, cruelty and fraud characterized a race
amongst whom no one was to be found capable of *creating* in form,
language or institution. The moral anomalies of such a state of society
are not justly to be charged upon any class of events immediately con-
nected with them, and those events are most entitled to our appro-
bation which could dissolve it most expeditiously. It is unfortunate for
those who cannot distinguish words from thoughts that many of these
anomalies have been incorporated into our popular religion.

It was not until the eleventh century that the effects of the poetry of
the Christian and the Chivalric systems began to manifest themselves.
The principle of equality had been discovered and applied by Plato in
his *Republic*, as the theoretical rule of the mode in which the materials
of pleasure and of power produced by the common skill and labour of

human beings ought to be distributed among them.° The limitations of this rule were asserted by him to be determined only by the sensibility of each, or the utility to result to all. Plato, following the doctrines of Timaeus and Pythagoras, taught also a moral and intellectual system of doctrine comprehending at once the past, the present and the future condition of man. Jesus Christ divulged the sacred and eternal truths contained in these views to mankind, and Christianity, in its abstract purity, became the exoteric° expression of the esoteric° doctrines of the poetry and wisdom of antiquity. The incorporation of the Celtic nations with the exhausted population of the South, impressed upon it the figure of the poetry existing in their mythology and institutions. The result was a sum of the action and reaction of all the causes included in it; for it may be assumed as a maxim that no nation or religion can supersede any other without incorporating into itself a portion of that which it supersedes. The abolition of personal and domestic slavery, and the emancipation of women from a great part of the degrading restraints of antiquity were among the consequences of these events.

The abolition of personal slavery is the basis of the highest political hope that it can enter into the mind of man to conceive. The freedom of women produced the poetry of sexual love. Love became a religion, the idols of whose worship were ever present. It was as if the statues of Apollo and the muses had been endowed with life and motion and had walked forth among their worshippers; so that earth became peopled by the inhabitants of a diviner world. The familiar appearances and proceedings of life became wonderful and heavenly; and a paradise was created as out of the wrecks of Eden. And as this creation itself is poetry, so its creators were poets; and language was the instrument of their art; 'Galeotto fu il libro, e chi lo scrisse'.° The Provençal Trouveurs,° or inventors, preceded Petrarch,° whose verses are as spells which unseal the inmost enchanted fountains of the delight which is in the grief of Love. It is impossible to feel them without becoming a portion of that beauty which we contemplate: it were superfluous to explain how the gentleness and the elevation of mind connected with these sacred emotions can render men more amiable, and generous, and wise, and lift them out of the dull vapours of the little world of self. Dante understood the secret things of love even more than Petrarch. His *Vita Nuova* is an inexhaustible fountain of purity of sentiment and language: it is the idealized history of that period, and those intervals of his life which were dedicated to love. His apotheosis of Beatrice in Paradise and the gradations of his own love and her loveliness, by which as by steps he feigns himself to have ascended to the throne of the Supreme Cause, is the most glorious imagination of modern poetry. The acutest critics have justly reversed the judgement of the vulgar and the order of the great acts of the 'Divine Drama'° in the measure of the admiration which they accord to the Hell, Purgatory and Paradise. The latter is a perpetual hymn to everlasting love. Love, which found a worthy poet in Plato° alone of all the ancients, has been celebrated by a chorus of the greatest writers of the renovated world; and the music has penetrated the caverns of society, and its echoes still drown the dissonance of arms, and superstition. At successive intervals Ariosto, Tasso, Shakespeare, Spenser, Calderon, Rousseau and the great writers of our own age have celebrated the dominion of love; planting as it were trophies in the human mind of that sublimest victory over sensuality and force. The true relation borne to each other by the sexes into which human kind is distributed has become less misunderstood; and if the error which confounded diversity with inequality of the powers of the two sexes has been partially recognized in the opinions and institutions of modern Europe, we owe this great benefit to the worship of which Chivalry was the law, and poets the prophets.

The poetry of Dante may be considered as the bridge thrown over the stream of time which unites the modern and the ancient world. The distorted notions of invisible things which Dante and his rival Milton have idealized are merely the mask and the mantle in which these great poets walk through eternity enveloped and disguised. It is a difficult question to determine how far they were conscious of the distinction which must have subsisted in their minds between their own creeds and that of the people. Dante at least appears to wish to mark the full extent of it by placing Riphaeus whom Virgil calls *justissimus unus* in Paradise,° and observing a most heretical caprice in his distribution of rewards and punishments. And Milton's poem contains within itself a philosophical refutation of that system of which, by a strange but natural antithesis, it has been a chief popular support. Nothing can exceed the energy and magnificence of the character of Satan as expressed in *Paradise Lost*. It is a mistake to suppose that he could ever have been intended for the popular personification of evil. Implacable hate, patient cunning, and a sleepless refinement of device to inflict the extremest anguish on an enemy: these things are evil; and although venial in a slave are not to be forgiven in a tyrant; although redeemed by much that ennobles his defeat in one subdued, are marked by all that dishonours his conquest in the victor. Milton's

Devil as a moral being is as far superior to his God as one who per-
severes in some purpose which he has conceived to be excellent in
spite of adversity and torture, is to one who in the cold security of
undoubted triumph inflicts the most horrible revenge upon his
enemy—not from any mistaken notion of inducing him to repent of a
perseverance in enmity, but with the alleged design of exasperating
him to deserve new torments.° Milton has so far violated the popular
creed (if this shall be judged to be a violation) as to have alleged no
superiority of moral virtue to his God over his Devil. And this bold
neglect of a direct moral purpose is the most decisive proof of the
supremacy of Milton's genius. He mingled as it were the elements of
human nature, as colours upon a single pallet, and arranged them into
the composition of his great picture according to the laws of epic
truth: that is, according to the laws of that principle by which a series
of actions of the external universe, and of intelligent and ethical beings
is calculated to excite the sympathy of succeeding generations of
mankind. The *Divina Commedia* and *Paradise Lost* have conferred
upon modern mythology° a systematic form; and when change and
time shall have added one more superstition to the mass of those
which have arisen and decayed upon the earth, commentators will be
learnedly employed in elucidating the religion of ancestral Europe,
only not utterly forgotten because it will have been stamped with the
eternity of genius.°

Homer was the first, and Dante the second epic poet: that is,
the second poet the series of whose creations bore a defined and intel-
ligible relation to the knowledge, and sentiment, and religion, and
political condition of the age in which he lived, and of the ages which
followed it: developing itself in correspondence with their develop-
ment. For Lucretius had limed the wings of his swift spirit in the
dregs of the sensible world:° and Virgil, with a modesty that ill became
his genius, had affected the fame of an imitator even whilst he created
anew all that he copied;° and none among the flock of mock-birds,°
though their notes were sweet, Apollonius Rhodius,° Quintus Calaber
Smyrnaeus,° Nonnus,° Lucan,° Statius° or Claudian° have sought
even to fulfil a single condition of epic truth. Milton was the third epic
poet: for if the title of epic in its highest sense be refused to the *Aeneid*
still less can it be conceded to the *Orlando Furioso*, the *Gerusalemme
Liberata*, the *Lusiad* or the *Fairy Queen*.°

Dante and Milton were both deeply penetrated with the ancient
religion of the civilized world; and its spirit exists in their poetry,
probably in the same proportion as its forms survived in the

unreformed worship of modern Europe. The one preceded and the other followed the Reformation at almost equal intervals. Dante was the first religious reformer, and Luther° surpassed him rather in the rudeness and acrimony than in the boldness of his censures of papal usurpation. Dante was the first awakener of entranced Europe; he created a language in itself music and persuasion out of a chaos of inharmonious barbarisms.° He was the congregator of those great spirits who presided over the resurrection of learning; the Lucifer° of that starry flock which in the thirteenth century shone forth from republican Italy, as from a heaven, into the darkness of the benighted world. His very words are instinct with spirit;° each is as a spark, a burning atom of inextinguishable thought; and many yet lie covered in the ashes of their birth, and pregnant with a lightning which has yet found no conductor. All high poetry is infinite; it is as the first acorn which contained all oaks potentially. Veil after veil may be undrawn and the inmost naked beauty of the meaning never exposed. A great Poem is a fountain forever overflowing with the waters of wisdom and delight; and after one person and one age has exhausted all its divine effluence° which their peculiar relations enable them to share, another and yet another succeeds, and new relations are ever developed, the source of an unforeseen and an unconceived delight.

The age immediately succeeding to that of Dante, Petrarch and Boccaccio was characterized by a revival of painting, sculpture, music and architecture. Chaucer caught the sacred inspiration, and the superstructure of English literature is based upon the materials of Italian invention.°

But let us not be betrayed from a defence into a critical history of poetry and its influence on society. Be it enough to have pointed out the effects of poets in the large and true sense of the word upon their own and all succeeding times, and to revert to the partial instances cited as illustrations of an opinion the reverse of that attempted to be established in the *Four Ages of Poetry*.

But Poets have been challenged to resign the civic crown to reasoners and mechanists° on another plea. It is admitted that the exercise of the imagination is more delightful, but it is alleged that that of reason is more useful. Let us examine as the ground of this distinction what is meant by Utility. Pleasure or good in a general sense, is that which the consciousness of a sensitive and intelligent being seeks, and in which when found it acquiesces. There are two kinds of pleasure, one durable, universal and permanent; the other transitory and particular. Utility may either express the means of producing the former, or the latter. In the former sense, whatever strengthens and purifies the affections, enlarges the imagination, and adds a spirit to sense, is useful. But the meaning in which the author of the *Four Ages of Poetry* seems to have employed the word utility is the narrower one of banishing the importunity of the wants of our animal nature, the surrounding men with security of life, the dispersing the grosser delusions of superstition, and the conciliating such a degree of mutual forbearance among men as may consist with the motives of personal advantage.

Undoubtedly the promoters of utility in this limited sense, have their appointed office in society. They follow the footsteps of poets, and copy the sketches of their creations into the book of common life. They make space and give time. Their exertions are of the highest value so long as they confine their administration of the concerns of the inferior powers of our own nature within the limits of what is due to the superior ones. But whilst the sceptic destroys gross superstititions, let him spare to deface, as some of the French writers° have defaced, the eternal truths charactered upon the imaginations of men. Whilst the mechanist° abridges, and the political economist combines, labour,° let them beware that their speculations, for want of a correspondence with those first principles which belong to the imagination, do not tend, as they have in modern England, to exasperate at once the extremes of luxury and want. They have exemplified the saying, 'To him that hath, more shall be given; and from him that hath not the little that he hath shall be taken away.'° The rich have become richer, and the poor have become poorer; and the vessel of the state is driven between the Scylla and Charybdis° of anarchy and despotism.° Such are the effects which must ever flow from an unmitigated exercise of the calculating faculty.

It is difficult to define pleasure in its highest sense; the definition involving a number of apparent paradoxes. For, from an inexplicable defect of harmony in the constitution of human nature, the pain of the inferior is frequently connected with the pleasures of the superior portions of our being. Sorrow, terror, anguish, despair itself are often the chosen expressions of an approximation to the highest good. Our sympathy in tragic fiction depends on this principle: tragedy delights by affording a shadow of the pleasure which exists in pain. This is the source also of the melancholy which is inseparable from the sweetest melody. The pleasure that is in sorrow is sweeter than the pleasure of pleasure itself. And hence the saying, 'It is better to go to the house of mourning, than to the house of mirth.'° Not that this highest species of pleasure is necessarily linked with pain. The delight of love and friendship, the ecstasy of the admiration of nature, the joy of the perception, and still more of the creation of poetry is often wholly unalloyed.

The production and assurance of pleasure in this highest sense is true utility. Those who produce and preserve this pleasure are poets or poetical philosophers. The exertions of Locke, Hume, Gibbon, Voltaire, Rousseau° and their disciples in favour of oppressed and deluded humanity are entitled to the gratitude of mankind. Yet it is easy to calculate the degree of moral and intellectual improvement which the world would have exhibited, had they never lived. A little more nonsense would have been talked for a century or two; and perhaps a few more men, women and children burnt as heretics. We might not at this moment have been congratulating each other on the abolition of the Inquisition in Spain.° But it exceeds all imagination to conceive what would have been the moral condition of the world, if neither Dante, Petrarch, Boccaccio, Chaucer, Shakespeare, Calderon, Lord Bacon, nor Milton had ever existed: if Raphael and Michelangelo had never been born; if the Hebrew poetry had never been translated; if a revival of a study of Greek Literature had never taken place; if no monuments of ancient sculpture had been handed down to us; and if the poetry of the religion of the ancient world had been extinguished together with its belief. The human mind could never, except by the intervention of these excitements, have been awakened to the invention of those grosser sciences, and that application of analytical reasoning to the aberrations of society, which it is now attempted to exalt over the direct expression of the inventive and creative faculty itself.

We have more moral, political and historical wisdom than we know how to reduce into practice: we have more scientific and economical knowledge than can be accommodated to the just distribution of the produce which it multiplies. The poetry, in these systems of thought, is concealed by the accumulation of facts and calculating processes. There is no want of knowledge respecting what is wisest and best in morals, government and political economy, or at least what is wiser and better than what men now practise and endure. But we 'let *I dare not* wait upon *I would*, like the poor cat in the adage'.° We want the creative faculty to imagine that which we know; we want the generous impulse to act that which we imagine; we want the poetry of life; our calculations have outrun conception; we have eaten more than we can digest. The cultivation of those sciences which have enlarged the limits of the empire of man over the external world, has, for want of the poetical faculty, proportionally circumscribed those of the internal world, and man, having enslaved the elements, remains himself a slave. To what but a cultivation of the mechanical arts in a degree disproportioned to the presence of the creative faculty which is the basis of all knowledge is to be attributed the abuse of all invention for abridging and combining labour, to the exasperation of the inequality of mankind? From what other cause has it arisen that the discoveries which should have lightened, have added a weight to, the curse imposed on Adam?° Poetry, and the principle of Self, of which money is the visible incarnation, are the God and the Mammon° of the world.

The functions of the poetical faculty are twofold: by one it creates new materials of knowledge, and power, and pleasure; by the other it engenders in the mind a desire to reproduce and arrange them according to a certain rhythm and order, which may be called the beautiful and the good. The cultivation of poetry is never more to be desired than at periods when from an excess of the selfish and calculating principle, the accumulation of the materials of external life exceed the quantity of the power of assimilating them to the internal laws of human nature. The body has then become too unwieldy for that which animates it.

Poetry is indeed something divine. It is at once the centre and circumference of knowledge;° it is that which comprehends all science, and that to which all science must be referred. It is at the same time the root and the blossom of all other systems of thought: it is that from which all spring, and that which adorns all; and that which if blighted denies the fruit and the seed, and withholds from the barren world the nourishment and the succession of the scions of the tree of life. It is the perfect and consummate surface and bloom of things; it is as the odour and the colour of the rose to the texture of the elements which compose it, as the form and splendour of unfaded beauty to the secrets of anatomy and corruption. What were Virtue, Love, Patriotism, Friendship—what were the scenery of this beautiful universe which we inhabit, what were our consolations on this side of the grave, and what were our aspirations beyond it, if Poetry did not ascend to bring light and fire from those eternal regions where the owl-winged faculty of calculation dare not ever soar? Poetry is not like reasoning, a power to be exerted according to the determination of the will. A man cannot say, 'I will compose poetry.' The greatest poet even cannot say it: for the mind in creation is as a fading coal which some invisible influence, like an inconstant wind, awakens to transitory brightness: this power arises from within like the colour of a flower which fades and changes as it is developed, and the conscious portions of our nature are unprophetic either of its approach or its departure. Could this influence be durable in its original purity and force, it is impossible to predict the greatness of the results: but when composition begins, inspiration is already on the decline, and the most glorious poetry that has ever been communicated to the world is probably a feeble shadow of the original conceptions of the poet. I appeal to the greatest Poets of the present day, whether it be not an error to assert that the finest passages of poetry are produced by labour and study. The toil and the delay recommended by critics can be justly interpreted to mean no more than a careful observation of the inspired moments, and an artificial connection of the spaces between their suggestions by the intertexture° of conventional expressions; a necessity only imposed by a limitedness of the poetical faculty itself. For Milton conceived the *Paradise Lost* as a whole before he executed it in portions. We have his own authority also for the Muse having 'dictated' to him 'the unpremeditated song'.° And let this be an answer to those who would allege the fifty-six various readings of the first line of the *Orlando Furioso*. Compositions so produced are to poetry what mosaic is to painting. This instinct and intuition of the poetical faculty is still more observable in the plastic and pictorial arts: a great statue or picture grows under the power of the artist as a child in the mother's womb, and the very mind which directs the hands in formation is incapable of accounting to itself for the origin, the gradations, or the media of the process.

Poetry is the record of the happiest and best moments of the happiest and best minds. We are aware of evanescent visitations of thought and feeling sometimes associated with place or person, sometimes regarding our own mind alone, and always arising unforeseen and departing unbidden, but elevating and delightful beyond all expression: so that even in the desire and the regret they leave there cannot but be pleasure, participating as it does in the nature of its object. It is as it were the interpenetration of a diviner nature through our own,° but its footsteps are like those of a wind over the sea, which the coming calm erases, and whose traces remain only as on the wrinkled sand which paves it. These and corresponding conditions of being are experienced principally by those of the most delicate sensibility and the most enlarged imagination. And the state of mind produced by them is at war with every base desire. The enthusiasm of virtue, love, patriotism and friendship is essentially linked with such emotions; and whilst they last self appears as what it is, an atom to an Universe. Poets are not only subject to these experiences as spirits of the most refined organization, but they can colour all that they combine with the evanescent hues of this ethereal world; a word, a trait in the representation of a scene or a passion will touch the enchanted chord, and reanimate in those who have ever experienced these emotions the sleeping, the cold, the buried image of the past. Poetry thus makes immortal all that is best and most beautiful in the world; it arrests the vanishing apparitions which haunt the inter-lunations° of life, and veiling them or in language or in form sends them forth among mankind bearing sweet news of kindred joy to those with whom their sisters abide—abide, because there is no portal of expression from the caverns of the spirit which they inhabit into the universe of things. Poetry redeems from decay the visitations of the divinity in man.

Poetry turns all things to loveliness: it exalts the beauty of that which is most beautiful, and it adds beauty to that which is most deformed: it marries exultation and horror, grief and pleasure, eternity and change; it subdues to union under its light yoke all irreconcilable things. It transmutes all that it touches, and every form moving within the radiance of its presence is changed by wondrous sympathy to an incarnation of the spirit which it breathes: its secret alchemy turns to potable° gold the poisonous waters which flow from death through life; it strips the veil of familiarity from the world, and lays bare the naked and sleeping beauty which is the spirit of its forms.

All things exist as they are perceived; at least in relation to the percipient—'The mind is its own place, and of itself can make a Heaven of Hell, a Hell of Heaven.'° But Poetry defeats the curse which binds us to be subjected to the accident of surrounding impressions. And whether it spreads its own figured curtain or withdraws life's dark veil from before the scene of things, it equally creates for us a being within our being. It makes us the inhabitants of a world to which the familiar world is as a chaos. It reproduces the common Universe of which we are portions and percipients, and it purges from our inward sight the film of familiarity° which obscures from us the wonder of our being. It compels us to feel that which we perceive, and to imagine that which we know. It creates anew the universe after it has been annihilated in our minds by the recurrence of impressions blunted by reiteration. It justifies that bold and true word of Tasso: *Non merita nome di creatore se non Iddio ed il Poeta.*°

A Poet, as he is the author to others of the highest wisdom, pleasure, virtue and glory, so he ought personally to be the happiest, the best, the wisest and the most illustrious of men. As to his glory, let Time be challenged to declare whether the fame of any other institutor of human life be comparable to that of a poet. That he is the wisest, the happiest and the best, inasmuch as he is a poet, is equally incontrovertible: the greatest Poets have been men of the most spotless virtue, of the most consummate prudence, and, if we would look into the interior of their lives, the most fortunate of men: and the exceptions, as they regard those who possessed the poetic faculty in a high yet inferior degree, will be found on consideration to confine rather than destroy the rule. Let us for a moment stoop to the arbitration of popular breath, and usurping and uniting in our own persons the incompatible characters of accuser, witness, judge and executioner, let us decide without trial, testimony or form that certain motives of those who are 'there sitting where we dare not soar'° are reprehensible. Let us assume that Homer was a drunkard, that Virgil was a flatterer, that Horace was a coward, that Tasso was a madman, that Lord Bacon was a peculator, that Raphael was a libertine, that Spenser was a poet laureate.° It is inconsistent with this division of our subject to cite living poets, but Posterity has done ample justice to the great names now referred to. Their errors have been weighed and found to have been dust in the balance; if their sins were as scarlet they are now as white as snow: they have been washed in the blood of the mediator and the redeemer Time. Observe in what a ludicrous chaos the imputations of real and of fictitious crime have been confused in the contemporary calumnies against poetry and poets; consider how little is as it appears, or appears as it is; look to your own motives, and judge not, lest ye be judged.°

Poetry, as has been said, differs in this respect from logic that it is not subject to the control of the active powers of the mind, and that its birth and recurrence has no necessary connection with consciousness or will. It is presumptuous to determine that these are the necessary conditions of all mental causation when mental effects are experienced insusceptible of being referred to them. The frequent recurrence of the poetical power, it is obvious to suppose, may produce in the mind an habit of order and harmony correlative with its own nature and with its effects upon other minds. But in the intervals of inspiration, and they may be frequent without being durable, a Poet becomes a man and is abandoned to the sudden reflux of the influences under which others habitually live. But as he is more delicately organized than other men, and sensible to pain and pleasure both his own and that of others in a degree unknown to them, he will avoid the one and pursue the other with an ardour proportioned to this difference. And he renders himself obnoxious° to calumny, when he neglects to observe the circumstances under which these objects of universal pursuit and flight have disguised themselves in one another's garments. But there is nothing necessarily evil in this error, and thus cruelty, envy, revenge, avarice, and the passions purely evil, have never formed any portion of the popular imputations on the lives of poets.

I have thought it most favourable to the cause of truth to set down these remarks according to the order in which they were suggested to my mind by a consideration of the subject itself, instead of following that of the treatise which excited me to make them public. Thus, although devoid of the formality of a polemical reply, if the view which they contain be just, they will be found to involve a refutation of the *Four Ages of Poetry*, so far at least as regards the first division of the subject. I can readily conjecture what should have moved the gall of the learned and intelligent author of that paper. I confess myself like him unwilling to be stunned by the *Theseids* of the hoarse Codri° of the day: Bavius and Maevius° undoubtedly are, as they ever were, insufferable persons. But it belongs to a philosophical critic to distinguish rather than confound.

The first part of these remarks has related to poetry in its elements and principles; and it has been shown, as well as the narrow limits assigned them would permit, that what is called poetry in a restricted sense has a common source with all other forms of order and of beauty according to which the materials of human life are susceptible of being arranged; and which is Poetry in an universal sense.

The second part will have for its object an application of these principles to the present state of the cultivation of Poetry, and a defence of the attempt to idealize the modern forms of manners and opinion, and compel them into a subordination to the imaginative and creative faculty. For the literature of England, an energetic development of which has ever preceded or accompanied a great and free development of the national will, has arisen as it were from a new birth. In spite of the low-thoughted envy° which would undervalue contemporary merit, our own will be a memorable age in intellectual achievements, and we live among such philosophers and poets as surpass beyond comparison any who have appeared since the last national struggle for civil and religious liberty. The most unfailing herald, companion and follower of the awakening of a great people to work a beneficial change in opinion or institution, is Poetry. At such periods there is an accumulation of the power of communicating and receiving intense and impassioned conceptions respecting man and nature. The persons in whom this power resides, may often as far as regards many portions of their nature, have little apparent correspondence with that spirit of good of which they are the ministers. But even whilst they deny and abjure, they are yet compelled to serve, the Power which is seated on the throne of their own soul. It is impossible to read the compositions of the most celebrated writers of the present day without being startled with the electric life which burns within their words. They measure the circumference and sound the depths of human nature with a comprehensive and all-penetrating spirit, and they are themselves perhaps the most sincerely astonished at its manifestations, for it is less their spirit than the spirit of the age. Poets are the hierophants° of an unapprehended inspiration, the mirrors of the gigantic shadows which futurity casts upon the present, the words which express what they understand not, the trumpets which sing to battle and feel not what they inspire: the influence which is moved not, but moves. Poets are the unacknowledged legislators of the World.°

NOTES

Bonca　　　　Teddi Chichester Bonca, *Shelley's Mirrors of Love: Narcissism, Sacrifice, and Sorority* (Albany, NY, 1999)

Brett-Smith　H. F. B. Brett-Smith (ed.), *Peacock's Four Ages of Poetry, Shelley's Defence of Poetry and Browning's Essay on Shelley* (Oxford, 1921)

BSM　　　　Donald H. Reiman (gen. ed.), *The Bodleian Shelley Manuscripts* (23 vols., New York, 1986–2002): vol. 1: *'Peter Bell the Third'* ... *Bodleian MS. Shelley adds. c. 5* ... *and 'The Triumph of Life'* ... *Bodleian MS. Shelley adds. c. 4, folios 18–58*, ed. Donald H. Reiman (1986); vol. 2: *Bodleian MS. Shelley adds. d. 7*, ed. Irving Massey (1987); vol. 3: *Bodleian MS. Shelley e. 4*, ed. P. M. S. Dawson (1988); vol. 4: *Bodleian MS. Shelley d. 1*, ed. E. B. Murray, 2 parts (1988); vol. 5: *The 'Witch of Atlas' Notebook* ... *Bodleian MS. Shelley adds. e. 6*, ed. Carlene Adamson (1997); vol. 6: *Shelley's Pisan Winter Notebook (1820–1821)* ... *Bodleian MS. Shelley adds. e. 8*, ed. Carlene Adamson (1992); vol. 7: *Shelley's Last Notebook* ... *Bodleian MS. Shelley adds. e. 20* ... *with Bodleian MS. Shelley adds. e. 15* ... *and Bodleian MS. Shelley adds. c. 4, folios 212–246*, ed. Donald H. Reiman and Hélène Dworzan Reiman (1990); vol. 8: *Bodleian MS. Shelley d. 3*, ed. Tatsuo Tokoo (1988); vol. 9: *The 'Prometheus Unbound' Fair Copies* ... *Bodleian MSS. Shelley e. 1, e. 2, and e. 3*, ed. Neil Fraistat (1991); vol. 10: *Mythological Dramas* ... *Bodleian MS. Shelley d. 2* ... *with 'Relation of the Death of the Family of the Cenci'* ... *Bodleian MS. Shelley adds. e. 13*, ed. Betty T. Bennett and Charles E. Robinson (1992); vol. 11: *The Geneva Notebook of* ... *Shelley* ... *Bodleian MSS. Shelley adds. e. 16 and adds. c. 4, folios 63, 65, 71, and 72*, ed. Michael Erkelenz (1992); vol. 12: *Shelley's 'Charles the First' Draft Notebook* ... *Bodleian MS. Shelley adds. e. 17*, ed. Nora Crook (1991); vol. 13: *Drafts for 'Laon and Cythna'* ... *Bodleian MSS. Shelley adds. e. 14 and adds. e. 19*, ed. Tatsuo Tokoo (1992); vol. 14: *Shelley's 'Devils' Notebook* ... *Bodleian MS. Shelley adds. e. 9*, ed. P. M. S. Dawson and Timothy Webb (1993); vol. 15: *The 'Julian and Maddalo' Draft Notebook* ... *Bodleian MS. Shelley adds. e. 11*, ed. Steven E. Jones (1990); vol. 16: *The 'Hellas' Notebook* ... *Bodleian MS. Shelley adds. e. 7*, ed. Donald H. Reiman and Michael C. Neth (1994); vol. 17: *Drafts for 'Laon and Cythna'*

... *Bodleian MS. Shelley adds. e. 10*, ed. Steven E. Jones (1994); vol. 18: *The Homeric Hymns and 'Prometheus' Draft Notebook ... Bodleian MS. Shelley adds. e. 12*, ed. Nancy Moore Goslee (1996); vol. 19: *The Faust Draft Notebook ... Bodleian MS. Shelley adds. e. 18*, ed. Nora Crook and Timothy Webb (1997); vol. 20: *The 'Defence of Poetry' Fair Copies ... Bodleian MSS. Shelley e. 6 and adds. e. 8*, ed. Michael O'Neill (1994); vol. 21: *Miscellaneous Poetry, Prose and Translations ... Bodleian MS. Shelley adds. c. 4, etc*, ed. E. B. Murray (1995); vol. 22, Part One: *Bodleian MS. Shelley adds. d. 6 ...*; vol. 22, Part Two: *Bodleian MS. Shelley adds. c. 5 ...*, ed. Alan M. Weinberg (1997); vol. 23: *Indexes to the Bodleian Shelley Manuscripts ...*, ed. B. C. Barker-Benfield and Tatsuo Tokoo (2001)

Butter P. H. Butter (ed.), *Percy Bysshe Shelley: Alastor and Other Poems; Prometheus Unbound with Other Poems; Adonais* (London, 1970)

Chernaik Judith Chernaik, *The Lyrics of Shelley* (Cleveland and London, 1972)

Clark David Lee Clark (ed.), *Shelley's Prose; Or, The Trumpet of a Prophecy* (corr. edn., Albuquerque, N. Mex., 1966)

Conc. F. S. Ellis (ed.), *A Lexical Concordance of the Poetical Works of Shelley* (London, 1892)

FQ Edmund Spenser, *The Faerie Queene*, ed. A. C. Hamilton (London, 1977)

Hogg Thomas Jefferson Hogg, *The Life of Shelley* (1858), in Humbert Wolfe (intro.), *The Life of Percy Bysshe Shelley* (2 vols., London, 1933)

Inf. *Inferno*

L Frederick L. Jones (ed.), *The Letters of Percy Bysshe Shelley* (2 vols., Oxford, 1964)

Locock C. D. Locock (ed.), *The Poems of Percy Bysshe Shelley* (2 vols., London, 1912)

Longman Kelvin Everest and G. M. Matthews (eds.), *The Poems of Shelley, 1804–1819* (2 vols. to date, Harlow, 1989, 2000)

Mary Jnl. Paula R. Feldman and Diana Scott-Kilvert (eds.), *The Journals of Mary Shelley 1814–1844* (2 vols., Oxford, 1987)

Massey Irving Massey (ed.), *Posthumous Poems of Shelley, Mary Shelley's Fair Copy Book, Bodleian MS. Shelley adds. d. 9* (Montreal, 1969)

Met. *Metamorphoses*; quotations are taken from A. D. Melville's Oxford World's Classics translation (Oxford, 1987)

Murray E. B. Murray (ed.), *The Prose Works of Percy Bysshe Shelley, Volume One* (Oxford, 1993)

MWSL	Betty T. Bennett (ed.), *The Letters of Mary Wollstonecraft Shelley* (3 vols., Baltimore, 1980–8)
MWS (1)	Mary Wollstonecraft Shelley (ed.), *The Poetical Works of Percy Bysshe Shelley* (4 vols., London, 1839)
MWS (2)	Mary Wollstonecraft Shelley (ed.), *The Poetical Works of Percy Bysshe Shelley* (1 vol., London, 1839)
MWS: Prose	Mary Wollstonecraft Shelley (ed.), *Essays, Letters from Abroad, Translations and Fragments by Percy Bysshe Shelley* (2 vols., London, 1840 [1839])
MYR: Shelley	Donald H. Reiman (gen. ed.), *Manuscripts of the Younger Romantics: Shelley* (9 vols., 1985–97). Relevant volumes: vol. 1: *The Esdaile Notebook*, ed. Donald H. Reiman (1985); vol. 2: *The Mask of Anarchy* (1985), ed. Donald H. Reiman; vol. 3: *Hellas: a Lyrical Drama* (1985), ed. Donald H. Reiman; vol. 4: *The Mask of Anarchy Draft Notebook . . . Huntington MS. HM 2177*, ed. Mary A. Quinn (1990); vol. 5: *The Harvard Shelley Poetic Manuscripts*, ed. Donald H. Reiman (1991); vol. 6: *Shelley's 1819–1821 Huntington Notebook . . . Huntington MS. HM 2176*, ed. Mary A. Quinn (1994); vol. 7: *Shelley's 1821–1822 Huntington Notebook . . . MS. HM 2111*, ed. Mary A. Quinn (1996); vol. 8: *Fair-Copy Manuscripts of Shelley's Poems in European and American Libraries*, ed. Donald H. Reiman and Michael O'Neill (1997)
Norton	Donald H. Reiman and Sharon B. Powers (eds.), *Shelley's Poetry and Prose*, Norton Critical Edition (New York, 1977)
Norton²	Donald H. Reiman and Neil Fraistat (eds.), *Shelley's Poetry and Prose*, Norton Critical Edition, 2nd edn. (New York, 2002)
Notopoulos	James A. Notopoulos, *The Platonism of Shelley: A Study of Platonism and the Poetic Mind* (Durham, NC, 1949)
Par.	*Paradiso*
PL	John Milton, *Paradise Lost* (Oxford Authors edition)
PP	Mary Wollstonecraft Shelley (ed.), *Posthumous Poems of Percy Bysshe Shelley* (London, 1824)
Purg.	*Purgatorio*
Rognoni	Francesco Rognoni (ed.), *Shelley: Opere* (Turin, 1995)
Rossetti	William Michael Rossetti (ed.), *The Poetical Works of Percy Bysshe Shelley* (2 vols., London, 1870)
SC	Kenneth Neill Cameron and Donald H. Reiman (eds.), *Shelley and His Circle 1773–1822* (Cambridge, Mass., 10 vols. to date, 1961–)
Sperry	Stuart M. Sperry, *Shelley's Major Verse: The Narrative and Dramatic Poetry* (Cambridge, Mass., 1988)
Webb	Timothy Webb (ed.), *Percy Bysshe Shelley: Poems and Prose*, with a critical selection by George E. Donaldson (London, 1995)

Aeschylus' *Prometheus Bound* and *The Persians* are quoted from Philip Vellacott's Penguin translation (1961); Ovid's *Metamophoses* are quoted from A. D. Melville's World's Classics translation (Oxford, 1987; 1986). Other Latin and Greek texts are cited from the relevant Loeb editions, unless indicated otherwise in the Notes. Dante is quoted from the Temple Classics series, Petrarch from E. H. Wilkins (trans.), *The Triumphs of Petrarch* (Chicago, 1962), Spenser from *FQ* and the Oxford Standard Authors edition, Shakespeare from *The Norton Shakespeare, Based on the Oxford Edition*, ed. Stephen Greenblatt (New York, 1997), and the Bible from the Authorized Version. Where possible, other writers are cited from the relevant Oxford Authors editions. Wordsworth's *Peter Bell* is quoted from the first edition (1819), as edited by John E. Jordan for the Cornell Wordsworth (1985). Shelfmarks for manuscripts in the Bodleian can be found by referring to the relevant volume in *BSM*; shelfmarks for other manuscripts are provided with the relevant facsimile volume.

1   '*A Cat in distress'*. Variously dated *c.*1802–11. First published *Hogg*. Text from an unpunctuated transcript by S.'s sister Elizabeth, photofacsimile in *SC* 4. 813–19. Perhaps S.'s earliest recorded poem, even if composed as late as 1810.

2   *To the Emperors of Russia and Austria Who Eyed the Battle of Austerlitz from the Heights whilst Buonaparte was Active in the Thickest of the Fight.* Composed 1810–13(?). Text from the unpublished *Esdaile Notebook*, transcript in *SC* 4. 937–9 (see *MYR: Shelley* 1). Napoleon defeated the combined Russian and Austrian armies at Austerlitz, in the Czech province of Moravia, on 2 Dec. 1805.

l. 26. *Exalt the high, abase the low. Longman* 1 thinks this line a slip on S.'s part, and prints instead 'Abase the high, exalt the low'.

3   l. 42. *Thou Northern chief.* The Russian Tsar, Alexander I (1777–1825).

l. 43. *Pale Austria.* Francis I, emperor of Austria (1768–1835).

l. 44. *The tyrant.* Napoleon, himself an emperor since 1804.

Zeinab and Kathema. Composed 1810–11(?). Text from *Esdaile Notebook*, transcript in *SC* 4. 1040–47 (see *MYR: Shelley* 1). The name 'Zeinab' derives from Southey's *Thalaba the Destroyer* (1801); 'Kathema' may have been suggested by 'Kehama' in Southey's *The Curse of Kehama* (1810). As *Longman* 1 points out, Sydney Owenson's (Lady Morgan's) anti-imperialist novel *The Missionary: an Indian Tale* (1811) is a probable source for the Cashmire setting, and Charlotte Dacre's (Mrs Byrne's) 'The Poor Negro Sadi' in *Hours of Solitude* (1805), 1. 117–22 is a probable source for the plot. The poem anticipates themes and images from *Laon and Cythna*.

l. 8. *where yonder Sun now speeds.* That is, to England.

6   l. 90. *motes.* Particles or specks of dust.

7   l. 132. *gibbet.* A gallows with an extended wooden arm from which the

bodies of executed criminals were hung in chains. There was a gibbet on Hounslow Heath, in Middlesex, near Shelley's first school, Syon House. 'Gibbeting' was legal in England until 1834.

7 l. 150. *turns to life*. That is, as the food of worms.

8 l. 164. *shriven*. 'Removed', as in Byron's 'To shrive from man his weight of mortal sin' (*Childe Harold* 2. 78, cited in *OED* 8b), which also makes play (though not ironic play, as here) with 'confessed' or 'absolved'.

l. 172. *matin prime*. Morning prayers.

Sonnet: On Launching Some Bottles Filled with Knowledge *into the Bristol Channel*. Composed mid-August 1812 in Lynmouth in Devon, at a time when S. was disseminating revolutionary writings in a variety of ways (see the following poem), to the consternation of the Home Office. Text from *Esdaile Notebook*, transcript in *SC* 4. 977 (see *MYR: Shelley* 1).

Title. 'Knowledge' refers to such propaganda pieces as 'The Devil's Walk: A Ballad' (1811–12), an attack on the Prince Regent in the manner of similar verses by Southey and Coleridge, and the prose broadsheet 'Declaration of Rights' (1812), modelled on comparable declarations adopted by the French National Assembly (1789). A copy of the latter was discovered in a bottle floating near the entrance of Milford Haven in Wales, presumably having crossed the Bristol Channel from Lynmouth.

l. 3. *stern*. Steer through or pass by (see *OED* 4), though *Longman* 1 calls this sense 'an improbable archaism' and, like some earlier editors, prints 'stem' instead.

9 l. 8. *west*. Because Liberty resides in the United States, without need of crown or elevated throne.

Sonnet: To a Balloon, Laden with Knowledge. See headnote to previous sonnet. Text from *Esdaile Notebook*, transcript in *SC* 4. 976–7 (see *MYR: Shelley* 1). No record survives of the sighting of one of these balloons.

Title. For 'Knowledge' see headnote to previous sonnet.

10 *Queen Mab; A Philosophical Poem with Notes*. Composed 1812–13, although conceived in December 1811. Printed in 1813 in an edition of 250 copies, but not published because of fears of prosecution (although S. distributed 70 copies to friends and fellow radicals, carefully removing his own name and address from the title-page). Our text is from the 1813 printing. A pirated edition of the poem was published in 1821 by William Clark, to S.'s disapproval. The poem influenced early trade union and Chartist movements; also, more generally, nineteenth- and twentieth-century radical working-class and British Marxist thinkers and activists. It draws on phrases, images, themes, and ideas from a range of radical sources, in particular Paine, Holbach, and Rousseau. For 'Queen Mab' herself see Mercutio's speech in *Romeo and Juliet* (1. 4. 55–94).

Epigraph 1. 'Crush superstition!' A frequent phrase in the correspondence of Voltaire (1694–1778); 'L'Infâme' might also signify 'fanaticism', 'religion', 'infamy', 'the infamous wretch', 'the demon'.

Epigraph 2. From *De Rerum Natura* ('On the Nature of Things'), a philosophical poem by the Roman Epicurean poet and philosopher Lucretius (*c*.99–*c*.55 BC). The epigraph comes from the beginning of book 4 (1–7; S. omits l. 4): 'A pathless country of the Pierides I traverse, where no other foot has ever trod. I love to approach virgin springs, and there to drink; I love to pluck new flowers [and to seek an illustrious chaplet for my head from fields] whence before this the Muses have crowned the brows of none: first because my teaching is of high matters, and I proceed to set free the mind from the close knots of superstition.'

Epigraph 3. 'Give me a place to stand, and I will move the earth', attributed to the Greek mathematician and scientist Archimedes (287–212 BC). *Longman* 1 cites the use of this saying by Paine and other radical writers of the Romantic period.

To Harriet * * * * *. Harriet Westbrook, S.'s first wife.

11 *Canto 1.* l. 27. *Ianthe.* The name of S.'s and Harriet's first child, born 23 June 1813.

12 l. 52. *that strange lyre.* An Aeolian harp or lyre, placed in a window or on a porch and played on by the wind (hence 'Aeolian', from Aeolus, Greek god of winds). Repeatedly alluded to in poetry of the Romantic period.

l. 53. *genii.* Attendant gods or spirits.

l. 61. *pennons.* Wings.

13 l. 94. *fibrous.* Formed of fibres or fibre-like; thus 'cirrus' (*Longman* 1).

ll. 98–9. *fair star . . . of morn.* The planet Venus, as the morning star.

l. 102. *purpureal.* Purple; though *Longman* 1 conjectures 'bright, beautiful', from Latin *purpureus.*

l. 108. *amaranth.* Mythic unfading flower, from the Greek word for 'unfading' or 'incorruptible'.

14 l. 140. *Wrapt.* We have retained the original spelling because of a possible pun on 'rapt'.

l. 149. *sempiternal.* Eternal, everlasting.

17 l. 235. *a belt.* 'The Milky Way' (*Longman* 1).

ll. 242–3. *The sun's . . . black concave.* See S.'s note (p. 71).

ll. 252–3. *Whilst . . . rolled.* See S.'s note (pp. 71–2).

l. 259. *Hesperus.* The planet Venus, as the evening star.

l. 260. *Some . . . with trains of flame.* Comets, with their fiery tails.

19 *Canto 2.* l. 21. *fane.* Temple.

l. 52. *for.* For all, despite.

20 l. 59. *meed.* Reward.

21 l. 110. *Palmyra's ruined palaces.* The city of Palmyra, in present-day Syria, grew powerful enough, under the princess Zenobia (*c.* AD 266), to challenge Rome, its protector. This challenge failed and Palmyra was totally destroyed in AD 273 by the Roman emperor Aurelian, although its impressive ruins are still visible today. Thomas Love Peacock, S.'s friend, had commemorated the city's lost glory in the poem *Palmyra* (1806), as had Constantin François Chassebœuf, Comte de Volney, in *Ruins of Empire* (1791), which influenced both Peacock and S.

22 l. 137. *Salem's haughty fane.* The Temple at Jerusalem, built by King Solomon ('Salem') in the ninth century BC, sacked by the Roman emperor Vespasian and his son Titus in AD 70. For the building of the Temple see 1 Kings 5–8 and 2 Chronicles 3–4.

l. 148. *dotard's.* King Solomon's.

l. 153. *Promiscuous.* Indiscriminately.

l. 155. *he.* Moses.

ll. 158–60. *tales . . . till terror credits.* The Old Testament stories retailed by priests (collectively 'imposture') to the Hebrews (collectively 'terror', presumably because terrorized, and thus 'crediting' out of fear).

23 l. 176. *tyrant's slave.* Since the current rulers of Greece are obedient to Turkish overlords.

ll. 179–81. *Where . . . deceives.* Rome, where worthy men like Cicero and Antoninus once lived, is now ruled by the Papacy. Cicero (106–43 BC) was a republican orator and sceptic. Antoninus is either the emperor and stoic philosopher Marcus Aurelius Antoninus (AD 121–80, who reigned AD 161–80), or the emperor Antoninus Pius (AD 86–161, who reigned AD 138–61).

l. 187. *a stately city.* Longman 1 conjectures Tenochtitlan (today's Mexico City), the capital of the Aztec empire, famed for botanical gardens, and built on islands in Lake Texococo (hence the 'ships' of l. 201). S., the same edition also conjectures, might have read of the city in D. F. S. Clavigero's *History of Mexico* (1787; 2nd edn. 1807), though he may also have been thinking of Southey's fictional 'Aztlan' in *Madoc* (1805), where the titular hero does battle with 'Aztecas'.

25 *Canto 3.* l. 17. *imbecility.* Feebleness, weakness, impotence.

26 l. 46. *palled.* Enfeebled.

28 l. 110. *mechanic's.* Manual labourer's. *hind.* Farm worker.

l. 111. *glebe.* Soil or earth.

29 l. 157. *impassive.* Invulnerable, unyielding, immovable.

30 l. 182. *lowered.* Frowned, looked darkly over.

l. 217. *aye.* Ever.

31 *Canto 4.* l. 10. *depend.* Hang down.

33 l. 66. *outsallying.* From the verb 'sally': 'to issue suddenly from a place of defence or retreat in order to make an attack' (*OED* 1).

l. 83. *poison-tree*. *Longman* 1 suggests a reference to the fabulous upas tree, alleged to have existed in Java, and so poisonous as to destroy all animal and vegetable life within 15 or 16 miles. An account of the tree appeared in the *London Magazine* in 1783, from which Erasmus Darwin drew in 'Loves of the Plants', book 2 of the *Botanic Garden* (1789), where its serpent-like and bleaching properties are reported.

34 l. 102. *But . . . glare*. That is, 'serving to highlight the terrible gulf between man and happiness, happiness being out of grasp, elusive, like a "meteor"'.

l. 122. *tenement*. The body, which houses the 'stranger-soul' or new-born child.

35 ll. 132-6. *The untainting . . . defencelessness*. An allusion in part to the exploitation of young children in factories, shut away from the 'untainting light of day'.

ll. 151-3. *Soul . . . arise*. That is, the soul is pure, like the beams of the sun, 'heaven's pure orb', at least until clouded over or 'tainted' (polluted?) by the earth's 'atmospheres'.

36 l. 174. *participate*. Participate in, share.

ll. 178-9. *These . . . throne*. See S.'s note (pp. 72-5).

37 ll. 203-20. *Then grave . . . power*. These lines were omitted by Mary S. from *MWS (1)*.

l. 240. *master*. Jesus.

38 l. 252. *unripe*. Premature.

ll. 260-5. *When . . . die?* Another reference to the upas tree (see note to 4. 83 above).

Canto 5. ll. 1-2. *Thus . . . the womb*. See S.'s note (p. 75).

ll. 4-6. *Even . . . soil*. See S's note (p. 75).

39 l. 34. *impassive*. 'Not susceptible of physical impression' (*OED* 2); hence 'by'.

40 l. 58. *The mob . . . kings*. See S's note (p. 75).

l. 80. *wealth of nations*. Alludes to Adam Smith's defence of *laissez-faire* capitalism in *An Inquiry into the Nature and Causes of the Wealth of Nations* (1776).

ll. 93-4. *And statesmen . . . wealth!* See S.'s note (p. 76).

41 ll. 112-13. *Or religion . . . mad*. See S.'s note (p. 76).

l. 135. *plastic*. Mouldable.

42 l. 140. *Cato*. The Roman senator Marcus Porcius Cato (234-149 BC), long-lived upholder of the Republic and its civic and moral virtues. *Longman* 1 quotes Cicero on Cato's active old age: 'The senate and the popular assembly never find my vigour wanting, nor do my friends, my dependants, or my guests' (*De Senectute*, 10. 32).

42 ll. 137–46. *How many . . . town!* This passage alludes to Gray's *Elegy Written in a Country Church Yard* (first publ. 1751), ll. 45–60, with its reference to 'some mute inglorious Milton' (l. 59) (quoted from David Fairer and Christine Gerrard (eds.), *Eighteenth-Century Poetry*, Oxford, 1999).

43 l. 189. *Even love is sold.* See S.'s note (pp. 76–8).

l. 194. *pestilence.* Venereal disease, though perhaps not exclusively.

44 l. 220. *his.* This pronoun should be 'its', referring to 'virtue' (l. 217); as it stands, it might refer to an implied 'that man' (*Longman* 1) or 'that virtuous man'.

l. 231. *commerce.* Selling (i.e. of virtue for material reward or 'human weal').

45 *Canto 6.* l. 4. *periods.* Sentences.

46 ll. 35–8. *The truths . . . death.* Norton cites 'Pliny and other natural historians of antiquity' for the belief that scorpions commit suicide if surrounded by fire.

l. 41. *Symphonious . . . spheres.* An allusion to the classical and Renaissance theory of the music produced by the spheres (the seven immortal planets) as they move through their revolutions. From this cosmic harmony earth is (though will not always be, S. is suggesting) excluded, being 'motionless at the centre or bottom of the universe . . . alone silent and corruptible' (*Longman* 1).

ll. 45–6. *To the red . . . there.* See S.'s note (p. 79).

47 l. 72. *Thou.* 'Religion' personified.

48 l. 111. *Earth . . . trembled.* An ironic allusion to *PL* 2. 787–9 ('I fled, and cried out Death; | Hell trembled at the hideous name, and sighed | From all her caves, and back resounded Death') and 9. 782–4 ('Earth felt the wound, and nature from her seat | Sighing through all her works gave signs of woe, | That all was lost').

l. 132. *horrent.* Shuddering.

49 l. 154. *sublunary.* Mortal, because subject to change or decay, like all things beneath the moon (e.g. Earth, as in the note to 6. 41).

ll. 171–3. *No atom . . . act.* See S.'s note (p. 79).

50 ll. 192–6. *Of all . . . see.* An allusion to Plato's allegory of the cave in *Republic*, 514a–521b.

l. 198. *Necessity . . . world!* See S.'s note (p. 79).

51 l. 231. *sensitive extension.* The meaning is uncertain, perhaps 'moral consciousness'.

ll. 54–238. *Now . . . strength.* Omitted by Mary S. from *MWS (1)*.

Canto 7. The whole of Canto 7 was omitted by Mary S. from *MWS (1)*.

l. 13. *There is no God!* See S.'s note (pp. 79–81).

52 l. 30. *Seeva . . . Lord.* Seeva is Shiva, the Hindu name for God as destroyer or transmuter (in the Hindu Trinity with Brahma and Vishnu); Buddh is Buddha; Foh, according to *Norton*, is the name used in England in S.'s day for Fu Hsi, the legendary or quasi-historical 'first king of China, who is said to have founded this empire soon after the deluge' (George Crabb, *Universal Historical Dictionary*, London, 1833), whilst *Longman* 1 cites Volney, *Ruins*, ch. 20, on 'one God, who under various names, is acknowledged by the nations of the East. The Chinese worship him under the name of *Fot*'; Jehovah is the Hebrew God ('Yahweh'); Lord (in Hebrew 'Adonai') is another name for Yahweh, used most frequently in invocations, suggesting authority, command, kingship.

ll. 33–6. *hosts . . . groans.* An allusion to the car of the Hindu god Vishnu (also called 'Jagannath', hence 'juggernaut') under which devotees are reputed to have thrown themselves to be crushed; *Brahmins* are the highest caste of Hindu.

l. 43. *religion's iron age.* The present, which in classical thought is the last and least noble of the four traditional ages of man: Golden, Silver, Bronze, and Iron.

l. 53. *Tablets.* Imagined as the Spirit's inner 'memoranda-book' (see *OED* 1c), on which are written eternal truths.

53 l. 65. *purblind.* Produced by defective vision; figuratively, 'obtuse', 'stupid'.

l. 66. *Ahasuerus.* The Wandering Jew. See S.'s note (p. 82).

l. 67. *wight.* Person.

54 l. 100. *A murderer.* Moses; see Exodus 2: 11–12.

55 ll. 135–6. *I will . . . world.* See S.'s note (p. 82).

56 l. 192. *ghastily.* Cited in *OED* as a rare form of 'ghastlily' or 'ghastly'.

l. 195. *Hell's freedom . . . heaven.* An allusion to Satan in *PL* 1. 263: 'Better to reign in hell, than serve in heaven.'

l. 208. *So.* That is, 'so also' or 'just so'.

57 l. 218. *winepress . . . wrath.* The image of the apocalyptic winepress comes from Revelation 14: 19–20.

58 *Canto 8.* l. 5. *half-devoured babes.* A reference to Cronus, Greek god commonly associated with time, who devoured his sons as soon as they were born.

60 l. 86. *basilisk.* A legendary reptile hatched by a snake from a cock's egg (also called a cockatrice, as in Isaiah 9: 8). Its breath and look killed.

61 l. 97. *vocal to.* Sounding of, resounding with.

l. 108. *consentaneous.* Mutual, agreeing.

ll. 124–6. *The lion . . . dreadless kid.* From Isaiah 11: 6–7 and Virgil's *Eclogues*, 4. 22. See our note on p. 811, on Shelley's Note on the final chorus in *Hellas*.

62 ll. 127–8. *custom's force*. As the lion grows accustomed to a meatless diet (having forgotten 'to thirst for blood') he grows pacific.

63 l. 183. *led to legal butchery*. *Longman* 1 thinks this a reference to being induced into the Egyptian campaigns of the Napoleonic War, 1798–1807.

ll. 184–6. *that burning sun . . . name of God*. Egypt is here conceived of as the birthplace of the linked tyrannies of priesthood and monarchy.

64 ll. 203–7. *Him . . . eternity*. See S.'s note (pp. 82–3), which begins with an alternative version of the lines in question: 'Him, (still from hope to hope the bliss pursuing, | Which, from the exhaustless lore of human weal | Dawns on the virtuous mind,) the thoughts that rise | In time-destroying infiniteness, gift | With self-enshrined eternity, &c.' This version is no clearer than that of the text. The subject of the sentence contained in either version is 'thoughts' (i.e. 'that rise | In self-destroying infiniteness'), the verb or predicate is 'gift', and the object is 'him' (i.e. 'the human being').

ll. 211–12. *no longer . . . face*. See S.'s note (pp. 83–8).

l. 222. *prune*. Preen.

Canto 9. l. 1. *'O . . . Heaven*. The Fairy continues to speak.

65 ll. 23–37. *Even Time . . . fall*. See S.'s letter to Elizabeth Hitchener of 14 February 1812 (*L* 1. 251–2), which, though written in prose, contains a strikingly similar passage (see *MYR* 8).

66 l. 48. *Nor . . . God*. This line was omitted by Mary S. from *MWS (1)* and, unlike other censored passages, was not restored in *MWS (2)*.

l. 76. *that sweet bondage*. Sexual love.

67 l. 86. *senselessness*. Absence of feeling.

68 l. 130. *wreck*. Trace, vestige; one meaning of 'wrack'.

71 *Notes to 'Queen Mab'*. S.'s Notes to *QM* are longer than the poem itself. They combine untranslated extracts from French, Latin, and Greek authors, and extended treatises on astronomy, religion, marriage, atheism, necessity, and vegetarianism, some of which are redactions of earlier printed texts, others of which were later published separately. When S. quotes directly and at length from another writer the reference alone will be given.

Note, 1. 242–3. Here, as in the Note to 1. 252–3, S.'s science is 'without serious error' (D. King-Hele, *Shelley: His Thought and Work* (London, 1960), 39).

72 *Note*. 1. 252–3. S.'s footnote to his Note here reads 'See Nicholson's Encyclopedia, art. Light', a reference to William Nicholson, *The British Encyclopedia*, 6 vols. (1807–9).

Note, 4. 178–9. *a little poem*. *Locock* suggests Coleridge's 'Fire, Famine, and Slaughter' (1798) as a model for 'Falsehood and Vice: A Dialogue', since both poems are written in the same octosyllabic metre and attack government abuse. *Longman* 1 identifies the second witches' scene in *Macbeth* (1. 3. 1–37) as the ultimate archetype of all such contemporary dialogues. Probably composed between December 1811 and March 1812.

76 *Note*, 5. 112–13. *Lucretius*. From *De Rerum Natura*, 3. 85–6: 'for often before now men have betrayed fatherland or beloved parents in seeking to avoid the regions of Acheron.'

77 *Note*, 5. 189. S.'s footnote to his Note here reads: 'The first Christian emperor made a law by which seduction was punished by death: if the female pleaded her own consent, she also was punished by death; if the parents endeavoured to screen the criminals, they were banished and their estates were confiscated; the slaves who might be accessory were burned alive, or forced to swallow melted lead. The very offspring of an illegal love were involved in the consequences of the sentence.' He cites as source Gibbon's *Decline and Fall of the Roman Empire* (1776–81), ch. 14, and refers also, 'for the hatred of the primitive Christians to love and even marriage', to Gibbon's ch. 15.

79 *Note*, 6. 198. S.'s lemma has a comma after 'Necessity'; the text has an exclamation mark.

Note, 7. 13. *A close examination.* From here to the paragraph ending 'no proof of the existence of a Deity' (p. 81), S. reproduces (with minor emendations and expansions) *The Necessity of Atheism*, published in 1811 by S. and his friend Thomas Jefferson Hogg at Oxford. This pamphlet eventually caused S.'s expulsion from the university. The differences between the Note and the pamphlet (mostly a matter of additions or expansions) are bracketed in our text. The Note ends with quotations from Bacon, Holbach (an extended selection of passages from the *Système de la Nature*), Pliny, and Spinoza.

80 *least.* 'Less' in the pamphlet.

But our idea of causation . . . reasoning experimentally. 'But what does this prove?' in the pamphlet.

81 *omnipotent being.* 'Almighty Being' in the pamphlet.

Hypotheses non fingo . . . non habent. From Newton's *Philosophiae Naturalis Principia Mathematica* (1687; 3rd edn. 1726), 3. 530): 'I do not make hypotheses, for whatever is not deduced from the phenomena must be called a hypothesis, and hypotheses, whether in metaphysics or physics, or occult qualities, or mechanics, have no place in philosophy.'

occult qualities . . . of Herschel. Peripatetics are followers of Aristotle's philosophical school. The chemist Robert Boyle (1627–91), who promoted a corpuscular or atomistic view of matter, applied the word 'effluvia' to material particles. The astronomer Sir Frederick William Herschel (1792–1871) used the words 'crinities' and 'nebulae' to refer to comets and distant star clusters.

praedicate in non. Negative proposition.

82 *Pour dire . . . lui-même.* The quotation comes from Holbach's *Système de*

la Nature (1781), where its author is unidentified. Also from Holbach is the following passage from Bacon's *Moral Essays* (1625), which S. translates back into English, and a further long passage in French, omitted here, consisting of selections from 2. 16–18, 27, 319–26. This is followed by comparably atheistic quotations in Latin from Pliny (*Naturalis Historia*, 2. 4. 14, 27, published after Pliny's death in AD 79), an assertion that 'The consistent Newtonian is necessarily an atheist' followed by refutation of Sir William Drummond (in *Academical Questions*, book 2, ch. 3) for apparently regarding the atheistic implications of Newton's 'system of gravitation' (S.'s phrase) as proof of the system's falsity, and a Latin passage from ch. 1 of Spinoza's *Tractatus Theologico-Politicus* (1670), arguing the indistinguishability of God and nature. These passages are also omitted.

82 *Note, 8. 203–7. Him, (still from hope . . .)* See note to the text of 8. 203–7, which S. has altered here in several respects.

83 *Dark flood of time! . . . unredeemed.* ll. 58–69 of 'To Harriet' ('It is not blasphemy to hope'), a poem of uncertain date of composition (*Longman* 1 conjectures late 1812), from the unpublished *Esdaile Notebook*. At the end of the Note, S. cites Godwin's *Political Justice* and Condorcet's *Esquisse d'un Tableau Historique des Progrès de l'Esprit Humain* (1793–4).

Note, 8. 211–12. This Note in its entirety varies only slightly from S.'s 1813 pamphlet *A Vindication of Natural Diet.* S. became a vegetarian in 1812, and for the most part remained one throughout his life. Probable sources for the Note include Joseph Ritson, *An Essay on Abstinence from Animal Food as a Moral Duty* (1802), William Lambe, *Reports on the effect of a peculiar regimen on scirrhous tumours and cancerous ulcers* (1811), from which are drawn 'all [S.'s] citations of Cuvier's *Leçons d'Anatomie Comparée*' (*Longman* 1), and John Frank Newton, *The Return to Nature; or, a Defence of the Vegetable Regimen* (1811). The note concludes with a lengthy quotation from Plutarch, *Moralia*, 'On the Eating of Flesh', omitted here.

Milton. PL 11. 477–88, where the speaker is Michael not Raphael.

84 *Horace. Odes,* 1. 3. 25–33: 'Bold to endure all things, mankind rushes even through forbidden wrong. Iapetus' daring son [Prometheus] by impious craft brought fire to the tribes of men. After fire was stolen from its home in heaven, wasting disease and a new throng of fevers fell upon the earth, and the doom of death, that before had been slow and distant, quickened its pace.'

mouflon. Wild sheep. This paragraph does not appear in the 1813 pamphlet.

85 *It is true . . . human evil.* This paragraph does not appear in the 1813 pamphlet.

if remote from . . . his inventions. S.'s footnote to his Note reads: 'The necessity of resorting to some means of purifying water, and the disease which arises from its adulteration in civilized countries, is sufficiently apparent—see Dr Lambe's Reports on Cancer. I do not assert that the use of water is in itself unnatural, but that the unperverted palate would swallow no liquid capable of occasioning disease.'

86 *Muley Ismael's.* Sultan of Morocco (1672–1727), surnamed 'the Bloodthirsty'.

88 *The labour . . . far lighter.* S.'s footnote to his Note reads: 'It has come under the author's experience, that some of the workmen on an embankment in North Wales, who, in consequence of the inability of the proprietor to pay them, seldom received their wages, have supported large families by cultivating small spots of sterile ground by moonlight. In the notes to Pratt's Poem, "Bread, or the Poor," is an account of an industrious labourer, who, by working in a small garden, before and after his day's task, attained to an enviable state of independence.' 'Pratt's Poem' is Samuel Jackson Pratt's *Bread; or, The Poor* (1802).

natural playfulness. S.'s footnote to his Note reads: 'See Mr Newton's book. His children are the most beautiful and healthy creatures it is possible to conceive; the girls are perfect models for a sculptor; their dispositions are also the most gentle and conciliating; the judicious treatment, which they experience in other points, may be a correlative cause of this. In the first five years of their life, of 18,000 children that are born, 7,500 die of various diseases; and how many more of those that survive are not rendered miserable by maladies not immediately mortal? The quality and quantity of a woman's milk are materially injured by the use of dead flesh. In an island near Iceland, where no vegetables are to be got, the children invariably die of tetanus, before they are three weeks old, and the population is supplied from the main land.—Sir G. Mackenzie's Hist. of Iceland.' S. also refers to Rousseau's *Émile* (1762), ch. i.

Stanzas.—April, 1814. Composed in April 1814 at Bracknell, the Berkshire village S. moved to in July 1813. Copy-text from *Alastor; or The Spirit of Solitude: And Other Poems* (1816) (henceforth *Alastor* (1816)). Though himself married (to Harriet Westbrook, since 1811), S. fell in love at Bracknell with the married Cornelia Turner, daughter of Harriet Collins de Boinville, the 'friend' of l. 6.

l. 8. *dereliction.* Presumably on the part of daughter and mother.

89 *'O! there are spirits of the air'.* Date of composition unknown, probably 1815. Published in *Alastor* (1816) under the Greek heading of the epigraph only (the text in this volume supplies our copy-text). According to Mary Shelley, who published the poem in *MWS (1)* under the heading 'To ****', 'The poem beginning "Oh, there are spirits in the air [*sic*]," was addressed in idea to Coleridge, whom he never knew; and at whose character he could only guess imperfectly, through his writings, and accounts he heard of him from some who knew him well. He regarded his change of opinions as rather an act of will than conviction, and believed

that in his inner heart he would be haunted by what Shelley considered the better and holier aspirations of his youth.' The poem explores the tensions between spiritual or ideal and earthly realms and the dangers of living purely 'in thine own mind', themes explored also in *Alastor*.

89 *Epigraph*. 'still my eyes shall be wet with tears | for your heartless doom' (trans. by David Grene, in *The Complete Greek Tragedies*, ed. David Grene and Richard Lattimore, 9 vols, Chicago, 1967, vol. 4). From Euripides, *Hippolytus* (1143–4), spoken by the Chorus about Hippolytus, who has been exiled by his father, Theseus, after his stepmother Phaedra's false accusations of rape.

90 *To Wordsworth*. Written in 1814 or 1815, published in *Alastor* (1816). S. never met Wordsworth, whose poetry he admired, but whose gathering political and religious conservatism he consistently deplored. He visited Keswick in the Lake District from November 1811 to January 1812, where he met Robert Southey. Subsequently, he suspected Southey (wrongly) of attacking his morality in an anonymous article in the *Quarterly Review*. The sonnet to Wordsworth may have been occasioned by a first reading of *The Excursion* in September 1814, or by a later reading in 1815, or after reading Wordsworth's *Poems* soon after their publication (in April 1815). It echoes Wordsworth's sonnet 'London, 1802', with its famous invocation: 'Milton! thou should'st be living at this hour' (e.g. in l. 7, 'Thou wert as a lone star', which recalls l. 9 of Wordsworth's sonnet: 'Thy soul was like a Star and dwelt apart').

92 *Alastor; or, The Spirit of Solitude*. Composed in the autumn and early winter of 1815, in a cottage in Bishopsgate (in Windsor Park), where S. and Mary had been living since August. Published in *Alastor*, from which our text is taken. The title, suggested by Thomas Love Peacock, comes from the Greek word *alastor* meaning 'evil genius' (also, according to *Longman* 1, 'avenging spirit or, more rarely, the victim of such a spirit'). Peacock explains in his *Memoirs of Shelley*: 'The poem treated the spirit of solitude as a spirit of evil' (*The Works of Thomas Love Peacock*, ed. H. F. B. Brett-Smith and C. E. Jones, 10 vols. (London, 1924–34), 8. 100), and the destructiveness of such a spirit is clear whether conceived of as supernatural agent (Peacock's view, supported, for example, in ll. 285 ff.) or imaginary creation (that is, of the poet-protagonist, as suggested, for example, in ll. 149 ff). The poet-protagonist has been variously associated with Wordsworth (to whose poetry S.'s Preface and poem explicitly allude on a number of occasions), Coleridge and S. himself. Mary S. and others attribute the poem's preoccupation with death to S.'s illness in the spring of 1815, when his doctor told him he was dying of consumption. The poem surrounds its account of the Poet's fate with opening and closing passages concerning the speaker. Much critical debate has taken place about the relation between the Narrator and the Poet, and between the poem and its Preface, and about the poem's view of the Poet, who has been seen as embodying the dangers of 'self-centred seclusion' (Preface) or as an admired if tragic questor after ideals.

93 *Preface. All else.* In complete contrast.

'The good ... socket!'. From Wordsworth, *The Excursion*, 1. 500–2, slightly misquoted.

Epigraph. 'I was not in love as yet, yet I loved to be in love, I sought about for something to love, loving still to be in love' (Augustine, *Confessions*, 3. 1). S. omits from the original, between 'amare amabam' and 'quaerebam', words which translate thus: 'and with a more secret kind of want, I hated myself having little want.'

l. 3. *natural piety.* See Wordsworth, 'My heart leaps up,' ll. 8–9: 'And I could wish my days to be | Bound each to each by natural piety.'

94 l. 26. *obstinate questionings.* See Wordsworth, 'Ode: Intimations of Immortality,' ll. 144–5: '... those obstinate questionings | Of sense and outward things.'

ll. 45–9. *I wait ... man.* See Wordsworth, 'Tintern Abbey,' ll. 96–103: 'a sense sublime | Of something far more deeply interfused, | Whose dwelling is the light of setting suns, | And the round ocean, and the living air, | And the blue sky, and in the mind of man, | A motion and a spirit, that impels | All thinking things, all objects of all thought, | And rolls through all things.'

l. 56. *cypress wreath.* Offered to the gods by mourners on behalf of the dead; see Ovid, *Met.* 10.

95 l. 85. *bitumen lakes.* Lakes of molten lava; as *Norton* points out, the exact phrase is found in Southey, *Thalaba*, 6. 15; 'bituminous' appears in *PL* 10. 562 and 12. 41, in descriptions of Hell.

l. 94. *chrysolite.* A greenish semi-precious gem.

96 l. 118. *daemons.* 'Intermediate spirits' (*Norton*) or minor deities capable of communicating between gods and men, from Greek mythology and Plato.

l. 120. *on the mute walls around.* Perhaps alluding to the temple of Isis at Dendera in Egypt, decorated (on the ceiling not the walls) with images of gods 'arranged within the pattern of the Zodiac' (*Norton*).

ll. 106–28. *His wandering step ... birth of time.* The Poet's journey in search of knowledge takes him round the eastern Mediterranean and up the Nile; he travels back in time from the Greeks (Athens) to the Phoenicians (Tyre, Balbec), to the Jews (Jerusalem), the Babylonians (Babylon), the Egyptians (Memphis, Thebes), to Ethiopia, described by Volney, *Ruins*, ch. 19, as the 'cradle of the sciences'.

97 l. 139. *Wildered.* Bewildered, lost.

ll. 140–5. *The Poet wandering ... vale of Cashmire.* A journey eastward through Arabia, Persia (including the Desert of Karmin, in the southeast), the Hindu Kush Mountains (setting of *Prometheus Unbound*, 1, and source of the rivers Indus and Oxus), to the vale of Kashmir in north-west India (in which *Prometheus Unbound*, 2. 1 is set).

97   l. 163. *numbers*. Verses.

99   l. 229. *precipitates*. Hastens.

l. 232. *aery*. Lofty.

l. 233. *shadow*. Image.

l. 240. *Till vast Aornos . . . Petra's steep*. Aornos was a mountain fortress on the Indus river; Petra is probably the Sogdian Rock, a steep summit above the Oxus river in Uzbekistan.

l. 242. *Balk*. An ancient Persian province south of the River Oxus, later the site of an independent Parthian kingdom; now Balkh, in Afghanistan.

100 l. 272. *Chorasmian*. The land between the Caspian and Aral Seas (about 175 miles) in what is now modern Russia; 'the lone Chorasmian shore' is either the eastern shore of the Caspian or the western shore of the Aral.

l. 299. *shallop*. Light open boat for shallow water.

101 l. 327. *ruining*. *Longman* 1 cites Latin *ruere*, 'to fall in disorder'. *MWS (1)* and *(2)* read 'running'; we have stayed with our copy-text.

102 l. 352. *etherial*. Here, high in the air.

103 l. 406. *yellow flowers*. Narcissi, recalling Narcissus, the youth in Greek mythology (Ovid, *Met.* 3), who pines away out of self-love, unresponsive to the love of others.

104 l. 425. *Mocking its moans*. Imitating the moans of the forest (l. 421) as the wind blows through it.

l. 426. *implicated*. Interwoven.

105 l. 490. *Two starry eyes*. These eyes recall the earlier 'beamy bending eyes' (l. 179).

106 l. 526. *lightsome*. Luminous.

l. 528. *windlestrae*. 'A dry thin withered stalk of grass, such as is left standing after the flower or seed is shed' (*OED*).

107 l. 546. *its precipice*. *Norton* explains this phrase as meaning the dell's 'headlong descent—*its* refers to *dell*, l.541'. 'Precipice' as 'headlong fall or descent' is the first definition offered in *OED*, but was already obsolete in S.'s time; nor does it help much in explaining ll. 547–8. If 'its' refers to 'stream' (l. 540) 'obscuring the ravine' makes more sense, but how a 'headlong descent' (whether of stream or dell) can 'disclos[e] above' 'toppling stones,' 'gulfs,' and 'caves,' remains unclear.

108 l. 585. *Red, yellow, or etherially pale*. See 'Ode to the West Wind': 'Yellow, and black, and pale, and hectic red' (l. 4).

109 l. 651. *meteor*. The moon; at this time the word 'meteor' applied to any phenomenon within the earth's atmosphere, including the moon (thought to be at the atmosphere's outer limit).

l. 654. *two lessening points of light*. Suggesting either the eyes of the dream-maid (ll. 179, 489–92) or the tips of a crescent moon.

110 l. 672. *Medea's wondrous alchemy*. Medea brewed a magic potion to revivify the aged Aeson, Jason's father; when she spilled some on the ground flowers and grass sprang up (see Ovid, *Met.* 7).

l. 677. *one living man*. Ahasuerus, the Wandering Jew; according to medieval legend he insulted Christ on the way to his crucifixion and was condemned to wander the earth as an outcast until the second coming. He appears as a character in *Queen Mab*, 7. 64–275.

l. 705. *senseless*. Unfeeling.

111 l. 713. *too 'deep for tears'*. See the last line of Wordsworth, 'Ode: Intimations of Immortality': 'Thoughts that do often lie too deep for tears.'

112 *Mutability*. Date of composition unknown, published in *Alastor* (1816), our copy-text.

1.5. *dissonant*. 'variously-sounding' (*Longman* 1); the wind lyre or Aeolian harp was repeatedly alluded to in the poetry of the period, frequently serving as an image for the mind, either in perception or creation; it is found also in *Alastor* (ll. 41–9, 663–8) and 'Ode to the West Wind'.

Verses Written on Receiving a Celandine in a Letter from England. Our copy-text is Mary S.'s transcription in the Smaller Silsbee Account Book at Harvard (MS Eng. 258.3; *MYR: Shelley*, 5). The poem was written in June/July 1816, and was not published until 1925. It expresses disenchantment with Wordsworth's growing conservatism. S. turns against Wordsworth the latter's own use of the celandine as an emblem of 'an altered Form' ('The Small Celandine', l. 10).

l. 2. *aery blue*. The celandine is yellow.

113 l. 29. *changed and withered*. See Wordsworth, 'The Small Celandine', ll. 18–19, where the poet says of the flower, 'It cannot help itself in its decay; | Stiff in its members, withered, changed of hue'.

l. 30. *Fallen . . . time*. See *PL* 7. 26: 'On evil days though fallen, and evil tongues.'

ll. 45–8. *That blood . . . celebrate*. Alludes to Wordsworth's poems celebrating the victory at Waterloo.

114 l. 59. *divine and simple song*. Poems such as those contained in *Lyrical Ballads*.

Hymn to Intellectual Beauty. Composed in the summer of 1816, the poem was first published by Leigh Hunt in the *Examiner*, 19 January 1817, and then in the *Rosalind and Helen* volume (1819). There is an intermediate fair copy in the Bodleian (*BSM* 11). Like 'Mont Blanc', the 'Hymn' also exists in a fair-copied version (in Mary S.'s hand) in the Scrope Davies Notebook, now in the British Library (*MYR: Shelley*, 8). S. probably lent this notebook, which came to light in 1976, to Byron in Switzerland. Byron, in turn, probably gave it to Scrope Davies for safe return to S. Since Davies did not return the notebook to S., the latter was obliged to finish both poems again, in all likelihood after returning to his drafts. We print both completed versions of the 'Hymn' and 'Mont

Blanc'; in each case copy-text for version B is the Scrope Davies fair copy, which we reproduce from the manuscript versions with some editorial intervention (some punctuation is added and spellings are modernized). Copy-text for version A of the 'Hymn' is based on the *Examiner* text, with corrections in S.'s hand (now at Harvard: see *MYR: Shelley* 5). 'Intellectual beauty' is a phrase S. could have met in writings by various authors, including William Godwin and Mary Wollstonecraft, and suggests a beauty of the mind or spirit; it is also used by him in his translation of Plato's *Symposium*. The 'Hymn' adapts the genre of the hymn to unorthodox ends. It responds to and reworks Spenser's 'An Hymne of Heavenly Beautie', Wordsworth's 'Ode: Intimations of Immortality', and Rousseau's epistolary novel *Julie; ou, La Nouvelle Héloïse* (with its emphasis on the protagonist's journey towards universal benevolence). It has affinities with passages in the poet's 'On Christianity' (1817) and the seven and a half stanzas beginning 'Frail clouds arrayed in sunlight lose their glory' (in *Longman* 2). The notes are keyed to version A of the poem.

114 l. 2. *some unseen Power.* See 'On Christianity' (1817): 'There is a power by which we are surrounded, like the atmosphere in which some motion-less lyre is suspended, which visits with its breath our silent chords, at will' (*Murray*, p. 251).

l. 5. *shower.* A verb governed by 'moonbeams'.

115 l. 17. *vale of tears.* Phrase in the Catholic prayer, 'Salve Regina'. See Keats in a letter of 1819: 'The common cognomen of this world among the misguided and superstitious is "a vale of tears"', *Letters*, ed. Hyder E. Rollins (2 vols., Cambridge, Mass., 1958), 2. 101.

l. 36. *grace and truth.* See John 1: 17: 'but grace and truth came by Jesus Christ.'

l. 37. *Love, Hope, and Self-esteem.* 'Self-esteem', by which S. means proper regard for one's human value, replaces 'faith' in St Paul's trinity of faith, hope, and charity (1 Corinthians 13: 13).

116 l. 45. *darkness . . . flame!* Though *Longman* 1 suggests that, in S.'s day, 'Strong light was believed to stifle a flame', the image is paradoxical and doubt-ridden.

l. 52. *Hopes . . . dead.* See James Thomson, 'Winter' (1746), ll. 431–2: 'There studious let me sit, | And hold high converse with the mighty dead'; quoted from *The Seasons*, ed. James Sambrook (Oxford, 1981).

ll. 53–4. *I called . . . I was not heard.* See the more direct attack on 'that false name' and 'the false name' in version B and the draft, respectively.

117 l. 84. *To fear himself.* To have due respect for his worth. *Longman* 1 cites Ecclesiastes 12: 13: 'Fear God, and keep his commandments: for this is the whole duty of man.'

120 *Mont Blanc.* Composed in July 1816 after S., Mary, and Claire Clairmont visited Chamonix and its Alpine environs (see S.'s account in

L 1. 495–502). Version B of the poem (copy-text supplied by the version in S.'s hand in the Scrope Davies Notebook) was completed by the time S. and his party left Geneva on 29 August. The text in *History of a Six Weeks' Tour* by Mary and P. B. Shelley (1817) provides the copy-text for version A. There is a draft in the Bodleian (*BSM* 11). In the Preface to *History* we are told that 'Mont Blanc' 'was composed under the immediate impression of the deep and powerful feelings excited by the objects which it attempts to describe' and that it is 'an undisciplined overflowing of the soul' which 'rests its claim to approbation on an attempt to imitate the untameable wildness and inaccessible solemnity from which those feelings sprang'. The poem's irregular rhyme-scheme, modelled on that of Milton's *Lycidas*, mimics the effort to give verbal form to these feelings. 'Mont Blanc' reads the Alpine landscape as sublime, but the sublimity it finds does not prove the existence of God, as it does in Coleridge's 'Hymn before Sun-Rise, in the Vale of Chamouni'. When Coleridge's poem was first printed (1802), it was accompanied by a note which included the exclamation, 'Who *would* be, who *could* be an Atheist in this valley of wonders!' In 'Mont Blanc' S., who had described himself (in Greek) in a number of Swiss hotel registers as a lover of mankind, democrat, and atheist, appears to respond to Coleridge's challenge, yet he is prepared (as in the 'Hymn') to invoke a heterodox 'power' (l. 127) or 'secret strength of things' (l. 139), possibly identifiable with the idea of Necessity. The poem begins with an emphasis on the power of the 'universe of things' (l. 1); it ends by pointing up (albeit in a question) the significance of 'the human mind's imaginings' (l. 143). The notes are keyed to version A.

l. 2. *the mind*. Has been read as the 'Universal Mind as distinct from the individual mind' (*Longman* 1), but S. is less explicit here than he is in 'The Daemon of the World' (a reworking, published in the *Alastor* volume, of parts of *Queen Mab*), 2. 248–51: 'For birth but wakes the universal Mind | Whose mighty streams might else in silence flow | Through the vast world, to individual sense | Of outward shows'.   *rolls . . . waves*. See Wordsworth, 'Tintern Abbey', l. 103: 'And rolls through all things'.

l. 6. *half its own*. See Wordsworth, 'Tintern Abbey', ll. 106–8: 'the mighty world | Of eye and ear, both what they half-create, | And what perceive'; the referent of 'its' is more likely to be 'The source of human thought' (l. 5) than the 'universe of things' (l. 1).

ll. 1–11. *The everlasting . . . raves*. The poem begins with a meditation on 'things' and 'thought' before it moves, in the second section, to the Alpine scene, read as illustrative ('Thus', l. 12) of the opening propositions.

l. 12. *Ravine of Arve*. The Arve flows through Chamouni into Lake Geneva.

l. 27. *unsculptured*. Both not sculptured (because natural) and still to be sculptured (awaiting the human mind's imaginings).

121 l. 43. *that or thou.* Throughout this part of section 2, the referents of S.'s pronouns are elusive as he struggles to render 'an unremitting interchange' (l. 39). Here, 'that' may refer back to 'My own, my human mind' (l. 37); 'thou' refers to the Ravine.

l. 45. *Seeking.* The likely subject is 'One legion of wild thoughts' (l. 41) or 'my human mind' (l. 37).

l. 47. *the breast.* Either the poet's or some supra-human source, such as the 'Power' (l. 16).

l. 53. *unfurled.* The usual sense of the word is 'unrolled', but some commentators agree with *Locock* that the intended meaning is 'drawn aside'.

122 l. 69. *tracks her there.* Version B has the more likely 'watches her'.

ll. 71–4. *Is this . . . silent snow?* Possible geological explanations for the Alpine scenery; ll. 73–4 refer to the theory proposed by the Comte de Buffon (1707–88) that the earth had begun as fluid heat and subsequently cooled. For S.'s awareness at this time of Buffon's ideas, see *L* 1. 499.

l. 77. *awful doubt, or faith so mild.* Awe-inducing scepticism about the existence of a benevolent creative deity, or trust in the existence of a 'Power' that differs from the Christian God by being indifferent to human existence and thus not exploitable by those who wish to find a divine sanction for oppressive forms of human authority ('Large codes of fraud and woe', l. 81).

l. 79. *But for such faith.* In version B, S. writes 'In such a faith', which makes more obvious sense. 'But for' may mean 'Only through'.

l. 86. *daedal.* Intricately wrought, after Daedalus, mythical inventor who built the Cretan labyrinth.

ll. 96–7. *Power . . . inaccessible.* See the Note to *Queen Mab*, 7. 13, where S. rejects the idea of 'a creative Deity' but not of 'a pervading Spirit coeternal with the universe' (p. 79). S.'s sense of 'Power' dwelling apart owes something to the Lucretian stricture against the belief 'that any holy abode of the gods exists in any part of the world' (*De Rerum Natura*, 5. 146–7).

l. 100. *adverting.* Attentive.

123 l. 105. *distinct.* Decorated (*OED* 4).

l. 120. *their place is not known.* See Job 7: 10: 'He shall return no more to his house, neither shall his place know him any more.'

ll. 120–2. *vast caves . . . welling.* There are echoes of Coleridge's 'Kubla Khan' here (see that poem's 'caverns measureless to man' (l. 4), 'deep romantic chasm' (l. 12), and river that 'sank in tumult to a lifeless ocean' (l. 28)): although S. did not receive his copy of Coleridge's *Christabel* volume (containing 'Kubla Khan') until late August 1816, he evidently knew 'Kubla Khan', possibly via Southey or Byron.

l. 123. *one majestic River*. The Rhône, fed by Lake Geneva into which the Arve flows.

l. 135. *Silently*. See Coleridge, 'Hymn before Sun-rise', ll. 6–7, describing how Mont Blanc 'Risest from forth thy silent sea of pines, | How silently!'

124 ll. 142–4. *And what . . . vacancy?* See S.'s comment in his journal-letter (22 June 1816) about visiting the Alps: 'All was as much our own as if we had been the creators of such impressions in the minds of others, as now occupied our own' (*L* 1. 497).

128 *To Constantia*. Composed between April 1817 and January 1818. First published in *Oxford University and City Herald*, 31 January 1818, which supplies our copy-text, though we have also consulted S.'s rough draft in the Bodleian (*BSM* 3) and his fair copy in the Smaller Silsbee Account Book at Harvard (MS Eng. 258.3; *MYR: Shelley* 5). Its first publication was under the pseudonym 'Pleyel', the name both of a contemporary pianist and composer, Ignaz Pleyel, Handel's pupil, and a character in the novel *Wieland, or the Transformation* (1798), by the American novelist Charles Brockden Brown. 'Constantia', S.'s name for Claire Clairmont, also comes from a novel by Brown, *Ormond; or the Secret Witness* (1799) about which Peacock wrote: 'The heroine of this novel, Constantia Dudley, held one of the highest places, if not the very highest, in Shelley's idealities of female character' (*Works*, ed. Brett-Smith and Jones, 8. 77).

l. 27. *cope of Heaven*. The roof or vault of Heaven, which the singing of St Cecilia, patron saint of music, was said to have the power of opening.

l. 32. *Nature's utmost sphere*. The orbit of the moon, thought to mark the atmosphere's outer limit (or 'verge'); all things below (that is, 'sublunary') belonged to the realm of nature.

129 l. 38. *Even . . . were*. This awkward line makes sense if the phrase 'its voice that were' is understood as appositional, describing the sounds which constitute the voice of the 'power' of l. 27; hence the surrounding commas, an editorial addition. S.'s first thought, in a notebook draft (though not the later fair copy), was: 'Even tho' the sounds which were its voice.'

130 From *Laon and Cythna; Or, The Revolution of the Golden City: A Vision of the Nineteenth Century. In the Stanza of Spenser*. The longest of S.'s poems (4,818 lines), composed in Great Marlow, Buckinghamshire, in spring, summer, and autumn 1817. Published by Charles Ollier in early December 1817 (though dated 1818), then immediately withdrawn and revised at Ollier's insistence, after protests from customers over its attacks on religion and the incestuous love of its title-characters. Republished in revised form in January as *The Revolt of Islam; A Poem, In Twelve Cantos*. Because S. agreed to revisions only as a last resort, our copy-text is the original published version, supplemented by surviving fair-copy manuscripts (of the Preface, Dedication, and 200 lines of Canto

9, in *BSM* 8) and notebook drafts of the poem as a whole (in *BSM* 8, 13, 17). *Laon and Cythna* derives from a period of intense political controversy and personal unhappiness (over the Lord Chancellor's decision in March to deny S. custody of his and Harriet's two children, S.'s own recurring fears of illness, and the recent suicides, in autumn 1817, of S.'s first wife Harriet and Mary's half-sister Fanny). Though S. identified the poem's 'Golden City' as Constantinople, its 'Revolution' is of a sort that 'might be supposed to take place in an European nation'. The poem is visionary, a '*beau ideal*' (*L* 1. 564) of the French Revolution, 'the master theme of the epoch' (*L* 1. 504). Its aim in part is to counter the disillusion of contemporaries such as Wordsworth, Coleridge, and Southey with the Revolution's failings. Though these failings are acknowledged and anatomized in *Laon and Cythna*, they are also seen from a wider and more optimistic perspective. As for the work's literary influences, these include the major poems of the heroic tradition, including those of Homer, Virgil, Lucan, Tasso, Spenser, and Milton, as well as contemporary works such as Volney's *Ruins* (1791); Peacock's *Ahrimanes* (1813), also written in Spenserian stanzas; Southey's Eastern narrative poems, *Thalaba the Destroyer* (1801) and *The Curse of Kehama* (1810); and Byron's *Childe Harold's Pilgrimage* (1812–18), which combines Eastern settings, the theme of political revolution, and romance motifs.

130   *Title*. 'Laon', the name of the poem's hero, comes from the Greek word for 'the people'; 'Cythna', his sister, may derive her name either from Cytherea, Aphrodite's surname (after the island Cythera), or from another Greek island, 'Cythnos', near Argolis, perhaps Laon and Cythna's original home (see l. 676; see *Longman* 2). The 'Stanza of Spenser' of the subtitle is the nine-line stanza of *FQ* (1590–6).

Epigraph. 'Give me a place to stand and I will move the earth' (see our note to third epigraph to *Queen Mab*, p. 707).

Preface. experiment. See Advertisement to Wordsworth and Coleridge's *Lyrical Ballads* (1798): 'The majority of the following poems are to be considered as experiments.'

enlightened and refined. The poem's intended audience, like that of *Queen Mab*, seems to have been chosen in part to avoid government prosecution, the fate of writers and publishers of comparably radical works written in a more popular idiom.

131   '*all . . . sun*'. See Ecclesiastes 4: 1: 'So I returned, and considered all the oppressions that are done under the sun: and behold the tears of such as were oppressed, and they had no comforter; and on the side of their oppressors there was power; but they had no comforter.'

confederacy . . . by foreign arms. Alludes to the restoration of the French monarchy in 1814 by the anti-revolutionary coalition of Austria, Great Britain, Prussia, and Russia.

scope. Intention.

132   *atrocities*. In subsequent sentences these atrocities are seen as con-

sequences of the oppressions and inequalities of pre-revolutionary France, an argument familiar from Paine's *Rights of Man* (1791). (See *Longman* 2.)

133 *Metaphysics*. S. adds a note: 'I ought to except Sir W. Drummond's "Academical Questions," a volume of very acute and powerful metaphysical criticism.' Sir William Drummond (1770–1828) was the author of *Academical Questions* (1805), a work of philosophical idealism which criticizes Kant's ideas and much influenced S.

like those. S. adds a note: 'It is remarkable, as a symptom of the revival of public hope, that Mr Malthus has assigned, in the later editions of his work, an indefinite dominion to moral restraint over the principle of population. This concession answers all the inferences from his doctrine unfavourable to human improvement, and reduces the "Essay on Population" to a commentary illustrative of the unanswerableness of "Political Justice."' Thomas Robert Malthus (1736–1834), an Anglican priest as well as a political economist, was the author of *Essay on the Principles of Population* (1798). In second and subsequent editions of the *Essay*, Malthus admitted 'moral restraint' (bk. IV, ch. 1) as a possible check to population growth.

infectious gloom. Such as is expressed, for example, in Byron's writings, notably *Manfred* (1817), which made S. feel 'dreadfully melancholy. . . . Why do you indulge such despondency?' (*L* 1. 547).

accidental education. That is, by experience, including not only the sorts of travels recounted in the next few sentences, which allude to S.'s expeditions with Mary and Claire Clairmont to the Vale of Chamonix in 1816 and through France, Switzerland and Germany two years previously, but S.'s personal relations with such 'men of genius' as Byron and Godwin.

134 *the Metaphysicians*. S. adds a note: 'In this sense there may be such a thing as perfectibility in works of fiction, notwithstanding the concession often made by the advocates of human improvement, that perfectibility is a term applicable only to science.' This Note alludes to contemporary controversies about improvement or perfectibility, including of the arts, sparked by Godwin's *Enquiry Concerning Political Justice* (1793).

age of Pericles. Pericles (*c*.495–429 BC) ruled Athens at the height of its prosperity and cultural achievement.

. . . and Lord Bacon. S. adds a note: 'Milton stands alone in the age which he illumined.'

Ford. John Ford (1586–?1639), dramatist, most famous for *'Tis Pity She's a Whore* and *The Broken Heart* (both 1633).

135 *alexandrine . . . in the middle of a stanza*. An alexandrine is a twelve-syllable line; there are at least two such lines in the poem, both in the fifth or middle lines of their respective stanzas (in Canto 4, stanza 27—not in this selection—and Canto 10, stanza 36).

system of criticism. S. is probably alluding to the influential rule-bound criticism of French neo-classicist critics such as Nicholas Boileau (1636–1711), also deplored by Keats in 'Sleep and Poetry' (1817).

135 *Longinus*. Supposed author of the literary treatise *On the Sublime* (first century AD), translated by Boileau in 1674.

anonymous censure. Most reviews in contemporary periodicals were unsigned.

my first serious appeal to the Public. A claim that S. might also have made for *Queen Mab* (1813) and the *Alastor* volume (1816) (see *Longman* 2).

136 *Lucretius*. For Lucretius and his poem *De Rerum Natura* see our note to epigraph 2 of *Queen Mab* (p. 707).

Ashtaroth. The Syrian moon-goddess Ashtoreth, or Astarte; the obscene behaviour of her priests was alluded to by S. in a review of Peacock's *Rhododaphne* (1818) (quoted in *Longman* 2).

unworthy successors of Socrates and Zeno. The Greek successors of Socrates (469–399 BC) and the Stoic philosopher Zeno (*c*.333–262 BC) were considered 'unworthy' because of their background as slaves of Rome and subjects of despotic rule in Asia; S. follows Lucan and other Roman writers in seeing their teachings as tainted by habits of subservience and submission (see *Longman* 2).

The latest . . . footsteps. That is, S. himself.

as many years. That is, in the six years since S.'s expulsion from Oxford on 25 March 1811.

express in the cruelty and malevolence of God. Replaced in *The Revolt of Islam* by 'entertain of the Deity, as injurious to the character of his benevolence', a revision signed by the printer Buchanan McMillan.

137 *The circumstance of which I speak . . . to promote*. S. adds a note: 'The sentiments connected with and characteristic of this circumstance, have no personal reference to the Writer.' This Note alludes to rumours concerning the supposed sexual entanglement of Byron, Claire Clairmont, Mary S. and S.

In the personal conduct of my Hero and Heroine . . . of the multitude. The entire concluding paragraph excised in *The Revolt of Islam*.

Dedication.

Epigraph. From *The Conspiracy of Charles Duke of Byron* (1608), a tragedy by George Chapman (?1599–1634).

Mary —— ——. 'Mary Wollstonecraft Shelley', as originally written, then cancelled (and replaced with dashes), in the notebook draft (*BSM* 8).

l. 3. *Knight of Faery*. One of Mary S.'s pet names for S. was 'Elfin Knight' (*Mary Jnl.* 1. 80).

138 l. 9. *thou Child of love and light*. A reference to Mary S.'s parents, Mary Wollstonecraft and William Godwin.

l. 16. *my lone boat*. See Mary S.'s 'Note on the Revolt of Islam,' in *MWS (1)*: 'The poem was written in his boat, as it floated under the beech-groves of Bisham, or during wanderings in the neighbouring country.'

l. 27. *of tyrants and of foes*. S.'s unhappiness at Eton, which he attended from 1804 to 1810, both with the masters ('tyrants') and with the fagging system (administered by older students, hence 'foes'), was attested to by all who knew him.

l. 38. *forbidden mines of lore*. Such as Godwin's *Political Justice*, first read while at Eton.

139   l. 47. *one*. That is, one person, the beloved.

l. 54. *clog*. Impediment, encumbrance, hindrance.

ll. 58–9. *In thy young wisdom . . . rend in twain*. Mary S. was 16 when she took the initiative and declared her love for the married S.

l. 61. *which . . . breathed*. 'Which' refers to the clouds (of detraction) 'breathed' (in the sense of 'breathed forth') by 'envious slaves', before Mary broke through them like a ray of 'light'.

l. 69. *Poverty*. In part a product of S.'s extravagance and generosity, among others to Godwin, Hunt, and Peacock.

l. 70. *Infamy*. Occasioned in part by the ruling of the Lord Chancellor in March 1817 depriving S. of custody of his two children by Harriet, on grounds of immorality, atheism, and political radicalism.

140   l. 77. *two gentle babes*. William S., born 24 January 1816, and Clara Evelina S., born 2 September 1817. S. omits a first child, a girl, born 22 February 1815 (died 6 March 1815).

l. 86. *Anarch*. Ruler over darkness and chaos (as in *PL* 2. 988 and Pope's *Dunciad* 4. 653), identified here with 'Custom'.

l. 88. *Amphion's*. That is, Amphion's lyre. Amphion, the son of Zeus and Antiope, was a poet and the father of music; his lyre was a gift from Hermes.

l. 90. *Death*. S. had twice been diagnosed with consumption and feared for his life during the time of the poem's composition.

l. 99. *vestal fire*. Vesta was the Roman goddess of the hearth; her flame was thought to bring prosperity to the state.

l. 102. *One*. Mary Wollstonecraft, who died on 10 September 1797, eleven days after giving birth to Mary S.

141   l. 108. *Sire*. William Godwin.

Epigraph. From the tenth Pythian Ode of the Greek lyric poet Pindar (*c*.522–443 BC): 'but among those glories that we of mortality attain to he goes | the whole way. Never on foot or ship could you explore | the marvelous road to the feast of the Hyperboreans' (*The Odes of Pindar*, trans. Richmond Lattimore, Chicago, 1976). The Hyperboreans were a mythic northern people, devoted to Apollo, who lived in a state of blessedness and harmony.

141 *Canto First*. l. 127. *trampled France*. After the defeat at Waterloo and the restoration of the Bourbon monarchy.

142 l. 135. *last wreck*. The Apocalypse (see Revelation 6.12–14).

l. 140. *complicating*. Intimately or intricately combining.   *steep*. Bathe, envelop like a flood.

l. 142. *keep*. Pervade, hold possession of (*Conc.*).

l. 146. *yawn*. A difficult image to visualize; the lightnings emerge from the sky like open or gaping mouths.

l. 156. *Fretted*. Both 'worn away' and 'agitated' (as by a storm or gust of wind).

143 l. 164. *rack*. Clouds, or a mass of cloud, driven before the wind in the upper air.

l. 172. *I could not choose but gaze*. Echoing 'He cannot choose but hear', from Coleridge, 'The Rime of the Ancient Mariner' (l. 18), the source also of 'A speck, a cloud, a shape' (l. 178), describing the distant 'bark' (l. 180), as in the Mariner's first glimpse of the spectre-ship: 'A speck, a mist, a shape, I wist' (l. 153).

l. 193. *An Eagle and a Serpent*. For S.'s use of snake–eagle imagery see *Alastor*, ll. 227–37; classical sources include *Iliad*, 12. 200–7, *Aeneid*, 11. 751–6, and *Met.* 4. 361–4, 714–17 (see *Longman* 2).

144 l. 207. *steadfast eye*. Alone among creatures, according to legend, the eagle is able to look directly into the sun.

l. 209. *clang*. As of armed combatants, but also, as *Longman* 2 points out, drawing on 'clang' as 'the loud harsh resonant cry or scream of certain birds' (*OED* 2).

l. 213. *eager*. Sharp, fierce, keen.

l. 224. *they*. Either 'talons' (l. 223) or 'foes' (l. 219).

145 l. 245. *unprevailing*. Without victor.   *event*. Outcome.

l. 246. *portentous*. Monstrous, ominous, prophetic (a portent or prophecy of the narrative to come, with its visionary rendering or '*beau ideal*' of the French Revolution).

l. 248. *lifeless*. Exhausted (since the serpent is alive at l. 280), taking 'stark,' the next word, as 'motionless' or 'desolate,' rather than 'rigid, stiff (in death)' (*OED* 4).

146 l. 269. *sea-mark*. Mark made by the tide.

l. 283. *immovable*. Fixed (on the Serpent) (*Longman* 2).

l. 290. *alone*. Only.

147 l. 304. *marmoreal*. Marble-like.

l. 325. *A boat of rare device*. 'It was a miracle of rare device, | A sunny pleasure-dome with caves of ice!', Coleridge, 'Kubla Khan', ll. 35–6.

148   ll. 331–3. *the mountains hang . . . we go.* It is hard to see how the mountains can 'hang and frown over' the 'starry deep that gleams below' unless by 'deep' S. means 'sea' (with reflected stars), making the phrase 'A vast and dim expanse' appositional; hence our comma after 'below', an editorial insertion.

l. 345. *urn.* 'Water-vessel, used figuratively for the source of a river or stream' (*Longman* 2).

l. 350. *Genii.* Plural of 'genius,' meaning tutelary spirit of a place, institution, etc.

l. 351. *Nought.* The 'chaos' of l. 353, taking chaos as 'formless void' (*OED* 2), as *Longman* 2 suggests.

l. 355. *jar.* Dissension or strife; also harsh sound, concussion, physical shock.

l. 356. *A blood-red Comet. Longman* 2 suggests an allusion to the red planet, Mars.

l. 359. *flood.* The chaos of the sublunary world.

149   l. 362. *which none may know.* Either 'none may know Power itself, only its "shapes" or manifestations', or 'none may know all Power's "shapes" or manifestations'.

l.368. *He.* The 'Fiend' of l. 363, our 'immortal foe' (l. 367).

l. 377. *In mockery.* Mocking the fact that the names of Good and Evil were misapplied.

l. 378. *own.* 'Yield obedience or submission to' (*OED* 6c).

150   l. 395. *beneath nether skies.* The skies of the underworld or 'hell' (l. 394).

l. 396. *blasting.* Infecting, blighting, as by a curse.

l. 405. *sanguine.* Bloody.

l. 413. *save.* Both preserve (in 'combat') and bring eternal happiness (presumably in contrast to the false 'Paradise' of religion promised after death).

l. 419. *hydra brood.* The Hydra was a mythical snake with poisonous breath and blood and numerous heads (hence 'brood').

151   l. 427. *garbage.* 'Offal of an animal used for food' (*OED* 1) (*Longman* 2).

l. 441. *unnatural.* Since infant sleep is meant to be untroubled by dream (as in line 261). (See *Longman* 2.)

l. 454. *A dying poet.* Recalls the youthful, dying poet of *Alastor.*

152   l. 466. *Hope's deep source.* Conceived of as an 'immortal urn' from which pours 'fresh light' in l. 647 (hence 'flows forth' here).

l. 485. *Morning Star.* The planet Venus.

153   l. 497. *speechless.* Defeating speech (too beautiful to be described).

153 l. 514. *that vast and peopled city*. Recalling Revolutionary Paris, where Mary Wollstonecraft—a spiritual guide for S., like the 'mortal maiden' (l. 505) whose 'strange and awful tale' (l. 334) is being recounted here— lived from late 1792 to 1795.

l. 522. *ruth*. Compassion.

154 l. 525. *others*. For example, as *Longman* 2 suggests, Coleridge and Wordsworth, both of whose poems echo in the following lines; Coleridge's 'France: An Ode' (1798) (stanza 1) in ll. 527–8, and Wordsworth's 'Ode: Intimations of Immortality', ll. 12–15, and 'Tintern Abbey', ll. 5–6, in ll. 530–1 and 533–4, respectively.

155 ll. 550–8. *And swift and swifter . . . far away*. See 'Rime of the Ancient Mariner', part 5, for several resemblances in this stanza, though 'the pole' of l. 553 is more likely the North than the South Pole, given the northern location of the temperate realm of the Hyperboreans (see our note to epigraph, Canto First, p. 727).

l. 568. *vast dome*. Of the heavens.

l. 578. *blosmy*. Blossomy, blooming.

l. 581. *aerial*. Elevated, but also etherial, ideal, imaginary.

156 l. 607. *mild, beautiful, and blind*. Identified in *Longman* 2 as the sightless poets Homer and Milton, indubitably 'Great' (l. 605) and 'beautiful' (as poets).

l. 621. *spherèd stars*. That is, the stars set in the 'hollow hemisphere' (l. 594) of the sky, the 'glorious roof' (l. 586) of the temple.

157 l. 625. *meteors*. Any atmospheric phenomenon, including, as suggested here, marsh gas, the *ignis fatuus* or will-o'-the-wisp.

l. 632. *a Form*. See Leigh Hunt's paraphrase of this episode in his review in the *Examiner* (1 February 1818): 'A magic and obscure circumstance then takes place, the result of which is, that the woman and serpent are seen no more, but that a cloud opens asunder, and a bright and beautiful shape, which seems compounded of both, is beheld sitting on a throne,— a circumstance apparently imitated from Milton' (a reference to *PL* 10. 441–584).

l. 635. *inform*. 'Pervade as a spirit, inspire, animate' (*OED* 2 3b).

l. 649. *one*. Laon, though not named until l. 791.

158 l. 659. *One*. Cythna, though not named until l. 855.

l. 662. *lines*. Rays of light.

Canto Second. l. 676. *Argolis*. A mountainous region in the north-eastern Peloponnesus.

159 ll. 691–2. *had given . . . in the grave*. 'Had given the state's priests, or ministers, power over them by accepting their authority in matters of divine judgement (about the afterlife, the life beyond the grave).'

l. 694. *bane*. Curse, poison.

l. 710. *the light which shows its worth*. Presumably an inner light, given the prevailing darkness; 'its' is 'Earth's' (from 'Earth', l. 703).

l. 716. *A deeper prison and heavier chains*. The constraints and fears of religion.

160 l. 718. *a stern Ruler*. Presumably a figure like Satan.

l. 719. *Terror and Time conflicting*. 'The contending fears of passing time and of punishment after death' (*Longman* 2).

l. 722. *a dark dwelling*. Like Hell.

l. 737. *fanes*. Temples.

l. 744. *polluted*. Sexually ('violated' in cancelled notebook draft: *BSM* 19).

l. 749. *even*. Evening.

161 l. 776. *glorious dead*. The ancient Greeks.

l. 778. *wingèd child*. Hope.

l. 783. *impious trust*. Ironic, since trust in the idol would have been pious before the called-for awakening.

163 l. 822. *his friend*. The most likely real-life model is Thomas Jefferson Hogg (1793–1862), co-author with S. of *The Necessity of Atheism* (1811), for which both were expelled from Oxford. Hogg was 'false' to S. by making advances to his first wife Harriet (in November 1811); the two friends reconciled in 1812, as will Laon and his friend (in Canto 5, stanzas 3–4).

l. 828. *had bled*. Either 'would have bled', taking 'for' as 'in place of,' or 'had bled' (i.e. in sympathy with the false friend), taking 'his own' as the friend's heart.

ll. 835–7. *but I betrayed it not . . . its wisdom blind*. A difficult passage. If 'it' refers to the 'great aim,' as opposed to 'sorrow' (both l. 829), and 'its' means 'sorrow's', then the meaning is something like: 'I did not betray the great aim, but selflessly, out of a love that needed no reciprocation, sought to disperse the clouds that blind, and thus falsify, the supposed wisdom of sorrow.'

l. 847. *I had . . . fair eyes*. Altered in *Revolt of Islam* to 'An orphan with my parents lived, whose eyes'.

l. 848. *lodestars*. Guiding-stars, especially the pole star.

165 l. 884. *sister*. In *Revolt of Islam* 'playmate'.

l. 885. *twelve years old*. Since the main public events in the poem are said (in Canto 4, l. 1509) to take place in seven years' time, Cythna will become a revolutionary at age 19, Mary S.'s age at the time of the poem's composition (see *Longman* 2).

l. 888. *cells*. Caves.

ll. 895–6. *It had . . . my toil*. 'The time spent with Cythna was not wasted, since it left me with a memory ("memorial") which braced ("strung") me to my struggle ("toil").'

165 l. 904. *pauses.* Cadences.

l. 912. *secret bird.* The nightingale (often heard but not seen, as in Keats's 'Ode to a Nightingale').

166 ll. 915–6. *strong . . . to be.* The meaning seems to be: '[the hymns are] more than capable of rousing a passion for freedom in others, the very passion that inspired me to compose them in the first place.'

ll. 937–45. *And this beloved child . . . had learned to trace.* 'One is reminded . . . of the atmosphere of Shelley's childhood at Field Place, the community of sympathy the poet sought to create for himself and his imaginative creations in the audience composed of his four younger sisters, especially Elizabeth, his intimate companion and poetical collaborator' (*Sperry*, p. 48).

168 l. 982. *coldly felt.* That is, by me (Laon).

l. 986. *mewed.* Shut up, confined, enclosed.

l. 992. *flushed o'er her.* Suffused her mind as a blush suffuses the cheek.

l. 1006. *The Golden City.* See note on the poem's title.

170 ll. 1048–52. *Can they . . . of woman.* 'Can men who oppress their wives ever be bold enough to overcome their own oppressors? The wives of such men will blight the home and the lives of their children, generating all the old crimes and religious frauds.'

171 l. 1081. *dare nor tremble.* 'Dare without trembling' (*Longman* 2).

From *Canto Sixth.* ll. 2578–9. *The autumnal winds . . . that recess.* After a prolonged and painful separation, and the revolution's seeming defeat, Laon and Cythna are reunited in a scene of sexual consummation. The transcendent as well as earthly nature of this consummation is signalled by the timeless character of its removed and paradisial mountain setting, in a hidden bower or 'recess | Which seasons none disturbed', a prefiguring of the bliss that awaits them after death.

172 l. 2581. *parasites.* Climbing plants, like ivy (mentioned in stanza 27).

l. 2585. *Whose.* Refers less to the 'blooms' of the 'flowering parasites' of l. 2581 (Longman 2) than to 'The wandering wind' of l. 2584.

l. 2596. *To the pure all things are pure!* A quotation from St Paul's Epistle to Titus, 1: 15.

l. 2610. *common blood.* In *Revolt of Islam* 'blood itself'.

l. 2612. *our very names.* In honour of her lost brother, Cythna adopted the name 'Laone' when she became a revolutionary.

173 l. 2617. *A wandering Meteor.* See note to l. 625.

l. 2620. *its blue hair.* That of the 'Meteor', as light from a flickering blue flame.

l. 2624. *ties.* 'Bands, plaits' (*Conc.*).

ll. 2633-4. *one interval | Made still.* Stopped for a moment.

174 l. 2649. *below.* On earth.

l. 2659. *It is the shadow.* Of the spirit. See the opening lines of 'Hymn to Intellectual Beauty': 'The awful shadow of some unseen Power | Floats though unseen amongst us.'

From *Canto Seventh.* l. 3091. *We live in our own world.* Cythna has been recounting her sufferings to Laon, which parallel Laon's own sufferings in the first half of the poem. Now she turns to the hopes that led her back to sanity and the renewed fight for liberty.

l. 3093. *Aye.* Ever, always.

l. 3095. *Such power.* The power to 'cast a lustre on' or illuminate departed hopes (thus gathering courage from them), rather than be cast down by ('darkened with') them (see *Longman* 2).

175 l. 3104. *One mind.* Revealed to Cythna by the exploration of her own mind; for ll. 3104-5 as a whole, see Coleridge, 'The Eolian Harp' (1795): 'O the one life within us and abroad, | Which meets all motion and becomes its soul' (ll. 26-7), lines added in a revised version of 1817.

ll. 3113-14. *truths which once . . . in old Crotona.* Perhaps alluding to the Pythagorean belief that number lay at the heart of material reality. Pythagoras lived and taught in Croton, in southern Italy, in the sixth century BC.

176 l. 3147. *Even.* Namely.

l. 3156. *there.* In the sea-cave, a sort of prison, to which Cythna was transported (see ll. 2929-30) after the most distressing of the experiences she recounts in this Canto, her rape (and impregnation) by the tyrant Othman.

l. 3160. *Scythian.* Scythia was an ancient region extending over most of European and Asiatic Russia.

177 From *Canto Eighth.* l. 3226. *What dream ye?* Cythna recalls how, as she sailed back to the City of Gold, she addressed the mariners who rescued her from imprisonment in the sea-cave at the end of Canto Seventh.

l. 3234. *that God.* In *Revolt of Islam* 'some Power', just as the next line's 'What then is God?' becomes 'What is that Power?'

178 l. 3251. *God has appointed Death.* 'That Power has chosen death' in *Revolt of Islam*; in next line 'his will' becomes 'it's [*sic*] laws.'

ll. 3253-5. *Men say . . . a rod.* 'Men say that they themselves have heard and seen, | Or known from others who have known such things, | A Shade, a Form, which Earth and Heaven between | Wields an invisible rod', in *Revolt of Islam.*

l. 3262. *that God.* In *Revolt of Islam* 'this Power'.

l. 3264. *And his red hell's undying snakes among.* 'And deepest hell, and deathless snakes among' in *Revolt of Islam*; where, in the next line, 'he' becomes 'is'.

179   l. 3275. *rests thereon.* That is, on opinion.

l. 3297. *To weep for crime.* But not to seek revenge, even for the blood of one's dearest friend.

180   ll. 3309–10. *For it is said . . . is made.* 'And as one Power rules both high and low, | So man is made . . .' in *Revolt of Islam*.

ll. 3330–3. *well ye know . . . to the oppressors flow.* 'You understand women because in oppressing them you also feel woe, the woe any oppressor feels when faced with the suffering of one he oppresses' (see also gloss in *Longman* 2).

181   l. 3361. *one human heart.* See Wordsworth, 'The Old Cumberland Beggar' (1800): 'That we have all of us one human heart' (l. 146).

l. 3368. *they.* Humankind (from l. 3366).

182   l. 3386. *Amphisbaena.* A mythic serpent, with a head at either end.

From *Canto Ninth.* l. 3649. *The blasts of autumn.* Cythna, addressing Laon, prophesies change and renewal, despite the collapse of the Revolution in the immediately preceding stanzas.

183   l. 3670. *germs.* Seeds.

l. 3674. *sanguine.* Bloody.

184   ll. 3688–91. *Spring comes, though we must pass . . . a broad sunrise.* 'Though we will not live to see the renewal of liberty for which we fought, our deaths presage that renewal, like mountain shadow dispersed by the coming sun' (see also gloss in *Longman* 2).

l. 3698. *thine own heart . . . a paradise.* Cythna advises Laon to look within, to the paradise of his own renovated consciousness, for a vision of the external spring or new age they may not live to see.

ll. 3708–11. *Necessity . . . divided never!* For S.'s views on the doctrine of necessity see *Queen Mab* 6. 146–238. In his lengthy Note on this passage (omitted in our edition), S. discusses the relation of necessity to liberty, morality and divinity, drawing on the writings of Hume, Holbach and Godwin. The Note does not, as here, suggest that good inevitably begets good (or bad bad), a view *Locock* and others trace to Aeschylus' *Agamemnon*, which S. was reading in late July 1817 (see *Longman* 2).

l. 3714. *prevailing Sages.* Those whose ideas have prevailed.

187   ll. 3788–91. *Fair star . . . its thousand eyes.* A loose translation of an epigram from Plato which Mary S. and S. cite as derived from the *Apologia* of Apuleius, a second-century AD rhetorician; also found in a passage marked by S. in *Lives of the Philosophers* by Diogenes Laertius, who lived in the third century AD. The epigram exists in a slightly different form in a fair-copy transcript by Mary S. (see *Longman* 1, pp. 581–2).

From *Canto Tenth.* l. 3937. *Day after day.* The Revolution has collapsed and in this extract the City of Gold and its environs suffer terribly under the renewed tyranny.

l. 3945. *Lethe's.* Lethe is the river of forgetfulness in Hades.

188   l. 3964. *blue Plague.* A reference to the blue spots commonly associated with plague.

l. 3980. *blains.* Blisters, pustules, swellings.

l. 3990. *Almighty God.* In *Revolt of Islam* 'the avenging Power'.

189   l. 3999. *Like forms . . . to agony.* An allusion to the Pygmalion story (see Ovid, *Met.* 10. 243–97).

ll. 4003–8. *Famine can smile . . . her prey.* A difficult passage, the main thrust of which seems to be that Plague, likened to a winged wolf, cannot be evaded by the rich or titled ('the throne'), whereas famine, likened to a house-dog (also a grey-haired courtier), can be, by being 'fed'. That Plague is winged and feeds on garbage ('offal', see note to l. 427) conforms to the theory that the disease originates from rotting meat and is carried on the wind.

l. 4010. *dight.* Clothed.

l. 4024. *Of their Amighty God, the armies wind.* 'The many-tongued and endless armies wind' in *Revolt of Islam*.

190   l. 4036. *O God Almighty!* 'O King of Glory' in *Revolt of Islam*.

l. 4055. *their own hearts' image.* A projection of their fears and inadequacies, like the 'Form' worshipped by the 'sophist' of ll. 3244–5, 'from his own soul upthrown.'

l. 4062. *God.* Lower-case 'god' in *Revolt of Islam*.

191   ll. 4063–4. *And Oromaze . . . and Foh.* Oromaze is the principle of Good in the dualistic theology of the Zoroastrians; 'Christ' becomes 'Joshua' (the Hebrew for Jesus, the learned would know) in *Revolt of Islam*; Brahm is Brahma, creator of the universe in the Hindu religion; Zerdusht is Zoroaster, founder of Zoroastrianism. For 'Foh' see our note to *Queen Mab*, 7. 30 (p. 711).

l. 4072. *He was a Christian Priest.* ''Twas an Iberian Priest' in *Revolt of Islam*; as, later, 'rebel Atheists' (l. 4075) and 'God' (l. 4080) become 'unbelievers' and 'Heaven'.

ll. 4094–5. *His cradled . . . creed.* 'The expiation, and the sacrifice, | That, though detested, Islam's kindred creed' in *Revolt of Islam*.

192   l. 4107. *And thrones . . . in God.* 'And kingly thrones, which rest on faith' in *Revolt of Islam*.

l. 4115. *the twain.* Laon and Cythna.

193   l. 4138. *God.* 'Heaven' in *Revolt of Islam*.

l. 4142. *speechless.* Unexpressed (his pride, that is, as opposed to his curses).

193 From *Canto Twelfth*. l. 4666. *When the consuming flames . . . round*. The speaker is Cythna's child, offspring of her rape by Othman, the tyrant ruler of the Golden City. She is recounting to Laon and Cythna (in the present of the poem, where they have been reunited in the Temple of the Spirit) what happened to her after their immolation.

l. 4674. *death-mark*. A blain or mark of plague (see l. 3980 and note).

194 l. 4705. *Atheists*. Laon and Cythna, whose calm death has helped to banish fear of tyranny, both political and religious; changed to 'unbelievers' ('In pain and fire have unbelievers gone') in *Revolt of Islam*.

l. 4714. *How Atheists . . . can die*. 'How those who love, yet fear not, dare to die' in *Revolt of Islam*.

195 l. 4739. *Between a chasm . . . riven*. See Coleridge, 'Kubla Khan', ll. 12–13: 'But oh! that deep romantic chasm which slanted | Down the green hill athwart a cedarn cover!'

196 l. 4762. *Cyclopean piles*. Huge buildings constructed by the Cyclops, giant figures famed as workmen of Hephaestus, the Greek god of fire and crafts.

ll. 4783–4. *Three days and nights . . . delightful hours*. The passage of days is calculated subjectively, since in their journey through celestial realms clock and calendar time do not apply.

197 l. 4799. *sunbows*. Rainbows formed by sun on spray or mist.

l. 4805. *on a line*. 'On one line' in both printed versions; frequently altered, as here, on grounds of meaning and metrical consistency (with the previous line).

l. 4813. *sphere*. See note to line 621.

l. 4818. *The charmèd boat . . . found*. Alludes to *FQ* 1.12.1, in which the poem is likened to a 'feeble barke'. The Canto opens: 'Behold I see the haven nigh at hand.' (This and subsequent references to *FQ* cite book, canto, and stanza.)

198 *Ozymandias*. Composed late 1817, as S.'s contribution to a competition with Horace Smith (see note to l. 250 of 'Letter to Maria Gisborne', p. 786). Smith visited S. in Marlow for two nights after Christmas 1817. First published in the *Examiner*, 11 January 1818, under the pseudonymn 'Glirastes', a jokey Latin and Greek compound meaning 'Dormouse lover' ('Dormouse' being one of S.'s pet names for Mary S.). 'Ozymandias' is the Greek name for Pharaoh Ramses II (reigned 1279–1213 BC), renowned as a model ruler, and for erecting many buildings and statues during his reign. No single source inspires the poem, though behind a range of possible sources lies the description of a monument to 'Osymandias' (the conventional spelling) quoted in the *Library of History* (*c*.60 BC to 30 BC), a forty-volume world history by the Greek Sicilian historian Diodorus Siculus. Our text is from *Rosalind and Helen* (1819), supplemented in places by S.'s pointing and capitalization in a careful fair copy in the Bodleian (*BSM* 3).

l. 8. *The hand*. The sculptor's.   *mocked*. Imitated, perhaps also derided.   *heart*. Ozymandias'.

Lines Written among the Euganean Hills. Begun in October 1818 while S. was staying in Byron's summer villa, 'I Cappucini', in the medieval fortress town of Este in the Euganean Hills, 40 miles south-west of Venice. Posted to Charles Ollier in December 1818 or January 1819 for inclusion in *Rosalind and Helen* (May 1819). 'Euganean' is pronounced in the English rather than Italian manner, with a stress on the third syllable. Our copy-text is *Rosalind and Helen* (1819) corrected, for ll. 56–112, from Huntington Library MS HM331 (*MYR: Shelley* 3) and, for ll. 165–205, from Tinker Library MS, Yale University (*MYR: Shelley* 8).

l. 2. *In the deep wide sea of Misery*. A condensed echo, the first of several, of Coleridge's 'Rime of the Ancient Mariner' (ll. 233–5); see also ll. 100–3, 238–40.

199 l. 34. *wreak*. Cause or effect.

l. 54. *sea-mews*. Seagulls.

200 ll. 45–65. *On the beach . . . nor murmurs not*. This passage, with its disturbing metaphor of the 'mariner, worn and wan' (l. 3) drifting towards 'the haven of the grave' (l. 26), has a suggestive power, but eludes biographical elucidation (though see *Norton*, pp. 582–4 for an allegorical interpretation). *Chernaik* quotes Sophocles' *Oedipus at Colonus* as a possible source: 'Think of some shore in the north the | Concussive waves make stream | This way and that in the gales of winter: | It is like that with him: | The wild wrack breaking over him | From head to foot, and coming on forever' (ll. 1239–44); *Chernaik* quotes from *The Complete Greek Tragedies*, ed. Grene and Lattimore, vol. 3.

l. 97. *Amphitrite's*. The daughter of Oceanus (the 'sire' of the next line) and wife of Poseidon, from Greek mythology.

201 ll. 111–14. *As the flames . . . Apollo spoke of old*. A reference to the Temple of Delphi, where there were sacrifices to the oracle of Apollo, god of light, prophecy, and art.

l. 117. *a darker day*. Once-conquering Venice had itself been conquered by Napoleonic France (1797); then ceded by France to Austria (1798); then retaken by France after the Battle of Austerlitz (1806); then returned to Austrian rule after Waterloo (1815).

l. 123. *slave of slaves*. S. means that Austria is the very epitome of tyranny, hence enslaved by its need to dominate. The reversal, whereby 'slave' is used of the 'tyrant', accords with S.'s sense that tyranny is a form of slavery.

202 l. 152. *Celtic Anarch's hold*. Refers to Austria's rule over Venice; 'Celtic' (pronounced 'Keltic') means northern or non-Mediterranean in this context; 'Anarch' means an author or agent of chaos (see *PL* 2. 988).

l. 174. *Swan*. Lord Byron, who had lived in and around Venice since 1816; swans were sacred to Apollo, associated with art and prophecy.

202 l. 177. *evil dreams.* The prurient rumour and scandal that drove Byron from England after his separation from his wife.

203 ll. 178–83. *and Ocean . . . terror.* Alludes to Byron's concluding apostrophe to the ocean in *Childe Harold*, canto 4, stanzas 179–84 (1817).

l. 195. *Scamander's.* Chief river of the Trojan plain, personified as a god in Homer's *Iliad*, where it fights and discomforts Achilles.

l. 200. *Petrarch's urn.* The tomb and remains of Francesco Petrarch (1304–74) were located in the village of Arqua, near Este, in the Euganean Hills, where the poet and humanist spent his last years.

204 l. 219. *In the garner of his foe.* The peasant's harvest is gathered for the Austrian overlord (the 'Celt' of l. 223); a 'garner' is a granary or storehouse.

l. 228. *foison.* Plentiful harvest.

ll. 238–48. *Son and Mother . . . Austrian.* For Sin and Death see *PL* 2; their dice game recalls Coleridge's 'Rime of the Ancient Mariner' (ll. 196–7); 'Ezzelin' is Ezzelino da Romano, tyrannical ruler ('Vice-Emperor' is partly a pun) of Padua, 'won' by death in 1259, after the death of his own protector, Emperor Frederick II ('the Mighty Austrian').

l. 257. *Padua.* Seat of one of Europe's oldest universities, founded in the eleventh century.

205 l. 258. *meteor.* Here with the properties of both shooting star and *ignis fatuus* or will-o'-the-wisp.

ll. 269–79. *As the Norway woodman . . . down in fear. Longman* 2 cites Letter 15 of Mary Wollstonecraft's *Letters Written . . . in Sweden, Norway, and Denmark* (1796) which describes a raging forest fire near Christiania (Oslo) begun after a sudden rising of the wind spread sparks from smaller fires set by farmers burning off 'roots of trees, stalks of beans, &c.'.

206 l. 323. *that one star.* Hesperus, the evening star (Venus).

207 l. 356. *The polluting multitude.* Those who 'must reap the things they sow' (l. 231).

l. 361. *heaves;. Longman* 2 substitute a comma for a semi-colon after 'heaves', to ensure that 'And the love' (l. 366) is understood to depend on 'subdued' (l. 357) rather than 'supplies' (l. 364), arguing that the latter reading 'would make the all-embracing love merely intermittent'. But love can be understood as implicit in the subduing influence of clime, winds, and leaves.

l. 371. *sprite.* Spirit or being.

ll. 352–73. *We may live . . . again.* The 'Paradise' S. imagines in the poem's concluding lines recalls Prospero's island in *The Tempest.*

208 *The Two Spirits—An Allegory.* Probably written in 1818, first published in *PP*. The only authoritative manuscript for this lyric is a rough draft in the Bodleian (*BSM* 18) (a later transcription by Mary S. in the Bodleian (*BSM* 2) is based on this manuscript), and the poem, an open-ended debate between an ardent, hopeful perspective and one that is fearful and admonitory, cannot be regarded as finished. Above and below the title S. wrote and cancelled the lines: 'Two genii stood before me in a dream | Seest [?] thou not the shades of even'; above those cancelled lines are the words: 'The good die first', the opening of the lines from Wordsworth's *Excursion* used as an epigraph for *Alastor*.

l. 1. *O.* Cancelled in the draft. We have kept for the metre; *Longman* 2 discards.

l. 3. *A.* Cancelled in the draft. 'Shadow' without an article is distinctly unusual; the 's' is not capitalized.

l. 6. *winds and beams.* No verb follows the phrase in the draft.

ll. 9–10. *The . . . night.—.* Punctuation as in draft; other editors point after l. 9, setting it off as a separate unit of sense. S.'s meaning includes: 'There is light—the light of the stars—should I venture into the night.'

l. 18. *Eclipse.* Written above 'The hail' (cancelled) and 'Hail' (uncancelled) in the draft.

l. 21. *And swift.* The start of this line is hard to decipher; the reading adopted is speculative.

209 l. 37. *languid.* Mary S.'s reading, and adopted here, but see *Longman* 2 which reads 'leagued'; in the draft the word seems to begin 'lea'.

Stanzas Written in Dejection—December 1818, near Naples. Composed in 1818, first published in *PP*. There is a rough draft in the Bodleian (*BSM* 15) and two fair copies in S.'s hand, one in the Pierpont Morgan Library (MA 406; *MYR: Shelley* 5) and one in the Bodleian (*BSM* 21). Our copy-text is the Bodleian fair copy, part of a booklet of S.'s 'saddest verses' (*L* 2. 246) sent to Ollier in November 1820. The poem emerges from a period of personal unhappiness for S. ('I have neither good health or spirits just now', he wrote to Leigh Hunt in December 1818; *L* 2. 68). Clara, his and Mary S.'s daughter, had died in September 1818. A further and possibly related cause of unhappiness was the mysterious case of S.'s 'Neapolitan charge' (*L* 2. 211), Elena Adelaide (who died in June 1820, not in the Shelleys' care). The baby, entered as S.'s and Mary's in the city's records, was not their child; it seems unlikely that S. was the father, and the child may have been adopted by him to comfort Mary in her loss. S. was also depressed by an attack on him (that did not name him) in a review in the *Quarterly Review* of Hunt's *Foliage* (see *L* 2. 66). The poem is written in modified Spenserian stanzas, and is influenced by Wordsworth's 'Resolution and Independence' and 'Ode: Intimations of Immortality' and Coleridge's 'Dejection: An Ode'.

ll. 10, 12. *I see.* See Coleridge, 'Dejection: An Ode', l. 38: 'I see, not feel, how beautiful they are!'

209   l. 10. *untrampled*. Cannot be walked upon (*Conc.*).

210   l. 22. *The sage*. S. is unspecific, but he may have Socrates in mind.

l. 27. *that cup*. A biblical metaphor for experience, often of suffering, as in Matthew 26: 39: 'O my Father, if it be possible, let this cup pass from me.'

l. 40. *this untimely moan*. In the draft S. replaced 'this' with 'such', but he returned to 'this' in both fair copies.

Sonnet ('Lift not the painted veil'). The poem's date of composition is uncertain, though likely to be between 1818 and 1819, possibly with later revisions (Mary S. includes it among 'Poems Written in 1818'). There is a draft in the Bodleian (*BSM* 18) and a fair copy (in S.'s hand) in the Pierpont Morgan Library (MA 406; *MYR: Shelley* 5). This fair copy differs verbally from the text of the poem's first publication, in *PP* (1824). In turn, the text in *PP* differs from that in *MWS (1)*. Our copy-text is based on *MWS (1)* since, as *Longman* 2 argues, 'this text probably derives from S.'s own best revised version'. Some punctuation has been modified in the light of the Morgan text. The poem inverts the usual pattern of the Petrarchan sonnet by placing the sestet before the octave.

l. 1. *painted veil*. The veil image suggests Plato, but no ideal world of forms rewards the questor.

211   l. 6. *Their . . . drear*. In *PP*, the line reads: 'The shadows, which the world calls substance, there.'

l. 13. *Upon . . . strove*. In the fair copy, the line reads: 'Cast on this gloomy world—a thing which strove'.

l. 14. *the Preacher*. The speaker in Ecclesiastes, who asserts that all is vanity.

212   *Julian and Maddalo*. Probably begun in September 1818 when S. was staying at Este and finished in 1819: a fair copy in S.'s hand in the Pierpont Morgan Library (MA 974; *MYR: Shelley* 8), our copy-text, was sent on 15 August 1819 to Hunt to give to Ollier for publication. In the event, the poem was not published until its appearance in *PP*. A draft exists in the Bodleian (*BSM* 15), which does not include 150 lines of the final version. The missing lines are from the Maniac's soliloquy. The poem was sparked into being by S.'s meeting with Byron in Venice in late August 1818 (see *L* 2. 36–7). Claire Clairmont wished to see Allegra, her daughter by Byron, and S. was negotiating with Byron on Claire's behalf. The two poets rode together on the Lido, discussing personal matters and literary topics, including the fourth canto of *Childe Harold*, stanzas of which Byron recited. S. would a few months later deplore the pessimistic tone of the canto, but he singled out the address to the Ocean at the close as proof that Byron was 'a great poet' (*L* 2. 58). Aspects of the Maniac's soliloquy may draw on S.'s and Mary's marital difficulties following the deaths of their children, Clara (in September 1818) and

William (in June 1819). The poem bears the impress of S.'s interest in the Italian poet, Torquato Tasso (1544–95), whose prison in Ferrara he visited in November 1818 and whose handwriting he analysed as 'the symbol of an intense & earnest mind exceeding at times its own depth' (*L* 2. 47); earlier in 1818 he told Peacock that he intended to write 'a tragedy on the subject of Tasso's madness' (*L* 2. 8). S. was conscious of *Julian and Maddalo* as written in a style 'quite opposed to the idealism' (*L* 2. 196) of *Prometheus Unbound*, and felt that it had something in common with Leigh Hunt's post-Wordsworthian attempts to 'express', in S.'s words to Hunt about *Julian and Maddalo*, 'the actual way in which people talk with each other whom education and a certain refinement of sentiment have placed above the use of vulgar idioms' (*L* 2. 108). S. goes on in the same letter to point out that vulgarity is not class-specific.

Epigraph. From Virgil's *Eclogues*, 10, translated at greater length (including these lines) by S. in June 1818 (see *Longman* 2 for a text).

[Preface]. *concentered.* Packed closely as round a centre (*OED* 2). See Byron, *Prometheus*, l. 57: 'Its own concentered recompense'.

Count Maddalo ... countries. Maddalo (stress on the first syllable) is modelled on Byron; S.'s description can be paralleled with comments he makes in letters about Byron.

213 *Julian ... serious.* Julian is based on S. himself. The name may allude, given Julian's 'heterodox opinions', to Julian the Apostate; Byron wrote an unfinished poem entitled 'Julian'.

the Maniac. The word 'Maniac' suggests mental derangement. S., who had written to Hunt that 'two of the characters [in the poem] you will recognize', remarked in the same letter that the third character (evidently the Maniac) was 'also in some degree a painting from nature, but, with respect to time and place, ideal' (*L* 2. 108).

l. 2. *bank of land.* The Lido.

l. 3. *Adria.* The Adriatic.

l. 17. *boundless.* A word that would suggest for S.'s contemporaries experence of the sublime: see Hugh Blair: 'Remove all bounds from any object, and you presently render it sublime,' quoted from Andrew Ashfield and Peter de Bolla (eds.), *The Sublime: A Reader in British Eighteenth-Century Aesthetic Theory* (Cambridge, 1996), 214.

l. 23. *the blue heavens were bare.* See Wordsworth, 'Ode: Intimations of Immortality', ll. 12–13: 'The moon doth with delight | Look round her when the heavens are bare'.

l. 25. *sound like delight.* See Coleridge, 'The Eolian Harp', l. 28: 'A light in sound, a sound-like power in light'.

214 ll. 39–45. *'twas forlorn ... achieve.* See *PL* 2. 555–61, where the fallen angels' debate, though 'sweet', leaves them 'in wandering mazes lost'.

214   l. 46. *descanted.* Talked lengthily and freely.

ll. 63–4. *As those . . . pilgrimage.* See *PL* 12. 1–2: 'As one who in his journey bates at noon, | Though bent on speed': a simile used of the Archangel Michael.

l. 67. *hoar.* Greyish-white.

215   l. 92. *Like fabrics . . . Heaven.* See *The Tempest,* 4. 1. 151: 'And like the baseless fabric of this vision'.

l. 95. *gondolieri.* Rowers of the gondola.

ll. 102–4. *hung . . . swung . . . tongue.* A triplet, reinforcing the impact of the bell's sound.

l. 107. *Shall be.* Maddalo is not simply pointing out a madhouse; he is also suggesting that what they observe might be interpreted as if it were a madhouse.

216   ll. 117–18. *if you can't swim . . . Providence.* S. could not swim, as Byron knew from their boat-trip round Lake Geneva in 1816: Byron admired S.'s composure and refusal to accept help when their boat was in danger of being capsized.

l. 143. *his child.* Based on Byron's daughter, Allegra, who died in 1822 at the age of 5.

217   l. 162. *saws.* Proverbial sayings, maxims.

l. 164. *a teachless nature.* A nature that cannot be taught the 'faith' (l. 165) on which Julian prides himself.

ll. 188–9. *those kings . . . blind.* Julian alludes to philosophers, such as Plato, Aristotle, and Socrates, who lived and thought before Christianity imposed, as he sees it, fetters on free thought.

ll. 190–1. *And those . . . religion.* Either 'Those who explain their compassion for others in religious terms', or 'Those whose capacity to feel for others is "as religion"'' (quoted phrase is from the draft).

218   l. 204. *"soul of goodness".* Julian quotes from *Henry V,* 4. 1. 4–5: 'There is some soul of goodness in things evil, | Would men observingly distil it out.'

l. 211. *spoke.* The only unrhymed line in the poem.

219   l. 244. *humourist.* Both 'subject to humours' and 'capable of humour' (see *Longman* 2).

ll. 263–5. *None . . . reverse.* Maddalo says that the Maniac has the same claim on him that he would have on 'all mankind', were he reduced to the Maniac's condition.

220   l. 282. *apart—.* The dash (the copy-text punctuation) connects the simile in ll. 283–4 to the account of the Maniac's grief-stricken smiling in ll. 281–2, even as that simile looks ahead to ll. 284–6 (see *Longman* 2).

l. 301. *jade.* Inferior or worn-out horse.

221 l. 337. *my spirit's mate*. There has been debate about whether this woman is the same as the figure addressed in ll. 384–5.

l. 350. *subdued*. See Shakespeare's Sonnet 111, ll. 6–7: 'And almost thence my nature is subdued | To what it works in, like the dyer's hand'.

222 l. 375. *red scaffold . . . bends*. The line alludes to execution and suggests the Maniac's fear of state punishment.

l. 384. *death's dedicated bride*. The draft identifies this figure as Laura, Tasso's beloved (see *BSM* 15).

223 l. 397. *I am left alone—*. The series of asterisks (*x*'s in the manuscript) following this line here and elsewhere serves to point up the 'unconnected' nature of the Maniac's 'exclamations' (Preface).

l. 405. *I loved . . . overthrow*. See Byron, '[Epistle to Augusta]', ll. 23–4: 'I have been cunning in mine overthrow | The careful pilot of my proper woe'.

ll. 416–18. *As the slow . . . ever-moving*. See *Othello*, 4. 2. 55–7: 'to make me | The fixed figure for the time of scorn | To point his slow and moving finger at'.

224 l. 433. *cearedst*. Embalmed; shut up. (We have kept S.'s spelling, rather than alter it to 'ceredst', because of the play on 'sear' it accommodates.)

l. 450. *The else unfelt oppressions of this earth*. See Ecclesiastes 4: 1: 'all the oppressions that are done under the sun'.

225 l. 476. *And from my pen*. The Maniac depicts himself as writing.

l. 499. *that sweet sleep*. Death.

228 l. 597. '*That*. We follow the copy-text in placing the opening quotation-mark at this point; the 'my' of the next line refers to Julian and not the speaker (Maddalo's daughter).

l. 614. *ceared*. See note to l. 433.

229 *Prometheus Unbound*. Composed at intervals between August or September 1818 and mid-1820; published by Charles Ollier in 1820, probably in August, as the title-poem of *Prometheus Unbound, with Other Poems*. S., who had not, despite his wishes, been sent proofs, regretted that 'the errors of the press' were 'so numerous' (*L* 2. 246). In the absence of Mary S.'s press transcript, we have taken the printed edition of 1820 as our copy-text, but have departed from it on numerous occasions after consulting Mary S.'s 1839 editions (incorporating some of S.'s 'errata' (*L* 2. 246)), the poet's fair copy in the Bodleian (*BSM* 9), and drafts in the Bodleian (*BSM* 18). The poem remodels genres and traditions to articulate S.'s most original and sublime imagining of freedom. Act 1 contains allusions to Aeschylus' *Prometheus Bound* and Milton's *PL*, as it depicts Prometheus overcoming his hatred for Jupiter while resisting the Furies' temptations to despair; subsequently the Spirits of the Human Mind offer visions of a more hopeful kind. Act 2 is

full of intimations of a world heading towards desired transformation. To help activate this change, Asia (the partner of Prometheus) and Panthea, her sister, descend into the Cave of Demogorgon. Demogorgon answers Asia's questions about the origin of evil and the nature of Jupiter in enigmatic ways, which serve to liberate her from needing explanations about ultimate reality. The 'destined hour' (2. 4. 128) arrives, and the act concludes with lyrics that depict Asia as an indefinable principle of beauty embarking on a voyage 'to a diviner day' (2. 5. 103). Act 3 depicts the overthrow of Jupiter, the freeing of Prometheus, the reuniting of the hero and Asia, and, often by descriptions that negate the negations of things as they are, change for the better among human beings. Act 4 evokes the cosmic dimension of the alteration imagined by the poem and builds on the analogy between love and forms of energy which S. articulates throughout.

229 *Lyrical Drama*. Suggests the work's mixture and reworking of genres.

Epigraph. 'Do you hear this, Amphiaraus, in your home under the earth?': a line from a lost play by Aeschylus (*Epigoni*) extant in Cicero's *Tusculan Disputations*. In a notebook (*BSM* 15) S. quotes the line below the words 'To the Ghost of Aeschylus'.

Preface. The 'Prometheus Unbound' . . . Hercules. S. alludes to a lost play of Aeschylus.

230 *One word is due*. The five paragraphs beginning here were added after S. read in October 1819 an adverse review of *The Revolt of Islam* (*Laon and Cythna*) in the *Quarterly Review*, attacking him for his heterodox 'system' and accusing him of being 'an unsparing imitator' who 'draws largely on the rich stores' of Wordsworth's poetry.

232 *a Scotch Philosopher*. Robert Forsyth, quoted from his *The Principles of Moral Science* (1805).

'a passion . . . world'. See Thomas Love Peacock's humorous portrait of S. as Scythrop Glowry in *Nightmare Abbey* (1818); Scythrop 'became troubled with the passion for reforming the world' (ch. 2).

Paley. William Paley (1743–1805), author of *The Principles of Moral and Political Philosophy*, a book disliked by S. (see *L* 1. 200).

Malthus. Thomas Malthus (1766–1834) argued, against Godwin and other advocates of human perfectibility, that population increase outstripped food supply and that, therefore, it needed checks.

233 *Act 1. Stage direction*. S. shifts the scene from the Caucasus mountains in Georgia to the Indian Caucasus, supposedly the place where civilization originated.

PROMETHEUS. In Greek mythology, one of the Titans, who gave men fire and was punished by Jupiter for withholding from him a secret (that the offspring of any marriage between Jupiter and Thetis would lead to a son who would be greater than his father).

l. 1. *Monarch*. Jupiter.　　　　*Daemons*. In Plato's *Symposium*, beings intermediary between the divine and the mortal.

l. 2. *One*. Prometheus. *Longman* 2 offers Demogorgon as another possibility.

l. 6. *knee-worship*. See *PL* 5. 782 ('Knee-tribute').

l. 7. *hecatombs*. Large sacrifices.

l. 9. *eyeless in hate*. See Milton's *Samson Agonistes*, l. 41: 'Eyeless in Gaza'. That the phrase goes with 'thou' (l. 10), but might also refer backwards to 'me' (l. 9), has a psychological and thematic appropriateness.

l. 20. *wall . . . mountain*. See *Prometheus Bound*, l. 15: 'this bitter, bleak ravine'.

234 ll. 44–7. *And yet to me . . . east*. See *Prometheus Bound*, ll. 23–5: 'Glad you will be to see the night | Cloaking the day with her dark spangled robe; and glad | Again when the sun's warmth scatters the frost at dawn.' S. departs from Aeschylus by having Prometheus voice his trust in an eventual overthrow of tyranny.

ll. 53–9. *Disdain? . . . recall*. Records a pivotal change in the hero, from hatred of Jupiter to pity for him.

l. 59. *recall*. The verb brings into play two meanings, 'remember' and 'revoke'.

235 ll. 82–3. *I had clothed . . . not their own*. Colour is produced by light; it is not an inherent property of material objects.

236 ll. 99–102. *By such dread words . . . blood*. Suggestive of the Crucifixion. See Luke 23: 44–6.

l. 121. *frore*. Frozen.

237 l. 135. *inorganic*. 'Not furnished with or acting by bodily or material organs' (*OED* 2, which cites this usage). Prometheus cannot trace the voice he hears to a bodily source.

l. 137. *And love*. 'And lovest'.

l. 141. *wheel of pain*. Both Ixion's wheel and the earth's axis.

238 l. 170. *Blue thistles*. Blue is often linked with disease in S. (See 'Blue Plague' in *Laon and Cythna*, 10. 20.)

l. 178. *contagion*. Here 'communication of disease', but the word can have good as well as bad connotations in S. (see 2. 3. 10 below).

l. 192. *Zoroaster*. Persian founder (also known as Zarathustra) of religion based on the idea of conflict between the spirit of good and light (Ormuzd) and the spirit of evil and darkness (Ahriman).

239 l. 202. *Terrible . . . shapes*. See Edmund Burke on Milton's description of Death in *PL*: 'all is dark, uncertain, confused, terrible, and sublime to the last degree' (*Philosophical Enquiry into the Origin of Our Ideas of the Sublime and Beautiful* (1757), ed. Adam Phillips (Oxford, 1990), 55).

239 l. 207. *Demogorgon*. A figure who resists allegorical translation; often connected by critics with Necessity, and sometimes with the people (his name might be read as meaning 'people [*Demos*] monster [*gorgon*]').

l. 221. *Phantasm of Jupiter*. Phantom, called up to utter Prometheus' former curse. There is a resemblance (see especially ll. 258–61) between the Phantasm and Prometheus before he expressed pity for Jupiter.

240 ll. 222, 231. *Ione ... Panthea*. Younger sisters of Asia, who perform a choric role and act as intermediaries between Prometheus and Asia while they are separated.

241 ll. 292–3. *Heap ... beholding good*. See *PL* 1. 209–20, where Satan is allowed to rise from 'the burning lake' (l. 210) only so as to 'Heap on himself damnation' (l. 215) and permit the workings of 'Infinite goodness' (l. 218): Milton's explanation is attacked by S. in 'On the Devil, and Devils' in a passage reworked in *A Defence of Poetry* (p. 692).

243 l. 325. *Mercury*. Messenger of the gods.

l. 331. *Jove's tempest-walking hounds*. The Furies. In Greek mythology, they are figures who torment someone guilty of crime (such as Orestes); S. builds on the Greek conception by making his Furies embody Prometheus' temptations to despair. They bring visions of physical pain (ll. 475–91); and then of war, the doomed fate of idealism (symbolized by the bloody outcome of the French Revolution and the perversion by institutionalized Christianity of the teachings of Christ), and the failure of nerve and will in the present generation (ll. 495–631).

l. 345. *streams of fire and wail*. Refers ('wail' is probably a noun) to two rivers in Hades, Phlegethon and Cocytus.

l. 346. *Geryon*. In Virgil (*Aeneid*, 6. 289) a monster with three heads.   *Gorgon*. Medusa, killed by Perseus; her gaze turned the onlooker to stone.

l. 347. *Chimaera*. A monster with lion's head, goat's body, and serpent's tail.   *Sphinx*. Winged monster of Thebes with woman's head and lion's body.

l. 348. *Unnatural love ... hate*. Oedipus solved a riddle put by the Sphinx; this led ('Unnatural love') to his marriage with Jocasta, his mother (though not known by Oedipus to be so) and to his cursing his two sons to kill one another ('unnatural hate').

245 l. 387. *thought-executing*. See the 'sulphurous and thought-executing fires' in *King Lear* (in the third or Conflated Text printed in *Norton Shakespeare*), 3. 2. 4. Here S. may mean both 'as speedy as thought' and 'putting a stop to thought'.

l. 398. *the Sicilian's ... sword*. Damocles was made by Dionysius I of Syracuse to dine under a sword hanging by a single horse-hair, so that he might experience the insecurity of being a ruler.

249 l. 530. *Kingly conclaves*. Alludes to the Congress of Vienna (1814–15),

when arrangements were made for the post-Napoleonic rule of Europe, arrangements which S. saw as reactionary.

250 l. 546. *One came forth.* Christ, whose 'words' (l. 548) have been used to justify actions at odds with the spirit of his teaching.

l. 563. *pillow of thorns.* Alludes to Christ's crown of thorns (Matthew 27: 29).

l. 567. *disenchanted nation.* France at the outset of the French Revolution, freed from an evil spell. For the same phrase, see Coleridge, 'France: An Ode', l. 28.

251 ll. 573–7. *See how … win.* Alludes to the Reign of Terror, the Revolutionary and Napoleonic wars, and the ultimate victory of the forces of reaction with the restoration of Bourbon monarchies in France and Spain after the Battle of Waterloo (1815).

252 l. 609. *ounces.* Leopards.

l. 631. *they know not what they do.* Christ's words on the cross (Luke 23: 34).

253 l. 658. *subtle and fair spirits.* Contrasting with the classical Furies, these 'spirits'—to be found within individual minds ('dim caves of human thought', l. 659) and the Zeitgeist ('world-surrounding ether', l. 660)— bear a resemblance to the angels who minister to Christ after he has been tempted by Satan (Matthew 4: 11).

255 ll. 718–22. *I alit … die.* S. sets this example of self-sacrifice against the malevolence of the 'Second Voice' in Byron's *Manfred* (1817) who describes causing a shipwreck and saving 'A traitor … and pirate' only so that he can 'wreak further havoc' (2. 3. 32, 33).

256 l. 765. *planet-crested.* Love, linked with 'lightning', wears the crest of Venus.

257 ll. 772–9. *Desolation … greet.* Draws on Plato's *Symposium*, 195, in which Love is described as 'the most delicate of all things, who touches lightly with his feet only the softest parts of those things which are the softest of all' (S.'s translation in *Notopoulos*, p. 435).

258 l. 825. *eastern star.* Venus.

259 *Act 2, Scene 1. Stage direction.* There has been debate about whether the action of the lyrical drama is simultaneous or sequential. As *Longman* 2 observes, support is given for the sequential view by the entrance of Panthea at this point; see also ll. 107–8 later in this scene.

260 l. 43. *erewhile.* A time before Prometheus' 'fall' (l. 40).

l. 44. *glaucous.* Dull greyish-green or blue.

262 l. 127. *shape.* Panthea's second dream (l. 61).

l. 135. *almond-tree.* An emblem of hope and expectation: see Jeremiah 1: 11–12. The Hebrew word for 'almond' also means 'hasten'.

l. 136. *Scythian wilderness.* The setting for *Prometheus Bound.*

262 l. 140. *Hyacinth.* A youth loved by Apollo and killed by Zephyrus out of jealousy; from Hyacinth's blood sprang up a flower whose petals were marked 'ai ai' (Greek for 'alas').

265 *Act 2, Scene 2.* l. 2. *cedar . . . yew.* See the wood in *PL* 4 surrounding Eden, 'A sylvan scene' made up of 'Cedar, and pine, and fir, and branching palm' (ll. 140, 139).

l. 10. *Hangs . . . flowers.* See *A Midsummer Night's Dream*, 2. 1. 14–15: 'I must go seek some dewdrops here, | And hang a pearl in every cowslip's ear'.

266 l. 50. *the destined.* Those who, wakened from 'talk or slumber' (l. 49) as a result of 'Demogorgon's mighty law' (l. 43), have a destiny to fulfil as harbingers of the coming revolutionary change; they believe that they 'obey' 'The sweet desires within' (l. 56). S. fuses notions of free-will and necessity.

l. 52. *breathing earth.* Vapours issuing out of the earth, especially as a result of volcanic activity: the volcano, a crucial image in the work, is associated by S. with revolution.

267 ll. 70–82. *I have heard . . . again.* Describes the hydrogen cycle, whereby hydrogen is released from plants in ponds, rises into the air and there ignites as 'meteors' (l. 79).

l. 90. *Silenus.* Aged, satyr-like tutor to Dionysus. His song is at the centre of Virgil, *Eclogues*, 6.   *thwart.* crossed, frustrated. *undrawn.* Unmilked.

268 *Act 2, Scene 3.* l. 3. *Like . . . chasm.* Alludes to exhalations from a volcano.

l. 4. *oracular vapour.* Vapour from a cleft in the earth inspired the priestess at the Delphic oracle to prophecy; Asia detects a comparable power at work here.

l. 9. *Maenads.* Female followers of Dionysus, driven to frenzy by their worship of the god.   *Evoe.* The cry associated with Maenads.

l. 10. *The voice . . . world.* Either 'the voice which conventional-minded people disapprove of as a kind of disease' or 'the voice which spreads enthusiasm throughout humanity'.

269 ll. 28–42. *And far . . . now.* Above a rough draft of these lines (*BSM* 21) S. wrote: 'This was suggested by the Xterly Review.' S.'s lines counter the attack on him in the *Quarterly Review*'s notice of Leigh Hunt's *Foliage*, by showing that it is possible to respond to sublime scenery in a different spirit (here of revolutionary hope) than that of Christian reverence. See Timothy Webb, ' "The Avalanche of Ages": Shelley's Defence of Atheism and *Prometheus Unbound*', *Keats–Shelley Memorial Bulletin*, 35 (1984), 1–39.

ll. 59–60. *Through . . . are.* Plato's distinction between shadows and reality is remodelled here: Asia and Panthea are 'descending into a cave . . .', whereas in Plato's myth [in the *Republic* 514a-521b]' what would be involved would be 'the ascent from the cave into the light of the sun' (*Butter*).

l. 70. *stone*. Lodestone.

270   l. 95. *the Eternal, the Immortal*. Demogorgon.

l. 97. *snake-like Doom*. Doom is 'fate' or 'destiny' (*OED* 4), imaged as a coiled snake waiting to be unloosed 'through life's portal' (l. 96). The unloosing of this 'Doom' will prove beneficial partly because of the hopes and 'sweet desires' of Asia and Panthea.   *throne*. A word associated with tyranny, but here given a positive meaning, implying an alternative rule to that of Jupiter.

Act 2, Scene 4. ll. 2–5. *I see . . . shapeless*. See the account of Death in *PL* 2. 666–70: 'The other shape, | If shape it might be called that shape had none | Distinguishable in member, joint, or limb, | Or substance might be called that shadow seemed, | For each seemed either; black it stood as night.' *Webb* suggests an accompanying allusion to God as 'Dark with excessive bright' (*PL* 3. 380).

271   ll. 20–2. *Which . . . heavily*. See S.'s description of '300 fettered criminals' with legs 'heavily ironed' in the square of St Peter's in Rome (*L* 2. 93).

272   l. 32. *Heaven and Earth*. Uranus and Gaia, parents of the Titans, including Saturn.

l. 52. *unseasonable seasons*. In the golden age preceding Jove's rule there was supposed to be perpetual spring.

l. 61. *Nepenthe*. A drug that dispelled care.   *Moly*. Plant given by Hermes to Odysseus to nullify Circe's potion. *Amaranth*. Unfading flower.

273   ll. 77–9. *And music . . . sound*. The lines imply a Christ-like ability to walk on water: see Matthew 14: 25–6.

l. 80. *mimicked*. Imitated.

ll. 83–4. *And mothers . . . race*. Pregnant women gazing on beautiful statues absorb a beauty which shows in their children.

l. 87. *implicated*. Entangled.

l. 88. *wide-wandering stars*. Planets or comets.

l. 89. *Changes his lair*. The sun seems to change its position with regard to the constellations.

l. 91. *interlunar*. The dark between the old and new moons.

l. 101. *immedicable*. Unhealable.

ll. 102–3. *Man . . . glorious*. Gives to human beings the power traditionally associated with God (see Genesis 1: 31: 'And God saw every thing that he had made, and behold, it was very good').

l. 107. *adamantine*. Unbreakable.

275   l. 142. *A spirit with a dreadful countenance*. Represents the element of potentially violent overthrow involved in revolution. It contrasts with the 'young spirit' at l. 159.

275 l. 157. *ivory shell*. Links Asia with Aphrodite (see below, 2. 5. 20–30).

276 *Act 2, Scene 5.* l. 2. *respire*. To breathe; here, to 'take a breather'.

l. 7. *Alas! it could not*. The arrival of the 'destined hour' cannot be speeded up by Asia.

ll. 11–14. *the light . . . sister*. Asia is the source of light.

l. 20. *Nereids*. Daughters of Nereus, the old sea-god.

l. 21. *hyaline*. Glass-like sea.

277 ll. 20–30. *The Nereids . . . within them*. Asia is associated with Aphrodite, carried on a shell to the island of Cythera after her birth from sea-foam; See Botticelli's *The Birth of Venus*, which S. may have seen in the Uffizi Gallery in Florence.

ll. 26–30. *love . . . them*. See Wordsworth's 'Tintern Abbey', ll. 94–103.

278 l. 70. *as I am failing*. The 'failing' of inspiration is a frequently dramatized event in S.'s poetry.

279 ll. 98–103. *We . . . day*. Whereas Wordsworth in 'Ode: Intimations of Immortality' describes the soul as moving from a pre-existent state to its earthly condition, Shelley reverses the process.

ll. 109–110. *And rest . . . melodiously!* 'We' (Asia and Prometheus) 'rest'; the 'shapes' which 'walk' and 'chant' are 'somewhat like thee' (Prometheus).

280 *Act 3, Scene 1.* l. 11. *pendulous air*. See *King Lear*, 3. 4. 64–5: 'Now, all the plagues that in the pendulous air | Hang fated o'er men's faults light on thy daughters!'

l. 12. *flake by flake*. Recalls with dramatic irony Asia's image for the coming of revolutionary change: see 2. 3. 39.

ll. 18–19. *Even now . . . child*. See *PL* 5. 603–4: 'This day I have begot whom I declare | My only son'.

l. 19. *That fatal child*. C. E. Pulos suggests that the 'child' might be the doctrines of Malthus (*PMLA* 67 (1952), 113–24).

l. 25. *Idaean Ganymede*. Ganymede was a youth taken from Mount Ida by Jupiter because of his beauty; he became the cup-bearer to the gods.

281 l. 36. *Thetis*. A sea-nymph who became the mother of Achilles and wife of Peleus.

ll. 37–9. *Insufferable . . . presence*. See the fate of Semele, destroyed in the act of love-making with Jupiter: Ovid, *Met.* 3: 'her mortal frame | Could not endure the tumult of the heavens; | That gift of love consumed her.'

ll. 40–1. *Like him . . . poison*. The allusion is to Lucan, *Pharsalia*, 9. 762–88; Sabellus, bitten by a fabled poisonous snake (seps) in the Numidian desert, 'dissolved' (l. 41).

l. 48. *Griding*. Cutting with a grating or strident sound. See *PL* 6. 329: 'The griding sword'.

l. 62. *Titanian*. Alludes to the imprisonment of the Titans underground in Tartarus after their defeat by Jupiter and the gods.

282 l. 79. *Ai! Ai!* A Greek cry of lament.

Act 3, Scene 2. Stage direction. Atlantis. Mythical island, scene of ideal commonwealth in Plato's *Critias*.

OCEAN. The god of the sea and source of all rivers (hence the stage direction, 'The mouth of a great river').

APOLLO. Greek god of the sun, poetry, medicine, and prophecy.

283 l. 19. *unstained with blood*. Wars at sea will be no more; S. may also allude to the end of the slave-trade (see l. 31).

l. 27. *sightless*. Invisible.

l. 49. *unpastured*. Unfed.

284 *Act 3, Scene 3.* l. 10. *a Cave*. Whereas in Plato (*Republic*, 514 ff) the image of a cave allegorizes the condition of ignorance, here it suggests a superior vantage-point from which Prometheus and his companions can 'sit and talk of time and change' (l. 23).

ll. 23-4. *Where . . . unchanged*. See *King Lear*, 5. 3. 8-19, where Lear describes to Cordelia how they might spend their time in prison.

285 l. 42. *Enna*. A meadow in Sicily from where Proserpina was taken by Dis (see Ovid, *Met.* 5).

l. 43. *Himera*. A town in Sicily.

ll. 49-53. *And lovely . . . reality*. See Diotima's explanation to Socrates in the *Symposium* of how the mind is nourished by 'contemplation of the beautiful' (S.'s translation in *Notopoulos*, p. 450).

l. 65. *Proteus*. Sea-god famous for shape-changing and prophecy; associated with elemental matter.

287 l. 124. *a Cavern*. Possibly the same as that described by Prometheus earlier in the scene (l. 10). In the past it has been a place of menacing oracle, its fumes inhaled by those who were thenceforward 'oracular' (l. 128) in misguided ways. Now its 'breath' (l. 131) is benign.

l. 136. *ivy*. Sacred to Dionysus (see later reference at l. 154).

288 l. 154. *Bacchic Nysa*. S.'s possible source, Arrian, *The Life of Alexander the Great*, trans. de Selincourt, 1958, mentions in book 5 'the city of Nysa, supposed to have been founded by Dionysus'.

l. 155. *beyond Indus . . . rivers*. Arrian (book 5) recounts Alexander's arrival at the Indus, then describes its tribute rivers.

l. 165. *Praxitelean*. Praxiteles was a Greek sculptor who lived in the fourth century BC.

ll. 168-70. *there the emulous . . . emblem*. The allusion is to the Lampadephoria, a race run in ancient Athens by young men carrying torches in remembrance of Prometheus' gift of fire to human beings. See Plato, *Republic*, 328a, and Lucretius, *De Rerum Natura*, 2. 78–9.

288   *Act 3, Scene 4. Stage direction. The SPIRIT OF THE EARTH.* Identified by various critics with electricity, the force which animates the physical universe in a way analogous to the operation of love in the moral universe.

l. 3. *A light . . . star.* Image may be borrowed from a Leyden jar, an early version of a battery, which gives off a green light.

289   l. 19. *dipsas.* A snake causing thirst though its bite.

290   ll. 65–7. *Those ugly . . . air.* Alludes to the Lucretian idea of *simulacra*, images that float off from the surfaces of things into the air. See *De Rerum Natura*, 4. 30–7.

l. 80. *halcyons.* Kingfishers, now vegetarian.

291   l. 112. *Phidian.* Phidias (fifth century BC) was the most famous sculptor in classical Greece.

292   l. 119. *amphisbaenic.* See note to *Laon and Cythna*, l. 3386 (p. 734).

l. 120. *mock.* Imitate as well as deride.

ll. 111–21. *And where . . . repose.* Based on S.'s sight in the Vatican Museum of a *biga* or chariot drawn by two horses yoked together by a two-headed snake.

l. 136. *'All . . . here'.* Quotation is from Dante, *Inf.* 3. 9, trans. by Henry Cary, *The Vision of Dante* (1814) exactly as in S.'s line.

l. 151. *unmeant hypocrisy.* See Coleridge, *Christabel*, l. 665: 'words of unmeant bitterness'.

293   l. 187. *unreclaiming tears.* Love's fate induces pity but no practical effort to 'reclaim' it.

294   l. 204. *inane.* A noun, meaning empty space.

295   *Act 4.* l. 14. *We . . . eternity.* S. implies not a complete escape from 'Time', but the burial of the past.

296   l. 34. *One.* Prometheus.

297   l. 58. *figured.* Embellished with patterns.

299   l. 110. *Delaying.* Time can be slowed down through the effort of acquiring 'Wisdom' (l. 109).

l. 116. *his.* The fair-copy reading appears to be 'her'.

300   l. 140. *clips.* Embraces.

301   l. 169. *gathering sphere.* Might allude to the theory of various scientists of the day that new planets are formed from clouds of dust and gases.

302   l. 213. *Regard like.* Look like (a rare usage).

ll. 219–24. *Within it . . . white light.* See Revelation 1: 14: 'His head and his hairs were white like wool, as white as snow; and his eyes were as a flame of fire.'

303 l. 230. *fire . . . brightness*. May refer to infra-red radiation discovered by Herschel and described by Humphry Davy.

ll. 236–7. *And . . . harmony*. See *PL* 6. 749: 'forth rushed with whirlwind sound'.

l. 246. *inter-transpicuous*. Visible through or between each other.

ll. 236–61. *And from . . . sense*. Influences on Panthea's vision of the Spirit of the Earth include the account of the 'living creatures' in Ezekiel 1: 5: 'the exalted wheels, . . . where the one movement smiteth on the other', Dante, *Par*. 10. 7–9; and the 'chariot of paternal deity' in *PL* 6. 750.

l. 261. *drowns the sense*. Overwhelms the capacity for sensuous response.

304 l. 269. *mocking*. Imitating, but possibly with a suggestion of lightly teasing.

l. 272. *tyrant-quelling myrtle*. The Greeks crowned triumphant soldiers with myrtle. The compound adjective, drawn from Coleridge's 'France: An Ode', l. 37, may refer to Harmodius and Aristogeiton who killed Hipparchus the Tyrant in 514 BC.

l. 281. *Valueless*. Cannot be valued.

305 ll. 270–318. *And from . . . no more*. This account of an uncovering of the earth's geology, history and prehistory is influenced by Keats, *Endymion*, 3. 119–41, part of which was singled out for praise by S. (see *L* 2. 252). It also shows the influence of contemporary geological theories, both evolutionary (as argued by James Hutton, who believed that change took place in long, gradual cycles, obedient to natural laws) and catastrophic (as argued by George Cuvier, who thought that successive phases of earth's prehistory bore witness to disasters such as floods). S. is also indebted to James Parkinson, *Organic Remains of a Former World* (1804–11), which he read in 1812.

ll. 314–18. *till . . . no more*. Two causes of extinction are suggested here: a flood or a comet.

307 ll. 388–93. *Leave . . . restored*. Alludes to the story of King Bladud, the mythical founder of Bath.

308 l. 415. *Orphic*. Orpheus was the archetypal poet, able to entrance all listeners, living, dead, animal, or inanimate.

309 ll. 444. *pyramid of night*. The conical shadow of the earth cast by the sun.

l. 474. *Agave*. Mother of Pentheus and daughter of Cadmus; in her unknowing frenzy she kills Pentheus in Euripides' *Bacchae*.

l. 475. *Cadmaean*. Pertaining to Cadmus, founder of Thebes.

310 l. 493. *And . . . weeps*. The Earth completes the Moon's lines, answering her for the first time.

311 l. 522. *The love . . . skies*. S.'s reworking of 'the Love that moves the sun and the other stars', in Dante, *Par*. 33. 145.

312 l. 539. *elemental Genii*. Personifications of the elements.

l. 555. *Earth-born's*. Prometheus'.

l. 556. *And Conquest . . . deep*. See Ephesians 4: 8: 'he led captivity captive'.

313 l. 575. *nor repent*. See *PL* 1. 94–6: 'yet not for those . . . do I repent or change'.

314 *The Cenci*. Written between May and August 1819; by late September 1819, 250 copies had been printed by the Italian firm of Glauco Masi to be shipped to England. S. hoped that the play would be performed in a London theatre, with Edmund Kean as the Count and Eliza O'Neill as Beatrice (*L* 2. 102–3). In the event, it was not accepted at Covent Garden (and possibly Drury Lane) 'on a plea', as S. put it wryly, 'of the story being too horrible', adding, '*I* believe it singularly fitted for the stage' (*L* 2. 178). The play also appeared in an authorized second edition (1821) incorporating errata in Mary S.'s hand (now pasted into a copy of the first edition in the Bodleian), presumably the same list as that mentioned by S. in a letter to Ollier (*L* 2. 188). We have taken the 1819 text as our copy-text, making corrections as warranted by the list of errata and by comparison with the second edition; we have also consulted the text in *Longman* 2 for its detailing of corrections made in a presentation copy of the 1819 edition given by S. to John Taaffe (see *Longman* 2, p. 724). Though *The Cenci* represents a conscious attempt on S.'s part to write for a popular audience, it broaches topics also addressed in *Prometheus Unbound*, including the theme of revenge, and has political resonances. S. drew on the translation in Mary S.'s hand of the Cenci story. Transcribed in *BSM* 10, this translation was first published in *MWS (2)*. The play explores Beatrice's response to the tyranny of her father, who subjects her to incestuous rape. Her decision to take revenge on her father gives rise in the audience, as S. notes, to a 'restless and anatomizing casuistry', an attempt to excuse what is felt to need excusing. In shaping his tragedy, S. made use of a wide range of models and analogues, including classical tragedy, Dante, various works by Byron, Coleridge's play *Remorse*, and (especially) Shakespeare's tragedies. The play was first produced by the Shelley Society in 1886; its first public staging in England took place in 1922, with Sybil Thorndike as Beatrice.

Dedication. sad reality. See S.'s letter of 15 December 1819 in which he speaks of poems whose subjects (like that of *Julian and Maddalo*) 'will all be drawn from dreadful or beautiful realities' (*L* 2. 164).

315 *Preface. Clement VIII*. Pope from 1592 until his death in 1605.

revenue. The errata say that the following sentence, in the main body of the Preface in the first edition, should be printed as a note: 'The Papal Government formerly took the most extraordinary precautions against the publicity of facts which offer so tragical a demonstration of its own wickedness and weakness; so that the communication of the MS had become, until, very lately, a matter of some difficulty.'

316 *Guido's picture . . . La Cenci.* S. alludes to a portrait of Beatrice Cenci by Guido Reni; it is now believed that the painting was not of Beatrice nor by Guido Reni.

317 *restless and anatomizing casuistry.* See the discussion in the Preface to *Prometheus Unbound* of the 'pernicious casuistry' provoked by the presentation of Satan in *PL*.

318 *nature.* S. keyed the following note: 'An idea in this speech was suggested by a most sublime passage in *El Purgatorio de San Patricio* of Calderon: the only plagiarism which I have intentionally committed in the whole piece.' (See this edition's note to 3. 1. 241–65.)

those modern critics. Principally Wordsworth and Coleridge in the Preface to *Lyrical Ballads* (1800).

the real language of men. The phrase is used in the Preface to *Lyrical Ballads* (1800). S.'s reservations about the Preface's programme are apparent in this sentence.

320 *Act 1, Scene 1.* l. 1. *matter of the murder.* Alludes to l. 23.

l. 3. *the Pincian gate.* Gate at the north end of the Via Veneto in Rome (*Norton*).

l. 16. *the nephew of the Pope.* 'Nephew' may be a euphemism for an ecclesiastic's illegitimate child; the word also suggests the Pope's network of nepotism (see *Longman* 2).

321 l. 57. *Aldobrandino.* Either the Pope, referred to by his family name (*Norton*), or the Pope's 'nephew' (l. 16) (*Longman* 2).

323 ll. 113. *bloody sweat of Christ.* Alludes to Christ in Gethsemane: see Luke 22: 44.

324 ll. 141–4. *Thou . . . intent!* See *Macbeth*, 2. 1. 56–8: 'Thou sure and firm-set earth, | Hear not my steps which way they walk, for fear | Thy very stones prate of my whereabout'.

326 *Act 1, Scene 2.* l. 85. *anatomize.* Analyse minutely.

327 *Act 1, Scene 3.* l. 4. *Anchorite.* Hermit.

328 l. 34. *dreadful ill.* See *Julian and Maddalo*, l. 525.

ll. 40–1. *God! | I thank thee.* An odd, possibly sardonic echo of Malvolio in *Twelfth Night*, 2. 5. 154: 'Jove, I thank thee.' See also note to 5. 3. 123–7.

ll. 58–61. *Rocco . . . Cristofano.* Cenci's sons.

329 l. 68. *the twenty-seventh of December.* The eve of the Feast of the Holy Innocents: the date points up Cenci's Herod-like conduct towards his children.

l. 73. *Infanta.* Daughter of the king of Spain.

l. 74. *El Dorado.* Fictitious city of gold.

l. 82. *like a sacrament.* Suggests Cenci's blasphemous mimicry of the Eucharist.

330 l. 109. *prone*. 'Ready in mind . . . eager' (for 'love' and 'reverence'): cited, as *Longman* 2 points out, in *OED* (a. 7).

l. 110. *it thus vanquish shame and fear*. As *Longman* 2 comments, 'shame and fear' govern the verb of which 'it' (that is, 'love' (l. 109)) is the object.

331 l. 126. *Prince Colonna*. The Colonna were a famous noble Roman family.

l. 151. *ill must come of ill*. A tragic topos at the play's thematic heart.

332 ll. 177–8. *The charm . . . done*. See *Macbeth*, 1. 3. 35 ('The charm's wound up') and several uses of 'done' in the same play (1. 4. 53; 1. 7. 1–2; 2. 1. 62).

334 *Act 2, Scene 1*. ll. 46–7. *Until . . . wrath*. See Lear to Kent in *King Lear*, 1. 1. 122: 'Come not between the dragon and his wrath.'

335 l. 86. *coil*. Turmoil.

336 l. 111. *that the earth would gape*. See Marlowe, *Doctor Faustus* ('Gape earth' in Faustus's last soliloquy; quoted from Charles Lamb, *Specimens of English Dramatic Poets* (1808)).

338 l. 177. garish. See *Romeo and Juliet*, 3. 2. 25: 'the garish sun'.

l. 181. *Come, darkness!* See *Macbeth*, 1. 5. 48: 'Come, thick night'.

ll. 184–5. *a bewildering mist | Of horror*. See John Webster, *The Duchess of Malfi* (quoted from Lamb, *Specimens*): 'Their life, a general mist of error; | Their death, a hideous storm of terror'.

339 *Act 2, Scene 2*. l. 14. *thrice-driven beds of down*. See *Othello*, 1. 3. 229: 'My thrice-driven bed of down'.

340 l. 49. *Visconti, Borgia, Ezzelin*. Three famous tyrants whom S. would have read about in Sismondi, *History of the Italian Republics in the Middle Ages* (1818). Galeazzo Visconti (1351–1402), leader of a well-known family in Milan; Cesare Borgia (1475–1507), the son of Pope Alexander VI; Ezzelino da Romano (1194–1259), leader of the Ghibelline faction in Lombardy (see *Norton*).

341 ll. 70–1. *And . . . death*. See Byron, *The Giaour*, ll. 422–38: 'The Mind, that broods o'er guilty woes, | Is like the Scorpion girt by fire . . .'.

342 l. 120. *fee*. Bribe.

343 l. 147. *I see . . . all*. See *Richard III*, 2. 4. 53: 'I see, as in a map, the end of all.'

344 *Act 3, Scene 1*. l. 13. *The beautiful . . . blood*. See Marlowe, *Doctor Faustus*: 'See [*sic*] where Christ's blood streams in the firmament' (quoted from *Specimens*).

345 ll. 36–7. *Like . . . father*. Beatrice's misery is so great it has 'killed' its 'father', that is, awareness of its cause.

l. 44. *hales*. Drags.

346 ll. 86–7. *something . . . not.* See *King Lear*, 2. 4. 275–7: 'I will do such things— | What they are, yet I know not; but they shall be | The terrors of the earth!' S. quoted Beatrice's words in a letter responding to news of the Peterloo massacre (*L* 2. 117).

348 ll. 132–4. *Self-murder . . . it.* See *Hamlet*, 1. 2. 131–2, where the hero wishes that 'the Everlasting had not fixed | His canon 'gainst self-slaughter'.

352 ll. 241–65. *But . . . night.* The passage mentioned by S. in the Preface as the only possible exception to his avoidance of 'mere poetry'. In fact, the passage bears on Cenci's moral wretchedness and, possibly, Beatrice's, too. In a footnote to the Preface S. suggests the influence on these lines of Calderón's *El Purgatorio de San Patricio*: the relevant passage occurs in Act 2, ll. 2019–26.

357 *Act 3, Scene 2.* ll. 8–18. *O . . . flesh.* Clearly modelled on *Othello*, 5. 2. 7–15.

358 l. 51. *relume.* See *Othello*, 5. 2. 12–13: 'I know not where is that Promethean heat | That can thy light relume'.

l. 62. *castellan.* Governor of a castle.

361 *Act 4, Scene 1.* l. 10. *her stubborn will.* Cenci seeks to make Beatrice will her own degradation, but see ll. 44–5 later in the scene when he appears to give up the wish 'To poison and corrupt her soul' (l. 45).

363 l. 83. *blazoned.* Proclaimed.

ll. 85–8. *She . . . others.* See Byron, *Manfred*, 2. 2. 204–5 ('But I can act even what I most abhor, | And champion human fears').

364 l. 115. *specious.* Fair or right on the surface but not in reality.

365 l. 131. *the Maremma's dew.* The Maremma is a low marshy area on the Tuscan coast from which pestilential vapours were supposed to rise.

l. 140. *That if she have a child.* As close as the play gets to describing explicitly Cenci's incestuous rape of Beatrice.

366 ll. 114–59. *God! . . . heaven.* Cenci curses the absent Beatrice in words that recall Lear's cursing of Goneril in *King Lear*, 1. 4. 252–66 and 2. 4. 155–7, 158–61. S. described Cenci's curse as 'a particular favourite with me' (*L* 2. 219).

ll. 187–9. *All good . . . quickened.* See *Macbeth*, 3. 2. 53–4: 'Good things of day begin to droop and drowse, | Whiles night's black agents to their preys do rouse'.

367 *Act 4, Scene 2.* l. 11. *recking.* Taking account of.

368 l. 33. *the Hell within him.* See *PL* 4. 20: 'The hell within him'.

370 *Act 4, Scene 3.* l. 8. *Did you not call? | When? | Now.* A strong reminiscence of *Macbeth*, 2. 2. 17.

370 l. 28. *equivocation*. A central theme in *Macbeth*; see 2. 3. 8–11.

371 l. 42. *light of life*. See *Prometheus Unbound*, 3. 3. 6; the phrase occurs in John 8: 12.

l. 43. *jellied*. Congealed.

373 *Act 4, Scene 4*. l. 23. *unappealable*. Cannot be appealed against.

l. 28. *warrant for his instant death*. S.'s ironic addition to the source-plot.

l. 49. *Free as . . . air*. See *Macbeth*, 3. 4. 22: 'As broad and general as the casing air'.

375 l. 76. *effortless*. Lifeless; with no sign of struggle.

380 *Act 5, Scene 1*. ll. 19–24. *O . . . desire*. See Coleridge, *Remorse*, 3. 2: 'O that I ne'er had yielded | To your entreaties'; quoted from *The Complete Poetical Works of Samuel Taylor Coleridge*, ed. E. H. Coleridge (2 vols., Oxford, 1912).

381 l. 56. *Put up your weapon*. See Jesus to Peter: 'Put up thy sword into the sheath' (John 18: 11).

382 l. 87. *misdeeming*. Misjudging.

l. 92. *that within*. See *Hamlet*, 1. 2. 85: 'But I have that within which passeth show.'

383 l. 99. *A word?* Another example of the play's obsession with the power and limits of language.

385 *Act 5, Scene 2*. ll. 49–54. *that fair . . . grief*. Mary S. remarks in her editorial note (*MWS (1)*) that these lines reflect the feelings which 'haunted' S. after the death of their son, William, in June 1819.

387 ll. 124–5. *that peace . . . heart*. See *Hamlet*, 3. 2. 65–6: 'I will wear him | In my heart's core, ay, in my heart of heart.'

388 l. 164. *pain*. The second edition reads 'pang'.

l. 169. *strain*. Sift.

389 ll. 172–5. *Who . . . one?* See Vittoria in Webster, *The White Devil* ('The arraignment of Vittoria', as Lamb calls the scene in question in *Specimens*): 'if you be my accuser | Pray cease to be my judge.' S., who could have read Lamb's account in *Specimens* of Vittoria's 'innocence-resembling boldness', may suggest likeness and unlikeness between his heroine and Webster's.

392 *Act 5, Scene 3*. l. 89. *No . . . word*. See Iago in *Othello*, 5. 2. 310: 'From this time forth I never will speak word.'

394 ll. 123–7. *Come . . . live*. See *Twelfth Night*, 2. 4. 42–5: there is an ironic contrast between Beatrice's situation (facing death) and that of Orsino and Viola (Cesario) (preoccupied with love).

395 *Act 5, Scene 4*. l. 13. *deprecation*. Disapproval.

396 ll. 47–9. *Oh . . . suddenly?* See Mary's translation of the Cenci story, where Beatrice says, 'How is it possible—oh my God—that I must so suddenly die!'

l. 56. *Let me not go mad!* See *King Lear*, 1. 5. 38: 'O, let me not be mad, not mad, sweet heaven!'

ll. 72–3. *Who ... realm?* See *Hamlet*, 3. 1. 80–2: 'death, | The undiscovered country from whose bourn | No traveller returns.'

ll. 47–75. *Oh ... whither.* See Claudio's speech beginning 'Ay, but to die, and go we know not where' in Shakespeare, *Measure for Measure*, 3. 1. 118–32.

ll. 77–8. *ere ... Paradise!* Alludes to Christ's words on the Cross to the 'good thief' in Luke 23: 43: 'Today shalt thou be with me in paradise.'

397 l. 80. *How tedious ... things.* See *Hamlet*, 1. 2. 133–4: 'How weary, stale, flat, and unprofitable | Seem to me all the uses of this world!'

l. 100. *narrow.* Brief.

398 l. 136. *Whose ... loves.* This line lacks a syllable: *Rossetti* emended by inserting 'as' before 'a bond'.

400 *The Mask of Anarchy.* Composed at Leghorn (Livorno) in September 1819 and sent on the 23rd to Leigh Hunt for publication in the *Examiner*, though it never appeared there (partly out of Hunt's fear of prosecution); published posthumously in an edition by Leigh Hunt (1832) and in *MWS (1)*. The poem is S.'s response, intended for a wide public audience, to the 'Peterloo Massacre' of 16 August 1819. 'Peterloo' (an ironic allusion to the defeat of the French at Waterloo) took place at St Peter's Fields, Manchester. Its occasion was a peaceful mass political protest in support of parliamentary reform. As the radical 'Orator' Henry Hunt was about to address a crowd of 60,000–80,000 men, women, and children, the assembly was brutally broken up, on orders from local magistrates, by regular cavalry and the Manchester Yeomanry (mounted militia, some of them drunk, mostly drawn from the city's industrial middle class). The militia panicked and charged the crowd, fifteen people were killed and 500 injured (by some estimates), and public revulsion at the unprovoked violence of the authorities provided opponents of the government with a powerful image of the cruelty of state repression. That this image also frightened the forces of established order, would lead, ironically, to increased repression: the 'Six Acts' of December 1819, limiting the right of assembly, reinforcing laws against 'Blasphemous and Seditious Libels', tightening the Press laws. The excuse for this new stringency was the threat of anarchy, which S.'s poem turns on its head. 'Mask' in the title means both masquerade, or allegorical pageant, and disguise or covering. The most important of the poem's political sources were Leigh Hunt's editorials about Peterloo in the issues of the *Examiner* for 22 and 29 August, the first of which pours scorn on 'these Men in the Brazen Masks of power'. Its literary models derive from poetical dream vision, a tradition stretching back to Chaucer, and popular ballad. Our copy-text is Mary S.'s press copy, with S.'s additions and corrections, in the Library of Congress (MMC 1399;

MYR: Shelley 2), though we have also consulted S.'s intermediate fair copy in the British Library (Ashley MS 4086; also in *MYR: Shelley* 2).

400   l. 1. *asleep in Italy*. Perhaps figurative and self-critical, implying S.'s lack of awareness of the political situation in England.

l. 6. *Castlereagh*. Robert Stewart, Viscount Castlereagh (1769-1822), Foreign Secretary (since 1812) and leader of the Tories in the House of Commons. Associated with suppression in Ireland and at home; also with support of the Napoleonic wars and the reactionary Holy Alliance.

l. 8. *seven bloodhounds*. *Norton* thinks this refers to the seven other nations (Austria, France, Russia, Prussia, Portugal, Spain, and Sweden) Britain allied itself with in 1815 when it agreed 'to postpone final abolition of the slave trade', and also points out that politicians who supported the war were frequently called 'bloodhounds' by its opponents.

l. 15. *Eldon*. John Scott, Baron Eldon (1751-1838), Lord Chancellor; in 1817 he had refused S. custody of his children by Harriet. His 'erminèd gown' marks his legal authority (and supposed 'purity', ermine being a symbol of purity). Though famous for public tears he also often separated parents from children in his Chancery judgements.

ll. 18-21. *And the little . . . by them*. See Luke 17: 2: 'It were better for him that a millstone were hanged about his neck, and he cast into the sea, than that he should offend one of these little ones.' Among the dead and wounded at Peterloo were several children.

l. 24. *Sidmouth*. Henry Addington, Viscount Sidmouth (1757-1844), Home Secretary (since 1812), and thus in charge of internal spying (a realm of 'shadows' and 'disguise'). In 1818 Sidmouth lobbied for a million pounds to be spent on churches for the poor in the new industrial towns, in hopes of quieting disorder among the labouring classes.

l. 25. *a crocodile*. Suggestive of hypocrisy.

401   l. 30. *Anarchy*. S.'s use of anarchy as a symbol of ultimate evil may derive from *PL* 2. 988, where Satan encounters Chaos, the 'anarch old,' ruler of the abyss. For details of Anarchy's personification see Revelation 6: 8: 'And I looked, and behold a pale horse; and his name that sat on him was Death, and Hell followed with him. And power was given unto them over the fourth part of the earth, to kill with sword, and with hunger, and with death, and with the beasts of the earth.' See also Benjamin West's painting *Death on the Pale Horse* (1783), in which Death, wearing a crown, and surrounded by sword-bearing followers, tramples a crowd.

402   l. 80. *globe*. The orb, along with sceptre and crown, a symbol of sovereignty.

l. 83. *Tower*. In addition to being a place of imprisonment, the Tower of London is the repository of the crown jewels; hence its coupling with the Bank of England.

l. 85. *pensioned*. Bribed or corrupted (as in the awarding of state pensions).

l. 97. *Misery, oh, Misery! Webb* cites Wordsworth's 'The Thorn' (1798): 'And to herself she cries, | "Oh misery! oh misery! | Oh woe is me! oh misery!"' (ll. 64–6).

403 l. 110. *a Shape.* The Shape's sudden materialization anticipates that of the 'glorious Phantom' in 'England in 1819'. Its association with a snake anticipates the imagery of ll. 227–9 (see note).

l. 115. *the Morning's.* The planet Venus, as the morning star.

404 l. 145. *accent.* Utterance.

l. 155. *Ye.* Here, as in the poem's final line, S. implies a gap, at once social and geographical, between himself and the audience he is addressing.

405 l. 169. *peak.* Droop, waste away, look sickly.

l. 176. *the Ghost of Gold.* Paper money, seen by S. as an imposture, a way of tricking the poor out of proper recompense for their labour. S. was influenced in this regard by the radical journalist William Cobbett (1763–1835), in *Paper Against Gold* (1815) and elsewhere.

406 l. 200. *When . . . air.* After this line, the following stanza is found in S.'s intermediate fair copy of the poem (and in Leigh Hunt's posthumous publication of it in 1832) but not in Mary S.'s press copy (which S. himself corrected): 'Horses, oxen, have a home, | When from daily toil they come; | Household dogs, when the wind roars, | Find a home within warm doors.' Either Mary S. forgot to transcribe the stanza or she convinced S. (or S. convinced her, on second thoughts) to omit it.

ll. 201–4. *Asses . . . hast none.* See Matthew 8: 20: 'The foxes have holes, and the birds of the air have nests; but the Son of man hath not where to lay his head.'

l. 216. *Fame.* Rumour.

l. 229. *That . . . snake.* 'This image had been used by the American Revolutionists in their "Don't Tread on Me" flag picturing a coiled rattlesnake' (*Norton*).

407 l. 241. *Gaul.* France, leagued against in 1793 by Britain, Austria, Prussia, Holland, Spain, and Sardinia.

ll. 246–7. *the rich . . . free.* Perhaps alluding to Mary Magdalen ('him' notwithstanding), whose kiss signalled repentence and submission (Luke 7: 45).

l. 257. *So . . . not.* S.'s intermediate holograph revised this line to read 'Such, they curse their Maker not.' What is not clear is whether this revision occurred after Mary S. had completed the press copy (which would make it the preferred reading), or whether Mary S. persuaded him against preferring the revision while she was making the press copy.

408 l. 282. *tares.* Weeds.

409 l. 301. *targes*. Shields.

l. 315. *scimitars*. Curved swords, especially associated with tyrannical 'Oriental' peoples (especially Turks and Persians).

l. 316. *sphereless stars*. That is, meteors, stars shooting from their fixed spheres in the heavens.

410 ll. 340–7. *And if then . . . away*. That S.'s advocacy of passive resistance could succeed as a political strategy is attested to by the examples of Gandhi, who was directly influenced by S.'s writings, and Martin Luther King.

411 l. 363. *A volcano . . . afar*. Volcanoes as images of rebellion against tyranny frequently occur in S.'s poetry.

412 *Ode to the West Wind*. Begun in Florence in October 1819; published in the 1820 volume, *Prometheus Unbound, with Other Poems*, which supplies our copy-text. There are drafts of different parts of the poem in the Bodleian (including drafts of stanzas 1–4 in *BSM* 18 and drafts of stanzas 4 and 5 in *BSM* 5) and the Huntington (MS HM 2176; *MYR: Shelley* 6). Each of the poem's five sections is a sonnet in *terza rima*, with a concluding couplet. The Ode is concerned with rebirth and regeneration in the personal and political spheres. Throughout, the wind is addressed as though it were a god-like force, but at the close it is the poet who asserts his poetic power. S. scrawled a line in Greek from Euripides, *Heracles*, l. 342, at the end of his draft in *BSM* 5; translated, it reads, 'In goodness I, though mortal, surpass you, a mighty god'. In 1820 the title is keyed to a note which reads: 'This poem was conceived and chiefly written in a wood that skirts the Arno, near Florence, and on a day when that tempestuous wind, whose temperature is at once mild and animating, was collecting the vapours which pour down the autumnal rains. They began, as I foresaw, at sunset with a violent tempest of hail and rain, attended by that magnificent thunder and lightning peculiar to the Cisalpine regions. The phenomenon alluded to at the conclusion of the third stanza is well known to naturalists. The vegetation at the bottom of the sea, of rivers, and of lakes, sympathizes with that of the land in the change of seasons, and is consequently influenced by the winds which announce it.'

ll. 2–3. *the leaves . . . | Are driven*. Fallen autumnal leaves are a traditional image for death or defeat: see Dante, *Inf.* 3. 112–17, and *PL* 1. 302–4.

l. 5. *Pestilence-stricken multitudes*. Throughout, S. treats the leaves figuratively as well as literally; here, they suggest crowds of people suffering from plague.

l. 9. *azure sister*. The warm west wind in spring, traditionally masculine in Greek and Latin mythology; S. makes it feminine.

l. 14. *Destroyer and Preserver*. Titles for the Hindu gods, Shiva (the Destroyer) and Vishnu (the Preserver); S.'s poem both revises Christian imagery and draws on Indian religion. *hear . . . hear!* See Psalm 61: 1: 'Hear my cry, O God: attend unto my prayer.'

l. 16. *Loose clouds*. Wispy, cirrus clouds.

l. 17. *tangled boughs*. S.'s metaphor is based on the exchange of water and vapour between sky and sea.

l. 18. *Angels*. Messengers.

l. 23. *locks . . . storm*. Dense clouds that run before the coming storm.

413   l. 32. *pumice isle*. Island formed from porous lava. *Baiae's bay*. Bay to the west of Naples, visited by the Shelleys in December 1818.

ll. 33–4. *And saw . . . day*. When S. visited the Bay of Baiae, he was able to see 'the ruins of its ancient grandeur standing like rocks in the transparent sea under our boat' (*L*. 2. 61).

ll. 51–2. *I would . . . sore need*. S. comes close to the posture and accents of biblical poetry here, a secular Psalmist or latter-day Job.

l. 54. *the thorns of life*. Possible sources include Keats, 'Sleep and Poetry', where he attacks poetry that merely 'feeds upon the burrs, | And thorns of life' (ll. 244–5).

414   l. 64. *new birth*. The phrase has a personal resonance since Mary S. was pregnant; Percy Florence Shelley was born on 12 November 1819.

ll. 69–70. *O . . . behind?* In a draft (*BSM* 5), S. finished with a statement: 'o Wind | When Winter comes Spring lags not far behind.'

415   *Peter Bell the Third*. Written sometime between July and 24 October 1819 in Leghorn (Livorno) and/or Florence (where S. moved on 2 October), inspired in part by reading (in the previous June) three pieces from Leigh Hunt's *Examiner*: Hunt's review of 2 May of Wordsworth's poem *Peter Bell* (published on 22 April 1819); a parody of the poem by John Hamilton Reynolds, entitled *Peter Bell: A Lyrical Ballad*, which appeared on 15 April (before Wordsworth's original had been published, but after rumours of its theme of sin and religious redemption had begun to circulate); and Keats's anonymous review of the Reynolds parody, which appeared on 25 April. Whether S. had read the Wordsworth poem itself in its entirety (as opposed to the excerpts in Hunt's review) is uncertain. The title of S.'s poem alludes to its place in a sequence: the Reynolds parody comes first (which is why S. calls it 'the antenatal Peter, | Wrapped in weeds of the same metre', ll. 3–4, Prologue); Wordsworth's poem is 'the second Peter' (l. 7, Prologue), because published after the parody; and S.'s poem is therefore 'Peter Bell the Third'. S.'s Peter is a Methodist (in Wordsworth's poem the sinful Peter's redemption is connected to his having overheard 'a pious Methodist' (l. 1134) urging sinners to repent) and a poet (whose career satirizes that of Wordsworth himself); in Wordsworth's poem Peter was an itinerant potter. S.'s poem takes as its starting point Hunt's

description of Wordsworth's poem as 'a didactic little horror', the moral of which was 'founded on the bewitching principles of fear, bigotry, and diseased impulse' (quoted in *Norton*). It opens with Peter's repentence, taking as the objects of its satire religion in general (and the political quietism, asceticism, and sexual guilt cultivated by Methodism in particular); the deficiencies of Wordsworth's perceptual imagination (ll. 268–82, 293–312, though these lines also acknowledge Wordsworth's characteristic strengths); Wordsworth's gathering conservatism (S. had recently deplored the poet's intervention on behalf of the Lowthers, his patrons and benefactors, against the reformer Henry Brougham in the Westmorland election of 1818); and the highly politicized culture of literary London and its reviews (S. having recently suffered at the hands of the conservative *Quarterly Review*, which not only abused *The Revolt of Islam*, in the issue of *c*.15 October, but accused S. of imitating Wordsworth). In its attack on literary culture the poem recalls Pope's *Dunciad* (1743), which it echoes in several ways. Its five-line iambic tetrameter stanzas are rhymed like the first five lines of a Spenserian stanza (though *abaab* rather than *ababb*); they also recall the knockabout *ottava rima* of Byron's *Don Juan* and *Beppo*. The radical nature of the poem's satire links it with S.'s political poems of autumn 1819, whose fate it shared: though sent to Hunt on 2 November 1819 to be passed on to Ollier and published anonymously, it only appeared posthumously, in *MWS (2)*. Our text for the poem is Mary S.'s press copy in the Bodleian (*BSM* 1), with headings, some notes, and corrections in S.'s hand.

415 *By Miching Mallecho, Esq.* See note to second epigraph.

First Epigraph. The fourth stanza from the end of Part First in the 1819 version of Wordsworth's poem, beginning after l. 515, a conjectured hallucination of Peter's, omitted in subsequent editions ('so as not to offend the pious', Wordsworth explained in a letter of 24 October 1828 to Barron Field (in *Letters of William and Dorothy Wordsworth: The Later Years 1821–1853*, ed. E. De Selincourt, rev. Alan G. Hill, 4 vols. (Oxford, 1978–88), 1. 312)).

Second Epigraph. From *Hamlet*, 3. 2. 123–5. The 'this' of Ophelia's question is the dumb-show, mounted by Hamlet to catch out Claudius; '*miching*' is sneaking, stealthy, secret, truant; '*mallecho*' (S. uses the Folio spelling) from the Spanish for misdeed or mischief.

Dedication. 'Thomas Brown, the Younger', was a pseudonym used by the popular Irish poet Thomas Moore (1779–1852) for a series of doggerel satires, including *The Fudge Family in Paris* (1818); 'H.F.' ('Historian of Fudges', according to *Norton*; '*Hibernicae Filius*', or 'Son of Ireland,' according to *Rossetti*) plays on Wordsworth's dedication of *Peter Bell* to 'Robert Southey, Esq., P.L.' (that is, 'Poet Laureate').

the Rat and the Apostate. The 'Rat' is Reynolds's Peter; Wordsworth's Peter, like his progenitor, was for S. a political apostate.

eleutherophobia. Fear of liberty (*eleutheros* is Greek for 'free').

Mr Murray's upper room. The *Quarterly Review*, the Tory rival of Hunt's *Examiner*, was edited in an upper room of the publishing house of John Murray ('our great friend') in Albemarle Street.

this monkey. Hunt.

two of the Mr Bells. Those of Reynolds's parody and Hunt's review of Wordsworth's poem.

416 *Proteus.* Greek god who could change shape at will.

ultra-legitimate. ultra-respectable.

White Obi. 'Obi' is a West Indian term for magic; 'White Obi' is Christianity or religion. The indented quotation immediately following is from Wordsworth's 'The French Revolution as It Appeared to Enthusiasts at Its Commencement' (1809), reprinted in *Poems* (1815).

six or seven days. Wordsworth had worked hard on *Peter Bell*, from 1798 to 1819, defiantly declaring (given its determinedly unelevated subject-matter and style) his aim, to quote from the poem's Dedication, 'to make the production less unworthy of a favourable reception; or, rather, to fit it for filling *permanently* a station however humble, in the Literature of my Country.' When S. sent his own poem to Hunt he claimed, in contrast, to 'have only expended a few days on this party squib' (*L* 2. 135).

417 *bitterns.* Marshland birds.

P.S. Pray excuse the date of place. 'Miching Mallecho' is ashamed to offer his address, as had been 'Tom Brown' in *The Fudge Family in Paris* (written from '245, Piccadilly'), because the street where he lodges is not 'respectable' or fashionable.

Prologue. l. 3. *antenatal Peter.* See headnote.

l. 10. *Aldric's themes.* Henry Aldrich (1647–1710) was the author of a standard school logic text, *Artis Logicae Compendium* (1691), from which come terms like 'proposition', 'mean of two extremes', and 'syllogism'.

l. 16. *his.* That is, the first or antenatal Peter's (whose 'antitype' is Wordsworth's Peter, a 'substantial' character, unlike Reynolds's Peter, who is only a 'shadow' or 'reflection').

418 l. 32. *predevote.* Predestined.

l. 35. *Cotter.* A peasant who lives in a cottage.

l. 36. *polygamic Potter.* Wordsworth's Peter was an itinerant potter, a maker and seller of pots; called 'polygamic' because, as Wordsworth tells us, 'He had a dozen wedded wives' (l. 256). S. adds a note of cod scholarship (in the manner of Pope's notes to *The Dunciad*): 'The oldest scholiasts read—A *dodecagamic* Potter. This is at once descriptive and more megalophonous—but the alliteration of the text had captivated the vulgar ears of the herd of later commentators.' ('Dodecagamic' here means married twelve times, from the Greek prefix 'dodeca-' (twelve); 'megalophonous' means great-sounding or high-sounding, from Greek 'mega-' (great)).

418　*Poem*. l. 8. *oiled his hair*. S.'s note reads: 'To those who have not duly appreciated the distinction between *whale* and *Russia* oil this attribute might rather seem to belong to the Dandy than the Evangelic. The effect, when to the windward, is indeed so similar, that it requires a subtle Naturalist to discriminate the animals. They belong however to distinct genera.' 'Russia oil', made from birch trees imported from Russia, was more expensive than whale oil, 'the common man's cheap substitute' (*Norton*).

419　l. 15. *the gravel*. A disease associated with pain and difficulty in passing urine, produced by 'an aggregation of urinary crystals which can be recognised as masses by the naked eye' (*OED* 4).

　　　l. 25. *The other . . . with you*. 'The other' is Peter's 'skin . . . of a brimstone hue' (which rhymes with 'you').

　　　l. 32. *Windermere*. The first of several Lake District sites, familiar from Wordsworth's life and writing, mentioned in the poem (see also ll. 56 and 60).

420　l. 66. *The Devil 'was' in it*. The devil's arrival in 'a black storm' (l. 61) echoes God's arrival to Job in a whirlwind (Job 38: 1) (Job is alluded to again in l. 459).

421　l. 81. *He is—what we are*. The devil exists only in the devilish behaviour of men, a theme reiterated throughout the poem.

　　　l. 84. *for sack*. The Poet Laureate (Robert Southey in 1819) was paid in sack, a type of wine; Wordsworth succeeded Southey as Poet Laureate in 1843.

　　　l. 86. *A thief . . . night*. An ironic allusion to Christ's second coming (1 Thess. 5:2).

　　　l. 92. *slop-merchant from Wapping*. A seller of cheap sailor's clothing; 'Wapping', located on the Thames in the East End of London, was a poor seamen's district.

　　　l. 94. *perk*. 'To assume . . . a lively, self-assertive, or self-conceited attitude or air' (*OED* 1).

　　　l. 96. *an upper Benjamin*. A short overcoat.

　　　ll. 108–10. *Each had . . . well*. Here and elsewhere S. deplores airy or fanciful abstraction ('an upper stream of thought'); l. 110 is ironic.

422　l. 116. *phiz*. Face (from 'physiognomy').

　　　l. 118. *clomb*. Climbed.

　　　l. 127. *Grosvenor square*. London's largest square, completed in 1837, 'inhabited by the *nouveaux riches*, including John Westbrook, the wealthy coffee-house owner who was Shelley's first father-in-law, and William Gifford, editor of the *Quarterly Review*' (*Norton*).

423　ll. 152–3. *There is . . . Castlereagh*. Hell's or London's inhabitants come from all political persuasions: John Castle ('Castles' in the press copy) was a government informer; George Canning (1770–1827) a liberal Tory

minister and polemicist; William Cobbett (1763–1835) a radical journal-
ist; and Castlereagh (for whom see note to *Mask of Anarchy*, l. 6) the
much-hated Foreign Secretary.

l. 154. *cozening*. Cheating.   *trepanning*. Catching in a trap,
swindling.

l. 157. *There is a * * **. In the press-copy, the asterisks are inserted above
'S–th–y', evidently a reference to Robert Southey.

l. 163. *Chancery Court*. Presided over in 1819 by Lord Eldon, the Lord
Chancellor (see *Mask of Anarchy*, l. 15 and note).

l. 167. *Paper money*. For S.'s attack on paper money see *Mask of
Anarchy*, l. 176 and note.

l. 174. *German soldiers*. Rumoured to be brought in by George III,
Elector of Hanover as well as King of England, to put down radical
dissent. *Webb* quotes S. to Leigh Hunt: 'The tremendous question is now
agitating, whether a military & judicial despotism is to be established by
our present rulers, or some form of government less unfavourable to the
real & permanent interests of all men is to arise from the conflict of
passions now gathering to overturn them' (*L* 2. 148).

l. 176. *methodism*. Methodism belongs with suicide because both, for S.,
as for Leigh Hunt in his review of Wordsworth's *Peter Bell*, grow from
despair.

424 l. 183. *amant misere*. Love miserably (they screech or 'caterwaul' when in
heat). S. adds a note: 'One of the attributes in Linnaeus's description of
the Cat. To a similar cause the caterwauling of more than one species of
this genus is to be referred;—except indeed that the poor quadruped is
compelled to quarrel with its own pleasures, whilst the biped is supposed
only to quarrel with those of others.'

l. 186. *chastity*. S. adds a note: 'What would this husk and excuse for a
Virtue be without its kernal prostitution, or the kernal prostitution
without this husk of a Virtue? I wonder the Women of the Town do
not form an association, like the Society for the Suppression of Vice,
for the support of what may be considered the "King, church, and
Constitution" of their order. But this subject is almost too horrible for a
joke.' The Society for the Suppression of Vice, founded in 1787 by the
Evangelicals William Wilberforce and Dr John Bowdler, discouraged
brothels, pornography, and Sunday games.

l. 187. *hobnobbers*. Those who drink together, or to each other, or are on
familiar terms.

l.190. *stock-jobbers*. Stockbrokers, speculators.

l. 197. *moiling*. Drudging, in dirt, mud, mire.

l. 202. *levees*. Assemblies held in the early afternoon, originally at court
and for men only; more generally, for and by persons of distinction.

l. 209. *Cretan-tonguèd*. Cretans were proverbial liars.

424 l. 210. *Alemannic*. German.

425 l. 212. *conversazioni*. Social gatherings at which art, literature, science, and culture are discussed.

l. 213. *Conventicles*. Meetings (or meeting-houses) of Dissenters or Nonconformists. More generally, 'a meeting (*esp.* a religious meeting) of a private, clandestine, or illegal kind' (*OED*).

ll. 220–3. *They are damned . . . 'God damns!'*. As the devil exists only in the devilish behaviour of men (l. 81), and Hell is 'a city much like London' (l. 147), so damnation is an exclusively human not divine punishment. The stanza of which ll. 220–22 are a part alludes to the poem's first epigraph, from Wordsworth's *Peter Bell*. S. adds the following note to l. 223: 'This libel on our national oath, and this accusation of all our countrymen of being in the daily practice of solemnly asseverating the most enormous falsehood I fear deserves the notice of a more active Attorney General than that here alluded to.'

l. 224. *flams*. Humbugs, deceptions.

l. 236. *stripe*. Stroke or lash-mark, of a whip or scourge.

l. 239. *Cobbett's snuff, revenge*. Cobbett's *Weekly Political Register* (1802–1835) could be accused of seeking to stir the poor to revenge against the ruling classes.

l. 242. *like we know who*. S. himself, and other like-minded reformers.

426 ll. 273–7. *All things . . . him*. An early allusion to what, after Keats, is often referred to as the Wordsworthian 'egotistical sublime'. Though S. himself could at times be accused of a comparable 'self-absorption', in the recently completed *Julian and Maddalo* and *The Cenci* he showed an ability to imagine situations from different points of view.

427 l. 285. *trim*. Character.

428 l. 320. *Diogenes*. The Cynic philosopher (*c*.400–325 BC), known for his espousal of asceticism, contempt for the body, and self-sufficiency.

ll. 328–9. *Bocca . . . luna*. 'A mouth kissed doesn't lose its freshness, for like the moon it always renews itself' (Boccaccio, *Decameron*, 2. 7, trans. G. H. McWilliam, Harmondsworth, 1972).

l. 341. *A toadlike lump*. An allusion to Satan 'Squat like a toad', *PL* 4. 800; Pope alludes to the same passage in his description of Sporus in 'Epistle to Dr Arbuthnot' (1735), l. 319.

429 l. 348. *wight*. Person.

l. 374. *petits soupers*. Intimate, informal suppers.

l. 375. *A man*. Based on Coleridge.

430 l. 407. *And . . . man*. A conflation of ll. 96–100 of Wordsworth's 'Tintern Abbey' and l. 203 of 'Ode: Intimations of Immortality' ('the human heart by which we live').

l. 411. *lie.* In the press copy, Mary S. wrote 'lie' and 'be', as though offering S. a choice (see *BSM* 1, p. 107 for commentary).

431   l. 421. *of rocks and trees.* See the concluding lines of Wordsworth's 'A Slumber Did My Spirit Seal': 'Rolled round in earth's diurnal course | With rocks and stones and trees.'

l. 429. *pedlars.* The Pedlar figures prominently in Wordsworth's *Excursion* (1814).

l. 447. *pipkins.* Small earthenware pots or pans.

ll. 448–9. *And Mr ——, the Bookseller,* | *Gave twenty pounds.* An allusion to Joseph Cottle, publisher of the *Lyrical Ballads* (who paid thirty guineas, not £20, for the copyright).

432   l. 459. *'O, that . . . book!'.* See Job 31: 35: 'Oh that one would hear me! behold, my desire is, that the Almighty would answer me, and that mine adversary had written a book.'

l. 463. *Peter's next new book.* Wordsworth's *Poems: In Two Volumes* (1807), much abused by the reviewers, famously by Francis Jeffrey in the *Edinburgh Review*.

l. 468. *seriatim.* In succession.

l. 470. *Mrs Foy's daughter.* Betty Foy is the mother of Wordsworth's 'Idiot Boy,' from *Lyrical Ballads*; she has no daughter in the poem. In the fair copy this stanza is followed by a crossed stanza reading: 'Another— "Impious Libertine! | That commits i——t with his sister. | In ruined Abbies—mighty fine | To write odes on *it*!"—I opine.'

l. 474. *Dr Willis.* Either Francis Willis (1718–1807) or his sons John (1751–1835) and Robert Darling Willis (1760–1821), all of whom treated George III for mental illness.

433   l. 500. *Emma.* The press-copy reading; S. asked Ollier to change 'Emma' to 'Betty' because, mistakenly, he thought that 'Emma' was 'the real name of the sister of a great poet who might be mistaken for Peter [i.e. Wordsworth]' (*L* 2. 196). *MWS* (2) reads 'Emma'.

l. 507. *Like . . . tune.* See *Hamlet*, 3. 1. 156–7: 'Now see that most noble and sovereign reason | Like sweet bells jangled out of tune and harsh.'

l. 512. *God's own voice.* S. adds a note: '*Vox populi, vox dei* [the voice of the people is the voice of God]. As Mr Godwin truly observes of a more famous saying, of *some merit as a popular maxim, but totally destitute of philosophical accuracy.*'

434   l. 519. *Born's . . . Kant's book.* F. G. Born's four-volume Latin translation of Kant, *Opera ad philosophiam criticam pertinentia* (1796–8). Immanuel Kant (1724–1824), German philosopher, was an influential opponent (for Coleridge in particular) of the empirical philosophy and atheistic tendencies of the eighteenth century.

l. 525. *furor verborum.* Inspired frenzy (especially of poets and prophets).

434   l. 532. *Sir William Drummond.* Author (1770–1828) of *Academical Questions* (1805), hereafter *AQ*, a book which criticizes Kant's ideas and much influenced S.

l. 534. *P. Verbovale Esquire.* S.'s note reads: 'Quasi, *Qui valet verba*:— *i.e.* all the words which have been, are, or may be expended by, for, against, with, or on him. A sufficient proof of the utility of this History. Peter's progenitor who selected this name seems to have possessed *a pure anticipated cognition* of the nature and modesty of this ornament of his posterity.' 'Pure anticipated cognition' is a phrase used jokily elsewhere by S. (see *L* 2. 438); Peacock pokes fun at Scythrop in *Nightmare Abbey* (1818) for his '*pure anticipated cognitions*' of female beauty (ch. 3), and the shared joke seems to have its origins in Sir William Drummond's attack on the 'admirers' of the 'Kantian system' 'who deduce truth from *anticipated cognitions*' (*AQ* 351, 352).

l. 538. *ex luce praebens fumum.* 'From light he then gives smoke', an inversion of ll. 143–4 of Horace's *Ars Poetica* (*c.*19 BC): 'His [a post-Homeric cyclic poet's] aim is not to have smoke after a flash, but light | emerging from smoke' (*Horace: Satires and Epistles; Persius: Satires*, trans. Niall Rudd (Harmondsworth, 1979)).

l. 541. *subter humum.* Underground.

435   l. 555. *Flibbertigibbet.* The name of a devil ('the foul fiend Flibberti-gibbet', *King Lear*, 3. 4. 106).

l. 566. *Deist.* A believer in 'natural religion'; one who rejects revelation, the divinity of Jesus, and the supernatural doctrines of Christianity.

l. 574. *Calvin and Dominic.* Calvin (1509–64), French theologian and reformer, and St Dominic (1170–1221), Spanish Catholic, founder of the Dominican order.

l. 583. *the Otter.* 'A famous river in the new Atlantis of the Dynasto-phylic Pantisocratists' (S.'s note). The River Otter passed by Coleridge's boyhood home and figures in his poetry; Pantisocracy was the name Coleridge, Southey, and their wives gave to the utopian movement they hoped to found on the banks of the Susquehanna River in Pennsylvania. According to *Norton*, '*Dynastophylic* refers to Southey's and Coleridge's later support of the established dynasties of Europe'.

436   ll. 584–8. *In the death hues . . . wish.* S.'s note reads: 'See the description of the beautiful colours produced during the agonizing death of a number of trout, in the fourth part of a long poem in blank verse [*The Excursion*, 8. 568–71], published within a few years. That Poem contains curious evidence of the gradual hardening of a strong but circumscribed sensibility, of the perversion of a penetrating but panic-stricken under-standing. The Author might have derived a lesson which he had probably forgotten from these sweet and sublime verses [the concluding lines of 'Hart-Leap Well', from the 1800 edition of *Lyrical Ballads*]: "This lesson, Shepherd, let us two divide, | Taught both by what She (Nature)

shews and what conceals, | Never to blend our measure or our pride | With sorrow of the meanest thing that feels."'

l. 603. *Sherry.* Richard Brinsley Sheridan (1751–1816), dramatist, wit, and Liberal MP; although a friend of George IV in George's days as Prince Regent, Sheridan was later shunned by him for his liberal political views.

l. 616. *George Colman.* George Colman, the Younger (1762–1836), dramatist and writer of farces, noted for his wit and bawdy good-humour.

l. 617. *male Molly.* Effeminate man.

437 ll. 636–7. *'May Carnage . . . daughter.* These lines allude to a notorious passage (ll. 106–9) in the first edition of Wordsworth's 'Ode, 1815', celebrating victory over Napoleon at Waterloo: 'But Thy most dreaded instrument, | In working out a pure intent, | Is Man—arrayed for mutual slaughter, | —Yea, Carnage is thy daughter.'

l. 644. *Slash . . . Manchester.* An allusion to the Peterloo Massacre.

l. 650. *Moloch.* A Canaanite god to whom children were sacrificed (see Leviticus 18: 21); also one of Milton's devils in *PL* 2. 43.

l. 652. *intent.* S.'s note reads: 'It is curious to observe how often extremes meet. Cobbett and Peter use the same language for a different purpose: Peter is indeed a sort of metrical Cobbett. Cobbett is however more mischievous than Peter because he pollutes a holy and now unconquerable cause with the principles of legitimate murder; while the other only makes a bad one ridiculous and odious. If either Peter or Cobbett should see this note, each will feel more indignation at being compared to the other than at any censure implied in the moral perversion laid to their charge.'

438 l. 655. *Lord MacMurderchouse's.* 'Chouse' means to cheat or swindle; as a noun, a cheat or swindler. Wordsworth received his government post in 1813, as Distributor of Stamps for Westmorland and Cumberland counties, a post in the revenue service, from William Lowther, Earl of Lonsdale.

l. 671. *Oliver.* A government spy (like Castle, l. 152), known as 'Oliver', thought by S. and other liberals to have worked as an *agent provocateur* in the Pentridge Rising of 1817; see S.'s *Address to the People on the Death of the Princess Charlotte*.

l. 679. *pelf.* Riches.

439 l. 688. *a house.* An allusion to Rydal Mount, the house Wordsworth purchased in 1813, after receiving his government post. The house was larger and more imposing than his previous house in Grasmere, Allan Bank; he lived there until his death in 1850.

l. 698. *curse.* Like the curse that visits Harry Gill in Wordsworth's 'Goody Blake and Harry Gill', in *Lyrical Ballads* (1798).

ll. 711–12. *the immortal . . . Swift.* An allusion to one of the Struldbrugs, who are endowed with immortality (which they find a misery), in Swift's *Gulliver's Travels* (1726), pt. 3, ch. 10.

440 l. 721-2 *Guatimozan . . . brass.* The successor of his uncle, the Aztec leader Montezuma; he led the failed Aztec attack against the Spaniards; after his capture he was tortured on a hot metal grid.

l. 725. *those famed seven.* Christian youths of Ephesus, sealed in a cave during the Decian persecution of AD 250, said to have awoken after a sleep of 187 years (according to Gibbon's calculation in *The History of the Decline and Fall of the Roman Empire*, ch. 33).

l. 733. *the drowsy curse.* Like the all-encompassing 'cosmic yawn' that settles over London at the end of Pope's *Dunciad*, resulting in that poem's final line: 'And universal darkness buries all.'

442 *Men of England: A Song.* Composed in Florence in late 1819 or early 1820, published posthumously in *MSW (1)*, this poem is probably one of a series of popular political verses referred to in a letter S. wrote to Leigh Hunt on 1 May 1820: 'I wish to ask you if you know of any bookseller who would like to publish a little volume of *popular songs* wholly political, & destined to awaken & direct the imagination of the reformers' (*L* 2. 191). Though this volume was never published, in a note to *MSW (1)* Mary S. refers to it: 'He had an idea of publishing a series of poems adapted expressly to commemorate . . . [the people's] circumstances and wrongs—he wrote a few, but in those days of prosecution for libel they could not be printed.' Three such poems, most scholars agree, are printed directly after *The Mask of Anarchy* in *MWS (1)*: 'Song, to the Men of England' (Mary S.'s retitling of the notebook version, 'Men of England: A Song'), 'Lines Written During the Castlereagh Administration' (titled 'England' in S.'s draft), and 'Similes' (a retitling of the notebook draft 'To S. and C.' (i.e. Sidmouth and Castlereagh), later expanded by Mary S. to 'Similes for Two Political Characters of 1819'). Among other poems subsequently associated with the series we print 'A New National Anthem', 'England in 1819', and 'What men gain fairly'. Our copy-text for 'Men of England: A Song' is S.'s fair copy in the Bodleian, originally part of the Larger Silsbee Notebook at Harvard (MS Eng. 258. 2; *MYR: Shelley* 5), supplemented by Mary S.'s text in *MSW(1)*.

443 *Lines Written during the Castlereagh Administration.* Composed in late 1819 or early 1820, published posthumously by Thomas Medwin, S.'s cousin, in the *Athenaeum*, 8 December 1832, where it first received this title, and by Mary S. in *MSW(1)*. For background see headnote to 'Men of England: A Song'. Our copy-text is taken from S.'s very lightly punctuated fair copy, titled 'To —', in Harvard fMS Eng. 822, folio 1b (*MYR: Shelley* 5), with some accidentals from S.'s intermediate fair copy, titled 'England', in Harvard MS Eng. 258.2 (*MYR: Shelley* 5) and *MSW (1)*. The poem is known by the Medwin title, which we have retained, despite Michael Scrivener's contention that it 'distances the political meaning for the 1832 audience' (*Radical Shelley* (Princeton, 1982), 227). For Castlereagh see note to *Mask of Anarchy*, l. 6.

l. 24. *Hell*. 'God' in the earlier Harvard MS (Eng. 258.2) and *MSW (1)*.

To S. and C. Composed late 1819 or early 1820, published posthumously in the *Athenaeum*, 25 August 1832 (where it was titled 'Similes') and in Mary S.'s 1839 editions. For background see headnote to 'Men of England: A Song'. Our copy-text is S.'s lightly punctuated draft in the Bodleian (*BSM* 18), supplemented by punctuation from Mary S.'s text in *MWS (2)*, which expands Medwin's title to 'Similes for Two Political Characters of 1819'. In the Harvard safe-keeping notebook the title is 'To Sxxxxxth and Cxxxxxxxxgh' (MS Eng. 258. 2; *MYR: Shelley* 5).

l. 1. *their*. Mary S.'s 1839 editions read 'an'.

l. 2. *wind*. Mary S.'s 1839 editions read 'sound'.

444 l. 7. *yew*. Mary S.'s 1839 editions read 'hue'.

l. 9. *moon*. Mary S.'s 1839 editions read 'morn'.

l. 20. *Two . . . one*. In another draft of stanza 4 of the poem in the Bodleian (*BSM* 7), its final line reads 'Two tangled snakes which are but one.'

'What men gain fairly'. Composed late 1819 or early 1820, published posthumously in *MWS (2)*; probably a fragment. For background see headnote to 'Men of England: A Song'. Our copy-text is S.'s holograph in the Huntington (MS. HM 2177; *MYR: Shelley* 4).

l. 7. *With those . . . strong*. This line omitted by Mary S.

A New National Anthem. Composed late 1819 or early 1820, published posthumously in the 'Note on Poems of 1819' (see headnote to 'Men of England: A Song') in *MWS (2)*. Our copy-text is S.'s draft in the Bodleian (*BSM* 5), which is not a fair copy; we have also consulted *MWS (2)*, especially for punctuation.

445 l. 13. *majestic*. Thus *MWS (2)*; the word in the draft is all but indecipherable; the transcription in *BSM* 5 reads '<approvative>'.

446 l. 42. *Queen*. After this word, two incomplete stanzas in the draft, one very difficult to decipher, have been omitted here, as in *MWS (2)*.

Sonnet: England in 1819. Composed in Florence in late 1819, sent to Leigh Hunt for publication on 23 December 1819, but only published posthumously, in *MWS (1)*. The poem may have been considered for the volume of 'popular songs' S. hoped to publish in 1820 (see headnote to 'Men of England: A Song'). *Webb* quotes the Westminster MP and parliamentary reformer Francis Burdett (1770–1844), in an Election Address of 11 October 1812, published in Hunt's *Examiner*: 'an army of spies and informers . . . a Phantom for a king; a degraded aristocracy; an oppressed people . . . vague and sanguinary laws.' Our copy-text is S.'s fair copy in the Bodleian (*BSM* 18).

l. 1. *King*. George III had reigned since 1760, had been insane since 1811, and was soon to die, aged 81, on 29 January 1820; his 'blindness' was metaphorical, Lear's rather than Gloucester's.

446 l. 2. *Princes.* George III's sons were notoriously dissolute.

l. 7. *A people . . . field.* An allusion to the Peterloo Massacre (see head-note to *Mask of Anarchy*).

l. 8. *liberticide.* The killing of liberty (S.'s coinage).

l. 10. *Golden and sanguine.* Gold and blood ('sanguine' here means bloody rather than hopeful or confident) recurrently symbolize the twin origins and underpinnings of tyranny in S.'s poetry: money and violence.

l. 12. *A senate . . . unrepealed.* The 'senate' here is the unreformed Parliament. 'Time's worst statute, unrepealed' refers to the Test and Corporations Acts which imposed disabilities upon Dissenters and Roman Catholics (and survived several attempts at repeal and modification).

Love's Philosophy. Published by Leigh Hunt in the *Indicator* in December 1819 and in *PP*; transcribed by S. in Harvard MS Eng. 258. 2 (*MYR: Shelley* 5) where it is entitled (possibly by Mary S.) 'An Anacreontic' and by S. for Sophia Stacey in a copy of the *Literary Pocket-Book for 1819* in Eton College Library (*MYR: Shelley* 8). This last manuscript supplies our copy-text (title added from *PP*). Sophia Stacey, a ward of S.'s uncle, shared the same boarding-house as the Shelleys in Florence, 1819; S. wrote a number of lyrics for her.

l. 7. *In . . . mingle.* 'In one another's being mingle', *PP*; Harvard.

447 l. 18. *What . . . worth.* 'What were these examples worth', Harvard; 'What are all these kissings worth,', *PP*.

Ode to Heaven. Composed in December 1819 and published in *Prometheus Unbound, with Other Poems*, which supplies our copy-text; we have also consulted the fair copy in the Bodleian (*BSM* 9) and the fair copy (by Mary S.) in the Larger Silsbee Notebook at Harvard (MS Eng. 258. 2; *MYR: Shelley* 5). In the Preface to *MWS: Prose*, Mary S. links the poem to the following account of S.'s metaphysical outlook: 'The creation, such as it was perceived by his mind—a unit in immensity, was slight and narrow compared with the interminable forms of thought that might exist beyond, to be perceived perhaps hereafter by his own mind; or which are perceptible to other minds that fill the universe, not of space in the material sense, but of infinity in the immaterial one'. The poem, written in trochaic tetrameters, shows S.'s interest in dialectic and perspective as its sections work through and set against each other different views of the idea of heaven.

First Spirit. 'Chorus of Spirits' in *BSM* 9.

ll. 1–27. *Palace-roof . . . alway!.* The First Spirit describes heaven in terms influenced by eighteenth-century astronomy and Deist theology; it equivocates about the existence of a 'Power' (l. 21), which may be only a human projection (ll. 21–2).

448 *Second Spirit.* 'A Remoter Voice' in *BSM* 9.

ll. 28–36. *Thou art ... dream.* The Second Spirit suggests that the human notion of heaven is an imperfect sketch of 'delights' (l. 33) that exceed conception.

Third Spirit. 'A Louder and Still Remoter Voice' in *BSM* 9.

l. 53. *millions. BSM* 9 has 'million'.

ll. 37–54. *Peace! . . . disappear!* The Third Spirit asserts that heaven and humans alike are insignificant in the scheme of things, yet that seemingly insignificant things can offer a glimpse of heaven, here 'an unimagined world' (l. 49).

To the Lord Chancellor. Dated 1819 by Mary S. but probably composed in 1820 (see *BSM* 14, pp. xviii–xix), 'To the Lord Chancellor' was published in part in Mary S.'s first 1839 edition and was published in full in her second 1839 edition. There is a draft in the Bodleian (*BSM* 14) and a later draft in Harvard MS Eng. 258. 2 (*MYR: Shelley* 5). A subsequent transcription by Mary S., with corrections by S., in Harvard fMS. Eng 822 (*MYR: Shelley* 5) provides our copy-text. After the death of his first wife, Harriet, S. had been refused custody of their children, Ianthe and Charles, in a Chancery case presided over by Lord Eldon, the Lord Chancellor. On 27 March 1817 Eldon decided against S. on the grounds that the latter's 'principles' would lead to the recommendation of 'conduct' that was 'immoral and vicious'. In her 'Note on Poems of 1819' Mary S. writes: 'No words can express the anguish he felt when his elder children were torn from him.' S. was also concerned that his children by Mary would be taken from him. For the idea of a curse and the poem's concluding twist, S. may be indebted to Byron's *Childe Harold*, 4. 132–5.

Title. The copy text has 'To Lxxd Exxxn', cancelled, presumably for prudential reasons, in favour of 'To ——'; the intermediate Harvard draft has 'To the Lord Chancellor', with the last two words cancelled. We have adopted the title in this intermediate draft before the cancellations, as did Mary S. and subsequent editors.

l. 4. *a buried form.* 'The Star-chamber' (Mary S. in her second 1839 edition).

449 ll. 21–4. *By . . . birth.* Cancelled in copy-text; S. then wrote in the right-hand margin 'Insert this'.

l. 36. *why not fatherless?* S. altered Mary S.'s transcription from 'yet not fatherless'.

450 l. 40. *tomb.* After this stanza, the copy-text has the following stanza cancelled with the instruction 'dele' (delete): 'By thy most impious Hell, and all its terror, | By all the grief, the madness, and the guilt | Which [*for* Of] thine impostures, which must be their error, | That sand on which thy crumbling Power is built'. The stanza is usually printed by editors (though not *Longman* 1) as part of the poem.

ll. 47–8. *And . . . men.* For Eldon's notorious weeping in court, see *Mask of Anarchy*, ll. 16–17.

450 *The Sensitive Plant.* Written in Pisa in the spring of 1820, *The Sensitive Plant* was included in the volume *Prometheus Unbound, with Other Poems* (1820). This text supplies our copy-text, though we have also consulted the fair copy in Mary S.'s hand in the Larger Silsbee Notebook at Harvard (MS Eng. 258. 2; *MYR: Shelley* 5); there is draft material in the Bodleian (*BSM* 18) and the Huntington (MS HM 2176; *MYR: Shelley* 6). Employing anapaestic tetrameters for its three Parts, before switching to octosyllabic iambics for its coda-like Conclusion, the poem questions whether our senses play us false in reporting that 'love, and beauty, and delight' are subject to decay. The poem may obliquely articulate S.'s political hopes and fears following the Cato Street Conspiracy of February 1820 in which an attempted assassination of ministers of the crown was foiled; S. regretted the attempted assassination as working against the cause of reform. S. draws on a variety of poems, most notably the account of the Garden of Adonis in Spenser's *FQ* 3. 6, and Milton's description of Eden in *PL*; he also returns to Erasmus Darwin's *The Loves of the Plants*, an early favourite. The sensitive plant, or *mimosa pudica*, was of interest in the period as occupying an ambiguous border between the vegetable and animal worlds, and had been made use of by William Cowper in his poem 'The Poet, the Oyster, and the Sensitive Plant' (1782). S. refers to himself in a letter of December 1821 as an 'Exotic . . . unfortunately belonging to the order of mimosa' (*L* 2. 368).

Part First. ll. 3–4. *And it opened . . . light.* See Erasmus Darwin, *The Loves of the Plants*, where the 'chaste MIMOSA' 'Shuts her sweet eye-lids to approaching night, | And hails with freshen'd charms the rising light' (1. 247, 253–4; quoted from Woodstock Books facsimile, 1991).

451 l. 12. *companionless.* The sensitive plant is an annual; all the other flowers in Part First are perennials.

l. 17. *pied.* Varied in colour.

l. 21. *Naiad-like.* Naiads were water nymphs, who incarnated the divinity of the springs and streams which they inhabited.

l. 25. *the hyacinth . . . sense.* The synaesthetic mingling of sound and odour here and elsewhere in Part First evokes a sense of harmony and interchange.

l. 29. *addressed.* Made ready.

l. 38. *blows.* Blooms; blossoms.

l. 42. *pranked.* Decked out; spangled.

452 l. 54. *fabulous asphodels.* Asphodels were flowers fabled to grow in the Elysian fields.

l. 58. *undefilèd Paradise.* In the draft S. wrote and cancelled 'this Republic of odours & hues'.

l. 63. *mine-lamps.* Humphry Davy had invented his safety-lamp for miners in 1815 (*Webb*).

453 ll. 76–7. *It loves . . . the beautiful!* See S.'s translation of Plato's *Symposium*: ' "It is conceded, then, that Love loves that which he wants but possesses not?"—"Yes, certainly."—"But Love wants and does not possess beauty?"—"Indeed it must necessarily follow" ' (*Notopoulos*, p. 440).

454 ll. 98–109. *And when evening . . . Sensitive Plant.* See *PL* 4. 598–604, which describes how when 'came still evening on' (l. 598) all beasts and birds went to sleep to the accompaniment of 'Silence' (l. 600)—'all but the wakeful nightingale; | She all night long her amorous descant sung' (ll. 602–3).

Part Second. l. 1. *a Power . . . place.* See Milton, *Arcades*, where the Genius of the Wood describes himself as 'the power | Of this fair wood' (ll. 44–5) and asserts that 'all my plants I save from nightly ill' (l. 48).

455 ll. 37–8. *lifted . . . bands.* See *PL* 9. 424–31, where Satan spies on Eve 'stooping to support | Each flower of slender stalk' (ll. 427–8).

l. 38. *osier.* Made of willow.

l. 43. *woof.* Woven fabric.

l. 49. *beam-like ephemeris.* Mayfly that sparkles like a line of light.

l. 51. *and harm not.* See *The Tempest*, 3. 2. 131, where Caliban describes 'sweet airs, that give delight and hurt not'.

l. 53. *antenatal.* Before birth. The idea of life before birth is central to the Platonic doctrine of reminiscence articulated in the *Phaedo*.

456 *Part Third.* l. 3. *Baiae.* A bay in the Gulf of Naples from which Mt. Vesuvius can be seen.

l. 4. *She.* The moon.

457 l. 54. *darnels.* Grass that can grow as a weed.

l. 55. *dock . . . hemlock.* 'Dock' is a coarse weed; 'henbane' and 'hemlock' are poisonous plants.

l. 56. *shank.* Lower part of leg, used metaphorically.

l. 60. *pulpous.* Pulpy.

l. 61. *Livid.* Of bluish leaden colour; discoloured as by bruise. *lurid.* Dingy yellowish brown.

458 l. 62. *agarics.* Gill mushrooms.   *mildew.* Destructive growth of minute fungi on plants.

ll. 66–9. *Their moss . . . by.* Cancelled in Mary S.'s transcription in *MYR: Shelley* 5 and omitted in her collected editions.

l. 70. *Spawn.* White fibrous matter from which mushrooms are produced.

l. 72. *flags.* Plant with bladed leaf growing on moist ground.

l. 78. *unctuous.* Greasy.

458 l. 82. *forbid*. Cursed. See *Macbeth*, I. 3. 20: 'He shall live a man forbid.'

l. 91. *One . . . lip*. See *Macbeth*, I. 3. 42–3: 'each at once her choppy finger laying | Upon her skinny lips.'

459 l. 103. *want*. Typical of this Part's ironic echoes of earlier Parts: here of 'love's sweet want' (I. II).

l. 113. *griff*. Claw.

l. 116. *mandrakes*. Poisonous plant with white or purple flowers and large yellow fruit; once thought to resemble human form and to shriek when plucked.

460 *Conclusion*. l. 12. *shadows of the dream*. Plato and Calderón (*Life is a Dream*) are likely influences.

l. 15. *own*. To admit; to concede something is the case. In drafts S. wrote 'think' and 'say'.

ll. 21–4. *For love . . . obscure*. The death and decay of love, beauty and delight are apparent, but not real: the result of failure on the part of our organs of perception and understanding.

An Exhortation. Composed in Pisa, April 1820 (place and date given in the fair copy in Mary S.'s hand in the Larger Silsbee Notebook at Harvard (MS Eng. 258. 2; *MYR: Shelley* 5)), sent to Maria Gisborne on 8 May 1820 ('a little thing about Poets . . . a kind of an excuse for Wordsworth' (*L* 2. 195)), and published in *Prometheus Unbound, with Other Poems* (1820). The 1820 published text supplies our copy-text. The poem represents a further stage in S.'s reflections on Wordsworth and, more generally, on the question that Wordsworth himself raises in the Preface to *Lyrical Ballads* (1802), 'What is a Poet?'

ll. 1–2. *Chameleons . . . fame*. Comparison and contrast between the shape-changing of chameleons and poets run through the poem.

461 l. 27. *the boon!* Possibly an ironic allusion to Wordsworth's sonnet, 'The world is too much with us', l. 4: 'We have given our hearts away, a sordid boon!'

The Cloud. Composed 1820 and published in *Prometheus Unbound, with Other Poems* (1820), which supplies our copy-text, though we have also consulted a draft in the Bodleian and fair copy of ll. 35–84 (both in *BSM* 5). *Norton* cites a work S. knew and admired, the song of the Nepheliads in part 2 of Leigh Hunt's 'The Nymphs', published in *Foliage* (1818), as the poem's most likely literary source; for a scientific source see the note to l. 18 below.

l. 7. *mother's*. The earth's.

l. 18. *pilot*. The positively charged electricity in the cloud, which reacts with the negatively charged electricity of 'Earth and Ocean', producing rain and thunderstorms. As the cloud is guided by the 'pilot', so 'Earth and Ocean' are guided by 'genii' (l. 23), 'the Spirit' (l. 28). *Norton* and

Webb cite Adam Walker's *A System of Familiar Philosophy*, 2 vols. (1799): 'water rises through the air, flying on the wings of electricity'. Walker had lectured both at Syon House Academy and Eton during S.'s years there.

l. 20. *at fits.* At intervals, randomly.

l. 23. *Lured by the love of the genii.* The attraction of 'pilot' and 'genii' is mutual, as suggested by this phrase, which refers both to the pilot's and the genii's love.

462 l. 33. *sailing rack.* Mass of clouds.

l. 34. *morning star.* The planet Venus (known as Hesperus, the evening star, at night).

l. 42. *depths.* The reading in the Bodleian fair copy; the copy-text has 'depth'.

l. 43. *airy nest.* A pun, the nest being both high in the air and made of air.

l. 44. *brooding dove.* An echo of the opening of *PL*, in which Milton invokes the 'Heavenly Muse' (identified with the Holy Spirit) which 'Dove-like sat'st brooding on the vast abyss | And mad'st it pregnant' (1. 21–2).

ll. 45–58. *That orbèd . . . moon and these.* See Wordsworth's 'A Night-Piece' in *Poems* (1815) for a comparable (and contrasting) scene of moon, stars, thinly textured cloud, and revelation.

l. 58. *paved with the moon and these.* The reflections of moon and stars ('these'), shining through 'rents' in the cloud, 'pave' the 'calm rivers, lakes, and seas'.

l. 59. *zone.* Belt or encircling band (like 'girdle' in next line).

463 l. 71. *sphere-fire.* The sun, a fiery sphere. The Bodleian fair copy and draft have 'sphere-fires', so there is a case for emendation.

l. 75. *pores.* Cloud-forming moisture (like 'sweat') is drawn from the earth's 'oceans and shores', as from the 'pores' of a body.   *oceans.* The reading in the fair copy. The copy-text has 'ocean'.

l. 79. *convex gleams.* From the cloud's perspective the rays of the sun ('gleams') would look curved ('convex') as they spread over the earth, since the earth's atmosphere bends or refracts them as they enter it.

l. 81. *cenotaph.* An empty tomb, the previous line's 'dome of blue air', 'unbuilt' in the last line by the cloud's return.

To a Skylark. Composed near Leghorn in summer 1820, published with *Prometheus Unbound, with Other Poems* (1820), which supplies our copy-text, though we have also consulted S.'s fair copy in the Larger Silsbee Notebook at Harvard (MS. Eng. 258. 2; *MYR: Shelley* 5). Skylarks sing only in flight, often when too high to be seen.

l. 8. *cloud of fire.* A cloud illuminated by the sun, fiery.

464 l. 22. *silver sphere.* The morning star (Venus).

465   l. 66. *Hymenaeal*. Pertaining to a wedding; Hymen is the Greek god of marriage.

466   ll. 86–7. *We look . . . what is not*. S. may be alluding to a comparable distinction between humans and animals in *Hamlet*, 4. 4. 23–9.

l. 103. *harmonious madness*. S. may have taken this view of the poet from Plato's *Phaedrus*, which he had read in May 1819.

Ode to Liberty. Composed between March and July 1820, published in *Prometheus Unbound, with Other Poems* (1820), as the final poem in the volume; this volume supplies our copy-text, though we have also consulted a rough draft in the Bodleian (*BSM* 5), a transcript of ll. 1–21 by Mary S. in the Larger Silsbee Notebook at Harvard (MS Eng. 258. 2; *MYR: Shelley* 5), and S.'s translation into Italian of stanzas 1–13 and 19 in the Bodleian (*BSM* 21). The poem's occasion was the success of the Spanish Revolution begun on 1 January and issuing in a string of liberal reforms, including suffrage to all literate males, biennial parliaments, freedom of the press, and abolition of the Inquisition. The poem follows the progress of Liberty through history in the manner of Thomas Gray's tracing of 'The Progress of Poetry,' in his Pindaric Ode of 1754.

Epigraph. Taken from Canto 4, stanza 98 of Byron's *Childe Harold* (1818), the last of 21 stanzas tracing the struggle of liberty against tyranny.

l. 1. *vibrated*. Made animate; more specifically, 'emitted the electric charge of revolution whose current links nation with nation' (*Webb*).   *again*. Perhaps referring to the earlier resistance of the Spanish people against the French in 1807–8.

467   l. 11. *Rapt it*. Made S.'s 'soul' (l. 5) rapt or awestruck.

ll. 5–15. *My soul . . . the same*. In these lines S.'s 'soul' is inspired in phrases drawn from both classical and biblical visionary poetry. *Webb* cites analogues from Pindar (*Nemeans*, 3. 80–82), Dante, and Revelation 16–17.

l. 18. *daedal*. Artfully constructed and adorned, like the work of Daedalus, master-craftsman of Greek mythology.

ll. 16–23. *The Sun . . . wert not*. A description of the Creation, described as 'a chaos and a curse' (l. 22) until redeemed by Liberty ('thou', l. 23).

468   l. 41. *sister-pest*. Religion; 'Pest' means pestilence, plague, curse.

l. 42. *pinions*. Wings.

l. 43. *Anarchs*. Tyrants, authors or agents of chaos, anarchy.

l. 47. *dividuous*. Broken up, or separated, one from the other, individual.

l. 58. *Parian stone*. The fine white marble favoured by Greek sculptors, quarried from the island of Paros.

l. 65. *Pave it . . . pavilions it*. The imagined city built by 'vision' (l. 61), likened to Athens.

l. 74. *that hill.* The Acropolis, site of the Parthenon and other public buildings decorated with sculptures of heroes and gods ('forms that mock the eternal dead | In marble immortality', ll. 73–4).

469 l. 92. *Maenad.* S.'s note, keyed to the end of this line, reads, 'See the Bacchae of Euripides'.

ll. 91–4. *Then Rome . . . unweanèd.* Though Athens ('thy dearest') was still devoted to Liberty ('From that Elysian food was yet unweaned'), Rome, too, drew inspiration ('the milk of greatness') from her, like one of the wolf cubs (the wolf was a symbol of Rome) suckled by Agave, Cadmus' daughter (hence 'Cadmaean'), and other ecstatic or possessed female followers of Dionysus ('Maenads') in Euripides' *Bacchae.*

l. 98. *Saintly Camillus . . . firm Atilius.* The general and statesman Marcus Furius Camillus, 'saviour of his country and second founder of Rome' (Livy, 5. 2), returned from voluntary exile to lead resistance to Rome's occupation by Gauls (*c.*390 BC); called 'saintly' because he refused an offer to use schoolchildren as hostages. 'Atilius' was Marcus Atilius Regulus (third century BC), Roman consul and a commander of the Roman expedition to Africa in the First Punic War; called 'firm' because, after he was captured by the Carthaginians and paroled to Rome to negotiate a peace, he kept his word and returned to them, despite advising the Romans to continue fighting and knowing his return meant certain death.

l. 100. *Capitolian throne.* The Capitoline hill in Rome, associated with the Republic.

ll. 103–4. *Palatinus sighed . . . Ionian song.* The Palatine hill, associated here with Empire, sighs in songs which echo those of Greek poets (as do the songs of Virgil and Horace, first poets of the Empire).

ll. 99–105. *But when tears . . . disown.* These lines trace Liberty's reluctant desertion of Rome as it grows from Republic to Empire.

l. 106. *Hyrcanian.* Refers to an area of Persia just south of the Caspian (Hyrcanian) Sea.

470 l. 115. *Scald's dreams . . . Druid's sleep.* Scalds (or 'skalds') were Norwegian and Icelandic poets; Druids were Celtic priests. Liberty plays no part in their dreams.

l. 119. *Galilean serpent.* The Christian religion.

l. 123. *Alfred's olive-cinctured brow.* King Alfred (848–99), king of the West Saxons from 871 to his death, poet and scholar; his brow is circled ('cinctured') with olive leaves, in ancient Greece the highest distinction of a citizen who deserved well of his country.

ll. 124–35. *And many . . . dome.* 'The rise of the communes, independent city-state republics in medieval Italy, led to the revival of the arts' (*Norton*). Presumably the 'warrior-peopled citadel[s]' of l. 124, likened to volcanoes rising out of the sea, are the republics of medieval Italy that fostered the arts.

470 l. 136. *Thou huntress . . . the Moon!* Liberty is swifter than Diana, goddess of the moon and of hunting.

l. 141. *Luther.* Martin Luther (1483–1546), leader of the Reformation in Germany, was partly a disciple of Liberty, helping to waken the nations from 'trance' (l. 143), but his lance, though capable of reflecting Liberty's 'lightning,' was 'leaden' (l. 142).

l. 145. *England's prophets.* See *A Philosophical View of Reform*: 'Shakespeare and Lord Bacon and the great writers of the age of Elizabeth and James I were at once the effects of this new spirit in men's minds, and the cause of its more complete development' (p. 638).

471 l. 149. *the sad scene.* The restoration of the Stuart monarchy.

l. 158. *the destroyer.* Death.

ll. 159–65. *When . . . eyes.* Liberty's rise, likened to that of the sun, is depicted in these lines as 'the Enlightenment and subsequent reform and revolutionary movements of the eighteenth century' (*Norton*).

l. 171. *Bacchanals of blood.* The excesses of the French Revolution, likened to those of the followers of Dionysus in Euripides' *Bacchae*.

l. 173. *Destruction's . . . brood!* The anti-revolutionary forces of Europe, both political ('sceptred slaves') and religious ('mitred brood').

l. 174. *one.* Napoleon.

472 l. 183. *Vesuvius wakens Etna.* 'The interconnection of the volcanic regions of the globe (which was first fully expounded by John Michell in 1760) provides a scientific basis for this image of a sympathetic network of revolutionary activity' (*Webb*).

ll. 185–6. *every Aeolian isle . . . Pelorus.* The islands from the Bay of Naples to Sicily. 'Aeolian' means wind-swept (from the Greek god of the winds, Aeolus). 'Pithecusa' is Ischia, west of Naples and Cumae; 'Pelorus' is Cape Faro, the north-east point in Sicily.

l. 189. *Her chains.* England's, 'threads' (in comparison to Spain's 'links of steel') because of her less tyrannical history.

l. 196. *Tomb of Arminius.* Germany; Arminius (18 BC–AD 19) was the Germanic tribal leader who freed Germany from Roman rule in AD 6.

l. 204. *thou.* Italy.

l. 216. *Ye.* 'The free' of l. 211.

l. 218. *gordian word.* 'KING' (l. 212); 'gordian' because difficult to undo, like the complicated knot of King Gordius of Phrygia; by cutting through it with his sword Alexander became emperor of Asia, as prophesied by an oracle (like the one heard by Liberty in l. 216).

473 l. 221. *The axes and the rods.* The *fasces* ('bundles', Lat.), a bundle of rods tied round with a red thong from which an axe projected, were assigned to the higher magistrates in ancient Rome as symbols of authority.

l. 224. *thou.* Liberty.

l. 233. *Power*. The nature of this power, a potential source of inspiration, is unspecified, though it is distinguished here from the 'aweless soul', an internal or human divinity.

l. 241. *He*. Either the 'aweless soul' or the 'Power unknown' of l. 233.

l. 252. *thy*. Art refers to itself as Nature's child; 'thy' means 'Nature's'.

l. 255. *thy gifts and hers*. Liberty's and Art's gifts.

474 l. 258. *Eoan*. Eastern, from Eos, the Greek name for Aurora, goddess of the dawn.

Sonnet ('Ye hasten to the grave!') Mary S. dates the poem to 1820. First published in *The Literary Pocket-Book for 1823* (1822). There is a transcription by S. in the Larger Silsbee Notebook at Harvard (MS Eng. 258. 2; *MYR: Shelley* 5) and one by S. in the Pierpont Morgan Library (MA 3223; *MYR: Shelley* 8). This latter transcription supplies our copy-text. The sonnet reverses the order of octave and sestet, and sustains its *b* rhyme from sestet to octave.

l. 1. *grave*. In Harvard MS, 'dead'; in copy-text, 'dead' and 'grave' are both cancelled.

475 l. 4. *Heart*. S.'s first thought was 'Sense'.

l. 5. *pale Expectation*. In Harvard, 'anticipation'.

Song ('Rarely, rarely comest thou'). Composed in Pisa, May 1820, according to S.'s note at the end of his transcription in the Larger Silsbee Notebook at Harvard (MS Eng. 258. 2; *MYR: Shelley* 5), which supplies our copy-text. The poem was first published in *PP*.

476 *Letter to Maria Gisborne*. The poem, written in June and posted in July 1820, was first published in incomplete form in *PP*. S.'s draft in the Bodleian can be consulted in *BSM* 14; there is also a transcription by Mary S. in the Huntington Library (HM 12338; *MYR: Shelley* 3), probably made in 1823, and a fair copy by John Gisborne in the Bodleian (Abinger Deposit d. 475), made in 1831, presumably from the copy sent by S. This last text serves as our copy-text, though we have also consulted the draft and Mary S.'s fair copy. *Letter to Maria Gisborne* was composed when the Shelleys were staying in the Leghorn house of their friends, John and Maria Gisborne, while the latter were visiting London. Maria had rejected a proposal of marriage by William Godwin after the death of Mary Wollstonecraft; she taught S. Spanish, principally so that the poet could read Calderón. Her son by an earlier marriage, Henry Reveley, was a nautical engineer. Helped by S., he had been designing a steamboat (which never materialized), and it is his workshop which S. describes in the poem. The poem only hints at the unhappiness that S. and Mary were experiencing in 1820. Mary was upset by Godwin's dire financial problems and attempts to borrow money. In a letter to the Gisbornes of 26 May 1820 S. describes Godwin as 'the only sincere enemy I have in the world' but asserts his 'admiration' for his father-in-law's 'intellectual powers, & even the moral

resources of his character' (*L* 2. 202, 203). Throughout, the poem asserts, through its very manner (which includes playful allusions to Spenserian romance), the improvisatory power of the creative imagination.

476 l. 1. *spider*. Jonathan Swift uses the spider as an emblem of the modern writer who spins meanings out of his own entrails (*The Battle of the Books*); S. reverses Swift's derogatory view of this activity.

l. 5. *whom . . . worm*. See Job 25: 6: 'How much less man, that is a worm? and the son of man, which is a worm?'

l. 7. *verse*. The reading in the draft and Gisborne fair copy; previous printed editions follow Mary S.'s 'rare' in the Huntington fair copy.

477 l. 10. *soft cell*. Cocoon from which S.'s winged 'living name' (l. 11) will emerge.   *that*. 'This decaying form' (l. 6).

l. 15. *I wist*. I know.

l. 16. *mechanist*. One skilled in mechanics.

l. 17. *Archimedean*. The adjective is formed from Archimedes (*c*.287–212 BC), the Greek scientist and inventor.

l. 19. *gin*. Mechanical contrivance or trap.

l. 20. *figured spells*. Draft has 'written spells'.

l. 21. *Its way . . . sea*. Alludes to the steamboat which Henry Reveley had been planning with S.'s financial support; it was planned that the steamboat should ply between Leghorn and Marseilles.

ll. 23–4. *Vulcan . . . the Titans*. At Jove's command Vulcan had made an ever-turning wheel on which Ixion was bound, as well as the chains that tied Prometheus (one of the Titans) to his mountain.

l. 25. *St Dominic*. Dominic (1170–1221) was the founder of the Dominicans and associated with the Inquisition.

l. 27. *philanthropic council*. Ironic allusion to councils of the Catholic Church, particularly the Council of Trent (1545–63) which launched the Counter-Reformation.

ll. 33–4. *lamp-like Spain . . . hearth*. Alludes to the virtually bloodless Spanish Revolution in 1820, when, in response to widespread revolt, King Ferdinand re-established the Constitution (see headnote to 'Ode to Liberty', p. 780).

ll. 36–7. *utmost crag . . . Cornwall*. Alludes to the defeat of the Spanish Armada (1588) when many ships were wrecked off the coast of Cornwall and off coasts as far north as the Orkneys.

l. 37. *the storm-encompassed isles*. Either islands off the Cornish coast or islands further north, such as the Orkneys. In the Bodleian draft S. cancelled 'the' in favour of 'its'.

l. 45. *Proteus*. Greek god who could change his shape at will.

478 l. 51. *Tubal Cain*. See Genesis 4: 22: 'an instructer of every artificer in brass and iron'.

l. 55. *knacks*. Ingenious contrivances.

l. 56. *catalogize*. Make a catalogue of.

l. 59. *swink*. Labour. A term found in Spenser (see 'Prosopopoia: or Mother Hubberds Tale', l. 163: 'For they doo swinke and sweate to feed the other').

l. 65. *rouse*. Draught of drink; drinking-bout. See *Hamlet*, 1. 2. 127: 'the King's rouse'.

l. 75. *a rude idealism*. A rough notion or version.

l. 83. *statical*. Concerned with statics, bodies at rest or in equilibrium.

l. 84. *rosin*. Resin.

479 l. 95. *Laplace*. Marquis Pierre Simon de Laplace (1749–1827). French mathematician and astronomer. S. alludes to him in a note to section 6 of *Queen Mab* (not included here).   *Saunderson*. Nicholas Saunderson (1682–1739), Cambridge mathematician, early teacher of Newtonian science, author of books on algebra and mathematical physics (see *Norton*).   *Sims*. *Norton* suggests either Thomas Simpson (1710–61), author of books on algebra, geometry, and trigonometry, or Robert Simson (1687–1768), author of books on geometry and conic sections.

l. 98. *Baron . . . Memoirs*. Baron François de Tott's *Memoirs sur les Turcs et les Tartares* (1784).

l. 103. *as . . . mo*. Mo (or moe) means more. See Spenser, *FQ* 4. 1. 24: 'And eke of private persons many moe'.

l. 104. *womb of time*. See *Othello*, 1. 3. 358–9: 'There are many events in the womb of time.'

l. 106. *Archimage*. Alludes ironically to Archimago, the evil enchanter in *FQ*.

l. 114. *Libeccio*. The south-west wind.

480 l. 132. *quaint*. Delicately odd, with something of the older meanings of the word, 'wise, knowing' (*OED* 1).

l. 137. *second-sighted*. Able to perceive future or distant occurrences.

l. 142. *sad enchantress*. Memory.

l. 149. *transverse*. In crosswise direction.

l. 168. *visionary rhyme*. See *The Witch of Atlas*, l. 8.

481 l. 175. *indued*. Put on; learned.

l. 176. *a land . . . free*. See note to ll. 33–4 above.

l. 180. *My name is Legion*. The words of an 'unclean spirit' in Mark 5: 9; legion means numberless.

481 l. 181. *Calderon*. Pedro Calderón de la Barca (1600–81), the Spanish dramatist, and author of many *autos sacramentales* (religious plays), was much admired by S., who translated scenes from *El mágico prodigioso*, and comments in a letter of November 1820, 'I am bathing myself in the light & odour of the flowery & starry Autos' (*L* 2. 250).

ll. 184–5. *thou . . . nurse*. S. learned Spanish with Maria Gisborne.

ll. 193–5. *that great sea . . . more*. The shipwreck imagery picks up that in ll. 36–7.

ll. 196–201. *That which . . . dumb*. S.'s portrait of William Godwin, his father-in-law, alludes to Milton's self-portrait in *PL* 7. 24–6 as singing 'with mortal voice, unchanged | To hoarse or mute, though fallen on evil days, | On evil days though fallen'.

482 l. 210. *salt of the earth*. Alludes to Matthew 5: 13: 'Ye are the salt of the earth.'

l. 213. *Shout*. Robert Shout was a London maker of plaster copies of antique statues. See Keats's 'Sleep and Poetry', ll. 354–91, for an 'inventory of the art garniture', as Charles Cowden Clarke called it, in Hunt's Hampstead cottage.

l. 220. *duns*. Debt-collectors.

ll. 209–25. *You will see Hunt . . . tenderness*. Leigh Hunt (1784–1859), dedicatee of *The Cenci*, was a poet, journalist, and editor: his familiar style is an influence on S.'s poem.

ll. 226–32. *You will see Hogg . . . deep*. Thomas Jefferson Hogg (1792–1862) was S.'s closest friend at Oxford, from where he was expelled with S. Hogg lived with Jane Williams after her return from Italy and wrote an entertaining but unreliable biography of the poet.

l. 240. *camelopard*. Giraffe.

ll. 232–47. *And there . . . expectation*. Thomas Love Peacock (1785–1866), a close friend of S., was a comic novelist, who worked for the East India Company (hence 'the Indian air', l. 235) and on 22 March 1822 had married Jane Gryffydh, who came from Snowdonia in Wales (hence l. 239).

483 l. 250. *Horace Smith*. (1779–1849), poet, parodist (the author, with his brother James, of *Rejected Addresses* (1812)), and stockbroker. Smith was admired by S., who, according to Hunt in his *Autobiography*, ed. J. E. Morpurgo, London, 1949, said of him, 'he writes poetry and pastoral dramas, and yet knows how to make money, and does make it, and is still generous!' (p. 190).

l. 266. *Hackney coaches*. Horse-drawn carriages for hire.

l. 267. *lordly*. The draft reading; copy-text and Huntington manuscript read 'lonely'.

l. 272. *Pollonia*. Alludes to Apollonia Ricci, one of the daughters of the Gisbornes' landlord at Leghorn; Mary S. teasingly refers to Apollonia's (and her sister Carlotta's) supposed fondness for Henry Reveley: 'the Miss Riccis . . . greatly lament the Caro Giovane' (*MWSL*, 1. 153).

ll. 272–3. *Or yellow-haired . . . thing*. This couplet is written in the margin of S.'s draft (*BSM* 14), and is not included in the Huntington manuscript; it was omitted from *PP* and Mary S.'s first 1839 edition.

l. 286. *contadino*. Italian peasant.

484 l. 294. *low-thoughted care*. See Milton, *Comus*, l. 6.

l. 305. *syllabubs*. A dish made of cream or milk flavoured, sweetened, and whipped to thicken it.

l. 308. *the Grand Duke's*. Belonging to Ferdinand III, Grand Duke of Tuscany.

l. 316. *they*. S.'s 'nerves' (l. 312).   *laudanum*. Preparation of opium in liquid form.

l. 317. *Helicon*. A mountain which contained a spring sacred to the Muses.   *Himeros*. 'A synonym of Love' (S.'s note).

l. 323. *'Tomorrow . . . new.'* S. quotes the last line (l. 193) of Milton's *Lycidas*.

To —— (Lines to a Reviewer). Published posthumously, under the signature [Σ], in *The Literary Pocket-Book* (1823), ed. Leigh Hunt (where it was titled 'To ——'); the poem is related to 'To —— (Lines to a Critic)' and the fragmentary 'Satire on Satire', both of which also reject hatred, and was probably composed in 1820 after S. exchanged letters with Southey, whom he suspected (incorrectly) of attacks on him in the *Quarterly Review*. Our copy-text is S.'s fair copy in the Bodleian on sheets torn—probably by Mary S. or Leigh Hunt—out of the Larger Silsbee Notebook at Harvard (see *MYR: Shelley* 5 for a photofacsimile). This fair copy is entitled 'To ——'. We have adopted this title, but appended to it in parentheses the title, 'Lines to a Reviewer', by which the poem is better known.

485 l. 12. *Narcissus*. S. is as unresponsive to the critic's hate as Narcissus was to Echo's love.

To —— (Lines to a Critic). Published posthumously in Hunt's *The Liberal*, No. 3, 1823 and in *PP*, where Mary Shelley dates it December 1817 (though recent editors date it rather later; it may have been composed in the wake of S.'s 1820 dispute with Southey; see headnote to 'To —— (Lines to a Reviewer)', above). There is a draft of the poem in the Bodleian (*BSM* 14), where it is entitled 'A Hate-Song'. Our copy-text is a fair copy in Mary S.'s hand, now in the Bodleian on sheets torn—probably by Mary S. or Leigh Hunt—from the Larger Silsbee Notebook at Harvard (see *MYR: Shelley* 5 for a photofacsimile of the manuscript). This fair copy is entitled 'To ——', the title we use, though we also append in parentheses the title of its first posthumous printing, by which it is better known. The poem was probably addressed to Southey, mentioned by name in 'Satire on Satire'.

485 l. 13. *prove*. S.'s draft has 'move'.

486 *The Witch of Atlas*. Written from 14 to 16 August 1820 after S. had
visited a shrine at the top of Monte San Pellegrino in the previous three
days. Sent to Ollier on 20 January 1821, with instructions that the poem
should be published. Ollier did not publish the poem, which appeared in
print for the first time in *PP* (without the introductory stanzas to Mary
S.). The text in *PP* supplies our copy-text for the main part of the poem;
the text in Mary S.'s 1839 editions supplies the copy-text for the intro-
ductory stanzas. Draft material survives in the Bodleian (*BSM* 5); there
is also an intermediate fair copy in S.'s hand in the Bodleian (*BSM* 4).
The Witch of Atlas is a comic epyllion (miniature epic poem). Its heroine
can be interpreted as 'a personification of the imaginative faculty in
its most airy abstractions' (Leigh Hunt, review of *PP*), but, as Hunt
points out, the poem is highly aware of 'reality'; moreover, S.'s playful,
metaphorical mode is at war with allegorical fixities of interpretation. If
the poem's synthesis of classical, Egyptian, and mythological materials
(drawn from Herodotus, Diodorus Siculus, Virgil, Ovid, Spenser,
Milton, and others) makes it a *tour de force*, its suggestion that it is
holding at arm's length 'the strife | Which stirs the liquid surface of
man's life' (ll. 543–4) gives it a latent pathos. The poem's humour and
use of *ottava rima* derive (and deviate) from two principal influences: the
Italian poet Niccolo Fortiguerri, whose *Ricciardetto* had been read by S.
and Mary in June and July 1820, and the Byron of *Beppo* (1818) and
Don Juan, cantos 1 and 2 (1819). Just before writing *The Witch of Atlas*,
S. composed his high-spirited *ottava rima* translation of Homer's 'Hymn
to Mercury'.

ON . . . INTEREST. See Samuel Johnson (in *Lives of the Poets*) on
PL: 'The want of human interest is always felt.'

l. 9. *the silken-wingèd fly*. See Spenser, *Muiopotmos*, l. 17, where the ill-
fated Clarion (a butterfly trapped by a spider) is said to be the most
'favourable' and 'fair' (l. 20) 'Of all the race of silver-winged Flies'
(l. 17).

l. 12. *the swan . . . dominions*. In classical mythology, the swan is sacred to
Apollo, god of the sun.

l. 17. *a wingèd Vision*. May allude to *Laon and Cythna* (*The Revolt of
Islam*) by whose reception S. had been disappointed.

487 l. 26. *Peter Bell*. See the notes to *Peter Bell the Third* (above).

l. 34. *Ruth or Lucy*. Female figures in Wordsworth's contributions to
Lyrical Ballads (1800).

l. 40. *'looped . . . raggedness.'* S. quotes from *King Lear*, 3. 4. 32.

l. 42. *hyperequatorial*. Extremely equatorial, that is, very hot.

l. 44. *Scaramouch*. In Italian farce, a boastful coward who is constantly
cudgelled by Harlequin.   *in hue Othello*. Black, like Othello.

l. 46. *Primate*. Archbishop.

l. 47. *shrive*. Perform the office of a confessor.

l. 49. *at one birth*. See Milton, 'L'Allegro', l. 14: 'at a birth'.

l. 55. *lady-witch*. S. uses 'witch' primarily to mean a fascinating figure capable of magic.   *Atlas' mountain*. Atlas, descended from the Titans, was forced by Zeus to bear the earth and heavens on his shoulders. He was changed into stone (and thus a mountain) by Perseus who showed him Medusa's head after Atlas had refused to give him shelter.

ll. 55–6. *A lady-witch . . . fountain*. Cf. the Massylian priestess, said by Dido to live 'where mightiest Atlas on his shoulders turns the sphere' (*Aeneid*, 4. 481–2) and to claim that 'her spells' can 'set free the hearts of whom she wills' or bring 'cruel love-pains' (4. 487–8).

488 l. 57. *Atlantides*. Daughters of Atlas and Hesperus, also known as the Hesperides, the Atlantides lived in a beautiful garden near Mt. Atlas.

ll. 58–64. *The all-beholding . . . away*. Modelled on the description in *FQ* 3. 6. 4–9 of how Chrysogonee was impregnated by the sun and gave birth to Belphoebe and Amoretta.

l. 70. *fit*. Capricious mood.

l. 73. *the Mother of the Months*. The moon.

ll. 73–4. *bent | Her bow*. Extended the curvature of its rim as it filled out from a crescent.

l. 74. *folding-star*. The evening star (Venus).

489 l. 89. *spotted camelopard*. A 'camelopard' is a giraffe. See Milton, *Comus*, l. 444, where Dian is said to tame 'the spotted mountain pard'.

l. 97. *The brinded lioness*. See Milton, *Comus*, l. 443 ('the brinded lioness'). 'Brinded' is an alternative of 'brindled', that is, brownish or tawny with streaks of other colour.

l. 99. *pard*. Leopard.

l. 105. *Silenus*. See note to *Prometheus Unbound*, 2. 2. 90 (p. 748).

l. 106. *wood-gods*. See *FQ* 1. 6. 9, where the 'wyld woodgods' pity Una; the episode is drawn on by S. elsewhere in this section of his poem.

l. 108. *Cicadae*. Transparent-winged, shrill-sounding insects.

l. 109. *Driope*. The consort of Faunus and beloved by Pan; see *FQ* 1. 6. 15.   *Faunus*. Ancient and legendary king of Italy; worshipped as a god.

l. 113. *Universal Pan*. God of the woods and shepherds; The phrase occurs in *PL* 4. 266.

l. 116. *want*. Norton suggests 'mole' (*OED*, sb1); in context, though, a more usual sense—'desire for thing held necessary'—seems appropriate.

490 l. 125. *Priapus*. God of procreation and fertility, gardens, and vineyards.

490   l. 130. *pastoral Garamant*. The Garamantes are an African people (north central Libya), described by Herodotus in his *Histories*, 4, as 'having no weapons of war' and living a twenty-day journey from the foot of Atlas.

l. 133. *Polyphemes*. One-eyed giants, after Polyphemus in Homer, *Odyssey*, 9.

l. 134. *Centaurs*. Fabled creatures, half-horse, half-man, born from Ixion and Juno in the form of a cloud: hence described by Ovid, *Met*. 12 as 'half-man centaurs' and 'cloud-born centaurs'.   *Satyrs*. Mythological woodland figures in human form with (in Roman accounts) goat's ears, tail, legs, and budding horns; associated with lechery.

ll. 135–6. *lumps . . . bird-footed*. See Herodotus' account of 'the dog-headed men and the headless that have their eyes in their breasts' (book 4).

ll. 145–7. *spindle . . . Long lines of light*. Possibly making playful use of a passage in Plato, *Republic*, 616b–c, where, in an account of the afterlife, there is mention of 'a straight shaft of light' and 'the spindle of Necessity' (see Robin Waterfield, trans. (Oxford, 1994), 454–6 for commentary).

l. 150. *belated*. Late-coming; tardy.

491   l. 156. *cells*. Small containers.

l. 169. *aviary*. Large cage or building for keeping birds.

l. 174. *vans*. Wings.

492   ll. 185–92. *Her cave . . . above*. These 'scrolls' were the work of a benevolent magician (the reverse of Spenser's malevolent Archimago in *FQ* 1), who lived in the Golden Age of Saturn, the loss of which led to the emergence of 'native vice', that is, evil that seems innate in human beings.

l. 195. *wizard*. Marvellous; magical.

493   l. 217. *Hamadryades*. Wood-nymphs.

l. 218. *Oreads*. Mountain-nymphs.   *Naiads*. Nymphs of fountains and streams.

ll. 217–20. *The Ocean-nymphs . . . rocks*. See *FQ* 1. 6. 18: 'The wooddy Nymphes, fair Hamadryades, | Her to behold do thither runne apace; | And all the troupe of light-foot Naiades | Flocke all about to see her lovely face.'

l. 226. *Naiades*. Alternative spelling of 'Naiads' (for metre).

ll. 225–32. *This . . . dust*. According to Plutarch, nymphs enjoyed unfading youth for 9,720 years.

494   l. 253. *woof*. The weft, transverse threads woven into the warp to make a web (*OED*).

l. 270. *withal*. In addition; moreover.

l. 271. *tenour*. Settled or prevailing course.

l. 276. *asphodel*. Immortal flower in Elysium.

495 l. 283. *bearded star*. Comet.

l. 289. *Boat*. Compare this boat with the narrator's 'little Boat' in Wordsworth's *Peter Bell* (l. 4); Wordsworth thinks of sporting 'amid the boreal morning' (l. 97), but his boat flies off, indignant at the poet's mock-reproof for forgetting 'What on the earth is doing' (l. 125), and Wordsworth proceeds to tell his earth-bound story.　　　　*Vulcan*. Blacksmith god, husband of Venus.

l. 292. *sphere*. 'Spheres' were revolving globe-shaped shells in which, according to the Ptolemaic system, heavenly bodies were supposed to be set.

l. 312. *circumfluous*. Flowing around; Ocean was thought in ancient times to be a stream flowing round the world.

496 l. 317. *Evan's feet*. Bacchus' feet.

l. 318. *Vesta's sceptre*. Vesta was a Roman goddess of the hearth, represented as holding a sceptre in her left hand.

ll. 321–3. *by strange art . . . love*. See the account in *FQ* 3. 8. 6 of the creation of the false Florimell by a malevolent Witch from 'purest snow in massie mould congeald'; S.'s Witch adds 'fire' (l. 321) and 'liquid love' (l. 323).

l. 328. *Pygmalion*. Pygmalion fell in love with a sculpture of a young woman he had made, and prayed to Venus that his bride should be its 'living likeness'. Venus granted his prayer by making the statue come to life (Ovid, *Met.* 10); hence, 'vital stone' (l. 327).

l. 329–31. *A sexless thing . . . sex*. The Witch's creation is a hermaphrodite (see l. 422). In classical myth Hermaphroditus was the son of Hermes (Mercury) and Aphrodite (Venus); his body was joined to that of a nymph, Salmacis, who lusted passionately after him (Ovid, *Met.* 4). Presented as 'both super- and non-human' (Michael O'Neill, *Human Mind's Imaginings* (Oxford, 1989), 154), the hermaphrodite suggests art's possibilities and limits.

l. 338. *seventh sphere*. Sphere to which the planet Saturn is fixed; see note to l. 292.

l. 339. *lightnings*. Here the word is trisyllabic (for the metre); in l. 445 'lightning' is disyllabic.

497 l. 345. *And down the streams*. The Witch's journey involves a descent from the head of the Nile, finally ending up in human habitation.

l. 349. *pinnace*. Small boat.

l. 369. *prone*. With downward slope.

l. 374. *besprent*. Sprinkled.

498 l. 377. *cataracts*. Waterfalls.

l. 382. *sunbows*. Produced by the rainbow-like effect given by sunlight on spray.

498 l. 399. *rime*. Frost formed from fog or cloud.

499 l. 421. *amain*. Vehemently; in haste.

l. 423. *the Austral waters*. Waters to the south.

l. 424. *Thamondocana*. The old name of Timbuctoo, an 'African El Dorado' (Frederick S. Colwell, *Rivermen* (Kingston, 1989), 177).

l. 428. *Canopus*. A brilliant star in the Carina (Keel) part of the constellation Argo Navis.

500 l. 451. *Hydaspes' banks*. Hydaspes, a river in what is now north-east Pakistan, gives its name to a famous victory of Alexander the Great.

l. 453. *quips and cranks*. See Milton, 'L'Allegro', l. 27: 'Quips and cranks, and wanton smiles'. By the phrase Milton means 'witty remarks' and 'verbal tricks' (Oxford Authors edn., p. 745); S. suggests non-verbal capers and games.

l. 462. *meteor flags*. See Satan's 'ensign' which 'Shone like a meteor streaming to the wind' (*PL* 1. 536, 537).

l. 464. *mere*. Lake.

ll. 465–6. *tent . . . exhalations*. See Milton's account of Pandaemonium: 'a fabric huge | Rose like an exhalation' (*PL* 1. 710–11).

l. 467. *lambent*. Softly radiant.

l. 469. *cressets*. Metal vessels for holding oil or coal, usually mounted on a pole. There are 'blazing cressets' in *PL* 1. 728.

501 l. 482. *crudded rack*. A rack of clouds that looks as though coagulated like curd.

l. 484. *like Arion . . . back*. In Herodotus (book 1) Arion was a Greek musician and poet who, about to be killed by the sailors of his ship, sang a song and threw himself into the sea; a dolphin bore him away to safety on its back. See *Twelfth Night*, 1. 2. 14: 'like Arion on the dolphin's back'.

l. 488. *fire-balls*. Balls of lightning.

l. 498. *Nilus*. The river Nile.

l. 500. *Axumè*. Mountain in north-east Ethiopia.

502 l. 505. *Moeris . . . lakes*. Lake Moeris is above the city of Memphis; Lake Mareotis is located in the lower Nile Delta.

l. 511. *the great Labyrinth*. See Diodorus Siculus, 1. 61 and 66 for an account of this intricate, huge, and beautiful Egyptian tomb.

l. 512. *Osirian feast*. According to Diodorus Siculus, Osiris, the son of Zeus and Hera and husband of the moon-goddess Isis, was a sun-god who became a wise Egyptian king, making 'mankind give up cannibalism'. Killed by Typhon, his dismembered body was recovered by Isis and honoured in 'rites and sacrifices' that anticipate, in their emphasis on fertility, the Greek 'festivals connected with Dionysus' (1. 14, 22).

l. 515. *And . . . ever*. See Wordsworth, 'Elegiac Stanzas, Suggested by a Picture of Peele Castle', l. 8: 'It trembled, but it never passed away.'

l. 519. *fanes*. Temples.

503 l. 552. *weltering*. Tossing and tumbling. See Milton, *Lycidas*, l. 13: 'and welter to the parching wind'.

504 ll. 577–8. *Aurora . . . grey*. Aurora, goddess of the dawn, fell in love with Tithonus, and asked Zeus to grant him immortality (which Zeus did), but she forgot to ask for eternal youth for him as well.

ll. 579–82. *Or how . . . pay*. Adonis, loved by Venus, was killed while hunting; Proserpina, queen of the underworld and wife of Hades, gave him back life on the condition that he spend half the year with her and half with Venus.

l. 584. *The Heliad*. The Witch of Atlas herself, daughter of the sun, or Helios.

ll. 587–8. *holy Dian . . . Endymion*. Diana, goddess of the moon, fell in love with the shepherd Endymion as he lay asleep on Mount Latmos: the theme of Keats's *Endymion*.

505 ll. 602–3. *shook . . . of*. Borrowed the light from.

l. 626. *Translating . . . Greek*. For S., Greek is the language of enlightened thought.

l. 627. *god . . . bull*. The holy bull or bull-god of Memphis, Apis was supposed to be the living manifestation of Osiris. S. may pun on 'bull' meaning 'expression containing contradiction in terms' (*OED*).

l. 631. *hawks . . . geese*. Diodorus Siculus comments that 'the Egyptians venerate certain animals exceedingly' (1. 83). The hawk was sacred to the Egyptian god, Horus. The Egyptian goddess, Bastet (equated by the Greeks with Diana), was cat-headed. As *Norton* suggests, the geese seem to be included for an effect of deliberate bathos.

506 ll. 633–40. *The king . . . same*. In Spenser, *Prosopopoia*, the Ape puts on the Lion's crown and is worshipped (with the support of the Fox) by the other animals: the two in turn govern corruptly (see ll. 967 ff).

l. 642. *somnambulism*. Sleep-walking.

l. 644. *Like . . . abysm*. Vulcan made arms for the gods and heroes, with the help of the Cyclopes, in his forge under Mt. Etna.

l. 645. *Beating . . . ploughshares*. Isaiah 2: 4: 'and they shall beat their swords into ploughshares.'

l. 647. *I wis*. I think or know. S. plays on 'iwis' (one word) meaning 'surely' and having nothing to do with 'I'.

l. 648. *Amasis* (570–526 BC). Diodorus Siculus remarks that 'Amasis . . . ruled the masses of the people with great harshness' (1. 60).

507 l. 670. *weird*. Uncanny, unearthly.

507 l. 671. *garish*. Obtrusively bright.

508 *Song of Apollo*. Composed in 1820 as part of Mary S.'s unpublished
blank-verse drama *Midas*, which, like its source, Ovid's *Met.* 11, tells
of a singing contest between Pan and Apollo. This contest is judged by
Tmolus, god of the mountain of the same name, who decides in Apollo's
favour; when Midas, King of Phrygia, questions Tmolus' verdict, Apollo
turns the king's ears into those of an ass. In Ovid, Pan sings first and
Apollo has the last word; in Mary S.'s play, order and outcome are
reversed. The songs were first published in *PP*. Our copy-texts for this
poem and for the 'Song of Pan' are supplied by S.'s drafts in the Bodleian
(*BSM* 5).

l. 22. *cinctured*. Girdled, encircled.

509 ll. 31–6. *I am the eye . . . belong*. Apollo describes himself as the god of
light, music, poetry, prophecy, and medicine; his haughty, self-satisfied
manner is traditional.

Song of Pan. See previous headnote. Pan, a late god in the Olympian
pantheon, is associated with universal nature ('pan' is the Greek word for
'all'); the fertility of flocks; mountains, caves, and lonely places; and
music, especially piping (whereas Apollo is associated with the lyre, as in
Ovid, *Met.* 11: 'Old Tmolus bade the reed bow to the lyre').

l. 11. See headnote to *Song of Apollo*; 'even old Tmolus', because Tmolus
will champion Apollo.

l. 13. *Peneus*. A river in Thessaly that flows through the valley of Tempe,
which lies between Mt. Olympus to the north-west and Mt. Ossa to the
south-east.

l. 15. *Pelion's*. A wooded mountain in Thessaly; in their attempt to scale
the heavens and overthrow the Olympians the Giants (see note to l. 27)
piled Mt. Pelion on Mt. Ossa and Mt. Ossa on Mt. Olympus. We have
retained this reading ('Pelion'), which is in *PP*, but see *BSM* 5, p. 373 for
a discussion of the difficulty of deciphering the word in question in the
copy-text.

l. 27. *giant wars*. The giants were sons of Gaia (Earth) and in post-
Homeric legend were involved in several battles with the Olympians, first
as allies (against the Titans) than as enemies; they were ultimately
defeated by the Olympians with the aid of Heracles (Hercules), a mortal.

l. 30. *Maenalus*. A mountain sacred to Pan, in Arcadia, a mountainous
region in the centre of the Peloponnese.

l. 31. *a maiden*. Syrinx, a nymph, was the maiden; when the gods turned
her into a reed to escape Pan's pursuit, he used the reed to construct an
elaborate musical pipe, which he named after her.

510 l. 34. *ye*. Apollo and Tmolus.

Sonnet: Political Greatness. Date of composition uncertain, probably
sometime after July 1820; first published in *PP*, under the title 'Political
Greatness'. There is draft material in the Bodleian (*BSM* 6). Our

copy-text is a fair copy in S.'s hand in the Bodleian (*BSM* 22), with the title 'Political Greatness'. An earlier fair copy in the Larger Silsbee Notebook at Harvard in S.'s hand, entitled 'To the Republic of Benevento' (MS Eng. 258. 2; *MYR: Shelley* 5), provides a clue to the poem's context. Benevento, a town north-east of Naples, briefly established itself as a 'republic' in the wake of a popular revolt in July 1820 against the despotic Bourbon Ferdinand, King of Naples. This revolt was crushed by Austria in the spring of 1821, as was the republic.

l. 1. *Nor . . . nor.* Neither . . . nor.

l. 7. *fleet.* Hurry or hasten.

The Indian Girl's Song. Our copy-text for this version of the poem, making clear that the speaker is not the poet, is based on a manuscript in S.'s hand in the Bibliotheca Bodmeriana, Cologny-Genève (see *MYR: Shelley* 8), a manuscript probably written in 1820–1. Under the title 'The Indian Serenade' different versions of the poem can be found in the Larger Silsbee Notebook at Harvard (MS Eng. 258. 2; *MYR: Shelley* 5) and the Pierpont Morgan Library (MA 814; *MYR: Shelley* 8). A version of the poem appears to have been given to Sophia Stacey in 1819. The poem was first published in the *Liberal* (1823) as 'Song. Written for an Indian Air' and in *PP* as 'Lines to an Indian Air'.

l. 11. *champak.* Highly fragrant species of magnolia.

512 *Epipsychidion.* Finished by 16 February 1821 when S. sent Ollier the poem with instructions that it should be published anonymously, as it was later in the year: this first edition supplies our copy-text. The poem was inspired by the predicament of Teresa Viviani (known as Emilia by the Shelleys). The daughter of the Governor of Pisa, she was confined to a convent while awaiting the outcome of marriage arrangements made on her behalf. Though some material had already been drafted in late 1819 to early 1820 (see *BSM* 6 and 18), the poem was brought to completion after S. met Viviani towards the end of 1820 and developed an intense friendship with her, involving the exchange on both sides of writings in Italian: Shelley translated parts of *Prometheus Unbound* and 'Ode on Liberty'; Viviani gave Shelley her essay *Il vero amore*, quoted in the epigraph. The poem's riddling title is modelled, ironically, given the attack on marriage in ll. 148–59, on 'Epithalamion' ('a song about a wedding'); by analogy, S.'s title means 'a song about a little soul' or 'little soul song'. Mary S., who did not comment on the poem in her 1839 Notes, summed up S.'s relationship with Viviani as 'Italian platonics' (*MWSL* 1. 223). S. called *Epipsychidion* 'an idealized history of my life and feelings' (*L* 2. 434). The description anticipates S.'s description in *A Defence of Poetry* of Dante's *Vita Nuova*, a major influence on the poem, as 'the idealized history of that period, and those intervals of [Dante's] life which were dedicated to love' (p. 690). S. asserted to John Gisborne that 'The Epipsychidion is a mystery—As to real flesh & blood, you know that I do not deal in those articles'; that the poem was being reduced to a tale of 'a servant girl & her sweetheart'; and that he intended

'to write a Symposium of my own to set all this right' (*L* 2. 363). This 'Symposium'—akin to Dante's *Convivio*—was never composed and S. soon grew disillusioned with the poem and its object (see *L* 2. 434), instructing Ollier to withdraw from circulation any remaining copies.

512 *Epigraph.* Quoted from Teresa Viviani, *Il vero amore*: 'The loving soul launches itself outside creation, and creates for itself in the infinite a world all its own, very different from this dark and frightening abyss' (editors' trans.).

Advertisement. the Sporades. Islands grouped together in the Aegean Sea; there are four main islands; round these, and mostly uninhabited, are many small islands and rocky outcrops.

Vita Nuova. S. read Dante's poem to Mary S. on 31 January 1821.

gran vergogna . . . intendimento. Quoted from *Vita Nuova*, section 25: 'deep shame were it to him who should rhyme under cover of a figure or of a rhetorical colour and, afterwards, being asked, knew not how to strip such vesture from his words, in such wise that they should have a real meaning.'

Voi . . . movete. The first line of the Canzone at the head of Dante's *Convivio*, 2: S. translated the Canzone, rendering the first line thus: 'Ye who intelligent the third Heaven move'.

513 *My Song . . . beautiful.* S.'s translation of the last stanza of 'Ye who intelligent the third Heaven move'. S.'s major change is the addition of the words 'tell them that they are dull'.

l. 1. *that orphan one.* Either S.'s or Mary S.'s spirit.

l. 2. *Whose . . . on.* Either (if the 'orphan one' refers to S.) the 'empire' of his name ('Percy' in Italian (*persi*) means 'lost') that provokes her compassionate tears. Or (if the 'orphan one' refers to Mary) the 'empire' of Mary's title as wife or Mrs Shelley, a title that provokes envious tears.

514 l. 44. *unvalued.* Both great and unmerited.

l. 45. *Would . . . mother!* See the Song of Solomon 8: 1: 'O that thou wert as my brother, that sucked the breasts of my mother!'

l. 55. *grey style.* The manner of traditional love-poetry.

l. 58. *A well . . . happiness.* See the Song of Solomon 4: 12, where the 'sister' is a 'spring shut up, a fountain sealed'.

l. 60. *A Star.* The pole star.

515 l. 72. *Stranger.* Shelley's draft has 'Reader'.

l. 85. *the sense.* The means by which sensation is experienced. See also l. 91.

l. 100. *quiver.* In the process of redrafting, Shelley failed to notice the lack of agreement between singular noun and plural verb.

516 l. 117. *the third sphere.* That of Venus.

l. 122. *Anatomy*. Skeleton.

517 l. 162–73. *Love . . . eternity*. With heterodox wit, the passage reworks Dante, *Purg.* 15. 46–75, where Virgil explains that in heaven love is unexclusive and infinite.

l. 185. *the eternal law*. See Keats's 'Hyperion', 2. 228–9: ''tis the eternal law | That first in beauty should be first in might.'

518 l. 213. *that best philosophy*. Refers to the ability to wrest value out of 'this cold common hell, our life' (l. 214) rather than to any philosopher's system of ideas.

l. 222. *Hesper's setting sphere*. The evening star.

519 l. 249. *wintry forest*. See the *selva oscura* (dark wood) in Dante, *Inf.* 1. 2.

520 l. 268. *idol of my thought*. 'Ideal image produced by and nurtured in my mind'. See S.'s 'On Christianity': 'Every human mind has, what Lord Bacon calls its *idola specus*, peculiar images which reside in the inner cave of thought' (*Murray*, p. 261).

l. 277. *One*. Usually identified with Mary S.

l. 295. *I was laid asleep*. An echo, ironic in effect, of Wordsworth's 'Tintern Abbey', ll. 46–7 ('we are laid asleep | In body, and become a living soul').

l. 304. *The wandering . . . mother*. Alludes to S.'s first wife Harriet Westbrook, whom he left for Mary S. in 1814, and by whom S. had two children, Ianthe and Charles; he was denied custody of the children after Harriet's suicide in 1816.

521 l. 312. *Tempest*. This may allude to Eliza Westbrook, older sister of Harriet S.; Shelley viewed her as hostile.   *She*. Probably alludes to Harriet Shelley.

ll. 308–19. *What . . . conceal*. This passage probably alludes, in a highly metaphorical way, to events in S.'s life in 1816 and 1817.

l. 345. *Twin Spheres*. Emily (the sun) and Mary (the moon).

522 ll. 368–73. *Thou . . . again!* Alludes to Claire Clairmont, Mary S.'s half-sister; she had a daughter, Allegra, by Byron, after a brief affair with him. Her presence in the Shelley household was the source of difficulty between her and Mary; as a result, she was living in Florence when the poem was being written. S. was close to Claire and negotiated on her behalf with Byron.

523 l. 412. *halcyons*. Seabirds mythically supposed to have the power to calm waves and winds.

l. 422. *Ionian*. Ionia was the name of the colony in western Asia Minor and neighbouring islands occupied by Hellenic settlers from Attica and the northern coast of the Peloponnesus.

524 l. 445. *peopled with sweet airs*. See *The Tempest*, 3. 2. 130–1, 'The isle is full of noises, | Sounds, and sweet airs, that give delight and hurt not.'

524 l. 459. *that wandering Eden Lucifer*. 'Lucifer' is Venus as the morning star, described with a flicker of irony (given Lucifer's other identity as the leader of the fallen angels), as 'that wandering Eden'.

525 l. 492. *sister and his spouse*. See the Song of Solomon 4: 9: 'Thou hast ravished my heart, my sister, my spouse.'

526 l. 507. *Parian*. Of the island of Paros in the Aegean, famed for white marble.

l. 540. *Conscious*. Aware, but also 'co-knowing', knowing as though they were one person.

528 l. 601. *Marina, Vanna, Primus*. Mary S.; Jane Williams; Edward Williams. Alludes to a sonnet from Dante to Cavalcanti, translated by S. (and included in the *Alastor* volume), in which Dante appeals to 'Vanna and Bice and my gentle love' (l. 10).

ll. 592–604. *Weak Verses . . . Love's*. This envoi is modelled on Dante's addresses to the poems of the *Vita Nuova*.

529 *Adonais*. Written between April 1821 and June 1821, *Adonais*, an elegy for John Keats, who had died in Rome in February 1821, was published in Pisa in July 1821. S. was pleased with the first edition (see *L* 2. 311), which, with a few emendations from *MWS (1)*, supplies our copy-text. There is a good deal of relevant manuscript material in the Bodleian (see *BSM* 7 and 14). S. saw Keats as persecuted and driven to an untimely death by hostile reviews, especially the review of *Endymion* in the *Quarterly Review* (April 1818), where the anonymous reviewer (John Wilson Croker) stigmatized Keats as 'a disciple of the new school . . . of Cockney Poetry' and asserts that 'our author . . . has no meaning'. Feeling himself to be similarly ill-used, S.'s anger at Keats's treatment duplicates the anger he felt on his own behalf. Yet the 'interposed stabs on the assassins of [Keats's] peace and of his fame' (*L* 2. 297) are only part of a poem described by S. as 'a highly wrought *piece of art*' (*L* 2. 294): this artistry shows in the original way that the poem (written in Spenserian stanzas) fulfils elegy's traditional task of supplying consolation in the last movement (stanzas 39–55) in which the idea of an afterlife for Adonais is evoked in language that reworks Platonic and Christian images and ideas, but locates permanence in the enduring significance of great poetry. The poem's title, as Earl Wasserman suggests in *Shelley: A Critical Reading* (Baltimore, 1971), probably conflates the Greek 'Adonis' with the Hebrew 'Adonai', meaning 'Lord'. Other influences include pastoral elegies by Bion and Moschus, Milton's *Lycidas*, and Spenser's *Astrophel*. Dante's *Paradiso* comes to the fore in the poem's closing stanzas. Extensive commentary is provided in Anthony D. Knerr (ed.), *Shelley's 'Adonais': A Critical Edition* (New York, 1984) (hereafter *Knerr*).

Epigraph. S. translated these lines as follows: 'Thou wert the morning star among the living, | Ere thy fair light had fled;— | Now, having died, thou art as Hesperus, giving | New splendour to the dead.'

Preface. The Greek is from Moschus' *Lament for Bion*, which translates: 'Poison, Bion, poison came to your lips, | and you took it. How could it touch | such lips without becoming nectar? | And what man on earth could be so vicious | as to mix poison and give it you | when you asked? He has poisoned music' (*Greek Pastoral Poetry*, trans. Anthony Holden (Harmondsworth, 1974)).

prove. Seemingly another instance of lack of agreement between noun and verb in S., but it is possible that an ellipsis ('should prove') is to be understood.

Hyperion. Published in Keats's *Lamia, Isabella, and Other Poems* (1820) and admired by S. as being 'in the very highest style of poetry' (*L* 2. 252–3).

on the —— of —— 1821. S. omits the precise date of Keats's death (23 February), presumably because he was not certain of it.

cemetery . . . protestants. The Cimitero Acattolico in Rome; S.'s son William was buried there (a fact alluded to in stanzas 49 and 51).

in love with death. See Keats's 'Ode to a Nightingale', l. 52: 'I have been half in love with easeful Death'.

530 *know not what they do*. See Luke 23: 34. One of a number of biblical allusions in the Preface turned ironically against those who disliked Keats's poetry, according to a cancelled draft of the Preface, solely because the poet was associated with Leigh Hunt, William Hazlitt, and 'other enemies of despotism & superstition'.

penetrable stuff. Ultimately *Hamlet*, 3. 4. 35; also quoted by Byron in his *English Bards and Scotch Reviewers* (l. 393; line number from Oxford Authors edn.) in a passage relevant to *Adonais*.

One . . . calumniator. Alludes to Robert Southey; S. mistakenly thought Southey was the author of a hostile review of *The Revolt of Islam* for the *Quarterly Review* in 1819.

Paris . . . Mr Howard Payne. *Paris in 1815* (1817) by George Croly (who gave *Adonais* a bad review in *Blackwood's*); *Woman*, a poem (1810) by Eaton Stannard Barrett; *Ilderim: A Syrian Tale*, part of *Eastern Sketches in Verse* (1816) by H. Galley Knight; *Mrs Lefanu*: possibly Alicia Lefanu (1753–1817), author of romances (see *Knerr*); *John Howard Payne*, an American dramatist who courted Mary S. after S.'s death.

the Rev. Mr Milman. Henry Hart Milman, author and contemporary of S. at Eton and Oxford; S. thought (incorrectly) that he might have written the review in the *Quarterly Review* mentioned above, after his suspicions had moved away from Southey (see *L* 2. 298–9).

What gnat . . . camels? See Matthew 23: 24: 'Ye blind guides, which strain at a gnat, and swallow a camel.'

Against . . . stone. See John 8: 7: 'He that is without sin among you, let him first cast a stone at her.'

530 *you have spoken . . . none.* See *Hamlet*, 3. 2. 366: 'I will speak daggers to her, but use none.'

The circumstances . . . press. S. refers to a letter from the Revd Robert Finch to John Gisborne, who passed it on to him.

Mr Severn. Joseph Severn (1793–1879), a painter and Keats's companion throughout his final months.

'such . . . of.' See *The Tempest*, 4. 1. 156–7: 'We are such stuff | As dreams are made on'.

531 ll. 1–2. *I weep . . . Adonais!* See Bion's *Lament for Adonis*, ll. 1–2: 'I mourn Adonis dead—loveliest Adonis— | Dead, dead Adonis'; S.'s translation (*MYR: Shelley* 8).

l. 5. *compeers.* Equals, peers. They are 'obscure' because, unlike the 'sad Hour', they have not been singled out ('selected', l. 3) for such duties of mourning.

l. 10. *mighty Mother.* Urania.

ll. 10–12. *Where . . . darkness?* See *Lycidas*, ll. 50–1: 'Where were ye nymphs when the remorseless deep | Closed o'er the head of your loved Lycidas?'

l. 12. *Urania.* Classical muse of astronomy, and also, more relevantly, the muse of sublime poetry for Dante and Milton (see *Purg.* 29. 41–2 and *PL* 7. 1–12). She assumes the place of Venus/Aphrodite in S.'s reworking of the original myth of Adonis.

l. 17. *corse.* Corpse.

l. 26. *Deep.* Abyss or pit—in effect, grave.

532 ll. 29–36. *He died . . . light.* These lines describe and praise Milton, isolated yet 'unterrified' after the Restoration. He is the 'third among the sons of light' because he is, for S., the greatest epic poet after Homer and Dante.

ll. 38–41. *happier they . . . perished.* Lesser poets whose 'tapers' still 'burn', unlike greater poets whose works have been lost.

ll. 48–9. *Like a pale flower . . . dew.* Alludes to the close of Keats's *Isabella* (1820).

l. 51. *extreme.* Utmost.

l. 55. *high Capital.* Rome, where Keats died. Milton (*PL* 1. 756) uses the phrase to describe Pandaemonium.

l. 63. *liquid.* Clear, undisturbed.

533 l. 72. *o'er . . . draw.* In the first printing, the relevant text read 'o'er his sleep the mortal curtain draw'.

l. 75. *flocks.* That is, the 'quick [living] Dreams' of l. 73, who take the place of the 'Loves' that mourn Adonis in Bion.

l. 80. *sweet pain.* The 'pain' is 'sweet' because the 'Dreams' have been imbued by Adonais with poetic 'music' (l. 77).

l. 84. *Our love . . . dead*. See *Lycidas*, l. 166: 'For Lycidas your sorrow is not dead'.

l. 94. *anadem*. Garland worn as a headband.

534   l. 100. *Splendour*. See Dante's 'splendori', in *Par.* (e.g. 9. 13) and discussed in the *Convivio*, 3. 14. 29–50, where 'splendour' is defined as reflected light.

l. 107. *clips*. 'Embraces' is the dominant sense, though 'cuts off' is another possible meaning.

535   ll. 132–5. *Since she . . . hear*. Alludes to the myth of Echo and Narcissus: Echo was a nymph who fell in love with Narcissus; when her love was not returned by Narcissus, who was in love with his reflection, she wasted away until she became merely a voice (see Ovid, *Met.* 3).

ll. 145–6. *Thy spirit's sister . . . pain*. Alludes to Keats's 'Ode to a Nightingale'; 'lorn' may allude to 'forlorn' in Keats's poem, ll. 70, 71.

l. 151. *Albion*. England.   *the curse of Cain*. Cain, the first murderer, was condemned by God to be 'a fugitive and a vagabond' (Genesis 4: 12).

l. 160. *brere*. Archaic form of 'briar'.

536   l. 177. *that alone which knows*. Consciousness, the mind.

ll. 178–9. *as a sword . . . lightning*. See Byron's *Childe Harold*, 3. 97, and his 'So, we'll go no more a roving'.

l. 179. *sightless*. Invisible, but also blind.

l. 195. *sister's song*. The Echo (ll. 15–18) repeating Adonais's 'melodies' (l. 16).

l. 198. *fading Splendour*. Urania.

537   l. 208. *Out of . . . Paradise*. Urania's journey to Adonais is modelled on Venus' journey to Adonis in Bion.

l. 212. *Palms*. Soles of the feet.

ll. 226–7. *Stay . . . live*. Like the whole stanza, these lines are close to Bion ('Wait yet a while, Adonis—oh, but once, | That I may kiss thee now for the last time'; S.'s translation).

l. 228. *heartless*. Having lost heart.

538   l. 238. *the unpastured dragon*. The hostile critic, responsible, in Shelley's view, for Keats's premature death; 'unpastured' means 'unfed'.

l. 240. *mirrored shield*. Alludes to Perseus' defence against Medusa, whose looks turned the beholder to stone.

l. 250. *The Pythian of the age*. Byron, who confronted the adverse reviewers of his *Hours of Idleness* volume in his satire *English Bards and Scotch Reviewers* in a way that is compared to the slaying by Apollo of the serpent Python (Apollo 'known | As Pythian from that serpent overthrown', Ovid, *Met.* 1). Apollo shot 'a thousand arrows'; Byron only needed 'one' (l. 250).

538   ll. 253–61. *'The sun . . . night.'* The 'sun' is a 'godlike mind' or great poet; the 'swarms' are lesser poets and critics who 'dimmed or shared its light' (l. 260); they vanish when the sun sinks and joins the 'immortal stars' (l. 261) (other great writers).

l. 262. *mountain shepherds.* Fellow-poets, as in other pastoral elegies, such as *Lycidas* with its 'woeful shepherds' (l. 165).

539   l. 264. *Pilgrim of Eternity.* Byron, who speaks in *Childe Harold*, 3. 70 of 'wanderers o'er Eternity | Whose bark drives on and on' (an image recalled in the final stanza of *Adonais*).

l. 268. *Ierne.* Ireland.

l. 269. *The sweetest lyrist.* Thomas Moore, author of *Irish Melodies*, a collection of lyrical poems (hence 'lyrist').

l. 271. *one frail Form.* Shelley himself.

l. 276. *Actaeon-like.* Actaeon, out hunting, saw the goddess Diana naked; she punished him by turning him into a stag, after which he was chased and killed by his own hounds (Ovid, *Met.* 3).

l. 280. *pardlike.* A 'pard' is a leopard, sacred to Dionysus.

l. 283. *superincumbent.* Lying on, pressing down upon.

l. 289. *pansies.* Associated with thoughts, as in *Hamlet*, 4. 5. 174.

ll. 291–2. *a light spear . . . grew.* Suggests the 'thyrsus', or staff carried by Dionysus and his followers.

l. 297. *A herd-abandoned . . . dart.* See William Cowper's self-portrait: 'I was a stricken deer, that left the herd | Long since' (*The Task*, 3. 108–9; quoted from *The Complete Poetical Works*, ed. H. S. Milford (London, 1905)).

540   l. 298. *partial.* Prejudiced. The 'frail Form' takes Adonais' part against the hostile reviewers; his doing so is motivated by fellow-feeling (see l. 300).

l. 306. *Cain's or Christ.* In a letter to John Taaffe, S. commented: 'The introduction of the name of *Christ* as an antithesis to *Cain* is surely any thing but irreverence or sarcasm' (*L* 2. 306).

l. 312. *He.* Leigh Hunt, who encouraged Keats and promoted his poetry.

l. 319. *nameless worm.* The anonymous reviewer of Keats's *Endymion* for the *Quarterly Review.*

l. 327. *noteless.* Without distinction.

541   l. 336. *wakes or sleeps.* S. takes a more unequivocal position in l. 343.

l. 337. *Thou . . . now.* See *PL* 4. 828–9: 'Know ye not me? Ye knew me once no mate | For you, there sitting where ye durst not soar'.

l. 338. *Dust to the dust!* The phrase occurs in the service for the Burial of the Dead in the Book of Common Prayer.

l. 339. *the burning fountain.* The image of spirit as fire derives from Plotinus and the Platonic tradition. See S.'s reference in 'On Christianity' to 'The unobscured irradiations from the fountain fire of all goodness' (*Murray*, p. 255).

l. 362. *Mourn not for Adonais.* Reverses the injunction in l. 2.

542 l. 372. *night's sweet bird.* The nightingale.

l. 381. *the one Spirit's plastic stress.* See Coleridge's 'The Eolian Harp', l. 47: 'Plastic and vast, one intellectual breeze'; 'plastic' means 'shaping' or 'moulding'.

ll. 381–3. *while . . . wear.* See S.'s essay 'On the Devil, and Devils': 'But the Greek philosophers . . . accounted for evil by supposing that . . . God in making the world . . . moulded the reluctant and stubborn materials ready to his hand into the nearest arrangement possible to the perfect archetype existing in his contemplation' (*Clark*, p. 266).

543 l. 397. *inheritors of unfulfilled renown.* Those who inherit the condition of incomplete fame, either because they died before receiving due recognition, or because they died before realizing their creative potential.

l. 399. *the Unapparent.* S. may have shaped his noun from *PL* 7. 103 ('the unapparent deep') or Wordsworth's *The Excursion*, 9. 605 ('the unapparent fount of glory'). *Chatterton.* Thomas Chatterton (1753–1770), to whose memory Keats dedicated *Endymion*, died at the age of 17; he was, until recently, supposed to have committed suicide.

l. 401. *Sidney.* Sir Philip Sidney (1554–86), poet, soldier, and courtier.

l. 404. *Lucan.* Roman poet (AD 39–65) and author of the *Pharsalia*; he committed suicide when his part in a conspiracy against Nero was discovered. *by his death approved.* The phrase probably distances S. from the view of Suetonius who accuses Lucan of having falsely incriminated his mother Attilla in a cowardly attempt to save himself.

l. 407. *effluence.* Literally 'flowing out'; influence.

l. 413. *an Heaven of song.* Alludes to and adapts the Ptolemaic system, used by Dante, according to which there are a series of heavens.

l. 414. *Vesper.* Hesperus. See the poem's epigraph.

l. 417. *pendulous.* Suspended, oscillating.

ll. 422–3. *And keep . . . brink.* Shelley urges the 'Fond wretch' (l. 416) to keep his heart light (remain light-hearted, cheerful) lest his hopes (probably of immortality, a world better than this) lure him dangerously towards 'the brink' (tempt him towards self-destruction).

l. 424. *Rome.* See S.'s letter (in December 1818): 'Rome is a city as it were of the dead, or rather of those who cannot die' (*L* 2. 59).

544 l. 439. *a slope of green access.* See S.'s acccount of the Protestant Cemetery as 'a green slope near the walls, under the pyramidal tomb of Cestius . . . the most beautiful & solemn cemetery I ever beheld' (*L* 2. 59–60).

544 l. 442. *grey walls*. Of Rome.

l. 444. *one keen pyramid*. The tomb of Caius Cestius, a Roman tribune during the first century BC (see Preface, second paragraph).

545 l. 463. *Stains*. Enriches or disfigures.

ll. 460–4. *The One remains . . . fragments*. See *Par.* 29. 142–5: 'See now the height and breadth of the eternal worth, since it hath made itself so many mirrors wherein it breaketh, remaining in itself one as before', and Southey's *Thalaba*, 5: 'The many-coloured domes | Yet wore one dusky hue'.

l. 477. *No more . . . together*. See Matthew 19: 6: 'What therefore God hath joined together, let not man put asunder.'

l. 478. *That Light . . . Universe*. See *Par.* 1. 1–2 ('The All-mover's glory penetrates through the universe').

l. 486. *Consuming . . . mortality*. See *Par.* 33. 31–3, where St Bernard prays to Mary on Dante's behalf that 'thou do scatter for him every cloud of his mortality with prayers of thine, so that the joy supreme may be unfolded to him'.

l. 487. *The breath . . . song*. Possibly alludes to the 'Ode to the West Wind'.

ll. 488–90. *my spirit's bark . . . given*. See *Par.* 2. 1–6: 'O ye who in your little skiff, longing to hear, have followed on my keel that singeth on its way, turn to revisit your own shores; commit you not to the open sea; for perchance, losing me, ye would be left astray.'

546 *To Night*. Composed 1821, first published in *PP*. Our copy-text is S.'s fair copy in the Larger Silsbee Notebook at Harvard (MS Eng. 258. 2; *MYR: Shelley* 5).

547 *The Aziola*. Probably composed in 1821, first published in *The Keepsake for 1829* (1828). There is a draft in S.'s hand of the first stanza and the last two lines in the Bodleian (*BSM* 21) and complete transcriptions by Mary S. in the Bodleian (*Massey*) and in the Pierpont Morgan Library (MS PM; *MYR: Shelley* 8), and an incomplete transcription by Mary S. in the Bodleian (*BSM* 2). Our copy-text is based on the Pierpont Morgan transcription; we have also consulted the draft. The title refers to the 'assiolo' or small owl.

548 *Hellas*. 'I am just finishing a dramatic poem called *Hellas* upon the contest now waging in Greece—a sort of imitation of the Persae of Aeschylus' (*L* 2. 363–4); so S. wrote to John Gisborne from Pisa on 22 October 1821. Sent to Ollier on 11 November, the poem was published in 1822, with some prudential cuts made by the publisher (S. had indicated that cuts to the Notes were permissible: see *L* 2. 365). S. received his copy in April and wrote to Gisborne that the poem was 'prettily printed, & with fewer mistakes than any poem I ever published' (*L* 2.

406); his short list of errata, sent to Ollier on 11 April, and the press copy manuscript are now in the Huntington Library (HM 329 and HM 20152; *MYR: Shelley* 3). The Bodleian holds drafts of the poem (*BSM* 16) and of some of the Notes and the title-page (*BSM* 21). We have taken the first edition as our copy-text, restoring suppressed material and consulting the drafts and the press copy manuscript. *Hellas* is dedicated to Prince Alexandros Mavrokordatos (Alexander Mavrokordato), the central figure of a group of Greeks exiled in Pisa; S. met him in December 1820. Mavrokordatos, who went in June 1821 to fight in the War of Greek Independence that broke out earlier that year, would later become prime minister of Greece after it had achieved independence. One of the purposes of *Hellas* was to mobilize British opinion on the side of the Greeks; at the outset of the war, the British were neutral. It is apparent from the finally discarded but extensive 'Prologue' (see Thomas Hutchinson (ed.), G. M. Matthews (corr.), *Shelley: Poetical Works* (London, 1970), for a text and *BSM* 16 for relevant draft material) that a point of departure for S. in conceiving *Hellas* was Goethe's *Faust*, part 1. But, as S. indicates, the structure of the published version (his second 'lyrical drama') is based on Aeschylus' *Persians*, in which the central figure is the Persian commander, Xerxes, who learns of the present and future defeats of his army through a series of messengers and the ghost of his predecessor, Darius. Like *Persians*, *Hellas* obeys the unities of time, action, and place, and explores the overthrow of tyranny from the perspective of the tyrant. The work sees history as a cycle of destruction and renewal, and offers a more favourable if strictly qualified view of Christianity than one finds elsewhere in S.'s poetry. Valuable information about the War of Greek Independence is provided in William St Clair, *That Greece Might Still Be Free* (London, 1972).

Epigraph. 'This day shall victory bring', Sophocles, *Oedipus at Colonus*, 1078.

Dedication. Hospodar. A word meaning 'lord', used for the governors of Wallachia and Moldavia.

549 *Preface. the prize . . . goat.* A goat is thought to have been the prize for the best tragedy (whose etymology has been traced to 'goat-song') at dramatic festivals in honour of Dionysus.

the Aristarchi . . . of the hour. Aristarchus of Samothrace (*c.*220–143 BC) was a notoriously harsh critic of Greek literature.

The only 'goat-song' . . . attempted. S. alludes to *The Cenci*.

display of newspaper erudition. In particular, S. relied on the *Examiner*, which was strongly pro-Greek and opposed to Britain's non-interventionist policy.

their defeat in Wallachia. At the battle of Dragashan ('battle | Of Bucharest', ll. 362–3); see ll. 373–457. Wallachia was a Turkish province north of the Danube, now part of Romania.

550 *Anastasius.* A novel by Thomas Hope, published anonymously in 1819: 'a faithful picture they say of modern Greek manners' (S. in *L* 2. 332).

551 *Should the English . . . foresee and dread.* This paragraph was left out of the first edition by Ollier.

Scene. Seraglio. The part of the Sultan's palace in which the women were secluded.

Chorus of Greek Captive Women. This chorus allows S. to voice 'lyrics of affirmation' (Carl Woodring, in *Norton*, p. 676). Aeschylus' chorus (by contrast) is Persian.

552 l. 16. *Samian.* From the island of Samos in the Aegean.

553 l. 50. *Imaus.* The Himalayas. In *PL* 3. 431, Satan is compared to 'a vulture on Imaus bred'.

l. 54. *Thermopylae.* Site of a heroic last stand (480 BC) by Leonidas of Sparta and his allies against the Persian army.   *Marathon.* A plain where the Greeks won a famous victory (490 BC) against a much larger Persian army.

l. 57. *Philippi.* Site of battle (42 BC) where Brutus and Cassius were defeated by Mark Antony and Caesar. Hence freedom only 'half-alighted' (l. 57).

l. 60. *Milan.* See S.'s Note, p. 584.

l. 70. *far Atlantis.* America.

l. 72. *sanguine streams.* The bloody excesses of the French Revolution.

554 l. 88. *lightnings.* Trisyllabic for the metre.

555 l. 116. *the Bosphorus.* The strait that links the Black Sea to the Sea of Marmara.

l. 123. *I am Mahmud still.* See Webster, *The Duchess of Malfi*, 4. 2. 134: 'I am Duchess of Malfi still'; the scene is in Lamb, *Specimens*.

556 ll. 149–51. *Some say . . . immortality.* Alludes to the Wandering Jew, the subject of an early long poem by S., and a figure in *Queen Mab*.

l. 152. *Enoch.* A biblical figure who did not die but was taken directly to heaven. See Genesis 5: 24: 'And Enoch walked with God: and he was not; for God took him.'

l. 164. *the Demonesi.* A group of nine islands in the Sea of Marmara, a few miles south-east of Constantinople (Istanbul).

557 l. 177. *Marmora.* Alternative spelling of Marmara.

558 l. 197. *Chorus.* See S.'s note (p. 584).

ll. 201–10. *But they . . . had cast.* Notopoulos finds an echo of an argument in Plato's *Phaedo*, 87–8: 'that the soul may pass through many bodies, just as the weaver may outlive many coats' (p. 304).

l. 211. *A power.* Jesus Christ.

l. 221. *The moon . . . of Mahomet.* The crescent moon, an emblem of Islam.

559   ll. 225–38. *Swift . . . golden years.* Alludes to Milton's account in 'On the Morning of Christ's Nativity' of the conquering of pagan gods by Christ; S.'s Chorus is overtly sympathetic to the victims of 'killing Truth' (l. 234).

l. 240. *The Janizars.* The janizaries were a body of Turkish infantry, forming the Sultan's guard and the chief part of the army (*OED*).

l. 245. *No hoary priests after that Patriarch.* See S.'s note (p. 585).

ll. 245–6. *that Patriarch . . . heart.* Gregorios, Patriarch of Constantinople, hanged by the Turks on 22 April 1821 in reprisal for the Greek revolt, even though he excommunicated the Greek rebels (l. 246). See S.'s Note, p. 585.

l. 252. *Solyman.* Suleiman I, the Magnificent, was Sultan 1520–66, and presided over Turkish victories and cultural achievements.

560   l. 266. *From . . . Ceraunia.* Mountain ranges that bounded the limits of the Turkish Empire: the Caucasus Mountains lie between the Black Sea and the Caspian Sea; the Ceraunian (or Acroceraunian) Mountains are in north-west Greece.

l. 277. *Sirocco's.* South-east wind from Africa, associated with fierce storms.

l. 281–2. *Phrygian . . . Mycale.* Mountains in Asia Minor.

l. 285. *Scala.* Scala Tyriorum, a promontory south of Tyre on the southern coast of Lebanon.

l. 289. *Moldavian.* Moldavia lies between Romania and Russia.

l. 290. *Allah-illa-Allah!.* A cry meaning 'There is no god but God!'

l. 294. *So were . . . the Danube's day!* Alludes to the defeat of Alexandros Ypsilantis in June 1821; Ypsilantis began the War of Greek Independence by crossing from Russia into Moldavia in March 1821; he fled to Austria, but the Austrians were allies of the Turks and imprisoned him until 1827.

l. 299. *The Anarchies of Africa.* Piratical states in North Africa: Algiers, Tunis, and Tripoli (*Norton*).

561   ll. 303–4. *the Queen | of Ocean.* Great Britain.

l. 312. *recreant.* Cowardly.

l. 329. *Anatolia.* The part of Turkey in Asia equivalent to the peninsula between the Black Sea and the Mediterranean.

l. 333. *One God . . . one Law.* See, to gauge S.'s irony here, *Mask of Anarchy*, l. 37.

562   l. 362–3. *battle . . . Bucharest.* A Turkish victory in a battle in June 1821 to the north-west of Bucharest; S. had read and been told how a group of Greek youths (the 'Sacred Legion') defended their standard bravely (see ll. 385–451).

563 l. 385. *the Pacha*. A title given to Turkish officers of high rank: here the army commander.

564 l. 422. *Ascribe to*. Enrol among.

565 ll. 470–1. *Latmos . . . Icarian isles*. Latmos and Ampelos are mountains in Asia Minor; Phanae is a promontory in Asia Minor. The Icarian isles are to the east of the island of Icaria.

566 l. 482. *Nauplia*. Nauplia lies on the east of the Peloponnesus (the peninsula to the south of mainland Greece and the Gulf of Corinth) at the head of the Gulf of Argolis; it fell to the Greeks in December 1822.

l. 485. *Hydriote*. Relating to the island of Hydra off the east coast of the Peloponnesus. Hydra joined the Greek rebels in April 1821, just after the War began.

l. 500. *Naxos*. Largest island of the Cyclades in the Aegean Sea.

567 l. 526. *Patmos*. An island to the east-north-east of Naxos.

ll. 476–527. *My presence . . . tempest*. This description is based on the destruction by the Greeks of a Turkish battleship. S., influenced by the Messenger's account of the battle of Salamis in *Persians*, aggrandizes the scale of the Turkish defeat.

ll. 528–9. *That Christian . . . the city*. The Russian Ambassador left Constantinople on 31 July 1821.

l. 531. *Hippodrome*. Course for chariot races.

l. 533. *planet-struck*. See *Coriolanus*, 2. 2. 109–110: 'struck | Coriolès like a planet'. Planets were supposed to induce bewilderment or terror.

ll. 546–7. *Tripolizza . . . Monembasia*. Tripolis, in the Peloponnesus, fell to the Greeks on 5 October 1821; some ten thousand Turks were killed in the ensuing massacre. *Mothon* (Methoni), *Navarin* (Pilos), which fell to the Greeks in August 1821, and *Monembasia* (Monemvasia), which fell to the Greeks in the same month, are also in the Peloponnesus. *Artas* (Arta) is in mainland Greece (Epirus).

568 ll. 554–5. *In deeds . . . light*. The 'deeds' appear to be those of the Greeks.

l. 555. *Patras*. On the north coast of the Peloponnesus (also called Patrai). Mavrocordato took part in the siege of Patras in August 1821.

l. 560. *oaths . . . Norway*. The British promised to restore the Genovese Republic, encouraging the Genovese to rebel against Napoleon, but the city was given to the kingdom of Sardinia. Norway, given to Sweden in 1814, rebelled and established a constitutional monarchy; but Britain, along with Austria, Russia, and Prussia, allowed Norway to be invaded by Sweden in 1818.

l. 563. *The freedman*. See S.'s Note, p. 585.

l. 564. *Attica*. The territory of Athens, bordering Boeotia and Megaris.

l. 565. *Negropont*. Euboea, an island off the coast of Attica.

l. 566. *Ali.* Ali (1741–1822) was a governor in Albania; *Yanina* (Ioannina) was the capital of his virtually autonomous state. His conflict with Mahmud, by whose army he was finally defeated, was among the catalysts of the War of Greek Independence.

l. 577. *Ypsilanti.* See note to l. 294.

l. 582. *Sennaar.* Sennaar (Sennar) is in the Sudan.

l. 587. *tribute.* Of females for the Sultan's harem.

569 l. 591. *Santons.* Islamic holy men, who pass their lives in fasting, meditation, and prayer.

l. 592. *prophesyings horrible.* See *Macbeth*, 2. 3. 53: 'prophesying with accents terrible'.

l. 595. *Dervise.* Muslim religious man devoted to poverty and austerity (*OED*).

ll. 598–9. *The Greeks . . . glory.* See Mark 13: 26: 'And then shall they see the Son of man coming in the clouds with great power and glory.'

l. 606. *Cydaris.* A small stream (now called Ali Bey Souyou), a northern tributary of the Golden Horn (a bay of water to the north of Constantinople).

l. 620. *Chelonites.* Westernmost point on the mainland of the Peloponnesus (*Norton*).

l. 621. *isles that groan.* The Ionian Islands, seven small islands in the Ionan Sea, became a British protectorate in 1815.

570 l. 627. *sulphureous.* S. uses this form of 'sulphurous' (see l. 829) for the metre.

l. 644. *Tomorrow and tomorrow.* Mahmud echoes Macbeth's 'Tomorrow, and tomorrow, and tomorrow' (5. 5. 18).

572 l. 688. *Thermae . . . Asopus.* Rivers close to which the Persians under Xerxes suffered defeats at Thermopylae (480 BC) and Plataea (479 BC) (*Norton*).

573 l. 728. *a small still voice.* See 1 Kings 19: 12: 'but the Lord was not in the fire: and after the fire a still small voice'.   *For.* Some editors have conjectured 'Fear', but there is no warrant for this in the press-copy manuscript or the draft.

l. 735. *the unknown God.* See Paul's rebuke to the Athenians for being 'too superstitious. For as I passed by, and beheld your devotions, I found an altar with this inscription, TO THE UNKNOWN GOD. Whom therefore ye ignorantly worship, him declare I unto you' (Acts 17: 22–3). Paul can identify God; S.'s Chorus suggests that God remains 'unknown'.

574 l. 742. *Frank.* Of western nationality.

l. 776. *Calpe.* Rock of Gibraltar.

l. 780. *all that it inherits.* See *The Tempest*, 4. 1. 154: 'all which it inherit'. Prospero's sense of life as illusion is re-articulated by Ahasuerus.

575   l. 781. *motes of a sick eye*. See *Hamlet*, 1. 1. 106.5: 'A mote it is to trouble the mind's eye.' Motes are small particles of dust.

l. 785. *Nought is . . . be*. See 'On Life', p. 635: 'nothing exists but as it is perceived.'

l. 793. *Dodona's forest*. Dodona was the location in Epirus (north-west Greece) of an oak grove containing an oracle sacred to Jupiter.

l. 804. *Knock . . . opened*. See Matthew 7: 7: 'knock, and it shall be opened unto you.'

ll. 807–8. *Mahomet . . . Stamboul*. Sultan Mahomet the Second conquered Constantinople (Stamboul or Istanbul) in 1453.

576   l. 829. Εν τούτῳ νίκη. 'In this [sign], victory': the Greek war-cry, set beside that of the Turks (see note to l. 290).

l. 838. *Tartarian barb*. Horse from Tartary (region in central Asia, peopled by Turks and Mongols, among others).

578   l. 903. *reversion*. The Hour will be enriched by what reverts to it on Mahmud's death.

579   ll. 918–20. *Were there such . . . fear?* See *Macbeth*, 1. 3. 81–3: 'Were such things here . . . Or have we eaten on the insane root | That takes the reason prisoner?'

l. 936. *Thule*. In ancient times, the northernmost part of the inhabitable world.   *the girdle of the world*. The Equator.

580   l. 948. *Russia's famished eagles*. 'The flag of Russia under the Romanov czars featured a double-headed eagle' (*Norton*).

l. 959. *lightning*. Trisyllabic for the metre.

l. 977. *contumely*. Scornful insolence.

581   l. 987. *Image of the Above*. The 'Image' is Liberty, the phrasing Platonic.

l. 991. *'The Sea! the Sea!'*. The cry is that of Greek troops retreating from Persia as described by Xenophon in *Anabasis*, 4. 7.

l. 993. *young Atlantis*. America.

l. 1006. *Amphionic music*. Amphion, legendary son of Zeus and Antiope, charmed the walls of Thebes into position through his music.

582   ll. 1016–17. *bought Briton . . . Islamite*. The British would not intervene with their navy.

l. 1019. *Othman*. Ottoman; Turkish.

l. 1030. *Evening land*. The West; specifically, America.

l. 1049. *Pranked*. Set, displayed.

583   l. 1059. *Chorus*. See S.'s note (p. 586).

ll. 1060–1. *The world's . . . return*. See Virgil, *Eclogues*, 4. 5–6: 'the great Sequence of the Ages starts afresh . . . and the rule of Saturn is restored' (E. V. Rieu, trans., Virgil, *The Pastoral Poems* (Harmondsworth, 1954)).

l. 1063. *winter weeds.* Garments; here snake-skin.

l. 1068. *Peneus.* River in Thessaly (north-central Greece) flowing through Tempe (l. 1070), a beautiful valley.

l. 1071. *Cyclads.* The Cyclades, a cluster of islands in the Aegean.

l. 1072. *Argo.* The ship in which Jason and the Argonauts sailed in their quest for the Golden Fleece.

ll. 1074–5. *Another Orpheus . . . dies.* Alludes to Orpheus' power of song, his love for Eurydice, his grief both at her loss and his failure to bring her out of the underworld (he looked back against Hades' order), and his death, torn to pieces by Maenads.

ll. 1075–6. *A new Ulysses . . . shore.* Alludes to the *Odyssey*, and to Odysseus' leaving of Calypso, the goddess-nymph with whom he stayed for seven years, for his home (in Ithaca) and wife (Penelope).

ll. 1072–7. *A loftier . . . shore.* Modelled on Virgil, *Eclogues*, 4. 34–6: 'a second Argo will set out . . . Wars even will repeat themselves, and the great Achilles will be despatched to Troy once more'. Virgil's words about repeated wars contribute to the sombre colouring of S.'s last two stanzas.

l. 1080. *Laian rage.* Warned by an oracle that he would be killed by his child, King Laius of Thebes ordered that his new-born son, Oedipus, should be exposed on a mountain. In Sophocles' version, *Oedipus the King*, the servant commanded to expose the baby gave it to shepherds. Oedipus grew up to fulfil the oracle, albeit unwittingly.

l. 1082. *Sphinx.* A monster with the face of a woman, the chest and feet of a lion, and wings like a bird of prey, who lived outside Thebes and posed riddles to passers-by, whom she devoured if they could not provide the right answer. Oedipus solved the riddles, and the Sphinx killed herself.

584   l. 1092. *One who rose.* See S.'s Note, p. 586.

l. 1094. *dowers.* A verb, meaning endows. In the draft it replaces the verbs 'wears' and 'vests'.

586   *Notes to 'Hellas'. Note*, ll. 814–15. *1453.* Corrected by editors since *Rossetti* from S.'s '1445'.

Phantom. S.'s draft has 'phantasm'.

master of. S.'s draft has 'master'.

Note, l. 1060. *magno nec proximus intervallo.* S. reworks a phrase from Virgil, *Aeneid*, 5. 320, *longo sed proximus intervallo* ('but next by a long distance'): S.'s meaning is 'and not next by a great distance', which appears to be assertive rather than deprecatory (but see *BSM* 21, where S.'s phrase is translated 'not near <but> at a great interval').

the 'lion shall lie down with the lamb'. A common misquotation of Isaiah 11: 6: 'The wolf also shall dwell with the lamb, and the leopard shall lie down with the kid.'

586 *omnis feret omnia tellus*. Virgil, *Eclogues*, 4. 39: 'each land makes all it needs' (editors' trans.).

Note, ll. 1090–1. *amerced*. Here, 'punished by being deprived'.

'the One who rose' . . . *worship*. Omitted from the first edition.

587 *Demon*. The press copy reading.

hecatombs. Sacrifices of many victims. S. refers to the slaughter committed in the name of the Christian religion.

The sublime . . . *torture*. Omitted from the first edition.

588 *Written on Hearing the News of the Death of Napoleon*. Composed sometime between the death of Napoleon, on 5 May 1821 (though news of the death would not have reached S. for several weeks), and 11 November 1821, the date he sent it, along with the manuscript of *Hellas*, to his publisher, Charles Ollier, with instructions to print it 'at the end' of the *Hellas* volume (1822), our copy-text, though we have also consulted the fair copy in the Huntington (HM 330; *MYR: Shelley* 3). For S. on Napoleon see also 'Ode to Liberty', *The Triumph of Life*, and 'Feelings of a Republican on the Fall of Buonaparte' (not included in this selection).

l. 10. *Hearth*. One of the names the Romans worshipped the earth under was Vesta; she was also the goddess of the hearth.

589 *'The flower that smiles today'*. Composed 1821–2. There are drafts and a fair copy in the Bodleian (*BSM* 16); the fair copy supplies our copy-text. G. M. Matthews argued that the lyric, drafted in the same notebook as *Hellas*, 'was evidently written for the opening of *Hellas*' (*Norton*, p. 690). But the manuscript evidence is inconclusive (see *BSM* 16, pp. liv–lv). The poem, first published in *PP* under the title 'Mutability', shares the concern of other late lyrics (such as 'When the lamp is shattered') with the brevity of 'delight' (l. 5) and with enduring after such delight has gone.

ll. 6–7. *Lightning* . . . *bright*. See *Romeo and Juliet*, 2. 1. 161–2: 'Too like the lightning which doth cease to be | Ere one can say it lightens'.

l. 12. *these*. Virtue, friendship, and love.

l. 13. *Survive their joy*. 'These' (see note to l. 12) persist but without joy once they have 'fallen' (see l. 12) from their original state.

590 *To* —— *('One word is too often profaned')*. Dated 1821 by Mary S. who published it in *PP*, under the title 'To ——', to which we have added in parentheses the first-line title by which the poem is often known. *PP* supplies our copy-text; there is also a transcription by Mary S. in the Bodleian (*BSM* 2).

'When the lamp is shattered'. Composed 1821–2, first published in full in *PP*. There is a draft in the Bodleian (*BSM* 19), a fair copy of the first three stanzas in Glasgow University Library (MS Gen. 505/34; *MYR: Shelley* 8), and a fair copy of the whole poem in the British Library (Add. MS 37232, f. 75; *MYR: Shelley* 8). The British Library manuscript

supplies our copy-text. The poem depends for its power on great rhythmic skill (mixing iambs and anapaests) and the movement from argument by analogy to the concentrated metaphoric force of the last stanza.

l. 2. *The light . . . dead.* As *Chernaik* notes, 'the "light in the dust" has not disappeared, but rather "lies dead"'.

591   l. 16. *That ring . . . knell.* See *The Tempest*, 1. 2. 406: 'Sea-nymphs hourly ring his knell' (*Rognoni*).

l. 17. *When . . . mingled.* Above this line in the Glasgow fair copy are the words 'second part'; S. may have thought of the poem at one stage as a debate, chorus-like lyric or part of a drama.

l. 25. *thee.* 'Love' (l. 21).

l. 32. *When . . . come.* The rhythm slows expressively (the result of stressed monosyllables).

To —— (*'The serpent is shut out from Paradise'*). Composed in January 1822, and a fair copy sent (our copy-text) to Edward Williams with an accompanying letter (referring to the 'dismal' (that is, 'sombre') nature of the verse); first published by Medwin (in corrupted form) in *Fraser's Magazine* (Nov. 1832). The fair copy and letter are now in the University of Edinburgh Library (Dc. 1. 100⁴; *MYR: Shelley* 8). The poem is written in *ottava rima*, with modified line-lengths, a possible gesture towards Byron whose nickname for S. ('The Snake') is adopted by the poet. If there is such a gesture, its purpose is to underscore Byron's far greater popularity: in the poem, S. refers not only to marital problems (see esp. l. 25) but also to the struggles of authorship (ll. 29–31).

592   l. 16. *its evil, good.* See Satan in *PL* 4. 110: 'Evil be thou my good.'

l. 18. *Dear friends, dear 'friend'.* Whether the 'friend' is Edward Williams or Jane Williams is left unclear.

l. 28. *scene.* We have retained the copy-text's full stop at the end of this line because it is expressive of the speaker's momentary, wearied halting.

l. 42. *No bird . . . nest.* See Matthew 8: 20: 'The foxes have holes, and the birds of the air have nests; but the Son of man hath not where to lay his head.'

593   *To Jane. The Invitation.* Composed in 1822 after S. had walked through a forest near Pisa to the sea with Mary S. and Jane Williams; first published (with 'To Jane—The Recollection') in *PP* as 'The Pine Forest of the Cascine, near Pisa'. This first publication was based on a transcription by Mary S. in the Bodleian (*BSM* 2). Mary must have copied from a draft in which the two poems were one. S. evidently decided to divide the poem into two. Our copy-text is supplied by his fair copy in the University Library, Cambridge (MS Add. 4444; *MYR: Shelley* 8). 'To Jane. The Invitation' was first published as a separate complete poem in *MWS (2)*.

The poem is written in tetrameters, mainly trochaic but occasionally iambic.

593   l. 6. *brake*. Thicket.

594   l. 48. *Awake . . . away*. See Satan in *PL* 1. 330: 'Awake, arise, or be forever fallen'.

     l. 58. *daisy-star*. Marguerite (ox-eye daisy).

595   l. 68. *seem*. The verb's cautiousness (S. could have written 'are') is appropriate for a poem that celebrates 'one moment's good' (l. 44).

     To Jane—The Recollection. (See the above headnote.) Composed 1822, first published as a separate complete poem in *MWS (2)*. Our copy-text is supplied by S.'s fair copy in the British Library (Add. MS 37538, ff. 40–1; *MYR: Shelley* 8), which contains below the title the date ('Feb. 2, 1822') of the walk through the pine forest mentioned in 'To Jane. The Invitation'. There is a draft of ll. 29–32 in the Bodleian (*BSM* 21).

     l. 6. *fled*. The reading in *BSM* 2 and *PP*; 'dead' in the fair copy is presumably a slip.

596   l. 45. *A spirit interfused*. See Wordsworth, 'Tintern Abbey', l. 97: 'something far more deeply interfused'.

597   l. 87. ———'*s mind*. The gap asks to be filled by 'Shelley'.

     The Magnetic Lady to Her Patient. Probably composed in 1822, first published (in corrupted form) by Medwin in 1832. Mary S. published an improved text in *MWS (2)*. S sent a fair copy to Jane and Edward Williams with the following notes: 'For Jane & Williams alone to see' (at the top of the page) and 'To Jane. Not to be opened unless you are alone, or with Williams' (on the outer wrapping). This fair copy, in the University Library, King's College, Aberdeen, supplies our copy-text (MS 937; *MYR: Shelley* 8). Given the personal nature of the poem (the 'chain' of the last line appears to refer to S.'s marriage), S. did not wish Mary S. to see it. Jane is a 'magnetic lady' because she has been mesmerizing the poet to alleviate the pain probably caused by a kidney stone.

598   l. 6. *like a sign*. Compare (and contrast) the 'Incantation' in Byron's *Manfred*, esp. 1. 201: 'With a power and with a sign'.

     l. 11. *he*. Edward Williams.

599   *With a Guitar. To Jane*. Composed 1822; ll. 43–90 first published by Medwin in the *Athanaeum*, 20 October 1832, and *The Shelley Papers* (1833); ll. 1–42 first published in *Fraser's Magazine* (1833). First complete corrected text published in *MWS (2)*. There is a draft of the first twelve lines (*BSM* 19) and a fair copy (*BSM* 21) in the Bodleian: the fair copy supplies our copy-text. S. had tried to buy a harp for Jane Williams; when that attempt failed, he gave her a Pisan guitar, now in the Bodleian. The poem, written in octosyllabic couplets and recalling seventeenth-

century lyrics by poets such as Robert Herrick, is spoken by S. in the guise of Ariel, the spirit in Shakespeare's *The Tempest* who was freed from a pine-tree by Prospero; Jane Williams is addressed as Miranda and Edward Williams as Ferdinand, from the same play. Covertly the poem reflects on the artist, art, and its audience.

l. 18. *As . . . tell.* See *The Tempest*, 5. 1. 317–21, where Ariel is charged by Prospero with the safe return to Naples of those on the island.

l. 27. *live again.* Alludes playfully to the notion of reincarnation.

601 *To Jane ('The keen stars were twinkling').* Our copy-text is the fair copy (now in the John Rylands University Library of Manchester: *MYR: Shelley* 8) sent by S. to Jane Williams in June 1822 with a note: 'I sate down to write some words for an ariette which might be profane. . . . I commit them to your secrecy & your mercy & will try & do better another time' (see *MYR: Shelley* 8). The poem was first published in truncated form by Medwin in the *Athenaeum*, 17 November 1832; it was first published in complete form in *MWS (2)*. There is a draft in the Bodleian (*BSM* 1). The poem's virtuoso rhythms and sound-patterns are attuned to the musicality of Jane Williams's singing, and to S.'s desire for 'some world far from ours'.

602 l. 24. *Are one.* The draft reads 'Are won'.

Lines Written in the Bay of Lerici. Composed in June 1822, first published by Richard Garnett in 1862. The only textual authority is a rough draft in the Bodleian (*BSM* 1), which supplies our copy-text. The poem typifies the psychological inwardness to be found in the late poems to Jane Williams.

ll. 1–14. *Bright . . . west.* Added (see *BSM* 1) after the main body of the poem had been drafted.

603 ll. 31–2. *The past . . . not.* S. means that past and present were forgotten as if the former had never been and the latter would never come to be.

l. 57. *pleasure.* There is no word after 'pleasure' in the draft.

l. 58. *Seeking . . . peace.* Any reading of the line is bound to be conjectural because of its unfinished state. *Chernaik* reads: 'Seeking life not peace'. *Norton* reads 'Destroying life alone not peace'. In the MS, 'Seeking' is written below 'Destroying'.

604 *The Triumph of Life.* Composed between May and July 1822, in the last months of S.'s life, and left uncompleted at his death, *The Triumph of Life* was first published from S.'s draft in the Bodleian (see *BSM* 1) by Mary S. in *PP*. This draft, in places very rough, supplies our copy-text. The title is ironic: 'Life' triumphs because it devastates those who live. The poem owes much to S.'s reading of Dante and Petrarch, and is written in the same verse form, *terza rima*, as Dante's *Commedia* and Petrarch's *Trionfi*; Dante's use of Virgil as a guide is echoed by S.'s use of Rousseau, while the central image of a Roman triumph recalls Petrarch's *Trionfi*, which is made up of successive triumphs, culminating in the triumph of Eternity. However, where Dante's quest is ordered, S.'s is

bewildering, and whether his poem would have followed a similar sequence to Petrarch's is doubtful. *The Triumph of Life* sees Rousseau as a figure associated with ideas that led to the French Revolution and as a precursor of Romanticism. Other texts drawn on by the poem include Lucretius' *De Rerum Natura*; *PL*; Goethe's *Faust* (parts of which S. translated in his final year); plays by Calderón (especially *La vida es sueño* [*Life is a Dream*]); Byron's *Childe Harold's Pilgrimage*, canto 3 (with its portraits of Napoleon, Voltaire, and Rousseau); and Wordsworth's 'Ode: Intimations of Immortality'. A further influence was probably the painting of the *Triumph of Death* in the Campo Santo in Pisa. *The Triumph of Life* re-explores the public themes of S.'s earlier work, but it lays emphasis on the apparent refusal of history to fulfil the hopes and desires of the revolutionary imagination.

604   l. 7. *orison.* Prayer.

ll. 26–8. *before . . . head.* The lines echo Goethe's *Faust*, part 1, ll. 1087–8: 'The day ahead, behind my back the night, | The sky above me and the waves below . . .' (trans. David Luke, Oxford, 1987). By contrast with Faust, S.'s narrator has his back to the day.

605   ll. 44–5. *a great stream | Of people.* Dante, *Inf.* 3. 55–7: 'behind it came so long a train of people, that I should never have believed death had undone so many.'

l. 54. *Some . . . feared.* See 'Tintern Abbey', ll. 71–2: 'more like a man | Flying from something that he dreads'.

606   l. 78. *light.* There is a blank space before 'light'; S.'s original thought (cancelled) was 'fascinating'; Mary S. inserted 'blinding' in *PP*.

l. 84. *The ghost . . . mother.* See Coleridge, 'Dejection: An Ode', first two lines of the epigraph ('Ballad of Sir Patrick Spens'): 'Late, late yestreen I saw the new Moon, | With the old Moon in her arms'.

l. 86. *a chariot.* Recalls and ironizes chariots in Ezekiel, esp. chs. 1 and 10; Dante, *Purg.* 29 (the car of the Church); and *PL* ('The chariot of paternal deity', 6. 750).

l. 91. *o'er . . . the head.* See *PL* 2. 672–3, where the phrase is used to describe Death; 'cloud', in our text, is the subject of 'Was bent' (l. 92), though the manuscript is difficult at this point, and other syntactical arrangements are possible.

607   l. 94. *Janus-visaged Shadow.* Refers, as l. 99 confirms, to 'Janus Quadrifrons', a figure with four faces.

ll. 111–16. *such seemed . . . bear.* The comparison is with a 'triumph' in 'Imperial Rome' (l. 113), marking the successful return of a military leader from war.

608   l. 126. *the great winter.* The conclusion of time.

l. 128. *the sacred few.* Principally 'they of Athens and Jerusalem' (l. 134), in particular Socrates and Jesus, both admired by S. as exemplary human beings.

l. 148. *her*. Establishes the gender of the Shape within the chariot.

609   l. 175. *And frost . . . those*. See *PL* 2. 594–5: 'the parching air | Burns frore, and cold performs the effect of fire.'

610   l. 190. *grim Feature*. See *PL* 10. 279, where the phrase is used of Death.

ll. 207. *A thousand . . . bore*. See Dante, *Purg*. 21. 94–6, where Statius speaks of the influence of Virgil's *Aeneid*: 'The sparks, which warmed me, from the divine flame whence more than a thousand have been kindled, were the seeds of my poetic fire.'

611   ll. 214–15. *And . . . evening*. See Petrarch, *Trionfo della Morte*, 1. 38–9: 'deaf and blind, night falls upon you ere 'tis eventide' (Death is speaking). Rousseau, speaking metaphorically, sees the victims of Life as undone by their inner chaos ('the mutiny within', l. 213) and their feigning of 'truth'; 'night' (the damage done to them by Life) occurs before their illusory 'morn of truth' can ripen into any resulting 'evening'.

ll. 235–6. *Voltaire . . . Leopold*. Figures from the Enlightenment, including so-called benevolent despots, Frederick the Great of Prussia (1712–86), Catherine the Great of Russia (1729–96), and Leopold II of Austria (1747–92), and intellectuals, Voltaire (1694–1778) and Immanuel Kant (1724–1804).

l. 237. *anarch*. A ruler who does not rule properly, because he governs despotically, and therefore gives rise to a state of 'anarchy'.

612   l. 243. *its object*. The object, in turn, of age, tears, infamy, and the tomb; to none of the objects of these things could Rousseau's heart be tempered.

l. 255. *his master*. Socrates, who did not succumb to sexual temptation, refusing the advances of Alcibiades (see the last section of Plato's *Symposium*).

l. 256. *That star . . . fair*. Alludes to the youth Aster, the Greek word for 'star', with whom Plato was believed to have fallen in love.

l. 261. *The tutor and his pupil*. Aristotle and Alexander the Great.

613   l. 274. *the great bards of old*. In the manuscript S. substitutes this phrase for the cancelled 'Homer & his brethren'.

ll. 276–80. *Their living . . . misery*. Rousseau contrasts the contained effect of poetry written by classical authors with the less controllable 'infection' spread by his own more confessional work.

l. 284. *Caesar's crime*. The building-up of state power under Julius Caesar.   *Constantine*. The Emperor who made Christianity the official state religion.

l. 288. *Gregory and John*. Possibly Pope Gregory VII (1073–85) and Pope John XXII (1316–34), but as likely to be used as generic names for successions of Popes.

613 l. 289. *Man and god*. The manuscript capital and lower-case reinforce S.'s heterodox meaning.

615 l. 338. *common Sun*. As Rousseau wakes from the 'oblivious spell' (l. 331), his language echoes that of Wordsworth's 'Ode: Intimations of Immortality', especially its reference to 'the light of common day' (l. 76) into which the 'vision splendid' (l. 73) is fated to 'die away' (l. 75).

l. 352. *shape all light*. The last and most enigmatic of S.'s female figures. The focus is on Rousseau's shifting apprehensions of her. For a complex analogue, see Dante's encounter with Matilda (*Purg.* 28) in the Earthly Paradise, a passage which S. translated.

l. 357. *Iris*. The goddess of the rainbow.

l. 359. *Nepenthe*. In Homer, *Odyssey*, 4, Helen of Troy give Menelaus the grief-dispelling drug, nepenthes, also alluded to in Milton's *Comus*, ll. 675–6.

l. 361. *palms*. Soles of the feet, as in *Adonais*, l. 212.

617 l. 422. *The Brescian shepherd*. In *PP*, Mary S. adds this footnote to the line: 'The favorite [*sic*] song, "Stanco di pascolar le peccorelle ['I am weary of pasturing my sheep']," is a Brescian national air.' Brescia is a city in northern Italy.

l. 424. *So knew I*. See the narrator's 'I knew | That I had felt' (ll. 33–4): one of several links between the narrator's and Rousseau's experiences.

618 l. 446. *atomies*. Tiny motes of dust.

619 l. 463. *Lethean*. Having the power to induce forgetfulness, a power attributed to the mythological river Lethe.

l. 471. *Behold a wonder*. See *PL* 1. 777.

l. 472. *him*. Dante.

l. 479. *The sphere*. The Third Heaven of Dante's *Paradiso*, the sphere of Venus.

ll. 488. *Shadows of shadows*. See the depiction in Lucretius, *De Rerum Natura*, 4. 30 ff. of *simulacra*, 'films' thrown off the surfaces of things.

620 l. 500. *anatomies*. Skeletons.

621 l. 533. *the car's creative ray*. Ironic; the car's ray is miscreative and distorting.

l. 544. *I said*. Revised from 'I cried' in the manuscript.

ll. 547–8. *'Happy . . . | Of*. Compare (and contrast) Petrarch's *Trionfi dell'Eternità*, ll. 46–8, 82–4, which employs the 'Happy' ('felice') formula to imagine the condition of those souls heading towards 'the final goal' (l. 83) (see Alan M. Weinberg, *Shelley's Italian Experience* (Basingstoke,1991), 241–2).

623 *An Address to the People on the Death of the Princess Charlotte*. Composed 11–12 November 1817, in response to the death in childbirth on 6 November of Princess Charlotte (b. 1796), daughter of the Prince

Regent, and the hanging and quartering on 7 November of Jeremiah Brandreth, Isaac Ludlam, and William Turner, three working men accused of treasonable utterances and actions as leaders of the 'Derbyshire Insurrection' or 'Pentridge Rising'. The death of Princess Charlotte, known to have liberal or reformist sympathies, was much lamented in pamphlets, poems (including canto IV of Byron's *Childe Harold's Pilgrimage*, stanzas 169–70) and the public press. The execution of the 'Pentridge Three' was controversial in part because of the leading role played by the government spy, 'William Oliver', who seems to have acted as an *agent provocateur*. S. argues that public mourning for the Princess ought more properly to be directed at the executed working men, entrapped by a government bent on suppressing liberty itself. Our copy-text is the only extant source of the pamphlet, an 1843 reprint, reproduced in *Murray*, pp. 229–39; we have used a copy of the reprint in Durham University Library. No copies of Ollier's original 1817 printing survive, in part because fear of prosecution seems to have limited their number to twenty (according to the publisher of the 1843 reprint), nor is there a surviving holograph or draft material. We follow our copy-text in leaving a line between each of the essay's numbered paragraphs.

The Hermit of Marlow. A pseudonym used also for the pamphlet *A Proposal for Putting Reform to the Vote* (1817); Marlow, in Buckinghamshire, had been S.'s residence since March 1817, though he actually wrote the *Address* in London.

Epigraph. A quotation from part 1 of Paine's *Rights of Man* (1791), in which Paine criticizes Burke's *Reflections* (1790) for pitying Marie Antoinette and the French aristocracy while wholly ignoring the plight of the people.

too deep for words. See the last line of Wordsworth, 'Ode: Intimations of Immortality': 'Thoughts that do often lie too deep for tears.'

624 *And have they no affections?* This question and the questions that follow recall *The Merchant of Venice*, 3.1. 49–56 ('Hath not a Jew eyes?' etc.).

illustrated. Shed lustre upon; made illustrious (see *OED* 4).

'that bourne . . . returns'. See *Hamlet*, 3. 1. 81–2: 'The undiscovered country from whose bourn | No traveller returns.'

Horne Took and Hardy. John Horne Tooke (1736–1812) and Thomas Hardy (1752–1832), radical reformers, acquitted of high treason in a notorious trial of 1794.

625 *Brandreth, Ludlam, and Turner.* The 'Pentridge Three'. Brandreth, a framework-knitter, was the most clearly culpable (he had killed a man, the only fatality of the uprising); Ludlam, part-owner of a stone quarry near Derby and a Methodist preacher, and Turner, a stone-mason, 'might well have been accused only of riot' (E. P. Thompson, *The Making of the English Working Class* (1963; repr. Harmondsworth, 1977), 727; and more generally pp. 723–34).

625 *She had accomplished nothing.* See *Murray*, pp. 452–3, for the 'rhetorical and relatively invidious' nature of S.'s criticism of the Princess.

626 *Her husband . . . brethren.* Charlotte had married Prince Leopold of Saxe-Coburg in May 1816; she was estranged from both her parents.

hurdle. A kind of sledge, on which convicted traitors would be carried to execution.

Who dares . . . grave? S. appends a note: ' "Your death has eyes in his head—mine is not painted so." Cymbeline.' S. quotes from *Cymbeline*, 5. 5. 268–9 (omitting 'then' after 'head' and substituting 'painted' for 'pictured').

depending on. Resulting from.

627 *circumstances.* Political and economic oppression (as detailed in the next section).

a check. 'S. probably refers to the institution of the Sinking Fund in 1786, which seemed to provide a mechanism for retiring the national debt but in fact provided an excuse for raising it' (*Murray*, p. 453).

fundamental defect. A limited or restricted suffrage.

sans . . . tache. Without fear and without stain.

gambling in the funds. Lending money to government.

'Corinthian . . . society'. Burke's description of the aristocracy in *Reflections* (singled out for censure in part 2 of Paine's *Rights of Man*).

628 *two chasms.* Anarchy (here meaning 'lawlessness') and misrule.

manufacturers. Factory workers.

helots. Slaves or serfs.

629 *spies were sent forth.* See Luke 20: 20: 'And they watched him, and sent forth spies'.

innocent and unsuspecting rustics. An inaccurate (perhaps 'rhetorical') characterization, according to Thompson, *The Making of the English Working Class*, 723–34.

extraordinary powers. In March 1817 Parliament passed the Seditious Meetings Act and suspended Habeas Corpus.

'OLIVER brought him to this'. S. appends a footnote here: 'These expressions are taken from the Examiner, Sunday, Nov. 9'; the italicized words three sentences later (*'while the executioner . . .'*) are also taken from the *Examiner*, as is the passage from 'when the stroke' to 'hosted'.

630 *the chaplain prevented.* For fear of what would be revealed about Oliver's role, according to liberal sentiment, thus denying the accused their right of last words.

631 *Phantom.* See 'England in 1819', 'A New National Anthem', ll. 110 ff. of *The Mask of Anarchy*, and *Laon and Cythna*, all of which imagine a rebirth of hope and liberty.

On Love. Composed at Bagni di Lucca in July 1818, probably between 20 and 25 July, after S. had finished his translation of Plato's *Symposium* (between 7 and 20 July) and before he began *A Discourse on the Manners of the Ancient Greeks Relative to the Subject of Love*, an essay that explores the difference between the ancient Greeks and modern Europeans 'in the regulations and the sentiments respecting sexual intercourse' (*Noto-poulos*, p. 407). First published in the *Keepsake for 1829* (1828). In 'On Love' S., influenced by Plato's impassioned rhetoric in the *Symposium*, explores love in a psychological analysis that recalls *Alastor* and looks ahead to *Epipsychidion*. Our copy-text for the essay, unpublished in S.'s lifetime, is his draft in the Bodleian (*BSM* 15).

sought. *MWS: Prose* reads 'sought sympathy', but there is no warrant for this addition in our copy-text. We have added a comma after 'sought'.

demandest what is Love. This is followed in the draft by the cancelled sentence: 'It is the sweet chalice of life whose dregs are bitterer than wormwood.'

airy children of our brain. S.'s cancelled alternative in his draft was 'creations of our mind'.

632 *We dimly see.* S. inserted an 'x' to key the following footnote (usually keyed to 'composed' in the next sentence): 'These words inefficient and metaphorical—Most words so—No help—'.

prototype. An original thing or person in relation to a copy, imitation, representation, later specimen, improved form (*OED*).

a soul within our soul. See *Epipsychidion*, l. 238 ('this soul out of my soul') and contrast the more other-centred account of love in *A Defence of Poetry* as 'a going out of our own nature' (p. 682).

antitype. That which a type or symbol represents (*OED*): here, 'not the person herself but rather the "soul within [her] soul"' (*Bonca*, p. 273 n. 31).

Sterne . . . cypress. See Laurence Sterne's *A Sentimental Journey through France and Italy* (1768): 'was I in a desert, I would find out wherewith in it to call forth my affections—If I could not do better, I would fasten them upon some sweet myrtle, or seek some melancholy cypress to connect myself to', ed. Graham Petrie (Harmondsworth, 1967), 51.

633 *On Life.* Written around late 1819 in the notebook in which S. drafted *A Philosophical View of Reform*; subsequently torn out of the notebook (in 1916); the manuscript is currently in the Pierpont Morgan Library (MA 408) and supplies our copy-text. A draft with cancellations, it presents some editorial problems, but it is the sole authority for a text unpublished in S.'s lifetime (it was first published by Medwin in 1832 and 1833, and, in a more accurate form, by Mary S. in *MWS: Prose*). Occasionally we follow Mary S.'s emendations. The work offers a short but important overview of S.'s metaphysical beliefs and allegiances, tracking his movement from materialism to the 'intellectual philosophy'. This philosophy

seems close in certain respects to the idealism of George Berkeley and his tenet, *esse est percipi aut percipere* (to be is to be perceived or to perceive); indeed, Mary S. writes in her Preface to her 1840 edition of Shelley's prose writings that 'Shelley was a disciple of the Immaterial Philosophy of Berkeley' (p. xii). But S. departs from Berkeley's belief in the mind of God as ultimately guaranteeing reality. The major influence on 'On Life' is *Academical Questions* (1805) (hereafter *AQ*) by Sir William Drummond, described by S. in a letter of November 1819 as 'the most acute metaphysical critic of the age' (*L* 2. 142). Drummond draws on David Hume's sceptical arguments about causality to reject the materialist argument that mind is subject to matter, and, indeed, to cast doubt upon the assumption 'that the objects of sense are different from the sensations, feelings, or perceptions, which exist in our own minds' (*AQ* 91). Out of this series of counter-intuitive doubts emerges 'the ideal system' (*AQ* 383), by which Drummond means acceptance of the view that we know only our ideas about things; we do not have direct knowledge of the world itself. Where S. differs from Drummond is his emphasis on 'unity' and the implicit trust he places in imagination as an escape from sceptical doubt: Drummond is quietly scornful of the way 'A poet saves himself by a metaphor' (*AQ* 96); S. is determined to heed 'high aspirations'.

633 *[of]*. The manuscript has 'by'.

[its]. Not in manuscript.

'*Non merita . . . Poeta*'. See note to *A Defence of Poetry*, p. 835.

634 *those philosophers . . . perceived*. Such as David Hume, quoted approvingly by Drummond as questioning the supposition that there is 'an external universe, which depends not on our perception' (*AQ* 397).

'*such stuff . . . made of*'. See *The Tempest*, 4. 1. 156–7: 'We are such stuff | As dreams are made on'.

'*looking . . . after*'. See *Hamlet*, 4. 4. 26–7 'Sure, he that made us with such large discourse, | Looking before and after'.

with. Cancelled in favour of 'whose' in the manuscript, but restored here, to make sense of the subsequent 'disclaiming', which is ungrammatical if 'whose' is kept.

'*thoughts . . . eternity*'. See Belial in *PL* 2. 146–8: 'for who would lose, | Though full of pain, this intellectual being, | Those thoughts that wander through eternity.'

change and extinction. Written above 'nothingness and dissolution' in the manuscript; neither pair of nouns is cancelled. We have included both pairs.

635 *misuse of . . . signs*. See *AQ* 407: 'the inaccuracies into which we are often betrayed in our habits of thinking from our habits of speaking.'

636 *preceded*. Other editors (though not *Norton²*) follow Mary S.'s 'produced'.

the basis. Written above 'the cause' in the manuscript; neither term is cancelled.

the manner in which two thoughts. In the manuscript S. seems to have written 'things' first, then to have written 'thoughts' above it. Neither word is cancelled; we have chosen what appears to have been S.'s latest choice.

A Philosophical View of Reform. Composition began towards the end of 1819 and continued into 1820. Described in a letter of 15 December 1819 to Charles Ollier as 'an octavo on reform. . . . I intend it to be an instructive and readable book, appealing from the passions to the reason of men' (*L* 2. 164). The original manuscript, unfinished and with many gaps and problematic insertions and alterations, was not published until 1920, though Mary S. transcribed a version, now in the Bodleian (*BSM* 22), with a view to its being 'published when [Shelley's] works assume a complete shape' (*MWS: Prose* 1, p. xviii). Our copy-text is the original manuscript, now in the Carl H. Pforzheimer Library, as transcribed in *SC* 6. All ellipses in square brackets are editorial; some omit incomplete sentences or passages, or sentences or passages which do not follow; in the case of more extended omissions or omissions of interest in themselves but disruptive of local arguments, we have paraphrased or quoted the omitted material in our endnotes.

1st. Sentiment . . . Desirable mode. These numbered headings are set out on the verso of the first page of the manuscript and may constitute an outline for the work as a whole; in l. 2, S. has written 'Probability' above 'Practicability' and 'Necessity' above 'Utility', without cancelling the originals.

637 *Epigraph.* Probably of S.'s devising; *MWS* and others add 'it' after 'that'.

two recent wars. Presumably the American and French Revolutions; Mary S.'s copy reads 'the French Revolution'.

The Republics and municipal governments of Italy. In 1176 the Lombard League of northern Italian communes overthrew the tyrannical rule of Frederick Barbarossa, leading to the Peace of Constance (1183) and greater autonomy for the Italian city-states. In later wars, between the popes and Holy Roman (German) emperors, Florence played a balancing role, preventing the dominance of either religious or political authority.

638 *The poor rose.* A reference to the Peasants' War (1522–5) in Germany.

The republic of Holland . . . even to death. According to Reiman, 'S. was thinking not only of Spinoza's writings but also of the numerous publications by French *philosophes* that were published (or purported to be published) in Holland during the seventeenth and eighteenth centuries' (*SC* 6. 966).

the strain of conquest. S. must be thinking only of Europe; by 1558, the date of the fall of Calais, at the time the last English stronghold on the continent, England no longer sought the conquest of France.

638 *exposition.* expulsion (*OED* 1), exposure (*OED* 2).

639 *one of those chiefs.* Charles I, about whom S. would later attempt to write a drama.

Revolution. The Glorious Revolution of 1688, in which James II was replaced by Mary and William III (of Orange).

those professing themselves established. 'The Pope, Luther, Calvin and others' (*Clark*).

this test was applied . . . this judgement formed. By measuring the doctrines and actions of Christ against those of religious authorities and interpreters (i.e. the 'established').

640 *Bayle.* Pierre Bayle (1647–1706), author of *Dictionaire historique et critique* (1695–97), a key influence on eighteenth-century French scepticism, also on S. and Byron.

Locke. John Locke (1632–1704), English philosopher and political theorist.

governments of Europe. Followed in the manuscript by a sentence S. subsequently brackets for exclusion, probably because he lifted it for use in the unfinished essay 'On Life', which he drafted in the back of this notebook at roughly the same time. The sentence reads: 'Philosophy went forth into the enchanted forest of the daemons of worldly power, as the pioneer of the overgrowth of ages.'

Berkeley and Hume and Hartley. George Berkeley, Bishop of Cloyne (1685–1755), David Hume (1711–76), and David Hartley (1705–57), English philosophers.

A crowd of writers in France. Preceded in the manuscript by a cancelled passage listing three philosophers, only the first of whom, Montesquieu, is French (the other two are the English philosophers Sidney and Harrington). Charles Louis de Secondat, Baron de la Brede et de Montesquieu (1689–1755) was the author of *L'Esprit des lois* (1748), the most influential political study of its time. Algernon Sidney (1622–83) was the author of the posthumously published *Discourses concerning Government* (1698), James Harrington (1611–77) of a comparably influential work of political theory, *The Commonwealth of Oceana* (1656).

641 *Bolingbroke.* Henry St John, Viscount Bolingbroke (1678–1751), Tory politician, political theorist, and friend of Pope, who versifies his ideas in *An Essay on Man* (1733–4).

642 *Utility.* The belief that society should be ordered to promote the 'happiness' of the greatest number of men, a view traced in Hume's *Enquiry concerning the Principles of Morals* (1751), Bentham's *Introduction to the Principles of Morals and Legislation* (1789), and Godwin's *Political Justice* (1793).

643 *These illustrious men.* The framers of the Constitution.

Court of Chancery. The institution which in March 1817 deprived S. of the care of his children, Ianthe and Charles, after the death of their mother, Harriet Westbrook Shelley.

644 *who have become.* S. appears to have missed out a word after 'become'; perhaps 'free' or 'freer'.

645 *their 'ills are interred with their bones'.* See *Julius Caesar*, 3. 2. 73: 'The good is oft interred with their bones.'

646 *at that period. [. . .].* We have here omitted several pages detailing the political histories of Germany, Spain, South America, Asia, India, and the Middle East.

Two nations. In 1819 there were two black nations in Haiti: an 'empire' in the north under Henri Cristophe and a 'republic' in the south under General Jean Pierre Boyer. The 'cautious measures' alluded to in the previous sentence were the Parliamentary acts of 1807 and 1811, the first abolishing the slave trade in British colonies (though not slavery itself), the second making slave-trading a felony; the phrase 'infection of the Spirit of Liberty' alludes to the efforts of Toussaint L'Ouverture (1743–1803), leader of the revolt of Haitian blacks, and other French West Indian revolutionaries.

since its last struggle for liberty. See the last paragraph of *A Defence of Poetry* for a revised version of this sentence; 'since its last struggle for liberty' means since the Renaissance and the religious turmoil which followed.

man and nature. We have omitted the following interpolated sentence (a later addition, crosswritten in darker ink) which Mary S. prints as a note: 'In this sense, Religion may be called Poetry, though distorted from the beautiful simplicity of its truth—Coleridge has said that every poet was religious, the converse, that every religious man must be a poet was more true—'.

of which it is the minister. 'It' refers to 'power' earlier in the sentence.

But although . . . their own soul. This sentence appears in the peroration to *A Defence of Poetry*, along with the more famous sentence beginning 'Poets and philosophers . . .', which appears twice in the paragraph in manuscript: in the sentence after next, and also as the final sentence of the paragraph (we include only the latter instance).

647 *On the Sentiment of the Necessity of Change.* This subtitle recalls point 2 from S.'s 'outline' at the beginning of the manuscript: '2nd. Practicability and Utility of such change.'

648 *The Parliament . . . of the people.* William and Mary were made sovereigns, 'with the acquiescence of a large part of the English public' (Reiman, *SC* 6. 998), by a 'Convention Parliament' that assembled on 22 January 1689, was declared a regular Parliament on 20 March 1689, and was not dissolved until October 1695; the 'Long Parliament', to which it is compared by S. in the next sentence, met from 3 November 1640 to late in 1648, when most of its members were expelled, leaving the

'Rump Parliament'. The Long Parliament was revived in 1659, after Cromwell's death, and dissolved itself to bring in new elections in a 'Convention Parliament'. This is the Parliament that recalled Charles II from Holland.

649 *the Commons.* 'In *The Black Book; or, Corruption Unmasked* (London, 1820), John Wade calculated (p. 423) that, of 658 members of the House of Commons, 300 were nominated by peers, 187 by rich commoners or by the government itself, and only 171 were returned by popular elections of any sort (many of which were also influenced by the same rich and powerful individuals)' (Reiman, *SC*, 6. 999).

650 *catchers of men.* See Luke 5: 10: 'from henceforth thou shalt catch men.'

public credit. The national debt came to prominence as an issue of public concern at the time of the chartering of the Bank of England in 1693, rose steadily over the next 125 years, and after Waterloo was calculated at '£885 million, with an annual interest of £32 million' (Reiman, *SC* 6. 1003).

651 *that they may rule by fraud [. . .].* We here omit several paragraphs on the history of public credit as a device of policy.

labour. [. . .]. At this point in the manuscript S. brackets the following passage, perhaps for use as a footnote: 'In a treatise devoted to general considerations it would be superfluous to enter into the *mode* in which this has been done; those who desire to see a full elucidation of that mode, may read Cobbett's *Paper Against Gold.* Our present business is with consequences. I would awaken, from a consideration that the present miseries of our country are nothing necessarily inherent of the stage of civilization at which we have arrived, foresight and hope.' William Cobbett's *Paper Against Gold* (1815, 2 vols.) reprints letters that had appeared in 1810–12 in the *Political Register.*

652 *There is something . . . merchant.* A bracketed sentence lower down on this page of the manuscript may be intended as a footnote to this sentence (or to follow it in the main text): 'As usual the first persons deceived are those who are the instruments of the fraud, and the merchant and the country gentleman may be excused for believing that their existence is connected with the permanence of the best practicable forms of social order.'

653 *amerced.* Punished by exacting an arbitrary fine.

poor-rates. Paid by working members of the community to support the poor, including widows, orphans, the aged, and the infirm. The Poor Laws were in effect from 1601. By 1819 they were under attack from merchants, industrialists, and urban taxpayers, in part because they were subject to abuse, in part because of pressures on the system caused by the rise of industrial cities (and resulting periods of mass unemployment) and an increase in the number of agricultural day-labourers (many of whom were often unemployed in the post-war period, after the return of foreign competition). In 1834 the Poor Laws were amended by

Parliament; the basic system was maintained but its administration was reformed and the conditions of the workhouses themselves were made as dehumanizing as possible, to encourage the poor to find employment.

655 *A writer of the present day ... excess of population.* Thomas Robert Malthus (1736–1834), author of *An Essay on the Principles of Population* (1798), was an Anglican priest as well as an economist.

656 *please.* The following sentence in the manuscript is bracketed by S.: 'The rights of all men are intrinsically and originally equal and they forgo the assertion of all of them only that they may the more securely enjoy a portion.'

657 *The national debt ... of the country.* See Godwin's *Political Justice*, book 5, ch. 16, for a similar analysis.

must be paid. These words are followed in the manuscript by an incomplete sentence bracketed by S., perhaps for use as a footnote: 'This sum cannot have amounted to less than two thousand millions; it would be a curious problem in political economy to calculate the precise degree of comfort and of ornament—'.

658 *persons of property.* These words are followed in the manuscript by a sentence bracketed by S., perhaps for use as a footnote: 'Such a gentleman must lose a third of his estate, such a citizen the fourth of his money in the funds; the persons who borrowed would have paid, and the juggling and complicated system of paper finance be suddenly at an end.'

former. 'latter' (i.e. the debtor) subsequent 'formers' and 'latters', and 'firsts' and 'seconds', are also confused; correct forms are given in square brackets.

660 *Lor[d Bacon].* The manuscript is blank here, and left so in Mary S.'s transcription; 'Lord Bacon' is Peck's editorial conjecture in the Julian edition of the *Complete Works* (1926–30), followed by *Clark*.

662 *argument [. . .].* The sentence is left incomplete in the manuscript.

then [. . .]. The sentence is left incomplete in the manuscript.

663 *[the people].* 'they' in the manuscript, those whose interests 'the advocates of universal suffrage' (at the beginning of the preceding paragraph) would advance.

Jesus Christ. This reading is preferred as more appropriate to the context than 'Moses', which in *SC* is described as a 'possible reading'.

a moral rather than political truth. This distinction was a familiar feature of contemporary political economy.

665 *voting by ballot.* S. means by secret ballot.

them. Motives.

vitality of [. . .]. S.'s sentence is incomplete in the manuscript.

666 *tempted, and betrayed.* By government spies and informers, presumably.

667 *triennial parliaments*. England had elected annual Parliaments (excepting numerous abridgements) from 1330 to 1676, when elections were made triennial; in 1715 Parliaments could be extended to seven years. S.'s proposal is to return to the middle position of triennial elections.

ulterior. Further (*OED* 1).

668 *16th of August*. Alludes to the Peterloo Massacre. See headnote to *Mask of Anarchy*.

670 *to examine [. . .]*. S.'s sentence is incomplete in the manuscript.

manufacturers. Factory workers.

inhabitants of London [. . .]. S.'s sentence is incomplete in the manuscript.

'pernicious to one touch'. A quotation from *PL* 6. 520 describing the Devil's invention of cannon.

671 *Godwin and Hazlitt and Bentham and Hunt*. Byron's name is cancelled in the manuscript. S.'s list 'may simply have been an attempt to name eloquent spokesmen for four reformist viewpoints. Note the absence of William Cobbett, whom he feared at this time as an incendiary influence upon ignorant people' (Reiman, *SC* 6. 1060).

672 *the reigning family*. A reference to the Act of Settlement of 1701, which brought in the House of Hanover.

673 *question at issue [. . .]*. S.'s sentence is incomplete in the manuscript.

674 *generous and [. . .]*. S.'s sentence is incomplete in the manuscript.

A Defence of Poetry. Composed in February and March 1821. A press copy in the Bodleian (*BSM* 20) transcribed by Mary S., with corrections in S.'s hand, was sent by S. to Charles Ollier on 20 March 1821; this press copy supplies our copy-text, though we have also consulted S.'s intermediate fair copy (*BSM* 7) and his draft (*BSM* 4). S. had intended to publish the essay in Ollier's *Literary Miscellany*, the first number of which appeared in 1820, containing Thomas Love Peacock's 'The Four Ages of Poetry'. This witty attack on the poet as 'a semi-barbarian in a civilized community' and on poetry as merely 'the mental rattle that awakened the attention of intellect in the infancy of civil society' (quoted from *Brett-Smith*) 'excited' S., as he put it in a letter to Peacock, 'to a sacred rage' and desire to vindicate 'the insulted Muses' (*L* 2. 261). However, Ollier's *Miscellany* folded after one issue. Subsequent attempts after S.'s death to publish his essay came to nothing, until it appeared (minus the references to Peacock) in *MWS: Prose*. On the last blank page of the press copy (a home-made notebook), S. gives as the full title: *A Defence of Poetry. Or Remarks Suggested by an Essay Entitled 'The Four Ages of Poetry'. Part 1*. In the text he states that the 'second part' (never written) will address 'the present state of the cultivation of Poetry' (p. 700). S. draws on a range of sources, including Plato's *Ion*, which he had translated in 1819–21, and Sir Philip Sidney's *The Defence of Poesy* (1595) (hereafter *Defence*), and recycles material from his other prose writings (the peroration is taken, with some revision, from *A Philo-sophical View of Reform*). What is original about the essay is inseparable from its 'vitally metaphorical' (p. 676) eloquence. It is at once aesthetic treatise and prose poem. S. turns Peacock's utilitarian arguments on their head; nothing is more useful than poetry because poetry, defined in both a 'general' and a 'restricted' way (pp. 675, 700), is the ordering principle at work in human creativity. S. also suggests that poetry is not left behind by the advance of civilization; rather, it is 'The most unfailing herald, companion and follower of the awakening of a great people to work a beneficial change in opinion or institution' (pp. 700–1).

Reason and Imagination. See S.'s draft letter to Ollier in which he says that Peacock 'would extinguish Imagination, which is the Sun of life, & grope his way by the cold & uncertain & borrowed light of [*that which is called*] the Moon which he calls Reason' (*L* 2. 273).

τὸ ποιειν . . . τὸ λογιζειν. The Greek words, transliterated, are *poiein* (making) and *logizein* (reasoning). For *poiein*, see Sidney, *Defence*, when he points out that the word 'poet' 'cometh of this word *poiein*, which is, to make'.

675 *'the . . . Imagination'.* The phrase seems to be S.'s own.

connate. Born at the same time.

676 *vitally metaphorical.* See S.'s comment to Leigh Hunt, 'Strong passion expresses itself in metaphor borrowed from objects alike remote or near, and casts over all the shadow of its own greatness' (*L* 2. 108).

'the same . . . world'. S.'s footnote to this quotation refers to Francis Bacon, *De Dignitate et Augmentis Scientiarum* (1623), 3. 1. In English translation, Bacon says that the connections he has drawn between different branches of knowledge are not 'only similitudes' but 'the same footsteps of nature, treading or printing upon several subjects or matters'; quoted from *The Works of Francis Bacon*, ed. J. Spedding and D. D. Heath (7 vols., London, 1857–9).

677 *the chaos . . . poem.* The material from which a 'cyclic poem', or series of epics, is made; these epics are probably those written by the 'cyclic poets' who followed Homer (p. 682).

Poets . . . prophets. See Sidney, *Defence*: 'Among the Romans a poet was called *vates*, which is as much as a diviner, foreseer, or prophet.'

the Book of Job. See S.'s account in 'On Christianity' of the way in which 'The sublime dramatic poem entitled *Job*, had familiarized his [Christ's] imagination with the boldest imagery afforded by the human mind' (*Murray*, p. 249).

678 *hieroglyphic.* Symbol.

679 *Plato . . . poet.* See S.'s 'On the *Symposium*, or Preface to the *Banquet* of Plato', where he finds in Plato 'the rare union of close and subtle logic, with the Pythian enthusiasm of poetry' (text from *Notopoulos*, p. 402);

see, too, Sidney, *Defence*: 'of all philosophers he [Plato] is the most poetical.'

679 *Cicero*. Roman statesman and author (106–43 BC), famous for his eloquent speeches in law-courts and senate.

Lord Bacon ... poet. S. keys the following footnote to 'poet': 'See the Filum Labyrinthi, and the Essay on Death particularly'. *Filum Labyrinthi* (1607) is a fragment in which Bacon, referring to himself in the third person, describes his empirical view of human knowledge. The essay *On Death* (1612) is a typical example of Bacon's memorably aphoristic style.

a story ... poem. Sidney, *Defence*, argues that for Aristotle (*Poetics*, 9) 'poetry' 'is more philosophical ... than history', since it 'dealeth with ... the universal consideration' and history with 'the particular'.

680 *epitomes*. Summaries.

have been called ... history. Alludes to Bacon, *The Advancement of Learning* (1605), 2: 'As for the corruptions and moths of history, which are Epitomes, the use of them deserveth to be banished.'

Herodotus. Greek historian (*c*.484–425 BC), known as 'the father of history' and author of the first Greek history in nine books.

Plutarch. Greek author (*c*.AD46–120) of the *Parallel Lives* of Roman and Greek figures.

Livy. Roman historian (*c*.59 BC–AD 17), author of a history of Rome in 142 books, 35 of which survive.

Poetry ... pleasure. See Coleridge, *Biographia Literaria*, ch. 14, where he defines a poem as 'proposing for its immediate object pleasure, not truth'.

impanelled. Be enrolled (for a jury).

681 *planetary music*. See Sidney, *Defence*: 'the planet-like music of poetry'.

the immorality of poetry. S. probably has in mind Plato's objections to 'representational poetry', such as the view that 'It has a terrifying capacity for deforming even good people' (*Republic*, 605c).

682 *his own conceptions ... wrong*. In his intermediate fair copy, S. pencilled the following comment: 'This was Mr Shelley's error in the Revolt of Islam [*Laon and Cythna*]. He has attempted to cure himself in subsequent publications but, except in the tragedy of the Cenci, with little success.'

many imperfections. Especially what S. in *A Discourse on the Manners of the Ancient Greeks* calls 'personal slavery and the inferiority of women' (*Clark*, p. 220).

683 *We know ... events*. Derives from David Hume's scepticism about causation; see S.'s direct reference to Hume in this context in *A Refutation of Deism* (*Murray*, p. 121).

idealisms. Here, representations informed by an idea and an ideal.

comedy . . . ideal. Comedy should be in keeping with the main 'idea' of the tragedy.

trilogies. Respectively, *Antigone*, *Oedipus the King*, and *Oedipus at Colonus* by Sophocles (though not strictly a trilogy), and *Agamemnon*, *Libation Bearers*, and *Eumenides* by Aeschylus.

684 *Calderon . . . Autos.* See the note to *Letter to Maria Gisborne*, l. 181, p. 786.

Philoctetes. A play by Sophocles, whose hero, like Agamemnon and Othello, is a warrior; S.'s metaphor humorously casts his debate with Peacock as a chivalric joust.

sophisms. Clever but fallacious arguments.

Paladins. The twelve peers of Charlemagne, alluded to by Peacock in 'The Four Ages of Poetry' as among 'the heroes of the iron age of chivalrous poetry'.

necromancers. Practitioners of black magic.

685 *The drama . . . mirror.* See *Hamlet*, 3. 2. 19–20: 'the purpose of playing, whose end . . . was and is to hold as 'twere the mirror up to nature.'

Cato. Tragedy (1713) by Joseph Addison; criticized by Samuel Johnson in his *Preface to Shakespeare* as containing 'nothing that acquaints us with human sentiments or human actions'.

Poetry . . . unsheathed. See Byron, *Childe Harold*, 3. 97: 'With a most voiceless thought, sheathing it as a sword' and his 'So, we'll go no more a roving', l. 5: 'For the sword outwears the sheath'.

686 *Machiavelli.* Niccolò Machiavelli (1469–1527), Florentine writer, author of *The Prince*, to which S. probably alludes here.

bucolic writers. These include Theocritus, Bion, and Moschus (S. translated from the last two of these poets).

687 *torpid.* Benumbed.

Astraea. Mythological goddess of justice; in Ovid, *Met.* 1, the last of the gods to leave the earth ('Justice, virgin divine, | The last of the immortals fled away').

luxurious. Sensually indulgent and wealthy.

The sacred links . . . all. This image derives from Plato's *Ion* (see Notopoulos, p. 472).

688 *Ennius.* Considered the father of Latin literature (*c.*239–170 BC); author of an influential epic, *Annales*.

Varro. Latin writer (*c.*116–27 BC); author of a great variety of works, and renowned for his learning.

Pacuvius. Tragic poet (*c.*220–130 BC) and nephew of Ennius.

Accius. Tragic poet (b. 170 BC).

Camillus. Defended Rome against the Gauls in the fourth century BC.

688 *Regulus.* See note to 'Ode to Liberty', l. 98 (p. 781).

the senators . . . Gauls. When the Gauls entered Rome in 390 BC they were met by senators so calm in their demeanour that they might have been mistaken for 'statues in some holy place' (Livy, *The Early History of Rome*, trans. Aubrey de Selincourt (Harmondsworth, 1960)). S. does not mention the fact that all the senators 'were butchered where they sat'.

battle of Cannae. In 216 BC, when the Roman army was destroyed by Hannibal.

quia . . . sacro. 'because they lack a sacred poet' (Horace, *Odes*, 4. 9. 28).

rhapsodist. One who declaims the works of poets, such as Ion in Plato's dialogue (while Socrates is probably ironic about the rhapsodist's 'inspired' state, S. appears not to be).

Moses . . . Isaiah. See Sidney, *Defence*, when he lists 'the poetical part of the Scripture' as including 'David in his Psalms; Solomon in his Song of Songs, in his Ecclesiastes, and Proverbs; Moses and Deborah in their Hymns; and the writer of Job'.

689 *the three . . . mind.* Plato distinguished between 'a ruling immortal soul, seated in the brain; a higher mortal soul, seated in the heart; and a lower appetitive soul, also ruled by the immortal but directly commanded by the higher mortal soul' (*Brett-Smith*, p. 95).

Light . . . rouse. Macbeth, 3. 2. 51–4. For S.'s 'And night's', Shakespeare has 'Whiles night's'. S. is agreeing with Peacock's ironical account of 'the dark ages' as a time 'in which the light of the Gospel began to spread over Europe, and in which, by a mysterious and inscrutable dispensation, the darkness thickened with the progress of light'.

Celtic conquerors. S. uses 'Celtic' to mean northern European.

690 *The principle . . . among them.* See Plato, *Republic*, 369, a passage translated by S.

exoteric. Intelligible to all. See S.'s description of *The Mask of Anarchy* 'as of the exoteric species' (*L* 2. 152).

esoteric. Intended only for the initiated. See S.'s comment that *Epipsychidion* 'is to be published simply for the esoteric few' (*L* 2. 263).

'Galeotto . . . scrisse'. 'Galeotto was the book, and he who wrote it' (editors' trans), Dante, *Inf.* 5. 137. The allusion is to the book which catalysed the illicit love of Paolo and Francesca, and to the name of the character who acted as messenger between Lancelot and Guinevere.

Trouveurs. The Troubadours, lyric poets (between the eleventh and thirteeenth centuries), writing mainly of love.

Petrarch. Italian poet (1304–74), admired by S. for his 'tender & solemn enthusiasm' (*L* 2. 20).

691 *Divine Drama.* Dante's *Divine Comedy*.

Love . . . Plato. See Agathon's speech about love in the *Symposium* (*Notopoulos*, pp. 434–7).

Dante . . . 'justissimus unus' in Paradise. Refers to Dante, *Par.* 20. 67–9 ('Who would believe, down in the erring world, the Trojan Ripheus in this circle to be the fifth of the holy lights') and Virgil, *Aeneid*, 2. 426 ('foremost in justice among the Trojans').

692 *alleged design . . . new torments*. See *PL* 1. 209–20.

modern mythology. Christianity.

And Milton's . . . eternity of genius. Much of this material, with variations, is taken from S.'s 'On the Devil, and Devils' (for a text see *Webb*, pp. 185–6). The earlier essay is more outspoken in its antagonism to 'the popular creed' (*Webb*, p. 185).

Lucretius . . . sensible world. Alludes to Lucretius' interest in atomic materialism. S. rejects a vision of reality as consisting only of that which is 'sensible' (that is, perceptible by the senses).

Virgil . . . copied. See Peacock, 'The Four Ages of Poetry': 'The imitative consists in recasting, and giving an exquisite polish to, the poetry of the age of gold: of this Virgil is the most obvious and striking example.'

mock-birds. Mocking-birds, that is, birds that mimic the notes of other birds.

Apollonius Rhodius. Alexandrian epic poet (b. 295 BC), author of *Argonautica*, read by S. in August 1820.

Quintus Calaber Smyrnaeus. Quintus Smyrnaeus wrote *Posthomerica*, a continuation in Greek of Homer in fourteen books; he was known as 'Calaber' because the manuscript of *Posthomerica* was found in Calabria (*Norton*).

Nonnus. Member of an epic school founded in Upper Egypt in the fifth century BC; author of *Dionysiaca*, a Greek epic in forty-eight books, ordered by S. in 1817 (see *L* 1. 575, 585) and praised by Peacock in 'The Four Ages of Poetry' as containing 'many passages of exceeding beauty in the midst of masses of amplification and repetition'.

Lucan. See note to *Adonais*, l. 404 (p. 803).

Statius. Epic poet (AD 45–96), author of the *Thebaid*.

Claudian. Latin poet (*c*.AD 370–404), author of a mythological epic on the rape of Proserpine (*Norton*).

Orlando Furioso . . . Fairy Queen. Epics written, respectively, by the Italian poets Ariosto (1474–1533) and Tasso (1544–95), the Portuguese poet Camões (1525–80), and the English poet Spenser.

693 *Luther*. See note to 'Ode to Liberty', l. 141 (p. 782).

Dante . . . barbarisms. In *De Vulgari Eloquentia* Dante argued in favour of an Italian (rather than Latin) literary language.

Lucifer. 'Bearer of light'; Venus as the morning star; Satan's name before he fell. S. alludes to *PL* 5. 708–10: 'His countenance, as the morning star that guides | The starry flock, allured them, and with lies | Drew after him the third part of heaven's host.'

693 *instinct with spirit.* See *PL* 6. 752: 'Itself instinct with spirit'.

effluence. Flowing out.

The age . . . invention. See Sidney, *Defence*, where he argues that poets are 'fathers in learning', refers to 'the poets Dante, Boccacio, and Petrarch' as the first 'in the Italian language . . . that made it aspire to be a treasure-house of science', and claims for 'Gower and Chaucer' a comparable distinction.

mechanists. Not merely makers of machines, unlike the use of 'mechanist' a little later in the essay (see below), but also those whose view of usefulness is narrowly mechanical.

694 *some of the French writers.* S. appears to have in mind writers such as Helvetius and Condorcet, and to be quarrelling with their intransigent materialism.

mechanist. Machine-maker.

combines, labour. Oversees organization of labour.

'To him . . . away.' S. quotes imprecisely from Mark 4: 25: 'For he that hath, to him shall be given; and he that hath not, from him shall be taken even that which he hath.'

Scylla and Charybdis. Sea-monster and whirlpool in Greek mythology, so positioned in the Straits of Messina that to avoid one was to risk the other.

anarchy and despotism. See S.'s comment in August 1819: 'But the change should commence among the higher orders, or anarchy will be only the last flash before despotism' (*L* 2. 115).

'It . . . mirth'. S. quotes inexactly from Ecclesiastes 7: 2: 'It is better to go to the house of mourning, than to go to the house of feasting.'

695 *Rousseau.* S. keys the following footnote: 'I follow the classification adopted by the author of the Four Ages of Poetry. But Rousseau was essentially a poet. The others, even Voltaire, were mere reasoners.' In 'The Four Ages of Poetry' Peacock speaks of Hume, Gibbon, Rousseau, and Voltaire as 'four extraordinary minds' that shook 'every portion of the reign of authority'.

Inquisition in Spain. The Inquisition was suppressed in 1820.

'I dare . . . adage'. Quoted from *Macbeth*, 1. 7. 44–5.

696 *the curse . . . Adam.* See Genesis 3: 17–19, where Adam is cursed to 'eat bread' 'In the sweat of thy face'.

Mammon. See Matthew 6: 24 and Luke 16: 13: 'Ye cannot serve God and mammon.'

the centre . . . knowledge. See Wordsworth, Preface to *Lyrical Ballads*: 'Poetry is the breath and finer spirit of all knowledge.'

697 *intertexture.* Matter that is woven in.

'dictated . . . song'. See *PL* 9. 23–4, where the poet's 'celestial patroness' (l. 21) 'inspires | Easy my unpremeditated verse'.

It is . . . own. See S.'s translation of Plato's *Ion*: 'For the authors of those great poems which we admire do not attain to excellence through the rules of any art but they utter their beautiful melodies of verse in a state of inspiration and, as it were, *possessed* by a spirit not their own' (*Notopoulos*, p. 472).

698 *interlunations.* Periods between the appearance of the moon.

potable. Drinkable.

'The mind . . . Heaven'. S. quotes from *PL* 1. 254–5, which reads 'in itself', not, as S. has it, 'of itself'.

film of familiarity. See Coleridge's 'film of familiarity' in *Biographia Literaria,* ch. 14.

Tasso: 'Non merita . . . Poeta'. The quotation comes from Tasso's *Discorsi del poema eroico* (S. may have met it in Pietro Serassi, *La vita di Torquato Tasso* (1785)) and translates as 'None merits the name of creator except God and the poet'.

699 *'there . . . soar'.* Adapted from *PL* 4. 829–30.

Homer . . . laureate. In S.'s ironic catalogue of poets' supposed moral failings, Homer might be described as a 'drunkard' because in the *Ion* poets are said to become 'like the Bacchantes' (S.'s translation, *Notopoulos*, p. 472); Virgil as a 'flatterer' because of his deference to the Emperor Augustus; Horace as a 'coward' because of his account of his retreat from the battle of Philippi (*Odes*, 2. 7); Tasso as a 'madman' because of his mental problems and imprisonment (see headnote to *Julian and Maddalo*, p. 741); Bacon as a 'peculator' (or embezzler) because he was convicted of receiving gifts from suitors in the court of Chancery; Raphael as a 'libertine' because of some remarks in Vasari's *Lives*; and Spenser as a 'poet laureate' because in *FQ* he extolled the virtues of Queen Elizabeth I.

Their errors . . . judged. Various biblical references occur here: they include Daniel 5: 27: 'Thou art weighed in the balances, and art found wanting'; Isaiah 1: 18: 'though your sins be as scarlet, they shall be as white as snow'; Revelation 7: 14: 'washed their robes, and made them white in the blood of the Lamb'; and Matthew 7: 1: 'Judge not, that ye be not judged.'

700 *obnoxious.* Liable.

Theseids . . . Codri. Juvenal (*Satires*, 1) refers to his being 'so often bored by the Theseid of the ranting Cordus'.

Bavius and Maevius. Types of the bad poet in Virgil, *Eclogues*, 3. 90: 'Maevius, I hope that anyone who can put up with Bavius's verse may fall for yours.'

700 *low-thoughted envy*. See Milton, *Comus*, l. 6: 'low-thoughted care'.

701 *hierophants*. Initiating priests; expounders of sacred mysteries. S. wrote 'priests' in the version of this passage in *A Philosophical View of Reform*.

Poets . . . World. In *A Philosophical View of Reform* S. wrote 'Poets and philosophers' (p. 647). In Samuel Johnson's *Rasselas* Imlac asserts that the poet 'must write as the interpreter of nature, and the legislator of mankind'.

FURTHER READING

Where an abbreviated title is used in the Notes, it is repeated here; see the head of the Notes for a full list of abbreviations.

EDITIONS

Stephen C. Behrendt (ed.), *Zastrozzi and St. Irvyne* (Oxford, 1986).

Betty T. Bennett (ed.), *The Letters of Mary Wollstonecraft Shelley* (3 vols., Baltimore, 1980–8) [*MWSL*].

H. F. B. Brett-Smith (ed.), *Peacock's Four Ages of Poetry, Shelley's Defence of Poetry and Browning's Essay on Shelley* (Oxford, 1921) [*Brett-Smith*].

P. H. Butter (ed.), *Percy Bysshe Shelley: Alastor and Other Poems; Prometheus Unbound with Other Poems; Adonais* (London, 1970) [*Butter*].

Kenneth Neill Cameron and Donald H. Reiman (eds.), *Shelley and His Circle 1773–1822* (Cambridge, Mass., 1961–   ; 10 vols. to date) [*SC*]. Contains important critical and biographical essays.

Judith Chernaik, *The Lyrics of Shelley* (Cleveland and London, 1972) [*Chernaik*]. Contains newly edited texts of shorter poems by Shelley as well as critical commentary.

David Lee Clark (ed.), *Shelley's Prose; Or, The Trumpet of a Prophecy* (corr. edn., Albuquerque, N. Mex., 1966) [*Clark*].

Kelvin Everest and G. M. Matthews (eds.), *The Poems of Shelley, 1804–1819* (2 vols. to date, Harlow, 1989, 2000) [*Longman* 1 and 2].

Paula R. Feldman and Diana Scott-Kilvert (eds.), *The Journals of Mary Shelley 1814–1844* (2 vols., Oxford, 1987) [*Mary Jnl.*].

H. Buxton Forman (ed.), *The Poetical Works of Percy Bysshe Shelley* (2nd edn., 2 vols., London, 1886).

Thomas Hutchinson (ed.), G. M. Matthews (corr.), *Shelley: Poetical Works* (London, 1970).

Roger Ingpen and Walter E. Peck (eds.), *The Complete Works of Percy Bysshe Shelley* (10 vols., London, 1926–30).

Frederick L. Jones (ed.), *The Letters of Percy Bysshe Shelley* (2 vols., Oxford, 1964) [*L*].

C. D. Locock (ed.), *The Poems of Percy Bysshe Shelley* (2 vols., London, 1912) [*Locock*].

E. B. Murray (ed.), *The Prose Works of Percy Bysshe Shelley, Volume One* (Oxford, 1993) [*Murray*].

James A. Notopoulos, *The Platonism of Shelley: A Study of Platonism and the Poetic Mind* (Durham, NC, 1949) [*Notopoulos*]. Contains texts of Shelley's translations from Plato as well as commentary.

Donald H. Reiman (gen. ed.), *Manuscripts of the Younger Romantics: Shelley* (9 vols., 1985–97) [*MYR: Shelley*].

Donald H. Reiman (gen. ed.), *The Bodleian Shelley Manuscripts* (23 vols., New York, 1986–2001) [*BSM*].

—— and Neil Fraistat (eds.), *The Complete Poetry of Percy Bysshe Shelley* (1 vol. to date, Baltimore, 2000).

—— and Sharon B. Powers (eds.), *Shelley's Poetry and Prose*, Norton Critical Edition (New York, 1977) [*Norton*].

—— and Neil Fraistat (eds.), *Shelley's Poetry and Prose*, Norton Critical Edition, 2nd edition (New York, 2002) [*Norton*^{2}].

Francesco Rognoni (ed.), *Shelley: Opere* (Turin, 1995) [*Rognoni*].

William Michael Rossetti (ed.), *The Poetical Works of Percy Bysshe Shelley* (2 vols., London, 1870) [*Rossetti*].

Mary Wollstonecraft Shelley (ed.), *Posthumous Poems of Percy Bysshe Shelley* (London, 1824) [*PP*].

—— (ed.), *The Poetical Works of Percy Bysshe Shelley* (4 vols., London, 1839) [*MWS (1)*].

—— (ed.), *The Poetical Works of Percy Bysshe Shelley* (1 vol., London, 1839) [*MWS (2)*].

—— (ed.), *Essays, Letters from Abroad, Translations and Fragments by Percy Bysshe Shelley* (2 vols., London, 1840 [1839]) [*MWS: Prose*].

Timothy Webb (ed.), *Percy Bysshe Shelley: Poems and Prose*, with a critical selection by George E. Donaldson (London, 1995) [*Webb*].

BIOGRAPHY, REFERENCE, AND 'LITERARY LIVES'

B. C. Barker-Benfield, *Shelley's Guitar* (Oxford, 1992).

Edmund Blunden, *Shelley: A Life Story* (1946; repr. London, 1965).

Kenneth Neill Cameron, *The Young Shelley: Genesis of a Radical* (New York, 1950).

—— *Shelley: The Golden Years* (Cambridge, Mass., 1974).

Richard Holmes, *Shelley: The Pursuit* (London, 1974).

Sylva Norman, *Flight of the Skylark: The Development of Shelley's Reputation* (London, 1954).

Michael O'Neill, *Percy Bysshe Shelley: A Literary Life* (Basingstoke, 1989).

—— 'Shelley', forthcoming in *New Dictionary of National Biography* (Oxford, 2004).

Donald H. Reiman, *Percy Bysshe Shelley: Updated Edition* (Boston, 1990).

Norman Ivey White, *Shelley* (2 vols., London, 1947).

Humbert Wolfe (intro.), *The Life of Percy Bysshe Shelley, as Comprised in 'The Life of Shelley' by Thomas Jefferson Hogg, 'The Recollections of Shelley and Byron' by Edward John Trelawny, 'Memoirs of Shelley' by Thomas Love Peacock* (London, 1933).

CRITICISM

Stephen C. Behrendt, *Shelley and His Audiences* (Lincoln, Nebr., 1989).

G. Kim Blank (ed.), *The New Shelley: Later Twentieth-Century Views* (Basingstoke, 1991).

Harold Bloom, *Shelley's Mythmaking* (Ithaca, NY, 1959).

Teddi Chichester Bonca, *Shelley's Mirrors of Love: Narcissism, Sacrifice, and Sorority* (Albany, NY, 1999) [*Bonca*].

Timothy Clark, *Embodying Revolution: The Figure of the Poet in Shelley* (Oxford, 1989).

Timothy Clark and Jerrold E. Hogle (eds.), *Evaluating Shelley* (Edinburgh, 1996).

Richard Cronin, *Shelley's Poetic Thoughts* (London, 1981).

Stuart Curran, *Shelley's Annus Mirabilis: The Maturing of an Epic Vision* (San Marino, Calif., 1975).

P. M. S. Dawson, *The Unacknowledged Legislator: Shelley and Politics* (Oxford, 1980).

David Duff, *Romance and Revolution: Shelley and the Politics of a Genre* (Cambridge, 1994).

Kelvin Everest (ed.), *Shelley Revalued: Essays from the Gregynog Conference* (Leicester, 1983).

—— (ed.), *Percy Bysshe Shelley: Bicentenary Essays: Essays and Studies 1992* (Cambridge, 1992).

Michael Ferber, *The Poetry of Shelley* (Harmondsworth, 1993).

Barbara Charlesworth Gelpi, *Shelley's Goddess: Maternity, Language, Subjectivity* (New York, 1992).

Paul Hamilton, *Percy Bysshe Shelley* (Tavistock, 2000).

Jerrold E. Hogle, *Shelley's Process: Radical Transference and the Development of His Major Works* (New York, 1988).

Steven E. Jones, *Shelley's Satire: Violence, Exhortation, and Authority* (DeKalb, Ill., 1994).

William Keach, *Shelley's Style* (New York, 1984).

Angela Leighton, *Shelley and the Sublime: An Interpretation of the Major Poems* (Cambridge, 1984).

Timothy Morton, *Shelley and the Revolution in Taste: The Body and the Natural World* (Cambridge, 1994).

Michael O'Neill, *The Human Mind's Imaginings: Conflict and Achievement in Shelley's Poetry* (Oxford, 1989).

—— (ed.), *Shelley*, Longman Critical Readers (London, 1993).

—— *Romanticism and the Self-Conscious Poem* (Oxford, 1997).

C. E. Pulos, *The Deep Truth: A Study of Shelley's Scepticism* (Lincoln, Nebr., 1954).

Tilottama Rajan, *Dark Interpreter: The Discourse of Romanticism* (Ithaca, NY, 1980).

Hugh Roberts, *Shelley and the Chaos of History: A New Politics of Poetry* (University Park, Pa. 1997).

Bryan Shelley, *Shelley and Scripture: The Interpreting Angel* (Oxford, 1994).

Stuart M. Sperry, *Shelley's Major Verse: The Narrative and Dramatic Poetry* (Cambridge, Mass., 1988) [*Sperry*].

Patrick Swinden (ed.), *Shelley: Shorter Poems and Lyrics, A Casebook* (London, 1976).

Ronald Tetreault, *The Poetry of Life: Shelley and Literary Form* (Toronto, 1987).

William A. Ulmer, *Shelleyan Eros: The Rhetoric of Romantic Love* (Princeton, 1990).

Earl R. Wasserman, *Shelley: A Critical Reading* (Baltimore, 1971).

Timothy Webb, *The Violet in the Crucible: Shelley and Translation* (Oxford, 1976).

—— *Shelley: A Voice Not Understood* (Manchester, 1977).

Alan M. Weinberg, *Shelley's Italian Experience* (Basingstoke, 1991).

Susan J. Wolfson, *Formal Charges: The Shaping of Poetry in British Romanticism* (Stanford, Calif., 1997).

ORDERING OF POEMS IN VOLUMES
PUBLISHED BY SHELLEY FROM
1816 TO 1822

(This list excludes volumes publishing only one poem and lists some poems not included in this selection.)

Alastor . . . and Other Poems *(1816)*

Alastor; or, the Spirit of Solitude
'O! there are spirits of the air'
Stanzas.—April, 1814
Mutability
'The pale, the cold, and the moony smile'
A Summer-Evening Churchyard
To Wordsworth
Feelings of a Republican on the Fall of Bonaparte
Superstition
Sonnet. From the Italian of Dante
Translated from the Greek of Moschus
The Daemon of the World

Rosalind and Helen: A Modern Eclogue;
with Other Poems *(1819)*

Rosalind and Helen
Lines Written among the Euganean Hills
Hymn to Intellectual Beauty
Ozymandias

Prometheus Unbound . . . with Other Poems *(1820)*

Prometheus Unbound
The Sensitive Plant
A Vision of the Sea
Ode to Heaven
An Exhortation
Ode to the West Wind
An Ode, Written, October, 1819, before the Spaniards Had
    Recovered Their Liberty
The Cloud
To a Skylark
Ode to Liberty

Hellas *(1822)*

Hellas
Written on Hearing the News of the Death of Napoleon

INDEX OF TITLES OF POEMS AND PROSE WORKS

'A Cat in distress' 1
A Defence of Poetry 674
Adonais 529
Alastor; or, The Spirit of Solitude 92
An Address to the People on the Death of the Princess Charlotte 623
A New National Anthem 444
An Exhortation 460
A Philosophical View of Reform 636
Epipsychidion 512
Hellas 548
Hymn to Intellectual Beauty (versions A and B) 114/117
Julian and Maddalo 212
Laon and Cythna 130
Letter to Maria Gisborne 476
Lines Written among the Euganean Hills 198
Lines Written During the Castlereagh Administration 443
Lines Written in the Bay of Lerici 602
Love's Philosophy 446
Men of England: A Song 442
Mont Blanc (versions A and B) 120/124
Mutability 112
Ode to Heaven 447
Ode to Liberty 466
Ode to the West Wind 412
On Life 633
On Love 631
'O! there are spirits of the air' 89
Ozymandias 198
Peter Bell the Third 415
Prometheus Unbound 229
Queen Mab 10
Song ('Rarely, rarely comest thou') 475
Song of Apollo 508
Song of Pan 509
Sonnet ('Lift not the painted veil') 210
Sonnet ('Ye hasten to the grave!') 474
Sonnet: England in 1819 446
Sonnet: On Launching Some Bottles Filled with *Knowledge* into the Bristol Channel 8
Sonnet: Political Greatness 510

Sonnet: To a Balloon, Laden with *Knowledge* 9
Stanzas.—April, 1814 88
Stanzas Written in Dejection—December 1818, near Naples 209
The Aziola 547
The Cenci 314
The Cloud 461
'The flower that smiles today' 589
The Indian Girl's Song 510
The Magnetic Lady to Her Patient 597
The Mask of Anarchy 400
The Sensitive Plant 450
The Triumph of Life 604
The Two Spirits—An Allegory 208
The Witch of Atlas 486
To —— (Lines to a Critic) 485
To —— (Lines to a Reviewer) 484
To —— ('One word is too often profaned') 590
To —— ('The serpent is shut out from Paradise') 591
To Constantia 128
To Jane ('The keen stars were twinkling') 601
To Jane. The Invitation 593
To Jane—The Recollection 595
To a Skylark 463
To Night 546
To S. and C. 443
To the Emperors of Russia and Austria Who Eyed the Battle of Austerlitz from the Heights whilst Bonaparte Was Active in the Thickest of the Fight 2
To the Lord Chancellor 448
To Wordsworth 90
Verses Written on Receiving a Celandine in a Letter from England 112
'What men gain fairly' 444
'When the lamp is shattered' 590
With a Guitar. To Jane 599
Written on Hearing the News of the Death of Napoleon 588
Zeinab and Kathema 3

INDEX OF FIRST LINES OF POEMS

A Cat in distress 1
A glorious people vibrated again 466
A Sensitive Plant in a garden grew 450
Alas, good friend, what profit can you see 484
An old, mad, blind, despised, and dying King; 446
Ariel to Miranda;—Take 599
As from their ancestral oak 443
As I lay asleep in Italy 400
Away! the moor is dark beneath the moon, 88

Before those cruel Twins, whom at one birth 487
Best and brightest, come away— 593
Bright ball of flame that through the gloom of even 9
Bright wanderer, fair coquette of Heaven, 602

Chameleons feed on light and air: 460
Corpses are cold in the tomb— 443
Coward Chiefs! who while the fight 2

'Do you not hear the Aziola cry? 547

Earth, ocean, air, beloved brotherhood! 93
From the forests and highlands 509

God prosper, speed, and save, 444

Hail to thee, blithe Spirit! 463
Honey from silkworms who can gather, 485
How, my dear Mary, are you critic-bitten 486
How wonderful is Death 11

I arise from dreams of thee 510
I bring fresh showers for the thirsting flowers, 461
I met a traveller from an antique land 198
In day the eternal universe of things 124

I rode one evening with Count Maddalo 213
I thought of thee, fair Celandine, 112
I weep for Adonais—he is dead! 531

Lift not the painted veil which those who live 210

Many a green isle needs must be 198
Men of England, wherefore plough 442
Monarch of Gods and Daemons, and all Spirits 233
My Song, I fear that thou wilt find but few 513

Nor happiness, nor majesty, nor fame, 510
Now the last day of many days, 595

O! there are spirits of the air, 89
O Thou who plumed with strong desire 208
O, wild West Wind, thou breath of Autumn's being, 412
One word is too often profaned 590

Palace-roof of cloudless nights! 447
Peter Bells, one, two and three, 417
Poet of Nature, thou hast wept to know 90

Rarely, rarely, comest thou, 475

'Sleep, sleep on, forget thy pain— 597
So now my summer-task is ended, Mary, 137
Sweet Spirit! Sister of that orphan one, 513
Swift as a spirit hastening to his task 604
Swiftly walk o'er the western wave, 546

That matter of the murder is hushed up 320

The awful shadow of some unseen Power 114

The everlasting universe of things 120

The flower that smiles today 589

The Fountains mingle with the River 446

The keen stars were twinkling 601

The lovely shadow of some awful Power 117

The serpent is shut out from Paradise— 591

The sleepless Hours who watch me as I lie 508

The spider spreads her webs, whether she be 476

The Sun is warm, the sky is clear, 209

Thy country's curse is on thee, darkest Crest 448

Thy voice, slow rising like a Spirit, lingers 128

Upon the lonely beach Kathema lay 3

Vessels of Heavenly medicine! may the breeze 8

We are as clouds that veil the midnight moon; 112

We strew these opiate flowers 551

What! alive and so bold, oh Earth? 588

What men gain fairly, that should they possess 444

When the lamp is shattered 590

When the last hope of trampled France had failed 141

Whose is the love that, gleaming through the world 10

Ye hasten to the grave! What seek ye there 474

JANE AUSTEN	Emma
	Mansfield Park
	Persuasion
	Pride and Prejudice
	Sense and Sensibility
MRS BEETON	Book of Household Management
LADY ELIZABETH BRADDON	Lady Audley's Secret
ANNE BRONTË	The Tenant of Wildfell Hall
CHARLOTTE BRONTË	Jane Eyre
	Shirley
	Villette
EMILY BRONTË	Wuthering Heights
SAMUEL TAYLOR COLERIDGE	The Major Works
WILKIE COLLINS	The Moonstone
	No Name
	The Woman in White
CHARLES DARWIN	The Origin of Species
CHARLES DICKENS	The Adventures of Oliver Twist
	Bleak House
	David Copperfield
	Great Expectations
	Nicholas Nickleby
	The Old Curiosity Shop
	Our Mutual Friend
	The Pickwick Papers
	A Tale of Two Cities
GEORGE DU MAURIER	Trilby
MARIA EDGEWORTH	Castle Rackrent

A SELECTION OF   **OXFORD WORLD'S CLASSICS**

GEORGE ELIOT   **Daniel Deronda**
The Lifted Veil and Brother Jacob
Middlemarch
The Mill on the Floss
Silas Marner

SUSAN FERRIER   **Marriage**

ELIZABETH GASKELL   **Cranford**
The Life of Charlotte Brontë
Mary Barton
North and South
Wives and Daughters

GEORGE GISSING   **New Grub Street**
The Odd Woman

THOMAS HARDY   **Far from the Madding Crowd**
Jude the Obscure
The Mayor of Casterbridge
The Return of the Native
Tess of the d'Urbervilles
The Woodlanders

WILLIAM HAZLITT   **Selected Writings**

JAMES HOGG   **The Private Memoirs and Confessions of a**
    Justified Sinner

JOHN KEATS   **The Major Works**
Selected Letters

CHARLES MATURIN   **Melmoth the Wanderer**

WALTER SCOTT   **The Antiquary**
Ivanhoe
Rob Roy

MARY SHELLEY   **Frankenstein**
The Last Man

A SELECTION OF OXFORD WORLD'S CLASSICS

ROBERT LOUIS
STEVENSON

Kidnapped and **Catriona**
**The Strange Case of Dr Jekyll and
   Mr Hyde** and **Weir of Hermiston**
Treasure Island

BRAM STOKER

Dracula

WILLIAM MAKEPEACE
THACKERAY

Vanity Fair

OSCAR WILDE

Complete Shorter Fiction
The Major Works
The Picture of Dorian Gray

DOROTHY WORDSWORTH

The Grasmere and Alfoxden Journals

WILLIAM WORDSWORTH

The Major Works

TROLLOPE IN   **OXFORD WORLD'S CLASSICS**

ANTHONY TROLLOPE

An Autobiography

The American Senator

Barchester Towers

Can You Forgive Her?

The Claverings

Cousin Henry

Doctor Thorne

The Duke's Children

The Eustace Diamonds

Framley Parsonage

He Knew He Was Right

Lady Anna

The Last Chronicle of Barset

Orley Farm

Phineas Finn

Phineas Redux

The Prime Minister

Rachel Ray

The Small House at Allington

The Warden

The Way We Live Now

A SELECTION OF   **OXFORD WORLD'S CLASSICS**

HANS CHRISTIAN ANDERSEN	**Fairy Tales**
J. M. BARRIE	**Peter Pan in Kensington Gardens** and **Peter and Wendy**
L. FRANK BAUM	**The Wonderful Wizard of Oz**
FRANCES HODGSON BURNETT	**The Secret Garden**
LEWIS CARROLL	**Alice's Adventures in Wonderland** and **Through the Looking-Glass**
CARLO COLLODI	**The Adventures of Pinocchio**
KENNETH GRAHAME	**The Wind in the Willows**
ANTHONY HOPE	**The Prisoner of Zenda**
THOMAS HUGHES	**Tom Brown's Schooldays**

The Oxford World's Classics Website

www.worldsclassics.co.uk

- Information about new titles
- Explore the full range of Oxford World's Classics
- Links to other literary sites and the main OUP webpage
- Imaginative competitions, with bookish prizes
- Peruse the Oxford World's Classics Magazine
- Articles by editors
- Extracts from Introductions
- A forum for discussion and feedback on the series
- Special information for teachers and lecturers

www.worldsclassics.co.uk

American Literature

British and Irish Literature

Children's Literature

Classics and Ancient Literature

Colonial Literature

Eastern Literature

European Literature

History

Medieval Literature

Oxford English Drama

Poetry

Philosophy

Politics

Religion

The Oxford Shakespeare

A complete list of Oxford Paperbacks, including Oxford World's Classics, Oxford Shakespeare, Oxford Drama, and Oxford Paperback Reference, is available in the UK from the Academic Division Publicity Department, Oxford University Press, Great Clarendon Street, Oxford OX2 6DP.

In the USA, complete lists are available from the Paperbacks Marketing Manager, Oxford University Press, 198 Madison Avenue, New York, NY 10016.

Oxford Paperbacks are available from all good bookshops. In case of difficulty, customers in the UK can order direct from Oxford University Press Bookshop, Freepost, 116 High Street, Oxford OX1 4BR, enclosing full payment. Please add 10 per cent of published price for postage and packing.